S0-BYQ-020

TV SEASON 76-77

Compiled and
Edited by
NINA DAVID

Operation Oryx, started more than 10 years ago at the Phoenix Zoo to save the rare white antelope — believed to have inspired the unicorn of mythology — has apparently succeeded.

An original herd of nine, put together through Operation Oryx by five world organizations, now numbers 34 in Phoenix with another 22 farmed out to the San Diego Wild Game Farm.

The operation was launched in 1962 when it became evident that the animals were facing extinction in their native habitat of the Arabian peninsula.

Published by The Oryx Press
3930 East Camelback Road
Phoenix, AZ 85018

Published simultaneously in Canada.

Printed and Bound in the United States of America

Library of Congress Card No. 77-94093
ISBN 0-912700-22-X

CONTENTS

INTRODUCTION

TV Season is an annual reference work of current and future value to researchers interested in the history of the medium, to television viewers, and to librarians and their patrons. The 1976–77 edition is the third of the series to be issued.

Information on each national TV program presented by the networks—ABC, CBS, NBC and PBS—as well as currently produced syndicated shows with national distribution, is given in the TV section. The listings are alphabetic by program name. Reruns in syndication are not listed. "See" references are used when a title is unclear.

Information on each regularly scheduled show includes name, network, type of show, descriptive material, and credits, such as executive producer, producer, director, writer, host, announcer, plus the stars and the characters they portray. For specials, e.g., variety shows, awards shows, parades, pageants, sports events and interviews, guests are noted; other specials, such as made-for-television movies, include cast names whenever possible. Feature films made originally for theater distribution do not list cast and credits. All individuals listed are included in the WHO'S WHO IN TV section.

Syndicated shows and shows on PBS air on different dates in different locations. For syndicated shows, the month of airing has been given; for most PBS shows, it is the first day or date a show is televised (occasionally, a month is used).

The editor has followed the networks' lead and designated Monday, September 20, 1976 as the first day of the 1976–77 season. This volume covers almost all shows originating between that date and September 12, 1977, the date chosen as the first day of the 1977–78 season. Therefore, *TV Season 76–77* covers 51 weeks of programming.

Exceptions to the rule include series still running as part of the 1975-76 season and those properly belonging to the 1977-78 season. In the first category fall programs such as *Grand Prix Tennis: Summer Tour '76* seen between 7/25/76-10/10/76 and *The Olympiad* which ended reruns as of 9/28/76. In the second category are series such as *Rafferty* which premiered 9/5/77 and the limited series *Washington: Behind Closed Doors* which inaugurated the 1977-78 season for ABC between 9/6/77-9/11/77.

The special lists encompass new shows, cancelled shows, new and cancelled shows, summer series and a list of shows captioned or translated for the hearing-impaired. As in previous years, *PBS series (which are usually of limited duration) and special shows are not found in these lists. The only exceptions are programs captioned for the hearing-impaired.*

The list of shows by program type has been expanded to include Western series. The category Limited Dramatic Series has been changed to Limited Series.

Emmy-award winning shows cover the period March 16, 1976–March 13, 1977.

All Emmy nominees are included; winners are noted with a star. The 1976 George Foster Peabody Broadcasting Awards for Television have also been listed.

The editor and publishers have used their best efforts to include all programs telecast in 1976–77 and to list all individuals connected to those programs, but have no legal responsibility for any omissions or errors. We will be grateful for any comments or suggestions, whether favorable or critical, for use on future editions.

Nina David
Santa Monica, California
November 1977

ACKNOWLEDGMENTS

This volume, like its predecessors, could not have been produced without the help and cooperation of many people in the television industry. In particular, I wish to thank the following people for enabling me to have ongoing access to present and future material: Mary Aladj, Public Information, Public Broadcasting Service; Michael Buchanan, Director of Press Information, CBS Television Network; Barbara Cronin, Public Relations, American Broadcasting Company; Pat Finn, Publicist, KCET-TV/Los Angeles; Tom Mackin, Director of Program Information, American Broadcasting Company.

Thanks also to the following individuals and organizations: Ralph Andrews, Executive Producer, Ralph Andrews Productions; John T. Blair, Producer, WITF-TV/Hershey, Pennsylvania; Beverlie Brewer, Executive Assistant, Show Biz, Inc.; Deborah Butler, Information Specialist, WBGY-TV/Springfield, Massachusetts; Julius Cain, Director of Programming, Mississippi Authority for Educational Television; John Cannon, National Academy of Television Arts and Sciences; Kathleen M. Cavalieri, D. L. Taffner, Ltd.; Jim Cooper, Director of Community Affairs, KOCE-TV/Huntington Beach, California; Kay Corcoran, Manager of Information Services, WETA-TV/Washington, D.C.; Margo Cozell, Public Broadcasting Service; Dennis Daych, WGBH-TV Sports/Boston; Mark Douglas, Supervisor of Public Information, Iowa Public Broadcasting Network; Paulette S. Evans, Editorial Assistant, South Carolina Educational Television; Janet Fede, Director of Promotion, KTTV-TV/Los Angeles; Deborah Feldstein, Administrative Secretary, National Academy of Television Arts and Sciences; James A. Gershman, Manager of Public Information, WSBE-TV/Providence, Rhode Island; Betty Goode, Press Department, MCA Television; Ken Horseman, Production Manager, Connecticut Public Television; Karen Johnson, Coordinator of Information Services, WGBH-TV/Boston; Kansas City Public Television; Carolyn Kowalski, Public Information Director, KAET-TV/Tempe, Arizona; Richard Krafsur, Awards Administrator, Academy of Television Arts and Sciences; Carole Krumland, Public Information, KQED-TV/San Francisco; KUHT-TV/Houston; Corrine Kunz, Promotion Director, WMVS-TV/Milwaukee; Chuck McConnell, Manager—TV, WXXI-TV/Rochester, New York: Joseph T. McDermott, Director of Information, Twin Cities Public Television; Skye McLeod, Promotion Director, Alabama Public Television Network; Pauline A. Mitchell, Director of Public Relations, Central Virginia Educational Television; Gail Y. Miyasaki, Promotions, Hawaii Public Television; Marcy Prince, Publicity, KLRN-TV/Austin, Texas; Jennifer Ralston, Promotion and Development, KAID-TV/Boise, Idaho; Stephen H. Schifrin, Publicity Department, Tandem/TAT; Screen Actors Guild; Owen S. Simon, Vice President, Creative Services, Group W Productions, Inc.; Joe Siegman, Producer, 7-10 Productions; Arthur J. Singer, Development Manager, WMHT-TV/Schenectady, New York;

Lester M. Soublet, Information Specialist, WYES-TV/New Orleans; Victoria Spencer, National Academy of Television Arts and Sciences (Los Angeles); Cheryl K. Stelmach, Assistant in Program and Operation, Maryland Center for Public Broadcasting; Robin Stickney, Information Services, WTTW-TV/Chicago; Frank E. Strand, Operation Manager, WVIZ-TV/Cleveland; Karen Summers, Filmation Associates; Deborah J. Sutro, The Cousteau Society; Robert Thurber, Producer, Thurber Productions; George Vescio, Sports Information, CBS Television Network; Gene Walsh, Vice President, Public Information, National Broadcasting Company; Gary L. Watts, WWVU-TV/Morgantown, West Virginia; WNYC-TV/New York.

Shows By Program Type

Animated Film Series

Children's Series

Comedy Series

Educational/Cultural Series

Feature Film Series

Game/Audience Participation Series

Limited Series

Limited Sports Series

Miscellaneous Series

Music/Comedy/Variety Series

Music/Dance Series

News Magazine Series

News Series

Shows Captioned or Translated for the Hearing Impaired

Cancelled Shows 1976-1977

New Shows 1976-1977

New & Cancelled Shows 1976-1977

Summer Shows 1976-1977

EMMY AWARDS

Presented by the
ACADEMY OF TELEVISION ARTS AND SCIENCES
for programs shown
March 16, 1976–March 13, 1977

All nominations are listed for each category; winners are starred.

PRIMETIME AWARDS

Outstanding Comedy Series [award(s) to executive producer(s) and/or producer(s)]

★ *The Mary Tyler Moore Show* Allan Burns, James L. Brooks, Executive Producers; Ed Weinberger, Stan Daniels, Producers (CBS)

All in the Family Mort Lachman, Executive Producer; Milt Josefsberg, Producer (CBS)

Barney Miller Danny Arnold, Executive Producer; Roland Kibbee, Danny Arnold, Producers (ABC)

The Bob Newhart Show Tom Patchett, Jay Tarses, Executive Producers; Michael Zinberg, Gordon Farr, Lynne Farr, Producers (CBS)

*M*A*S*H* Gene Reynolds, Executive Producer; Allan Katz, Don Reo, Burt Metcalfe, Producers (CBS)

Outstanding Drama Series [award(s) to executive producer(s) and/or producer(s)]

★ *Upstairs, Downstairs,* Masterpiece Theatre; John Hawkesworth, Joan Sullivan, Producers (PBS)

Baretta Anthony Spinner, Bernard Kowalski, Leigh Vance, Executive Producers; Charles E. Dismukes, Producer (ABC)

Columbo, NBC Sunday Mystery Movie; Everett Chambers, Producer (NBC)

Family Aaron Spelling, Leonard Goldberg, Mike Nichols, Executive Producers; Nigel McKeand, Carol Evan McKeand, Producers (ABC)

Police Story David Gerber, Executive Producer; Liam O'Brien, Producer; Mel Swope, Co-producer (NBC)

Outstanding Comedy-Variety or Music Series [award(s) to executive producer(s) and/or producer(s) and star(s), if applicable]

★ *Van Dyke and Company* Byron Paul, Executive Producer; Allan Blye, Bob Einstein, Producers; Dick Van Dyke, Star (NBC)

The Carol Burnett Show Joe Hamilton, Executive Producer; Ed Simmons, Producer; Carol Burnett, Star (CBS)

Evening at Pops William Cosel, Producer; Arthur Fiedler, Star (PBS)

The Muppet Show Jim Henson, David Lazer, Executive Producers; Jack Burns, Producer; The Muppets—Frank Oz, Richard Hunt, Dave Goelz, Eren Ozker, John Lovelady, Jerry Nelson, Stars (SYN)

NBC's Saturday Night Lorne Michaels, Producer (NBC)

Outstanding Limited Series [award(s) to executive producer(s) and/or producer(s)]

★ *Roots,* ABC Novel for Television; David L. Wolper, Executive Producer; Stan Margulies, Producer (ABC)

The Adams Chronicles Jac Venza, Executive Producer; Virginia Kassel, Series Producer; Robert Costello, Coordinating Producer; Fred Coe, James Cellan-Jones, Producers (PBS)

Captains and the Kings, NBC's Best Seller; Roy Huggins, Executive Producer; Jo Swerling, Jr., Producer (NBC)

Madame Bovary, Masterpiece Theatre; Richard Beynon, Producer (PBS)

The Moneychangers, NBC World Premiere Movie, The Big Event; Ross Hunter, Jacque Mapes, Producers (NBC)

Outstanding Special—Drama or Comedy [award(s) to executive producer(s) and/or producer(s)]

★ *Eleanor and Franklin: The White House Years,* ABC Theatre; David Susskind, Executive Producer; Harry R. Sherman, Producer. Shown March 13, 1977 (ABC)

★ *Sybil,* NBC World Premiere Movie, The Big Event; Peter Dunne, Philip Capice, Executive Producers; Jacqueline Babbin

Producer. Shown November 14 & 15, 1976 (NBC)

Harry S. Truman: Plain Speaking David Susskind, Producer. Shown October 5, 1976 (PBS)

Raid on Entebbe, The Big Event; Edgar J. Sherick, Daniel H. Blatt, Executive Producers. Shown January 9, 1977 (NBC)

21 Hours at Munich, The ABC Sunday Night Movie; Edward S. Feldman, Executive Producer; Frank von Zerneck, Robert Greenwald, Producers. Shown November 7, 1976 (ABC)

Outstanding Special—Comedy-Variety or Music [award(s) to executive producer(s) and/or producer(s) and star(s), if applicable]

★ *The Barry Manilow Special* Miles Lourie, Executive Producer; Steve Binder, Producer; Barry Manilow, Star. Shown March 2, 1977 (ABC)

Doug Henning's World of Magic Jerry Goldstein, Executive Producer; Walter C. Miller, Producer; Doug Henning, Star. Shown December 23, 1976 (NBC)

The Neil Diamond Special Jerry Weintraug, Executive Producer; Gary Smith, Dwight Hemion, Producers; Neil Diamond, Star. Shown February 21, 1977 (NBC)

The Shirley MacLaine Special: Where Do We Go From Here? George Schlatter, Producer; Shirley MacLaine, Star. Shown March 12, 1977 (CBS)

Sills and Burnett at the Met Joe Hamilton, Producer; Beverly Sills, Carol Burnett, Stars. Shown November 25, 1976 (CBS)

Outstanding Classical Program in the Performing Arts [for a special program, or for a series (excluding drama) award(s) to executive producer(s) and/or producer(s) and star(s), if applicable]

★ *American Ballet Theatre: Swan Lake Live from Lincoln Center,* Great Performances; John Goberman, Producer. Shown June 30, 1976 (PBS)

American Ballet Theatre: Dance in America, Great Performances; Jac Venza, Executive Producer; Emile Ardolino, Series Coordinating Producer; Merrill Brockway, Series Producer. Shown December 15, 1976 (PBS)

Arthur Rubenstein at 90 Great Performances; Jac Venza, Executive Producer; Klaus Hallig, Herbert Kloiber, Executive Producers; David Griffiths, Fritz Buttenstadt, Producers; Arthur Rubenstein, Star. Shown January 26, 1977 (PBS)

The Bolshoi Ballet: Romeo and Juliet Lothar Bock, Executive Producer; Alvin Cooperman, Producer. Shown June 27, 1976 (CBS)

Martha Graham Dance Company Dance in America, Great Performances; Jac Venza, Executive Producer; Emile Ardolino, Series Coordinating Producer; Merrill Brockway, Series Producer; Martha Graham, Star. Shown April 7, 1976 (PBS)

Outstanding Children's Special [for specials which were broadcast during the evening award(s) to executive producer(s) and producer(s)]

★ *Ballet Shoes Parts 1 & 2,* Piccadilly Circus; John McRae, Joan Sullivan, Producers. Shown December 27 & 28, 1976 (PBS)

It's Arbor Day Charlie Brown Lee Mendelson, Executive Producer; Bill Melendez, Producer. Shown March 16, 1976 (CBS)

Peter Pan, Hallmark Hall of Fame, The Big Event; Gary Smith, Dwight Hemion, Executive Producers; Gary Smith, Producer. Shown December 12, 1976 (NBC)

Pinocchio Bernard Rothman, Jack Wohl, Producers. Shown March 27, 1976 (CBS)

The Little Drummer Boy—Book II Arthur Rankin, Jr., Jules Bass, Producers. Shown December 13, 1976 (NBC)

Outstanding Lead Actor in a Comedy Series

★ Carroll O'Connor *All in the Family* (CBS)
Jack Albertson *Chico and the Man* (NBC)
Alan Alda *M*A*S*H** (CBS)
Hal Linden *Barney Miller* (ABC)
Henry Winkler *Happy Days* (ABC)

Outstanding Lead Actor in a Drama Series

★ James Garner *The Rockford Files* (NBC)
Robert Blake *Baretta* (ABC)
Peter Falk *Columbo* (NBC)
Jack Klugman *Quincy, M.E.* (NBC)
Karl Malden *The Streets of San Francisco* (ABC)

Outstanding Lead Actor in a Limited Series

★ Christopher Plummer *The Moneychangers,* NBC World Premiere, The Big Event (NBC)

Stanley Baker *How Green Was My Valley,* Masterpiece Theatre (PBS)

Richard Jordan *Captains and the Kings,* NBC's Best Seller (NBC)

Steven Keats *Seventh Avenue,* NBC's Best Seller (NBC)

Outstanding Lead Actor in a Drama or Comedy Special

★ Ed Flanders *Harry S. Truman: Plain Speaking*. Shown October 6, 1976 (PBS)
Peter Boyle *Tail Gunner Joe,* NBC World Premiere Movie, The Big Event. Shown February 6, 1977 (NBC)
Peter Finch *Rain on Entebbe,* The Big Event. Shown January 9, 1977 (NBC)
Edward Herrmann *Eleanor and Franklin: The White House Years,* ABC Theatre. Shown March 13, 1977 (ABC)
George C. Scott *Beauty and the Beast,* Hallmark Hall of Fame. Shown December 3, 1976 (NBC)

Outstanding Lead Actor for a Single Appearance in a Drama or Comedy Series

★ Louis Gossett, Jr. *Roots—Part 2*. Shown January 24, 1977 (ABC)
John Amos *Roots—Part 5*. Shown January 27, 1977 (ABC)
Levar Burton *Roots—Part 1*. Shown January 23, 1977 (ABC)
Ben Vereen *Roots—Part 6*. Shown January 28, 1977 (ABC)

Outstanding Lead Actress in a Comedy Series

★ Beatrice Arthur *Maude* (CBS)
Valerie Harper *Rhoda* (CBS)
Mary Tyler Moore *The Mary Tyler Moore Show* (CBS)
Suzanne Pleshette *The Bob Newhart Show* (CBS)
Jean Stapleton *All in the Family* (CBS)

Outstanding Lead Actress in a Drama Series

★ Lindsay Wagner *The Bionic Woman* (ABC)
Angie Dickinson *Police Woman* (NBC)
Kate Jackson *Charlie's Angels* (ABC)
Michael Learned *The Waltons* (CBS)
Sada Thompson *Family* (ABC)

Outstanding Lead Actress in a Limited Series

★ Patty Duke Astin *Captains and the Kings,* NBC's Best Seller (NBC)
Susan Flannery *The Moneychangers,* NBC World Premiere Movie, The Big Event (NBC)
Dori Brenner *Seventh Avenue,* NBC's Best Seller (NBC)
Eva Marie Saint *How the West was Won* (ABC)
Jane Seymour *Captains and the Kings,* NBC's Best Seller (NBC)

Outstanding Lead Actress in a Drama or Comedy Special

★ Sally Field *Sybil,* The Big Event. Shown November 14 & 15, 1976 (NBC)
Jane Alexander *Eleanor & Franklin: The White House Years,* ABC Theatre. Shown March 13, 1977 (ABC)
Susan Clark *Amelia Earhart,* NBC Monday Night at the Movies. Shown October 25, 1976 (NBC)
Julie Harris *The Last of Mrs. Lincoln,* Hollywood Television Theatre. Shown September 16, 1976 (PBS)
Joanne Woodward *Sybil,* The Big Event. Shown November 14 & 15, 1976 (NBC)

Outstanding Lead Actress for a Single Appearance in a Drama or Comedy Series

★ Beulah Bondi *The Pony Cart,* The Waltons. Shown December 2, 1976 (CBS)
Susan Blakely *Rich Man, Poor Man—Book II*. Shown September 21, 1976 (ABC)
Madge Sinclair *Roots—Part 4*. Shown January 26, 1977 (ABC)
Leslie Uggams *Roots—Part 6*. Shown January 28, 1977 (ABC)
Jessica Walter *'Til Death Us Do Part,* The Streets of San Francisco. Shown November 18, 1976 (ABC)

Outstanding Continuing Performance by a Supporting Actor in a Comedy Series [for a regular or limited series]

★ Gary Burghoff *M*A*S*H* (CBS)
Edward Asner *The Mary Tyler Moore Show* (CBS)
Ted Knight *The Mary Tyler Moore Show* (CBS)
Harry Morgan *M*A*S*H* (CBS)
Abe Vigoda *Barney Miller* (ABC)

Outstanding Continuing Performance by a Supporting Actor in a Drama Series [for a regular or limited series]

★ Gary Frank *Family* (ABC)
Noah Beery *The Rockford Files* (NBC)
David Doyle *Charlie's Angels* (ABC)
Tom Ewell *Baretta* (ABC)
Will Geer *The Waltons* (CBS)

Outstanding Continuing or Single Performance by a Supporting Actor in Variety or Music [for a continuing role in a regular or limited series; or a one-time appearance in a series; or a special]

★ Tim Conway *The Carol Burnett Show*. Entire Series (CBS)
John Belushi *NBC's Saturday Night,* with Candice Bergen. Shown December 11, 1976 (NBC)

Chevy Chase *NBC's Saturday Night,* with Elliott Gould. Shown May 29, 1976 (NBC)
Harvey Korman *The Carol Burnett Show.* Entire Series (CBS)
Ben Vereen *The Bell Telephone Jubilee.* Shown March 26, 1976 (NBC)

Outstanding Performance by a Supporting Actor in a Comedy or Drama Special

★ Burgess Meredith *Tail Gunner Joe,* The Big Event. Shown February 6, 1977 (NBC)
Martin Balsam *Raid on Entebbe,* The Big Event. Shown January 9, 1977 (NBC)
Mark Harmon *Eleanor and Franklin: The White House Years,* ABC Theatre. Shown March 13, 1977 (ABC)
Yaphet Kotto *Raid on Entebbe,* The Big Event. Shown January 9, 1977 (NBC)
Walter McGinn *Eleanor and Franklin: The White House Years,* ABC Theatre. Shown March 13, 1977 (ABC)

Outstanding Single Performance by a Supporting Actor in a Comedy or Drama Series [**for a one-time appearance in a regular or limited series**]

★ Edward Asner *Roots—Part 1.* Shown January 23, 1977 (ABC)
Charles Durning *Captains and the Kings—Chapter 2,* NBC's Best Seller. Shown October 7, 1976 (NBC)
Moses Gunn *Roots—Part 1.* Shown January 23, 1977 (ABC)
Robert Reed *Roots—Part 5.* Shown January 27, 1977 (ABC)
Ralph Waite *Roots—Part 1.* Shown January 23, 1977 (ABC)

Outstanding Continuing Performance by a Supporting Actress in a Comedy Series [**for a regular or limited series**]

★ Mary Kay Place *Mary Hartman, Mary Hartman* (SYN)
Georgia Engel *The Mary Tyler Moore Show* (CBS)
Julie Kavner *Rhoda* (CBS)
Loretta Swit *M*A*S*H* (CBS)
Betty White *The Mary Tyler Moore Show* (CBS)

Outstanding Continuing Performance by a Supporting Actress in a Drama Series [**for a regular or limited series**]

★ Kristy McNichol *Family* (ABC)
Meredith Baxter Birney *Family* (ABC)
Ellen Corby *The Waltons* (CBS)
Lee Meriwether *Barnaby Jones* (CBS)
Jacqueline Tong *Upstairs, Downstairs,* Masterpiece Theatre (PBS)

Outstanding Continuing or Single Performance by a Supporting Actress in Variety of Music [**for a continuing role in a regular or limited series; or a one-time appearance in a series; or a special**]

★ Rita Moreno *The Muppet Show* (SYN)
Vicki Lawrence *The Carol Burnett Show* Entire Series (CBS)
Gilda Radner *NBC's Saturday Night,* with Steve Martin. Shown February 26, 1977 (NBC)

Outstanding Performance by a Supporting Actress in a Comedy or Drama Special

★ Diana Hyland *The Boy in the Plastic Bubble,* The ABC Friday Night Movie. Shown November 12, 1976 (ABC)
Ruth Gordon *The Great Houdinis,* The ABC Friday Night Movie. Shown October 8, 1976 (ABC)
Rosemary Murphy *Eleanor and Franklin: The White House Years,* ABC Theatre. Shown March 13, 1977 (ABC)
Patricia Neal *Tail Gunner Joe,* The Big Event. Shown February 6, 1977 (NBC)
Susan Oliver *Amelia Earhart,* NBC Monday Night at the Movies. Shown October 25, 1976 (NBC)

Outstanding Single Performance by a Supporting Actress in a Comedy or Drama Series [**for a one-time appearance in a regular or limited series**]

★ Olivia Cole *Roots—Part 8.* Shown January 30, 1977 (ABC)
Sandy Duncan *Roots—Part 5.* Shown January 27, 1977 (ABC)
Eileen Heckart *Lou Proposes,* The Mary Tyler Moore Show. Shown November 20, 1976 (CBS)
Cicely Tyson *Roots—Part 1.* Shown January 23, 1977 (ABC)
Nancy Walker *The Separation,* Rhoda. Shown September 20, 1976 (CBS)

Outstanding Writing in a Drama Series [**a single episode of a regular or limited series with continuing characters and/or theme**]

★ Ernest Kinoy, William Blinn *Roots—Part 2.* Shown January 24, 1977 (ABC)
James Lee *Roots—Part 5.* Shown January 27, 1977 (ABC)
Roger O. Hirson *Charles Francis Adams: Minister to Great Britain,* The Adams Chronicles. Shown March 30, 1976 (PBS)
M. Charles Cohen *Roots—Part 8.* Shown January 30, 1977 (ABC)
Tad Mosel *John Quincy Adams: President,* The Adams Chronicles. Shown March 16, 1976 (PBS)

Outstanding Writing in a Comedy Series [a single episode of a regular or limited series with continuing characters and/or theme]

★ Allan Burns, James L. Brooks, Ed Weinberger, Stan Daniels, David Lloyd, Bob Ellison *The Last Show,* The Mary Tyler Moore Show. Shown March 19, 1977 (CBS)

Alan Alda *Dear Sigmund,* M*A*S*H. Shown November 9, 1976 (CBS)

Danny Arnold, Tony Sheehan *Quarantine—Part 2,* Barney Miller. Shown October 7, 1976 (ABC)

David Lloyd *Mary Midwife,* The Mary Tyler Moore Show. Shown September 25, 1976 (CBS)

Earl Pomerantz *Ted's Change of Heart,* The Mary Tyler Moore Show. Shown October 23, 1976 (CBS)

Outstanding Writing in a Comedy-Variety or Music Series [a single episode of a regular or limited series]

★ Anne Beatts, Dan Aykroyd, Al Franken, Tom Davis, James Downey, Lorne Michaels, Marilyn Suzanne Miller, Michael O'Donoghue, Herb Sargent, Tom Schiller, Rosie Shuster, Alan Zweibel, John Belushi, Bill Murray *NBC's Saturday Night* (with Sissy Spacek). Shown March 12, 1977 (NBC)

Jim Henson, Jack Burns, Marc London, Jerry Juhl *The Muppet Show* (with Paul Williams). Syndicated (SYN)

Anne Beatts, Chevy Chase, Al Franken, Tom Davis, Lorne Michaels, Marilyn Suzanne Miller, Michael O'Donoghue, Herb Sargent, Tom Schiller, Rosie Shuster, Alan Zweibel *NBC's Saturday Night* (with Elliott Gould). Shown May 29, 1976 (NBC)

Ed Simmons, Roger Beatty, Elias Davis, David Pollock, Rick Hawkins, Liz Sage, Adele Styler, Burt Styler, Tim Conway, Bill Richmond, Gene Perret, Dick Clair, Jenna McMahon *The Carol Burnett Show* (with Eydie Gorme). Shown February 12, 1977 (CBS)

Bob Einstein, Allan Blye, George Burditt, Garry Ferrier, Ken Finkelman, Mitch Markowitz, Don Novello, Pat Proft, Leonard Ripps, Mickey Rose, Aubrey Tadman, Dick Van Dyke, Paul Wayne *Van Dyke & Company* (with John Denver). Shown October 7, 1976 (NBC)

Outstanding Writing in a Comedy-Variety or Musical Special

★ Alan Buz Kohan, Ted Strauss *America Salutes Richard Rodgers: The Sound of His Music.* Shown December 9, 1976 (CBS)

Alan Thicke, Don Clark, Susan Clark, Ronny Pearlman, Steve Binder, Barry Manilow, Bruce Vilanch *The Barry Manilow Special.* Shown March 2, 1977 (ABC)

Bill Dyer, Ntozake Shange *An Evening with Diana Ross,* The Big Event. Shown March 6, 1977 (NBC)

Ken Welch, Mitzi Welch, Kenny Solms, Gail Parent *Sills and Burnett at the Met.* Shown November 25, 1976 (CBS)

Digby Wolfe, George Schlatter *John Denver and Friend.* Shown March 29, 1976 (ABC)

Outstanding Writing in a Special Program —Drama or Comedy—Original Teleplay

★ Lane Slate *Tail Gunner Joe,* The Big Event. Shown February 6, 1977 (NBC)

Barry Beckerman *Raid on Entebbe,* The Big Event. Shown January 9, 1977 (NBC)

James Costigan *Eleanor and Franklin: The White House Years,* ABC Theatre. Shown March 13, 1977 (ABC)

Ernest Kinoy *Victory at Entebbe.* Shown December 13, 1976 (ABC)

Douglas Day Stewart, Teleplay, Joe Morgenstern and Douglas Day Stewart, Story *The Boy in the Plastic Bubble,* The ABC Friday Night Movie. Shown November 12, 1976 (ABC)

Outstanding Writing in a Special Program —Drama or Comedy—Adaptation

★ Stewart Stern *Sybil,* The Big Event. Shown November 14 & 15, 1976 (NBC)

William Bast *The Man in the Iron Mask,* The Bell System Presents. Shown January 17, 1977 (NBC)

John McGreevey *Judge Horton and the Scottsboro Boys,* NBC World Premiere. Shown April 22, 1976 (NBC)

Carol Sobieski *Harry S. Truman: Plain Speaking.* Shown October 5, 1976 (PBS)

Steven Gethers *A Circle of Children.* March 10, 1977 (CBS)

Outstanding Directing in a Comedy Series [a single episode of a regular or limited series with continuing characters and/or theme]

★ Alan Alda *Dear Sigmund,* M*A*S*H. Shown November 9, 1976 (CBS)

Paul Bogart *The Draft Dodger,* All in the Family. Shown December 25, 1976 (CBS)

Joan Darling *The Nurses,* M*A*S*H. Shown October 19, 1976 (CBS)

Alan Rafkin *Lt. Radar O'Reilly,* M*A*S*H. Shown October 12, 1976 (CBS)

Jay Sandrich *The Last Show,* The Mary Tyler Moore Show. Shown March 19, 1977 (CBS)

Outstanding Directing in a Drama Series [a single episode of a regular or limited series with continuing characters and/or theme]

★ David Greene *Roots—Part 1*. Shown January 23, 1977 (ABC)

Marvin Chomsky *Roots—Part 3*. Shown January 25, 1977 (ABC)

Fred Coe *John Quincy Adams: President,* The Adams Chronicles. Shown March 16, 1976 (PBS)

John Erman *Roots—Part 2* (Second Hour). Shown January 24, 1977 (ABC)

Gilbert Moses *Roots—Part 6* (Second Hour). Shown January 28, 1977 (ABC)

Outstanding Directing in a Comedy-Variety or Music Series [a single episode of a regular or limited series]

★ Dave Powers *The Carol Buenwrr Show* (with Eydie Gorme). Shown February 12, 1977 (CBS)

John C. Moffitt *Van Dyke and Company* (with John Denver). Shown October 7, 1976 (NBC)

Dave Wilson *NBC's Saturday Night* (with host—Paul Simon). Shown November 20, 1976 (NBC)

Outstanding Directing in a Comedy-Variety or Music Special

★ Dwight Hemion *America Salutes Richard Rodgers: The Sound of His Music*. Shown December 9, 1976 (CBS)

Steve Binder *The Barry Manilow Special*. Shown March 2, 1977 (ABC)

Tony Charmoli *The Shirley MacLaine Special: Where Do We Go From Here?*. Shown March 12, 1977 (CBS)

Walter C. Miller *Doug Henning's World of Magic*. Shown December 23, 1976 (NBC)

David Powers *Sills and Burnett at the Met*. Shown November 25, 1976 (CBS)

Outstanding Directing in a Special Program —Drama or Comedy

★ Daniel Petrie *Eleanor and Franklin: The White House Years,* ABC Theatre. Shown March 13, 1977 (ABC)

Fielder Cook *Judge Horton and the Scottsboro Boys,* NBC World Premiere. Shown April 22, 1976 (NBC)

Tom Gries *Helter Skelter*. Shown April 1, 1976 (CBS)

Irvin Kershner *Raid on Entebbe,* The Big Event. Shown January 9, 1977 (NBC)

Jud Taylor *Tail Gunner Joe,* The Big Event. Shown February 6, 1977 (NBC)

ENTERTAINMENT AREAS
(Possibility of one award, more than one award or no award)

Special Classification of Outstanding Program Achievement [An award for unique program achievements, which does not fall into a specific category, or is not otherwise recognized]

The Tonight Show Starring Johnny Carson Fred De Cordova, Producer; Johny Carson, Star. Series (NBC)

Outstanding Achievement in Coverage of Special Events—Individual [An award for individual achievement. A special event is a single program presented as live coverage; i.e., parades, pageants, awards presentations, salutes and coverage of other live events which were not covered by the news division.]

John C. Moffitt (Director) *The 28th Annual Emmy Awards*. Shown May 17, 1976 (ABC)

CREATIVE TECHNICAL ARTS

Outstanding Achievement in Music Composition for a Series (Dramatic Underscore) [for a single episode of a regular or limited series]

★ Quincy Jones, Gerald Fried *Roots—Part 1*. Shown January 23, 1977 (ABC)

Elmer Bernstein *Captains and the Kings—Chapter 8,* NBC's Best Seller. Shown November 25, 1976 (NBC)

Gerald Fried *Roots—Part 8*. Shown January 30, 1977 (ABC)

Dick De Benedictis *Monster Manor,* Police Story. Shown November 30, 1976 (NBC)

Jack Urbont *The Vigilante,* Bronk. Shown March 28, 1976 (CBS)

Outstanding Achievement in Music Composition for a Special (Dramatic Underscore)

★ Alan Bergman, Leonard Rosenman, Marilyn Bergman *Sybil,* The Big Event. Shown November 14 & 15, 1976 (NBC)
John Barry *Eleanor and Franklin: The White House Years,* ABC Theatre. Shown March 13, 1977 (ABC)
Fred Karlin *Minstrel Man*. Shown March 2, 1977 (CBS)
David Shire *Raid on Entebbe,* The Big Event. Shown January 9, 1977 (NBC)
Billy Goldenberg *Helter Skelter*. Shown April 1 & 2, 1976 (CBS)

Outstanding Achievement in Music Direction [for a single episode of a series, or a special program, whether it be variety or music]

★ Ian Fraser *America Salutes Richard Rodgers: The Sound of His Music*. Shown December 9, 1976 (CBS)
Andre Previn *Previn and the Pittsburgh Mozart as Keyboard Prodigy*. Shown February 27, 1977 (PBS)
Jack Urbont *The Vigilante,* Bronk. Shown March 28, 1976 (CBS)
Peter Matz *Sills and Burnett at the Met*. November 27, 1976 (CBS)
Rafael Kubelik *New York Philharmonic: Rafael Kubelik Live from Lincoln Center,* Great Performances. Shown November 20, 1976 (PBS)

Outstanding Cinematography in Entertainment Programming for a Series [for a single episode of a regular or limited series]

★ Ric Waite *Captains and the Kings—Chapter 1,* NBC's Best Seller. Shown September 30, 1976 (NBC)
Joseph Biroc *The Moneychangers,* NBC World Premiere Movie, The Big Event. Shown December 4, 1976 (NBC)
John J. Jones *Once an Eagle—Part 1,* NBC's Best Seller. Shown December 2, 1976 (NBC)
William Jurgensen *Dear Sigmund,* M*A*S*H. Shown November 9, 1976 (CBS)
Sherman Kunkel *Soldier in the Jungle,* Baretta. Shown January 5, 1977 (ABC)
Stevan Larner *Roots—Part 2*. Shown January 24, 1977 (ABC)
Sol Negrin, A.S.C. *A Shield for Murder—Part 2,* Kojak. Shown November 21, 1976 (CBS)
Joseph M. Wilcots *Roots—Part 7*. Shown January 29, 1977 (ABC)

Outstanding Cinematography in Entertainment Programming for a Special [for a special or a feature length program made for television]

★ William Butler *Raid on Entebbe,* The Big Event. Shown January 9, 1977 (NBC)
James Crabe *Eleanor and Franklin: The White House Years,* ABC Theatre. Shown March 13, 1977 (ABC)
Mario Tosi *Sybil,* The Big Event. Shown November 14 & 15, 1976 (NBC)
Ted Voigtlander, A.S.C. *The Loneliest Runner*. Shown December 20, 1976 (NBC)
Ric Waite *Tail Gunner Joe,* The Big Event. Shown February 6, 1977 (NBC)

Outstanding Film Editing in a Comedy Series [for a single episode of a regular or limited series]

★ Douglas Hines, A.C.E. *Murray Can't Lose,* The Mary Tyler Moore Show. Shown November 27, 1976 (CBS)
Stanford Tischler, A.C.E., Samuel E. Beetley, A.C.E. *Dear Sigmund,* M*A*S*H. Shown November 9, 1976 (CBS)

Outstanding Film Editing in a Drama Series [for a single episode of a regular or limited series]

★ Neil Travis *Roots—Part 1*. Shown January 23, 1977 (ABC)
James T. Heckert *Roots—Part 8*. Shown January 30, 1977 (ABC)
Peter Kirby *Roots—Part 3*. Shown January 25, 1977 (ABC)
Jerrold Ludwig *Rich Man, Poor Man—Book II*. Shown October 5, 1976 (ABC)
Neil Travis, James Heckert *Roots—Part 2*. Shown January 24, 1977 (ABC)

Outstanding Film Editing for a Special [for drama, comedy or music-variety special or film made for television]

★ Rita Roland, A.C.E., Michael S. McLean *Eleanor and Franklin: The White House Years,* ABC Theater. Shown March 13, 1977 (ABC)
Byron "Buzz" Brandt, A.C.E., Bud Isaacs, A.C.E. *Helter Skelter*. Shown April 1 & 2, 1976 (CBS)
Ronald J. Fagan, A.C.E. *21 Hours at Munich,* The ABC Sunday Night Movie. Shown November 7, 1976 (ABC)
Bud S. Isaacs, A.C.E., Art Seid, A.C.E., Nick Archer, A.C.E. *Raid on Entebbe,* The Big Event. Shown January 9, 1977 (NBC)
John L. Loeffler *The Loneliest Runner*. Shown December 20, 1976 (NBC)

Outstanding Achievement in Film Sound Editing for a Series [for a single episode of a regular or limited series]

★ Larry Carow, Larry Neiman, Don Warner, Colin Mouat, George Fredrick, Dave Pettijohn, Paul Bruce Richardson *Roots —Part 2*. Shown January 24, 1977 (ABC)

Dale Johnston, James A. Bean, Carl J. Brandon, Joe Divitale, Don Tomlinson, Don Weinman, Gene Craig *The Return of Bigfoot—Part 1,* The Six Million Dollar Man. Shown September 19, 1976 (ABC)

Douglas H. Grindstaff, Richard Raderman, Sid Lubow, Hans Newman, Al Kajita, Luke Wolfram, Don V. Isaacs, Hank Salerno, Larry Singer, Stanley M. Gilbert. *Atlantium,* Fantastic Journey. Shown February 10, 1977 (NBC)

Jerry Rosenthal, William L. Stevenson, Michael Corrigan *The Mexican Connection,* Charlie's Angels. Shown September 29, 1976 (ABC)

Outstanding Achievement in Film Sound Editing for a Special

★ Bernard F. Pincus, Milton C. Burrow, Gene Eliot, Don Ernst, Tony Garber, Don V. Isaacs, Larry Kaufman, William L. Manger, A. David Marshall, Richard Oswald, Edward L. Sandlin, Russ Tinsley *Raid on Entebbe,* The Big Event. Shown January 9, 1977 (NBC)

Douglas H. Grindstaff, Don V. Isaacs, Larry Kaufman, Bob Human, Buzz Cooper, Jack A. Finley, Marvin I. Kosberg, Horold Lee Chaney, Dick Friedman, Bill Andrews, Larry Singer, Stanley M. Gilbert, Hank Salerno *The Quest,* NBC Thursday Night at the Movies. Shown May 13, 1976 (NBC)

Richard Harrison *Eleanor and Franklin: T White House Years,* ABC Theatre. Shown March 13, 1977 (ABC)

Jerry Rosenthal, William Phillips, John Strauss, William Jackson, James Yant, Jerry Pirozzi, Bruce Bell *The Boy in the Plastic Bubble,* The ABC Friday Night Movie. Shown November 12, 1976 (ABC)

Outstanding Achievement in Film Sound Mixing [for a single episode of a regular o limited series; or for a special program]

★ Alan Bernard, George E. Porter, Eddie J. Nelson, Robert L. Harman *The Savage Bees,* NBC Monday Night at the Movies. Shown November 22, 1976 (NBC)

Willie D. Burton, George E. Porter, Eddie J. Nelson, Robert L. Harman *Roots—Part 4*. Shown January 26, 1977 (ABC)

Hoppy Mehterian, George E. Porter, Eddie J. Nelson, Arnold Braun *Roots—Part 7*. Shown January 29, 1977 (ABC)

George E. Porter, Eddie J. Nelson, Robert L. Harman, Arnold Braun *Roots—Part 8*. Shown January 30, 1977 (ABC)

Richard Portman, David Ronne, Donald W. MacDougall, Edward "Curly" Thirlwell *Eleanor and Franklin: The White House Years,* ABC Theatre. Shown March 13, 1977 (ABC)

Bill Varney, Leonard Peterson, Robert Litt, Willie D. Burton *Roots—Part 1*. Shown January 23, 1977 (ABC)

Outstanding Art Direction or Scenic Design for a Comedy Series [for a single episode of a regular or limited series]

★ Thomas E. Azzari, Art Director *The Really Longest Day,* Fish. Shown February 5, 1977 (ABC)

Seymour Klate, Art Director; Mary Ann Biddle, Set Decorator *The Happy Hooker,* Sirota's Court. Shown January 29, 1977 (NBC)

C. Murawski, Art Director *Walter's Crisis,* Maude. Shown October 11, 1976 (CBS)

Don Roberts, Art Director *The Unemployment Story—Part 2,* All in the Family. Shown October 13, 1976 (CBS)

Roy Christopher, Art Director; Mary Ann Biddle, Set Decorator *The Americanization of Michi,* Mr. T & Tina Shown October 2, 1976 (ABC)

Outstanding Art Direction or Scenic Design for a Drama Series [for a single episode of a regular or limited series]

★ Tim Harvey, Scenic Designer *The Pallisers*. Shown January 24, 1977 (PBS)

John Corso, Art Director; Jerry Adams, Set Decorator *Captains and the Kings—Chapter 2,* NBC's Best Seller. Shown October 7, 1976 (NBC)

Joseph R. Jennings, Art Director; Solomon Brewer, Set Decorator *Roots—Part 6*. Shown January 28, 1977 (ABC)

Jan Scott, Art Director; Charles Bennett, Set Decorator *Roots—Part 2*. Shown January 24, 1977 (ABC)

Ed Wittstein, Production Designer *John Quincy Adams: Congressman,* The Adams Chronicles. Shown March 23, 1976 (PBS)

Outstanding Art Direction or Scenic Design for a Comedy-Variety or Music Series [for a single episode of a regular or limited series]

★ Romain Johnston, Art Director *The Mac*

Davis Show, (with Susan St. James, The Pointer Sisters, Shields & Yarnell). Shown May 17, 1976 (NBC)

Paul Barnes, Bob Sansom, Art Directors; Bill Harp, Set Decorator *The Carol Burnett Show,* (with Glen Campbell). Shown January 15, 1977 (CBS)

Bill Bohnert, Art Director; John Told, Set Decorator *Donny and Marie,* (with Chad Everett, Florence Henderson). Shown October 1, 1976 (ABC)

Eugene Lee, Leo Yoshimura, Franne Lee *NBC's Saturday Night,* (with Sissy Spacek). Shown March 12, 1977 (NBC)

Outstanding Art Direction or Scenic Design for a Dramatic Special

★ Jan Scott, Art Director; Anne D. McCulley, Set Decorator *Eleanor and Franklin: The White House Years,* ABC Theatre. Shown March 13, 1977 (ABC)

William H. Tuntke, Art Director; Richard Friedman, Set Decorator *Amelia Earhart,* NBC Monday Night at the Movies. Shown October 25, 1976 (NBC)

Roy Christopher, Art Director; Beulah Frankel, Set Decorator *The Last of Mrs. Lincoln,* Hollywood Television Theatre. Shown September 16, 1976 (PBS)

Trevor Williams, Art Director; Robert Checchi, Set Decorator *Eccentricities of a Nightingale,* Theater in America, Great Performances. Shown June 16, 1976 (PBS)

Outstanding Art Direction or Scenic Design for a Comedy-Variety or Music Special

★ Robert Kelly, Art Director *America Salutes Richard Rodgers: The Sound of His Music.* Shown December 9, 1976 (CBS)

Jac Venza, Scenic Designer *Billy the Kid,* American Ballet Theatre Dance in America. Shown December 15, 1976 (PBS)

Roy Christopher, Art Director; John Hueners, Set Decorator *The George Burns Comedy Special.* Shown December 1, 1976 (CBS)

William Mickley, Art Director *Les Patineurs,* American Ballet Theatre Dance in America, Great Performances. Shown December 15, 1976 (PBS)

Outstanding Achievement in Graphic Design and Title Sequences [for a single episode of a series; or for a special program this includes animation only when created for use in titling]

★ Eytan Keller, Stu Bernstein *Bell Telephone Jubilee.* Shown March 26, 1976 (CBS)

Phill Norman *The Moneychangers—Part 1,* NBC Saturday Night at the Movies. Shown December 4, 1976 (NBC)

Gene Piotrowsky *Visions,* The Gardener's Son. Shown January 6, 1977 (PBS)

Martine Scheon, David Summers *Previn and the Pittsburgh Mozart as Keyboard Prodigy.* Shown February 27, 1977 (PBS)

Outstanding Achievement in Costume Design for a Drama Special

★ Joe I. Tompkins *Eleanor and Franklin: The White House Years,* ABC Theatre. Shown March 13, 1977 (ABC)

Olga Lehmann *The Man in the Iron Mask,* A Bell System Special. Shown January 17, 1977 (NBC)

Albert Wolsky *Beauty and the Beast,* Hallmark Hall of Fame. Shown December 3, 1976 (NBC)

Outstanding Achievement in Costume Design for Music-Variety [for a single episode of a series, or for a special program]

★ Jan Skalicky *The Barber of Seville,* Live from Lincoln Center, Great Performances. Shown November 3, 1976 (PBS)

Bill Hargate *Neil Sedaka Steppin' Out.* Shown September 17, 1976 (NBC)

Frank Thompson *America Salutes Richard Rodgers: The Sound of His Music.* Shown December 9, 1976 (CBS)

Ret Turner, Bob Mackie *The Sonny & Cher Show,* (with Barbara Eden and the Smothers Brothers). Shown October 3, 1976 (CBS)

Bob Mackie *An Evening with Diana Ross,* The Big Event. Shown March 6, 1977 (NBC)

Outstanding Achievement in Costume Design for a Drama or Comedy Series [for a single episode of a regular or limited series]

★ Raymond Hughes *The Pallisers,* Episode No. 1. Shown January 24, 1977 (PBS)

Alvin Colt *Henry Adams: Historian,* The Adams Chronicles. Shown April 6, 1976 (PBS)

Jack F. Martell *Roots—Part 1.* Shown January 23, 1977 (ABC)

Joan Ellacott *Madame Bovary,* Episode No. 3, Masterpiece Theatre. Shown October 24, 1976 (PBS)

Grady Hunt *Prairie Woman,* The Quest. Shown November 10, 1976 (NBC)

Outstanding Achievement in Make-Up [for a single episode of a series, or for a special program]

★ Ken Chase, Make-Up Design; Joe DiBella, Make-Up Artist *Eleanor and Franklin: The White House Years,* ABC Theatre. Shown March 13, 1977 (ABC)

Del Acevedo, John Chambers, Dan Striepeke *Beauty and the Beast,* Hallmark Hall of Fame. Shown December 3, 1976 (NBC)

Dick Smith *Harry S. Truman: Plain Speaking*. Shown October 6, 1976 (PBS)

Michael G. Westmore, Ed Butterworth, Charlie Schram *The Million Dollar Rip-Off,* NBC World Premiere Movie, NBC Wednesday Night at the Movies. Shown September 22, 1976 (NBC)

Stan Winston *An Evening with Diana Ross,* The Big Event. Shown March 6, 1977 (NBC)

Outstanding Achievement in Choreography [for a single episode of a series or a special program]

★ Ron Field *America Salutes Richard Rodgers: The Sound of His Music*. Shown December 9, 1976 (CBS)

David Blair *Swan Lake,* Live from Lincoln Center, Great Performances. Shown June 30, 1976 (PBS)

Ernest O. Flatt *The Carol Burnett Show,* (with The Pointer Sisters). Shown November 27, 1976 (CBS)

Alan Johnson *The Shirley MacLaine Special: Where Do We Go From Here?*. Shown March 12, 1976 (CBS)

Donald McKayle *Minstrel Man*. Shown March 2, 1976 (CBS)

Outstanding Achievement in Lighting Direction [for a single episode of a regular or limited series, or for a special program]

★ William M. Klages, Peter Edwards *The Dorothy Hamill Special*. Shown November 17, 1976 (ABC)

Imero Fiorentino, Scott Johnson *The Neil Diamond Special*. Shown February 21, 1977 (NBC)

George Riesenberger, William Knight *John Quincy Adams: President,* The Adams Chronicles. Shown March 16, 1976 (PBS)

Dick Weiss, William Knight *Henry Adams: Historian,* The Adams Chronicles. Shown April 6, 1976 (PBS)

Ken Dettling, Leard Davis *Gold Watch,* Visions. Shown November 11, 1976 (PBS)

Outstanding Achievement in Tape Sound Mixing [for a single episode of a regular or limited series; or for a special program]

★ Doug Nelson *John Denver and Friend*. Shown March 29, 1976 (ABC)

Michael T. Gannon, Jerry Clemans, Tom Huth, Phil Serretti *Ice Time,* Police Story. Shown March 8, 1977 (NBC)

Doug Nelson, Norman H. Schwartz, John Black *The American Music Awards*. Shown January 31, 1977 (ABC)

Emil Neroda *John Quincy Adams: President,* The Adams Chronicles. Shown March 16, 1976 (PBS)

Outstanding Achievement in Video Tape Editing for a Series

★ Roy Stewart *The War Widow,* Visions. Shown October 28, 1976 (PBS)

Terry Pickford *Meeting of Minds*. Shown January 24, 1977 (PBS)

Ken Denisoff, Stowell Werden *Sharkey Boogies on Down,* C.P.O. Sharkey. Shown February 23, 1977 (NBC)

Jimmy B. Frazier *Ice Time,* Police Story. Shown March 8, 1977 (NBC)

Outstanding Achievement in Video Tape Editing for a Special

★ Gary H. Anderson *American Bandstand's 25th Anniversary*. Shown February 4, 1977 (ABC)

Thomas Klein, Bill Breshears *The Barry Manilow Special*. Shown March 2, 1977 (ABC)

Susan Jenkins, Manual Martinez *The Captain and Tennille Special*. Shown August 17, 1976 (ABC)

Jimmy B. Frazier, Danny White *The Dorothy Hamill Special*. Shown November 17, 1976 (ABC)

James McElroy, Mike Gavaldon, David Saxon *Victory at Entebbe*. Shown December 13, 1976 (ABC)

William Breshears, Barbara Babcock *The Neil Diamond Special*. Shown February 21, 1977 (NBC)

Outstanding Achievement in Technical Direction and Electronic Camerawork [for a single episode of a regular or limited series; or for a special program]

★ Karl Messerschmidt, Technical Director; Jon Olson, Bruce Gray, John Gutierrez, Jim Dodge, Wayne McDonald, Cameramen *Doug Henning's World of Magic*. Shown December 23, 1976 (NBC)

Ernie Buttelman, Technical Director; David Hilmer, James Balden, Jack Denton, Mayo Partee, Cameramen *A Special*

Olivia Newton-John. Shown November 17, 1976 (ABC)

Gene Crowe, Technical Director; Sam Dowlen, Tom Doakes, Larry Heider, Bob Keys, Wayne Orr, Bill Philbin, Ron Sheldon, Cameramen *The Neil Diamond Special*. Shown February 21, 1977 (NBC)

Ken Lamkin, Technical Director; Lew Adams, Mike Keeler, Gary Stanton, Samuel E. Dowlen, Cameramen *Victory at Entebbe*. Shown December 13, 1976 (ABC)

Ken Anderson, Technical Director; Arthur G. Vogel, Jr., Cameraman *Harry S. Truman: Plain Speaking*. Shown October 5, 1976 (PBS)

Creative Arts in Entertainment Areas [possibility of one award, more than one award or no award)

Outstanding Individual Achievement in Children's Programming [for a single episode of a series; or for a special program]

★ Jean De Joux (Videoanimation), Elizabeth Savel (Videoanimation) *Peter Pan,* Hallmark Hall of Fame, The Big Event. Shown December 12, 1976 (NBC)

★ Bill Hargate (Costume Designer) *Pinocchio*. Shown March 27, 1976 (CBS)

★ Jerry Greene (Video Tape Editor) *Pinocchio*. Shown March 27, 1976 (CBS)

Outstanding Individual Achievement In Children's Programming [for a single episode of a series; or for a special program]

★ Jean De Joux (Videoanimation) Elizabeth Savel (Videoanimation) *Peter Pan,* Hallmark Hall of Fame, The Big Event. Shown December 12, 1976 (NBC)

★ Bill Hargate (Costume Designer) *Pinocchio*. Shown March 27, 1976 (CBS)

★ Jerry Greene (Video Tape Editor) *Pinocchio*. Shown March 27, 1976 (CBS)

Outstanding Individual Achievement in any Area of Creative Technical Crafts [an award for individual technical craft achievement which does not fall into a specific category, and is not otherwise recognized.]

★ Emma Di Vittorio (Hairstylist) Vivienne Walker (Hairstylist) *Eleanor and Franklin: The White House Years,* ABC Theatre. Shown March 13, 1977 (ABC)

Special Classification of Outstanding Individual Achievement [an award for unique individual achievements, which does not fall into a specific category, or is not otherwise recognized]

★ Allen Brewster, Bob Roethle, William Lorenz, Manuel Martinez, Ron Fleury, Mike Welch, Jerry Burling, Walter Balderson, Chuck Droege (Video Tape Editing) *The First Fifty Years,* The Big Event. Shown November 21, 1976 (NBC)

Outstanding Achievement in Coverage of Special Events—Individuals [an award for individual achievement. A special event is a single program presented as live coverage; i.e., parades, pageants, awards presentations, salutes and coverage of other live events which were not covered by the news division.]

★ Brian C. Bartholomew, Keaton S. Walker (Art Directors) *The 28th Annual Emmy Awards*. Shown May 17, 1976 (ABC)

DAYTIME EMMYS

Presented by the
NATIONAL ACADEMY OF TELEVISION
ARTS AND SCIENCES
for programs shown
March 16, 1976–March 13, 1977

Outstanding Daytime Talk, Service, or Variety Series [emmy(s) to executive producer(s) and producer(s)]

★ *The Merv Griffin Show* Bob Murphy, Producer (SYN)
Dinah! Henry Jaffe and Carolyn Raskin, Executive Producers; Fred Tatashore, Producer (SYN)
The Gong Show Chuck Barris, Executive Producer; Gene Banks, Producer (NBC)
The Mike Douglas Show David Salzman, Executive Producer; Jack Reilly, Producer (SYN)

Outstanding Host or Hostess in a Talk, Service or Variety Series

★ Phil Donahue *Donahue* (SYN)
Mike Douglas *The Mike Douglas Show* (SYN)
Merv Griffin *The Merv Griffin Show* (SYN)
Dinah Shore *Dinah!* (SYN)

Outstanding Individual Director for a Daytime Variety Program [for a single episode]

★ Donald R. King *Mike in Hollywood with Ray Charles & Michel Le Grand,* The Mike Douglas Show. (SYN)
Dick Carson *Merv Griffin in Israel,* TheMerv Griffin Show. (SYN)
John Dorsey *The Gong Show.* Shown November 23, 1976 (NBC)
Glen Swanson *Dinah from Australia,* Dinah! (SYN)

Outstanding Game or Audience Participation Show [for daytime and nighttime programs emmy(s) to executive producer(s) and producer(s)]

★ *Family Feud* Howard Felsher, Producer (ABC)
The $20,000 Pyramid Bob Stewart, Executive Producer; Anne Marie Schmitt, Producer (ABC)
Hollywood Squares Robert Quigley and Merrill Heatter, Executive Producers; Jay Redack, Producer (NBC)
Match Game '76 Ira Skutch, Producer (CBS)
Tattletales Ira Skutch, Executive Producer; Paul Alter, Producer (CBS)

Outstanding Host or Hostess in a Game or Audience Participation Show [for daytime or nighttime programs]

★ Bert Convy *Tattletales* (CBS)
Dick Clark *The $20,000 Pyramid* (ABC)
Gene Rayburn *Match Game '76* (CBS)

Outstanding Individual Director for a Game or Audience Participation Show [for a single episode of a daytime or nighttime series]

★ Mike Gargiulo *The $20,000 Pyramid* (with Tony Randall & Jo Anne Worley). Shown August 10, 1976 (ABC)
Joseph Behar *Let's Make a Deal.* Shown May 5, 1976 (ABC)

Outstanding Entertainment Children's Series [emmy(s) to executive producer(s) and producer(s)]

★ *Zoom* Cheryl Susheel Bibbs, Executive Producer; Monia Joblin and Mary Benjamin, Producers (PBS)
Captain Kangaroo Jim Hirschfeld, Producer (CBS)
David Copperfield Once Upon A Classic; Jay Rayvid, Executive Producer; John McRae and Don Coney, Producers (PBS)
Heidi Once Upon A Classic; Jay Rayvid, Executive Producer; John McRae and Don Coney, Producers (PBS)
The Prince and the Pauper Once Upon A Classic; Jay Rayvid, Executive Producer; Barry Letts and Don Coney, Producers (PBS)

Outstanding Entertainment Childrens Special [emmy(s) to executive producer(s) and producer(s)]

★ *Big Henry and the Polka Dot Kid* Special Treat; Linda Gottlieb, Producer. Shown November 9, 1976 (NBC)

Blind Sunday ABC Afterschool Specials; Daniel Wilson, Producer. Shown April 21, 1976 (ABC)

Francesca Baby ABC Afterschool Specials; Martin Tahse, Producer. Shown October 6, 1976 (ABC)

Luke was There Special Treat; Linda Gottlieb, Executive Producer; Richard Marquand, Producer. Shown October 5, 1976 (NBC)

The Original Rompin' Stompin' Hot and Heavy, Cool and Groovy All Star Jazz Show The CBS Festival of Lively Arts for Young People; Ron Kass and Edgar Bronfman, Jr., Executive Producers; Gary Keys, Producer. Shown April 13, 1976 (CBS)

P. J. and the President's Son ABC Afterschool Specials; Danny Wilson, Executive Producer; Fran Scars, Producer. Shown November 10, 1976 (ABC)

Outstanding Informational Children's Series [emmy(s) to executive producer(s) and producer(s)]

★ *The Electric Company* Samuel Y. Gibbon, Jr., Executive Producer (PBS)

ABC Minute Magazine Thomas H. Wolf, Producer (ABC)

America Rock Tom Yohe, Executive Producer; Radford Stone, Producer (ABC)

Animals Animals Animals Lester Cooper, Executive Producer; Peter Weinberg, Producer (ABC)

Outstanding Informational Children's Special [emmy(s) to executive producer(s) and producer(s)]

★ *My Mom's Having a Baby* ABC Afterschool Specials; David H. DePatie and Friz Freleng, Executive Producers; Bob Chenault, Producer. Shown February 16, 1977 (ABC)

How to Follow the Election Sid Darion, Producer. Shown October 31, 1976 (ABC)

Outstanding Instructional Children's Programming—Series and Specials [emmy(s) to executive producer(s) and producer(s)]

★ *Sesame Street* Jon Stone, Executive Producer; Dulcy Singer, Producer. Series (PBS)

Villa Alegre Claudio Guzman, Executive Producer; Larry Gottlieb, Producer. Series (PBS)

Outstanding Actress in a Daytime Drama Series

★ Helen Gallagher *Ryan's Hope* (ABC)
Nancy Addison *Ryan's Hope* (ABC)
Beverlee McKinsey *Another World* (NBC)
Mary Stuart *Search For Tomorrow* (CBS)
Ruth Warrick *All My Children* (ABC)

Outstanding Program and Individual Achievement in Daytime Drama Specials

★ *The American Woman: Portraits of Courage* Gaby Monet, Producer. Shown May 20, 1976 (ABC)

★ Lois Nettleton, Performer *The American Woman: Portraits of Courage*. Shown May 20, 1976 (ABC)

★ Gaby Monet, Anne Grant, Writers *The American Woman: Portraits of Courage*. Shown May 20, 1976 (ABC)

Outstanding Instructional Children's Programming—Series and Specials [emmy(s) to executive producer(s) and producer(s)]

★ *Sesame Street* Jon Stone, Executive Producer; Dulcey Singer, Producer. Series (PBS)

Villa Alegre Claudio Guzman, Executive Producer; Larry Gottlieb, Producer. Series (PBS)

Mary Stuart *Search For Tomorrow* (CBS)
Ruth Warrick *All My Children* (ABC)

Outstanding Writing for a Daytime Drama Series [for a single episode of a series; or for the entire series]

★ Claire Labine, Paul Avila Mayer, Mary Munisteri *Ryan's Hope*. Series (ABC)

William J. Bell, Pat Falken Smith, William Rega, Kay Lenard, Margaret Stewart *Days of Our Lives*. Series (NBC)

Harding Lemay, Tom King, Peter Swet, Barry Berg, Jan Merlin, Arthur Giron, Kathy Callaway *Another World*. Series (NBC)

Agnes Nixon, Wisner Washam, Kathryn McCabe, Mary K. Wells, Jack Wood *All My Children*. Series (ABC)

Robert Soderberg, Edith Sommer, Ralph Ellis, Eugenie Hunt, Theodore Apstein, Gillian Spencer *As The World Turns*. Shown October 27, 1976 (CBS)

Outstanding Actor in a Daytime Drama Series

★ Val Dufour *Search For Tomorrow* (CBS)
Farley Granger *One Life to Live* (ABC)
Larry Haines *Search For Tomorrow* (CBS)
Lawrence Keith *All My Children* (ABC)
James Pritchett *The Doctors* (NBC)

Outstanding Individual Director for a Daytime Drama Series [for a single episode]
★ Lela Swift *Ryan's Hope*. Shown February 8, 1977 (ABC)
Joseph Behar *Days Of Our Lives*. Shown March 8, 1977 (NBC)
Ira Cirker *Another World*. Shown November 10, 1976 (NBC)
Paul E. Davis, Leonard Valenta *As The World Turns*. Shown January 14, 1977 (CBS)
Al Rabin *Julie and Doug's Wedding,* Days Of Our Lives. Shown October 1, 1976 (NBC)
John Sedwick *The Edge Of Night*. Shown August 6, 1976 (ABC)

Outstanding Daytime Drama Series [**emmy(s) to executive producer(s) and producer(s)**]
★ *Ryan's Hope* Paul Avila Mayer and Claire Labine, Executive Producers; Robert Costello, Producer (ABC)
All My Children Bud Kloss and Agnes Nixon, Producers (ABC)
Another World Paul Rauch, Executive Producer; Mary S. Bonner and Joseph H. Rothenberger, Producers (NBC)
Days Of Our Lives Mrs. Ted Corday, Executive Producer; H. Wesley Kenney and Jack Herzberg, Producers (NBC)
The Edge of Night Erwin Nicholson, Producer (ABC)

Outstanding Individual Achievement in any Area of Creative Technical Crafts [**an award for individual technical craft achievement which does not fall into a specific category, and is not otherwise recognized**]
★ Emma Di Vittorio (Hairstylist), Vivienne Walker (Hairstylist) *Eleanor and Franklin: The White House Years,* ABC Theatre. Shown March 13, 1977 (ABC)

Special Classification of Outstanding Individual Achievement [**an award for unique individual achievements, which does not fall into a specific category, or is not otherwise recognized**]
★ Allen Brewster, Bob Roethle, William Lorenz, Manuel Martinez, Ron Fleury, Mike Welch, Jerry Burling, Walter Balderson, Chuck Droege (Video Tape Editing) *The First Fifty Years,* The Big Event. Shown November 21, 1976 (NBC)

Outstanding Achievement in Coverage of Special Events—Individuals [**an award for individual achievement. A special event is a single program presented as live coverage; i.e., parades, pageants, awards presentations, salutes and coverage of other live events which were not covered by the news division.**]
★ Brian C. Bartholomew, Keaton S. Walker (Art Directors) *The 28th Annual Emmy Awards*. May 17, 1976 (ABC)

Outstanding Directing in Sports Programming
Chet Forte *ABC NFL Monday Night Football*. Shown September 19–December 17, 1976 (ABC)

Outstanding Live Sports Special [**emmy(s) to executive producer(s) and/or producer(s)**]
1976 Olympic Games/ Montreal, Canada Roone Arledge, Executive Producer; Chuck Howard, Don Ohlmeyer, Chet Forte, Dennis Lewin, Bob Goodrich, Geoffrey Mason, Terry Jastrow, Eleanor Riger, Ned Steckel, Brice Weisman, John Wilcox, Doug Wilson, Producers. Shown July 17–August 1, 1976 (ABC)

Outstanding Live Sports Series [**emmy(s) to executive producer(s) and/or producer(s)**]
The NFL Today, NFL Football on CBS, Barry Frank, Executive Producer; Mike Pearl, Hal Classon, Sid Kaufman, Producers (CBS)

Outstanding Edited Sports Special [**emmy(s) to executive producer(s) and/or producer(s)**]
A Special Preview of the 1976 Olympic Games from Montreal, Canada Roone Arledge, Executive Producer; Chuck Howard, Don Ohlmeyer, Chet Forte, Dennis Lewin, Bob Goodrich, Geoffrey Mason, Terry Jastrow, Eleanor Riger, Ned Steckel, Brice Weisman, John Wilcox, Doug Wilson, Producers. Shown July 17, 1976 (ABC)

Outstanding Edited Sports Series [**emmy(s) to executive producer(s) and/or producer(s)**]
The Olympiad Cappy Petrash Greenspan, Executive Producer; Bud Greenspan, Producer (PBS)

Outstanding Sports Personality
Frank Gifford *ABC Sports Programs* (ABC)

Creative Arts in Entertainment Areas
(Possibility of one award, more than one award or no award)

Outstanding Individual Achievement in Daytime Programming [for a single episode of a series; or for a special program]

Vicenzo Cilurzo, Lighting Director *The Merv Griffin Show*. Shown October 13, 1976 (SYN)

Outstanding Individual Achievement in Religious Programming

Chuck Murawski, Art Director; Bill Harp, Set Decorator *Insight, Jesus B.C.* (SYN)

Doc Siegel, Film Sound Mixer *This is the life, The Healer* (SYN)

Outstanding Individual Achievement in Sports Programming

Peter Henning, Harvey Marrison, Harry Hart, D'Arcy March, Don Shapiro, Don Shoemaker, Joe Valentine, Cinematographers *1976 Olympic Games*. Shown July 17–August 1, 1976 (ABC)

John Peterson, Angelo Bernarducci, Irwin Krechaf, Margaret Murphy, Vincent Reda, Anthony Zaccaro, Film Editors *1976 Olympic Games*. Shown July 17–August 1, 1976 (ABC)

Outstanding Individual Achievement in Sports Programming [for a single episode of a series, or for a special program]

Engineering supervisors: Julius Barnathan, Phil Levens, Joe Debonis, Joe Maltz, Ben Greenberg, William H. Johnson, Abdelnour Tadros, Jack Neitlich, Herb Kraft, Jacques Lesgards, Bob Czinke, Frank Genereux, Dick Horan, Mel Morehouse, Mort Romanoff, Jack Wilkey. Technical directors: Ernie Buttleman, Bill Morris, Dave Smith, Gene Affrunti, Bob Myers, Vic Bary, John Allen, John Broderick, Charlie Giles, Tom Sumner, Werner Gunther. Bob Bernthal, Joe Nesi. Electronic cameramen: Keith Brock, Evan Baker, John Lee, Bill Sullivan, Simon Melrose, Jim Angel, Andy Armentani, John Cronin, Drew Derosa, Jack Dorfman, Sal Folino, Charlie Hennegahan, William Karvelas, Mort Levin, John Morreale, Steve Nikifor, Roger Pierce, Mike Rebich, Joe Sapienza, Joe Scarpa, Joe Stefhnoni, Larry Stenman, Joe Talosi, Dale Walsh, *1976 Olympic Games*. Shown July 17–August 1, 1976 (ABC)

Associate directors: Carol Lehti, Dick Buffinton, Jeff Cohan, Vince De Dario, John De Lisa, Lou Frederick, Jack Gallivan, Jim Jennett, Bob Lanning, Jean Mac Lean, Dave Malenofski, Norm Samet, Howard Shapiro, Stan Spiro. Video tape editors: Emil Rich, John Stevens, Mike Raffaele, Ron Ackerman, Harry Allen, Harvey Beal, Ronald Blachut, Barbara Bowman, Bud Crowe, Peter Fritz, Charles Gardner, Vito Gerardi, Nick Giordano, James Hepper, Jacob Hierl, Hector Kicelian, Conrad Kraus, Fred Labib, Hal Lea, Pat Malik, Ed Mc Carthy, Peter Mecca, Alex Moskovic, Harvey Otto, Nicholas Pantelakis, Chester Pawlak, Carl Pollack, Douglas Ridsdel, Erskin Roberts, Danny Rosenson, Winston Sadoo, Gene Smejkal, Leo Stephen, Ted Summers, Martin Thibeau, Arthur Volk Mike Wenig, Mike Biondi, Rocco Cotugno, John Florence, Marvin Gench Victor Gonzalez, Frank Guigliano, Galen Halloway, Emerson Lawson, Nick Mazur, Merrit Roesser, Nathan Rogers, Mario Schenoman, Truett Smith, Charles Stephenson, George Stevens, Tom Wight, Hector Kierl, Ken Klingbeil, *1976 Olympic Games*. Shown July 17–August 1, 1976 (ABC)

The 1976 George Foster Peabody Broadcasting Awards

TELEVISION

WLBT-TV, Jackson, Mississippi, for *Power Politics in Mississippi,* an example of greatly needed documentary reporting in an area seemingly untouched in the recent past.

FRANKLIN MCMAHON, WBBM-TV, Chicago, for *Primary Colors, An Artist on the Campaign Trail,* showing how an artist can serve as a reporter on the Presidential Campaign trail, lending a new dimension to political reporting.

CHARLES BARTHOLD, WHO-TV, Des Moines, Iowa for his filming of a powerful and destructive tornado in action as it struck and demolished the small town of Jordan, Iowa.

HUGHES RUDD AND BRUCE MORTON OF *The CBS Morning News,* for their inventive and creative writing coupled with their reporting of significant and insignificant events through pointed humorous features.

SY PEARLMAN, NBC-TV, New York, as producer of *Weekend's 'Sawyer Brothers',* segment, an outstanding example of the power of television to investigate and uncover new facts resulting in a reexamination of criminal justice in this case.

KCET/28, Los Angeles, for *Visions,* for giving extensive new opportunities to writers and independent filmmakers to display their talents before sizeable audiences.

NBC-TV, New York for *Sybil,* one of the truly outstanding dramatic programs of the year.

ABC-TV, New York for *Eleanor and Franklin,* a well written, superbly acted, capably directed, moving treatment of a segment of the lives of two of America's best known historical personalities.

ABC NEWS, New York, for *Animals Animals Animals,* a quality mixture of graphics, animation and live actions focusing on a particular animal in each segment as seen through the eyes of man.

ABC SPORTS, New York, for *The 1976 Winter Olympic Games, Innsbruch, Austria* and *The 1976 Summer Olympic Games, Montreal, Canada,* for reaching new heights in television sports journalism.

TOMORROW ENTERTAINMENT, INC., New York, for *Judge Horton and the Scottsboro Boys,* a program representative of the excellence one has come to expect from Thomas W. Moore and his associates.

WETA-TV, Washington, D.C., for *In Performance at Wolf Trap,* a superb example of the use of television to expand exponentially the audience for great cultural events to all America.

PERRY COMO, with especial reference to the NBC-TV presentation of *Perry Como's Christmas in Austria,* which provided viewers with a sparkling and moving musical experience.

CBS NEWS, for *In The News,* which enables children to better understand events, people, and concepts they encounter during the course of their daily lives.

KERA-TV, Dallas, for *A Thirst in the Garden,* an incisive look at the problems produced by the handling of water in one of the most productive farming areas in the world.

JIM KARAYN AND THE LEAGUE OF WOMEN VOTERS, Washington, D.C., for *'76 Presidential Debates* for persistence against formidable obstacles which resulted in a series of joint appearances of the Presidential and Vice Presidential Candidates during the 1976 political campaign.

WNET/13, New York, for *The Adams Chronicles,* an impressive endeavor which enabled Americans to more realistically comprehend the great contributions to the American heritage by one of the great patriots of the founding days of this Nation.

CBS NEWS, New York, for *In Celebration of US* which significantly highlighted the nation's 200th birthday with their most extensive coverage on any single day since man landed on the moon.

ABC NEWS, New York, for *Suddenly An Eagle,* documenting how key events, ideas, and problems led ultimately to the Revolutionary War and the founding of the United States of America.

WETA-TV, Washington, D.C. and WNET/13, New York for *A Conversation with Jimmy Carter* in which principal reporter, Bill Moyers, demonstrated the tremendous impact through which television brought Candidate Jimmy Carter to the attention of the American people.

CBS NEWS, New York, for *60 Minutes,* as a program which clearly indicates there is a large and important audience for serious broadcast journalism.

TV Programs 1976-1977

1 **AAU Junior Olympic National Multi-Sports Championships** NBC
Program Type Sports Special
90 minutes each day. Coverage of the AAU Junior Olympics from the University of Nebraska at Lincoln 8/13/77 and 8/14/77.
Executive Producer Don Ohlmeyer
Producer Mike Weisman
Company NBC Sports
Director Ken Fouts
Host Jim Simpson
Announcer Marv Albert
Commentators Willie Davenport, Micki King, Charlie Jones, Bill Toomey, Nancy Theis, Allyson Johnson

2 **ABC Afterschool Specials** ABC
Program Type Children's Series
60 minutes. Wednesdays. Premiere date: 10/72. Fifth season premiere: 10/6/76. Young people's specials presented during the school year. The Bank Street School of Education (New York City) serves as consultant for the series. 14 shows aired during the 1976-77 season: "The Amazing Cosmic Awareness of Duffy Moon," "Blind Sunday," "Dear Lovey Hart (I Am Desperate!)" "Fawn Story," "Francesca, Baby," "The Horrible Honchos," "It Must Be Love, ('Cause I Feel So Dumb!)" "Me & Dad's New Wife," "Mighty Moose and the Quarterback Kid," "My Mom's Having a Baby," "The Pinballs," "P.J. and the President's Son," "The Shaman's Last Raid," "Very Good Friends." (*See* individual titles for credits.)

3 **ABC Evening News With Harry Reasoner and Barbara Walters** ABC
Program Type News Series
30 minutes. Mondays-Fridays. Premiere date: 10/4/76. Successor to "ABC News With Harry Reasoner." Jeff Gralnick became senior producer in March 1977; Av Westin succeeded Robert Siegenthal as executive producer 7/11/77.
Executive Producer Robert Siegenthaler/Av Westin
Senior Producers David Jayne, Richard Richter/Jeff Gralnick
Company ABC News
Anchors Harry Reasoner, Barbara Walters
Commentator Howard K. Smith

4 **The ABC Friday Night Movie** ABC
Program Type Feature Film Series – TV Movie Series
90 minutes/two hours. Fridays. Season premiere 9/24/76. A combination of made-for-television films and theatrically released motion pictures. The TV films are: "The Boy in the Plastic Bubble," "Bridger," "Death at Love House," "Delta County, U.S.A.," "Dog and Cat" (pilot), "Fantasy Island," "The Feather & Father Gang - Never Con a Killer," "The Great Houdinis," "High Risk," "The Last Dinosaur," "Look What's Happened to Rosemary's Baby," "The Love Boat," "The Love Boat II," "Lucan," "The Night That Panicked America," "Nightmare in Badham County," "One of My Wives Is Missing," "The Quinns," "Revenge for a Rape," "The San Pedro Bums," "Smash-Up on Interstate 5," "SST - Death Flight," "Strange New World," "Sweet Hostage," "Time Travelers," "Wanted: The Sundance Woman," "The Woman Who Cried Murder," "Young Pioneers' Christmas." (*See* individual titles for credits.) The feature films are: "Aloha, Bobby and Rose" (1976) shown 5/6/77, "Bang the Drum Slowly" (1973) shown 4/8/77, "The Brain" (1969) shown 6/24/77, "Brother John" (1971) shown 7/1/77, "Cooley High" (1975) shown 4/1/77, "Dirty Mary Crazy Larry" (1974) shown 2/18/77, "The Double Con" (1973—released theatrically as "Trick Baby") shown 7/8/77, "Gordon's War" (1973) shown 7/29/77, "The Great American Cowboy" (1974) shown 6/10/77, "A Gunfight" (1971) shown 7/15/77, "Hands of the Ripper" (1971) shown 6/24/77, "Hard Driver" (1973—released theatrically as "The Last American Hero") shown 5/27/77, "Jenny" (1970) shown 6/17/77, "The Legend of Hell House" (1973) shown 8/5/77, "Let's Scare Jessica to Death" (1971) shown 3/11/77, "Lovin' Molly" (1974) shown 6/10/77, "The Neptune Disaster" (1973—released theatrically as "The Neptune Factor") shown 5/27/77, "Star Spangled Girl" (1971) shown 6/17/77, "Summer of

The ABC Friday Night Movie *Continued* '42" (1971) shown 8/19/77, "Walking Tall-Part II" (1975) shown 9/24/76, "What's Up, Doc?" (1972) shown 12/10/76 and 8/12/77, "Yours, Mine and Ours" (1968) shown 12/24/76.

5 **ABC Minute Magazine** ABC
Program Type Children's Series
60 seconds. Sundays. Premiere date: 1/30/77. Evening series for young people designed to broaden their understanding of world events in the news.
Producer Thomas H. Wolf
Company ABC News
Hosts Various

6 **The ABC Monday Comedy Special** ABC
Program Type Comedy Series
30 minutes. Mondays. Premiere date: 5/16/77. Last show: 9/5/77. Half-hour comedy pilots plus several "Blansky's Beauties" episodes and two "Holmes & Yoyo" episodes. Pilots aired: "Bumpers," "The Chopped Liver Brothers," "Constantinople," "Great Day," "MacNamara's Band," "Mason," "The Primary English Class," "Sheehy and the Supreme Machine," "Stick Around," "Walkin' Walter." (*See* individual titles for credits.)

7 **The ABC Monday Night Movie** ABC
Program Type Feature Film Series – TV Movie Series
Times vary. Mondays. Premiere date: 1/3/77. Last show: 7/18/77. Irregularly scheduled made-for-television dramas and commercially released motion pictures. The television films are: "Charlie's Angels" (pilot), "Green Eyes," "How the West Was Won," "Roger & Harry." (*See* individual titles for credits.) The commercially released motion pictures are: "From Russia With Love" (1963) shown 2/21/77 and "The Man With the Golden Gun" (1974) shown 1/10/77.

8 **ABC News Closeup** ABC
Program Type Documentary/Informational Series
60 minutes each. Premiere date: 10/18/73. Fourth season premiere: 12/16/76. Ten documentary specials shown during the 1976–77 season: "ABC News Closeup—Cuba: The Castro Generation," "ABC News Closeup—Divorce: For Better Or For Worse," "ABC News Closeup: The Equality Conflict," ABC News Closeup—ERA: The War Between the Women," "ABC News Closeup: Justice on Trial," "ABC News Closeup: Madness and Medicine," "ABC News Closeup—Nuclear Power: Pro & Con," "ABC News Closeup: On Camera," "ABC News Closeup—Sex For Sale: The Urban Battleground," "ABC News Closeup: What's Happened Since . . ." (*See* individual titles for credits.)

9 **ABC News Closeup—Cuba: The Castro Generation**
ABC News Closeup ABC
Program Type Documentary/Informational Special
60 minutes. Premiere date: 3/4/77. A report on life in Cuba under Fidel Castro.
Producer Arthur Holch
Company ABC News
Director Arthur Holch
Writer Arthur Holch
Cinematographers Erik Durschmied, Steve Stanford
Film Editors Walter Essenfeld, Harold Popik
Special Consultant Fred Ward
Correspondent/Commentator Howard K. Smith

10 **ABC News Closeup—Divorce: For Better Or For Worse**
ABC News Closeup ABC
Program Type Documentary/Informational Special
60 minutes. Premiere date: 12/16/76. An examination of divorce and the divorce business.
Producer James Benjamin
Company ABC News
Director James Benjamin
Writer James Benjamin
Cinematographers William Birch, Bryan Anderson, Larry Mitchell
Film Editor Nils Rasmussen
Correspondents Steve Bell, Margaret Osmer

11 **ABC News Closeup: The Equality Conflict**
ABC News Closeup ABC
Program Type Documentary/Informational Special
60 minutes. Premiere date: 8/27/77. An examination of legal and moral problems arising from "reverse discrimination."
Producer Stephen Fleischman
Company ABC News
Director Stephen Fleischman
Writers Stephen Fleischman, Debra Kram
Cinematographers Terry Morrison, Dick Mingalone
Film Editors Nils Rasmussen, Victor Kanefsky
Correspondent Frank Reynolds

12 **ABC News Closeup—ERA: The War Between the Women**
ABC News Closeup ABC
Program Type Documentary/Informational Special
60 minutes. Premiere date: 1/22/77. An examination of the support for and opposition to the Equal Rights Amendment.
Producer Stephen Fleischman
Company ABC News
Director Stephen Fleischman
Writer Stephen Fleischman
Cinematographers Murray Alvey, Larry Johnson, Terry Morrison, Brianne Murphy, Chuck Pharris
Film Editors Zina Voynow, Alison Berkley
Correspondent/Commentator Howard K. Smith

13 **ABC News Closeup: Justice on Trial**
ABC News Closeup ABC
Program Type Documentary/Informational Special
60 minutes. Premiere date: 1/7/77. An investigative report on the inequities in criminal sentencing around the country. A segment from the play "Short Eyes" by Miguel Pinero performed by the Los Angeles Actors Theatre.
Producer Richard Gerdau
Company ABC News
Director Richard Gerdau
Writer Richard Gerdau
Cinematographers Dick Roy, Bryan Anderson, Murray Alvey
Film Editor Molly Smollett
Correspondent/Commentator Howard K. Smith

14 **ABC News Closeup: Madness and Medicine**
ABC News Closeup ABC
Program Type Documentary/Informational Special
60 minutes. Premiere date: 5/26/77. A look at three major methods of treatment of the mentally ill: drugs, electric shock and psychosurgery.
Producer Phil Lewis
Company ABC News
Director Phil Lewis
Writers Phil Lewis, Anne Pedersen
Cinematographers Bryan Anderson, Sidney Dobish, Bob Cirace
Film Editor Samuel Cohen
Correspondent/Commentator Howard K. Smith

15 **ABC News Closeup—Nuclear Power: Pro & Con**
ABC News Closeup ABC
Program Type Documentary/Informational Special
60 minutes. Premiere date: 6/7/77. Two-part program examining the arguments in favor of nuclear power and those against it.

The Case For Nuclear Power
Producer James Benjamin
Company ABC News
Director James Benjamin
Writers James Benjamin, Jules Bergman
Cinematographer William Birch
Film Editor Walter Essenfeld
Correspondent/Commentator Howard K. Smith
Reporter Jules Bergman

The Case Against Nuclear Power
Producer Tony Batten
Company ABC News
Director Tony Batten
Writers Tony Batten, Christopher Koch
Cinematographer Bryan Anderson
Film Editor Harold Popik
Researchers Betty Odabashian, Susan Steiger
Correspondent/Commentator Howard K. Smith
Reporter Roger Peterson

16 **ABC News Closeup: On Camera**
ABC News Closeup ABC
Program Type Documentary/Informational Special
60 minutes. Premiere date: 7/21/77. Three major stories: the people of Enewetak, sufferers of Joseph's Disease and Michael Price of the Goodspeed Opera House plus a short look at flag-raising at the U.S. Capitol.
Senior Producer William Peters
Producers William Peters, Ene Riisna, Aram Boyajian
Company ABC News
Director Jack Sameth
Writers William Peters, Peter Jennings
Correspondents Peter Jennings, Sandy Hill

17 **ABC News Closeup—Sex For Sale: The Urban Battleground**
ABC News Closeup ABC
Program Type Documentary/Informational Special
60 minutes. Premiere date: 4/22/77. An investigation of sex businesses and their impact on American cities.
Producer Pamela Hill
Company ABC News
Director Pamela Hill
Writer Pamela Hill
Cinematographers Bryan Anderson, Richard Kuhne
Film Editors James Flanagan, Nils Rasmussen
Correspondent/Commentator Howard K. Smith
Reporter James Walker

18 **ABC News Closeup: What's Happened Since . . .**
ABC News Closeup ABC
Program Type Documentary/Informational Special
60 minutes. Premiere date: 8/4/77. Follow-up report to eight stories seen on previous "ABC News Closeups" from October 1973-January 1977.
Producer Alice Herb
Company ABC News
Director Alice Herb
Writer Alice Herb
Cinematographers Sidney Dobish, Richard V. Norling
Film Editor Henriette Huehne
Researcher Betty Odabashian
Correspondent/Commentator Howard K. Smith

ABC News With Harry Reasoner *see* ABC Evening News With Harry Reasoner and Barbara Walters

19 **ABC Newsbrief** ABC
Program Type News Series
60 seconds. Daily. Premiere date: 3/14/77. Evening report from Washington, D.C. covering late-breaking news developments.
Producer Steve Steinberg
Company ABC News
Anchor Tom Jarriel

20 **ABC Newsbrief (Daytime)** ABC
Program Type News Series
60 seconds. Monday-Fridays. Premiere date: 4/25/77. Afternoon report from Washington, D.C. covering latebreaking news.
Company ABC News
Anchors Steve Bell (Monday-Wednesday), Tom Jarriel (Thursday-Friday)

21 **ABC Saturday News With Ted Koppel** ABC
Program Type News Series
30 minutes. Saturdays. Premiere date: 7/5/75. Continuous. Regular features: "Saturday Closeup, " "Perspective."
Senior Producer Phil Bergman
Company ABC News
Anchor Ted Koppel

22 **ABC Short Story Specials** ABC
Program Type Children's Series
30 minutes. Saturdays. Premiere date: 1/29/77. Adaptations of short stories for young people. Four stories aired during the 1976-77 season: "The Haunted Trailer," "Homer and the Wacky Doughnut Machine," "My Dear Uncle Sherlock," "Valentine's Second Chance." (*See* individual titles for credits.)

23 **The ABC Sunday Night Movie** ABC
Program Type Feature Film Series – TV Movie Series
90 minutes/two hours (occasionally longer). Sundays. Season premiere: 9/19/76. A combination of feature films and made-for-television movies. The TV movies are: "The Boy in the Plastic Bubble," "Good Against Evil," "Having Babies," "How the West Was Won," "Little Ladies of the Night," "Lucan," "Murder at the World Series," "Operation Petticoat," "Secrets," "21 Hours at Munich." (*See* individual titles for credits.) The feature films are: "Airport" (1970) shown 5/1/77, "The Bridge at Remagen" (1969) shown 7/24/77, "Catch-22" (1970) shown 12/5/76, "Diamonds Are Forever" (1971) shown 12/26/76, "Emperor of the North" (1973) shown 8/7/77, "A Fistful of Dollars" (1967) shown 8/28/77, "For a Few Dollars More" (1967) shown 4/24/77, "The Gambler" (1974) shown 3/6/77, "High Plains Drifter" (1973) shown 5/15/77, "I Never Sang For My Father" (1970) shown 6/19/77, "Jeremiah Johnson" (1972) shown 12/19/76, "JW Coop" (1971) shown 7/31/77, "Lawrence of Arabia" (1962) shown 8/21/77, "Little Fauss and Big Halsy (1970) shown 8/14/77, "Live and Let Die" (1973) shown 10/31/76, "The Long Goodbye" (1973) shown 7/17/77, "Paper Chase" (1974) shown 6/26/77, "Patton" (1970) shown 11/14/76, "The Reincarnation of Peter Proud" (1975) shown 1/9/77, "The Scalphunters" (1968) shown 7/10/77, "The Seven-Ups" (1974) shown 12/12/76, "Sky Terror" (1972—released theatrically as "Skyjacked") shown 9/19/76, "Sleuth" (1973) shown 7/3/77, "The Stepford Wives" (1975) shown 10/24/76, "Suicide Run" (1970) shown 6/12/77, "Survive!" (1976) shown 2/27/77, "The Ten Commandments" (1957) shown 4/10/77, "Thunderbolt and Lightfoot" (1974) shown 11/21/76, "The Way We Were" (1973) shown 10/3/76, "W. W. and the Dixie Dancekings" (1974) shown 1/2/77, "You Only Live Twice" (1967) shown 4/3/77.

24 **ABC Thanksgiving Funshine Festival** ABC
Program Type Children's Special
Five hours. Premiere date: 11/25/76. A special Thanksgiving Day lineup of the regular ABC Saturday shows for children: "The Tom & Jerry/Grape Ape/Mumbly Show," "Jabberjaw," "The Scooby Doo/Dynomutt Hour," "The Krofft Supershow," and "Junior Almost Anything Goes." (*See* individual titles for credits.)

Original material produced on location at Kings Island entertainment center.
Executive Producers William Hanna, Joseph Barbera
Company Hanna-Barbera Productions
Director Lawrence Einhorn
Writers Duane Poole, Dick Robbins
Host Soupy Sales

25 **ABC Theatre** ABC
Program Type Dramatic Special
Two specials seen during the 1976-77 season: "Eleanor and Franklin: The White House Years" and "Green Eyes." (*See* individual titles for credits.)

26 **The ABC Tuesday Night Movie** ABC
Program Type Feature Film Series – TV Movie Series
Two hours. Tuesdays. Premiere date: 6/28/77. Last show: 8/30/77. A combination of made-for-television films and theatrically released motion pictures. The TV films are: "Fantasy Island," "Griffin and Phoenix: A Love Story," "Having Babies," "Love Boat II," "Smash-Up on Interstate 5." (*See* individual titles for credits.) The theatrically released motion pictures are: "For Pete's Sake" (1974) shown 8/16/77, "Goodbye, Columbus" (1969) shown 8/2/77, "Love Story" (1970) shown 7/19/77, "Sleeper" (1973) shown 7/12/77, "The Wrecking Crew" (1968) shown 7/26/77.

27 **ABC Weekend News** ABC
Program Type News Series
15 minutes. Saturdays and Sundays. Late night broadcasts anchored on Saturdays at first by various national and local newscasters, then by Tom Jarriel and on Sundays by Bill Beutel.
Senior Producer Phil Bergman
Producer Marge Lipton
Company ABC News
Anchors Tom Jarriel, Bill Beutel

28 **ABC's Championship Auto Racing** ABC
Program Type Sports Special
Live coverage of two stock car races: the Daytona "500" and the Atlanta "500." Coverage of the Trenton "200" aired as part of "ABC's Wide World of Sports"; the Indianapolis "500" seen as special (*see* credits.)

Daytona "500"
90 minutes. Live coverage of the 19th annual Daytona "500" 2/20/77.
Executive Producer Roone Arledge
Producer Chet Forte
Company ABC Sports
Director Roger Goodman
Announcer Jim McKay
Expert Commentators Chris Economaki, Jackie Stewart

Atlanta "500"
60 minutes. Live coverage of the Atlanta "500" 3/20/77.
Executive Producer Roone Arledge
Producer Chet Forte
Company ABC Sports
Director Don Ohlmeyer
Announcer Keith Jackson
Expert Commentators Chris Economaki, Jackie Stewart

29 **ABC's Monday Night Baseball** ABC
Program Type Limited Sports Series
18 live primary and secondary telecasts of major league baseball. Monday nights. Premiere date: 4/12/76. Second season premiere: 4/11/77. Produced through the end of the regular baseball season in September 1977.
Executive Producer Roone Arledge
Producers Chuck Howard, Dennis Lewin, Bob Goodrich, Terry O'Neil, Joe Aceti
Company ABC Sports
Directors Chet Forte, Roger Goodman, Joe Aceti, Lou Volpicelli, Larry Kamm
Play-By-Play Announcers Keith Jackson, Al Michaels, Warner Wolf
Expert Commentators Bob Uecker, Bill White, Bob Gibson, Howard Cosell

30 **ABC's Wide World of Sports** ABC
Program Type Sports Series
90 minutes. Saturdays (year round)/Sundays (winter-spring). Saturday premiere date: 4/29/61. Continuous. Fourth Sunday premiere. 1/2/77. Last Sunday show: 4/24/77. Coverage of all types of sports events held throughout the world, including the "World Series of Auto Racing," the Little League Baseball World Series, the Hula Bowl Classic and the Pro Football Hall of Fame Game.
Executive Producer Roone Arledge
Coordinating Producer Dennis Lewin
Producers Various
Company ABC Sports
Directors Various
Host Jim McKay
Announcers Howard Cosell, Bill Flemming, Frank Gifford, Keith Jackson, Jim Lampley, Jim McKay, Al Michaels, Bud Palmer, Chris Schenkel, Jackie Stewart, Warner Wolf

31 **About Us: A Deep South Portrait** PBS
Program Type Documentary/Informational

About Us: A Deep South Portrait
Continued

Special

60 minutes. Premiere date: 7/19/77. Special focusing on the changes in the South. Filmed in eight southern states as part of an Auburn University project on "Technology, Human Values and the Southern Future." Presented by the Alabama Public Television Network. Funding provided in part by the National Endowment for the Humanities.

Executive Producers Dr. W. David Lewis, Dr. B. Eugene Griessman
Producer Roger Hagan
Company Roger Hagan and Associates
Director Roger Hagan
Writer Roger Hagan
Cinematographer Roger Hagan
Narrator Roger Hagan

32 Academy Awards ABC
Program Type Parades/Pageants/Awards Special

Live coverage of the 49th annual Awards of the Academy of Motion Picture Arts and Sciences 3/28/77 from the Dorothy Chandler Pavilion of the Los Angeles Music Center.

Producer William Friedkin
Company The Academy of Motion Picture Arts and Sciences
Director Marty Pasetta
Writers Hal Kanter, Ray Bradbury
Musical Director Bill Conti
Choreographer Donald McKayle
Costume Designer Theoni V. Aldredge
Masters of Ceremonies Warren Beatty, Ellen Burstyn, Jane Fonda, Richard Pryor
Presenters Pearl Bailey, James Caan, Neil Diamond, Tamara Dobson, Marty Feldman, Louise Fletcher, Lillian Hellman, William Holden, Marthe Keller, Norman Mailer, Jeanne Moreau, Jack Nicholson, Tatum O'Neal, Roy Scheider, Red Skelton, Sylvester Stallone, Cicely Tyson, Liv Ullmann
Performers Eddie Albert, Ann-Margret, Barbra Streisand, Tom Jones, Ben Vereen, Lea Vivante

33 Academy of Country Music Awards
Thursday Night Special ABC

Program Type Parades/Pageants/Awards Special

90 minutes. Premiere date: 2/24/77. 12th annual country music awards taped at the Shrine Auditorium in Los Angeles 2/27/77.

Hosts Pat Boone, Patti Page, Jerry Reed
Presenters LeVar Burton, Ren Woods, Carol Channing, Donny Most, Anson Williams, Shelly Novack, Abe Vigoda, Connie Stevens, Lynne Marta, Joe Campanella, Claude Akins, Marty Robbins, Larry Mahan, T. G. Shepherd, Larry Gatlin, Freddie Hart, Kenny Rogers, Loretta Lynn
Performers Jerry Reed, Pat Boone, Patti Page, Freddy Fender, Mickey Gilley, Don Williams, Donna Fargo, Mel Tillis, Crystal Gayle

34 The Adams Chronicles PBS
Program Type Limited Series

60 minutes. Premiere date: 1/20/76. Repeats shown Mondays as of 9/20/76. 13-part series dramatizing the Adams family from 1750-1900. Conceived and created by Virginia Kassel with the collaboration of The Adams Papers, the Massachusetts Historical Society and the Harvard University Press. Series made possible by grants from the National Endowment for the Humanities, the Andrew W. Mellon Foundation and the Atlantic Richfield Company. Captioned for the hearing impaired. (Cast list in alphabetical order.)

Executive Producer Jac Venza
Producers Various
Company WNET-TV/New York
Directors Various
Story Editor Anne Howard Bailey
Writers Various
Script Consultant Jacqueline Babbin
Coordinating Producer Robert Costello

CAST

Andrew Jackson	Wesley Addy
Charles Francis Adams	John Beal
John Quincy Adams (age 36–48)	David Birney
Henry Adams	Peter Brandon
Samuel Adams	W. B. Brydon
Mrs. Charles Francis Adams	Nancy Coleman
Abigail Adams (age 44–73)	Leora Dana
John Quincy Adams (age 50–81)	William Daniels
John Hancock	Curt Dawson
John Adams	George Grizzard
Henry Clay	George Hearn
Jay Gould	Paul Hecht
George Washington	David Hooks
Jeremiah Gridley	John Houseman
Tsar Alexander I	Christopher Lloyd
Abigail Adams II	Lisa Lucas
Mrs. Smith	Nancy Marchand
Mrs. Henry Adams	Gilmer McCormick
Abraham Lincoln	Stephen D. Newman
Mrs. John Quincy Adams	Pamela Payton-Wright
John Quincy Adams II	Nicholas Pryor
Charles Francis Adams II	Charles Siebert
Thomas Jefferson	Albert Stratton
Alexander Hamilton	Jeremiah Sullivan
Benjamin Franklin	Robert Symonds
Brooks Adams	Charles Tenney
King George III	John Tillinger
Abigail Adams (age 18–44)	Kathryn Walker

The Adventures of Frontier Fremont *see* NBC Movie of the Week

35 **Aetna World Cup Tennis** PBS
Program Type Sports Special
Four hours each. Live coverage of singles and doubles matches 3/12/77 and 3/13/77 between the United States and Australia. Program made possible by a grant from United Technologies.
Producers Ken Horseman, Greg Harney
Company Connecticut Public Television
Director Greg Harney
Announcers Donald Dell, Bud Collins

36 **AFC Championship Game** NBC
Program Type Sports Special
Live coverage of the AFC championship between the Pittsburgh Steelers and the Oakland Raiders from the Oakland-Alameda Coliseum 12/26/76.
Producers Ted Nathanson, George Finkel
Company NBC Sports
Director Ted Nathanson
Announcer Curt Gowdy
Analyst Don Meredith

37 **AFC Play-Offs (Game I)** NBC
Program Type Sports Special
Live coverage of the play-off game between the Oakland Raiders and the New England Patriots from Oakland, Calif. 12/18/76.
Company NBC Sports
Announcer Curt Gowdy
Analyst Don Meredith

38 **AFC Play-Offs (Game II)** NBC
Program Type Sports Special
Live coverage of the play-off game between the Pittsburgh Steelers and the Baltimore Colts in Baltimore 12/19/76.
Company NBC Sports
Announcer Jim Simpson
Analyst John Brodie

39 **The African Queen** CBS
Program Type Dramatic Special
60 minutes. Premiere date: 3/18/77. Adventure-drama set in Africa during World War I based on the 1951 motion picture version of the C. M. Forester story. Music by John Murtaugh. Filmed on location in the Florida Everglades.
Executive Producer Mark Carliner
Producer Leonard B. Kaufman
Company Mark Carliner Productions in association with Viacom
Director Richard Sarafian
Writer Irving G. Neiman
Art Director Don Ivey

CAST

Charlie Allnot .... Warren Oates
Rosie Sayer .... Mariette Hartley
Jogana .... Johnny Sekka
Kaninu .... Tyrone Jackson
Sgt. Abuttu .... Clarence Thomas
Lt. Biedemeyer .... Wolf Roth
Pvt. Heinke .... Frank Schuller
Maj. Strauss .... Albert Paulsen

40 **Africa's Defiant White Tribe**
NBC Reports NBC
Program Type Documentary/Informational Special
60 minutes. Premiere date: 7/27/77. An examination of the racial situation in South Africa.
Producer Robert Rogers
Company NBC News
Director Robert Rogers
Writers Garrick Utley, Robert Rogers
Cinematographer Richard V. Norling
Film Editor Desmond McElroy
Reporter Garrick Utley

41 **After Hours: From Janice, John, Mary and Michael, With Love** CBS
Program Type Music/Dance Special
60 minutes. Premiere date: 12/8/76. Afternoon special of music and dance. Special musical material by Billy Barnes.
Producer John Conboy
Company CBS Television Network
Director Bill Glenn
Musical Director John Berkman
Choreographer Carl Jablonski
Costume Designer Pete Menefee
Art Director James J. Agazzi
Stars Janice Lynde, John McCook, Michael Nouri, Mary Stuart

42 **After Hours: Getting To Know Us** CBS
Program Type Music/Dance Special
60 minutes. Premiere date: 5/26/77. Second musical-variety show with daytime television stars. Special musical material by Billy Barnes.
Producer Bob Henry
Company CBS Television Network
Director Bob Henry
Writers Ed Hider, Stephen Spears
Musical Director Nick Perito
Choreographer Bob Thompson
Costume Designer Bill Belew
Art Director Romain Johnston
Stars Michael Allinson, Meg Bennett, David Hasselhoff, Kathryn Hays, Don Stewart, Tudi Wiggins

Against a Crooked Sky *see* NBC Saturday Night at the Movies

43 **The Age of Uncertainty** PBS
Program Type Educational/Cultural Series
60 minutes. Thursdays. Premiere date: 5/19/77. 13-part series exploring 200 years of political economics and social thought. Regular feature: rebuttal essay called "Another View" seen at the conclusion of each episode. Programs made possible by grants from Public Television Stations, the Ford Foundation and the Corporation for Public Broadcasting.
Executive Producer Adrian Malone
Senior Producer Dick Gilling
Producers David Kennard, Mick Jackson
Company The British Broadcasting Corporation, KCET-TV/Los Angeles, the Canadian Broadcasting Corporation and the Ontario Educational Communications Authority
Writer John Kenneth Galbraith
Narrator John Kenneth Galbraith
Project Coordinator Greg Andorfer

44 **Agronsky at Large** PBS
Program Type Public Affairs Series
30 minutes. Fridays. Premiere date: 11/5/76. (60-minute show). Interviews with political figures and newsworthy personalities from around the world. Series made possible by grants from Public Television Public Affairs Fund, the European Economic Community and the German Marshall Fund of the United States.
Producer John Larkin
Company WETA-TV/Washington
Host Martin Agronsky

45 **Ah, Wilderness!**
Theater in America/Great Performances PBS
Program Type Dramatic Special
Two hours. Premiere date: 10/13/76. The Long Wharf Theatre of New Haven in a production of the 1932 comedy by Eugene O'Neill about an adolescent boy at a turn-of-the-century Fourth of July. Program made possible by grants from Exxon Corporation, the Corporation for Public Broadcasting, the Ford Foundation and Public Television Stations.
Executive Producer Jac Venza
Producer Lindsay Law
Company WNET-TV/New York
Director Arvin Brown
Writer Eugene O'Neill

CAST

Richard .... Richard Backus
Nat .... William Swetland
Essie .... Geraldine Fitzgerald
Sid .... John Braden
Lily .... Joyce Ebert
Belle .... Suzanne Lederer
Muriel .... Swoosie Kurtz
Arthur .... Victor Garber
Mildred .... Christina Whitmore
Tommy .... Anthony Petrillo
Nora .... Linda Hunt
McComber .... Ralph Drischell
Salesman .... Don Gantry
Bartender .... Stephen Mendillo
Wint Selby .... Sean Griffin

46 **Ailey Celebrates Ellington**
The CBS Festival of Lively Arts for Young People CBS
Program Type Children's Special
60 minutes. Premiere date: 11/28/74. Repeat date: 4/23/77. Six modern dance works inspired by the music of Duke Ellington. Narration written by Stanley Dance.
Executive Producer Herman Krawitz
Producer Robert Weiner
Company Jodav and Ring-Ting-A-Ling Productions
Director Joshua White
Writer Stanley Dance
Choreographer Alvin Ailey
Host Gladys Knight
Guest Artists Fred Benjamin, Marleane Furtick
Dancers Alvin Ailey American Dance Center Repertory Workshop Dancers

Airport *see* The ABC Sunday Night Movie

Airport 1975 *see* NBC Monday Night at the Movies/NBC Saturday Night at the Movies

The Alamo *see* CBS Special Film Presentations

47 **Alan King Tennis Classic at Caesars Palace** ABC
Program Type Sports Special
Live coverage of the tournament from Caesars Palace in Las Vegas, Nev. 4/30/77 and 5/1/77.
Executive Producer Roone Arledge
Producer Chet Forte
Company ABC Sports
Director Roger Goodman
Host Howard Cosell
Expert Commentators Arthur Ashe, Pancho Gonzalez

48 **Alan King's Final Warning** ABC
Program Type Comedy Special
60 minutes. Premiere date: 4/12/77. Comedy sketches about survival in the modern world. Sound effects by Ralph Emerson.
Executive Producers Alan King, Rupert Hitzig
Company King-Hitzig Productions
Director Bill Persky

Writers Harry Crane, George Bloom, Jeremy Stevens, Tom Moore, Alan King, Bill Persky
Costume Designer Frank Thompson
Art Director Charles Lisanby
Star Alan King
Guest Stars Angie Dickinson, Abe Vigoda, Don Knotts, Linda Lavin
Additional Cast Arlene Golonka, Bella Bruck, Ed Barth, Sam Denoff, Elliott Reed, Alex Rocco, John Lupton, Darryl Hickman, Phoebe Dorin, Dolores Morris

49 **Alan King's Pleasures of Rome**
Thursday Night Special ABC
Program Type Documentary/Informational Special
90 minutes. Premiere date: 3/24/77. A tour of Rome with famous residents and guests.
Executive Producer Alan King
Producer Rupert Hitzig
Company A King-Hitzig Production
Director Jerry Weisman
Host Alan King

Alexander Nevsky *see* PBS Movie Theater

50 **Alexander: The Other Side of Dawn**
NBC Monday Night at the Movies NBC
Program Type TV Movie
Two hours. Premiere date: 5/16/77. Sequel to "Dawn: Portrait of a Teenage Runaway" (*see* credits). Based on a story by Walter Dallenbach and Dalene Young. Music by Fred Karlin.
Executive Producer Douglas S. Cramer
Producer W. L. Baumes
Company Douglas Cramer Productions in association with NBC-TV
Director John Erman
Writer Walter Dallenbach
Art Director Carl Anderson

CAST

Alexander .... Leigh J. McCloskey
Dawn .... Eve Plumb
Ray Church .... Earl Holliman
Myra .... Juliet Mills
Landlady .... Jean Hagen
Eddie .... Lonny Chapman
Charles .... Alan Feinstein
Buddy .... Asher Brauner

Ali the Fighter *see* NBC Night at the Movies

51 **Alice** CBS
Program Type Comedy Series
30 minutes. Wednesdays/Saturdays (as of 11/6/76). Premiere date: 9/29/76. Comedy about a would-be-singer working as a waitress in Mel's Cafe outside Phoenix. Based on the 1974 film "Alice Doesn't Live Here Any More" by Robert Getchell. Pilot for series aired 8/31/76.
Executive Producers William P. D'Angelo, Harvey Bullock, R. S. Allen
Producer Bruce Johnson
Company Warner Bros. Television
Directors Various
Executive Story Editor Arnold Kane
Story Editor Lloyd Garver
Writers Various
Art Director Scott Ritenour

CAST

Alice Hyatt .... Linda Lavin
Mel .... Vic Tayback
Flo .... Polly Holliday
Vera .... Beth Howland
Tommy Hyatt .... Philip McKeon

52 **Alice Through the Looking Glass**
Piccadilly Circus PBS
Program Type Dramatic Special
90 minutes. Premiere date: 11/25/76. Adaptation of the classic novel by Lewis Carroll with live action and animation based on the drawings of Sir John Tenniel. Music by Herbert Chappell. Presented by WGBH-TV/Boston, produced by Joan Sullivan, and made possible by a grant from Mobil Oil Corporation.
Producer Rosemary Hill
Company MCA Television and the British Broadcasting Corporation
Director James MacTaggart
Writer James MacTaggart
Host Jeremy Brett

CAST

Alice .... Sarah Sutton
White Queen .... Brenda Bruce
White King .... Richard Pearson
Red Queen .... Judy Parfitt
Red King .... John Scott Martin
White Knight .... Geoffrey Bayldon
Humpty Dumpty .... Freddie Jones
Haigha .... Stephen Moore
Hatta .... Doughas Milvain
Tweedledum .... Anthony Collin
Tweedledee .... Raymond Mason
Walrus .... Bruce Purchase
Carpenter .... Stanley Lebor
Unicorn .... Nicholas Jones
Lion .... Robin Wentworth
Gnat .... Ian Trigger
Frog .... Jeffrey Segal
Tiger Lily .... June Watson
Rose .... Vivienne Moore
Daisy .... Samantha Gate
Another Daisy .... Sylvia O'Donnell
Beamish Boy .... Richard Speight

53 All Creatures Great and Small
Hallmark Hall of Fame/All Specials Night NBC

Program Type Dramatic Special
90 minutes. Premiere date: 2/4/75. Repeat date: 3/29/77. Dramatization of the veterinary experiences of James Herriot adapted from his book of the same name. Filmed on location in Yorkshire. Music composed by Wilfred Josephs.
Producers David Susskind, Duane C. Bogie
Company Talent Associates Ltd. in association with FCB Productions
Director Claude Whatham
Writer Hugh Whitemore

CAST

James Herriot	Simon Ward
Siegfried Farnon	Anthony Hopkins
Helen Alderson	Lisa Harrow
Tristan Farnon	Brian Stirner
Soames	T. P. McKenna
Mr. Alderson	John Collin
Mrs. Harbottle	Brenda Bruce
Dean	Burt Palmer
Connie	Jane Collins

54 All in the Family CBS
Program Type Comedy Series
30 minutes. Wednesdays/Saturdays (as of 11/6/76). Premiere date: 1/12/71. Seventh season premiere: 9/22/76 (60-minute episode). Comedy about a working-class bigot set in Queens, N.Y. Based on "Till Death Do Us Part" created for the British Broadcasting Corporation by Johnny Speight. Developed by Norman Lear. "Those Were the Days" by Lee Adams and Charles Strouse; "Remembering You" by Roger Kellaway and Carroll O'Connor.
Executive Producer Mort Lachman
Producer Milt Josefsberg
Company Tandem Productions, Inc.
Director Paul Bogart
Executive Story Editors Mel Tolkin, Larry Rhine
Story Editors Douglas Arango, Phil Doran
Writers Various
Script Supervisors Milt Josefsberg, Mort Lachman

CAST

Archie Bunker	Carroll O'Connor
Edith Bunker	Jean Stapleton
Mike Stivic	Rob Reiner
Gloria Stivic	Sally Struthers
Teresa Betancourt	Liz Torres

55 All in the Family (Daytime) CBS
Program Type Comedy Series
30 minutes. Mondays–Fridays. Premiere date: 12/1/75. Continuous. Morning reruns of evening series. For credit information, *see* "All in the Family."

56 All My Children ABC
Program Type Daytime Drama Series
30 minutes/60 minutes (as of 4/25/77). Mondays–Fridays. Premiere date: 1/5/70. Continuous. Created by Agnes Nixon. Set in Pine Valley, U.S.A.; story concentrates on the Martin and Tyler families. Julia Barr replaced Elissa Leeds as Brooke English. Cast list is alphabetical.
Producer Bud Kloss
Company Creative Horizons
Directors Del Hughes, Henry Kaplan
Head Writer Agnes Nixon
Writers Wisner Washam, Kathryn McCabe, Mary K. Wells, Jack Wood

CAST

Ann Tyler Martin	Judith Barcroft
Brooke English	Julia Barr
Philip Brent	Nick Benedict
Kate Martin	Kay Campbell
Dr. Franklin Grant	John Danelle
Caroline Murray	Pat Dixon
Donna Beck	Candice Early
Ruth Martin	Mary Fickett
Benny Sago	Larry Fleischman
Dr. Charles Tyler	Hugh Franklin
David Thornton	Paul Gleason
Tara Martin Brent	Karen Gorney
Clay Watson	Reuben Green
Mona Kane	Frances Heflin
Myrtle Lum	Eileen Herlie
Kitty Tyler	Francesca James
Nick Davis	Lawrence Keith
Dan Kennicott	Daren Kelly
Mark Dalton	Mark LaMura
Philip Tyler	Brian Lima
Erica Kane Brent	Susan Lucci
Dr. Joe Martin	Ray MacDonnell
Paul Martin	William Mooney
Dr. Jeff Martin	Robert Perault
Dr. Christina Karras	Robin Strasser
Chuck Tyler	Richard Van Vleet
Phoebe Tyler	Ruth Warrick
Lincoln Tyler	Peter White
Nancy Grant	Lisa Wilkinson

57 All Specials Night/Multi-Special Night NBC
Program Type Miscellaneous Series
Various specials ranging from dramas to music/comedy/variety shows to theatrically released motion pictures preempting most or all regular primetime programming. The motion pictures are: "Give 'Em Hell, Harry!" (1975) shown 1/20/77 and introduced by Mrs. Margaret Truman Daniel and "Godzilla Vs. Megalon" (1976) shown in a specially edited version 3/15/77 and introduced by John Belushi. Specials seen during the 1976–77 season are: "Africa's Defiant White Tribe," "All Creatures Great and Small," "The All-Star Gong Show Special," "Ann-Margret . . . Rhinestone Cowgirl," "The Chevy Chase Show," "Dead of Night," "Dean Martin Celebrity Roast: Danny Thomas," "The First Easter Rabbit," "Highlights of Ringling Bros. and Bar-

num & Bailey Circus," "The John Davidson Christmas Show," "Johnny, We Hardly Knew Ye," "King of the Beasts," "The Last Voyage of the Argo Merchant," "The Little Drummer Boy Book II," "Look Out World," "The Mac Davis Christmas Special . . . When I Grow Up," "Mac Davis . . . Sounds Like Home," "MONSTERS! Mysteries or Myths?" "The Parenthood Game," "Perry Como's Christmas in Austria," "The Richard Pryor Special?" "Texaco Presents Bob Hope's Comedy Christmas Special," "Tut: The Boy King." (*See* individual titles for credits.)

58 **All-Star Game** NBC
Program Type Sports Special
Live coverage of the 48th annual baseball all-star game from Yankee Stadium in New York City 7/19/77.
Executive Producer Scotty Connal
Producer Roy Hammerman
Company NBC Sports
Director Harry Coyle
Announcers Joe Garagiola, Tony Kubek

59 **The All-Star Gong Show Special**
All-Specials Night NBC
Program Type Game/Audience Participation Special
60 minutes. Premiere date: 4/26/77. Special nighttime version of the daily "Gong Show" with guest stars and 26 acts seen on the daytime show.
Executive Producer Chuck Barris
Producer Gene Banks
Company Chuck Barris Productions
Director John Dorsey
Musical Director Milton Delugg
Host Chuck Barris
Guest Stars Tony Randall, Rosey Grier, Aretha Franklin, Ray Charles, Ben Vereen, Sen. Alan Cranston, UCLA Marching Band
Celebrity Panel Arte Johnson, Jamie Farr, Jaye P. Morgan

60 **All Star Softball** CBS
Program Type Sports Special
60 minutes. Premiere date: 2/19/77. Second annual All Star Softball game between the National and American Leagues at Innisbrook Resort, Florida.
Producer Perry Smith
Company CBS Network Sports
Director Bernie Hoffman
Announcer Vin Scully
Expert Analyst Frank Robinson
Umpire Brent Musburger
Interviewer Phyllis George

61 **All-Star Swing Festival** PBS
Program Type Music/Dance Special
60 minutes. Premiere date: 11/29/72 (on NBC). Repeat dates (on PBS): 3/77 and 8/77. Peabody Award-winning jazz concert special taped in October 1972 at Lincoln Center in New York City. Program made possible by a grant from Westinghouse Corporation.
Executive Producers Burt Rosen, David Winters
Producers Bernard Rothman, Jack Wohl
Director Grey Lockwood
Writer Donald Ross
Host Doc Severinsen
Guest Stars Duke Ellington, Count Basie, Ella Fitzgerald, Benny Goodman, Lionel Hampton, Gene Krupa, Dizzy Gillespie, Bobby Hackett, Teddy Wilson, Max Kaminsky, Joe Williams, the Dave Brubeck Quartet, Willie "The Lion" Smith, Paul Desmond, Earl "Fatha" Hines, Barney Bigard, Tyree Glenn, Jimmy Hamilton, Cootie Williams, Arvell Shaw, Barrett Deems, Tommy Flanagan, Harry Carney, Paul Gonsalves

62 **An All-Star Tribute to John Wayne**
ABC
Program Type Music/Comedy/Variety Special
60 minutes. Premiere date: 11/26/76. A tribute to the actor under the auspices of Variety Clubs International.
Producer Paul W. Keyes
Co-Producer Marc London
Company A Paul W. Keyes Production
Director Dick McDonough
Writers Paul W. Keyes, Marc London
Musical Director Nelson Riddle
Art Directors E. Jay Krause, Bob Keene
Host Frank Sinatra
Guest of Honor John Wayne
Guest Stars Charles Bronson, John Byner, Glen Campbell, Sammy Davis, Jr., Angie Dickinson, Monty Hall, Bob Hope, Ron Howard, Dick Martin, Lee Marvin, Maureen O'Hara, Dan Rowan, James Stewart, Claire Trevor, Henry Winkler

63 **All That Glitters** Syndicated
Program Type Comedy Series
30 minutes. Mondays–Fridays. Premiere date: 4/18/77. Last show: 7/15/77. Late-night comedy about women in executive positions at Globetron Corporation and men at home or in clerical jobs. "Genesis Revisited" composed by Alan Bergman and Marilyn Bergman.
Executive Producer Stephanie Sills
Producer Viva Knight
Company TAT Communications Co.
Distributor TAT Syndication
Supervising Director Jim Frawley
Executive Script Consultant Richard Powell

All That Glitters *Continued*
Executive Story Consultant Harry Cauley
Special Consultant Eve Merriam

CAST

Christina Stockwood .... Lois Nettleton
Nancy Bankston .... Anita Gillette
L. W. Carruthers .... Barbara Baxley
Glen Bankston .... Wes Parker
Bert Stockwood .... Chuck McCann
Michael McFarland .... David Haskell
Linda Murkland .... Linda Gray
Peggy Horner .... Vanessa Brown
Andrea Martin .... Louise Shaffer
Grace Smith .... Marte Boyle Slout
Dan Kincaid .... Gary Sandy
Jeremy Stockwood .... Jim Greenleaf
Joan Hamlyn .... Jessica Walter
Ma Packer .... Eileen Brennan

64 **All's Fair** CBS
Program Type Comedy Series
30 minutes. Mondays. Premiere date: 9/20/76. Last show: 8/15/77. Comedy about a conservative political columnist and a liberal freelance photographer in Washington, D.C. Created by Rod Parker, Bob Weiskopf and Bob Schiller; developed by Norman Lear.
Executive Producer Rod Parker
Producers Bob Schiller, Bob Weiskopf
Company T.A.T. Communications Company
Director Bob Claver
Writers Various
Art Director Edward Stephenson

CAST

Richard C. Barrington .... Richard Crenna
Charlotte "Charley" Drake .... Bernadette Peters
Al Brooks .... J. A. Preston
Ginger .... Judy Kahan
Lucy .... Lee Chamberlin
Sen. Wayne Joplin .... Jack Dodson

65 **Almaden Grand Masters** PBS
Program Type Sports Special
Four hours. Live coverage of the tennis tournament held at Palmas Del Mar, Puerto Rico on 11/21/76. Program made possible by a grant from Owens-Illinois Glass Company.
Producer Greg Harney
Company WGBH-TV/Boston
Director Greg Harney
Announcers Bud Collins, Jack Kramer

Almos' a Man *see* Soldier's Home/Almos' a Man

Aloha, Bobby and Rose *see* The ABC Friday Night Movie

66 **The Alternatives** NBC
Program Type Religious/Cultural Special
30 minutes. Premiere date: 7/17/77. A discussion of the alternatives to abortion with Jean Garton.
Producer Doris Ann
Company NBC Television Religious Programs Unit in association with the Lutheran Church-Missouri Synod
Director Walter Kravetz
Interviewer Betty Rollin

67 **The Amazing Cosmic Awareness of Duffy Moon**
ABC Afterschool Specials ABC
Program Type Children's Special
60 minutes. Premiere date: 2/4/76. Repeat date: 3/23/77. Comedy adventure of sixth grader with unusual powers. Based on the novel "The Strange But Wonderful Cosmic Awareness of Duffy Moon" by Jean Robinson. Music by Joe Weber; lyrics by Zoey Wilson.
Producer Daniel Wilson
Company Daniels Wilson Productions, Inc.
Director Larry Elikann
Writer Thomas Baum

CAST

Peter Finley .... Lance Kerwin
Duffy Moon .... Ike Eisenmann
Dr. Flamel .... Jim Backus
Mr. Finley .... Jerry Van Dyke
Photographer .... Basil Hoffman
Aunt Peggy .... Jane Connell
Uncle Ralph .... Jack Collins
Old Lady .... Merie Earle
Mrs. Varner .... Carol Worthington
Brian Varner .... Sparky Marcus
Andrew Varner .... Tommy Crebbs
Mrs. Charles .... Peggy Rea
Mrs. Toby .... Dodo Denney
Boots McAfee .... Alexa Kenin

68 **Amazing Grace—America in Song**
Great Performances PBS
Program Type Music/Dance Special
90 minutes. Premiere date: 10/27/76. The American spirit expressed in song. Program presented by WNET-TV/New York and made possible by grants from the National Endowment for the Arts, Exxon Corporation, the Corporation for Public Broadcasting, the Ford Foundation and Public Television Stations.
Executive Producer Jac Venza
Producer Allan Miller
Company The Music Project for Television, Inc.
Director Allan Miller
Film Editor David Hanser
Project Coordinator Sonya Haddad
Guest Stars Lena Horne, the Allman Brothers, Aaron Copland, Phyllis Curtin, Donald Gramm

69 The Amazing Howard Hughes CBS

Program Type Dramatic Special

Four hours. Premiere dates: 4/13/77 and 4/14/77 (two hours each). Biographical drama based on the book "Howard, the Amazing Mr. Hughes" by Noah Dietrich and Bob Thomas. Music by Laurence Rosenthal. Aviation coordination by Tallmantz Aviation.

Executive Producer Roger Gimbel

Producer Herbert Hirschman

Company A Roger Gimbel Production for EMI Television Programs, Inc.

Director William A. Graham

Writer John Gay

CAST

Howard Hughes .... Tommy Lee Jones
Noah Dietrich .... Ed Flanders
Wilbur Peterson .... James Hampton
Katharine Hepburn .... Tovah Feldshuh
Billie Dove .... Lee Purcell
George .... Jim Antonio
Mayor La Guardia .... Sorrell Booke
Jimmy .... Lee Jones-de Broux
Production Manager .... Roy Engel
Barnes .... Arthur Franz
Shirley .... Denise Galik
Jenks .... Howard Hesseman
Irene .... Tannis G. Montgomery
Henry Kaiser .... Garry Walberg
Jean Peters .... Carol Bagdasarian
Robert Maheu .... Bart Burns
Odlum .... Thayer David
Forbes .... Ray Ballard
Lewis .... Robert Baron
Asst. Cutter .... James Beach
Lewis Milestone .... Marty Brill
Ella Hughes .... Morgan Brittany
Jean Harlow .... Susan Buckner
P.R. Man .... Ray Buktenica
Gresham .... Sid Conrad
Chauffeur .... Jack Denbo
Cutter .... John Dennis
Harris .... Steve Doubet
Butler .... Shay Duffin
Doctor .... S. John Launer
M.C. .... Joel Lawrence
Major .... John Lupton
Graves .... Jim McKrell
Gen. Hap Arnold .... Walter O. Miles
Stunt Pilot .... Glenn Miller
Air Show Announcer .... Myron Natwick
Arlene .... Kim O'Brien
Roy Cruickshank .... Andy Romano
Greta Nissen .... Jette Seear
Sen. Brewster .... Barry Atwater
Jim Bacon .... Jim Bacon
Station Attendant .... John Bellah
Guard .... Thom Carey
DeMarco .... Peter Dane
Sen. Ferguson .... William Dozier
Reeves .... Hal England
Newsreel Announcer .... Art Gilmore
Dr. Palmer .... Ben Hammer
Gene Handsaker .... Gene Handsaker
Russ .... Ed Harris
Attorney .... Ted Hartley
Dr. Bergman .... Wayne Heffley
Sheriff .... Russ McGinn
Marvin Miles .... Marvin Miles
Saunders .... Barney Phillips
McKenna .... John S. Ragin
Hospital Administrator .... Ken Sansom
Vernon Scott .... Ken Scott
Government Official .... Dave Shelley
Wayne Thomis .... Wayne Thomis
Counsel .... Jerome Thor
Mr. Hardesty .... Bert Williams

70 Amelia Earhart

NBC Monday Night at the Movies NBC

Program Type Dramatic Special

Three hours. Premiere date: 10/25/76. A biography of Amelia Earhart. Music composed by David Shire. Aerial sequences staged by Frank Tallman.

Producer George Eckstein

Company Universal Television in association with NBC-TV

Director George Schaefer

Writer Carol Sobieski

Costume Designer Edith Head

Art Director William H. Tuntke

CAST

Amelia Earhart .... Susan Clark
George Putnam .... John Forsythe
Paul Mantz .... Stephen Macht
Snookie .... Susan Oliver
Pidge .... Catherine Burns
Amy .... Jane Wyatt
Mr. Earhart .... Charles Aidman
Radio Operator .... David Huffman
Sid Isaacs .... Ed Barth
Fred Noonan .... Bill Vint
David .... Lance Kerwin
Railey .... Robert Ridgely
Bradford .... Kip Niven
Stultz .... Jack Colvin
Miss Perkins .... Florida Friebus

71 America Salutes Richard Rodgers: The Sound of His Music CBS

Program Type Music/Comedy/Variety Special

Two hours. Premiere date: 12/9/76. A retrospective on the career of Richard Rodgers. Special musical material by Larry Grossman.

Executive Producers Jack Haley, Jr., David Susskind

Producers Gary Smith, Dwight Hemion

Company A 20th Century-Fox presentation in association with Talent Associates and Smith-Hemion Productions

Director Dwight Hemion

Writers Buz Kohan, Ted Strauss

Musical Director Ian Fraser

Choreographer Ron Field

Costume Designer Frank Thompson

Art Director Bob Kelly

Hosts Gene Kelly (as Oscar Hammerstein II), Henry Winkler (as Lorenz Hart)

Guest Stars Diahann Carroll, Vic Damone,

America Salutes Richard Rodgers: The Sound of His Music *Continued*
Sammy Davis, Jr., Sandy Duncan, Lena Horne, Cloris Leachman, Peggy Lee, John Wayne

72 **American Airlines Tennis Games** NBC
Program Type Sports Special
Live coverage of the semi-finals and final matches of the American Airlines Tennis Games from the Mission Hills Golf and Country Club in Palm Springs, Calif. 2/26/77 and 2/27/77.
Company NBC Sports
Commentators Bud Collins, John Newcombe

American Athletic Union *see* AAU

73 **American Ballet Theatre**
Dance in America/Great Performances PBS
Program Type Music/Dance Special
60 minutes. Premiere date: 12/15/76. The American Ballet Theatre in two dances from their repertoire: "Billy the Kid" with music by Aaron Copland and "Les Patineurs" with music by Giacomo Meyerbeer. Program funded by grants from Exxon Corporation, the National Endowment for the Arts and the Corporation for Public Broadcasting.
Executive Producer Jac Venza
Producer Emile Ardolino
Company WNET-TV/New York
Director Merrill Brockway

Billy the Kid
Choreographer Eugene Loring
Scenic Designer Jac Venza
Narrator Paul Newman

CAST
Billy .... Terry Orr
Pat Garrett .... Frank Smith
Alias .... Clark Tippet
Sweetheart/Mother .... Marianna Tcherkassky
Prospector .... Victor Barbee
Mailman .... Michael Owen
Dance Hall Girls .... Marie Johansson, Ruth Mayer, Patricia Wesche
Cowboy in Red .... Kirk Peterson
Mexican Girls .... Francia Kovak, Christine Spizzo

Les Patineurs (The Skaters)
Choreographer Frederick Ashton
Scenic Designer William Mickley

CAST
The Girl in Pink .... Karena Brock
The Girl in Yellow .... Kristine Elliott
Skating Couples .... Elizabeth Ashton, Susan Jones, Cathryn Rhodes, Denise Warner, Warren Conover, Charles Maple, Richard Schafer, Michael Owen
The Boy in Green .... Fernando Bujones
The Lovers .... Nanette Glushak, Charles Ward
The Friends .... Jolinda Menendez, Janet Shibata

74 **American Ballet Theatre's "Giselle"**
Live from Lincoln Center/Great Performances PBS
Program Type Music/Dance Special
Two hours. Premiere date: 6/2/77. Live performance by the American Ballet Theatre of "Giselle" with music by Adolphe Adam and staged by David Blair. Telecast from the Metropolitan Opera House at Lincoln Center for the Performing Arts in New York City. Program made possible by grants from Exxon Corporation, the National Endowment for the Arts and the Corporation for Public Broadcasting.
Producer John Goberman
Company WNET-TV/New York in collaboration with Lincoln Center
Conductor John Lanchbery
Costume Designer Peter Hall
Scenic Designer Oliver Smith
Host Dick Cavett
Announcer Martin Bookspan

CAST
Giselle .... Natalia Makarova
Count Albrecht .... Mikhail Baryshnikov
Myrtha .... Martine Van Hamel
Hilarion .... Frank Smith
Bathilde .... Berthica Prieto
Berthe .... Ruth Mayer
Peasants .... Marianna Tcherkassky, Kirk Peterson

75 **American Bandstand** ABC
Program Type Music/Dance Series
60 minutes. Saturdays. Premiere date: 8/5/57. Season premiere: 9/11/76. Annual dance contest. Winners chosen by viewers. Judy Price succeeded as producer in January 1977 by Barry Glazer and Larry Klein.
Executive Producer Barry Glazer
Producers Judy Price/Barry Glazer and Larry Klein
Company Dick Clark Productions in association with the ABC Television Network
Director Barry Glazer
Host Dick Clark

76 **American Bandstand's 25th Anniversary** ABC
Program Type Music/Comedy/Variety Special
Two hours. Premiere date: 2/4/77. Special celebrating "American Bandstand's" 25th year on television. Taped at the Santa Monica (Calif.) Civic Auditorium with highlights of the show from the 1950s through the 1970s.
Executive Producers Dick Clark, Bill Lee
Producer Judy Price
Company Dick Clark Teleshows, Inc.
Director Barry Glazer

Writers Robert Arthur, Bill Lee
Musical Director H. B. Barnum
Choreographer Ron Poindexter
Costume Designers Rickie Hansen, Warden Neil
Art Director Ray Klausen
Host Dick Clark
Guest Stars Chuck Berry, David Brenner, The Captain & Tennille, Chubby Checker, Barry Manilow, Tony Orlando, Johnnie Ray, Jim Stafford, Frankie Valli and the Four Seasons, Stevie Wonder

77 **The American Condition** ABC
Program Type Documentary/Informational Special
60 minutes. Premiere date: 12/26/76. A look at how Americans see themselves and their future.
Coordinating Producer Tom Bywaters
Producers Tom Bywaters, Tony Batten, Debra Kram
Company ABC News Public Affairs
Directors C. Harper Heinz, Tom Bywaters, Tony Batten
Cinematographers Sidney Dobish, Larry Johnson, Bryan Anderson
Film Editors Jo Ann Caplin, Henriette Huehne, Joseph Burton
Narrator Harry Reasoner

78 **The American Film Institute Salute to Bette Davis** CBS
Program Type Parades/Pageants/Awards Special
90 minutes. Premiere date: 3/21/77. Testimonial program and presentation of the fifth American Film Institute Life Achievement Award to Bette Davis. Film segments produced by Marshall Flaum. Taped 3/1/77 at the Beverly Hilton Hotel in Beverly Hills, Calif.
Executive Producer George Stevens, Jr.
Supervising Producer Perry Lafferty
Producer Robert Scheerer
Company Filmways in association with the American Film Institute
Director Robert Scheerer
Writer Rod Warren
Musical Director Nelson Riddle
Art Director Ray Klausen
Host Jane Fonda
Participating Celebrities Bette Davis, Olivia de Havilland, Peter Falk, Geraldine Fitzgerald, Henry Fonda, Paul Henreid, Celeste Holm, Joseph L. Mankiewicz, Martin Manulis, Liza Minnelli, George Stevens, Jr., Robert Wagner, Natalie Wood, William Wyler

79 **American Indian Artists** PBS
Program Type Educational/Cultural Series
30 minutes. Six-program series. Premiere date: 8/3/76. Series repeats shown Tuesdays as of 1/11/77. Profiles of Indian artists and their work. Narrative poetry written by James McGrath. Series funded by the Corporation for Public Broadcasting.
Producer Jack Peterson
Company KAET-TV/Tempe, Ariz.
Directors Allan Houser, Don Cirillo, Tony Schmitz
Cinematographer Don Cirillo
Narrator Rod McKuen

80 **American League Championship (Baseball)** ABC
Program Type Sports Special
Live coverage of the American League Championship games between the New York Yankees and the Kansas City Royals beginning 10/9/76. Special feature: "Up Close and Personal" profiles of the athletes.
Executive Producer Roone Arledge
Producer Bob Goodrich
Company ABC Sports
Director Chet Forte
Announcers Bob Uecker (first game)/Keith Jackson
Color Commentator Howard Cosell
Expert Analyst Reggie Jackson

81 **The American Music Awards** ABC
Program Type Parades/Pageants/Awards Special
Two hours. Live coverage of the fourth annual music awards from the Santa Monica (Calif.) Civic Auditorium 1/31/77.
Executive Producer Dick Clark
Producer Al Schwartz
Company Dick Clark Teleshows, Inc.
Director John Moffitt
Musical Director Nelson Riddle
Hosts Glen Campbell, Lou Rawls, Helen Reddy
Presenters The Captain & Tennille, Donny Osmond, Marie Osmond, Merv Griffin, Michael Jackson, Dionne Warwick, Freddy Fender, Donna Summer, Doc Severinsen, Dolly Parton, Engelbert Humperdinck, Herb Alpert, Lani Hall, Bobby Vinton, Charley Pride, Tammy Wynette, George Jones, Seals and Crofts, Peter Frampton, Aretha Franklin

82 **The American Short Story** PBS
Program Type Drama Series
60 minutes/90 minutes. Tuesdays. Premiere date: 4/5/77. Six-part series dramatizing famous American short stories: "Bernice Bobs Her Hair/I'm a Fool," "The Blue Hotel," "The Displaced Person," "The Music School," "Parker Adderson, Philosopher/The Jolly Corner," "Soldier's Home/Almos' a Man." (*See* individual ti-

The American Short Story *Continued*
tles for credits.) Programs presented by South Carolina Educational Television and made possible by a grant from the National Endowment for the Humanities.

83 **The American Sportsman** ABC
Program Type Limited Sports Series
60 minutes. Sunday afternoons. Show premiered in 1965. 13th season premiere: 1/2/77. Last show of season: 5/22/77. Nine shows with celebrities and outdoor experts in varied nature programs.
Executive Producer Roone Arledge
Coordinating Producer Robert Duncan
Supervising Producer John Wilcox
Producers Pat Smith, Curt Gowdy
Company ABC Sports
Directors Various
Writers Pat Smith and others
Host Curt Gowdy

84 **Americana** PBS
Program Type Documentary/Informational Series
30 minutes. Fridays/Sundays (as of 7/10/77). Premiere date: 12/3/77. Documentaries produced by local PBS stations and some independent filmmakers. Programs seen during the 1976–77 season are: "Amiotte," "Baymen—Our Waters Are Dying," "Bethlehem," "A Blind Teacher in a Public School," "Boley, Oklahoma—Alive and Well," "The Eleventh Year," "From These Roots," "The Great Iowa Bike Race," "In and Out of Maine: The New People," "James Michael Curley: He Did It for a Friend," "A Matter of Size," "National Tractor Pull 1976," "A New Generation: Shades of Gray," "Number Our Days," "Oneida," "Seconds to Play," "See How They Run," "Stonewall Joe," "A Storyteller's Town," "Sweet Land of Liberty," "These Faces I've Seen," "A Thirst in the Garden," "Thomas Hart Benton's 'The Sources of Country Music,'" "Through All Time," "Two Ball Games." (*See* individual titles for credits.)

85 **Americans All** ABC
Program Type Documentary/Informational Special
5 minutes each. Two mini-documentaries highlighting the achievements of minority group individuals. Shows aired on 3/11/77 and 8/19/77 following the "ABC Friday Night Movie." Series premiered during the 1973–74 season.
Executive Producer Marlene Sanders
Company ABC News Television Documentaries

86 **America's Junior Miss Pageant** CBS
Program Type Parades/Pageants/Awards Special
60 minutes. Premiere date: 5/9/77. Finale of the 20th annual pageant from Mobile, Ala.
Executive Producers Saul Ilson, Ernest Chambers
Producer Harry Waterson
Director Jeff Margolis
Writers Brian Alison, J. Mendelson
Musical Director Bob Rosario
Choreographer Kevin Carlisle
Costume Designer Bill Hargate
Art Director Rene Lagler
Host Michael Landon

87 **America's Last King** PBS
Program Type Documentary/Informational Special
30 minutes. Premiere date: 9/28/76. A conversation between H. R. H. Prince Charles of Great Britain and Alistair Cooke about King George III. Filmed at Windsor Castle in England. Program made possible by a grant from the Xerox Corp.
Producer Colin Clark
Company WGBH-TV/Boston
Director Colin Clark

88 **AMF Grand Prix of Bowling** NBC
Program Type Sports Special
Live coverage of the finals of the first AMF Grand Prix of Bowling from the Thunderbowl Lanes in Allen Park, Mich. 12/4/76.
Producer Larry Cirillo
Company NBC Sports
Director Harry Coyle
Announcer Jack Buck

89 **Amiotte**
Americana PBS
Program Type Documentary/Informational Special
30 minutes. Premiere date: 6/10/77. The story of Arthur Amiotte, a Sioux Indian artist, after his return to the Pine Ridge Reservation in western South Dakota. Program made possible by grants from the Jerome Hill Foundation and the Corporation for Public Broadcasting.
Producer Bruce Baird
Company South Dakota Public Television
Director Richard Muller
Cinematographer Richard Muller

90 **The Amish: People of Preservation**
Documentary Showcase PBS
Program Type Documentary/Informational Special
60 minutes. Premiere date: 6/10/77. A profile of the Amish community of Lancaster, Pennsylvania. Program presented by WITF-TV/Hershey, Pennsylvania and made possible by a grant from the Corporation for Public Broadcasting.
Producer John L. Ruth
Company Heritage Productions, Inc.
Cinematographer Burton Buller

91 **Andre Kostelanetz—Nutcracker**
In Performance at Wolf Trap PBS
Program Type Music/Dance Special
60 minutes. Premiere date: 12/23/74. Repeat date: 12/20/76. Music by Peter Ilich Tchaikovsky performed by the National Symphony Orchestra. "Nutcracker" verses by Ogden Nash recited by Rohan McCullough. Program made possible by a grant from the Atlantic Richfield Company.
Executive Producer David Prowitt
Company WETA-TV/Washington, D.C.
Conductor Andre Kostelanetz
Host David Prowitt

92 **Andre Watts**
Live from Lincoln Center/Great Performances PBS
Program Type Music/Dance Special
Two hours. Premiere date: 11/28/76. Live solo recital by pianist Andre Watts from Avery Fisher Hall at Lincoln Center for the Performing Arts in New York City. Concert stereo-simulcast on local FM radio stations. Program made possible by grants from Exxon Corporation, the National Endowment for the Arts, the Corporation for Public Broadcasting and the Charles A. Dana Foundation.
Producer John Goberman
Company WNET-TV/New York in collaboration with Lincoln Center
Host Dick Cavett
Announcer Martin Bookspan

Androcles and the Lion *see* PBS Movie Theater

93 **The Andros Targets** CBS
Program Type Drama Series
60 minutes. Mondays. Premiere date: 1/31/77. Last regular show: 5/16/77. Two repeat episodes aired 7/2/77 and 7/9/77. Action drama about an investigative reporter for a large daily newspaper, the New York Forum. Filmed on location in and around New York City.
Executive Producers Bob Sweeney, Larry Rosen
Producer Edward H. Feldman
Company CBS Television Network
Directors Various
Executive Story Consultant Jerome Coopersmith
Writers Various
Journalistic Consultant Nicholas Gage

CAST

Mike Andros .... James Sutorius
Sandi Farrell .... Pamela Reed
Chet Reynolds .... Roy Poole
Norman Kale .... Alan Mixon
Wayne Hillman .... Ted Beniades

94 **Andy** Syndicated
Program Type Music/Comedy/Variety Series
30 minutes. Weekly. Premiere date: 9/76. One-season music/variety show.
Executive Producer Pierre Cossette
Producer Robert Scheerer
Company Pierre Cossette Company
Distributor Grey Productions
Director Robert Scheerer
Writers Jeremy Stevens, Tom Moore
Musical Director George Wyle
Star Andy Williams
Regular Wayland Flowers

95 **Andy Williams San Diego Open** CBS
Program Type Sports Special
Coverage of the final two rounds from Torrey Pines Golf Club, La Jolla, Calif. 1/29/77 and 1/30/77.
Producer Frank Chirkinian
Company CBS Television Network Sports
Directors Bob Dailey, Frank Chirkinian
Commentators Vin Scully, Pat Summerall, Jack Whitaker, Ben Wright, Ken Venturi

96 **Animal World** Syndicated
Program Type Science/Nature Series
30 minutes. Weekly. Premiered on NBC 6/68; went into syndication 1/73. Tenth season premiere: 9/76. Animal life and survival.
Producer Betty Bettino
Company Bill Burrud Productions, Inc.
Distributor Les Wallwork & Associates
Writer Miriam Birch
Host Bill Burrud

97 **Animals Animals Animals** ABC
Program Type Children's Series
30 minutes. Sunday mornings. Premiere date: 9/12/76. Magazine-format show focusing on a single animal in art, history, legend, music and religion plus film of the animal as it exists today. Music by Michael Kamen, Stan Davis and Lester Cooper. Animation by Folio One Productions, Ltd.

Animals Animals Animals *Continued*
Executive Producer Lester Cooper
Producer Peter Weinberg
Company ABC News Public Affairs
Director Lester Cooper
Writer Lester Cooper
Host Hal Linden
Regulars Lynn Kellogg, Roger Caras
Voices Estelle Parsons, Mason Adams

98 **The Animals Nobody Loved**
National Geographic Special PBS
Program Type Science/Nature Special
60 minutes. Premiere date: 2/10/76. Repeat date: 6/14/77. A look at the controversy surrounding coyotes, rattlesnakes and wild mustangs. Program funded by a grant from Gulf Oil Corporation and presented by WQED-TV/Pittsburgh.
Executive Producer Dennis B. Kane
Producer Christine Z. Wiser
Company National Geographic Society in association with Wolper Productions
Directors Christine Z. Wiser, Wolfgang Bayer
Writer Nicolas Noxon
Narrator Hal Holbrook

99 **Ann-Margret . . . Rhinestone Cowgirl**
All-Specials Night NBC
Program Type Music/Comedy/Variety Special
60 minutes. Premiere date: 4/26/77. A salute to country music. Taped at the Grand Ole Opry House, Nashville, Tenn. Special musical material by Larry Grossman.
Executive Producers Roger Smith, Allan Carr
Producers Gary Smith, Dwight Hemion
Company A Smith-Hemion Production in association with Roger Smith Video Productions
Director Dwight Hemion
Writer Buz Kohan
Musical Director Bill Walker
Choreographer Rob Iscove
Costume Designers Bob Mackie, Ret Turner
Art Director Tom H. John
Star Ann-Margret
Guest Stars Perry Como, Minnie Pearl, Chet Atkins
Special Guest Star Bob Hope

100 **Another World** NBC
Program Type Daytime Drama Series
60 minutes. Mondays–Fridays. Premiere date: 5/4/64. Continuous. Became first regularly scheduled 60-minuted daytime drama on television as of 1/6/75. Revolves around the Matthews, Cory and Carrington families in Bay City, U.S.A. William B. Williams appeared on the program 10/7/76 as an art restorer. Credit information as of April 1977. Cast listed alphabetically.
Executive Producer Paul Rauch
Producers Mary S. Bonner, Joseph H. Rothenberger
Company Procter & Gamble Productions
Directors Ira Cirker, Melvin Bernhardt, Paul Lammers
Head Writer Harding Lemay
Writers Barry Berg, Jan Merlin, Peter Swet, Arthur Giron, Kathy Callaway

CAST

Dr. David Gilchrist	David Ackroyd
Dr. Russ Matthews	David Bailey
Sven Petersen	Roberts Blossom
Rocky Olsen	John Braden
Corinne Seton	Pamela Brook
Clarice Hobson	Gail Brown
Nancy McGowan	Danielle Jean Burns
Raymond Gordon	Gary Carpenter
Liz Matthews	Irene Dailey
Jamie Frame	Bobby Doran
Daryll Stevens	Richard Dunne
Ada McGowan	Constance Ford
Scott Bradley	Michael Goodwin
Sally Frame	Cathy Greene
Jeff Stone	Dan Hamilton
Dennis Carrington	Mike Hammett
Alice Frame	Susan Harney
Sharlene Matthews	Laurie Heineman
Vera Finley	Carol Mayo Jenkins
Evan Webster	Barry Jenner
Michael Randolph	Lionel Johnston
Angela Perrini	Maeve Kinkead
Olive Gordon	Jennifer Leak
Gwen Parrish	Dorothy Lyman
Brooks	Joseph Maher
Jim Matthews	Hugh Marlowe
Iris Carrington	Beverlee McKinsey
Louise Goddard	Anne Meacham
Molly Randolph	Rolanda Mendels
Marianne Randolph	Ariane Munker
Pat Randolph	Beverly Penberthy
Ted Bancroft	Eric Roberts
Burt McGowan	William Russ
Willis Frame	Leon Russom
John Randolph	Michael M. Ryan
Brian Bancroft	Paul Stevens
Helga Lindemann	Helen Stenborg
Mackenzie Cory	Douglass Watson
Rachel Cory	Victoria Wyndham

101 **Antiques** PBS
Program Type Educational/Cultural Series
30 minutes. Premiere date: 10/5/75. Program repeats began Tuesday mornings 6/7/77 and again 9/6/77. 26-part series devoted to practical information on antique collecting. Funded by the Corporation for Public Broadcasting, the Ford Foundation and Public Television Stations.
Producers George Michael, Sam Price
Company WENH-TV/Durham for the New Hampshire Network
Director Sam Price
Host George Michael

102 **Antonia: A Portrait Of a Woman** PBS

Program Type Documentary/Informational Special

60 minutes. Premiere date: 4/20/76. Repeat date: 1/24/77. The 1975 award-winning documentary about Antonia Brico. Presented by WNET-TV/New York through a grant from the Corporation for Public Broadcasting and the National Endowment for the Arts.

Producer Judy Collins
Company Rocky Mountain Productions, Inc.
Directors Judy Collins, Jill Godmilow

103 **Anyone for Tennyson?** PBS

Program Type Educational/Cultural Series

30 minutes. Wednesdays. Premiere date: 1/5/76. Second season premiere: 2/9/77. Second series repeats began 5/29/77 and again 9/14/77. 15 programs of dramatized poetry by The First Poetry Quartet: George Backman, Cynthia Herman, Norman Snow and Jill Tanner plus weekly guests. Programs made possible by grants from the Corporation for Public Broadcasting, the Ford Foundation and Public Television Stations.

Executive Producer William Perry
Producer Marshall Jamison
Company Nebraska Educational Television Network in association with The Great Amwell Company, Inc.
Director Marshall Jamison
Writer Jane Iredale
Research Consultant Laurie Zwicky

104 **The Appalshop Show**
Documentary Showcase PBS

Program Type Documentary/Informational Special

90 minutes. Premiere date: 1/28/77. Appalachia's struggle for survival as shown in excerpts from 12 Appalshop films and interviews with filmmakers. Program made possible by a grant from the Corporation for Public Broadcasting.

Executive Producer Perry Miller Adato
Company WNET-TV/New York and Appalshop, Inc.
Directors William Richardson, Herb E. Smith
Film Editors William Richardson, Herb E. Smith

Ara Parseghian's Sports *see* Ara's Sports World

105 **Ara's Sports World** Syndicated

Program Type Sports Series

30 minutes. Weekly. Premiere date: 9/76. Highlights of youth sports competitions plus interviews. Show changed names mid-season to "Ara Parseghian's Sports."

Executive Producer Jack Jones
Producers Jeffrey Pill, Russ Lunday, Phil Harmon
Company Herb Golden Organization
Distributor Viacom Enterprises
Director Herb Golden
Writer Herb Golden
Host Ara Parseghian

106 **Archie** ABC

Program Type Comedy Special

60 minutes. Premiere date: 12/19/76. Repeat date: 5/18/77. Pilot based on the comic strip characters created by John L. Goldwater. Music by Stu Gardner and Larry Farrow.

Executive Producer James Komack
Producer Perry Cross
Co-Producers Eric Cohen, George Yanok
Company The Komack Company, Inc.
Director Robert Scheerer
Writers Eric Cohen, George Yanok, Beverly Bloomberg, Peter Gallay, Mickey Rose, Neil Rosen, George Tricker

CAST

Archie .... Dennis Bowen
Betty .... Audrey Landers
Veronica .... Hilary Thompson
Reggie .... Mark Winkworth
Jughead .... Derrel Maury
Moose .... Jim Boelsen
Midge .... Susan Blu
Big Ethel .... Tifni Twitchell
Mr. Andrews .... Gordon Jump
Mr. Weatherbee .... Byron Webster
Miss Grundy .... Jane Lambert
Mrs. Lodge .... Amzie Strickland
Mr. Lodge .... Whit Bissell
Little Jinx .... Michelle Stacy
Larry .... Bill Mumy
Phil .... Paul Gordon
Aunt Helen .... Mae Marmy

107 **Arizona, Here We Come!**
CBS Reports CBS

Program Type Documentary/Informational Special

60 minutes. Premiere date: 2/22/77. A look at Arizona, the fastest growing state in the nation.

Executive Producer Howard Stringer
Producer Janet Roach
Co-Producer Leslie Waring Flynn
Company CBS News
Director Janet Roach
Writers Bill Moyers, Janet Roach
Cinematographer Skip Brown
Researcher Madeline Nelson
Reporter Bill Moyers

108 **Ark II** CBS
Program Type Children's Series
30 minutes. Saturday mornings. Premiere date: 9/11/76. Live-action children's adventure set in 2476 A.D. concerning the efforts of a group of young people to reestablish a civilization in a world destroyed by atomic war. Created by Martin Roth.
Executive Producers Lou Scheimer, Norm Prescott
Producer Richard Rosenbloom
Company Filmation Associates
Directors Ted Post, Hollingsworth Morse
Story Editor Robert Specht
Writers Various

CAST

Jonah .... Terry Lester
Ruth .... Jean Marie Hon
Samuel .... Jose Flores

109 **Arlo Guthrie and Pete Seeger in Concert** PBS
Program Type Music/Dance Special
60 minutes. Premiere date: 7/16/77. Folk music concert taped at the Saratoga (N.Y.) Performing Arts Center. Program made possible by a grant from the New York State Council on the Arts.
Producer Joan Lapp
Company WMHT-TV/Schenectady, N.Y.
Director Bob Shea
Stars Arlo Guthrie, Pete Seeger

110 **Arthur Fiedler With the Boston Pops From Carnegie Hall**
Monsanto Night Syndicated
Program Type Music/Dance Special
60 minutes. Premiere date: 12/25/76. Christmas special from Carnegie Hall in New York City with music performed by the Boston Pops Orchestra.
Producer Jack Sobel
Company York Enterprises
Director Clark Jones
Writers Ed Haas, Jack Sobel
Conductor Arthur Fiedler
Guests Lena Horne, Richard Morse, Rasa Allen, Barnette Ricci Dancers

111 **Arthur Rubinstein at 90**
Fine Music Specials/Great Performances PBS
Program Type Music/Dance Special
90 minutes. Premiere date: 1/26/77. Arthur Rubenstein in conversation at his Paris home and in performance with the London Symphony Orchestra at Fairfield Halls, Croyden, England. Special in honor of his 90th birthday. Program presented by WNET-TV/New York and made possible by grants from Exxon Corporation, the Corporation for Public Broadcasting, the Ford Foundation and Public Television Stations.
Producers David Griffiths, Fritz Buttenstedt
Company Unitel Productions
Director Hugo Kach
Conductor Andre Previn
Host Robert MacNeil

112 **The Arts and Crafts of China** PBS
Program Type Documentary/Informational Special
30 minutes. Premiere date: 1/18/74. Repeat date: 12/28/76. Special filmed largely at the Peking (China) Comprehensive Arts and Crafts Factory. Program made possible by grants from the Corporation for Public Broadcasting and the Office of the Governor of the State of Hawaii.
Company KHET-TV/Honolulu
Director David Allen Silvian
Writer Charles Stubblefield
Cinematographer Joe Konno
Narrator Charles Stubblefield
Special Advisor/Consultant Kogi Ariyoshi

113 **As Long As We're Together** PBS
Program Type Documentary/Informational Special
60 minutes. Premiere date: 10/2/76. Repeat date: 2/27/77. An award-winning documentary about an American family in Micronesia in 1971 and their thoughts about it four years later. Music by Chuck Mangione. Presented by WXXI-TV/Rochester.
Executive Producer Joseph C. Wilson
Producers Stirlin Harris, Victoria Harris
Company Harris and Fischel Films, Inc.
Directors Stirlin Harris, Victoria Harris

114 **As the World Turns** CBS
Program Type Daytime Drama Series
60 minutes. Mondays–Fridays. Premiere date: 4/2/56. Continuous. Became 60-minute show 12/1/75. Drama of the closely-related Hughes, Lowell and Stewart families in Oakdale, U.S.A. Theme music by Charles Paul. Don MacLaughlin and Helen Wagner are original cast members.
Producer Joe Willmore
Company Proctor & Gamble Productions
Directors Leonard Valenta, John Litvack, Robert Myhrum
Head Writers Robert Soderberg, Edith Sommer
Writers Ralph Ellis, Eugenie Hunt, Ted Apstein

CAST

Marion Connelly .... Clarice Blackburn
Ellen Stewart .... Patricia Bruder
Dr. John Dixon .... Larry Bryggman
Natalie Hughes .... Judith Chapman
Teddy Ellison .... Joseph Christopher
Dr. Dan Stewart .... John Colenback
Tom Hughes .... C. David Colson

Jay Stallings .... Dennis Cooney
Betsy Stewart .... Suzanne Davidson
Annie Stewart .... Martina Deignan
Laurie Keaton .... Laurel Delmar
Grant Colman .... James Douglas
Dr. David Stewart .... Henderson Forsythe
Lisa Colman .... Eileen Fulton
Franny Hughes .... Maura Gilligan
Emmy Stewart .... Jenny Harris
Dr. Bob Hughes .... Don Hastings
Kim Dixon .... Kathryn Hays
Dr. James Strasfield .... Geoffrey Horne
Beau Spencer .... Wayne Hudgins
Dick Martin .... Ed Kemmer
Chris Hughes .... Don MacLaughlin
Dr. Susan Stewart .... Marie Masters
Dee Stewart .... Marcia McClain
Valerie Conway .... Judith McConnell
Carol Stallings .... Rita McLaughlin
Kevin Thompson .... Michael Nader
Pat Holland .... Melinda Peterson
Alma Miller .... Ethel Remey
Joyce Colman .... Barbara Rodell
Sandy Garrison .... Barbara Rucker
Nancy Hughes .... Helen Wagner
Don Hughes .... Martin West
Mary Ellison .... Kelly Wood

115 **Ask President Carter** PBS
Program Type Public Affairs Special
Two hours. Tape-delayed broadcast of Pres. Jimmy Carter's CBS Radio call-in from the White House 3/5/77.
Executive Producer Emerson Stone
Producers Tony Brunton, Dick Reeves, Jon Ward
Company CBS Radio Network
Host Walter Cronkite

116 **Asmat—The Cannibal Craftsmen of New Guinea** PBS
Program Type Documentary/Informational Special
60 minutes. Premiere date: 3/77. An examination of Stone Age headhunters living in the jungles of Indonesian New Guinea. Originally televised on the BBC series, "The World Around Us."
Producers Bill Leimbach, Claire Leimbach
Company British Broadcasting Corporation
Directors Bill Leimbach, Claire Leimbach
Cinematographers Bill Leimbach, Claire Leimbach
Narrator David Attenborough

117 **At the Top** PBS
Program Type Music/Dance Series
60 minutes. Thursdays. Premiere date: 2/17/75. Third season premiere: 6/23/77. Eight programs of jazz performed in a nightclub or concert hall setting. Programs funded by grants from the Corporation for Public Broadcasting, the Ford Foundation and Public Television Stations.
Executive Producer James A. DeVinney
Producers Jim Dauphinee, Elliott Mitchell
Company WXXI-TV/Rochester
Directors Jim Dauphinee, Elliott Mitchell

118 **Attack on Terror: The FBI Versus the Ku Klux Klan** CBS
Program Type Dramatic Special
Four hours. Premiere dates: 2/20/75 and 2/21/75. Repeat dates: 8/22/77 and 8/24/77 (two hours each). Drama of three young civil rights workers murdered in Mississippi. Case taken from the files of the FBI. Originally entitled "The FBI Story: The FBI Versus the Ku Klux Klan."
Executive Producer Quinn Martin
Producer Philip Saltzman
Company Quinn Martin Productions in association with Warner Bros. Television
Director Marvin Chomsky
Writer Calvin Clements
Narrator William Conrad

CAST

Dep. Sheriff Ollie Thompson .... Ned Beatty
George Greg .... John Beck
Dave Keene .... Billy Green Bush
Paul Mathison .... Dabney Coleman
Insp. Ryder .... Andrew Duggan
Atty. Ralph Paine .... Ed Flanders
Atty. Clay .... George Grizzard
Roy Ralston .... L. Q. Jones
Sheriff Ed Duncan .... Geoffrey Lewis
Jean Foster .... Marlyn Mason
Dan Foster .... Wayne Rogers
Ben Jacobs .... Peter Strauss
Glen Tuttle .... Rip Torn
Dee Malcom .... Mills Watson
Harry Dudley .... James Hampton
Linn Jacobs .... Sheila Larken
Steve Bronson .... Andrew Parks
Charles Gilmore .... Hilly Hicks
Aaron Cord .... Luke Askew
Jailer Sutton .... John McLiam
Bea Sutton .... Martine Bartlett
Thurston Carson .... Logan Ramsey

119 **Austin City Limits** PBS
Program Type Music/Dance Series
60 minutes. Mondays. Premiere date: 1/2/76. Second season premiere: 5/16/77. Progressive country music series. Program made possible by grants from the Corporation for Public Broadcasting, the Ford Foundation and Public Television Stations.
Executive Producers Howard Chalmers, Bill Arhos
Producer Charles Vaughn
Company KLRN-TV/San Antonio-Austin
Director Charles Vaughn

120 **Austin City Limits—Country Music and Then Some** PBS

Program Type Music/Dance Special

60 minutes. Premiere date: 2/15/77. Repeat date: 8/77. Six country music performers in a night club-like setting. Program made possible by grants from Public Television Stations, the Corporation for Public Broadcasting, the Ford Foundation and the Lone Star Brewing Company.

Executive Producer Howard Chalmers
Producer Bill Arhos
Company KLRN-TV/San Antonio-Austin
Director Bruce Scafe
Performers Earl Scruggs, Larry Gatlin, Willie Nelson, Guy Clark, the Amazing Rhythm Aces, Clarence "Gatemouth" Brown

121 **The Author of Beltraffio**
Piccadilly Circus PBS

Program Type Dramatic Special

60 minutes. Premiere date: 2/8/77. Repeat date: 9/11/77. Adaptation of a short story by Henry James. Program presented by WGBH-TV/Boston, produced by Joan Sullivan, and made possible by a grant from Mobil Oil Corporation.

Producer Stephen Bayly
Company Scott Free Enterprises Production in cooperation with O.R.T.F., Cosmovision, Technisonor, of Paris, Bavaria Film, of Munich
Director Tony Scott
Writer Robin Chapman
Art Director Marianne Ford
Host Jeremy Brett

CAST
Mark Ambient .... Tom Baker
Beatrice Ambient .... Georgina Hale
James Sinclair .... Michael J. Shannon
Gwendolen Ambient .... Catherine Willmer
Dolcino .... Stefan Gates
Additional Cast Gary Rich, John Moore, Rynagh O'-Grady, Rosamund Greenwood, Preston Lockwood

122 **Avalanche**
Once Upon a Classic PBS

Program Type Children's Special

60 minutes. Premiere date: 1/1/77. Story about youngsters on a skiing holiday in the Austrian Tirol. Music by John Shakespeare and Derek Warne. Filmed on location. Program captioned for the hearing-impaired. Presented by WQED-TV/Pittsburgh and made possible by grants from McDonald's Local Restaurants Association and McDonald's Corporation.

Coordinating Producer John Coney
Producer Harry Field
Company Telstar Specialised Productions, Ltd. for Children's Film Foundation/London
Director Frederic Goode
Writer Wally Bosco
Host Bill Bixby

CAST
David .... Michael Portman
Rob .... David Ronder
Hans .... Norbert Gleirscher
Sheena .... Ann Mannion
Pam .... Bernadette Winship
Mr. Goring .... David Dundas
Karl Muller .... Karl Span

123 **Baa Baa Black Sheep** NBC

Program Type Drama Series

60 minutes. Tuesdays. Premiere date: 9/21/76 (two-hour special). Last show: 8/30/77. Based on the exploits of World War II ace Gregory "Pappy" Boyington as told in "Baa Baa Black Sheep." Boyington appeared in two episodes 1/18/77 and 3/8/77 in the role of Gen. Kenley. Music by Mike Post and Peter Carpenter.

Executive Producer Stephen J. Cannell
Supervising Producer Philip DeGuere, Jr.
Company Universal Television in association with NBC-TV
Directors Various
Writers Stephen J. Cannell, Philip DeGuere, Jr., Ken Pettus, Milt Rosen
Technical Consultant Gregory "Pappy" Boyington

CAST
Maj. Gregory "Pappy" Boyington .... Robert Conrad
Gen. Moore .... Simon Oakland
Col. Lard .... Dana Elcar
Capt. Gutterman .... James Whitmore, Jr.
Lt. J. Bragg .... Dirk Blocker
Lt. T. J. Wiley .... Robert Ginty
Lt. Bob Anderson .... John Larroquette
Lt. L. Casey .... W. K. Stratton
French .... Jeff MacKay
Boyle .... Larry Manetti
Hutch .... Joey Aresco
Sgt. Andy Micklin .... Red West
Meatball .... True Grit (bull terrier)

124 **Baa Baa Blacksheep (Special)**
Childhood/Great Performances PBS

Program Type Dramatic Special

60 minutes. Premiere date: 2/16/77. Repeat date: 8/31/77. Adapted from the story by Rudyard Kipling. Memory-play about his move from India to a foster home in Victorian England. Presented by WNET-TV/New York. Program made possible by a grant from Exxon Corporation with additional support from member stations of PBS.

Executive Producer Jac Venza
Coordinating Producer Ann Blumenthal
Producer James Brabazon
Company Granada Television
Director Mike Newell
Writer Arthur Hopcraft
Host Ingrid Bergman

CAST

Punch .... Max Harris
Judy .... Claudia Jessop
Alice Lockwood .... Gillian Hawser
Lockwood .... Paul Freeman
Auntie Rosa .... Eileen McCallum
Uncle Harry .... Freddie Jones
Harry .... Anthony McCaffrey
Dr. Inverarity .... Tom Watson
Jane .... Dinah Glaskin
Emily .... Jane Carr
Emily's Boyfriend .... Jim Whelan
The Ayah .... Charubala Chokshi
Meeta .... Tariq Yunus
Mr. Birtles .... Gerry Cowan
Ringleader .... David Menashe
Little Boy .... Adam Hertz

Badlands *see* The CBS Friday Night Movies

125 **Ball Four** CBS

Program Type Comedy Series

30 minutes. Wednesdays. Premiere date: 9/22/76. Last show: 10/27/76. Series created by Jim Bouton, Marvin Kitman and Vic Ziegel based on "Ball Four" by Jim Bouton and edited by Leonard Shecter. "Ball Four Theme" by Harry Chapin. Comedy about life in the locker room and bull pen of the Washington Americans (a major league baseball club); revolves around relief pitcher Jim Barton.

Producer Don Segall

Company CBS Television Network Production

Directors Various

Executive Story Editor Jay Sommers

Writers Various

Creative and Technical Supervisor Jim Bouton

CAST

Jim Barton .... Jim Bouton
Manager "Cap" Capogrosso .... Jack Somack
Bill Westlake .... David-James Carroll
"Rhino" Rhinelander .... Ben Davidson
Coach "Pinky" Pinkney .... Bill McCutcheon
Lenny "Birdman" Siegel .... Lenny Schultz
Rayford Plunkett .... Marco St. John
Orlando Lopez .... Jaime Tirelli
C. B. Travis .... Sam Wright

126 **Ballet Shoes**

Piccadilly Circus PBS

Program Type Dramatic Special

90 minutes each. Premiere dates: 12/27/76 and 12/28/76. Adaptation of the classic by Noel Streatfeild about three orphan girls in the 1930s depression who blossom at a school for dance and drama. Program presented by WGBH-TV/Boston, produced by Joan Sullivan, and made possible by a grant from Mobil Oil Corporation.

Company British Broadcasting Corporation

Host Jeremy Brett

CAST

Pauline .... Elizabeth Morgan
Petrova .... Jane Slaughter
Posy .... Sarah Prince
Sylvia .... Angela Thorne
Nana .... Barbara Lott
Madame Fidolia .... Mary Morris
Simpson .... Terence Skelton
Theo Dane .... Joanna David

127 **The Banana Co.** CBS

Program Type Comedy Special

30 minutes. Premiere date: 8/25/77. Comedy pilot about combat correspondents in the South Pacific during World War II. Created by Milton Sperling.

Executive Producers Carroll O'Connor, Terry Becker

Producer Ronald Rubin

Company O'Connor-Becker Productions

Director Bruce Bilson

Writers Ronald Rubin, Bob Klane, Bernard Kahn

Art Director Perry Ferguson

CAST

Capt. Harry Gill .... John Reilly
Maj. Platt .... Ted Gehring
Sgt. Muldoon .... Ron Masak
Lt. David Segal .... Sam Chew, Jr.
Capt. Seebring .... Eddie Quillan
Pfc. Peebles .... Gailard Sartain
Ned Turner .... Robert Brown
Aussie .... John Archer
Young Marine .... Ben Marley

Bang the Drum Slowly *see* The ABC Friday Night Movie

128 **Bar Mitzvah Boy** PBS

Program Type Dramatic Special

75 minutes. Premiere date: 3/77. Repeat date: 8/77. Original British television play about a Jewish boy reaching his 13th birthday. Originally shown on the BBC series "Play for Today."

Producer Graeme McDonald

Company British Broadcasting Corporation

Director Michael Tuchner

Writer Jack Rosenthal

CAST

Eliot Green .... Jeremy Steyn
Leslie Green .... Adrienne Posta
Mrs. Green .... Maria Charles
Mr. Green .... Bernard Spear
Rabbi Sherman .... Jack Lynn
Grandad .... Cyril Shaps
Boyfriend .... Jonathan Lynn

129 **The Barbara Walters Special (First Special)** ABC

Program Type Documentary/Informational Special

60 minutes. Premiere date: 12/14/76. Interviews

The Barbara Walters Special (First Special) *Continued*
with President-Elect Jimmy Carter and Rosalynn Carter and with Barbra Streisand and Jon Peters.
Producer Lucy Jarvis
Company ABC
Director John Desmond
Researcher Peter Jarvis
Interviewer Barbara Walters

130 **The Barbara Walters Special (Second Special)** ABC
Program Type Documentary/Informational Special
60 minutes. Premiere date: 4/6/77. Repeat date: 7/28/77. Interviews with Elizabeth Taylor and John Warner, Shah Mohammed Reza Pahlevi and Empress Farah Diba Pahlevi of Iran, and Rep. Barbara Jordan.
Producer Daniel Wilson
Company A Barwall Production, Inc.
Director Don Mischer
Interviewer Barbara Walters

131 **The Barbara Walters Special (Third Special)** ABC
Program Type Documentary/Informational Special
60 minutes. Premiere date: 5/31/77. Interviews with Bob Hope, Bing Crosby and Redd Foxx.
Producer Daniel Wilson
Director Don Mischer
Interviewer Barbara Walters

132 **The Barber of Seville**
Great Performances PBS
Program Type Music/Dance Special
2 1/2 hours. Premiere date: 1/7/76. Repeat date: 4/20/77. Based on the La Scala Opera production designed by Jean-Pierre Ponnelle of the 1816 comic opera by Gioacchino Rossini. Music performed by the La Scala Opera Orchestra. Program made possible by a grant from Exxon Corporation. Presented by WNET-TV York.
Coordinating Producer David Griffiths
Company Unitel Productions
Director Jean-Pierre Ponnelle
Conductor Claudio Abbado

CAST
Figaro .... Hermann Prey
Rosina .... Teresa Berganza
Count Almaviva .... Luigi Alva
Bartolo .... Enzo Dara
Basilio .... Paolo Montarsolo
Additional Cast Renato Cesari, Stefania Malagu, La Scala Opera Chorus

133 **The Barber of Seville (Live Performance)**
Live from Lincoln Center/Great Performances PBS
Program Type Music/Dance Special
Three hours. Premiere date: 11/3/76. Live performance of the regularly scheduled production of "The Barber of Seville" by Gioacchino Rossini. Performed by the New York City Opera at Lincoln Center for the Performing Arts in New York City. Stereo-simulcast on local FM radio stations. Program made possible by grants from the Corporation for Public Broadcasting, the National Endowment for the Arts, Exxon Corporation and the Charles A. Dana Foundation.
Producer John Goberman
Company WNET-TV/New York in collaboration with Lincoln Center
Director Sarah Caldwell
Conductor Sarah Caldwell
Costume Designer Jan Skalicky
Scenic Designers Helen Pond, Herbert Senn
Host Dick Cavett
Announcer Martin Bookspan

CAST
Rosina .... Beverly Sills
Dr. Bartolo .... Donald Gramm
Figaro .... Alan Titus
Almaviva .... William Harness
Don Basilio .... Samuel Ramey
Berta .... Diane Curry

134 **Baretta** ABC
Program Type Crime Drama Series
60 minutes. Wednesdays. Premiere date: 1/17/75. Third season premiere: 9/22/76. Adventures of undercover police detective with pet cockatoo, Fred. Series created by Stephen J. Cannell. Theme "Keep Your Eye on the Sparrow" with music by Dave Grusin, lyrics by Morgan Ames, sung by Sammy Davis, Jr..
Executive Producer Anthony Spinner
Producer Charles E. Dismukes
Company Public Arts/Roy Huggins/Universal Production
Directors Various
Writers Various

CAST
Tony Baretta .... Robert Blake
Billy Truman .... Tom Ewell
Lt. Hal Brubaker .... Ed Grover
Rooster .... Michael D. Roberts

135 **Baretta (Late Night)** ABC
Program Type Crime Drama Series
60 minutes. Fridays. Premiere date: 4/22/77. Late-night repeat presentations of the primetime series. For credit information, *see* "Baretta."

136 **Barnaby Jones** CBS
Program Type Crime Drama Series
60 minutes. Thursdays. Premiere date: 1/28/73. Fifth season premiere: 10/7/76. Crime drama of private investigator, daughter-in-law/girl Friday and nephew. Theme by Jerry Goldsmith.
Executive Producer Quinn Martin
Producer Philip Saltzman
Company Quinn Martin Productions
Directors Various
Writers Various

CAST
Barnaby Jones .... Buddy Ebsen
Betty Jones .... Lee Meriwether
J. R. Jones .... Mark Shera

137 **Barney Miller** ABC
Program Type Comedy Series
30 minutes. Thursdays. Premiere date: 1/23/75. Third season premiere: 9/23/76. Comedy about detectives in New York City's 12th police precinct. Series created by Danny Arnold and Theodore J. Flicker. Music by Jack Elliott and Allyn Ferguson. February 1977 spinoff: "Fish."
Executive Producer Danny Arnold
Producer Roland Kibbee
Company Four D Productions
Directors Noam Pitlik, Bruce Bilson and others
Story Editor Tony Sheehan
Writers Various

CAST
Capt. Barney Miller .... Hal Linden
Det. Phil Fish .... Abe Vigoda
Det. Wojehowicz .... Max Gail
Det. Nick Yemana .... Jack Soo
Det. Harris .... Ron Glass
Insp. Luger .... James Gregory
Det. Arthur Dietrich .... Steve Landesberg
Officer Carl Levitt .... Ron Carey

138 **The Barry Manilow Special** ABC
Program Type Music/Comedy/Variety Special
60 minutes. Premiere date: 3/2/77. Barry Manilow's first television special.
Executive Producer Miles Lourie
Producer Steve Binder
Company Kamakazi Music Corporation Production
Director Steve Binder
Writers Alan Thicke, Don Clark, Susan Clark, Ron Pearlman, Barry Manilow, Steve Binder, Bruce Vilanch
Musical Director Gerald Alters
Choreographer Joe Tremaine
Costume Designers Pete Menefee, Patrick Elliot
Art Director Tom H. John
Star Barry Manilow
Guest Stars Penny Marshall, Lady Flash

139 **The Baseball Business**
CBS Reports CBS
Program Type Documentary/Informational Special
60 minutes. Premiere date: 4/26/77. A report on the business of baseball.
Executive Producer Howard Stringer
Producer Paul Greenberg
Company CBS News
Writers Paul Greenberg, Bill Moyers
Cinematographer Dan Lerner
Film Editors Maurice Murad, Lee Reichenthal
Reporter Bill Moyers

140 **Baseball Game-of-the-Week** NBC
Program Type Limited Sports Series
Live coverage of 26 regular-season major league baseball games. Saturdays. 12th season premiere: 4/9/77. One Saturday evening game shown 7/2/77.
Executive Producer Scotty Connal
Company NBC Sports
Announcers Joe Garagiola and Tony Kubek (primary game)/Jim Simpson or Dick Enberg and Maury Wills (secondary game)

141 **The Baseball World of Joe Garagiola** NBC
Program Type Limited Sports Series
15 minutes. Premiered in 1973. Show preceded the All-Star Game 7/19/77 and the four World Series games 10/16/76–10/20/76. *See also* "the Changing Face of Baseball," 60-minute special 3/27/77.
Executive Producer Don Ellis
Producer Ginny Seipt
Company NBC Sports in cooperation with Joe Garagiola Enterprises
Writer Frank Slocum
Host Joe Garagiola

Battle For the Planet of the Apes *see* The CBS Friday Night Movies

142 **Battle For the White House**
Political Spirit of '76 ABC
Program Type Public Affairs Series
Premiere date: 9/3/76. Last show: 10/29/76. Seven campaign and election special reports.
Senior Producer Jeff Gralnick
Company ABC News Special Events Unit
Anchors Howard K. Smith, Harry Reasoner, Barbara Walters
Pollster/Voter Analyst Louis Harris

143 **The Battle of Billy's Pond**
Once Upon a Classic PBS
Program Type Children's Special
60 minutes. Premiere date: 3/26/77. Story about the pollution of a lake pitting two boys against a tanker. Story by Michael Abrams and Harley Cokliss. Music by Harry Robinson. Special effects by Arnold Jackson. Filmed on location in Hertfordshire, England. Captioned for the hearing-impaired. Presented by WQED-TV/Pittsburgh and made possible by grants from McDonald's Local Restaurants Association and McDonald's Corporation.
Coordinating Producer John Coney
Producer Mark Forstater
Company Mark Forstater Productions Ltd./Irit Films Ltd. for the Children's Film Foundation Ltd.
Director Harley Cokliss
Writer Howard Thompson
Art Director Tim Hutchinson
Host Bill Bixby

CAST

Billy .... Ben Buckton
Gobby .... Andrew Ashby
Mr. Pugh .... Talfryn Thomas
Mrs. Bateson .... Ann Beach
Mr. Bateson .... Keith James
Tanker Driver .... Geoff Hinsliff
Driver's Mate .... Derek Ware
1st Policeman .... Geoffrey Palmer
2nd Policeman .... Andrew Bradford
Tour Guide .... Miriam Margoyles
Sally .... Linda Robson

144 **Battle of the Network Stars** ABC
Program Type Sports Special
Two hours. Premiere date: 11/13/76. First contest pitting teams of stars from ABC, CBS, and NBC against each other in athletic events (*see also* "Challenge of the Network Stars.")
Executive Producer Roone Arledge
Producer Don Ohlmeyer
Company Trans World International, Inc. in association with ABC Sports
Director Roger Goodman
Host Howard Cosell
Commentators Bruce Jenner, Mark Spitz, Cathy Rigby, Reggie Jackson, Bob Rosburg
Stars from ABC Gabriel Kaplan (captain), Darleen Carr, Lynda Carter, Farrah Fawcett-Majors, Richard Hatch, Robert Hegyes, Ron Howard, Hal Linden, Penny Marshall, John Schuck
Stars from CBS Telly Savalas (captain), Adrienne Barbeau, Gary Burghoff, Kevin Dobson, Pat Harrington, Bill Macy, Lee Meriwether, Mackenzie Phillips, Loretta Swit, Jimmie Walker
Stars from NBC Robert Conrad (captain), Melissa Sue Anderson, Karen Grassle, Tim Matheson, Ben Murphy, Barbara Parkins, Joanna Pettet, Kevin Tighe, Bobby Troup, Demond Wilson

145 **The Bay City Amusement Company**
Comedy Time NBC
Program Type Comedy Special
30 minutes. Premiere date: 7/28/77. Comedy pilot about writers, actors and a producer trying to put on a television show in the San Francisco area.
Executive Producer Norman Steinberg
Producer Bo Kaprall
Company Universal Television
Directors Norman Steinberg, Gary Shimokawa
Writers Ken Levine, David Isaacs

CAST

Clifford .... Terry Kiser
Alan .... Dennis Howard
Ann .... Barrie Youngfellow
Howie .... Pat McCormick
Gail .... June Gable
Bradshaw .... Ted Gehring
Warren .... Jim Scott

146 **Baymen—Our Waters Are Dying**
Americana PBS
Program Type Documentary/Informational Special
30 minutes. Premiere date: 2/11/77. Repeat dates: 3/22/77 and 8/21/77. A look at the plight of eastern Long Island's clam diggers. Program made possible by grants from the National Endowment for the Arts, Creative Artists Public Service Program and the Corporation for Public Broadcasting.
Producer Anne Belle
Company WGBH-TV/Boston
Director Anne Belle
Cinematographer Peter Aaron

147 **Be Glad Then America . . . A Documentary** PBS
Program Type Documentary/Informational Special
60 minutes. Premiere date: 7/4/77. A behind-the-scenes look at the events contributing to the world premiere of the Bicentennial opera, "Be Glad Then America: A Decent Entertainment From the Thirteen Colonies."
Producer Gary Perdue
Company WPSX-TV/University Park, Pa.

148 **Be My Valentine, Charlie Brown**
CBS
Program Type Animated Film Special
30 minutes. Premiere date: 1/28/75. Repeat date: 2/14/77. Based on the comic strip created by Charles M. Schulz. Music by Vince Guaraldi.
Executive Producer Lee Mendelson

Producer Bill Melendez
Company Lee Mendelson-Bill Melendez Production in cooperation with United Feature Syndicate, Inc. and Charles M. Schulz Creative Associates
Director Phil Roman
Writer Charles M. Schulz
Music Supervisor John Scott Trotter

VOICES

Charlie Brown	Duncan Watson
Linus	Stephen Shea
Lucy	Melanie Kohn
Schroeder	Greg Felton
Violet	Linda Ercoli
Sally	Lynn Mortensen

149 **Beauty and the Beast**
Hallmark Hall of Fame NBC
Program Type Dramatic Special
90 minutes. Premiere date: 12/3/76. New adaptation of the classic love story. Filmed in England at Knebworth House, Salisbury Hall and Sudeley Castle. Music composed by Ron Goodwin. Special make-up by Del Acevedo.
Executive Producer Thomas M. C. Johnston
Producer Hank Moonjean
Company Palm Productions, Inc.
Director Fielder Cook
Writer Sherman Yellen
Conductor Ron Goodwin
Costume Designer Albert Wolsky
Art Director Elliott Scott
Set Decorator Terry Parr

CAST

The Beast	George C. Scott
Belle	Trish Van Devere
Lucy	Virginia McKenna
Beaumont	Bernard Lee
Anthony	Michael Harbour
Nicholas	William Relton
Susan	Patricia Quinn

150 **Beauty and the Beast (Children's Special)** PBS
Program Type Children's Special
30 minutes. Premiere date: 12/23/73. Repeat date: 12/21/76. The classic fairy tale presented by the Zapletal Puppets.
Producer Peter Zapletal
Company Mississippi Center for Educational Television
Puppeteers Peter Zapletal, Jarmila Zapletal

Beauty and the Beast (Feature Film) *see* PBS Movie Theater

151 **Behind the Fence—Albert Paley: Metalsmith** PBS
Program Type Documentary/Informational Special
30 minutes. Premiere date: 2/23/77. Documentary following the construction of an 80-foot iron fence for the Hunter Museum of Art in Chattanooga, Tenn. by Albert Paley.
Company KUED-TV/Salt Lake City
Cinematographer David Darby

152 **Bell System Family Theatre** NBC
Program Type Miscellaneous Series
Specials of various types. Premiere date: 9/12/70. Seventh season premiere: 12/12/76. Programs broadcast during the 1976–77 season are: "The Man in the Iron Mask," "Our Town," "The Tiny Tree." (*See* individual titles for credits.)

153 **The Belle of Amherst** PBS
Program Type Dramatic Special
90 minutes. Premiere date: 12/29/76. One-woman show about Emily Dickinson based on her poems, notes and letters. Recorded before a live audience. Program made possible by a grant from IBM.
Producers Mike Merrick, Don Gregory
Company A Dome/Creative Image Production in association with KCET-TV/Los Angeles
Director Charles S. Dubin
Writer William Luce
Costume Designer Theoni V. Aldredge
Production Designer H. R. Poindexter
Artistic Advisor Charles Nelson Reilly
Compiler Timothy Helgeson

CAST

Emily Dickinson	Julie Harris

Ben Hur *see* CBS Special Film Presentations

154 **Benny and Barney: Las Vegas Undercover**
NBC Movie of the Week NBC
Program Type TV Movie
90 minutes. Premiere date: 1/19/77. Repeat date: 5/29/77. Pilot drama centered around two Las Vegas undercover policemen. Created by Glen A. Larson.
Executive Producer Glen A. Larson
Producer Ron Satlof
Company A Glen A. Larson Production in association with Universal Television and NBC-TV
Director Ron Satlof
Writer Glen A. Larson

CAST

Benny Kowalski	Terry Kiser

Benny and Barney: Las Vegas Undercover *Continued*

Barney Tuscom .... Timothy Thomerson
Lt. Callan .... Jack Colvin
Margie .... Jane Seymour
Mickey Doyle .... Jack Cassidy
Davis .... Hugh O'Brian
Joey Gallion .... Pat Harrington
Manager .... Rodney Dangerfield
Higgie .... Marty Allen
Drunk .... George Gobel
Sgt. Ross .... Michael Pataki
Paul Mizener .... Bobby Troup
Will Dawson .... Dick Gautier

155 Bernice Bobs Her Hair/I'm a Fool

The American Short Story PBS
Program Type Dramatic Special

Bernice Bobs Her Hair

45 minutes. Premiere date: 4/5/77. Adaptation of the short story by F. Scott Fitzgerald set in the Midwest circa 1919. Music by Dick Hyman. Program funded by a grant from the National Endowment for the Humanities. Presented by South Carolina Educational Television.
Executive Producer Robert Geller
Producer Paul R. Gurian
Company Learning in Focus, Inc.
Director Joan Micklin Silver
Writer Joan Micklin Silver
Costume Designer Robert Pusilo
Scenic Designer Stuart Wurtzel
Host Colleen Dewhurst

CAST

Bernice .... Shelly Duvall
Marjorie .... Veronica Cartwright
Warren .... Bud Cort
Mrs. Harvey .... Polly Holliday
Additional Cast Dennis Christopher, Gary Springer, Lane Binkley, Mark LaMura, Murray Moston, Patrick Byrne, Mark Newkirk, Leslie Thorsen, Claudette Warlick

I'm a Fool

36 minutes. Adaptation of a short story by Sherwood Anderson set in the early 1900s. Music by Ed Bogas.
Executive Producer Robert Geller
Producer Dan McCann
Company Learning in Focus, Inc.
Director Noel Black
Writer Ron Cowen
Costume Designer Marianne DeFina
Scenic Designer Don DeFina
Host Colleen Dewhurst

CAST

Andy .... Ron Howard
Lucy .... Amy Irving
Burt .... Santiago Gonzales
George .... John Tidwel
Wilbur .... John Light
Additional Cast Randi Kallan, Otis Calef

156 Bernstein and the New York Philharmonic

Great Performances PBS
Program Type Music/Dance Special
60 minutes. Premiere date: 11/26/75. Repeat date: 8/28/77. The Symphony No. 4 by Peter Ilich Tchaikovsky performed by the New York Philharmonic Orchestra. Program made possible by a grant from Exxon Corporation. Presented by WNET-TV/New York.
Executive Producers Klaus Hallig, Harry Kraut
Producer David Griffiths
Company Unitel-Amberson
Conductor Leonard Bernstein

157 Bernstein and the New York Philharmonic in London

Great Performances PBS
Program Type Music/Dance Special
60 minutes. Premiere date: 7/12/76. Repeat date: 7/3/77. A concert of American music performed by the New York Philharmonic Orchestra: the overture to "Candide" by Leonard Bernstein, "Rhapsody in Blue" by George Gershwin, "A Lincoln Portrait" by Aaron Copland with text recited by William Warfield and "The Stars and Stripes Forever" by John Philip Sousa. Taped in London. Program presented by WNET-TV/New York and made possible by a grant from Exxon Corporation.
Executive Producers Harry Kraut, Herbert Kloiber
Coordinating Producer David Griffiths
Producer Derek Bailey
Company Unitel Productions and Amberson Productions in association with London Weekend Television
Director Derek Bailey
Conductor Leonard Bernstein

158 Bernstein Conducts Boston Symphony

Fine Music Specials/Great Performances PBS
Program Type Music/Dance Special
90 minutes. Premiere date: 7/13/77. The Boston Symphony Orchestra and Tanglewood Festival Chorus in a performance of "A Faust Symphony" by Franz Liszt, Program simulcast in stereo on local FM radio stations. Presented by WNET-TV/New York and made possible by grants from Exxon Corporation, the Corporation for Public Broadcasting, the Ford Foundation and Public Television Stations.
Executive Producers Harry Kraut, Klaus Hallig
Coordinating Producer David Griffiths
Company Unitel-Amberson Productions
Director Humphrey Burton
Conductor Leonard Bernstein

Choral Director John Oliver
Soloist Kenneth Riegel

159 **Bernstein Conducts Mahler**
Fine Music Specials/Great Performances PBS
Program Type Music/Dance Special
90 minutes. Premiere date: 2/9/77. Repeat date: 9/25/77. The Israel Philharmonic taped at the Frederic Mann Auditorium in Tel Aviv, Israel in a performance of "Das Lied von der Erde" ("The Song of the Earth") by Gustav Mahler. Program stereo-simulcast on local FM radio stations. Presented by WNET-TV/New York and made possible by grants from Exxon Corporation, the Corporation for Public Broadcasting, the Ford Foundation and Public Television Stations.
Executive Producer Fritz Buttenstedt
Producer David Griffiths
Company Unitel Production in association with Amberson Productions
Director Humphrey Burton
Conductor Leonard Bernstein
Featured Soloists Christa Ludwig, Rene Kollo

160 **Best Friends** CBS
Program Type Comedy Special
30 minutes. Premiere date: 7/19/77. Comedy pilot about teenagers "hanging around" in an apartment building basement on Chicago's Northwest Side. Music composed and performed by Flo & Eddie.
Producer Alan Sacks
Company Warner Bros. Television
Director Jerry Paris
Writers Peter Meyerson, Stanley Ralph Ross
Scenic Designer John Hueners

CAST

Nick Ryan .... James Canning
Arthur .... Bill Henry Douglass
Mountain Man .... Gary Epp
Gypsy .... Barry Pearl
Kathy .... Sherry Hursey
Aunt Maggie .... Gloria LeRoy
Oupensky .... Cliff Osmond
Lionel "Big O" Lapidus .... Ray Sharkey

161 **The Best of Donny & Marie** ABC
Program Type Music/Comedy/Variety Series
60 minutes. Wednesdays/Fridays (as of 8/12/77). Premiere date: 6/1/77. Last show: 8/26/77. Repeat presentations of "Donny & Marie". (*See* "Donny & Marie" for credit information.)

162 **The Best of Ernie Kovacs** PBS
Program Type Comedy Series
30 minutes. Tuesdays. Premiere date: 4/12/77. Ten programs featuring black-and-white videotape and kinescope footage from the "Ernie Kovacs" shows of the 1950s seen on NBC and ABC. Put together by John Lollos of the Video Tape Network. Programs made possible by grants from the Corporation for Public Broadcasting, the Ford Foundation and Public Television Stations.
Producer David Erdman
Company WTTW-TV/Chicago
Host Jack Lemmon
Star Ernie Kovacs

163 **The Best of Police Story** NBC
Program Type Crime Drama Series
60 minutes. Tuesdays. Premiere date: 5/10/77. Last show: 8/23/77. Repeats of shows from 1973–1977. For credit information, *see* "Police Story."

164 **The Best of "The Waltons"** CBS
Program Type Drama Series
60 minutes. Thursdays. Premiere date: 6/16/77. Last show: 9/7/77. Selected rebroadcasts of the family drama. For credit information *see* "The Waltons."

Best Sellers *see* NBC's Best Seller

165 **Bethlehem**
Americana PBS
Program Type Documentary/Informational Special
30 minutes. Premiere date: 4/29/77. Repeat date: 9/11/77. A "cinema verite" documentary about life in an institution for juvenile delinquents. Filmed at the Bethlehem Lutheran Home for Children in New York. Program made possible by a grant from the Corporation for Public Broadcasting and presented by WPBT-TV/Miami.
Producer Robert Thurber
Company Thurber Productions, Inc.
Director Robert Thurber
Cinematographer Robert Thurber
Film Editor Robert Thurber

166 **The Better Sex** ABC
Program Type Game/Audience Participation Series
30 minutes. Mondays–Fridays. Premiere date: 7/18/77. A bluffing game between one team of six men and a second of six women.
Executive Producer Ira Skutch
Producer Robert Sherman
Company Goodson-Todman Productions
Director Paul Alter
Hosts Bill Anderson, Sarah Purcell

167 **Beyond Niagara** NBC
Program Type Religious/Cultural Special
60 minutes. Premiere date: 2/20/77. A look at Canada's historical, cultural and religious development. Filmed on location in various parts of Canada.
Producer Doris Ann
Company NBC Television Religious Programs Unit in association with the Southern Baptist Radio and Television Commission
Director Joseph Vadala
Writer Philip Scharper
Film Editor Ed Williams
Host/Narrator Alexander Scourby

168 **Beyond the Horizon**
Theater in America/Great Performances PBS
Program Type Dramatic Special
Two hours. Premiere date: 1/14/76. Repeat date: 7/20/77. Television premiere of the Pulitzer Prize winning play as performed by The McCarter Theatre, Princeton, N.J. Music by Bill Brohn. Program made possible by grants from Exxon Corporation, Public Television Stations, the Corporation for Public Broadcasting and the Ford Foundation. (Cast list in order of appearance.)
Executive Producer Jac Venza
Producer Lindsay Law
Company WNET-TV/New York
Directors Michael Kahn, Rick Hauser
Writer Eugene O'Neill
Costume Designer Jane Greenwood
Art Director David Jenkins
Host Hal Holbrook

CAST

Robert Mayo .... Richard Backus
Kate Mayo .... Kate Wilkinson
James Mayo .... John Randolph
Andrew Mayo .... Edward J. Moore
Ruth Atkins .... Maria Tucci
Capt. Scott .... James Broderick
Mrs. Atkins .... Geraldine Fitzgerald
Mary .... Kathy Koperwhats
Ben .... Michael Houlihan
Dr. Fawcett .... John Houseman

169 **A Bicentennial Christmas Liturgy** ABC
Program Type Religious/Cultural Special
60 minutes. Premiere date: 12/25/76. Christmas candlelight celebration from the Cathedral of Saints Peter and Paul in Providence, R.I. featuring music by Dr. C. Alexander Peloquin and the Peloquin Chorale. The Most Reverend Louis E. Gelineau, Bishop of Providence, principal celebrant. Program produced in cooperation with the United States Catholic Conference.
Producer Sid Darion
Company ABC News Public Affairs
Conductor Dr. C. Alexander Peloquin

170 **Bicentennial Hall of Fame** PBS
Program Type Drama Series
90 minutes each. Three-part series in honor of the Bicentennial dealing with Presidents Washington, Lincoln and Truman: "Valley Forge," "The Rivalry" and "Truman At Potsdam." (*See* individual titles for credits.) Programs originally shown on NBC during the 1975–76 season. Presented to PBS by Hallmark Cards, Inc. Interview segments between Elie Abel and Dr. Daniel J. Boorstin funded by a grant from the Corporation for Public Broadcasting.

171 **Bicentennial Minutes** CBS
Program Type Educational/Cultural Series
Daily narration of an incident of American history as it happened "200 years ago today." Premiere date: 7/4/74. Originally scheduled to conclude on the Bicentennial 7/4/76, it was extended with the same format. Last show: 12/31/76. 60 seconds every night. Different narrator each night. For concluding show, Pres. Gerald R. Ford was the narrator.
Executive Producer Robert Markell
Producer Paul Waigner
Company CBS News
Director Sam Sherman
Story Editor Jerome Alden

172 **Big Blue Marble** Syndicated
Program Type Children's Series
30 minutes. Weekly. Premiere date: 9/74. Third season premiere: 9/76. Magazine format focusing on children from all over the world. Regular feature: "Dear Pen Pal." Show is a public service of I.T.T. Corporation. Created by Henry Fownes, Robert L. Garrison, Ken Snyder.
Producer Henry Fownes
Company Alphaventure
Distributor Media International
Directors Various
Writers Various
Musical Director Norman Paris
Animation Director Ron Campbell

The Big Country *see* The CBS Friday Night Movies

173 **The Big Event** NBC
Program Type Miscellaneous Series
Times vary. Sundays (usually). Premiere date: 9/26/76. A combination of dramas, musical-variety shows, documentaries, sporting events and motion pictures. The theatrically released motion pictures shown on "The Big Event" are: "Earthquake" (1974—with FM simulcast to duplicate Sensurround) shown in two parts 9/26/76 and 10/3/76, "Gone With the Wind"

(1939) shown in two parts 11/7/76 and 11/8/76, "The Hindenburg" (1975) shown 9/6/77 and "2001: A Space Odyssey" (1968) shown 2/13/77. The sporting event, the second game of the World Series, was shown live 10/17/76 (*see* "World Series" for credits.) The other specials are: "The Big Party," "The Billion Dollar Movies," "Christmas Around the World," "The Emmy Awards," "An Evening With Diana Ross," "The Father Knows Best Reunion," "The First Fifty Years," "In the Glitter Palace," "Irwin Allen's Production of Fire!" "Jesus of Nazareth," "Life Goes to the Movies," "Live from the Mardi Gras, It's Saturday Night on Sunday" (*see* "NBC's Saturday Night"), "The National Disaster Survival Test," "Once Upon a Time . . . Is Now the Story of Princess Grace," "Raid on Entebbe," "The Spell," "Sybil," "Tail Gunner Joe," "That Was the Year That Was," "US Against the World." (*See* individual titles for credits.)

174 **Big Henry and the Polka Dot Kid**
Special Treat NBC
Program Type Children's Special
60 minutes. Premiere date: 11/9/76. Dramatization based on the story "Luke Baldwin's Vow" by Morley Callaghan about a 10-year-old orphan and a blind dog. Music by Carl Davis.
Executive Producer George A. Heinemann
Producer Linda Gottlieb
Company Learning Corporation of America
Director Richard Marquand
Writer W. W. Lewis
Scenic Designer Robert Lachman
Dog Trainers Leonard Brook, Bunny Brook

CAST

Big Henry .... Ned Beatty
Luke Baldwin .... Chris Barnes
Edwina Kemp .... Estelle Parsons
Aunt Helen .... Estelle Omens
Conductor .... Robert Gerringer
Telegraph Man .... Paul Benedict
Stokey Andrews .... Barry Corbin
Veterinarian .... Fred Stuthman
Sam Carter .... William Duell
Dan .... Wolfie

Big Jake *see* NBC Night at the Movies/NBC Saturday Night at the Movies

175 **Big John, Little John** NBC
Program Type Children's Series
30 minutes. Saturday mornings. Premiere date: 9/11/76. Last show: 9/3/77. Comedy about a 45-year-old high school teacher who keeps changing into a 12-year-old boy and back again. Created by Sherwood Schwartz.
Executive Producer Sherwood Schwartz
Producer Lloyd Schwartz
Company A Redwood Production in association with D'Angelo/Bullock/Allen Productions
Directors Various
Writers Various

CAST

Big John .... Herb Edelman
Little John .... Robbie Rist
Additional Cast Joyce Bulifant, Mike Darnell, Olive Dunbar, Christoff St. John, Cari Anne Warder, Stephen Cassidy

176 **The Big Party**
The Big Event NBC
Program Type Music/Comedy/Variety Special
90 minutes. 9/26/76. Live "salute" from three New York City locations to the 1976–77 sports, performing arts and motion picture seasons.
Executive Producer Alvin Cooperman
Producer John Gilroy
Company National Broadcasting Company
Director Clark Jones
Writers Harvey Jacobs, Brian McConnachie
Musical Director Elliot Lawrence

From Sardi's and Shubert Alley
A salute to the new Broadway season, including scenes from the all-black revival of "Guys and Dolls."
Host George C. Scott
Stars Marvin Hamlisch, Hal Linden, Ethel Merman
Special Guest Star Joanne Woodward

From the Top of the Park Restaurant
A salute to new films.
Hosts Lauren Bacall, Leonard Nimoy

From the Felt Forum at Madison Square Garden
A salute to sports.
Host Dick Cavett
Stars Blood, Sweat and Tears
Guests Muhammad Ali, Ken Norton
NBC Blimp Anchormen Bob and Ray (Bob Elliot and Ray Goulding)

Bigfoot, the Mysterious Monster *see* NBC Night at the Movies

177 **Bikes, Bikes, Bikes** PBS
Program Type Documentary/Informational Special
30 minutes. Premiere date: 10/25/76. A chronicle of the bicycle. Captioned for the hearing-impaired by Daniel B. Glisson, Jr. Program funded by a grant from the U.S. Bureau of Education for the Handicapped.
Company WGBH-TV Caption Center/Boston

178 **Bill Russell Raps** PBS
Program Type Documentary/Informational Special
30 minutes. Premiere date: 10/24/76. Film excerpted from the high school lectures and informal conversations of Bill Russell with teenagers. Program made possible by a grant from the American Telephone and Telegraph Company.
Executive Producer William F. Russell (Bill Russell)
Company WNET-TV/New York

179 **The Billion Dollar Movies**
The Big Event NBC
Program Type Documentary/Informational Special
90 minutes. Premiere date: 5/15/77. Highlights of the highest-grossing motion pictures released since 1927.
Producers Lee Mendelson, Karen Crommie
Company Lee Mendelson Productions, Inc.
Directors Lee Mendelson, Karen Crommie
Writer Lee Mendelson
Cinematographers Chuck Barbee, David Crommie
Film Editors Paul Preuss, Ben Maiden
Researcher E. J. Muller
Music Coordinators Ed Bogas, Larry Finlayson
Host/Narrator David Niven

Billy Jack *see* NBC Saturday Night at the Movies

180 **Bing! . . . A 50th Anniversary Gala** CBS
Program Type Music/Comedy/Variety Special
90 minutes. Premiere date: 3/20/77. Music-variety special celebrating Bing Crosby's 50 years in show business. Special musical material by Ray Charles. Film sequences by Stu Bernstein and Eytan Keller. Taped at the Ambassador College Auditorium in Pasadena, Calif. 3/3/77.
Executive Producer Frank Konigsberg
Producer Marty Pasetta
Company The Konigsberg Company
Director Marty Pasetta
Writer Buz Kohan
Musical Director Nick Perito
Choreographer Robert Sidney
Art Director Roy Christopher
Star Bing Crosby
Special Guest Star Bob Hope
Guest Stars Paul Anka, Pearl Bailey, Joe Bushkin, Rosemary Clooney, Kathryn Crosby, Harry Crosby, Mary Frances Crosby, Nathaniel Crosby, Sandy Duncan, the Mills Brothers, Donald O'Connor, Martha Raye, Debbie Reynolds, Anson Williams, Bette Midler

181 **Bing Crosby National Pro-Am** ABC
Program Type Sports Special
Live coverage of the final two rounds of the golf championship from the Pebble Beach (Calif.) Golf Links 1/22/77 and 1/23/77.
Executive Producer Roone Arledge
Producer Chuck Howard
Company ABC Sports
Directors Jim Jennett, Terry Jastrow
Hosts Bing Crosby, Jim McKay
Anchor Jim McKay
Expert Commentators Peter Alliss, Dave Marr, Bob Rosburg

182 **Bing Crosby's White Christmas Special** CBS
Program Type Music/Comedy/Variety Special
60 minutes. Premiere date: 12/1/76. Bing Crosby's 41st annual Christmas show. Special musical material by Ray Charles. Program taped in London.
Executive Producer Frank Konigsberg
Producer Norman Campbell
Director Norman Campbell
Writer Herbert Baker
Musical Director Peter Knight
Choreographer Norman Maen
Art Director Ken Wheatley
Stars Bing Crosby, Bernadette Peters, Kathryn Crosby, Mary Frances Crosby, Harry Crosby, Nathaniel Crosby
Special Guest Jackie Gleason

183 **The Bionic Woman** ABC
Program Type Crime Drama Series
60 minutes. Wednesdays. Premiere date: 1/14/76. Second season premiere: 9/22/76 (as the conclusion to a two-part episode which started 9/19/76 on "The Six Million Dollar Man.") Last show on ABC: 5/4/77. (On NBC during the 1977–78 season.) Spin-off from "The Six Million Dollar Man." Action adventure of bionic schoolteacher/Office of Scientific Information (OSI) agent. Created for television by Kenneth Johnson; based on the novel "Cyborg" by Martin Caidin. Music by Joe Harnell.
Executive Producer Harve Bennett
Producer Kenneth Johnson
Company Harve Bennett Productions in association with Universal Television
Directors Various
Executive Story Consultant Arthur Rowe
Writers Various

CAST

Jaime Sommers .... Lindsay Wagner
Oscar Goldman .... Richard Anderson
Rudy Wells .... Martin E. Brooks

184 **The Birth and Death of a Star** PBS
Program Type Science/Nature Special
30 minutes. Premiere date: 1/29/73. Repeat date: 1/4/77. Documentary tracing the evolution of a great star. Program made with the cooperation of Hale Observatories, Kitt Peak National Observatory, the National Astronomy and Ionospheric Center and the National Radio Astronomy Observatory. Program made possible by a grant from the National Science Foundation.
Executive Producer Dr. Richard S. Scott
Producer Bert Shapiro
Company KCET-TV/Los Angeles in association with the American Institute of Physics and the National Science Foundation
Director Bert Shapiro
Writer Bert Shapiro
Host/Commentator Dr. John A. Wheeler
Guests Dr. Don Hall, Dr. Jesse L. Greenstein, Dr. Beverly T. Lynds, Dr. Frank D. Drake, Dr. John A. Ball

185 **Black Filmmakers Hall of Fame** PBS
Program Type Parades/Pageants/Awards Special
90 minutes. Premiere date: 4/9/77. The fourth Oscar Micheaux Awards ceremony honoring blacks in motion pictures. Taped 2/20/77 at the Paramount Theatre in Oakland, Calif. Program made possible by a grant from the Corporation for Public Broadcasting.
Executive Producer Christopher Lukas
Producer Carol Munday Lawrence
Company KQED-TV/San Francisco
Director Robert N. Zagone
Hosts Lou Gossett, Denise Nicholas
Guest Stars James Earl Jones, Cicely Tyson, LeVar Burton, Brock Peters, Roscoe Lee Browne, Roxie Roker, Bee Freeman, Bernard Johnson, Maidie Norman

186 **Black Journal** PBS
Program Type Public Affairs Series
30 minutes. Mondays. Premiere date: 6/68. Ninth season premiere: 2/7/77. Repeats began 5/9/77. 13-part series examining "how Afro-American events, personalities, issues and movements have influenced American life." Magazine format. Series made possible by a grant from the Pepsi-Cola Company.
Executive Producer Tony Brown
Company WNET-TV/New York
Director Bud Myers
Musical Director Bob Thomas
Host Tony Brown

187 **Black Perspective On the News** PBS
Program Type Public Affairs Series
30 minutes. Thursdays. Third season premiere: 9/2/76. Taped around the country with black media journalists interviewing newsmakers. Series funded by the Ford Foundation, the Corporation for Public Broadcasting and Public Television Stations.
Producers Reginald Bryant, Acel Moore
Company WHYY-TV/Wilmington/Philadelphia
Director J. M. Van Citters
Research Associate Shirley Jones
Host/Moderator Reginald Bryant

188 **Blackout**
CBS News Special Report CBS
Program Type News Special
30 minutes. Premiere date: 7/14/77. A look at the power loss in New York City and an examination of the possibilities of a similar situation elsewhere.
Executive Producer Leslie Midgley
Company CBS News
Anchor Morton Dean

189 **Blackout in New York City**
NBC News Special NBC
Program Type News Special
30 minutes. Premiere date: 7/14/77. Special report on the New York City blackout of 7/13/77
Producer Patrick Trese
Company NBC News
Anchor Edwin Newman
Commentators/Reporters Jackson Bain, Carole Simpson, Fred Francis, George Lewis, John Marshall, Robert Bazell

190 **Blansky's Beauties** ABC
Program Type Comedy Series
30 minutes. Saturdays. Premiere date: 2/12/77. Last regular show: 5/21/77. Several shows subsequently seen on "The ABC Monday Comedy Special" on 6/6/77, 6/27/77 and 7/11/77. Comedy about the producer of shows at the Las Vegas Oasis Hotel created by Garry K. Marshall, Bob Brunner and Arthur Silver. "I Want It All" music by Charles Fox, lyrics by Norman Gimbel, sung by Cyndi Grecco.
Executive Producers Garry K. Marshall, Edward K. Milkis, Thomas L. Miller
Producers Bruce Johnson, Tony Marshall, Nick Abdo
Company Miller-Milkis Productions, Inc. and Henderson Production Company, Inc. in association with Paramount Television
Directors Jerry Paris, Alan Rafkin
Writers Various
Choreographer Gary Menteer

Blansky's Beauties *Continued*
Costume Designer Jack Bear

CAST

Nancy Blansky .... Nancy Walker
Bambi Benton .... Caren Kaye
Joey DeLuca .... Eddie Mekka
Anthony DeLuca .... Scott Baio
Hillary S. Prentiss .... Taaffe O'Connell
Arkansas .... Rhonda Bates
Horace "Stubs" Wilmington .... George Pentecost
Ethel "Sunshine" Akalino .... Lynda Goodfriend
Lovely Carson .... Bond Gideon
Sylvia Silver .... Antonette Yuskis
Misty Karamazov .... Jill Owens
Gladys "Cochise" Littlefeather .... Shirley Kirkes
Jackie Outlaw .... Gerri Reddick
Bridget Muldoon .... Elaine Bolton
Arnold .... Pat Morita
Blackjack (a Great Dane) .... Blackjack

191 **Blind Sunday**
ABC Afterschool Specials ABC
Program Type Children's Special
60 minutes. Premiere date: 4/21/76. Repeat date: 10/27/76. Young people's drama of a friendship between a blind girl and a sighted boy. Music by Michel Legrand.
Producer Daniel Wilson
Company Daniel Wilson Productions, Inc.
Director Larry Elikann
Writers Arthur Barron, Fred Pressburger

CAST

Mrs. Hays .... Betty Beaird
Eileen .... Jewel Blanch
Jeff .... Leigh J. McCloskey
Jeff's Father .... Robert Ridgely
Lifeguard .... Corbin Bernsen
Ticket Taker .... Ivan Bonar
Marge .... Cindy Eilbacher
Cab Driver .... Bill Elliot
Pam .... Debi Storm
Erik .... Steve Tanner
Math Teacher .... Carol Worthington

192 **A Blind Teacher In a Public School**
Americana PBS
Program Type Documentary/Informational Special
30 minutes. Premiere date: 4/22/77. Repeat date: 9/4/77. A look at David Ticchi, a blind 7th grade English teacher in Newton, Massachusetts. Program made possible by grants from Braille Services Club, Inc., Frederick E. Weber Charities Corporation, Maurice Falk Medical Foundation, Reader's Digest Foundation and Polaroid Foundation.
Producer Pauline McCance
Company WGBH-TV/Boston

The Blue Angel *see* PBS Movie Theater

193 **The Blue Hotel**
The American Short Story PBS
Program Type Dramatic Special
60 minutes. Premiere date: 4/19/77. Adaptation of a short story by Stephen Crane set in a rustic inn at the edge of a Nebraska town in the 1880s. Program presented by South Carolina Educational Television and made possible by a grant from the National Endowment for the Humanities.
Executive Producer Robert Geller
Producer Ozzie Brown
Company Learning in Focus, Inc.
Director Jan Kadar
Writer Harry M. Petrakis
Costume Designer Juul Haalmeyer
Scenic Designer Charles Rosen
Host Colleen Dewhurst

CAST

Swede .... David Warner
Journalist .... Geddeth Smith
Cowboy .... John Bottoms
Scully .... Rex Everhart
Johnnie .... James Keach
The Stranger .... Tom Aldredge
Additional Cast Red Sutton, Lisa Pelikan, Cynthia Wright

194 **The Blue Knight** CBS
Program Type Crime Drama Series
60 minutes. Wednesdays. Premiere date: 12/17/75. Second season premiere: 9/22/76. Last show: 10/20/76. Based on the 1972 novel "The Blue Knight" by Joseph Wambaugh and 5/9/75 TV special. Story of a veteran cop on the beat in a big-city integrated neighborhood. Theme music by Henry Mancini.
Executive Producers Lee Rich, Philip Capice
Producer Robert Schlitt
Company Lorimar Productions
Directors Various
Story Editor James Hirsch
Writers Various
Production Consultant Joseph Wambaugh

CAST

Bumper Morgan .... George Kennedy

Blue Water, White Death *see* NBC Saturday Night at the Movies

195 **The Boarding House** PBS
Program Type Music/Dance Series
30 minutes. Tuesdays. Premiere date: 8/7/74. Repeats shown as of 9/7/76. Six-part series of music concerts taped at The Boarding House in San Francisco. Programs made possible by a grant from the Corporation for Public Broadcasting.
Executive Producer Zev Putterman
Company KQED-TV/San Francisco

Director Robert N. Zagone
Guests Mary McCreary, Esther Phillips, The Pointer Sisters, Leo Sayer, Taj Mahal, Wendy Waldman

196 **Bob Hope Desert Classic** NBC
Program Type Sports Special
Live coverage of the final two rounds of the 18th annual five-day pro-am golf tournament from the La Quinta (Calif.) Country Club 2/12/77 and 2/13/77.
Producer Larry Cirillo
Company NBC Sports
Director Harry Coyle
Host Bob Hope
Anchors Jim Simpson, Cary Middlecoff
Commentators Bruce Devlin, Fran Tarkenton, John Brodie

197 **The Bob Newhart Show** CBS
Program Type Comedy Series
30 minutes. Saturdays. Premiere date: 9/16/72. Fifth season premiere: 9/25/76. Series created by David Davis and Lorenzo Music. Story centers around Chicago psychologist. Music by Pat Williams.
Executive Producers Tom Patchett, Jay Tarses
Producers Michael Zinberg, Gordon Farr, Lynne Farr
Company MTM Enterprises, Inc.
Directors Various
Story Editor Sy Rosen
Writers Various

CAST

Bob Hartley .... Bob Newhart
Emily Hartley .... Suzanne Pleshette
Jerry Robinson .... Peter Bonerz
Howard Bordon .... Bill Daily
Carol Kester Bondurant .... Marcia Wallace
Elliott Carlin .... Jack Riley
Mr. Peterson .... John Fiedler
Mrs. Bakerman .... Florida Friebus
Michelle .... Renee Lippin
Larry Bondurant .... Will MacKenzie

198 **The Bobby Goldsboro Show** Syndicated
Program Type Music/Comedy/Variety Series
30 minutes. Weekly. Season premiere: 9/76. Pop/country music-variety show.
Executive Producer Bill Graham
Producers Bill Hobin, Jane Dowden, J. Reginald Dunlap
Company Show Biz, Inc.
Distributor Show Biz, Inc.
Director Bill Hobin
Writer Ed Hider
Musical Director Timmy Tappan
Host Bobby Goldsboro

199 **The Bobby Vinton Show** Syndicated
Program Type Music/Comedy/Variety Series
30 minutes. Weekly. Premiere date: 9/75. Second (last) season premiere: 9/76. Filmed in Toronto.
Executive Producers Allan Blye, Chris Bearde
Producer Alan Thicke
Company Chuck Barris Productions and Allan Blye-Chris Bearde Productions in association with CTV
Distributor Station Program Sales
Director Mike Steele
Host Bobby Vinton

200 **The Body Human: The Miracle Months** CBS
Program Type Documentary/Informational Special
60 minutes. Premiere date: 3/16/77. Informational special on human birth with the emphasis on problem pregnancies. Music by Teo Macero.
Executive Producer Thomas W. Moore
Producer Alfred R. Kelman
Co-Producer Vivian R. Moss
Company Tomorrow Entertainment/Medcom Company
Director Alfred R. Kelman
Writer Robert E. Fuisz, M.D.
Cinematographer Robert Elfstrom
Film Editor Peter Eliscu
Narrator Alexander Scourby

201 **Boley, Oklahoma—Alive and Well**
Americana PBS
Program Type Documentary/Informational Special
30 minutes. Premiere date: 6/3/77. A look at one of the oldest all-Black towns in the United States now famous for its annual rodeo.
Producer Ed Clay
Company Nebraska Educational Television Network
Director Ed Clay
Cinematographer Drew Suss
Host Mal Adams

202 **Bonnie Raitt and Mose Allison**
In Performance at Wolf Trap PBS
Program Type Music/Dance Special
60 minutes. Premiere date: 10/20/75. Repeat date: 11/1/76. Two separate concerts of blues and jazz performed by Bonnie Raitt and Mose Allison at the Wolf Trap Farm Park in Arlington, Va. Program made possible by a grant from the Atlantic Richfield Company.
Executive Producer David Prowitt
Producer Ruth Leon
Company WETA-TV/Washington, D.C.
Hosts Beverly Sills, David Prowitt
Executive-in-Charge Jim Karayn

203 **Book Beat** PBS
Program Type Educational/Cultural Series
30 minutes. Wednesdays. Premiered in 1965. Continuous. Weekly interview show with authors. Series funded by grants from the Corporation for Public Broadcasting, the Ford Foundation and Public Television Stations.
Producer Chuck Tyler
Company WTTW-TV/Chicago
Director Chuck Tyler
Host Robert Cromie

204 **Born Again**
CBS Reports CBS
Program Type Documentary/Informational Special
60 minutes. Premiere date: 7/14/77. A look at Evangelical Christianity in the United States.
Executive Producer Howard Stringer
Producers Janet Roach, Judy Crichton
Company CBS News
Directors Janet Roach, Judy Crichton
Writers Bill Moyers, Janet Roach
Cinematographers Skip Brown, William J. Wagner
Film Editors Larry Silk, Joseph Fackovec
Researcher Susan D. Werbe
Reporter Bill Moyers

Born Losers *see* NBC Saturday Night at the Movies

205 **The Boston Pops in Hollywood** PBS
Program Type Music/Dance Special
90 minutes. Premiere date: 3/8/76. Repeat date: 12/14/76. The first performance of the Boston Pops Orchestra on the West Coast. Filmed at the Century Plaza Hotel in Los Angeles 9/13/75. Special lyrics to "California Here I Come" by Sammy Cahn performed by the Johnny Mann Singers. Program made possible by a grant from Gulf Oil Corporation.
Executive Producer Loring d'Usseau
Producer William Cosel
Company KCET-TV/Los Angeles
Director William Cosel
Writer Marc London
Conductor Arthur Fiedler
Host Charlton Heston
Guest Stars Edgar Bergen, Anthony Paratore, Joseph Paratore

206 **Boxing Doubleheader** CBS
Program Type Sports Special
Two hours. Premiere date: 10/15/76. Heavyweight fight between George Foreman and Dino Dennis and the World Boxing Association Lightweight Championship fight between Roberto Duran and Alvaro Rojas from the Hollywood (Fla.) Sportorium.
Producer Frank Chirkinian
Company CBS Television Network Sports
Director Frank Chirkinian
Host Jack Whitaker
Commentators Tom Brookshier, Jerry Quarry (heavyweight fight)/Brent Musburger, Sugar Ray Leonard (lightweight fight)

207 **Boxing Special** CBS
Program Type Sports Special
60 minutes. Premiere date: 3/20/77. Howard Davis, Jr. vs. Rick Craney, Leon Spinks vs. Jerry McIntyre, Lee Canalito vs. Bill Jackson from Louisville, Ky.
Producer David Fox
Company CBS Television Network Sports
Director Tony Verna
Commentators Tom Brookshier, Ken Norton

208 **Boxing Tripleheader** CBS
Program Type Sports Special
Two hours. Live coverage of three fights from the Miami Beach (Fla.) Convention Hall 7/17/77: Mike Rossman vs. Marcel Clay; Howard Davis, Jr. vs. Dom Monaco; Ronnie "Mazel" Harris vs. Frank Reiche.
Producer David Fox
Company CBS Television Network Sports
Director Bob Dailey
Commentators Tom Brookshier, Jerry Quarry

209 **Bowl Preview—1976–77** ABC
Program Type Sports Special
30 minutes. Premiere date: 12/19/76. A look at the top college football teams competing in the 1976–77 season bowl games.
Executive Producer Roone Arledge
Producer Joe Aceti
Company ABC Sports
Director Norm Samet
Host Keith Jackson

210 **The Boy In the Plastic Bubble**
Star The ABC Friday Night Movie/The ABC Sunday Night Movie ABC
Program Type TV Movie
Two hours. Premiere date: 11/12/76. Repeat date: 5/8/77. Story by Joseph Morgenstern and Douglas Day Stewart. Concerns a boy born without immunities and forced to live in an incubator-like environment. Music by Mark Snow, "What Would They Say?" composed and sung by Paul Williams.
Executive Producers Aaron Spelling, Leonard Goldberg
Producers Joel Thurm, Cindy Dunne

Company Spelling/Goldberg Productions
Director Randal Kleiser
Writer Douglas Day Stewart
Art Director Paul Sylos

CAST

Tod Lubitch	John Travolta
Gina Biggs	Glynnis O'Connor
Johnny Lubitch	Robert Reed
Mickey Lubitch	Diana Hyland
Martha Biggs	Karen Morrow
Pete Biggs	Howard Platt
Dr. Gunther	Ralph Bellamy
Roy Slater	John Friedrich
Col. Edwin E. "Buzz" Aldrin, Jr.	Col. Edwin E. "Buzz" Aldrin, Jr.

A Boy Named Charlie Brown *see* CBS Special Film Presentations

211 **The Brady Bunch Hour** ABC
Program Type Music/Comedy/Variety Series
60 minutes. Sundays (every fifth week)/Mondays (weekly) as of 3/21/77. Premiere date: 1/23/77. Last regular show: 4/25/77. One extra show 5/25/77. Musical/variety show with the characters from "The Brady Bunch" in California starring in a television series.
Executive Producers Sid Krofft, Marty Krofft
Producer Lee Miller
Co-Producer Tom Swale
Company Sid and Marty Krofft Production in association with Paramount Television
Director Jack Regas
Writing Supervisor Carl Kleinschmitt
Writers Ronny Graham, Bruce Vilanch, Steve Bluestein, Mike Kagan
Musical Director George Wyle
Choreographer Joe Cassini
Costume Designer Pete Menefee

CAST

Carol Brady	Florence Henderson
Mike Brady	Robert Reed
Greg Brady	Barry Williams
Marcia Brady	Maureen McCormick
Peter Brady	Christopher Knight
Bobby Brady	Mike Lookinland
Cindy Brady	Susan Olsen
Jan Brady	Geri Reischl
Alice	Ann B. Davis
Merrill	Rip Taylor

Regulars Krofftette Dancers, Water Follies

212 **The Brady Bunch Variety Hour** ABC
Program Type Music/Comedy/Variety Special
60 minutes. Premiere date: 11/28/76. The stars of "The Brady Bunch" series (9/69–8/74) in a comedy/music pilot for "The Brady Bunch Hour."
Executive Producers Sid Krofft, Marty Krofft
Producers Lee Miller, Jerry McPhie
Company A Sid & Marty Krofft Television Production in association with Paramount Television
Director Art Fisher
Writers Carl Kleinschmitt, Ronny Graham, Terry Hart, Steve Bluestein
Guests Donny Osmond, Marie Osmond, Tony Randall

CAST

Mike Brady	Robert Reed
Carol Brady	Florence Henderson
Greg Brady	Barry Williams
Marcia Brady	Maureen McCormick
Peter Brady	Christopher Knight
Jan Brady	Geri Reischl
Bobby Brady	Mike Lookinland
Cindy Brady	Susan Olsen
Alice	Ann B. Davis

The Brain *see* The ABC Friday Night Movie

213 **The Brandywine Tradition** PBS
Program Type Documentary/Informational Special
30 minutes. Premiere date: 12/24/76 (captioned.) A look at an illustrator at work. Captioned for the hearing-impaired by Lucinda Winslow at WGBH-TV/Boston. Program made possible by a grant from the U.S. Bureau of Education for the Handicapped.
Company WITF-TV/Hershey, Pa.

Brannigan *see* The CBS Friday Night Movies

214 **Bravo Two** CBS
Program Type Dramatic Special
30 minutes. Premiere date: 3/25/77. Action-adventure pilot about the exploits of the Los Angeles Harbor Patrol. Created by Guerdon Trueblood. Filmed in part on location in Marina del Rey, Calif.
Executive Producers Lee Rich, Philip Capice
Producers Robert Stambler, Guerdon Trueblood
Company Lorimar Productions
Director Ernest Pintoff
Writer Leo Gordon

CAST

Wiley Starrett	Bruce Fairbairn
Bud Wizzer	David Gilliam
Lt. O'Brien	James Hampton
T. J. Phillips	Cooper Huckabee
Mr. Morgan	Don Matheson
Mrs. Morgan	Lynn Carlin
Eddie Morgan	Matthew Laborteaux
Lucy	Lucy Saroyan

215 **Break the Bank** Syndicated
Program Type Game/Audience Participation Series
30 minutes. Weekly. Premiere date: 9/76. New version of game show which originally premiered in 1948.
Producer Dan Enright
Company Barry & Enright Productions
Distributor Dick Colbert Company
Director Richard Kline
Host Jack Barry

Breakout *see* NBC Monday Night at the Movies/NBC Saturday Night at the Movies

Breezy *see* NBC Monday Night at the Movies

The Bridge at Remagen *see* The ABC Sunday Night Movie

216 **Bridger**
The ABC Friday Night Movie ABC
Program Type TV Movie
Two hours. Premiere date: 9/10/76. Repeat date: 7/15/77. Based on the true-life adventures of the legendary mountain man in the 1830s. Filmed in part in the Sierra Madre mountains in California.
Producer David Lowell Rich
Company Universal Television
Director David Lowell Rich
Writer Merwin Gerard
Costume Designer Charles Waldo
Set Decorator Joseph J. Stone

CAST

Jim Bridger .... James Wainwright
Kit Carson .... Ben Murphy
Joe Meek .... Dirk Blocker
Jennifer Melford .... Sally Field
Sen. Daniel Webster .... William Windom
Pres. Andrew Jackson .... John Anderson
David Bridger .... Claudio Martinez
Shoshone Woman .... Margarita Cordova
Doctor .... Tom Middleton
Modoc Leader .... Robert Miano
Paiute Chief .... Skeeter Vaughan
Crow Chief .... X Brands
Army Lieutenant .... W. T. Zacha
Presidential Aide .... Keith Evans

Brief Encounter *see* PBS Movie Theater

217 **Bristol-Myers Mixed Doubles Classic** NBC
Program Type Sports Special
Two hours. Live coverage of the Mixed Doubles Classic from the Woodlands Inn and Country Club near Houston, Tex. 4/24/77.
Producer Dick Auerbach
Company NBC Sports
Director Ken Fouts
Announcer Bud Collins
Analyst John Newcombe
Reporter Barbara Hunter

218 **British Open Golf Championship** ABC
Program Type Sports Special
Two hours. Live satellite coverage of the final round of the 106th British Open Golf Championship from Turnberry, Ayrshire, Scotland 7/9/77.
Executive Producer Roone Arledge
Producer Chuck Howard
Company ABC Sports
Director Jim Jennett
Announcer Jim McKay
Expert Commentators Dave Marr, Bob Rosburg

Brother John *see* The ABC Friday Night Movie

219 **The Bugs Bunny Easter Special** CBS
Program Type Animated Film Special
60 minutes. Premiere date: 4/7/77. Animated special with Easter theme tying together segments from ten classic Warner Bros. cartoons featuring Bugs Bunny, Daffy Duck, Sylvester the Cat, Pepe Le Pew, Foghorn Leghorn, Yosemite Sam and Granny.
Executive Producer Hal Geer
Company DePatie-Freleng Productions
Supervising Director Friz Freleng
Directors Bob McKimson, Gerry Chiniquy, Chuck Jones
Voices Mel Blanc, June Foray

220 **Bugs Bunny in Space** CBS
Program Type Animated Film Special
30 minutes. Premiere date: 9/6/77. Animated adventures of Bugs Bunny in space drawn from previously released productions.
Executive Producer Hal Geer
Company Warner Bros., Inc.
Animation Directors Chuck Jones, Friz Freleng
Voices Mel Blanc

221 **The Bugs Bunny/Road Runner Hour** CBS
Program Type Animated Film Series
60 minutes. Saturday mornings. Premiere date: 9/6/75. Second season premiere: 9/11/76. Reruns of old cartoons from the Warner Bros. cartoon library featuring Yosemite Sam, Daffy

Duck, Porky Pig, Sylvester Jr., Elmer Fudd and others. Main voice characterizations by Mel Blanc.
Company Warner Bros.

222 **Bumpers**
The ABC Monday Comedy Special ABC
Program Type Comedy Special
30 minutes. Premiere date: 5/16/77. Comedy pilot about a Detroit automobile assembly line worker.
Producers David Davis, Charlotte Brown
Company MTM Enterprises, Inc.
Director James Burrows
Writers David Davis, Charlotte Brown

CAST

Joey Webber .... Richard Masur
Rozzie Webber .... Stephanie Faracy
Andy .... Michael L. McManus
Murphy .... Jack Riley
Jay .... Tim Reid
Jennifer .... Zane Buzby
Mr. Dickey .... Ray Buktenica
Ernie Stapp .... Brian Dennehy

223 **Bunco** NBC
Program Type TV Movie
60 minutes. Premiere date: 1/13/77. Pilot drama of bunco squad investigators. Created by Jerry Ludwig.
Executive Producers Lee Rich, Philip Capice
Producer Jerry Ludwig
Company Lorimar Production in association with NBC-TV
Director Alexander Singer
Writer Jerry Ludwig

CAST

Gordean .... Tom Selleck
Walker .... Robert Urich
Lt. Hyatt .... Milt Kogan
Frankie .... Donna Mills
Dixon .... Michael Sacks
Sonny .... Alan Feinstein
Winky .... Will Geer
Yousha .... Arte Johnson

Buona Sera, Mrs. Campbell *see* NBC Monday Night at the Movies

224 **Busting Loose** CBS
Program Type Comedy Series
30 minutes. Mondays/Wednesdays (as of 7/27/77). Premiere date: 1/17/77. Show preempted as of 5/2/77. Returned 7/27/77. Comedy about a 22-year-old in search of independence and a career. Created by Mark Rothman and Lowell Ganz. "Busting Loose" theme by Mark Rothman. Music by Jack Elliott.
Executive Producers Mark Rothman, Lowell Ganz
Producer Lawrence Kasha
Company Paramount Television
Directors Various
Writers Various
Story Consultant Greg Antonacci

CAST

Lenny Markowitz .... Adam Arkin
Sam Markowitz .... Jack Kruschen
Pearl Markowitz .... Pat Carroll
Melody Feebeck .... Barbara Rhoades
Lester Bellman .... Danny Goldman
Allan Simmonds .... Stephen Nathan
Vinnie Mordabito .... Greg Antonacci
Woody Warshaw .... Paul Sylvan
Ralph Cabell .... Paul B. Price
Raymond St. Williams .... Ralph Wilcox

Butch Cassidy and the Sundance Kid *see* Special Movie Presentation

225 **Byron Nelson Golf Classic** ABC
Program Type Sports Special
Live coverage of the final rounds of the 1977 golf classic from the Preston Trail Golf Club in Dallas, Tex. 5/7/77 and 5/8/77.
Executive Producer Roone Arledge
Producer Bob Goodrich
Company ABC Sports
Directors Jim Jennett, Terry Jastrow
Anchors Chris Schenkel, Bill Flemming
Expert Commentators Bob Rosburg, Dave Marr, Verne Lundquist

The Cabinet of Dr. Caligari *see* PBS Movie Theater

226 **The Cabot Connection** CBS
Program Type TV Movie
60 minutes. Premiere date: 5/10/77. Adventure pilot about a jet-set socialite-turned-undercover agent. Music by George Romanis.
Executive Producer Barry Weitz
Producer Robert Mintz
Company Columbia Pictures Television
Director E. W. Swackhamer
Writer George Kirgo
Art Director John Beckman

CAST

Marcus Cabot .... Craig Stevens
Olivia Cabot .... Cathie Shirriff
Muffin Cabot .... Jane Actman
Stephen Kordiak .... Chris Robinson
Dolly Foxworth .... Gloria DeHaven
Heinz Vogel .... Alf Kjellin
Victor Kreindler .... Curt Lowens
Brom Loomis .... Dirk Benedict
Bozuffi .... James Luisi
Harold O'Hara .... Warren Kemmerling
Essie .... Matilda Calnan
Rosenfeld .... Frank Downing
Wendell .... Ivor Barry

The Cabot Connection *Continued*

Clerk .... Llynn Storer
Wharfman .... Glenn R. Wilder
Bidder No. 1 .... Walter O. Miles
Bidder No. 2 .... Bill Smillie
Bidder No. 3 .... Bill Morey
Customer .... Ted Stanhope

Caesar and Cleopatra *see* PBS Movie Theater

227 **Cage Without a Key**
The CBS Wednesday Night Movies CBS
Program Type TV Movie
Two hours. Premiere date: 3/14/75. Repeat date: 2/2/77. Drama of teenager in a jail for juvenile criminal offenders. Filmed in part at the Las Palmas School for Girls, City of Commerce, Calif.
Executive Producer Douglas S. Cramer
Producer Buzz Kulik
Company Douglas S. Cramer Company in association with Columbia Pictures Television
Director Buzz Kulik
Writer Joanna Lee

CAST

Valerie Smith .... Susan Dey
Ben Holian .... Michael Brandon
Tommy .... Jonelle Allen
Buddy Goleta .... Sam Bottoms
Joleen .... Anne Bloom
Betty Holian .... Karen Carlson
Angel Perez .... Edith Diaz
Suzy .... Suesie Elene
Sarah .... Dawn Frame
Mrs. Little .... Katherine Helmond
Jamie .... Vicky Huxtable
Mrs. Turner .... Karen Morrow
Noreen .... Lani O'Grady
Wanda Polsky .... Margaret Willock

Cahill, U. S. Marshall *see* CBS Special Film Presentations/The CBS Wednesday Night Movies

228 **The California Dream: A Search For Community** PBS
Program Type Documentary/Informational Special
30 minutes. Premiere date: 10/15/76. An in-depth examination of California—its past, present and future. Program made possible by a grant from Title I of the Higher Education Act.
Producer Paul Cabbell
Company KOCE-TV/Huntington Beach, Calif.
Director Harry Ratner
Writer Paul Cabbell
Reporter Paul Cabbell

229 **Call It Macaroni** Syndicated
Program Type Children's Series
30 minutes each. Monthly. Premiere date: 1/75. Second season premiere: 6/76. Twelve programs each season showing the real-life adventures of youngsters in different parts of the country. "Anything Is Possible" music by David Lucas; lyrics by Gail Frank and Stephanie Meagher.
Executive Producer George Moynihan
Producers Gail Frank, Stephanie Meagher
Company Group W Productions, Inc.
Directors Gail Frank, Stephanie Meagher

230 **The Call of the Wild**
NBC Thursday Night at the Movies NBC
Program Type TV Movie
Two hours. Premiere date: 5/22/76. Repeat date: 1/6/77. Drama based on the novel by Jack London of two men searching for gold in the Klondike with the dog, Buck. Filmed on location in the High Sierras of California, in Southern California and in Wyoming. Music by Peter Matz.
Executive Producer Charles Fries
Producer Malcolm Stuart
Company Charles Fries Productions, Inc., in association with NBC-TV
Director Jerry Jameson
Writer James Dickey
Costume Designer Chad M. Harwood
Art Director Joel Schiller
Dog Trainers Frank Weatherwax, Carl Spitz

CAST

Thornton .... John Beck
Francois .... Bernard Fresson
Prospector .... John McLiam
Simpson .... Donald Moffat
Stranger .... Michael Pataki
Rosemary .... Penelope Windust
Guitar Player .... Johnny Tillotson
Redsweater .... Billy Green Bush
Will .... Raymond Guth
Stony .... Dennis Burkley

231 **Calling Dr. Storm, M.D.**
Comedy Time NBC
Program Type Comedy Special
30 minutes. Premiere date: 8/25/77. Comedy pilot about a surgical resident trying to cope with politics at All Fellows Hospital.
Executive Producer Stirling Silliphant
Producer Frank Konigsberg
Company A Silliphant-Konigsberg Company Production in association with Warner Bros. Television and NBC-TV
Director James Burrows
Writers Lawrence J. Cohen, Fred Freeman

CAST

Jim Storm .... Larry Linville
Patti Storm .... Sharon Spelman
Paul Sloane .... Stephen Parr
Nate Nateman .... Richard Libertini

Bart Burton .... James Sikking
Maggie Barbour .... Marian Mercer
Sarah Baynes .... P. J. Soles
Ilko Stendak .... Bruce Gordon
Vanessa Stendak .... Mary Louise Weller
Glenn Puber .... Robert Hogan

Camelot *see* NBC Monday Night at the Movies/NBC Saturday Night at the Movies

232 **Camera Three** CBS
Program Type Educational/Cultural Series
30 minutes. Sundays. Local premiere on WCBS-TV/New York: 5/16/53. National premiere date: 1/22/56. 21st season network premiere: 9/12/76. Experimental series dealing with "a variety of people, ideas, performances and new directions in the arts and sciences."
Executive Producer John Musilli
Producers John Musilli, Roger Englander and others
Company WCBS-TV/New York
Directors John Musilli, Roger Englander and others

233 **The Campaign and the Candidates**
Decision '76 NBC
Program Type Public Affairs Series
30 minutes. Premiere date: 9/12/76. Last show: 10/23/76. Seven special pre-election programs focusing on the candidates and issues of the 1976 campaign with various correspondents anchoring the programs.
Executive Producer Gordon Manning
Producer Earl Ubell
Company NBC News Special Broadcast Unit
Anchors John Chancellor, David Brinkley, Catherine Mackin, Edwin Newman, Linda Ellerbee

234 **Campaign '76 (Series)** CBS
Program Type Public Affairs Series
Special weekly series covering the presidential campaign and the election issues. 30 minutes. Fridays. Special 60-minute premiere: 9/3/75. Last show: 10/29/76.
Executive Producer Leslie Midgley
Producer Ernest Leiser
Company CBS News
Anchor Walter Cronkite

235 **Campaign '76: Election Night** CBS
Program Type News Special
Live coverage of election results 11/2/76–11/3/76 beginning 7 p.m.–4:49 a.m. (Eastern time).
Executive Producer Russ Bensley
Senior Producer David Buksbaum
Company CBS News
Director Arthur Bloom
Anchor Correspondent Walter Cronkite
Analysis Correspondents Eric Sevareid, Bill Moyers
Regional Correspondents Roger Mudd, Dan Rather, Lesley Stahl, Mike Wallace
Trend Desk Correspondent Bruce Morton
Remote Correspondents Ed Rabel, Ed Bradley, Bruce Hall, David Dick, Robert Pierpoint, Bob Schieffer, Phil Jones, Fred Graham, Barry Serafin, Eric Engberg, Marya McLaughlin, Sylvia Chase, Morton Dean, Randy Daniels, Chris Kelly, Bill Plante, Jed Duvall, Terry Drinkwater, Richard Wagner

236 **Campaign '76: Election Preview** CBS
Program Type News Special
60 minutes. 10/31/76. A pre-election special report on major races and issues throughout the country.
Executive Producer Russ Bensley
Senior Producer David Buksbaum
Company CBS News
Director Arthur Bloom
Anchor Walter Cronkite

237 **Campaign '76: The Presidential Debates—Analysis (First Debate)** CBS
Program Type News Special
30 minutes. 9/23/76. CBS News Special Report analyzing the first debate from Philadelphia.
Executive Producer Russ Bensley
Company CBS News
Anchor Walter Cronkite
Analysts Eric Sevareid, Bob Schieffer, Ed Bradley
Reporters Roger Mudd, Phil Jones, Ed Rabel

238 **Campaign '76: The Presidential Debates—Analysis (Second Debate)** CBS
Program Type News Special
25 minutes. 10/6/76. CBS News Special Report analyzing the second debate from San Francisco.
Executive Producer Russ Bensley
Company CBS News
Anchor Walter Cronkite
Analysts Eric Sevareid, Bob Schieffer, Ed Bradley
Reporters Roger Mudd, Lesley Stahl, Phil Jones, Ed Rabel

239 **Campaign '76: The Presidential Debates—Analysis (Third Debate)** CBS
Program Type News Special
25 minutes. 10/22/76. CBS News Special Report analyzing the last presidential debate from Williamsburg, Va.

Campaign '76: The Presidential Debates —Analysis (Third Debate) *Continued*
Executive Producer Russ Bensley
Company CBS News
Anchor Walter Cronkite
Analysts Eric Sevareid, Bob Schieffer, Ed Bradley
Reporters Roger Mudd, Lesley Stahl, Phil Jones, Ed Rabel

240 **Campaign '76: The Vice-Presidential Debate—Analysis** CBS
Program Type News Special
15 minutes. 10/15/76. CBS News Special Report analyzing the debate between the vice-presidential candidates.
Executive Producer Russ Bensley
Company CBS News
Anchor Walter Cronkite
Analysts Eric Sevareid, Bill Plante, Barry Serafin
Reporters Bruce Morton, Lesley Stahl, Jed Duvall, Eric Engberg

241 **Campaign '76: What Happened Last Night** CBS
Program Type News Special
60 minutes. 11/3/76. A post-election special report analyzing the results of the elections throughout the country.
Executive Producer Russ Bensley
Senior Producer David Buksbaum
Company CBS News
Director Arthur Bloom
Anchor Walter Cronkite

242 **Canadian Open** CBS
Program Type Sports Special
Live and taped coverage of the final two rounds of the Canadian Open golf championship at Glen Abbey Golf Club in Toronto, Canada 7/23/77 and 7/24/77.
Producer Frank Chirkinian
Company CBS Television Network Sports
Producer Bob Dailey
Commentators Vin Scully, Pat Summerall, Ben Wright, Frank Glieber, Jack Whitaker, Ken Venturi

243 **Candide**
Classic Theatre: The Humanities in Drama PBS
Program Type Dramatic Special
90 minutes. Premiere date: 10/30/75. Repeat date: 3/24/77. Adapted from the play by Voltaire. Live action and cartoon backgrounds. Program made possible by grants from the National Endowment for the Humanities and Mobil Oil Corporation. Presented by WGBH-TV/Boston; Joan Sullivan, producer.
Producer Cedric Messina
Company British Broadcasting Corporation
Director James MacTaggart
Writer James MacTaggart

CAST

Voltaire .... Frank Finlay
Candide .... Ian Ogilvy
Dr. Pangloss .... Emrys James
Cunegonde .... Angela Richards
Cocambo .... Clifton Jones

244 **The Canonization of Bishop John Neumann** CBS
Program Type Religious/Cultural Special
60 minutes. Premiere date: 6/19/77. Highlights of the canonization of Bishop John Neumann transmitted via satellite from St. Peter's Square in the Vatican.
Executive Producer Pamela Ilott
Producer Chalmers Dale
Company CBS News Religious Broadcast
Commentators Charles Osgood, Father Francis X. Murphy

245 **The Captain & Tennille** ABC
Program Type Music/Comedy/Variety Series
60 minutes. Mondays. Premiere date: 9/20/76. Last show: 3/14/77. Regular feature: "Masterjoke Theatre" with pie-in-the-face conclusion. In January 1977 the production staff changed completely.
Executive Producers Alan Bernard/Dick Clark and Mace Neufeld
Producer Bob Henry/Bill Lee
Company Moonlight & Magnolias, Inc. and Bob Henry Productions/Moonlight & Magnolias, Inc. and Dick Clark Teleshows
Director Tony Charmoli/John Moffitt
Head Writers John Boni and Norman Stiles/Ray Jessel
Writers Stephen Spears, Thad Mumford, Tom Dunsmuir, Ed Hider, Ruth Merithew/Lennie Ripps, Robert Sand, Robert Illes, James R. Stein, April Kelly, George Geiger
Musical Director Lenny Stack
Choreographer Bob Thompson
Costume Designer Bill Belew
Art Director Romain Johnston
Stars Daryl Dragon, Toni Tennille (The Captain & Tennille)

246 **Captain Kangaroo** CBS
Program Type Children's Series
60 minutes. Monday–Friday mornings. Premiere date: 10/3/55. 22nd season premiere: 9/27/76. Created by Bob Keeshan. Set in "the Captain's Place." Cosmo Allegretti is the voice of many characters: Dancing Bear, Mr. Moose, Bunny

Rabbit, Miss Frog, etc. Hugh "Lumpy" Brannum plays various characters: Percy, Mr. Bainter, the Painter, The Professor, etc.
Producer Jim Hirschfeld
Company Robert Keeshan Associates, Inc.
Director Peter Birch
Head Writer Bob Colleary
Costume Designer Hugh Holt
Puppeteer Cosmo Allegretti

CAST

Captain Kangaroo .... Bob Keeshan
Mr. Green Jeans .... Hugh "Lumpy" Brannum
Dennis, the Apprentice .... Cosmo Allegretti
Mr. Baxter .... Jimmy Wall
Debbie .... Debbie Weems

247 **Captains and the Kings**
NBC's Best Seller NBC
Program Type Limited Series
Ten hours. Thursdays. Premiere date: 9/20/76. Repeats began: 3/31/77. Dramatization of the novel by Taylor Caldwell about an Irish immigrant's rise to power between 1857 and 1912. Special 60-minute recapitulation of the first five hours shown 11/4/76.
Executive Producer Roy Huggins
Producer Jo Swerling, Jr.
Company Roy Huggins/Public Arts in association with Universal Television
Director Douglas Heyes, Allen Reisner
Writer Douglas Heyes

CAST

Joseph Francis Xavier Armagh .... Richard Jordan
Young Joseph .... Johnny Doran
Sean Armagh (as a child) .... Kristopher Marquis
Mary Armagh (as a child) .... Missy Gold
Moira Armagh/Mary Armagh .. Katherine Crawford
R. J. Squibbs .... Ray Bolger
Sister Angela .... Celeste Holm
Mrs. Finch .... Ann Sothern
Katherine Hennessey .... Joanna Pettet
Tom Hennessey .... Vic Morrow
Young Bernadette .... Elizabeth Cheshire
Martinique .... Barbara Parkins
Miss Emmy .... Beverly D'Angelo
Haroun (Harry) Zeff .... Harvey Jason
Ed Healey .... Charles Durning
Elizabeth .... Blair Brown
Clair Montrose .... Peter Donat
O'Herlihy .... Neville Brand
Strickland .... Joe Kapp
Father Hale .... John Carradine
Charles Desmond .... Robert Vaughn
Col. Braithwaite .... Pernell Roberts
Sean Armagh .... David Huffman
Rory Armagh .... Perry King
Honora Armagh .... Jenny Sullivan
Claudia Armagh .... Cynthia Sikes
Sen. Enfield Bassett .... Henry Fonda
Marjorie Chisholm .... Jane Seymour
Courtney Wickersham .... Terry Kiser
Kevin Armagh .... Douglas Heyes, Jr.
"Old Syrup" .... Burl Ives
Bernadette Armagh .... Patty Duke Astin
Anne-Marie Armagh .... Ann Dusenberry
Judge Chisholm .... John Houseman
Brian Armagh .... Cliff De Young
Theodore Roosevelt .... Lee Jones-de Broux

248 **Captioned ABC Evening News** PBS
Program Type News Series
30 minutes. Mondays–Fridays. ABC (7 p.m.) news captioned for the hearing-impaired at WGBH-TV/Boston. Program funded by the U.S. Department of Health, Education and Welfare—Bureau of Education for the Handicapped. (*See* "ABC Evening News With Harry Reasoner and Barbara Walters" for credits.)

249 **Captioned Elliot Norton Reviews** PBS
Program Type Educational/Cultural Special
30 minutes. Premiere date: 5/30/77. A discussion about the National Theatre for the Deaf with David Hays and Elliot Norton. Captioned for the hearing-impaired with funds provided by the U.S. Office of Education—Bureau of Education for the Handicapped.
Company WGBH-TV/Boston

The Carey Treatment *see* The CBS Friday Night Movies

250 **The Carnival of the Animals** CBS
Program Type Children's Special
30 minutes. Premiere date: 11/22/76. A live-action and animation special based on the music of Camille Saint-Saens and verses by Ogden Nash.
Producer Chuck Jones
Company A Chuck Jones Enterprises Production
Director Chuck Jones
Writer Chuck Jones
Musical Director Michael Tilson Thomas
Animation Director Herbert Klynn
Live Action Director Gerry Woolery
Musical Supervisor Dean Elliott
Dual Pianists Zita Carno, Kathryn Ando (as Bugs Bunny and Daffy Duck)

VOICES

Bugs Bunny/Daffy Duck/Porky Pig .... Mel Blanc

251 **Carnivore**
Documentary Showcase PBS
Program Type Documentary/Informational Special
60 minutes. Premiere date: 12/3/76. Repeat date: 8/5/77 (with closed captions for the hearing-impaired.) An objective look at America's meat eating habits.
Producer John Beyer
Company Iowa Public Broadcasting Network

Carnivore *Continued*
Director John Beyer
Writer John Beyer
Cinematographer Ron Burnell
Film Editor Ron Burnell
Narrator Matthew James Faison

252 **The Carol Burnett Show** CBS
Program Type Music/Comedy/Variety Series
60 minutes. Saturdays. Premiere date: 9/11/67. Tenth season premiere: 9/25/76. Regular features include "Mrs. Wiggins and Mr. Tudball," "As the Stomach Turns" and "The Family" sketches and musical salutes. Show takes an annual summer vacation. Special 90-minute show celebrating ten years and 200 episodes aired 4/2/77.
Executive Producer Joe Hamilton
Producer Ed Simmons
Company Punkin Productions, Inc.
Director Dave Powers
Head Writer Ed Simmons
Writers Ed Simmons, Roger Beatty, Bill Richmond, Gene Perret, Dick Clair, Jenna McMahon, Bert Styler, Adele Styler, Elias Davis, David Pollock, Rick Hawkins, Liz Sage
Musical Director Peter Matz
Choreographer Ernest Flatt
Costume Designer Bob Mackie
Art Directors Paul Barnes, Bob Sanson
Star Carol Burnett
Regulars Harvey Korman, Tim Conway, Vicki Lawrence, Ernest Flatt Dancers

253 **The Carpenters** ABC
Program Type Music/Comedy/Variety Special
60 minutes. Premiere date: 12/8/76. The first television special for the Carpenters. Musical material written by Ken Welch and Mitzi Welch.
Executive Producer Jerry Weintraub
Producers Rich Eustis, Al Rogers
Director Bill Davis
Writers Jim Mulligan, Ray Jessel, Ronny Graham, April Kelly, George Geiger, Rich Eustis, Al Rogers
Musical Director Eddie Karam
Costume Designer Bill Belew
Art Director Ken Johnson
Stars The Carpenters (Richard Carpenter, Karen Carpenter)
Guest Stars John Denver, Victor Borge
Creative Consultant Joe Layton

254 **Carrascolendas** PBS
Program Type Children's Series
30 minutes. Saturdays. Premiere date: 10/72. Last season premiere: 10/9/76. 39 Spanish-English musical plays set in the village of Carrascolendas. Music composed by Raoul Gonzalez. Series made possible by grants from the U.S. Department of Health, Education and Welfare—Office of Education, Emergency School Aid Act (ESAA TV).
Executive Producer Aida Barrera
Producers Jose Villarreal, Daniel Wilcox
Company KLRN-TV/San Antonio-Austin
Director James Field
Head Writer Daniel Wilcox
Writers Robert Rafferty, Richard Smith, Vicki Kodama, Joel Quinones-Garza, Joe Garza, Paul Papanek, Mike Sullivan, Raoul Gonzalez, Jose Villarreal
Musical Director Nick Fryman
Costume Designer Karen Hudson
Art Director Brent Ramsey
Artistic Director Erick Santamaria

CAST

Agapito	Harry Frank Porter
Cleofas	Luis Avalos
Rita the Roofer	Boots Harvey
Dona Paquita	Eloise Campos
Don Jose	Adolph Aguilar
Benito Vendetodo	Erick Santamaria
Benjamin	Benjamin Lopez
Chelo	Cristine Beato
Campamocha	Mike Gomez
Josefina	Iraida Polanco
Chuchin	Ramiro "Ray" Ramirez
Paco	Francisco Vela III
Gloria	B. Natalia Dowd
Alice	Anne Galvan

255 **Carter Abroad: An Assessment**
NBC News Special NBC
Program Type News Special
30 minutes. Premiere date: 5/10/77. Coverage of President Carter's trip to England and Europe covered via satellite from London.
Executive Producer Gordon Manning
Producer Ray Lockhart
Company NBC News
Director Walter Kravetz
Anchor David Brinkley

256 **The Carter Report Card** ABC
Program Type Public Affairs Special
30 minutes. Premiere date: 8/14/77. An evaluation of the Carter Administration based on two ABC News/Louis Harris Polls plus an interview about the polls with Pres. Jimmy Carter.
Executive Producer Elliot Bernstein
Producer Bob Roy
Company ABC News Special Events
Anchor Harry Reasoner
Interviewers Harry Reasoner, Sam Donaldson

Casque D'Or *see* PBS Movie Theater

257 **Cat on a Hot Tin Roof**
NBC Monday Night at the Movies/Laurence Olivier Presents a Tribute to American Theatre NBC
Program Type Dramatic Special
Two hours. Premiere date: 12/6/76. Adaptation of the Pulitzer Prize-winning play by Tennessee Williams. Theme music by Henry Purcell arranged by Michael Lankester; incidental music by Derek Hilton.
Producers Derek Granger, Laurence Olivier
Company Granada Television in association with NBC-TV
Director Robert Moore
Writer Tennessee Williams
Costume Designer Jane Robinson
Scenic Designer Peter Phillips

CAST

Big Daddy .... Laurence Olivier
Margaret .... Natalie Wood
Brick .... Robert Wagner
Big Mama .... Maureen Stapleton
Gooper .... Jack Hedley
Mae .... Mary Peach
Dixie .... Heidi Rundt
Sonny .... Sean Saxon
Buster .... Mark Taylor
Trixie .... Elizabeth Caparros
Polly .... Jennifer Hughes
Lacey .... Sam Manseray
Daisy .... Gladys Taylor
Brightie .... Nadia Catouse
Sookey .... George Harris
Small .... Mel Taylor
Doc Baugh .... David Healy

Catch-22 *see* The ABC Sunday Night Movie

258 **Caught In the Act** PBS
Program Type Music/Dance Series
30 minutes. Thursdays. Premiere date: 10/7/74. Series repeats began 9/9/76. Seven-part program of musical concerts.
Executive Producer Peter Anderson
Company New Jersey Public Broadcasting Authority
Directors Various
Guest Artists The Bottle Hills Boys, Boys of the Lough, Jonathan Edwards, Raun MacKinnon and Jeremiah Burnheim, Murphy and Salt, The Persuasions, Arthur Prysock

259 **CBS All-American Thanksgiving Day Parade** CBS
Program Type Parades/Pageants/Awards Special
Three hours. 11/25/76. Live coverage of the 50th annual New York City Macy's Parade, the 57th Philadelphia Gimbels Parade and the 50th Detroit J. L. Hudson Parade; taped coverage of the 72nd Toronto Eaton's Santa Claus Parade and the 4th Hawaii Aloha Floral Parade.
Executive Producer Mike Gargiulo
Producers Wilf Fielding, Clarence Schimmel, Jim Hirschfeld, Mal Wienges, Vern Diamond
Company CBS Television
Writers Beverly Schanzer, Carolyn Miller, Betty Cornfeld, Chuck Horner
Host William Conrad
Parade Hosts Richard Crenna, Kevin Dobson, Michael Learned, Jack Lord, Gavin MacLeod, Mackenzie Phillips, Isabel Sanford, Loretta Swit

260 **The CBS Children's Film Festival** CBS
Program Type Children's Series
30 minutes/60 minutes (as of 4/9/77). Saturday mornings. Premiered in 1967. Tenth season premiere: 9/11/76. Films for children from around the world.
Company CBS Television Network Presentation
Hosts Fran Allison and Kukla, Fran and Ollie
Puppeteer Burr Tillstrom

261 **CBS Evening News (Saturday Edition)** CBS
Program Type News Series
30 minutes. Saturday evenings. Continuous. Bob Schieffer succeeded Dan Rather in November 1976.
Executive Producer Joan Richman
Company CBS News
Anchor Dan Rather/Bob Schieffer

262 **CBS Evening News (Sunday Edition)** CBS
Program Type News Series
30 minutes. Premiere date: 1/25/76. Continuous. Early Sunday evening news. Morton Dean succeeded Bob Schieffer in November 1976.
Executive Producer Joan Richman
Company CBS News
Anchor Bob Schieffer/Morton Dean

263 **CBS Evening News With Walter Cronkite** CBS
Program Type News Series
30 minutes. Premiere date: 9/2/63. Mondays–Fridays. Continuous. First 30-minute evening news program on television. Regular feature "On the Road" with Charles Kuralt returned 8/5/77 after being seen on "Who's Who."
Executive Producer Burton Benjamin
Company CBS News
Anchor Walter Cronkite
Regular Substitute Roger Mudd
Commentator Eric Sevareid

264 **The CBS Festival of Lively Arts for Young People** CBS
Program Type Children's Series
60 minutes. Monthly (Saturdays). Music, dance, poetry, and opera specials. Shows seen during the 1976–77 season are: "Ailey Celebrates Ellington," "Dance of the Athletes," "Fanfares and Fugues," "Gianni Schicchi," "Henry Winkler Meets William Shakespeare," "Making Pictures With Music," "Music for Young Performers," "The Original Rompin' Stompin' Hot and Heavy, Cool and Groovy All Star Jazz Show," "You're a Poet and Don't Know It! . . . The Poetry Power Hour." (*See* individual titles for credits.)

265 **The CBS Friday Night Movies** CBS
Program Type Feature Film Series – TV Movie Series
Two hours/three hours. Fridays. Season premiere: 9/24/76. Last show: 1/7/77. Return date: 5/6/77. Last show: 9/9/77. A combination of made-for television films and theatrically released motion pictures. The TV movies are: "Foster and Laurie," "The Hostage Heart," "I Want to Keep My Baby!" "Mayday at 40,000 Feet," "Smile, Jenny, You're Dead." (*See* individual titles for credits.) The theatrically released motion pictures are "Badlands" (1974) shown 10/29/76, "Battle for the Planet of the Apes" (1973) shown 6/17/77, "The Big Country" (1958) shown 7/8/77, "Brannigan" (1975) shown 10/8/76 and 5/20/77, "The Carey Treatment" (1972) shown 8/19/77, "Class of '44" (1973) shown 4/29/77, "Fear Is the Key" (1973) shown 5/13/77, "French Connection II" (1975) shown 11/26/76, "Hawaii" (1966) shown 7/1/77, "It's a Mad, Mad, Mad, Mad World" (1963) shown 12/31/76, "Magnum Force" (1973) shown 9/24/76, "Man on a Swing" (1974) shown 1/7/77, "The Other" (1972) shown 7/22/77, "Paper Moon" (1973) shown 10/1/76, "Play It Again, Sam" (1972) shown 11/5/76, "Pocket Money" (1972) shown 12/17/76, "Report to the Commissioner" (1975) shown 12/10/76, "The Russians Are Coming, the Russians Are Coming" (1966) shown 7/15/77, "Sharks' Treasure" (1975) shown 8/26/77, "Support Your Local Gunfighter" (1971) shown 5/6/77, "The Terminal Man" (1974) shown 12/3/76, "They Call Me Mister Tibbs" (1970) shown 8/5/77, "West Side Story" (1961) shown 6/24/77.

266 **CBS Galaxy** CBS
Program Type Music/Comedy/Variety Special
60 minutes. Premiere date: 9/5/77. Preview of the 1977–78 CBS series in a musical-comedy format. Special musical material by Artie Malvin and Dick Williams.
Executive Producer Joe Hamilton
Producer Rich Eustis
Director Dave Powers
Writers Bill Richmond, Gene Perret, Roger Beatty
Musical Director Peter Matz
Choreographer Joe Bennett
Costume Designer Bob Mackie
Art Director Ken Johnson
Host Dick Van Dyke
Stars Betty White, John Hillerman, Bob Newhart, Suzanne Pleshette, Peter Bonerz, Bill Daily, Linda Lavin, Beatrice Arthur, Bill Macy, Valerie Harper, Isabel Sanford, Sherman Hemsley, Carroll O'Connor, Jean Stapleton, Bess Armstrong, Lynnie Greene, Alan Alda, Jimmie Walker, Bonnie Franklin, Mackenzie Phillips, Pat Harrington, Adam Arkin, Oliver Clark, Beverly Archer, Tom Poston, Tony Randall, Gregory Harrison, Heather Menzies, Edward Asner, Telly Savalas, Buddy Ebsen, Jack Lord, James MacArthur, Robert Wagner, Eddie Albert, Bert Kramer, Mariclare Costello, Rick Moses, Lynda Carter, Patrick McGoohan, Ralph Waite, Michael Learned, Carol Burnett

267 **The CBS Invitational Tennis Championship** CBS
Program Type Sports Special
Two tennis events with 16 players.

Part I
90 minutes. Live coverage from Ocean City, Md. 2/19/77.
Producer Bob Rowe
Company CBS Television Network Sports
Director Bob Dailey
Commentators Pat Summerall, Tony Trabert

Part II
Highlights of the second event from Virginia Beach, Va. shown on the "CBS Sports Spectacular" 4/23/77.
Producer Perry Smith
Company CBS Television Network Sports
Director Bob Dailey
Commentator Pat Summerall

268 **The CBS Late Movie** CBS
Program Type Feature Film Series – TV Movie Series
A combination of made-for-television films and theatrically released features. Monday–Friday nights. Included are repeats of television series: "Kojak" scheduled twice weekly, plus recurring episodes of "Columbo," "McCloud" and "McMillan & Wife."

269 **CBS Mid-Day News With Douglas Edwards** CBS
Program Type News Series
Five minutes. Mondays–Fridays. Premiere date: 10/2/61. Continuous. Douglas Edwards has anchored the news since February 1969.
Company CBS News
Anchor Douglas Edwards

270 **CBS Morning News With Hughes Rudd and Bruce Morton** CBS
Program Type News Series
60 minutes. Monday–Fridays. Premiere date: 9/2/63. Continuous. Hughes Rudd anchors from New York; Bruce Morton from Washington, D.C. Rod MacLeish became commentator November 1976.
Executive Producer David F. Horwitz
Company CBS News
Anchors Hughes Rudd, Bruce Morton
Regulars Ray Brady, Ray Gandolf
Commentator Rod MacLeish

271 **CBS News Specials** CBS
Program Type News Series – Documentary/Informational Series
Special news and documentary broadcasts presented throughout the year. Programs shown during the 1976–77 season are: "Blackout," "Conversations With Eric Sevareid," "Energy: The Facts ... The Fears ... The Future," "Friends, Romans, Communists," "Inside CBS News," "Meet the New Senators," "Mr. Rooney Goes to Work," "On the Road With Charles Kuralt," "Our Happiest Birthday," "Presidential Address to a Joint Session of Congress," "Presidential Address to the Nation," "The Presidential Inauguration," "The Retirement Revolution," "Space Shuttle: The First Voyage," "State of the Union Address," "When Television Was Live," "Who's Ahead? The Debate Over Defense," "Who's Got a Right to Rhodesia." (*See* individual titles for credits.)

272 **CBS Reports** CBS
Program Type Documentary/Informational Series
60 minutes/two hours. Special documentary broadcasts presented throughout the year. Programs shown during the 1976–77 season are: "Arizona, Here We Come!" "The Baseball Business," "Born Again," "CBS Reports Special," "The CIA's Secret Army," "The Fire Next Door," "The People V. Gary Gilmore." (*See* individual titles for credits.)

273 **CBS Reports Special**
CBS Reports CBS
Program Type Documentary/Informational Special

The West Bank
30 minutes. Premiere date: 8/16/77. A report on the occupied West Bank of the Jordan River.
Executive Producer Howard Stringer
Producer Paul Greenberg
Company CBS News
Reporter Bill Moyers

Mad City
30 minutes. Premiere date: 8/16/77. A look at New York City during the summer of '77.
Executive Producer Howard Stringer
Producer Janet Roach
Company CBS News
Reporter Bill Moyers

274 **CBS Salutes Lucy—The First 25 Years** CBS
Program Type Comedy Special
Two hours. Premiere date: 11/28/76. Film and videotape highlights of Lucille Ball series, specials and guest appearances. Music by Peter Matz.
Producer Gary Morton
Co-Producer Sheldon Keller
Company Lucille Ball Productions, Inc.
Directors William Asher, Marc Breaux, Dick Carson, Jack Carter, Hal Collins, Marc Daniels, Jack Donohue, Greg Garrison, Jack Haley, Jr., Ron Jacobs, James V. Kern, George Marshall, John Moffitt, Jerry Paris, Dave Powers, Bobby Quinn, Coby Ruskin, Maury Thompson
Writer Sheldon Keller
Contributing Writers Herbert Baker, Bob Carroll, Jr., Madelyn Davis, Milt Josefsberg, Bob O'Brien, Jess Oppenheimer, Bob Schiller, Al Schwartz, Ray Singer, Bob Weiskopf, Ken Welch, Mitzi Welch
Star Lucille Ball
Guest Stars Desi Arnaz, Sr., Milton Berle, Carol Burnett, Richard Burton, Johnny Carson, Sammy Davis, Jr., Gale Gordon, Bob Hope, Danny Kaye, Dean Martin, James Stewart, Danny Thomas, Vivian Vance, Dick Van Dyke, John Wayne

275 **CBS Special Film Presentations** CBS
Program Type Feature Film Series – Feature Film Specials
Times vary. Feature films seen on an irregular basis until 5/1/77, then weekly (Sundays) through 5/22/77 and again between 7/24/77–9/18/77. The films are: "The Alamo" (1960)

CBS Special Film Presentations
Continued
shown 5/1/77, "Ben Hur" (1959) shown 5/22/77, "A Boy Named Charlie Brown" (1969) shown 4/29/77, "Cahill, U.S. Marshall" (1973) shown 9/11/77, "Charlotte's Web" (1971) shown in two parts 11/26/76 and 12/3/76, "The Cheyenne Social Club" (1970) shown 5/24/77, "Cold Turkey" (1971) shown 5/16/77, "The Getaway" (1972) shown 9/4/77, "Hannie Caulder" (1971) shown 7/31/77, "Hello, Dolly!" (1970) shown 5/23/77, "Juggernaut" (1974) shown 11/3/76, "The Life and Times of Judge Roy Bean" (1972) shown 9/18/77, "Logan's Run" (1976) shown 9/6/77, "Paper Moon" (1973) shown 5/15/77, "Snoopy, Come Home" (1972) shown 11/5/76, "Super Cops" (1974) shown 8/21/77, "The Taking of Pelham One Two Three" (1974) shown 7/24/77, "That's Entertainment!" (1974) shown 1/9/77, "Tom Sawyer" (1973) shown in two parts 12/14/76 and 12/21/76, "Vanishing Point" (1971) shown 8/7/77, "The Way West" (1967) shown 3/25/77, "White Lightning" (1973) shown 5/8/77, "The Wilby Conspiracy" (1975) shown 8/14/77, "The Wizard of Oz" (1939) shown 3/20/77.

276 **CBS Sports Spectacular** CBS
Program Type Sports Series
90 minutes. Saturdays. Coverage of sports events from around the world, including the 109th Belmont Stakes, the 36th Daytona "200" Motorcycle Race and the first Stuntmen's Competition and Awards Championships.
Coordinating Producer Perry Smith
Producers Various
Company CBS Television Network Sports
Directors Various
Host Pat Summerall
Commentators Gary Bender, Tom Brookshier, Don Criqui, Phyllis George, Brent Musburger, Lindsey Nelson, Vin Scully, Ken Squier, Jack Whitaker, Frank Wright

277 **CBS Sunday Night News** CBS
Program Type News Series
15 minutes. Late Sunday nights. Premiere date: 4/29/62. Continuous. Ed Bradley succeeded Morton Dean November 1976.
Executive Producer Joan Richman
Company CBS News
Anchor Morton Dean/Ed Bradley

278 **The CBS Wednesday Night Movies** CBS
Program Type Feature Film Series – TV Movie Series
Two hours. Wednesdays. Season premiere: 11/10/76. A combination of theatrically released motion pictures and made-for-television films. The TV movies are "Cage Without a Key" and "Red Alert." (*See* individual titles for credits.) The feature films are "Cahill, U. S. Marshall" (1973) shown 12/22/76, "Chinatown" (1974) shown 11/17/76, "Chisum" (1970) shown 3/30/77, "The Cowboys" (1972) shown 5/11/77, "The Deadly Trackers" (1973) shown 8/3/77, "Death Wish" (1974) shown 11/10/76, "The Deserter" (1971) shown 1/5/77, "Dillinger" (1973) shown 8/10/77, "El Condor" (1970) shown 4/27/77, "The French Connection" (1971) shown 11/24/76, "The Getaway" (1972) shown 12/15/76, "In the Heat of the Night" (1967) shown 7/20/77, "Made for Each Other" (1971) shown 7/13/77, "The Magnificent Seven Ride!" (1972) shown 8/17/77, "A Man Called Horse" (1970) shown 2/16/77, "McCabe & Mrs. Miller" (1971) shown 6/22/77, "Mr. Majestyk" (1974) shown 3/9/77, "The Parallax View" (1974) shown 2/23/77, "Posse" (1975) shown 3/23/77, "Race With the Devil" (1975) shown 5/4/77, "Red Sun" (1971) shown 5/25/77, "Rollerball" (1975) shown 2/9/77, "Save the Tiger" (1973) shown 12/8/76, "Scarecrow" (1973) shown 6/15/77, "The Secret of Santa Vittoria" (1969) shown 7/6/77, "Smile" (1975) shown 12/29/76, "Soylent Green" (1973) shown 6/8/77, "A Warm December" (1973) shown 6/29/77, "When the Legends Die" (1972) shown 7/27/77.

279 **CBS Youth Invitational ... Frisbee** CBS
Program Type Children's Special
30 minutes. Premiere date: 8/27/77. Eight of the top junior and senior frisbee champions in competition. Taped 7/12/77 and 7/13/77 at Six Flags Over Georgia in Atlanta, Ga.
Executive Producer Jack Dolph
Producer Jim Cross
Company Jack Dolph Associates, Inc.
Director Jim Cross
Host Tom Brookshier
Expert Commentator Peter Bloeme

280 **CBS Youth Invitational ... Skateboarding** CBS
Program Type Children's Special
30 minutes. Premiere date: 2/12/77. Six teenage skateboarders in three events. Taped at The Dark Continent, Busch Gardens, Tampa, Florida.
Executive Producers Jack Dolph, Bill Riordan
Producer Jim Cross
Company Jack Dolph Associates, Inc.
Director Jim Cross
Host Tom Brookshier
Expert Analyst Denis Shufeldt

281 **Celebrating a Century** PBS
Program Type Documentary/Informational Special
30 minutes. Premiere date: 5/11/77. Repeat date (captioned for the hearing-impaired): 7/4/77. A recreation of the 1876 Philadelphia Exposition celebrating the 100th birthday of the United States. Music by Oscar Brand. Presented by WHYY-TV/Phildelphia-Wilmington. Program made possible by grants from the National Science Foundation and the Smithsonian Institution. Funds for captioning for the hearing-impaired provided by the Bureau of Education for the Handicapped to WGBH-TV/Boston.
Producer Karen Loveland
Company Smithsonian Institution
Director John Hiller
Writer Benjamin W. Lawless
Narrator James Whitmore

282 **Celebrity Bowling** Syndicated
Program Type Sports Series
30 minutes. Daily and weekly. Preceded by "The Celebrity Bowling Classic" in 1969. In syndication since 1/71. Four guest celebrities in team bowling.
Producers Joe Siegman, Don Gregory
Company 7–10 Productions
Distributor Syndicast Services, Inc.
Director Don Buccola
Host Jed Allan

283 **Celebrity Challenge of the Sexes** CBS
Program Type Sports Special
Two hours. Premiere date: 4/17/77. Variation of "Challenge of the Sexes" with male and female celebrities in competition in a variety of events.
Producers Jay Michaels, Rudy Tellez
Company Trans World International
Director Tony Verna
Hosts Vin Scully, Phyllis George
Co-Hosts/Celebrity Coaches Penny Marshall, Rob Reiner
Competitors Bill Cosby, Farrah Fawcett-Majors, Connie Stevens, Flip Wilson, Susan Howard, Gabriel Kaplan, Dan Haggerty, Kristy McNichol, Robert Conrad, Penny Marshall, Phyllis George, O. J. Simpson, Redd Foxx, Roz Kelly, Edward Asner, Lola Falana, Lloyd Bridges, Cindy Williams, Kathryn Crosby, McLean Stevenson, Elliott Gould, Brenda Vaccaro, Stefanie Powers, Tony Randall

284 **Celebrity Sweepstakes** NBC
Program Type Game/Audience Participation Series
30 minutes. Mondays–Fridays. Premiere date: 4/1/74. Last show: 10/1/76. Contestants bet on the knowledge of six guest celebrities.
Executive Producer Ralph Andrews
Producer George Vosburgh
Company Ralph Andrews Productions in association with Burt Sugarman Productions and NBC-TV
Director Dick McDonough
Host Jim McKrell
Announcer Bill Armstrong
Regular Carol Wayne

285 **Celebrity Sweepstakes (Evening)** Syndicated
Program Type Game/Audience Participation Series
30 minutes. Weekly. Premiere date: 9/74. Last season premiere: 9/76. Evening version of daytime game.
Executive Producer Ralph Andrews
Producer George Vosburgh
Company Ralph Andrews Productions
Distributor 20th Century-Fox Television
Director Dick McDonough
Host Jim McKrell
Announcer Bill Armstrong

286 **Celebrity Tennis** Syndicated
Program Type Sports Series
30 minutes. Weekly. Four guest celebrities in doubles matches.
Producers Joe Siegman, Don Gregory
Company 7–10 Productions
Distributor Syndicast Services, Inc.
Director Don Buccola
Host Bobby Riggs

287 **Challenge of the Network Stars** ABC
Program Type Sports Special
Two hours. Premiere date: 2/28/77. Second contest pitting teams of stars from ABC, CBS and NBC against each other in athletic events (*see also* "Battle of the Network Stars.")
Executive Producer Roone Arledge
Producer Don Ohlmeyer
Company Trans World International, Inc. in association with ABC Sports
Director Chet Forte
Host Howard Cosell
Expert Commentators O. J. Simpson, Bruce Jenner
Stars from ABC Gabriel Kaplan (captain), LeVar Burton, Darleen Carr, Richard Hatch, Ron Howard, Lawrence-Hilton Jacobs, Hal Linden, Penny Marshall, Kristy McNichol, Jaclyn Smith
Stars from CBS Telly Savalas (captain), Sonny Bono, Kevin Dobson, Mike Farrell, Loretta

Challenge of the Network Stars
Continued
Swit, David Groh, Linda Lavin, Lee Meriwether, Rob Reiner, Marcia Wallace
Stars from NBC Robert Conrad (captain), Elizabeth Allen, Carl Franklin, Lynda Day George, Karen Grassle, Dan Haggerty, Art Hindle, Kurt Russell, Jane Seymour, W. K. Stratton

288 **Challenge of the Sexes** CBS
Program Type Limited Sports Series
45 minutes. Sundays. Premiere date: 1/10/76. Second season premiere: 1/16/77. Last show of series: 4/3/77 ("Best of Challenge of the Sexes"). Top male and female athletes competing against each other in a variety of sports. Taped at Mission Viejo, Calif. and Mt. Tremblant, Quebec, Canada. (*See also* "Celebrity Challenge of the Sexes.")
Producers Jay Michaels, Rudy Tellez
Company Trans World International
Director Tony Verna
Hosts Vin Scully, Phyllis George

289 **The Changing Face of Baseball** NBC
Program Type Sports Special
60 minutes. Premiere date: 3/27/77. A report on the business of baseball in 1977.
Executive Producers Don Ellis, Joe Garagiola
Producer Ginny Seipt
Company NBC Sports in cooperation with Joe Garagiola Enterprises
Director Steve Rosen
Writer Frank Slocum
Scenic Designer Kathy Ankers
Host Joe Garagiola
Reporters Tony Kubek, Jim Simpson, Maury Wills, Barbara Hunter, Don Drysdale

290 **A Charlie Brown Christmas** CBS
Program Type Animated Film Special
30 minutes. Premiere date: 12/9/65. Repeat date: 12/18/76. Created by Charles M. Schulz. Music by Vince Guaraldi.
Executive Producer Lee Mendelson
Producers Lee Mendelson, Bill Melendez
Company A Lee Mendelson–Bill Melendez Production in cooperation with United Feature Syndicate, Inc.
Director Bill Melendez
Writer Charles M. Schulz
Musical Director Vince Guaraldi
Music Supervisor John Scott Trotter

VOICES

Charlie Brown .... Peter Robbins
Lucy .... Tracy Stratford
Linus .... Christopher Shea
Schroeder .... Chris Doran
Patti .... Sally Dryer
Sally .... Cathy Steinberg
Frieda .... Ann Altieri

291 **A Charlie Brown Thanksgiving** CBS
Program Type Animated Film Special
30 minutes. Premiere date: 11/20/73. Repeat date: 11/22/76. Created by Charles M. Schulz. Music by Vince Guaraldi.
Producers Lee Mendelson, Bill Melendez
Company A Lee Mendelson–Bill Melendez Production in cooperation with United Feature Syndicate, Inc., and Charles M. Schulz Creative Associates
Directors Bill Melendez, Phil Roman
Writer Charles M. Schulz
Musical Director Vince Guaraldi
Music Supervisor John Scott Trotter

VOICES

Charlie Brown .... Todd Barbee
Linus .... Stephen Shea
Peppermint Patty .... Christopher Defaria
Lucy .... Robin Kohn
Sally .... Hilary Momberger
Marcie .... Jimmy Ahrens
Franklin .... Robin Reed

292 **Charlie Cobb: Nice Night for a Hanging**
NBC Movie of the Week NBC
Program Type TV Movie
Two hours. Premiere date: 6/9/77. Dramatic pilot about a private eye in the West of the 1870s. Based on a story by Peter Fischer, Richard Levinson and William Link.
Executive Producers Richard Levinson, William Link
Producer Peter Fischer
Company Fairmount/Foxcroft Production in association with Universal Television and NBC-TV
Director Richard Michaels
Writer Peter Fischer

CAST

Charlie Cobb .... Clu Gulager
McVea .... Ralph Bellamy
Charity .... Blair Brown
Martha .... Stella Stevens
Sheriff .... Pernell Roberts
Waco .... Christopher Connelly
Angelica .... Tricia O'Neil
Conroy .... George Furth

293 **Charlie's Angels** ABC
Program Type Crime Drama Series
60 minutes. Wednesdays. Premiere date: 9/22/76. Action-adventure about three private investigators working for a never-seen boss who communicates with them by phone. Created by Ivan Goff and Ben Roberts. Pilot aired 3/21/76 and 9/14/76. Music by Jack Elliott and Allyn Ferguson.

Executive Producers Aaron Spelling, Leonard Goldberg
Producers Rick Husky, Barney Rosenzweig
Company A Spelling/Goldberg Production
Directors Various
Story Editors Jack V. Fogarty, Edward J. Lakso
Writers Various

CAST

Sabrina Duncan .... Kate Jackson
Jill Munroe .... Farrah Fawcett-Majors
Kelly Garrett .... Jaclyn Smith
Bosley .... David Doyle

294 **Charlie's Angels (Pilot)**

The ABC Monday Night Movie ABC
Program Type TV Movie
90 minutes. Premiere date: 3/21/76. Repeat date: 5/2/77. Pilot for 1976–77 season series about three female detectives. Filmed in part in Napa and Palmdale, Calif. Music by Barry De-Vorzon.
Executive Producers Aaron Spelling, Leonard Goldberg
Producers Ivan Goff, Ben Roberts
Company Spelling/Goldberg Productions
Director John Llewellyn Moxey
Writers Ivan Goff, Ben Roberts
Art Director Paul Sylos

CAST

Sabrina .... Kate Jackson
Jill .... Farrah Fawcett-Majors
Kelly .... Jaclyn Smith
Bosley .... David Doyle
Woodville .... David Ogden Stiers
Rachel .... Diana Muldaur
Beau Creel .... Bo Hopkins
Bancroft .... John Lehne
Aram .... Tommy Lee Jones
Wilder .... Grant Owens
Clerk .... Ken Sansom
Miguel .... David Nunez
Hicks .... Ron Stein
Hawkins .... Bill Erwin
Bathing Beauty .... Colette Bertrand
Sheriff .... Russ Grieve

Charlotte's Web *see* CBS Special Film Presentations

295 **A Chat With Country Music Artist Doc Williams** PBS

Program Type Documentary/Informational Special
30 minutes. Premiere date: 7/23/77. An interview with Doc Williams.
Producer David R. Hopfer
Company WWVU-TV/Morgantown, W. Va.
Director David R. Hopfer
Interviewer Carl Fleischhauer

296 **The Chevy Chase Show**

Multi-Special Night NBC
Program Type Music/Comedy/Variety Special
60 minutes. Premiere date: 5/5/77. Chevy Chase's first television special. Special musical material by Paul Shaffer.
Executive Producer Martin Erlichman
Producer Bob Finkel
Company Cornelius Productions
Director Art Fisher
Writers Chevy Chase, Stuart Birnbaum, Brian Doyle-Murray, Thomas Leopold, Lane Sarasohn
Musical Director Alan Copeland
Costume Designer Warden Neil
Art Director Bill Bohnert
Star Chevy Chase
Special Guest Star Tim Conway
Guests Jack LaLanne, Dr. Joyce Brothers, Stuff, Ken Norton, Duane Bobick, Jimmy Ellis, Dave Stockton, the Shapiro Sisters, Moore's Mongrel Revue, Jacqueline Chase
Additional Cast Burten Carraher, Brian Doyle-Murray, Chris Guest, Bob Harks, David Hayward, Kevin Kishler, Thomas Leopold, Edie McClurg, Wendie Jo Sperber, Bunny Summers, Arno Vigen, Bill Zuckert, Dick Tufeld

The Cheyenne Social Club *see* CBS Special Film Presentations

297 **The Chicago Soul Special** NBC

Program Type Music/Dance Special

Part I

90 minutes. Premiere date: 3/12/77 (1–2:30 a.m.). Music special taped in October 1976 at the Amphitheater in Chicago during the Rev. Jesse Jackson's "Push for Excellence" campaign.
Producer Cal Burton
Company Avandi II Production
Director Martin Morris
Art Director Carlos Berben
Hosts Don Cornelius, The Spinners
Guests Ronnie Dyson, Walter Jackson, Johnnie Taylor, the Brothers Johnson, D. J. Rogers, Eddie Kendricks, Bill Withers, B. T. Express

Part II

90 minutes. Premiere date: 4/16/77 (1–2:30 a.m.). More songs from the October 1976 special.
Producer Cal Burton
Company Avandi II Production
Director Martin Morris
Art Director Carlos Berben
Host Don Cornelius
Guests The Spinners, D. J. Rogers, the Dramatics, Johnnie Taylor, Walter Jackson, Ronnie Dyson, the Chi-lites, Bill Withers, Brass Construction

298 **Chicago Symphony Orchestra: Solti Conducts Wagner** PBS
Program Type Music/Dance Special
60 minutes. Premiere date: 3/1/77. Repeat date: 6/26/77. The orchestral opera music of Richard Wagner performed by the Chicago Symphony Orchestra. Presented by WTTW-TV/Chicago. Program made possible by a grant from Kraftco.
Executive Producer Klaus Hallig
Producer David Griffiths
Company Unitel
Director Humphrey Burton
Conductor Sir Georg Solti

299 **Chico and the Man** NBC
Program Type Comedy Series
30 minutes. Fridays. Premiere date: 9/13/74. Third season premiere: 10/1/76. Comedy series about a garage owner in the barrio of East Los Angeles and his young Chicano partner. Music by Jose Feliciano. Created by James Komack.
Executive Producer James Komack
Supervising Producer Hal Kanter
Producer Michael Morris
Company The Komack Company, Inc. in association with the Wolper Organization and NBC-TV
Director Jack Donohue
Executive Story Editor George Bloom
Writers Various
Art Director Roy Christopher
Executive Script Supervisor Marty Nadler

CAST

Ed Brown .... Jack Albertson
Chico .... Freddie Prinze
Della Rogers .... Della Reese
Louie Wilson .... Scatman Crothers

300 **Chico and the Man (Daytime)** NBC
Program Type Comedy Series
30 minutes. Mondays–Fridays. Premiere date: 5/9/77. Morning reruns of the evening series. For credit information, *see* "Chico and the Man."

301 **Childhood**
Great Performances PBS
Program Type Drama Series
60 minutes. Wednesdays. Premiere date: 2/16/77. Series repeats began 8/31/77. Adaptations of five stories told from a child's point of view: "Baa Baa Blacksheep," "Easter Tells Such Dreadful Lies," "A Great Day For Bonzo," "An Only Child," "Possessions." (*See* individual titles for credits.) Series made possible by a grant from Exxon Corporation with additional support from member stations of PBS.

302 **Chinatown**
Documentary Showcase PBS
Program Type Documentary/Informational Special
60 minutes. Premiere date: 12/10/76. Repeat date: 7/29/77 (with captions for the hearing-impaired). A videotaped look at the plight of New York City's poverty-stricken Chinese community. Program made possible by grants from the Corporation for Public Broadcasting and the New York State Council on the Arts.
Executive Producer David Loxton
Producers Jon Alpert, Keiko Tsuno, Yoko Maruyama
Company Downtown Community Television Center and the Television Laboratory at WNET-TV/New York
Directors Jon Alpert, Keiko Tsuno, Yoko Maruyama
Writers Jon Alpert, Keiko Tsuno, Yoko Maruyama
Narrator Jon Alpert

Chinatown (Feature Film) *see* The CBS Wednesday Night Movies

Chisum *see* The CBS Wednesday Night Movies

303 **The Chopped Liver Brothers**
The ABC Monday Comedy Special ABC
Program Type Comedy Special
30 minutes. Premiere date: 6/20/77. Comedy pilot about two men trying to make it as a comedy team.
Executive Producers Tom Patchett, Jay Tarses
Producer Michael Zinberg
Company MTM Enterprises, Inc.
Director Hugh Wilson
Writers Tom Patchett, Jay Tarses, Hugh Wilson
Art Director Sydney Z. Litwack

CAST

Tom Van Brocklin .... Tom Patchett
Jay Luckman .... Jay Tarses
Sally Van Brocklin .... Gwynne Gilford
Mr. Ruth .... Philip Bruns
Duffy .... Robert Emhardt
Kelso .... Michael Pataki
Nathan Brailoff .... Phil Roth
Receptionist .... Madeleine Fisher
Impressionist .... Rick Podell

304 **Christmas Around the World**
The Big Event NBC
Program Type Music/Comedy/Variety Special
90 minutes. Premiere date: 12/19/76. Special showing how various Christmas celebrations have become part of the American tradition. Filmed around the world.

Executive Producer Lee Mendelson
Producer Karen Crommie
Company A Lee Mendelson Film Production in association with Crommie & Crommie Inc.
Directors Karen Crommie, Lee Mendelson
Writers Karen Crommie, Lee Mendelson
Musical Director Ed Bogas
Cinematographers Chuck Barbee, Terry Morrison, Al Niggemeyer
Film Editor Paul Preuss
Researcher Debbie Muller
Stars Vikki Carr, William Conrad, Gene Kelly, Marcel Marceau, Marilyn McCoo and Billy Davis, Jr., Liv Ullmann, Dick Van Dyke, Jonathan Winters
Featuring Scott Beach, Larry Finlayson

305 **Christmas at Washington Cathedral** NBC
Program Type Religious/Cultural Special
60 minutes. Premiere date: 12/25/76. Live coverage of the Christmas Day Service from the Washington (D.C.) National Cathedral celebrated by the Rt. Rev. William F. Creighton. Christmas message by the Very Rev. Francis B. Sayre, Jr..
Producer Doris Ann
Company NBC Television Religious Programs Unit in association with the National Council of Churches
Director Richard Cox
Musical Director Dr. Paul Callaway
Organist William Stokes

306 **A Christmas Carol**
Famous Classic Tales CBS
Program Type Animated Film Special
60 minutes. Premiere date: 12/13/70. Repeat date: 12/18/76. Adaptation of the Christmas story by Charles Dickens. Music composed by Richard Bowden.
Producer Walter J. Hucker
Company Air Programs International
Writer Michael Robinson
Animation Director Zoran Janjic

307 **A Christmas Celebration** PBS
Program Type Music/Dance Special
30 minutes. Premiere date: 12/20/76. The traditions and customs of the Christmas season traced through music and historical narrative. Music performed by the Hofstra University Collegium Musicum and the Renaissance Street Trio. Taped at the Cloisters in New York City. Program made possible by a grant from the Corporation for Public Broadcasting.
Producers Gail Macandrew, Gail Jansen
Company WNET-TV/New York
Director Jon Merdin
Host Richard Kiley

308 **Christmas Chester Mystery Play**
Great Performances PBS
Program Type Dramatic Special
90 minutes. Premiere date: 12/22/76. An adaptation of eight 14th century mystery plays originally performed by a group of craft guilds in the city of Chester, England. Program presented by WNET-TV/New York and made possible by grants from Exxon Corporation, the Corporation for Public Broadcasting, the Ford Foundation and Public Television Stations.
Company British Broadcasting Corporation
Host Hal Holbrook

309 **Christmas Eve Service** CBS
Program Type Religious/Cultural Special
60 minutes. Premiere date: 12/25/76 (midnight to 1 a.m.) Christmas services from Grace Baptist Church in Mount Vernon, N.Y. led by the Rev. W. Franklin Richardson.
Executive Producer Pamela Ilott
Producer Chalmers Dale
Company CBS News Religious Broadcast
Director Alvin Thaler

310 **Christmas in Disneyland** ABC
Program Type Children's Special
60 minutes. Premiere date: 12/8/76. Story of an old grouch who finds the Christmas spirit at Disneyland. Filmed on location at Disneyland in Anaheim, California. Special musical material by Alan Copeland.
Producer Marty Pasetta
Company Pasetta Productions, Inc.
Director Marty Pasetta
Writer Buz Kohan
Conductors Jack Elliott, Allyn Ferguson

CAST

Gramps/Dr. Wunderbar .... Art Carney
Disneyland Visitor/Grandpa Jesse/ Santa Claus .... Glen Campbell
Disneyland Tour Guide .... Sandy Duncan
Terri .... Terri Lynn Wood
Brad .... Brad Savage
Additional Cast The Kids of the Kingdom, the Mitchell Boys Choir

311 **Christmas in New York** ABC
Program Type Music/Comedy/Variety Special
90 minutes. Premiere date: 12/24/74. Repeat date: 12/24/76. Music, ice skating and storytelling in a Christmas special. Filmed in part at Rockefeller Center.
Musical Director Elliot Lawrence
Host John Lindsay
Stars The King Sisters, the King Cousins, the

Christmas in New York *Continued*
Voices of East Harlem, Diahann Carroll, Lucien Meyer and His Skating Chimps, Albert Lucas, David Lucas, the Ice Capades Corps de Ballet

312 **Christmas Rome 1976** NBC
Program Type Religious/Cultural Special
75 minutes. Premiere date: 12/25/76 (12 midnight to 1:15 a.m.). The Christmas Eve Midnight Mass from St. Peter's Basilica in Vatican City celebrated by Pope Paul VI. English language commentary by the Rev. Agnellus Andrew, O.F.M.
Executive Producer Doris Ann
Producer Martin Hoade
Company NBC Television Religious Programs Unit in association with the Office for Film and Broadcasting of the United States Catholic Conference
Director Martin Hoade

313 **Christopher Closeup** Syndicated
Program Type Religious/Cultural Series
30 minutes. Weekly. Premiere date: 10/52. Interview-talk show originally produced by Father James Keller, M.M., founder of the Christophers. Interpreter for the hearing impaired: Carol Tipton.
Executive Producer Rev. Richard Armstrong
Producer Jeanne Glynn
Company A Christopher Production
Director Raymond J. Hoesten
Hosts Rev. Richard Armstrong, Jeanne Glynn

314 **Church Rights and Human Rights** NBC
Program Type Religious/Cultural Special
30 minutes. Premiere date: 7/3/77. Discussion of church and human rights.
Executive Producer Doris Ann
Company NBC Television Religious Programs Unit in association with the American Council of Christian Churches
Director George Charles
Participants The Rev. O. R. Harbuziuk, Dr. George J. Hess, the Rev. B. Robert Biscoe

315 **The CIA's Secret Army**
CBS Reports CBS
Program Type Documentary/Informational Special
Two hours. Premiere date: 6/10/77. An examination of U.S. secret policies toward Cuba.
Executive Producer Howard Stringer
Producers Judy Crichton, George Crile III
Company CBS News
Director Judy Crichton
Writers George Crile III, Bill Moyers
Cinematographer William J. Wagner
Film Editor Joseph Fackovec
Researchers Leslie Danoff, Teresa Styles
Reporter Bill Moyers

316 **Cinderella** PBS
Program Type Music/Dance Special
60 minutes. Premiere date: 12/25/76. The ballet by Sergei Prokofiev performed by the Columbia City Ballet of South Carolina with recorded music by the Moscow Symphony.
Company South Carolina Educational Television Network
Director Sidney Palmer
Production Designer Ann Brodie

CAST

Cinderella	Mimi Wortham
Prince Charming	Henry Everett
Fairy Godmother	Lou Martin

317 **A Circle of Children** CBS
Program Type Dramatic Special
Two hours. Premiere date: 3/10/77. Drama about emotionally disturbed children based on the book by Mary MacCracken. Music by Nelson Riddle. "A Circle of Children" music by Steve Hines, lyrics by Steven Gethers, sung by Carmen McRae.
Executive Producers Edgar J. Scherick, Daniel H. Blatt
Producer Steven Gethers
Company Edgar J. Scherick Productions, Inc., in association with 20th Century-Fox Television
Director Don Taylor
Writer Steven Gethers
Art Director Lawrence G. Paull

CAST

Mary MacCracken	Jane Alexander
Helga	Rachel Roberts
Dan Franklin	David Ogden Stiers
Doris Fleming	Nan Martin
Brian O'Connell	Matthew Laborteaux
Larry MacCracken	Peter Brandon
Chris	Jason Tyler
Sarah	Kyle Richards
Elizabeth	Susan Pratt
Mrs. O'Connell	Judy Lewis

Circles *see* The Tapestry/Circles

318 **Circus Lions, Tigers and Melissas Too** NBC
Program Type Music/Comedy/Variety Special
60 minutes. Premiere date: 5/21/77. Performances by circus acts from around the world.
Producers Joseph Cates, Gilbert Cates
Company Joseph Cates Company, Inc.
Directors Joseph Cates, Gilbert Cates
Writer Frank Slocum

Art Director Molly Joseph
Hosts Melissa Sue Anderson, Melissa Gilbert
Performers Pablo Noel, Katherine Blanckhardt, Dickie Chipperfield, Miss Josephine

319 **The Circus Moves On in Calabria**
Piccadilly Circus PBS
Program Type Documentary/Informational Special
60 minutes. Premiere date: 5/10/76. Repeat date: 8/7/77. The life of a traveling family circus in Italy. Program made possible by a grant from Mobil Oil Corporation. Presented by WGBH-TV/Boston; Joan Sullivan, producer,
Producer John Bird
Company British Broadcasting Corporation
Host Jeremy Brett

320 **Circus of the Stars** CBS
Program Type Music/Comedy/Variety Special
Two hours. Premiere date: 1/10/77. Repeat date: 6/6/77. American and French entertainers in circus acts taped at the Santa Monica (Calif.) Civic Auditorium.
Executive Producer Bob Stivers
Production Executive Julian Bercovici
Producers Bill Watts, Dan Kibbee, Dominique Perrin
Director Sidney Smith
Writers Herbert Baker, Dan Kibbee
Musical Director Harper Mackay
Costume Designer Pete Menefee
Creative Consultant Mark Wilson
Technical Advisors Bob Yerkes, Parley Baer, Ralph Helfer, Carol Lille
Ringmasters Jean Pierre Aumont, Jack Cassidy, George Hamilton, Bernadette Peters
Stars Marty Allen, Edward Asner, Billy Barty, Jane Birkin, Karen Black, Claudia Cardinale, Lynda Carter, Gary Collins, Niki Dantine, David Doyle, Anny Duperrey, Totie Fields, The Firemen of Paris, Peter Fonda, John Forsythe, Rosey Grier, Joey Heatherton, David Janssen, Jack Klugman, Janet Leigh, Peter Marshall, Rue McClanahan, Liza Minnelli, Mary Ann Mobley, Lilliane Montevecchi, Pat Morita, David Nelson, Paul Newman, Beth Nufer, Valerine Perrine, Deborah Raffin, Regine, Rusty Rock and Patty Rock, Wayne Rogers, Shields and Yarnell, Jean Stapleton, John Travolta, Bobby Van, Jackie Vernon, Abe Vigoda, Joanne Woodward, Jo Anne Worley

321 **The City**
NBC Movie of the Week NBC
Program Type TV Movie
90 minutes. Premiere date: 1/12/77. Pilot police drama set in Los Angeles.
Executive Producer Quinn Martin
Producer John Wilder
Company Quinn Martin Productions in association with NBC-TV
Director Harvey Hart
Writer John Wilder
Musical Director John Elizalde

CAST

Lt. Matt Lewis	Robert Forster
St. Brian Scott	Don Johnson
Capt. Lloyd Bryant	Ward Costello
Wes Collins	Jimmy Dean
Eugene Banks	Mark Hamill
Burt Frescura	Paul Cavonis
Carol Carter	Susan Sullivan
Dr. Hank Cullen	Felton Perry
Girl at Hospital	Leslie Ackerman
Jed Haynes	Paul Fix
Mel Greenwall	Joby Baker

322 **City Center Joffrey Ballet**
Dance in America/Great Performances PBS
Program Type Music/Dance Special
60 minutes. Premiere date: 1/21/76. Repeat date: 1/19/77. Excerpts from "Remembrances" choreographed by Robert Joffrey, "Olympics" by Gerald Arpino, "Parade" by Leonide Massine (with sets and costumes by Pablo Picasso), "The Green Table" by Kurt Jooss and the complete "Trinity" by Gerald Arpino as danced by the City Center Joffrey Ballet. Program taped at KRLN-TV/Austin. Funded by grants from Exxon Corporation, the National Endowment for the Arts and the Corporation for Public Broadcasting.
Executive Producer Jac Venza
Producer Emile Ardolino
Company WNET-TV/New York
Director Jerome Schnur
Series Producer Merrill Brockway
Principal Dancers Charthel Arthur, Dermot Burke, Adix Carman, Francesca Corkle, Paul Sutherland, Jan Hanniford

Class of '44 *see* The CBS Friday Night Movies

323 **Classic Theatre Preview: The Humanities in Drama** PBS
Program Type Educational/Cultural Series
30 minutes. Tuesdays. Premiere date: 9/22/75. Program repeats began 2/15/77. 13-week series of interviews and discussions with the producers, stars and/or scholars of the plays presented on "Classic Theatre: The Humanities in Drama." Programs made possible by a grant from the National Endowment for the Humanities.
Producer Joan Sullivan
Company WGBH-TV/Boston
Director David Atwood

324 **Classic Theatre: The Humanities in Drama** PBS
Program Type Drama Series
Times vary. Thursdays. Premiere date: 9/25/75. Series repeats began 2/17/77. 13-weeks of classic plays from the 16th to the 20th century. Programs seen during the 1976–77 season: "Candide," "The Duchess of Malfi," "Edward II," "Hedda Gabler," "Macbeth," "Mrs. Warren's Profession," "Paradise Restored," "The Playboy of the Western World," "The Rivals," "She Stoops to Conquer," "The Three Sisters," "Trelawney of the 'Wells'," "The Wild Duck." (*See* individual titles for credits.) Series funded by grants from the National Endowment for the Humanities and Mobil Oil Corporation. Presented by WGBH-TV/Boston. Producer for WGBH: Joan Sullivan.

325 **Clay Courts Championships** CBS
Program Type Sports Special
2 1/4 hours. Live coverage of the 67th Clay Courts Championship from Indianapolis, Ind. 8/14/77.
Producer E. S. "Bud" Lamoreaux
Company CBS Television Network Sports
Director Perry Smith
Commentator Gary Bender

326 **Cleo Laine and John Dankworth**
In Performance at Wolf Trap PBS
Program Type Music/Dance Special
60 minutes. Premiere date: 11/15/76. Jazz concert by Cleo Laine, John Dankworth and the Dankworth Ensemble (Ken Clare, Brian Torff and Paul Hart) performed at the Wolf Trap Farm Park for the Performing Arts in Arlington, Va. Program made possible by a grant from the Atlantic Richfield Company.
Executive Producer David Prowitt
Producer Ruth Leon
Company WETA-TV/Washington, D.C.
Director Stan Lathan
Conductor John Dankworth

327 **Clinton Asks the President** ABC
Program Type News Special
Two hours. Premiere date: 3/16/77. Tape-delayed telecast of the 3/16/77 town meeting in Clinton, Massachusetts with Pres. Jimmy Carter.
Producer Bob Roy
Company ABC News Special Events Unit
Anchor Frank Reynolds
Correspondents Sam Donaldson, Jim Kincaid

328 **Clue Club** CBS
Program Type Animated Film Series
30 minutes. Saturday mornings. Premiere date: 8/14/76. Last show: 9/3/77. Crime-solving animated adventures of a group of teenagers and their dogs.
Executive Producers Joseph Barbera, William Hanna
Producer Iwao Takamoto
Company Hanna-Barbera Productions
Director Charles A. Nichols
Story Editor Sid Morse
Musical Director Hoyt Curtin

VOICES

Larry .... David Jolliffe
D. D. .... Bob Hastings
Pepper .... Patricia Stich
Dottie .... Tara Talboy
Woofer .... Paul Winchell
Wimper .... Jim MacGeorge
Sheriff Bagley .... John Stephenson

329 **C'mon, Saturday!** NBC
Program Type Children's Special
60 minutes. Premiere date: 9/9/77. Primetime preview of the NBC children's programming for the 1977–78 season. Music arranged by Elliot Lawrence; special lyrics by Martin Charnin.
Executive Producer Ken Greengrass
Producer Martin Charnin
Director Martin Charnin
Writer Tom Meehan
Conductor Elliot Lawrence

CAST

A. M. .... Andrea McArdle
Mr. Wister .... Leonard Nimoy
A. M.'s Mother .... Ruth Buzzi
Tyrone .... Arte Johnson
Muhammad Ali .... Muhammad Ali
Young Executives .... Stephen Grober, Tony Holmes, Michael McArdle, Joe Meehan, Tarn Menzies, David Reed, Carl Tramon

330 **Code Name: Diamond Head** NBC
Program Type TV Movie
90 minutes. Premiere date: 5/3/77. Adventure-drama pilot of a U.S. counterintelligence agent. Music composed by Morton Stevens. Filmed in Honolulu and other locations in Hawaii.
Executive Producer Quinn Martin
Producer Paul King
Company Quinn Martin Productions in association with NBC-TV
Director Jeannot Szwarc
Writer Paul King
Art Director George B. Chan

CAST

Johnny Paul .... Roy Thinnes
Tso-Tsing .... France Nuyen
Zulu .... Zulu
Capt. MacIntosh .... Ward Costello
H. K. Muldoon .... Don Knight
Sean Donavan .... Ian McShane
Ernest Graeber .... Eric Braeden
Cmdr. Yarnell .... Dennis Patrick
Edward Sherman .... Alex Henteloff

Sakai .... Frank Michael Liu
Father Murphy .... Eric Christmas
Yamamoto .... Ernest Harada
Dr. En-Ping .... Harry Endo
Tanner .... Lee Stetson

331 **Code R** CBS
Program Type Drama Series
60 minutes. Fridays. Premiere date: 1/21/77. Last show: 6/10/77. Adventure drama dealing with emergency rescue operations on a small island off the coast of Southern California. Created by Edwin Self. Music by Lee Holdridge.
Producer Edwin Self
Company Warner Bros. Television
Directors Various
Executive Story Consultant Dan Ullman
Writers Various
Art Director Robert Kinoshita
Story Consultant John Groves
CAST
Rick Wilson .... James Houghton
George Baker .... Martin Kove
Walt Robinson .... Tom Simcox
Suzy .... Susanne Reed
Milbank .... Ben Davidson
Harry .... W. T. Zacha
Bobby .... Robbie Rundle

Cold Turkey *see* CBS Special Film Presentations

332 **Colgate-Dinah Shore Winners Circle Golf Championship** ABC
Program Type Sports Special
Live coverage of the final two rounds of the Colgate-Dinah Shore Winners Circle Golf Championship from the Mission Hills Golf & Country Club in Palm Springs, Calif. 4/2/77 and 4/3/77.
Executive Producer Roone Arledge
Company ABC Sports
Host Dinah Shore

333 **Colgate-Hall of Fame Golf Classic** ABC
Program Type Sports Special
Live coverage of the final rounds of the first Colgate-Hall of Fame Golf Classic from the Pinehurst (N.C.) Country Club 8/27/77 and 8/28/77.
Executive Producer Roone Arledge
Producer Bob Goodrich
Company ABC Sports
Directors Jim Jennett, Roger Goodman
Anchor Jim McKay
Expert Commentators Dave Marr, Peter Alliss, Bob Rosburg, Bill Flemming

334 **Colgate Inaugural** NBC
Program Type Sports Special
Two hours. Live coverage of the singles finals and highlights of the pro-celebrity mixed doubles tennis competition from the Mission Hills Country Club in Palm Springs, Calif. 10/23/76.
Producer Dick Auerbach
Company NBC Sports
Director Ken Fouts
Announcer Bud Collins
Expert Analyst Julie Anthony
Reporter Barbara Hunter

335 **Colgate Triple Crown** ABC
Program Type Sports Special
90 minutes. Live coverage of the final round of the Colgate Triple Crown women's golf championship from the Mission Hills Country Club in Palm Springs, Calif. 1/16/77.
Executive Producer Roone Arledge
Producer Chuck Howard
Company ABC Sports
Directors Jim Jennett, Terry Jastrow
Anchor Jim McKay
Expert Commentators Carol Mann, Bob Rosburg, Laura Baugh, Marlene Floyd

336 **College Basketball '77 (NCAA Basketball)** NBC
Program Type Limited Sports Series
Live coverage of 88 regular-season national and regional college basketball games. Saturdays and Sundays. Season premiere: 1/2/77. Last regular season game: 3/6/77. Dick Enberg and Billy Packer cover national games.
Executive Producer Scotty Connal
Producers Various
Company NBC Sports in association with TVS
Directors Various
Announcers Dick Enberg, Dick Stockton, Marv Albert, Merle Harmon, Jay Randolph, Marty Brennaman, Ross Porter, Tom Hedrick, John Ferguson, Frank Glieber, Phil Samp, Bob Barry, Fred White, Monte Moore, Connie Alexander, Larry Conley, Curt Gowdy
Color Analysts John Wooden, Billy Packer, Bucky Waters, Fred Taylor, Gary Thompson, Steve Bassett, Tom Hawkins, Gary Griffith, Joe Dean, Frank Fallon, John Andariese, Omar Williams, Bob Boozer, Steve Grad, Bill Strannigan, Bill O'Donnell

337 **College Football '77: It's Anybody's Ballgame** ABC
Program Type Sports Special
60 minutes. Premiere date: 9/1/77. Primetime special focusing on the top college football teams in the six NCAA geographical regions.
Executive Producer Roone Arledge

College Football '77: It's Anybody's Ballgame *Continued*
Producer Terry O'Neil
Company ABC Sports
Director Ric LaCivita
Host Keith Jackson

338 **College Football '76** ABC
Program Type Limited Sports Series
60 minutes. Sundays. Season premiere: 9/12/76. Last show of season: 12/5/76. 13-week series. Highlights of the important collegiate games and players of the week.
Executive Producer Richard Giannini
Producer Kemper Peacock
Company NCAA Films
Director Kemper Peacock
Host Bill Flemming

339 **Colonial National Invitation** CBS
Program Type Sports Special
Final two rounds of the $200,000 Colonial National Invitation from the Colonial Country Club in Fort Worth, Tex. 5/14/77 and 5/15/77.
Producer Perry Smith
Company CBS Television Network Sports
Director Bob Dailey
Commentators Vin Scully, Jack Whitaker, Pat Summerall, Frank Glieber, Ben Wright, Ken Venturi

340 **Columbo**
NBC Sunday Mystery Movie NBC
Program Type Crime Drama Series
90 minutes. Sundays. Broadcast irregularly as part of the "NBC Sunday Mystery Movie." Premiere date: 9/15/71. Sixth season premiere: 10/10/76. Original pilots: "Prescription: Murder" shown 2/20/68 and "Ransom for a Dead Man" shown 3/1/71. Created and written by Richard Levinson and William Link. Series revolves around a slow-moving detective in a rumpled raincoat. Richard Alan Simmons succeeded Everett Chambers as producer in February 1977.
Producer Everett Chambers/Richard Alan Simmons
Company Universal Television in association with NBC-TV
Directors Various
Writers Various

CAST
Lt. Columbo .... Peter Falk

341 **Comedy Time** NBC
Program Type Comedy Series
30 minutes. Days vary. Premiere date: 7/6/77. Last show: 9/1/77. Comedy pilots produced for NBC. Programs seen during the 1976–77 season are: "The Bay City Amusement Company," "Calling Dr. Storm, M.D.," "Daughters," "Good Penny," "Instant Family," "Look Out World," "The Natural Look," "Riding High," "The Rubber Gun Squad," "Susan and Sam." (*See* individual titles for credits.)

342 **Commercial Union Masters** PBS
Program Type Sports Special
Four hours each day. Live coverage of the finals of the singles and doubles competition of the Commercial Union Masters Tennis Tournament held at Houston, Texas 12/11/76 and 12/12/76. Program made possible by a grant from Fieldcrest Mills, Inc.
Executive Producer Greg Harney
Producer Greg Harney
Company WGBH-TV/Boston
Director Greg Harney
Announcers Bud Collins, Donald Dell

343 **A Community Called Earth** PBS
Program Type Documentary/Informational Special
60 minutes. Premiere date: 1/17/77. An examination of our natural resources and how we must use them to survive. Program made possible by grants from the Northwest Regional Foundation, the German Marshall Fund, the Bolton Institute, the U.S. Office of Education and the Corporation for Public Broadcasting.
Executive Producer Mike McElreath
Producers Rita Pastore, Prentiss Childs
Company KWSU-TV/Pullman, Wash.
Writers Rita Pastore, Prentiss Childs
Host Hugh Downs

344 **Concentration** Syndicated
Program Type Game/Audience Participation Series
30 minutes. Mondays–Fridays (daytime). In syndication since 9/73. Game show for prizes.
Executive Producer Howard Felsher
Producer Buck D'Amore
Company Goodson-Todman Productions
Distributor Jim Victory Television, Inc.
Director Ira Skutch
Host Jack Narz
Announcer Johnny Olson

345 **Constantinople**
The ABC Monday Comedy Special ABC
Program Type Music/Dance Special
30 minutes. Premiere date: 7/25/77. Music from rock 'n' roll to country-western.
Executive Producer Grant Tinker
Producer Jack Good
Company MTM Enterprises, Inc.

Director Rita Gillespie
Writer Jack Good
Musical Director Ray Pohlman
Conductor H. B. Barnum
Choreographer Andre Tayir
Costume Designer Bill Belew
Performers H. B. Barnum Blues and Boogie Band, Lance LeGault, John Valenti, the Manhattan Transfer, Doug Kershaw with Slidin' Jake, Kathie Epstein, Mark Atkinson, Tina Turner, Ian Whitcomb

346 **Consumer Survival Kit** PBS
Program Type Educational/Cultural Series
30 minutes. Sundays. Premiere date: 1/9/75. Third season premiere: 1/9/77. Program repeats began 7/13/77 (Wednesdays). 26-week consumer series with a variety format. Regular feature: national and local recourses. Program funded by the Corporation for Public Broadcasting, the Ford Foundation and Public Television Stations.
Executive Producer Donna Faw
Producer Anne Jarrell
Company Maryland Center for Public Broadcasting
Director Tom Barnett
Host Lary Lewman
Regulars Rhea Feikin, Fran Johanson, Bob Smith

347 **A Conversation With Dr. Philip A. Potter** NBC
Program Type Religious/Cultural Special
30 minutes. Premiere data: 10/31/76. A conversation with the General Secretary of the World Council of Churches, Dr. Philip A. Potter.
Producer Doris Ann
Company NBC Television Religious Programs Unit
Director Jack Dillon
Interviewer Edwin Newman

348 **A Conversation With Isaac Bashevis Singer**
Eternal Light NBC
Program Type Religious/Cultural Special
30 minutes. Premiere date: 12/12/76. A conversation with author Isaac Bashevis Singer in honor of Hanukkah.
Producer Doris Ann
Company NBC Television Religious Programs Unit in association with the Jewish Theological Seminary of America
Director Jack Dillon
Interviewer Rabbi Jules Harlow

349 **A Conversation With Itzhak Perlman**
Eternal Light NBC
Program Type Religious/Cultural Special
60 minutes. Premiere date: 11/7/76. Repeat date: 7/31/77. An interview with violinist Itzhak Perlman.
Producer Doris Ann
Company NBC Television Religious Programs Unit in association with the Jewish Theological Seminary of America
Director Jack Dillon
Interviewer Martin Bookspan

350 **A Conversation With Professor Sydney Ahlstrom** NBC
Program Type Religious/Cultural Special
60 minutes. Premiere date: 2/6/77. A conversation with Prof. Sydney Ahlstrom.
Producer Doris Ann
Company NBC Television Religious Programs Unit in association with the National Council of Churches
Director Jack Dillon
Interviewer Philip Scharper

351 **A Conversation With Rabbi Louis Finkelstein**
Eternal Light NBC
Program Type Religious/Cultural Special
30 minutes. Premiere date: 10/3/76. A discussion with Rabbi Louis Finkelstein in honor of Yom Kippur.
Producer Doris Ann
Company NBC Television Religious Programs Unit in association with the Jewish Theological Seminary of America
Director Robert Priaulx
Moderator Sol M. Linowitz

352 **Conversations On a Farm** PBS
Program Type Documentary/Informational Special
60 minutes. Premiere date: 11/28/76. A look at a dairy farm family in New York State. Program made possible by grants from the Corporation for Public Broadcasting and the Norwich Pharmacal Division of Morton-Norwich Products, Inc.
Producer Patricia Stanley
Company WMHT-TV/Schenectady, N.Y.
Director Dennis Remick

353 **Conversations With Eric Sevareid**
CBS News Special CBS
Program Type Documentary/Informational Special

Conversations With Eric Sevareid *Continued*
60 minutes. Premiere date: 5/27/77. A conversation with Anne Morrow Lindbergh.
Executive Producer Perry Wolff
Producer Perry Wolff
Co-Producer Christina Barnes
Company CBS News
Cinematographers Robert J. Clemens, William J. Wagner, Karl Malkames
Film Editor Nobuko Oganesoff
Researcher Gail Eisen
Interviewer Eric Sevareid

Cooley High *see* The ABC Friday Night Movie

354 **Copland Conducts Copland**
Music in America/Great Performances PBS
Program Type Music/Dance Special
60 minutes. Premiere date: 3/17/76. Repeat date: 8/21/77. First "Music in America" concert. Aaron Copland conducts the Los Angeles Philharmonic Orchestra in a selection of his own works. Roger Wagner directs the Los Angeles Master Chorale. Taped at the Dorothy Chandler Pavilion in the Music Center in Los Angeles, Calif. January 1976. Program funded by a grant from the Exxon Corporation.
Executive Producers Jac Venza, Klaus Hallig
Producer David Griffiths
Company WNET-TV/New York and International Television Trading Corporation
Conductor Aaron Copland
Guest Soloist Benny Goodman

355 **Copland on America** PBS
Program Type Music/Dance Special
90 minutes. Premiere date: 2/1/77. A concert of music by American composers performed by the Minnesota Orchestra. Taped 7/4/76 at Orchestra Hall in Minneapolis. Program made possible by a grant from Honeywell, Inc.
Producer Larry Morrisette
Company KTCA-TV/St. Paul-Minneapolis
Director Larry Morrisette
Conductor Aaron Copland
Featured Soloist Berj Zamkochian

356 **Corey: For the People**
NBC Movie of the Week NBC
Program Type TV Movie
90 minutes. Premiere date: 6/12/77. Dramatic pilot about a young assistant district attorney who prosecutes a socialite in a capital case. Created by Alvin Boretz.
Executive Producer Buzz Kulik
Producer Jay Daniel
Company Jeni Production in association with Columbia Pictures Television
Director Buzz Kulik
Writer Alvin Boretz

CAST

Dan Corey	John Rubinstein
D. A. Patrick Shannon	Eugene Roche
Harriet Morgan	Carol Rossen
Det. Gilman	Wynn Irwin
Dr. Paul Hanley	Ronny Cox
Janet Hanley	Lana Wood
Laura Casey	Ann Sweeny
Nick Wolfe	Stephen Pearlman
Katie Ryan	Joan Pringle
Sam Myers	Stephen Burleigh
Judy Corey	Deborah Ryan
Judge Taylor	Joseph Campanella

357 **COS** ABC
Program Type Children's Series
60 minutes. Sundays. Premiere date: 9/19/76. Last show: 10/31/76. Children's variety series with regular features "Outrageous" and "Kids Will Be Kids."
Producer Chris Bearde
Co-Producer Alan Thicke
Company Jemmin Productions
Director Jeff Margolis
Writers Jeremy Stevens, Tom Moore, Rick Kellard, Bob Comfort, Sandra Harmon, China Clark, Kevin Hartigan, David Garber, Stuart Bloomberg, Gina Goldman, Nita Schroeder, John Donley, Nance McCormick
Choreographer Kevin Carlisle
Art Director Ed LaPorta
Announcer John Wilson
Star Bill Cosby
Regulars Jeff Altman, Willie Bobo, Mauricio Jarrin, Buzzy Linhart, Marion Ramsey, Timothy Thomerson

358 **Cotton Bowl** CBS
Program Type Sports Special
Three hours. Live coverage of the Cotton Bowl football game between the University of Maryland Terrapins and the University of Houston Cougars in Dallas, Tex. 1/1/77.
Company CBS Television Network Sports
Announcer Lindsey Nelson
Analyst Paul Hornung

359 **Cotton Bowl Festival Parade** CBS
Program Type Parades/Pageants/Awards Special
90 minutes. 1/1/77. Live coverage of the 21st annual parade from Dallas, Texas.
Executive Producer Mike Gargiulo
Company CBS Television
Director Mike Gargiulo
Writer Beverly Schanzer
Host William Conrad

Hosts/Commentators Kevin Dobson, Bernadette Peters

360 **Counterpoint: The U-2 Story**
Documentary Showcase PBS
Program Type Documentary/Informational Special
60 minutes. Premiere date: 3/11/77. Repeat date: 7/15/77 (with captions for the hearing-impaired). A look at Francis Gary Powers, the U-2 pilot, and Selmar Nilsen, a Norwegian spy for Russian intelligence, in a documentary about the 1960 cold war incident. Program presented by WITF-TV/Hershey, Pa. and made possible by a grant from the Corporation for Public Broadcasting.
Producer Peter Davis
Company Swedish Television
Directors Peter Davis, Staffan Lamm
Cinematographers Peter Davis, Staffan Lamm
Film Editors Peter Davis, Staffan Lamm
Narrator Barry Callaghan

361 **Country Moods** PBS
Program Type Music/Dance Special
30 minutes. Premiere date: 7/23/77. A concert by Doc Williams and The Border Riders of Wheeling, W. Va.: Chickie Williams, vocalist; Karen McKenzie, vocalist; Roy Scott, vocalist, fiddler and guitarist; Randy Bethune, banjoist; Marion Martin, cordovoxist; Billy Miedel, drummer.
Producer David R. Hopfer
Company WWVU-TV/Morgantown, W. Va.
Director David R. Hopfer

362 **Country Music Association Awards** CBS
Program Type Parades/Pageants/Awards Special
90 minutes. Tenth annual awards presentation 10/11/76 from the Grand Old Opry House in Nashville, Tenn.
Producer Robert Precht
Company Country Music Association
Director Walter C. Miller
Writers Donald K. Epstein, Bud Wingard
Musical Director Bill Walker
Art Director Don Shirley
Hosts Johnny Cash, Roy Clark
Performers/Presenters Chet Atkins, June Carter Cash, Freddy Fender, Tennessee Ernie Ford, Crystal Gayle, Johnny Gimble, Merle Haggard, Emmylou Harris, Loretta Lynn, C. W. McCall, Charlie McCoy, Barbara Mandrell, Ronnie Milsap, Willie Nelson, Dolly Parton, Minnie Pearl, Charley Pride, Hargus "Pig" Robbins, Hank Snow, Red Sovine, Mel Tillis, Conway Twitty, Tammy Wynette

363 **Country Music Hit Parade** NBC
Program Type Music/Dance Special
90 minutes. Premiere date: 5/3/77. Performances of the top 20 songs of the year (5/1/76–5/1/77) in country music as compiled by the Gavin Report. Taped at the Grand Ole Opry in Nashville, Tenn.
Executive Producer Joseph Cates
Producer Chet Hagan
Company Joseph Cates Company, Inc. Production
Director Walter C. Miller
Writers Frank Slocum, Chet Hagan, Joseph Cates
Musical Director Bill Walker
Art Director Jim Stanley
Host Jimmy Dean
Guest Stars Donna Fargo, Freddy Fender, Larry Gatlin, Crystal Gayle, Jan Howard, George Jones, Ronnie Milsap, the Nitty Gritty Dirt Band, the Oak Ridge Boys, the Statler Brothers, Ray Stevens, Mel Tillis, Don Williams, Tammy Wynette
Special Guest Star Tennessee Ernie Ford

364 **Cousteau/Oasis in Space** PBS
Program Type Science/Nature Series
30 minutes. Saturdays. Premiere date: 11/13/76. Series repeats began 6/4/77. Six programs about the global environment. Series made possible by grants from the Corporation for Public Broadcasting, the Ford Foundation and Public Television Stations.
Executive Producer Philippe Cousteau
Producer Andrew W. Solt
Company The Cousteau Society in association with Andrew Solt Productions and in cooperation with KAMU-TV/College Station, Texas
Directors Philippe Cousteau, Andrew W. Solt
Writer Andrew W. Solt
Host Philippe Cousteau

365 **Cover Girls**
NBC Movie of the Week NBC
Program Type TV Movie
90 minutes. Premiere date: 5/18/77. Action-adventure pilot about two high fashion models /undercover espionage agents. Music by Richard Shores.
Executive Producer David Gerber
Producers Charles B. FitzSimons, Mark Rodgers
Company Columbia Pictures Television in association with the NBC Television Network
Director Jerry London
Writer Mark Rodgers
Costume Designer Grady Hunt
Art Directors Ross Bellah, Robert Peterson

CAST
Linda Allen .... Cornelia Sharpe
Monique Lawrence .... Jayne Kennedy

Cover Girls *Continued*

Bradner .... Vince Edwards
James Andrews .... Don Galloway
Michael .... George Lazenby
Football Player .... Bill Overton
Ziggy .... Ellen Travolta
Fritz Porter .... Jerry Douglas
Paul Reynolds .... Michael Baseleon
Karl .... Deveren Bookwalter
Sven .... Sean Garrison
Johnny Wilson .... Don Johnson

366 **Cowboys**
Documentary Showcase PBS
Program Type Documentary/Informational Special
60 minutes. Premiere date: 2/1/76 (as part of "Bill Moyers' Journal"). Repeat date: 2/4/77. A look at the lives of today's cowboys in Colorado.
Executive Producer Charles Rose
Producer Martin Clancy
Company WNET-TV/New York
Host Bill Moyers

The Cowboys (Feature Film) *see* The CBS Wednesday Night Movies

367 **Coxon's Army** PBS
Program Type Music/Dance Special
30 minutes. Premiere date: 4/3/76. Repeat date: 11/9/76. Pop music concert by Phil Coxon and his band.
Executive Producer Walter McGhee
Producer Bob Jones
Company WCVE-TV/Richmond, Va.
Director Donna Sanford

368 **CPO Sharkey** NBC
Program Type Comedy Series
30 minutes. Wednesdays. Premiere date: 12/1/76. Last show of the season: 8/31/77. Scheduled for return during the 1977–78 season. Comedy about a chief petty officer in command of a training unit at the San Diego Naval Training Center. Created by Aaron Ruben.
Executive Producer Aaron Ruben
Producer Gene Marcione
Company R & R Production
Director Peter Baldwin
Writer Aaron Ruben

CAST

CPO Sharkey .... Don Rickles
Capt. Quinlan .... Elizabeth Allen
Chief Robinson .... Harrison Page
Seaman Pruitt .... Peter Isacksen
Daniels .... Jeff Hollis
Kowalski .... Tom Ruben
Skolnick .... David Landsberg
Mignone .... Barry Pearl
Lt. Whipple .... Jonathan Daly
Rodriguez .... Richard Beauchamp

369 **Crockett's Victory Garden** PBS
Program Type Educational/Cultural Series
30 minutes. Saturdays. Premiere date: 4/11/76. Second season premiere: 4/9/77. Weekly series on gardening of plants and vegetables. Programs made possible by a grant from Public Television Stations.
Producer Russ Morash
Company WGBH-TV/Boston
Director Russ Morash
Writer James Underwood Crockett
Host James Underwood Crockett
Gardener Gary Mottau

370 **The Cross-Wits** Syndicated
Program Type Game/Audience Participation Series
30 minutes. Mondays–Fridays. Premiere date: 12/75. Second season premiere: 9/76. Two teams of three players each try to guess words in a crossword puzzle. Four guest celebrities weekly.
Executive Producer Ralph Edwards
Producers Ray Horl, Ed Bailey
Company Ralph Edwards Productions
Distributor Metromedia Producers Corporation
Director Richard Gottlieb
Host Jack Clark
Announcer John Harlan

371 **Cyrano de Bergerac**
Theater in America/Great Performances PBS
Program Type Dramatic Special
2 1/2 hours. Premiere date: 2/6/74. Repeat date: 12/29/76. The American Conservatory Theatre of San Francisco in a performance of the classic romance by Edmond Rostand. Translated by Brian Hooker. Music by Lee Hoiby. Program made possible by grants from Exxon Corporation and the Corporation for Public Broadcasting.
Executive Producer Jac Venza
Producers Matthew N. Herman, Dennis Powers
Company WNET-TV/New York
Directors William Ball, Bruce Franchini
Writer Dennis Powers
Costume Designer Robert Fletcher
Host Hal Holbrook

CAST

Cyrano .... Peter Donat
Roxane .... Marsha Mason
Christian .... Marc Singer
Rageuneau .... Robert Mooney
De Guiche .... Paul Shenar
Duenna .... Elizabeth Huddle
Le Bret .... Earl Boen
Bellerose .... Roger Aaron Brown
Capuchin .... Andy Backer
Orange Girl .... Janie Atkin
Meddler .... Joseph Bird
Lord/Poet .... Robert Chapline
Valvert .... Patrick Crean
Lise .... Kathryn Crosby

Montfleury ..... Charles Hallahan
Cut Purse ..... John Hancock
Ligniere ..... Henry Hoffman
Musician/Page ..... Daniel Kern
Chavigny ..... E. Kerrigan Prescott
Jodelet ..... Howard Sherman
Mother Marguerite ..... Shirley Slater
Musketeer ..... Steven White

372 **Dan August** ABC
Program Type Crime Drama Series
60 minutes. Thursdays/Mondays (as of 1/3/77). Premiere date: 9/23/76. Last show: 4/18/77. Late night repeats of primetime show that aired on ABC during the 1970–71 season and was repeated on CBS during the summer (1975–76 summer) 1975–76 season.
Executive Producer Quinn Martin
Supervising Producer Adrian Samish
Producer Anthony Spinner
Company Quinn Martin Productions
Directors Various
Writers Various

CAST

Dan August ..... Burt Reynolds
Sgt. Wilentz ..... Norman Fell
Chief Untermeyer ..... Richard Anderson
Sgt. Rivera ..... Ned Romero
Katy Grant ..... Ena Hartman

373 **Dance in America**
Great Performances PBS
Program Type Music/Dance Series
60 minutes. Special dance performances by leading American companies. Programs presented during the 1976–77 season are: "American Ballet Theatre," "City Center Joffrey Ballet," "Martha Graham Dance Company," "Merce Cunningham and Dance Company," "The Pennsylvania Ballet," "Pilobolus Dance Theatre," "Trailblazers of Modern Dance," "Twyla Tharp & Dancers." (*See* individual titles for credits.)

374 **Dance of the Athletes**
The CBS Festival of Lively Arts for Young People CBS
Program Type Children's Special
60 minutes. Premiere date: 9/26/76. A young people's special focusing on the similarities shared by sports figures and dancers. Music by Gordon Lowry Harrell.
Producer Edward Villella
Company Prodigal Productions
Director David Saperstein
Writer Douglas Howard Gray
Choreographer Edward Villella
Costume Designer John Rager
Art Director Michael Dennison
Star Edward Villella
Athletes Tom Seaver, Jerry Grote, Bob Griese, Virginia Wade, George McGinnis, Muriel Grossfeld
Principal Dancers Edward Villella, Anna Aragno
Dancers Stephen Caras, Bart Cook, Elise Flagg, Laura Flagg, Susan Hendl, Jay Jolley, Laurence Matthews, Susan Pilarre, Bryan Pitts, Marjorie Spohn

375 **Dance Theatre of Harlem**
Great Performances PBS
Program Type Music/Dance Special
60 minutes. Premiere date: 3/23/77. The Dance Theatre of Harlem in performance and behind-the-scenes in rehearsals: "Forces of Rhythm" choreographed by Louis Johnson with music by Rufus Thomas and Donny Hathaway, "Bugaku" choreographed by George Balanchine, excerpts from "Holberg Suite" by Arthur Mitchell, "The Beloved" by Lester Horton and "Dougla" by Geoffrey Holder. Program made possible by grants from the National Endowment for the Arts, the Corporation for Public Broadcasting and Exxon Corporation.
Executive Producer Jac Venza
Producer Emile Ardolino
Company WNET-TV/New York
Director Merrill Brockway
Principal Dancers Homer Bryant, Virginia Johnson, Paul Russell, Gayle McKinney, Roman Brooks, Melva Murray-White, Ronald Perry

376 **Danger in Paradise**
NBC Movie of the Week NBC
Program Type TV Movie
Two hours. Premiere date: 5/12/77. Drama about a man fighting to keep his father's ranch estate in Hawaii. Pilot for 1977–78 season series "Big Hawaii." Music by Jack Elliott and Allyn Ferguson. Filmed in part on location in Hilo, Hawaii and Las Vegas, Nevada.
Executive Producer Perry Lafferty
Producers Bill Finnegan, Pat Finnegan
Company Finnegan & Associates and Filmways Television Production in association with NBC-TV
Director Marvin Chomsky
Writer William Wood

CAST

Mitch Fears ..... Cliff Potts
Marla Fears ..... Ina Balin
Barrett Fears ..... John Dehner
Karen ..... Lucia Stralser
Bobby ..... Michael Mullins
Oscar ..... Bill Lucking
Reva ..... Jean Marie Hon
Stephen ..... Harry Moses
Big Lulu ..... Elizabeth Smith
Garfield ..... Moe Keale

377 **Danger! Radioactive Waste**
NBC Reports NBC
Program Type Documentary/Informational Special
60 minutes. Premiere date: 1/26/77. An examination of the problems involved in disposing of nuclear waste.
Producer Joan Konner
Company NBC News
Director Joan Konner
Writer Joan Konner
Cinematographers Houseton Hall, Henry Kokojan, Charles Ray, Aaron Fears, Fred Gutman
Film Editors George Johnson, Clay Cassell
Researchers Jewel Curvin, Martha Elliott
Consultants Harry Woolf, Ph.D., Howard Seliger, Ph.D.
Reporter Floyd Kalber

378 **Dark Victory**
NBC Monday Night at the Movies NBC
Program Type TV Movie
Three hours. Premiere date: 2/5/76. Repeat date: 7/4/77. Modernized version of the 1932 play by George Emerson Brewer, Jr. and Bertram Bloch which became a 1939 motion picture. Drama of a morning TV talk show producer dying of a brain tumor. Music composed by Billy Goldenberg.
Executive Producer Richard Irving
Producer Jules Irving
Company Universal Television
Director Robert Butler
Writer M. Charles Cohen
Art Director William H. Tuntke
Set Decorator John Franco

CAST

Katherine Merrill .... Elizabeth Montgomery
Dr. Michael Grant .... Anthony Hopkins
Dolores .... Michele Lee
Eileen .... Janet MacLachlan
Manny .... Michael Lerner
Jeremy .... John Elerick
Dr. Kassirer .... Herbert Berghof
Archie .... Vic Tayback
Sandy .... Mario Roccuzzo
Veronica .... Julie Rogers

379 **The Daughter of the Regiment**
In Performance at Wolf Trap PBS
Program Type Music/Dance Special
Two hours. Premiere date: 10/14/74. Repeat date: 9/13/77. English-language version of Gaetano Donizetti's comic opera. Performed at Wolf Trap Farm Park in Arlington, Va. with members of the Wolf Trap Company Chorus. Program made possible by a grant from the Atlantic Richfield Company.
Executive Producer David Prowitt
Company WETA-TV/Washington, D.C.
Director Kirk Browning
Conductor Charles Wendelken-Wilson
Costume Designer Beni Montresor
Scenic Designer Beni Montresor
Host David Prowitt

CAST

Marie .... Beverly Sills
Marquise .... Muriel Costa-Greenspun
Tonio .... William McDonald
Sgt. Sulpice .... Spiro Malas
Hortensius .... Stanley Wexler

380 **Daughters**
Comedy Time NBC
Program Type Comedy Special
30 minutes. Premiere date: 7/20/77. Comedy pilot about a police chief trying to bring up three daughters alone.
Executive Producers Paul Junger Witt, Tony Thomas
Producer Susan Harris
Company Witt/Thomas/Harris Productions
Director Bob Claver
Writer Susan Harris

CAST

Dominick .... Michael Constantine
Diane .... Olivia Barash
Terry .... Robin Groves
Cookie .... Judy Landers
Rosa .... Julie Bovasso

381 **David Copperfield**
Once Upon a Classic PBS
Program Type Children's Series
30 minutes. Saturdays. Premiere date: 1/8/77. Ten-part dramatization of the 1850 novel by Charles Dickens. Filmed in England. Captioned for the hearing-impaired. Presented by WQED-TV/Pittsburgh and made possible by grants from McDonald's Local Restaurants Association and McDonald's Corporation.
Executive Producer Jay Rayvid
Coordinating Producer John Coney
Producer John McRae
Company British Broadcasting Corporation and Time-Life Television
Director Joan Craft
Writer Hugh Whitemore
Host Bill Bixby

CAST

David Copperfield (as a young boy) .. Jonathan Kahn
David Copperfield (older) .... David Yelland
Mr. Micawber .... Arthur Lowe
Miss Betsey Trotwood .... Patience Collier
Uriah Heep .... Martin Jarvis
Steerforth .... Anthony Andrews
Thomas Traddles .... Peter Bourke
Peggotty .... Pat Keen
Mr. Peggotty .... Ian Hogg
Mr. Dick .... Timothy Bateson
Ham Peggotty .... David Troughton
Agnes Wickfield .... Gail Harrison
Dora Spenlow .... Beth Morris
Little Emily .... Melanie Hughes

Mrs. Micawber	Patricia Routledge
Clara	Colette O'Neil
Mr. Murdstone	Gareth Thomas
Barkis	Edward Sinclair
Mr. Creakle	Clifford Kershaw
Wickfield	Godfrey Kenton
Rosa	Jacqueline Pearce

382 **David Hartman . . . Gamblers: Winners and Losers**
Thursday Night Special ABC
Program Type Documentary/Informational Special
90 minutes. Premiere date: 3/17/77. Interviews with people involved with legal gambling. Taped in Las Vegas.
Executive Producer David Hartman
Producer Gary Hoffman
Company Rodman-Downs Ltd. Inc.
Director Gary Hoffman
Host David Hartman

383 **The David Soul and Friends Special** ABC
Program Type Music/Dance Special
60 minutes. Premiere date: 8/18/77. David Soul's first musical special. Filmed in part in England during his concert tour and in part in Hollywood.
Executive Producer Dick Clark
Producer Robert Arthur
Company Dick Clark Teleshows, Inc.
Directors Perry Rosemond, Steve Turner
Writers Phil Hahn, Robert Arthur
Star David Soul
Guest Stars Donna Summer, Ron Moody, England Dan & John Ford Coley, Dick Clark, Lynne Marta

384 **The Davis Cup Special** CBS
Program Type Sports Special
60 minutes. Premiere date: 12/18/76. Tennis action between the U.S. and Mexican teams. Highlights also seen during half-time of the National Football League NFC playoffs 12/18/76 and 12/19/76. Tennis action between the U.S. and South African teams seen 4/16/77.
Producer Frank Chirkinian
Company CBS Television Network Sports
Director Bob Dailey
Commentator Gary Bender

385 **Davy Crockett on the Mississippi**
Famous Classic Tales CBS
Program Type Animated Film Special
60 minutes. Premiere date: 11/20/76. Adventures of the American folklore hero during his days as a frontiersman. "Davy Crockett" theme by Gairden Cooke and Hoyt Curtin. Graphics by Iraj Paran.
Executive Producers William Hanna, Joseph Barbera
Producer Iwao Takamoto
Company Hanna-Barbera Productions, Inc.
Director Charles A. Nichols
Writer Sid Morse
Musical Director Hoyt Curtin
Animators Carlos Alfonso, Oliver E. Callahan, Ken Muse, Juan Pina, Carlo Vinci
Voices Mike Bell, Ron Feinberg, Randy Gray, Kip Niven, Pat Parris, John Stephenson, Ned Wilson

386 **The Dawn of Laurel and Hardy** PBS
Program Type Feature Film Series
30 minutes each. Ten programs with excerpts from 26 silent films of Stan Laurel and Oliver Hardy. Shown in March 1976. Repeat date: March 1977.
Producer Hal Roach
Company Roach Studios

387 **Dawn: Portrait of a Teenage Runaway**
NBC Monday Night at the Movies NBC
Program Type TV Movie
Two hours. Premiere date: 9/27/76. Drama of a 15-year-old runaway who becomes a prostitute. Music by Fred Karlin; lyrics by Meg Karlin. "Comin' Home Again" sung by Shaun Cassidy. Filmed on location in southern California and Tucson, Arizona.
Producer Douglas S. Cramer
Company The Douglas S. Cramer Company in association with NBC-TV
Director Randal Kleiser
Writer Dalene Young
Costume Designers Tom Welsh, Jo Ann Haas
Art Director James Hulsey

CAST

Dawn	Eve Plumb
Swan	Bo Hopkins
Alexander	Leigh J. McCloskey
Donald Umber	Georg Stanford Brown
Frankie Lee	Marguerite De Lain
Dawn's Mother	Lynn Carlin
Harry	William Schallert
Susie	Joan Prather
Dr. Roberts	David Knapp
Counter Woman	Anne Seymour
Randy	Stephanie Burchfield
Melba	Kaaren Ragland

388 **The Day After Tomorrow**
Special Treat NBC
Program Type Children's Special
60 minutes. Premiere date: 12/9/75. Repeat date: 1/11/77. Drama special illustrating Ein-

The Day After Tomorrow *Continued*
stein's theory of relativity: a trip into outer space in a ship traveling at almost the speed of light. Special effects by Brian Johnson. Filmed at Pinewood Studios in England.
Executive Producer George A. Heinemann
Producer Gerry Anderson
Director Charles Crichton
Writer John Byrne
Scientific Advisor Prof. John Taylor

CAST

Capt. Harry Masters .... Nick Tate
Jane Masters .... Katherine Levy
Tom Bowen .... Brian Blessed
Anna Bowen .... Joanna Dunham
David Bowen .... Martin Lev

The Day of the Dolphin *see* NBC Saturday Night at the Movies

389 **A Day With President Carter**
NBC Reports NBC
Program Type Documentary/Informational Special
60 minutes. Premiere date: 4/14/77. A look at how the White House is organized and operates plus an interview with Pres. Jimmy Carter taped on the day of the broadcast.
Executive Producer Gordon Manning
Producer Ray Lockhart
Company NBC News
Director Ray Lockhart
Reporter/Interviewer John Chancellor

390 **Days of Our Lives** NBC
Program Type Daytime Drama Series
60 minutes. Mondays–Fridays. Premiere date: 11/8/65. Continuous. Second regularly scheduled 60-minute daytime drama (as of 4/21/75). Created by Ted Corday, Irna Phillips and Allan Chase. Series revolves around the Horton family of Salem, U.S.A. Macdonald Carey, Frances Reid and John Clarke are original cast members. Ten-year retrospective showing the evolution of current characters seen in September 1976. Credit information as of April 1977. Cast list is alphabetical.
Executive Producers Betty Corday, H. Wesley Kenney
Producer Jack Herzberg
Company Corday Productions, Inc. and Columbia Pictures Television in association with NBC-TV
Directors Joseph Behar, Alvin Rabin, Frank Pacelli, Richard Sandwick, Alan Pultz
Story Editor William J. Bell
Head Writer Ann Marcus
Writers Rocci Chatfield, Michael Robert David, Raymond Goldstone, Joyce Perry, Elizabeth Harrower, Laura Olsher

CAST

Don Craig .... Jed Allan
Valerie Grant .... Tina Andrews
Dr. Greg Peters .... Peter Brown
Rebecca LeClare .... Brooke Bundy
Dr. Tom Horton .... Macdonald Carey
Mickey Horton .... John Clarke
Robert LeClare .... Robert Clary
Phyllis Curtis .... Corinne Conley
Danny Grant .... Michael Dwight-Smith
Michael Horton .... Wesley Eure
Dr. Laura Horton .... Rosemary Forsyth
Amanda Peters .... Mary Frann
Dr. Neil Curtis .... Joseph Gallison
David Banning .... Richard Guthrie
Dr. Marlena Evans .... Deidre Hall
Doug Williams .... Bill Hayes
Julie Williams .... Susan Seaforth Hayes
Johnny Collins .... Paul Henry Itkin
Brooke Hamilton .... Adrienne La Russa
Helen Grant .... Ketty Lester
Dr. Tommy Horton, Jr. .... John Lupton
Dr. Bill Horton .... Edward Mallory
Linda Phillips .... Margaret Mason
Alice Horton .... Frances Reid
Maggie Horton .... Suzanne Rogers
Hope Williams .... Natasha Ryan
Mary Anderson .... Barbara Stanger
Jeri Clayton .... Kaye Stevens
Bob Anderson .... Mark Tapscott
Trish Clayton .... Patty Weaver

391 **The Daytime Emmy Awards** NBC
Program Type Parades/Pageants/Awards Special
90 minutes. Premiere date: 5/12/77. Live telecast of the fourth annual daytime Emmy awards from the New York (City) Shakespeare Festival's Delacorte Theater in Central Park. Special material written by Donald K. Epstein and Carmen Finestra.
Producer Walter C. Miller
Director Walter C. Miller
Writers Mel Brez. Ethel Brez
Musical Director Elliot Lawrence
Choreographer Judith Haskell
Costume Designer Robert Anton
Scenic Designer Leon Munier
Hosts Jack Gilford, Peter Marshall, Soupy Sales, Chuck Woolery, Victoria Wyndham
Presenters Chuck Barris, Peggy Cass, Dick Clark, Tony Craig, Richard Dawson, Patricia Estrin, Mary Fickett, Al Freeman, Jr., Eileen Fulton, Gerald Gordon, Judy Graubart, Arte Johnson, Lance Kerwin, Kristy McNichol, Melba Moore, Rita Moreno, David O'Brien, Fred Rogers, Don Stewart, Beatrice Straight, Susan Sullivan, Edward Villella, Tudi Wiggins, Jo Anne Worley

392 **Dead of Night**
All-Specials Night NBC
Program Type TV Movie
90 minutes. Premiere date: 3/29/77. Trilogy of dramas about the effect of the supernatural on the mind. "Second Chance" based on a story by Jack Finney. Music by Robert Cobert.
Executive Producer Dan Curtis
Producer Robert Singer
Company Dan Curtis Productions in association with NBC-TV
Director Dan Curtis
Writer Richard Matheson
Art Director Trevor Williams

No Such Thing As a Vampire
CAST
Michael Vares .... Horst Bucholz
Alexis Gheria .... Anjanette Comer
Dr. Gheria .... Patrick Macnee
Karel .... Elisha Cook

Second Chance
CAST
Frank .... Ed Begley, Jr.
Helen .... Christina Hart
Mrs. McCauley .... Ann Doran
Mr. McCauley .... E. J. Andre

Bobby
CAST
Alma .... Joan Hackett
Bobby .... Lee Montgomery

393 **The Deadliest Season** CBS
Program Type Dramatic Special
Two hours. Premiere date: 3/16/77. Drama of a professional hockey player determined to succeed any cost. Story by Ernest Kinoy and Tom King. Music by Dick Hyman. Filmed on location in Hartford, Conn.
Executive Producer Herbert Brodkin
Producer Robert Berger
Company Titus Productions, Inc.
Director Robert Markowitz
Writer Ernest Kinoy
Costume Designer Joseph Aulisi
Art Director Richard Bianchi
Hockey Consultant Ned Dowd
CAST
Gerry Miller .... Michael Moriarty
George Graff .... Kevin Conway
Tom Feeney .... Sully Boyar
Carole Eskanazi .... Jill Eikenberry
Horace Meade .... Walter McGinn
Sharon Miller .... Meryl Streep
Al Miller .... Andrew Duggan
Bertram Fowler .... Patrick O'Neal
Dave Eskanazi .... Paul D'Amato
Bill Cairns .... Mason Adams
Coach Bryant .... Mel Boudrot
Trainer Doyle .... Tom Quinn
Judge Reinhardt .... Ronald Weyand
Referee Merritt .... Dino Narizzano
Pres. MacCloud .... George Petrie
Bobby Miller .... Eddie Moran
Rene Beavois .... Frank Bongiorno
Waiter .... Rudy Hornish
Det. Forscher .... Alan North

394 **The Deadly Tower**
NBC Saturday Night at the Movies NBC
Program Type TV Movie
Two hours. Premiere date: 10/18/75. Repeat date: 1/15/77. Drama based on the 1966 University of Texas sniper killings of 13 people. Filmed on location in Baton Rouge, La. Music by Don Ellis. Special effects by Cliff Wenger.
Executive Producer Richard Caffey
Producer Antonio Calderon
Company MGM Television in association with NBC-TV
Director Jerry Jameson
Writer William Douglas Lansford
Narrator Gilbert Roland
CAST
Charles Whitman .... Kurt Russell
Ramiro Martinez .... Richard Yniguez
Crum .... Ned Beatty
Lt. Forbes .... John Forsythe
Lt. Lee .... Pernell Roberts
Capt. Ambrose .... Clifton James
Tim Davis .... Alan Vint
C. T. Foss .... Paul Carr
Mano .... Pepe Serna
Vinnie Martinez .... Maria-Elena Cordero

The Deadly Trackers *see* The CBS Wednesday Night Movies

395 **The Deadly Triangle**
NBC Movie of the Week NBC
Program Type TV Movie
90 minutes. Premiere date: 5/19/77. Crime drama pilot about a former Olympic skier who becomes sheriff of the resort town of Sun Valley. Filmed on location in Sun Valley, Idaho.
Producer Robert Stambler
Company A Barry Weitz Production in association with Columbia Pictures Television and NBC-TV
Director Charles S. Dubin
Writer Carl Gottlieb
CAST
Bill Stedman .... Dale Robinette
Charles Cole .... Robert Lansing
Edith Cole .... Diana Muldaur
Archie Sykes .... Taylor Lacher
Joanne Price .... Linda Scruggs Bogart
Red Bayliss .... Geoffrey Lewis
Merrie Leonard .... Maggie Wellman
Dwight Thatcher .... James Coleman
Wayne .... Tom McFadden
Ernst Haag .... Norbert Weisser

396 **Dean Martin Celebrity Roast: Angie Dickinson** NBC
Program Type Comedy Special
60 minutes. Premiere date: 2/8/77. Special honoring Angie Dickinson. Taped at the MGM Grand Hotel in Las Vegas.
Producer Greg Garrison
Company A Sasha Production in association with Greg Garrison Productions
Director Greg Garrison
Writers Harry Crane, Larry Markes, Martin Ragaway, Arthur Phillips, Mel Chase, Bob Mills, Mike Marmer, Stan Burns, Howard Albrecht, Sol Weinstein
Host Dean Martin
Guest of Honor Angie Dickinson
Celebrities Red Buttons, Foster Brooks, Earl Holliman, Ruth Buzzi, LaWanda Page, Cathy Rigby, Juliet Prowse, Jimmie Walker, Rex Reed, Cindy Williams, Orson Welles, Eve Arden, Scatman Crothers, Joey Bishop, James Stewart, Jackie Mason

397 **Dean Martin Celebrity Roast: Danny Thomas** NBC
Program Type Comedy Special
60 minutes. Premiere date: 12/15/76. Special honoring Danny Thomas. Taped at the MGM Grand Hotel in Las Vegas.
Producer Greg Garrison
Company A Sasha Production in association with Greg Garrison Productions
Director Greg Garrison
Writers Harry Crane, Bill Daley, Larry Markes, Bob Keane, Martin Ragaway, Arthur Phillips, Mel Chase, Bob Mills, Mike Marmer, Stan Burns
Host Dean Martin
Guest of Honor Danny Thomas
Celebrities Lucille Ball, Gene Kelly, Milton Berle, Orson Welles, Jimmie Walker, Charo, Red Buttons, Charlie Callas, Dena Dietrich, Jan Murray, Don Knotts, Ruth Buzzi, Nipsey Russell, Howard Cosell, Sandi Herdt, Harvey Korman

398 **Dean Martin Celebrity Roast: Gabe Kaplan** NBC
Program Type Comedy Special
60 minutes. Premiere date: 2/21/77. Special honoring Gabriel Kaplan. Taped at the MGM Grand Hotel in Las Vegas.
Producer Greg Garrison
Company A Sasha Production in association with Greg Garrison Productions
Director Greg Garrison
Writers Harry Crane, Bill Daley, Larry Markes, Bob Keane, Martin Ragaway, Arthur Phillips, Mel Chase, Bob Mills, Mike Marmer, Stan Burns
Host Dean Martin
Guest of Honor Gabriel Kaplan
Celebrities Jimmie Walker, Johnny Bench, Liz Torres, Ed Bluestone, Charo, Abe Vigoda, Billy Crystal, Howard Cosell, Joe Garagiola, Orson Welles, Alice Ghostley, Red Buttons, Nipsey Russell, Charlie Callas, George Kirby, Milton Berle

399 **Dean Martin Celebrity Roast: Jackie Gleason** NBC
Program Type Comedy Special
60 minutes. Premiere date: 2/27/75. Repeat date: 5/25/77. Roast honoring Jackie Gleason taped at the MGM Grand Hotel in Las Vegas.
Producer Greg Garrison
Company A Sasha Production in association with Greg Garrison Productions
Director Greg Garrison
Writers Harry Crane, George Bloom, Tom Tenowich, Milt Rosen, Peter Gallay, Howard Albrecht, Sol Weinstein, Nick Arnold, Jeffrey Barron
Host Dean Martin
Guest of Honor Jackie Gleason
Celebrities Phyllis Diller, Milton Berle, Danny Thomas, Audrey Meadows, Gene Kelly, Nipsey Russell, Sid Caesar, Sheila MacRae, Art Carney, Frank Gorshin, Foster Brooks

400 **Dean Martin Celebrity Roast: Joe Garagiola** NBC
Program Type Comedy Special
60 minutes. Premiere date: 5/25/76. Repeat date: 8/18/77. Special taped at the MGM Grand Hotel in Las Vegas.
Producer Greg Garrison
Director Greg Garrison
Host Dean Martin
Guest of Honor Joe Garagiola
Celebrities Jack Carter, Mickey Mantle, Orson Welles, Charlie Callas, Pat Henry, Hank Aaron, Yogi Berra, Shirley Jones, Charlie Finley, Norm Crosby, Luis Tiant, Jackie Gayle, Stan Musial, Nipsey Russell, Willie Mays, Red Buttons, Maury Wills, Gabriel Kaplan

401 **Dean Martin Celebrity Roast: Peter Marshall** NBC
Program Type Comedy Special
60 minutes. Premiere date: 5/2/77. Special honoring Peter Marshall. Taped at the MGM Grand Hotel in Las Vegas.
Producer Greg Garrison
Company A Sasha Production in association with Greg Garrison Productions
Director Greg Garrison

Writers Harry Crane, Larry Markes, Martin Ragaway, Arthur Phillips, Mel Chase, Bob Mills, Mike Marmer, Stan Burns, Howard Albrecht, Sol Weinstein
Host Dean Martin
Guest of Honor Peter Marshall
Celebrities Red Buttons, Foster Brooks, Rip Taylor, Vincent Price, Karen Valentine, Paul Lynde, Jimmie Walker, Jack Carter, Jackie Gayle, Rose Marie, Orson Welles, Zsa Zsa Gabor, Wayland Flowers and Madam, Joey Bishop, Ed Bluestone

402 **Dean Martin Celebrity Roast: Redd Foxx** NBC
Program Type Comedy Special
60 minutes. Premiere date: 11/26/76. First "roast" of the season. Taped at the MGM Grand Hotel in Las Vegas.
Producer Greg Garrison
Company A Sasha Production in association with Greg Garrison Productions
Director Greg Garrison
Writers Harry Crane, Bill Daley, Larry Markes, Bob Keane, Martin Ragaway, Arthur Phillips, Mel Chase, Bob Mills, Mike Marmer, Stan Burns
Art Director Robert Fletcher
Host Dean Martin
Guest of Honor Redd Foxx
Celebrities Steve Allen, Slappy White, Norm Crosby, Milton Berle, Liz Torres, Orson Welles, George Kirby LaWanda Page, Marty Allen, Abe Vigoda, Jimmie Walker, Joe Garagiola, Isaac Hayes, Isabel Sanford, Nipsey Russell, Don Rickles

403 **Dean Martin Celebrity Roast: Ted Knight** NBC
Program Type Comedy Special
60 minutes. Premiere date: 3/2/77. Special honoring Ted Knight. Taped at the MGM Grand Hotel in Las Vegas.
Producer Greg Garrison
Company A Sasha Production in association with Greg Garrison Productions
Director Greg Garrison
Writers Harry Crane, Larry Markes, Martin Ragaway, Arthur Phillips, Mel Chase, Bob Mills, Mike Marmer, Stan Burns, Howard Albrecht, Sol Weinstein
Host Dean Martin
Guest of Honor Ted Knight
Celebrities Red Buttons, Foster Brooks, Georgia Engel, Paul Williams, LaWanda Page, Gavin MacLeod, Edward Asner, Jimmie Walker, Jack Carter, Julie McWhirter, Harvey Korman, Orson Welles, Jackie Mason, Scatman Crothers, Willie Tyler, James Stewart, Kelly Monteith, Dr. Renee Richards

404 **Dean Martin's Red Hot Scandals of 1926** NBC
Program Type Music/Comedy/Variety Special
60 minutes. Premiere date: 11/8/76. Comedy-variety special with 1920s theme. Taped in part at the Biltmore Hotel, Los Angeles and the Mayfair Music Hall, Santa Monica, Calif.
Executive Producer Greg Garrison
Producer Lee Hale
Co-Producer Robert Fletcher
Company A Sasha Production in association with Greg Garrison Productions
Directors Greg Garrison, Robert Sidney
Writers Mike Marmer, Stan Burns
Conductor Les Brown
Choreographer Robert Sidney
Costume Designer Robert Fletcher
Production Designer Robert Fletcher
Star Dean Martin
Guest Stars Jonathan Winters, Dom DeLuise, Hermione Baddeley, Abe Vigoda, Georgia Engel, Charlene Ryan, the Golddiggers

405 **Dean Martin's Red Hot Scandals Part Two** NBC
Program Type Music/Comedy/Variety Special
60 minutes. Premiere date: 4/4/77. Second comedy-variety special with 1920s theme. Taped in part at the Biltmore Hotel, Los Angeles and the Mayfair Music Hall, Santa Monica, Calif.
Executive Producer Greg Garrison
Producer Lee Hale
Co-Producer Robert Fletcher
Company A Sasha Production in association with Greg Garrison Productions
Directors Greg Garrison, Robert Sidney
Writers Mike Marmer, Stan Burns
Conductor Les Brown
Choreographer Robert Sidney
Costume Designer Robert Fletcher
Scenic Designer Robert Fletcher
Star Dean Martin
Guest Stars Jonathan Winters, Dom DeLuise, Hermione Baddeley, Abe Vigoda, Georgia Engel, Charlene Ryan, the Golddiggers

406 **Dear Lovey Hart (I Am Desperate!)**
ABC Afterschool Specials ABC
Program Type Children's Special
60 minutes. Premiere date: 5/19/76. Repeat date: 1/26/77. Young people's comedy-drama about a high school newspaper editor and his secret lonely hearts columnist. Based on the novel by Ellen Conford.
Executive Producer Martin Tahse
Producer Fred W. Bennett

Dear Lovey Hart (I Am Desperate!) *Continued*
Company Martin Tahse Productions, Inc.
Director Larry Elikann
Writer Bob Rodgers
Art Director Ray Markham

CAST

Carrie Wasserman .... Susan Lawrence
Skip Custer .... Meegan King
Susan .... Barbara Timko
Linda .... Elyssa Davalos
Mar .... Del Hinkley
Bernice .... Bebe Kelly
Jeff Wasserman .... Al Eisenmann
Marty .... Stephen Liss
Bob .... Benny Medina
Barker .... Craig Hundley
Sam .... John Starr
2nd Tennis Player .... Helene T. Nelson
1st Tennis Player .... Sheri Jason
Freddie .... Bruce Caton

407 **Dear Mr. Gable** NBC
Program Type Documentary/Informational Special
60 minutes. Premiere date: 3/5/68. Repeat date: 11/4/76. The life and career of Clark Gable. Title song sung by Judy Garland in the 1938 motion picture "Broadway Melody of 1938." Original music by Gerald Fried.
Executive Producer Irwin Rosten
Producer Nicolas Noxon
Company Metro-Goldwyn-Mayer Television for NBC-TV
Writer Nicolas Noxon
Conductor Gerald Fried
Narrator Burgess Meredith

408 **Death at Love House**
The ABC Friday Night Movie ABC
Program Type TV Movie
90 minutes. Preimere date: 9/3/76. Repeat date: 6/3/77. Suspense melodrama about the obsession of a young writer for a long-dead movie queen. Filmed in part at the Harold Lloyd estate in Beverly Hills. Music by Laurence Rosenthal.
Executive Producers Aaron Spelling, Leonard Goldberg
Producer Hal Sitowitz
Company A Spelling-Goldberg Production
Director E. W. Swackhamer
Writer Jim Barnett
Art Director Paul Sylos

CAST

Joel Gregory, Jr./Joel Gregory, Sr. .. Robert Wagner
Donna Gregory .... Kate Jackson
Mrs. Josephs .... Sylvia Sidney
Lorna Love (in flashback) .... Mariana Hill
Marcella .... Joan Blondell
Conan Carroll .... John Carradine
Denise .... Dorothy Lamour
Oscar .... Bill Macy
Bus Driver .... Joseph Bernard
Eric .... John A. Zee
The Director .... Robert Gibbons
The Policeman .... Al Hansen
Actor in Film .... Crofton Hardester

409 **The Death of Richie**
NBC Monday Night at the Movies NBC
Program Type TV Movie
Two hours. Premiere date: 1/10/77. Fact-based drama based on "Richie"by Thomas Thompson about the effect of a teenager's drug addiction on his family. Music by Fred Karlin.
Executive Producer Charles B. FitzSimons
Producer Michael Jaffe
Company Henry Jaffe Enterprises, Inc. in association with NBC-TV
Director Paul Wendkos
Writer John McGreevey
Art Director James Hulsey

CAST

George Werner .... Ben Gazzara
Richie Werner .... Robby Benson
Carol Werner .... Eileen Brennan
Russell Werner .... Lance Kerwin
Brick .... Charles Fleischer
Peanuts .... Clint Howard
Mark .... Harry Gold
Sheila .... Susan Neher
Mrs. Norlon .... Shirley O'Hara
Elaine .... Jennifer Rhodes

Death Scream *see* The Woman Who Cried Murder

410 **Death Trap** NBC
Program Type Science/Nature Special
60 minutes. Premiere date: 4/28/77. A photographic study of carnivorous insects, reptiles and plants. Original music by John Scott
Company Oxford Scientific Films and Swan Productions Limited
Distributor Juno Films Limited
Directors Hugh Falkus, Bill Travers, James Hill
Writers Hugh Falkus, Bill Travers, James Hill
Cinematographers Sean Morris, Peter Parks
Researchers Sean Morris, Peter Parks
Narrator Vincent Price

Death Wish *see* The CBS Wednesday Night Movies

411 **Debate: Is School Desegreation Working?** PBS
Program Type Public Affairs Special
60 minutes. Premiere date: 11/7/76. A debate based on the report of the U.S. Commission on Civil Rights on desegregation in American schools. Program made possible by grants from

the Corporation for Public Broadcasting, the Ford Foundation and Public Television Stations.
Executive Producers Wallace Westfeldt, Robert Ferrante
Producers Lou Wiley, Susan Mayer
Company WGBH-TV/Boston and WETA-TV/Washington
Moderator Jim Lehrer

412 **Decades of Decision** PBS
Program Type Drama Series
60 minutes. Premiere date: 3/17/76. Repeats shown 1/7/77 and 5/15/77. Five-part series dramatizing little-known facts about the American Revolution. Program made possible in part by a grant from the Mobil Oil Corporation.
Producer Tom Cherrones
Company National Geographic Society in association with WQED-TV/Pittsburgh
Director M. von Braunitsch
Host Henry Fonda
Project Designers Louis B. Wright, M. von Braunitsch
Project Director Thomas Skinner

413 **Decision '76** NBC
Program Type News Special – Public Affairs Special
News and public affairs specials seen during the election year. Programs include "The Campaign and the Candidates" (series), "Election Eve Special Report," "Election '76 Coverage," "Election '76: The President from Plains," "The Presidential Candidates Debate—Post Debate Wrap-Up," "The Vice-Presidential Debate—Wrap Up." (*See* individual titles for credits.)

414 **Delta County, U.S.A.**
The ABC Friday Night Movie ABC
Program Type TV Movie
Two hours. Premiere date: 5/20/77. Drama of young people in the new South. Filmed in southern California. Music by Jack Elliott and Allyn Ferguson.
Executive Producer Leonard Goldberg
Producers Robert Greenwald, Frank von Zerneck
Company Leonard Goldberg Productions in association with Paramount Television
Director Glenn Jordan
Writer Thomas Rickman
Art Director Jack Collins

CAST

Jack the Bear .... Jim Antonio
Terry Nicholas .... Jeff Conaway
Bo .... Robert Hays
Val Nicholas .... Ed Power
Kate McCain Nicholas .... Joanna Miles
John McCain, Jr. .... Peter Donat
Dossie Wilson .... Lola Albright
Josie Wilson .... Michele Carey
Vonda .... Leigh Christian
Capt. McCain .... John McLiam
Bevo .... James Crittenden
McCain Nicholas .... Doney Oatman
Joe Ed .... Joe Penny
Robbie Jean .... Tisch Raye
Billy Wingate .... Peter Masterson
Doris Ann .... Morgan Brittany
Biggie .... Dennis Burkley

415 **Delvecchio** CBS
Program Type Crime Drama Series
60 minutes. Sundays. Preview date: 9/9/76. Premiere date: 9/26/76. Last show: 7/17/77. Crime drama about a metropolitan police detective. Created by Joseph Polizzi and Sam Rolfe.
Executive Producer William Sackheim
Producer Steven Bochco, Michael Rhodes
Directors Various
Writers Various
Art Director John E. Chilberg II

CAST

Sgt. Dominick Delvecchio .... Judd Hirsch
Shonski .... Charles Haid
Lt. Macaven .... Michael Conrad
Tomaso Delvecchio .... Mario Gallo

The Deserter *see* The CBS Wednesday Night Movies

416 **The Devil's Work**
Ourstory PBS
Program Type Dramatic Special
30 minutes. Premiere date: 1/20/76. Repeat date: 11/26/76. Dramatization of the life and work of an itinerant theater company in the mid-1800s. Music by Dave Conner. Filmed in part at Old Bethpage Village Restoration, Nassau County, N.Y. Funded by a grant from the National Endowment for the Humanities.
Executive Producer Don Fouser
Producer Ron Finley
Company WNET-TV/New York
Director Ron Finley
Writer Stephen Jennings
Costume Designer John Boxer
Art Director Stephen Hendrickson
Host Bill Moyers

CAST

Joseph Jefferson .... Jerry Mayer
Cornelia Jefferson .... Betty Buckley
Joe Jr. .... John Dunn
Will McBride .... Frederick Coffin
Ella McBride .... Elizabeth Farley
Tom .... Bobby Grober
Abe Lincoln .... Stephen Keep
Rev. Scanlon .... Gil Rogers
Mayor Peebles .... John C. Becher
Mr. Fitch .... Tom Spratley
Mrs. Powell .... Elaine Eldridge
Ned .... Sam McMurray

The Devil's Work *Continued*

Eustace .... Christopher Curry
Wagon Driver .... Richard Hamilton

417 **Diamond Rivers** PBS

Program Type Documentary/Informational Special

30 minutes. Premiere date: 6/1/77. A look at an 80-year-old diamond prospector in the Brazilian state of Bahia. Program made possible by a grant from Sandgren & Murtha, Inc.

Producer Bill Benenson

Company WNET-TV/New York

Diamonds Are Forever *see* The ABC Sunday Night Movie

418 **Dickens of London**

Masterpiece Theatre PBS

Program Type Limited Series

60 minutes. Sundays. Premiere date: 8/28/77. Ten-part series dramatizing the life of Charles Dickens. Music by Monty Norman. Filmed in England. Presented by WGBH/TV/Boston; Joan Sullivan, series producer. Series made possible by a grant from Mobil Oil Corporation.

Executive Producer David Cunliffe

Producer Marc Miller

Company Yorkshire Television

Director Marc Miller

Writer Wolf Mankowitz

Host Alistair Cooke

CAST

John Dickens/Charles Dickens .... Roy Dotrice
Charles Dickens (as a boy) .... Simon Bell
Charles Dickens (as a youth) .... Gene Foad
Mrs. Dickens .... Diana Coupland
Maria .... Karen Dotrice
Hogarth .... Richard Leech
Catherine Hogarth .... Adrienne Burgess
Mary .... Lois Baxter
Fred .... Graham Faulkner
Forster .... Trevor Bowen
Chapman .... John Ringham
Edgar Allan Poe .... Seymour Matthews
Dolby .... John Landry
Clerk .... Bob Sessions

419 **Die Fledermaus (The Bat)**

Opera Theater PBS

Program Type Music/Dance Special

Two hours. Premiere date: 5/25/76. Repeat date: 8/30/77. English-language version of the light opera by Johann Strauss, translated by Christopher Hassal and Edmund Tracey, and featuring the New Philharmonic Orchestra. Program made possible by grants from the Ford Foundation, the Corporation for Public Broadcasting and Public Television Stations. Presented by WNET-TV/New York.

Coordinating Producers Linda Krisel, David Griffiths

Producer Cedric Messina

Company British Broadcasting Corporation and WNET-TV/New York

Director John Gorrie

Conductor Raymond Leppard

Choreographer Geoffrey Cauley

CAST

Gabriel von Eisenstein .... David Hillman
Alfredo .... David Hughes
Rosalinda .... Sheila Armstrong
Frank .... Eric Shilling
Prince Orlofsky .... Ann Howard
Adele .... Anne Pashley
Dr. Falke (The Bat) .... David Bowman
Dr. Blind .... Francis Egerton

Dillinger *see* The CBS Wednesday Night Movies

420 **Dinah!** Syndicated

Program Type Talk/Service/Variety Series

90 minutes. Mondays-Fridays. Premiere date: 10/21/74. Continuous. Successor to "Dinah's Place."

Producers Henry Jaffe, Carolyn Raskin

Producer Fred Tatashore

Company Winchester Productions

Distributor 20th Century-Fox Television

Director Glen Swanson

Musical Director John Rodby

Host Dinah Shore

Announcer Johnny Gilbert

421 **Dionne Warwick**

In Performance at Wolf Trap PBS

Program Type Music/Dance Special

60 minutes. Premiere date: 12/1/75. Repeat date: 11/29/76. A concert by Dionne Warwick performed at the Wolf Trap Farm Park in Arlington, Va. Program made possible by a grant from the Atlantic Richfield Company.

Executive Producer David Prowitt

Producer Ruth Leon

Company WETA-TV/Washington, D.C.

Director Clark Santee

Hosts Beverly Sills, David Prowitt

Executive-in-charge Jim Karayn

422 **Directions** ABC

Program Type Religious/Cultural Series

30 minutes. Sundays. Premiere date: 11/13/60. 17th season premiere: 11/7/76. Became 52-week show during 1976–77 season. Continuing theme: "Conscience of America" begun during the 1975–76 season.

Executive Producer Sid Darion

Producers Various

Company ABC News Public Affairs
Directors Various
Writers Various

Dirty Harry *see* NBC Saturday Night at the Movies

Dirty Mary Crazy Larry *see* The ABC Friday Night Movie

423 **The Disappearance of AIMEE**
Hallmark Hall of Fame NBC
Program Type Dramatic Special
Two hours. Premiere date: 11/17/76. Drama based on the disappearance of Aimee Semple McPherson in 1926. Filmed on location in Denver, Col. and near Marina del Rey, Calif.
Executive Producer Thomas W. Moore
Producer Paul Leaf
Company Tomorrow Entertainment
Director Anthony Harvey
Writer John McGreevey
Musical Director Steve Byrne
Costume Designer Edith Head
Art Director Chuck Rosen

CAST

Aimee Semple McPherson .... Faye Dunaway
Minnie Kennedy .... Bette Davis
D.A. Asa Keyes .... James Sloyan
Joseph Ryan .... James Woods
Capt. Cline .... John Lehne
Emma Shaffer .... Lelia Goldoni
S. I. Gilbert .... Severn Darden
Kenneth Ormiston .... William Jordan
Judge Blake .... Sandy Ward
Wallace Moore .... Barry Brown
Benedict .... Irby Smith
Clerk .... Hartley Silver
Williams .... Harlan Knudson
Jameson .... Lucian Berrier
Ahern .... Rena Andrews
Engineer .... Paul Felix
Reporter No. 1 .... Richard Jamison
Reporter No. 2 .... Jerry Reitmeyer
Reporter No. 3 .... Dusty Saunders
Nurse .... Liz Jury
Bailiff .... Lester Palmer

424 **Disco '77** Syndicated
Program Type Music/Dance Series
30 minutes. Weekly. Premiere date: Spring 1977. Short-lived music/dance show taped at a discotheque in Ft. Lauderdale, Fla. Different guest hosts weekly.
Producers Steve Marcus, Arnie Wohl, Lou Sposa
Company Marcus Productions
Distributor Vitt Media
Director Steve Marcus

425 **The Displaced Person**
The American Short Story PBS
Program Type Dramatic Special
60 minutes. Premiere date: 4/12/77. Adaptation of a short story by Flannery O'Connor set in the late 1940s on a Georgia farm. Music by Bill Conti. Program presented by South Carolina Educational Television and funded by a grant from the National Endowment for the Humanities.
Executive Producer Robert Geller
Producer Matthew N. Herman
Company Learning in Focus, Inc.
Director Glenn Jordan
Writer Horton Foote
Costume Designer Joseph Aulisi
Scenic Designer Charles Bennett
Host Colleen Dewhurst

CAST

Mrs. McIntyre .... Irene Worth
Father Flynn .... John Houseman
Mr. Guizac .... Noam Yerushalmi
Mrs. Shortley .... Shirley Stoler
Mr. Shortley .... Lane Smith
Field Hand .... Robert Earl Jones

426 **Doc** CBS
Program Type Comedy Series
30 minutes. Saturdays. Premiere date: 9/13/75. Second season premiere: 9/25/76. Last show: 10/30/76. Created by Ed. Weinberger and Stan Daniels. In second season series set in New York City's Westside Community Clinic.
Executive Producers Ed. Weinberger, Stan Daniels
Producers Martin Cohan, Laurence Marks
Company MTM Enterprises, Inc.
Directors Various
Writers Various

CAST

Doc Joe Bogert .... Barnard Hughes
Janet Scott .... Audra Lindley
Stanley Moss .... David Ogden Stiers
Woody Henderson .... Ray Vitte
Teresa Ortega .... Lisa Mordente

427 **Doc and Gladys Celebrate** NBC
Program Type Music/Dance Special
Three hours. Premiere date: 1/1/77 (1–4 a.m.) New Year's Eve musical special.
Executive Producer Burt Sugarman
Producer Stan Harris
Director Stan Harris
Hosts Gladys Knight and the Pips, Doc Severinsen
Announcer Wolfman Jack
Guests Bay City Rollers, Loretta Lynn, Elvin Bishop, Jim Stafford, Orleans, Fred Travalena, Jeff Kutash and the Dancin' Machine

Doctor *see* Dr.

428 **The Doctors** NBC

Program Type Daytime Drama Series

30 minutes. Mondays-Fridays. Premiere date: 4/1/63. Continuous. Series revolves around the Powers, Aldrich and Dancy families. Set primarily in Hope Memorial Hospital in Madison, U.S.A. Special 60-minute show 3/8/77. Cast list is alphabetical.

Producer Jeff Young

Company Channelex, Inc.

Directors Norman Hall, Gene Lasko

Head Writer Douglas Marland

Writers Robert Cessna, Elizabeth David, Nancy Franklin

CAST

Dr. Erich Aldrich .... Keith Blanchard
Dr. Maggie Powers .... Lydia Bruce
Dr. Paul Sommers .... Paul Carr
Jason Aldrich .... Glenn Corbett
Dr. Ann Larimer .... Geraldine Court
Dr. Hank Iverson .... Palmer Deane
Penny Davis .... Julia Duffy
Wendy Conrad .... Kathy Eckles
Billy Allison .... David Elliott
Martha Allen .... Sally Gracie
Nola Dancy .... Kathryn Harrold
Jerry Dancy .... Jonathan Hogan
Greta Powers .... Jennifer Houlton
Dr. Althea Davis .... Elizabeth Hubbard
Virginia Dancy .... Elizabeth Lawrence
Mona Croft .... Meg Mundy
Dr. Steve Aldrich .... David O'Brien
Dr. Matt Powers .... James Pritchett
Stacy Sommers .... Leslie Ann Ray
Carolee Aldrich .... Jada Rowland
Eleanor Conrad .... Lois Smith
Lew Dancy .... Frank Telfer
M.J. Match .... Lauren White

429 **Documentary Showcase** PBS

Program Type Documentary/Informational Series

60 minutes. Fridays. Premiere date: 11/5/76. A collection of documentaries produced by different PBS stations and independent producers. Programs captioned for the hearing-impaired in repeat showings. Programs shown during the 1976–77 season are: "The Amish: People of Preservation," "The Appalshop Show," "Carnivore," "Chinatown," "Counterpoint: The U-2 Story," "Cowboys," "The 81st Blow," "Full Moon Lunch," "Galveston: The Gilded Age of the Golden Isle," "Giving Birth," "Going Past Go: An Essay on Sexism," "Guess Who's Pregnant?" "I.F. Stone's Weekly," "Kitty Hawk to Paris," "Murder One," "The Others," "Song at Twilight: An Essay on Aging," "South Africa: The White Laager," "Teton: Decision and Disaster," "To Expect To Die: A Film About Living," "TVTV Looks at the Oscars," "Two Stones," "Waiting for Fidel," "Winners and Losers: Poverty in California," "Work, Work, Work," "The World's Worst Air Crash: The Avoidable Accident?" "You Should See What You're Missing." (*See* individual titles for credits.)

430 **Dog and Cat** ABC

Program Type Crime Drama Series

60 minutes. Saturdays. Premiere date: 3/5/77. Last show: 5/14/77. Action-adventure about a male plainclothes cop teamed with a female rookie officer. Created by Walter Hill. Music by Barry Devorzon.

Executive Producer Lawrence Gordon

Producer Robert Singer

Company A Largo Production

Directors Various

Writers Various

Art Director Ray Beal

CAST

Sgt. Jack Ramsey .... Lou Antonio
Officer J.Z. Kane .... Kim Basinger
Lt. Kipling .... Matt Clark

431 **Dog and Cat (Pilot)**

The ABC Friday Night Movie ABC

Program Type TV Movie

90 minutes. Premiere date: 7/22/77. Pilot for police drama series not previously shown.

Executive Producer Lawrence Gordon

Producer Robert Singer

Company A Largo Production

Director Robert Kelljan

Writers Walter Hill, Owen Morgan, Henry Rosenbaum, Haywood Gould

CAST

Jack Ramsey .... Lou Antonio
J. Z. Kane .... Kim Basinger
Lt. Kipling .... Matt Clark
Travan .... Charles Cioffi
Shirley .... Richard Lynch
Storey .... Geoffrey Scott
Evans .... Dale Robinette
Roeanne .... Janit Baldwin
Velman .... Leslie Wood
Gonzo .... Matt Bennett
Trog .... Walt Davis

432 **Dolly** Syndicated

Program Type Music/Comedy/Variety Series

30 minutes. Weekly. Premiere date: 9/76. One-season musical/variety show with guests.

Executive Producer Bill Graham

Producer J. Reginald Dunlap

Company Show Biz, Inc.

Distributor Show Biz, Inc.

Director Bill Turner

Writers Bill Graham, Paul Elliott

Musical Director Jerry Whitehurst

Star Dolly Parton

433 **The Don Ho Show** ABC
Program Type Music/Comedy/Variety Series
30 minutes. Mondays-Fridays. Premiere date: 10/25/76. Last show: 3/4/77. Daytime variety show from the Cinerama Reef Hotel, Waikiki Beach, Honolulu, Hawaii.
Executive Producer Bob Banner
Producer Brad Lachman
Company Bob Banner Associates, Inc.
Director Jack Regas
Writers George Atkins, Jay Burton
Musical Director Johnny Todd
Art Director Bill Bohnert
Set Decorator Wally White
Star Don Ho
Regulars Sam Kapu, Jr., Pat Swalli, Angel Pablo, Tokyo Joe

434 **Don Kirshner's Rock Concert** Syndicated
Program Type Music/Dance Series
90 minutes. Weekly. Premiere date: 9/73. Fourth season Premiere: 9/76. Late night show with different rock stars weekly. Introductions by Don Kirshner. First show to use radio simulcasts.
Executive Producer Don Kirshner
Producer David Yarnell
Company Don Kirshner Productions
Distributor Viacom International, Inc.
Host Don Kirshner

435 **Donahue** Syndicated
Program Type Talk/Service/Variety Series
60 minutes. Mondays-Fridays. Premiere date: 11/6/67 (as "The Phil Donahue Show.") Continuous. Hourlong discussion show with questions from the studio audience.
Executive Producer Richard Mincer
Producer Patricia McMillen
Company Avco Broadcasting
Distributor Multimedia Program Sales
Director Ron Weiner
Host Phil Donahue

436 **Donny & Marie** ABC
Program Type Music/Comedy/Variety Series
60 minutes. Fridays. Premiere date: 1/23/76. Second season premiere: 9/24/76. Music and variety. Regular features: skating act, country/rock concerts. (*See also* "The Best of Donny & Marie.")
Executive Producers Raymond Katz, The Osmond Brothers
Producers Sid Krofft, Marty Krofft
Company An Osmond Production in association with Sid & Marty Krofft Productions
Director Art Fisher
Writing Supervisor Arnie Kogen
Writers Bill Larkin, Chet Dowling, Sandy Krinski, Rod Warren, April Kelly, Tom Chapman
Choreographer David Winters
Costume Designer Madeline Graneto
Art Director Bill Bohnert
Stars Donny Osmond, Marie Osmond
Announcer George Fenneman
Regulars The Ice Vanities
Ice Choreographer Bob Paul

437 **Doral Eastern Open** CBS
Program Type Sports Special
Final two rounds of the 16th Open from the Doral Country Club in Miami, Fla. 3/12/77 and 3/13/77.
Producer Frank Chirkinian
Company CBS Television Network Sports
Directors Frank Chirkinian, Bob Dailey
Commentators Vin Scully, Pat Summerall, Jack Whitaker, Ben Wright, Frank Glieber, Ken Venturi

438 **The Dorothy Hamill Special** ABC
Program Type Music/Comedy/Variety Special
60 minutes. Premiere date: 11/17/76. An ice skating/variety special. Special musical material and choral direction by Ray Charles.
Executive Producer Jerry Weintraub
Producers Gary Smith, Dwight Hemion
Company Smith-Hemion Productions
Director Dwight Hemion
Writer Buz Kohan
Musical Director Ian Fraser
Choreographer Rob Iscove
Costume Designer David Doucette
Art Director Ray Klausen
Star Dorothy Hamill
Special Guest Star Gene Kelly
Guest Stars Jim McKay, Carrie Weber

439 **The Dorothy Hamill Winter Carnival Special** ABC
Program Type Music/Comedy/Variety Special
60 minutes. Premiere date: 3/2/77. Ice-skating/variety special filmed in and around Quebec City and at the Quebec Winter Carnival. Special musical material by Ray Charles.
Executive Producer Jerry Weintraub
Producers Rich Eustis, Al Rogers
Company Jon-Jer Productions, Inc.
Director Bill Davis
Writers Rich Eustis, Al Rogers
Musical Director Ian Fraser
Choreographer Edward Villella
Costume Designer David Doucette
Art Director Ken Johnson
Star Dorothy Hamill
Special Guest Stars The Carpenters
Guest Stars Beau Bridges, Edward Villella

The Double Con *see* the ABC Friday Night Movie

440 **Double Dare** CBS
Program Type Game/Audience Participation Series
30 minutes. Mondays–Fridays. Premiere date: 12/13/76. Last show: 4/29/77. A game of knowledge in which contestants "dare" and "double dare" each other to answer correctly.
Executive Producer Jay Wolpert
Producer Jonathan Goodson
Company Goodson-Todman Productions
Director Marc Breslow
Music Supervisor Bart Eskander
Creative Consultant Theodore Cooper
Host Alex Trebek

441 **Doug Henning's World of Magic**
Mobil Showcase Presentation NBC
Program Type Music/Comedy/Variety Special
60 minutes. Premiere date: 12/23/76. Live magic show with ten original illusions created by Doug Henning. Magic consultant: Charles Reynolds.
Executive Producer Jerry Goldstein
Producer Walter C. Miller
Company Doug Henning's Magic, Inc.
Director Walter C. Miller
Writer Buz Kohan
Musical Director Peter Matz
Choreographer Charlene Painter
Costume Designer Karen Katz
Art Director Charles Lisanby
Star Doug Henning
Host Michael Landon
Guests Joey Heatherton, Ricky Jay

442 **Dr. Seuss' Horton Hears a Who** CBS
Program Type Animated Film Special
30 minutes. Premiere date: 3/19/70. Repeat date: 5/13/77. Created by Theodor Geisel. Music by Eugene Poddany; lyrics by Theodor Geisel.
Producers Theodor Geisel, Chuck Jones
Director Chuck Jones
Writer Theodor Geisel
Narrator Hans Conried

443 **Dr. Seuss' How the Grinch Stole Christmas** CBS
Program Type Animated Film Special
30 minutes. Premiere date: 12/18/66. Repeat date: 12/18/76. Based on the book by Theodor Geisel. Music by Albert Hague; lyrics by Theodor Geisel.
Producers Theodor Geisel, Chuck Jones
Company MGM Television
Director Chuck Jones
Writer Theodor Geisel
Narrator Boris Karloff

VOICES
Christmas Spoiler .... Boris Karloff

444 **Dr. Seuss' the Lorax** CBS
Program Type Animated Film Special
30 minutes. Premiere date: 2/14/72. Repeat date: 7/19/77. Based on the book by Theodor Geisel. Music by Dean Elliott; lyrics by Theodor Geisel.
Executive Producer David H. DePatie
Producers Friz Freleng, Theodor Geisel
Company DePatie-Freleng Production
Director Hawley Pratt
Writer Theodor Geisel
Narrator Eddie Albert
Voices Bob Holt, Helen Carraher

Dreams *see* PBS Movie Theater

445 **Drink, Drank, Drunk** PBS
Program Type Documentary/Informational Special
60 minutes. Premiere date: 10/21/74. Repeat date: 10/24/76. Skits and practical advice for families, friends and employers of alcoholics. Program made possible by a grant from the 3M Company.
Executive Producer Thomas Skinner
Producer Charlie Hauck
Company WQED-TV/Pittsburgh
Directors Jack Kuney, Joe Hamilton
Writers Joe Bologna, Renee Taylor, John Boni, Charlie Hauck, Jack B. Weiner
Host Carol Burnett
Guests Larry Blyden, Joe Bologna, Ron Carey, Morgan Freeman, Stanley Grover, Linda Hopkins, Ellen Madison, E. G. Marshall, Maeve McGuire, Renee Taylor

446 **Drum Corps International Championships—1977** PBS
Program Type Sports Special
Four hours. Live coverage of the sixth annual Drum Corps International Championship from the Mile High Stadium in Denver, Colorado 8/19/77. Program made possible in part by a grant from public television stations.
Producer Syrl Silberman
Company WGBH-TV/Boston
Hosts Gene Rayburn, Helen Rayburn, Peter Emmons

447 **The Duchess of Malfi**
Classic Theatre: The Humanities in Drama
PBS
Program Type Dramatic Special
Two hours. Premiere date: 10/9/75. Repeat date: 3/3/77. 1614 play filmed at Chastleton House and in the Cotswolds countryside of England. Program made possible by grants from the National Endowment for the Humanities and from Mobil Oil Corporation. Presented by WGBH-TV/Boston; Joan Sullivan, producer.
Producer Cedric Messina
Company British Broadcasting Corporation
Director James MacTaggart
Writer John Webster

CAST

The Duchess of Malfi .... Eileen Atkins
Daniel de Bosola .... Michael Bryant
Duke Ferdinand .... Charles Kay
The Cardinal .... T. P. McKenna
Antonio Bologna .... Gary Bond
Julia .... Jean Gilpin

448 **Duffy** CBS
Program Type Comedy Special
30 minutes. Premiere date: 5/6/77. Comedy pilot about an almost human dog adopted by a school as its mascot.
Producer George Eckstein
Company Universal Television
Director Bruce Bilson
Writer Richard DeRoy

CAST

Cliff Sellers .... Fred Grandy
Thomas N. Tibbles .... Roger Bowen
Marty Carter .... Lane Binkley
Happy Jack .... George Wyner
Postman .... Dick Yarmy
Mrs. Dreifuss .... Jane Lambert
Neighbor .... Jane Dulo
Friendly Bum .... Robert E. Ball
Nick .... John Sheldon
Craig .... John Herbsleb
Josh .... Stephen Manley
Danny .... Jarrod Johnson

449 **Dying** PBS
Program Type Documentary/Informational Special
Two hours. Premiere date: 4/29/76. Repeat date: 7/18/77. Filmed over two years, documentary follows three people terminally ill with cancer. Program made possible through grants from the National Endowment for the Humanities and Polaroid Corporation.
Executive Producer Michael Ambrosino
Producer Michael Roemer
Company WGBH-TV/Boston
Director Michael Roemer
Cinematographer David Grubin

450 **An Eames Celebration** PBS
Program Type Documentary/Informational Special
90 minutes. Premiere date: 2/3/75. Repeat date: 10/26/76. A profile of Charles Eames and Ray Eames. Program made possible by grants from the National Science Foundation and IBM.
Producer Perry Miller Adato
Company WNET-TV/New York
Director Perry Miller Adato

Earth *see* PBS Movie Theater

Earthquake *see* The Big Event/NBC Saturday Night at the Movies

451 **East-West Shrine Football Game**
Syndicated
Program Type Sports Special
Live coverage of the 52nd annual Shrine football game from Palo Alto, Calif. 1/2/77.
Producer Robert Wold
Company The Robert Wold Company
Distributor The Robert Wold Company
Announcer Ray Scott
Color Commentator John McKay

452 **The Easter Bunny Is Comin' To Town** ABC
Program Type Animated Film Special
60 minutes. Premiere date: 4/6/77. Animated musical special about Easter customs using dimensional stop-motion photography. Music by Maury Laws; lyrics by Jules Bass.
Producers Arthur Rankin, Jr., Jules Bass
Company A Rankin/Bass Production
Directors Arthur Rankin, Jr., Jules Bass
Writer Romeo Muller
Musical Director Bernard Hoffer
Narrator Fred Astaire

VOICES

Sunny the Easter Bunny .... Skip Hinnant
Chugs .... Robert McFadden
Hallelujah Jones .... Ron Marshall
King Bruce .... James Spies
Lilly Longtooth .... Meg Sargent
Additional Voices Allen Swift, Jill Choder, Ray Owens, Karen Dahle, Michael McGovern, Laura Dean, George Brennan, Gia Andersen, Stacey Carey

453 **Easter Chester Mystery Play**
Great Performances PBS
Program Type Dramatic Special
60 minutes. Premiere date: 4/6/77. Adaptation of five 14th century Easter mystery plays originally performed by a group of craft guilds in the city of Chester, England. Program presented by WNET-TV/New York and made possible by

Easter Chester Mystery Play *Continued*
grants from Exxon Corporation, the Corporation for Public Broadcasting, the Ford Foundation and Public Television Stations.
Producer Cedric Messina
Company British Broadcasting Corporation
Director Piers Haggard

CAST

Christ .... Tom Courtenay
God .... Michael Hordern
Additional Cast Joe Gladwin, Brian Glover, Fiona Gray, Christopher Guard, Christine Hargreaves, David Jackson, Terence Scully

454 **Easter Seal Telethon** Syndicated
Program Type Telethon
20 hours. Premiere dates: 3/26/77–3/27/77. Live coverage of the sixth annual telethon of the National Easter Seal Society for Crippled Children and Adults telecast from Los Angeles.
Executive Producer Woody Fraser
Company National Easter Seal Society
Host Michael Landon

455 **Easter Tells Such Dreadful Lies**
Childhood/Great Performances PBS
Program Type Dramatic Special
60 minutes. Premiere date: 3/2/77. Repeat date: 9/14/77. Adaptation of a story by Barbara Waring about a nine-year-old girl with an overactive imagination. Presented by WNET-TV/New York. Program made possible by a grant from Exxon Corporation with additional support from member stations of PBS.
Executive Producer Jac Venza
Coordinating Producer Ann Blumenthal
Producer James Brabazon
Company Granada Television
Director June Howson
Writer Barbara Waring
Host Ingrid Bergman

CAST

Easter Braden .... Rosalind McCabe
Harry .... Simon Griffiths
Mrs. Braden .... Diana Fairfax
Dr. Braden .... Bernard Horsfall
Nancy Thomas .... Rosemary Martin
Mrs. Thomas .... Betty Hardy
Mademoiselle .... Miriam Margoyles
Mary .... Fiona Mathieson

456 **Easter Worship Services** CBS
Program Type Religious/Cultural Special
60 minutes. Premiere date: 4/10/77. Live coverage of Easter services from the First Baptist Church in Washington, D.C. Sermon delivered by the Rev. Dr. Charles A. Trentham.
Executive Producer Pamela Harper
Producer Alan Harper
Company CBS News Religious Broadcast

457 **Ecce Homo (Behold This Is Man!)** NBC
Program Type Religious/Cultural Special
60 minutes. Premiere date: 1/5/69. Repeat date: 7/10/77. Award-winning documentary portraying man's past and "the riddle of his future."
Producer Doris Ann
Company NBC Television Religious Programs Unit in association with the Southern Baptist Convention's Radio and Television Commission
Director Joseph Vadala
Writer Philip Scharper
Cinematographer Joseph Vadala

458 **Eccentricities of a Nightingale**
Theater in America/Great Performances PBS
Program Type Dramatic Special
Two hours. Premiere date: 6/16/76. Repeat date: 12/1/76. Another version of "Summer and Smoke" by Tennessee Williams. Produced in collaboration with San Diego's Old Globe Theater Company. Program funded by grants from Exxon Corporation, the Corporation for Public Broadcasting, the Ford Foundation and Public Television Stations.
Executive Producer Jac Venza
Producers Lindsay Law, Glenn Jordan
Company WNET-TV/New York
Director Glenn Jordan
Writer Tennessee Williams
Host Hal Holbrook

CAST

Alma Winemiller .... Blythe Danner
Rev. Winemiller .... Tim O'Connor
Mrs. Winemiller .... Louise Latham
John Buchanan, Jr. .... Frank Langella
Mrs. Buchanan .... Neva Patterson
Roger Doremus .... Lew Horn
Vernon .... Tobias Andersen
Mrs. Bassett .... Priscilla Morrill
Rosemary .... Lois Foraker
Traveling Salesman .... Carl Weintraub

459 **Eddie and Herbert** CBS
Program Type Comedy Special
30 minutes. Premiere date: 5/30/77. Comedy pilot about the friendship of two blue-collar workers and their wives. Music by Ray Charles.
Executive Producer Perry Lafferty
Supervising Producer Duke Vincent
Producer Richard Rosenbloom
Company Filmways Production
Writer Sam Bobrick
Art Director Ray Klausen

CAST

Eddie Scanlon .... Jeffrey Tambor
Herbert Draper .... James Cromwell
Madge Scanlon .... Marilyn Meyer
Dorine Draper .... Candy Azzara

460 **The Edge of Night** ABC
Program Type Daytime Drama Series
30 minutes. Mondays-Fridays. Premiere date: 4/2/56. Continuous. "The Edge of Night" and "As the World Turns" were the first two 30-minute daytime dramas. Moved from CBS to ABC 12/1/75. Crime detection and intrigue set in the fictional midwest city of Monticello. Created by Irving Vendig. Theme music by Paul Taubman. Cast listed alphabetically.
Producer Erwin Nicholson
Company Procter & Gamble Productions, Inc.
Directors Allen Fristoe, John Sedwick
Head Writer Henry Slesar
Writer Frank Salisbury

CAST

Steve Guthrie .... Denny Albee
Molly O'Connor .... Helena Carroll
Raven Alexander .... Juanin Clay
Mike Karr .... Forrest Compton
Tracy Micelli .... Pat Conwell
Laurie Dallas .... Linda Cook
Draper Scott .... Tony Craig
Danny Micelli .... Lou Criscuolo
Lt. Luke Chandler .... Herb Davis
Kevin Jamison .... John Driver
Deborah Saxon .... Frances Fisher
Nancy Karr .... Ann Flood
John (the Whitney Butler) .... George Hall
Trudy (the Whitney Maid) .... Mary Hayden
Geraldine Whitney .... Lois Kibbee
Chief Bill Marceau .... Mandel Kramer
Johnny Dallas .... John LaGioia
Adam Drake .... Donald May
Nicole Travis Drake .... Maeve McGuire
Clay Jordan .... Niles McMaster
Timmy Faraday .... Doug McKeon
Dr. Hugh Lacey .... Brooks Rogers
Tony Saxon .... Louis Turenne

461 **Edison: The Old Man** PBS
Program Type Documentary/Informational Special
30 minutes. Premiere date: 2/26/74. Repeat dates: 12/28/76 and 9/5/77 (captioned for the hearing-impaired). A pictorial biography of Thomas Alva Edison.
Producer Robert Garthwaite
Company WNJT-TV/Trenton, N.J.

462 **Edward II**
Classic Theatre: The Humanities in Drama PBS
Program Type Dramatic Special
Two hours. Premiere date: 10/2/75. Repeat date: 2/24/77. 1969 Edinburgh Festival production recreated and filmed at London's Piccadilly Theatre. Music by Carl Davis. Program made possible by grants from the National Endowment for the Humanities and Mobil Oil Corporation. Presented by WGBH-TV/Boston; Joan Sullivan, producer.
Producer Mark Shivas
Company British Broadcasting Corporation
Director Tony Robertson
Writer Christopher Marlowe
Costume Designer Dinah Collin
Set Designer Kenneth Powell

CAST

King Edward .... Ian McKellen
Young Mortimer .... Timothy West
Queen Isabella .... Diane Fletcher
Piers Gaveston .... James Laurenson
Lightborn .... Robert Eddison
Edmund of Kent .... Peter Bourne
Elder Mortimer .... Michael Spice
Warwick .... Paul Hartwick
Additional Cast Trevor Martin, Colin Fisher

The Effect of Gamma Rays on Man-in-the-Moon Marigolds *see* Special Movie Presentation

The Eiger Sanction *see* NBC Monday Night at the Movies

463 **Eight Is Enough** ABC
Program Type Drama Series
60 minutes. Tuesdays (through 5/3/77) /Wednesdays (as of 8/10/77). Preview date: 3/15/77 (with slightly different cast). Premiere date: 3/22/77. Comedy-drama about a couple with eight children. Based on the book "Eight Is Enough" by Thomas Braden. Created by William Blinn. Originally shown as a six-week series.
Executive Producers Lee Rich, Philip Capice
Producer Robert L. Jacks
Company Lorimar Productions, Inc.
Directors Various
Executive Story Consultant William Blinn
Writers Various

CAST

Tom Bradford .... Dick Van Patten
Joan Bradford .... Diana Hyland
David Bradford .... Grant Goodeve
Mary Brady .... Lani O'Grady
Joannie Brady .... Lauri Walters
Susan Brady .... Susan Richardson
Nancy Brady .... Dianne Kay
Elizabeth Brady .... Connie Newton
Tommy Brady .... Willie Aames
Nicholas Brady .... Adam Rich
Dr. Maxwell .... Michael Thoma
Daisy Maxwell .... Virginia Vincent
Donna .... Jennifer Darling

Eight on the Lam *see* NBC Thursday Night at the Movies

464 The 81st Blow

Documentary Showcase PBS

Program Type Documentary/Informational Special

90 minutes. Premiere date: 4/1/77. Repeat date: 6/22/77. Israeli-made documentary on the horrors of the Nazi Holocaust. Hebrew narration with English subtitles provided by Michael B. Styer in cooperation with Haim Gouri. Edited from two hours by Michael Styer. Program presented by the Maryland Center for Public Broadcasting and made possible by a grant from the Corporation for Public Broadcasting.

Executive Producer Michael B. Styer

Producers Jacquot Ehrlich, David Bergman, Haim Gouri

465 84, Charing Cross Road PBS

Program Type Dramatic Special

75 minutes. Premiere date: 8/76. Repeat date: 12/76. Based on the 1970 account by Helene Hanff of her 20-year correspondence with the London bookshop of Marks & Co. Program made possible by grants from Polaroid Corporation and Public Television Stations.

Producer Mark Shivas

Company British Broadcasting Corporation

Director Mark Cullingham

Writer Hugh Whitemore

CAST

Helene Hanff .... Anne Jackson
Frank Doel .... Frank Finlay

El Condor *see* The CBS Wednesday Night Movies

466 El Corrido

Visions PBS

Program Type Dramatic Special

90 minutes. Premiere date: 11/4/76. Repeat date: 2/3/77. Original television play in which farm workers see their lives paralleled in a ballad about a Mexican laborer. Program made possible by grants from the Ford Foundation, the National Endowment for the Arts and the Corporation for Public Broadcasting.

Producer Barbara Schultz

Company KCET-TV/Los Angeles

Directors Kirk Browning, Luis Valdez

Writers Luis Valdez in collaboration with El Teatro Campesino

Musical Director Daniel Valdez

Costume Designer Diane Rodriguez

Art Directors John Retsek, Bob Morales

Musicians Daniel Valdez, Noe Montoya, Edgar Sanchez, Luis Moreno

CAST

Beto .... Daniel Valdez
Old Man .... Luis Valdez
Jesus Rasquachi .... Felix Alvarez
Truck Driver/Devil .... Jose Delgado
Foreman/Death .... Socorro Cruz
Madre .... Della Gonzales
Maria Rasquachi .... Lily Alvarez
Gonzales .... Daniel Camacho
Senora .... Olivia Chumacero
Senor .... Julio Gonzales
Mother .... Armida Valdez
Sons .... Manuel Serna, Felippe Serna
Senors .... Edgar Sanchez, Guadalupe Serna
Senora .... Julia Serna
Compadres .... Ernesto Hernandez, Rosa Moreno
Jose Rasquachi .... Andres Gutierrez
Rose Rasquachi .... Diane Rodriguez
Luis Rasquachi .... Chris Valdez
Mack Rasquachi .... Noe Montoya
Bracero/Chuco .... Rojelio Rojas
Bracero/Wino .... Robert Morales
Huelgustas .... Phil Esparza, Lupe Valdez
Priest .... Luis Moreno
Nun .... Roberta Esparza

467 Eleanor and Franklin: The White House Years

ABC Theatre ABC

Program Type Dramatic Special

Three hours. Premiere date: 3/13/77. Dramatization of the lives of Eleanor and Franklin Delano Roosevelt from 1932–1945. Based on the biography "Eleanor and Franklin" by Joseph P. Lash. Music by John Barry. Filmed in part in Washington, D.C., Hyde Park, N.Y. and Pasadena, Calif.

Executive Producer David Susskind

Producer Harry R. Sherman

Company A Talent Associates Ltd. Production

Director Daniel Petrie

Writer James Costigan

Conductor John Barry

Costume Designer Joe I. Tompkins

Production Designer Jan Scott

Story Consultants Franklin Delano Roosevelt, Jr., Joseph P. Lash

CAST

Eleanor Roosevelt .... Jane Alexander
Franklin Delano Roosevelt .... Edward Herrmann
Missy Lehand .... Priscilla Pointer
Louis Howe .... Walter McGinn
Sara Delano Roosevelt .... Rosemary Murphy
Anna Roosevelt .... Blair Brown
Theodore Roosevelt .... David Healy
Grace Tully .... Peggy McCay
Harry Hopkins .... Donald Moffat
Malvina Thompson .... Toni Darnay
Dr. Carr .... John Beal
Marian Anderson .... Barbara Conrad
Plog .... Morgan Farley
Robert Dunlap .... Mark Harmon
Laura Delano .... Anna Lee
Lucy Mercer .... Linda Kelsey
Ike Hoover .... Colin Hamilton
James Roosevelt .... Ray Baker
John Roosevelt .... Brian Patrick Clarke
Elliott Roosevelt .... Don Howard

Franklin D. Roosevelt, Jr. .... Joseph Hacker
Irvin McDuffie .... Charles Lampkin

468 **Election Eve Special Report**
Decision '76 NBC
Program Type News Special
60 minutes. 11/1/76. A preview of the national, state and local election contests.
Executive Producer Gordon Manning
Company NBC News
Anchors John Chancellor, David Brinkley
Correspondents Catherine Mackin, Tom Brokaw, John Hart, Tom Pettit, Edwin Newman, Douglas Kiker

469 **Election '76 Coverage**
Decision '76 NBC
Program Type News Special
Live coverage 11/2/76–11/3/76 of the 1976 elections from 7 p.m.—4:43 a.m. (Eastern time).
Executive Producer Gordon Manning
Producers Lester M. Crystal, Ray Lockhart
Company NBC News
Anchors John Chancellor, David Brinkley
Correspondents Catherine Mackin, Tom Brokaw, Marilyn Berger, Bob Jamieson, Douglas Kiker, Garrick Utley, Linda Ellerbee, Don Oliver, Judy Woodruff, Kenley Jones, Charles Quinn, Edwin Newman, John Hart
Chief Elections Consultant Richard M. Scammon
Statistical Consultant Dr. Richard Link

470 **Election '76 Preview** PBS
Program Type Public Affairs Special
30 minutes. Premiere date: 11/1/76. Program designed to help the hearing-impaired analyze national trends developing during election day (11/2/76). Program signed by Tim Medina and captioned. Funded by a grant from the U.S. Bureau of Education for the Handicapped.
Executive Producer Philip L. Collyer
Producers Jeff Hutchins, Deborah Popkin
Company WGBH-TV Caption Center/Boston
Director Jeff Hutchins
Host Tim Medina

471 **Election '76: The President from Plains**
Decision '76 NBC
Program Type News Special
60 minutes. 11/3/76. An analysis of the 1976 election and its implications.
Executive Producer Gordon Manning
Company NBC News
Directors Walter Kravetz, Enid Roth
Anchors John Chancellor, David Brinkley
Correspondents John Hart, Tom Pettit, Don Oliver, Kenley Jones, Catherine Mackin, Judy Woodruff, Richard Hunt
Chief Elections Consultant Richard M. Scammon

472 **The Electric Company** PBS
Program Type Children's Series
30 minutes. Mondays-Fridays (usually twice daily). Premiere date: 10/25/71. Sixth season premiere: 10/18/76. Informational series teaching basic reading skills to second through fourth graders. Skits, music, audience involvement in a magazine format. Teen rock group Short Circus members: June Angela, Todd Graff, Rejane Magloire, Janina Mathews, Rodney Lewis. Funded by grants from the U.S. Office of Education - Dept. of Health, Education and Welfare, Public Television Stations, the Ford Foundation, the Corporation for Public Broadcasting, and the Carnegie Corporation of New York.
Executive Producer Samuel Y. Gibbon, Jr.
Producer Andrew B. Ferguson, Jr.
Company Children's Television Workshop
Director Robert S. Schwarz
Head Writer Tom Whedon
Writers John Boni, Sara Compton, Tom Dunsmuir, Thad Mumford, Jeremy Stevens, Jim Thurman
Musical Director Dave Conner
Choreographers Patricia Birch, Liz Thompson
Costume Designer Mostoller
Production Designer Ronald Baldwin
Set Decorator Nat Mongioi

CAST

Dr. Doolots/Pedro .... Luis Avalos
Paul the Gorilla/Blue Beetle/
J. Arthur Crank .... Jim Boyd
Easy Reader .... Morgan Freeman
Jennifer of the Jungle/
Julia Grownup .... Judy Graubart
Fargo North, Decoder .... Skip Hinnant
Pandora the Brat/Movie Director/
Millie-the-Helper .... Rita Moreno
Spider-Man .... Danny Seagren
The Fox/Valerie the Librarian .... Hattie Winston
Milkman/Ken Kane .... Bill Cosby
Vi .... Lee Chamberlin

473 **The Eleventh Year**
Americana PBS
Program Type Documentary/Informational Special
30 minutes. Premiere date: 1/21/77. An interview with Robert La Pierre, paroled from the Bordentown Reformatory after eleven years in jail for murder.
Executive Producer Betty Adams
Company New Jersey Public Television/Trenton
Director Louis Presti
Interviewer Betty Adams

474 **Eliza**

Ourstory PBS

Program Type Dramatic Special

30 minutes. Premiere date: 10/6/75. Repeat date: 11/5/76. Dramatization of the life of Eliza Lucas Pinckney who cultivated the first American indigo on her 18th century South Carolina plantation. Music composed by Luther Henderson. Filmed at the Middleburg Plantation and the Heyward-Washington House, Charleston, S.C. Program funded by a grant from the National Endowment for the Humanities.

Executive Producer Don Fouser
Producer Marcia Speinson
Company WNET-TV/New York
Director Don Fouser
Writer Don Fouser
Musical Director Luther Henderson
Costume Designer John Boxer
Art Director William Ritman
Host Bill Moyers
Set Decorator Charles Bennett

CAST

Eliza .... Tovah Feldshuh
Mrs. Lucas .... Polly Holliday
Col. Charles Pinckney .... Tom Klunis
Quash .... Howard E. Rollins, Jr.
Nicholas Cromwell .... Stephan Weyte
Young Officer .... Cyrus Newitt
Newspaper Publisher .... Mariett Wicks
Musicians .... Lucien De Groote, Suzanne G. Rollins, Larry Long
Messenger .... Quentin McGown IV
Polly .... Lee Gibbs
Little Girls .... Carletta Ball, Cleo Lyles
Slaves .... Charles Seabrook, Leroy Singleton, Myra Bennett
Field Hands .... Pamela Robinson, Louise J. Waring

Additional Cast Fay King, Wendy Wofford, Jan Jenkins, Lenore Bender, Peggy Roehsler, Bill Bender, Norman Weber

475 **Ellington Is Forever** CBS

Program Type Religious/Cultural Special

60 minutes. Premiere date: 11/28/76. Highlights of a tribute to Duke Ellington filmed at the Cathedral of St. John the Divine in New York City 4/29/76.

Executive Producer Pamela Ilott
Producer Bernard Seabrooks
Company CBS News Religious Broadcast
Conductor Mercer Ellington
Performers The Duke Ellington Orchestra, Dave Brubeck, Charles Mingus, Anita Moore, Sarah Vaughn, Joe Williams, the Hampton Institute Choir

476 **Elton John: In Concert**

Thursday Night Special ABC

Program Type Music/Dance Special

90 minutes. Premiere date: 2/3/77. Highlights of a concert held in Edinburgh, Scotland in September 1976.

Producer John Reid
Company John Reid Enterprises, London
Director David Bell
Star Elton John

Elvis on Tour *see* NBC Night at the Movies

477 **Emergency!** NBC

Program Type Drama Series

60 minutes. Saturdays. Premiere date: 1/22/72. Sixth season premiere: 9/25/76. Last show: 9/3/77. The operations of the paramedics of Engine Company 51 of the Los Angeles County Fire Department and their liaison with Ramparts General Hospital. Created by Harold Jack Bloom and Robert A. Cinader. Music by Billy May. Filmed in cooperation with the Los Angeles Fire Department.

Executive Producer Robert A. Cinader
Company Mark VII Ltd. Productions, in association with Universal Television and NBC-TV
Directors Various
Writers Various

CAST

John Gage .... Randolph Mantooth
Roy DeSoto .... Kevin Tighe
Dr. Kelly Brackett .... Robert Fuller
Dr. Joe Early .... Bobby Troup
Nurse Dixie McCall .... Julie London
Capt. Stanley .... Michael Norell
Fireman Chet Kelly .... Tim Donnelly
Fireman Stoker .... Mike Stoker
Dr. Morton .... Ron Pinkard
Fireman Lopez .... Marco Lopez

478 **Emily, Emily**

Hallmark Hall of Fame NBC

Program Type Dramatic Special

90 minutes. Premiere date: 2/7/77. Sequel to the 1969 "Hallmark Hall of Fame" play "Teacher, Teacher" about a retarded boy. Original score by John Rubinstein.

Executive Producer Henry Jaffe
Production Executive David Lawrence
Producer Michael Jaffe
Company Henry Jaffe Enterprises, Inc.
Director Marc Daniels
Writer Allan Sloane
Costume Designer Jane Greenwood
Art Director Ben Edwards

CAST

Freddie .... Thomas Hulce
Niles Putnam .... John Forsythe
Terry .... Karen Grassle
Emily Ward .... Pamela Bellwood
Joe Crane .... James Farentino
JoJo .... Ilana Frank
Frank .... Carl Marchand

Jimmy .... Bob Park
Kevin .... Jerome Pascaris
Frannie .... Marianne Skanks
Jesse .... Paul-Emile Frappier

479 **The Emmy Awards**
The Big Event NBC
Program Type Parades/Pageants/Awards Special
Live coverage of the 29th annual Emmy Awards from the Pasadena (Calif.) Auditorium 9/11/77.
Producer Don Ohlmeyer
Company NBC Television Network
Director Bill Carruthers
Writer Marty Farrell
Musical Director Doc Severinsen
Hosts Robert Blake, Angie Dickinson

Emmy Awards (Daytime) *see* Daytime Emmy Awards

Emperor of the North *see* The ABC Sunday Night Movie

480 **End of Summer**
Theater in America/Great Performances PBS
Program Type Dramatic Special
Two hours. Premiere data: 6/15/77. The Charles MacArthur Center for American Theater in association with the Asolo State Theater in a production of the 1930's drawing-room comedy by S. N. Behrman. Program presented by WNET-TV/New York and made possible by grants from Exxon Corporation, the Corporation for Public Broadcasting, the Ford Foundation and Public Television Stations.
Executive Producer Richard Fallon
Producer Ken Campbell
Company The Charles MacArthur Center for American Theater in association with the Asolo State Theater of Sarasota, Florida
Directors Stephen Porter, Ken Campbell
Host Helen Hayes

CAST

Leonie .... Lois Nettleton
Mrs. Wyler .... Helen Hayes
Paula .... Pamela Lewis
Will .... Dennis Michaels
Dr. Rice .... Paul Shenar
Dennis .... Paul Rudd
Sam .... Alan Mixon
Boris .... Robert Strane
Robert .... Bradford Wallace

481 **Enemies**
Theater in America/Great Performances PBS
Program Type Dramatic Special
Two hours. Premiere data: 1/23/74. Repeat date: 11/28/76. The Repertory Theater of Lincoln Center in a production of the drama by Maxim Gorky; translated by Jeremy Brooks. Taped along New York's Hudson River; set on an estate in provincial Russia in 1905. Program made possible by grants from Exxon Corporation and the Corporation for Public Broadcasting.
Executive Producer Jac Venza
Producer Bo Goldman
Company WNET-TV/New York
Directors Ellis Rabb, Kirk Browning
Host Hal Holbrook

CAST

Zakhar Bardin .... Peter Donat
Paulina Bardin .... Frances Sternhagen
Yakov Bardin .... Ellis Rabb
Tatiana Bardin .... Carrie Nye
Kleopatra Skrobotov .... Kate Reid
Madya .... Susan Sharkey
Gen. Pechenegov .... Rick Woods
Kon .... Will Lee
Michail Skrobotov .... Stefan Gierasch
Nikolai Skrobotov .... Josef Sommer
Agrafena .... Jane Rose
Pologgy .... George Pentecost
Sinstove .... Dan Sullivan

482 **Energy: Another View**
NBC News Special NBC
Program Type Public Affairs Special
30 minutes. Premiere date; 6/2/77. A Republican response to Pres. Carter's energy proposals.
Company NBC News
Guests Gerald R. Ford, Ronald Reagan

483 **Energy: The Facts ... The Fears ... The Future**
CBS News Special CBS
Program Type Documentary/Informational Special
Three hours. Premiere date: 8/31/77. An in-depth look at the energy issue. Pres. Jimmy Carter answered videotaped questions about energy in one segment anchored by Bob Schieffer.
Executive Producer Leslie Midgley
Senior Producers Russ Bensley, Ernest Leiser
Producers Bernard Birnbaum, David Buksbaum, Bill Crawford, Hal Haley, Judith Hole, Mark Kramer, George Murray, Charles Thompson, Kenneth Witty
Company CBS News
Director Arthur Bloom
Writers Russ Bensley, John Mosedale
Researchers Meg Clarke, Mariana Edmunds, Margaret Ershler, Angela LeJuge, A. Lawrence Maraynes, O. R. Tuckerman, Dyan Wiley
Anchor/Reporter Walter Cronkite
Correspondents Nelson Benton, Eric Engberg, Richard Wagner, Morton Dean, George Herman, Charles Collingwood, Bruce Dunning,

Energy: The Facts . . . The Fears . . . The Future *Continued*

Mike Lee, Phil Jones, Bob Schieffer, David Culhane

484 **Energy: The President's Proposals** ABC

Program Type News Special
30 minutes. Live coverage of Pres. Jimmy Carter's address to the nation on energy and the economy 4/18/77.
Executive Producer Elliot Bernstein
Company ABC News Special Events
Anchor Frank Reynolds

485 **Energy: The Republican View** ABC

Program Type Public Affairs Special
30 minutes. Premiere date: 5/6/77. The Republican view of the Carter energy proposals.
Executive Producer Elliot Bernstein
Producer Daryl Griffin
Company ABC News Special Events
Anchor Frank Reynolds
Guests William Simon, William Coleman, Sen. Howard Baker, Rep. John Rhodes, Sen. Ted Stevens, Rep. Barber Conable

486 **Enigma** CBS

Program Type TV Movie
60 minutes. Premiere date: 5/27/77. Action-adventure pilot about a secret agent for Triangle, a larger-than-life organization with a global charter to fight crime. Created by Sam Rolfe. Music by Harry Sukman.
Producer Sam Rolfe
Company 20th Century-Fox Television
Director Michael O'Herlihy
Writer Sam Rolfe
Art Director Bell Creber
Stunt Coordinator Dick Butler

CAST

Andrew Icarus	Scott Hylands
Maurice Mockcastle	Guy Doleman
Mei San Gow	Soon-Teck Oh
Miranda Larawa	Barbara O. Jones
Dora Herren	Melinda Dillon
Peter McCauley	Peter Coffield
Idi Ben Yousef	Percy Rodrigues
Kate Valentine	Sherry Jackson
Col. Valentine	Jim Davis
Wolf	Bill Fletcher
Benjamin Herren	Morgan Farley
Dr. Beverly Golden	Melodie Johnson
Marsha	Judith Brown

487 **The Enterprise** NBC News Special NBC

Program Type News Special
30 minutes. Live coverage of the first manned free flight of the space shuttle *Enterprise* 8/12/77.
Executive Producer Gordon Manning
Producers Ray Lockhart, Ray Cullin
Company NBC News
Anchor Jack Perkins
Commentator/Reporter Roy Neal

488 **The Entertainer of the Year Awards** CBS

Program Type Parades/Pageants/Awards Special
90 minutes. 1/16/77. Seventh annual AGVA (American Guild of Variety Artists) Awards to its top performers. Taped at Caesars Palace, Las Vegas.
Producer Robert Precht
Company Sullivan Productions
Director John Moffitt
Writers Robert Arthur, Martin Ragaway, Arthur Phillips, Walter Stone
Musical Director Ray Bloch
Art Director Bill Bohnert
Host Jackie Gleason
Presenters Milton Berle, George Burns, Redd Foxx, Jack Haley, Sr., Steve Lawrence Bobby Short, Phil Silvers

489 **The Epic That Never Was** PBS

Program Type Documentary/Informational Special
60 minutes. Premiere data: March 1977. Documentary on the unfinished production of "I, Claudius" in 1937.
Producer Bill Duncalf
Company British Broadcasting Corporation
Narrator Dirk Bogarde

490 **Eric**

NBC Thursday Night at the Movies NBC
Program Type Dramatic Special
Two hours. Premiere data: 11/10/75. Repeat data: 7/21/77. Based on the memoir by Doris Lund of her son's last years. Music by Dave Grusin. Filmed in part in Seattle, Wash. Originally presented as a "Hallmark Hall of Fame" special.
Executive Producer Lee Rich
Producer Herbert Hirschman
Company Lorimar Productions, Inc., in association with NBC-TV
Director James Goldstone
Writers Nigel McKeand, Carol Evan McKeand
Art Director Phil Barber
Set Decorator Robert de Vestel

CAST

Eric	John Savage
Doris	Patricia Neal
Sydney	Claude Akins
Mary Lou	Sian Barbara Allen

Mark .... Mark Hamill
Lisa .... Eileen McDonough
Dr. Duchesnes .... Nehemiah Persoff
Tom .... James Richardson

491 **The Erie War**
Ourstory PBS
Program Type Dramatic Special
30 minutes. Premiere date: 3/22/76. Repeat date: 12/3/76. A dramatization of Cornelius Vanderbilt's attempt to buy control of the Erie Railroad in 1868. Funded by grants from the National Endowment for the Humanities, the Arthur Vining Davis Foundations and the George Gund Foundation.
Executive Producer Don Fouser
Producer Ron Finley
Company WNET-TV/New York
Director Ron Finley
Writer John Crowley
Costume Designer John Boxer
Art Director Stephen Hendrickson
Host Bill Moyers
Cartoonist Frank Springer

CAST

Cornelius Vanderbilt .... Gil Rogers
Jim Fisk .... Ron Faber
Jay Gould .... Lewis J. Stadlen
Daniel Drew .... Fred Stuthman
Thomas Nast .... Marshall Efron
Josie Mansfield .... Patricia Elliott
Erie Secretary .... Roy K. Stevens
Broker .... Gary Allen
Vanderbilt's Secretary .... William Duell
Office Boy .... Miles Chapin
Reporters .... Robert B. Silver, Page Johnson

Escape from Colditz *see* NBC Thursday Night at the Movies

492 **Eternal Light** NBC
Program Type Religious/Cultural Series
30 minutes/60 minutes. Sundays. Religious-cultural programs presented by the Jewish Theological Seminary of America. Programs seen during the 1976–77 season are: "A Conversation With Isaac Bashevis Singer," "A Conversation With Itzhak Perlman," "A Conversation With Rabbi Louis Finkelstein," "Home for Passover," "The Israel Museum: A Living Legacy," "Woman of Valor." (*See* individual titles for credits.)

493 **The European vision of America**
PBS
Program Type Documentary/Informational Special
60 minutes. Premiere date: 12/19/76. A guide through a 350-piece art exhibit from 13 countries portraying America from the arrival of Columbus to the end of the 19th century. Photographed at the Cleveland Museum of Art. Program made possible by grants from the National Endowment for the Arts and the Corporation for Public Broadcasting.
Company WVIZ-TV/Cleveland
Director Richard Siemanowski
Writer Richard Siemanowski
Cinematographer Frank Boll
Narrator Peter Ustinov

494 **Evel Knievel's Death Defiers** CBS
Program Type Music/Comedy/Variety Special
90 minutes. Premiere date: 1/31/77. Live and taped special of daredevil acts from the Chicago Amphitheater, from Miami Beach and from the Lincolnshire (Ill.) Resort.
Executive Producer Marty Pasetta
Producer Michael Seligman
Company Marty Pasetta Productions, Inc.
Director Marty Pasetta
Writers Don Clark, Susan Clark
Musical Director Nick Perito
Hosts Telly Savalas, Jill St. John
Guest Stars Evel Knievel, Karl Wallenda, Dave Merrifield, Joe Gerlach, Orvall Kisselburg, Ron Phillips

495 **Evening at Pops** PBS
Program Type Music/Dance Series
60 minutes. Sundays. Seventh season premiere: 7/10/77. 13-week series featuring the Boston Pops Orchestra in concert with guest singers, dancers and musicians. Programs funded by a grant from Martin Marietta Corporation.
Producer William Cosel
Company WGBH-TV/Boston
Director David Atwood
Conductor Arthur Fiedler

496 **Evening at Symphony** PBS
Program Type Music/Dance Series
60 minutes/90 minutes. Sundays. Premiere date: 10/6/74. Third season premiere: 10/10/76. Program repeats began 1/9/77. 13-part series featuring the Boston Symphony Orchestra and guest conductors and soloists. Programs made possible by grants from Raytheon Corporation, Public Television Stations, the Ford Foundation and the Corporation for Public Broadcasting.
Producer Jordan Whitelaw
Company WGBH-TV/Boston
Directors David Atwood, William Cosel
Musical Director Seiji Ozawa
Guest Conductors Colin Davis, Erich Leinsdorf, William Steinberg, Michael Tilson Thomas

497 **An Evening of Championship Skating (1976)** PBS

Program Type Sports Special

60 minutes. Premiere date: 12/4/76. Repeat date; 3/26/77. The fourth annual exhibition of championship ice skating taped at Watson Rink, Harvard University in November 1976. Program made possible by a grant from the Champion Spark Plug Company.

Producer Syrl Silberman

Company WGBH-TV/Boston

Director Russ Fortier

Host John Powers

Performers Judi Genovesi and Kent Weigle, Janet Hominuke and Mark Hominuke, David Santee, Wendy Burge, Barbie Smith, Jim Sladky and Judy Sladky, Lorna Whilton and John Dowling

498 **An Evening With Diana Ross**

The Big Event NBC

Program Type Music/Dance Special

90 minutes. Premiere date: 3/6/77. Show tracing the life and career of Diana Ross through music. Music consultant: Gil Askey; music coordinator: D'Vaughn Pershing; additional musical arrangements: Nick Perito. Special makeup designed by Stan Winston. "The Ladies" written by Ntozake Shange.

Producer Joe Layton

Company Motown Productions

Director Norman Campbell

Writer Bill Dyer

Musical Director Billy Goldenberg

Choreographer Joe Layton

Costume Designer Bob Mackie

Production Designer Tom H. John

Star Diana Ross

Featuring Motown Ballet: Ka-Ron Sowell Brown, Gary Chapman, Michael Peters and the Richmond Shepard Mime Company: Stewart Fischer, Hayward Coleman, Don McLeod

499 **Executive Suite** CBS

Program Type Drama Series

60 minutes. Mondays/Fridays (as of 1/14/77). Premiere date: 9/20/76. Last show: 2/11/77. Drama about the personnel of the Cardway Corporation based on the novel of the same name by Cameron Hawley and produced as a 1954 MGM feature film. Developed for television by Stanley Rubin and Norman Felton. Music by Billy Goldenberg. Rita Lakin succeeded Norman Felton and Stanley Rubin as executive producer; Buck Houghton succeeded Don Brinkley as producer; Art Lewis succeeded Peter Allan Fields as executive story consultant.

Executive Producers Norman Felton and Stanley Rubin/Rita Lakin

Producer Don Brinkley/Buck Houghton

Company Stanley Rubin/Arena Productions in association with MGM Television

Directors Various

Executive Story Consultant Peter Allan Fields /Art Lewis

Story Editors Barbara Avedon, Barbara Corday

CAST

Don Walling .... Mitchell Ryan
Howell Rutledge .... Stephen Elliott
Helen Walling .... Sharon Acker
Brian Walling .... Leigh J. McCloskey
Mark Desmond .... Richard Cox
Astrid Rutledge .... Gwyda Donhowe
Tom Dalessio .... Paul Lambert
Pearce Newberry .... Byron Morrow
Yvonne Holland .... Trisha Noble
Stacey Walling .... Wendy Phillips
Glory Dalessio .... Joan Prather
Hilary Madison .... Madlyn Rhue
Malcolm Gibson .... Percy Rodrigues
Anderson Galt .... William Smithers
Marge Newberry .... Maxine Stuart
Summer Johnson .... Brenda Sykes
Harry Ragin .... Carl Weintraub
B. J. Koslo .... Moosie Drier
Nick Koslo .... Scott Marlowe
Leona Galt .... Patricia Smith

500 **Exo-Man**

NBC Saturday Night at the Movies NBC

Program Type TV Movie

Two hours. Premiere date: 6/18/77. Adventure pilot about a paralyzed physics professor who creates an exo-suit making him mobile again.

Executive Producer Richard Irving

Producer Lionel E. Siegel

Company Universal Television in association with NBC-TV

Director Richard Irving

Writers Martin Caidin, Howard Rodman

CAST

Nicholas Conrad .... David Ackroyd
Emily Frost .... Anne Schedeen
Raphael Torres .... A Martinez
Travis .... Harry Morgan
Kermit Haas .... Jose Ferrer
D.A. Kamenski .... Kevin McCarthy
Martin .... Jack Colvin
Eddie Rubenstein .... Jonathan Segal
Dominic Leandro .... John Moio
Jim Yamaguchi .... Richard Narita

501 **Face the Nation** CBS

Program Type Public Affairs Series

30 minutes. Sundays. Original premiere: 11/7/54. Ran through 4/20/61. Current series premiere: 9/15/63. Continuous. Interviews with people in the news. Generally originates live from Washington.

Producer Mary O. Yates

Company CBS News
Director Robert Vitarelli
Moderator George Herman

502 **Faces of Hope**
Under God NBC
Program Type Religious/Cultural Special
60 minutes. Premiere date: 1/25/76. Repeat date: 10/3/76. Documentary on Yugoslavia including its religious life.
Executive Producer Doris Ann
Company NBC Television Religious Programs Unit in association with the Radio and Television Commission of the Southern Baptist Convention
Director Joseph Vadala
Writer Philip Scharper
Cinematographer Joseph Vadala
Film Editor Ed Williams
Narrator Alexander Scourby

503 **Failing to Learn—Learning to Fail**
NBC Reports NBC
Program Type Documentary/Informational Special
60 minutes. Premiere date: 8/30/77. A look at learning disabilities and their relation to delinquent behavior
Producer Mike Gavin
Company NBC News
Director Mike Gavin
Writers Betty Rollin, Mike Gavin
Cinematographers Dexter Alley, Vo Huynh
Film Editor Gary Raschella
Researcher Mamye Smith
Consultant Grace Hechinger
Reporter Betty Rollin

504 **Family** ABC
Program Type Drama Series
60 minutes. Tuesdays. Premiere date: 3/9/76 (as six-week series.) Premiere date: 9/28/76 (as regular series). Story of a closely knit family in Pasadena, California. Created by Jay Presson Allen. Music by Pete Rugolo; theme by John Rubinstein.
Executive Producers Mike Nichols, Aaron Spelling, Leonard Goldberg
Producers Nigel McKeand, Carol Evan McKeand
Company An Icarus Production in association with Spelling-Goldberg Productions
Directors Various
Executive Story Consultant Mark Rydell
Writers Various
Story Consultant Jay Presson Allen

CAST

Kate Lawrence .... Sada Thompson
Doug Lawrence .... James Broderick
Nancy Lawrence Maitland .. Meredith Baxter Birney
Willie Lawrence .... Gary Frank
Letitia "Buddy" Lawrence .... Kristy McNichol
Salina Magee .... Season Hubley

505 **Family Circle Magazine Cup** NBC
Program Type Sports Special
90 minutes each day. Live coverage of semi-final and final matches of the $110,000 women's tennis tournament from Sea Pines Plantation on Hilton Head Island, S.C. 4/2/77 and 4/3/77.
Company NBC Sports
Commentators Bud Collins, Julie Anthony

506 **Family Feud** ABC
Program Type Game/Audience Participation Series
30 minutes. Mondays-Fridays. Premiere date: 7/12/76. Continuous. Question-and-answer game in which two families compete trying to match answers given by respondents in a nationwide survey.
Producer Howard Felsher
Company Goodson-Todman Productions
Director Paul Alter
Host Richard Dawson

507 **The Family Holvak** CBS
Program Type Drama Series
60 minutes. Tuesdays. Premiere date: 9/7/75 (on NBC). Returned 5/31/77 (to CBS). Last show: 6/28/77. Drama of a preacher's family in the rural South during the depression of the 1930s. Based on the novel "Ramey" by Jack Farris and pilot "The Greatest Gift" by Abby Mann which aired 11/4/74. Music by Dick De Benedictis.
Executive Producers Roland Kibbee, Dean Hargrove
Producer Richard Collins
Company A Universal Television Production
Directors Various
Writers Various
Costume Designer Yvonne Wood

CAST

Rev. Tom Holvak .... Glenn Ford
Mrs. Elizabeth Holvak .... Julie Harris
Ramey Holvak .... Lance Kerwin
Julie Mae Holvak .... Elizabeth Cheshire

The Family Way *see* NBC Monday Night at the Movies

508 **Famous Classic Tales** CBS
Program Type Animated Film Series
60 minutes. A series of animated specials for children based on classic tales. Programs shown during the 1976–77 season are: "A Christmas Carol," "Davy Crockett on the Mississippi," "Master of the World," "The Mysterious Island." (*See* individual titles for credits.)

509 **Fanfares and Fugues**
The CBS Festival of Lively Arts for Young People CBS
Program Type Children's Special
60 minutes. Premiere date: 10/10/76. A New York Philharmonic Young People's Concert from Avery Fisher Hall at Lincoln Center for the Performing Arts in New York City. Special illustrates two dramatic forms in music, the fanfare and the fugue, with music by Debussy, Copland, Wagner and Bach.
Producer Robert Myhrum
Company CBS Television Network
Director Robert Myhrum
Writer Michael Tilson Thomas
Conductor Michael Tilson Thomas
Narrator Michael Tilson Thomas

510 **The Fantastic Journey** NBC
Program Type Science Fiction Series
60 minutes. Thursdays. Premiere date: 2/3/77 (90-minute special). Last show: 6/16/77. Science-fiction drama about people from different time periods trapped in a time/space warp trying to find their way back to their homes. Music by Robert Prince.
Executive Producer Bruce Lansbury
Producer Leonard Katzman
Company Bruce Lansbury Productions, Ltd. in association with Columbia Pictures Television and NBC-TV
Directors Various
Writers Various
Story Consultants Dorothy Fontana, Calvin Clements, Jr.

CAST
Varian .... Jared Martin
Liana .... Katie Saylor
Dr. Fred Walters .... Carl Franklin
Scott Jordan .... Ike Eisenmann
Jonathan Willoway .... Roddy McDowall

511 **Fantasy Island**
The ABC Friday Night Movie/The ABC Tuesday Night Movie ABC
Program Type TV Movie
Two hours. Premiere date: 1/14/77. Repeat date: 7/5/77. Drama of three people living out their fantasies at an island paradise. Music by Laurence Rosenthal.
Producers Aaron Spelling, Leonard Goldberg
Company A Spelling-Goldberg Production
Director Richard Lang
Writer Gene Levitt
Art Director Paul Sylos

CAST
Roarke .... Ricardo Montalban
Arnold Greenwood .... Bill Bixby
Franchesca .... Sandra Dee
Grant Baines .... Peter Lawford
Liz Hollander .... Carol Lynley
Henley .... Hugh O'Brian
Eunice Baines .... Eleanor Parker
Michelle .... Victoria Principal
Charles Hollander .... Dick Sargent
Connie Raymond .... Christina Sinatra
Tattoo .... Herve Villechaize
Hunter 1 .... John McKinney
Hunter 2 .... Cedric Scott
Hunter 3 .... Peter MacLean
Bartender .... Ian Abercrombie
Barmaid .... Elizabeth Dartmoor

512 **Far Out Space Nuts** CBS
Program Type Children's Series
30 minutes. Sunday mornings. Premiere date: 9/6/75. Second season premiere: 9/12/76 (in reruns). Last show: 9/4/77. Live-action comedy series about two Cape Kennedy food concessionaires and their interplanetary adventures.
Producers Sid Krofft, Marty Krofft, Al Schwartz
Company Sid and Marty Krofft Productions
Directors Various
Writers Various

CAST
Junior .... Bob Denver
Barney .... Chuck McCann
Honk .... Patty Maloney

513 **Farewell to Manzanar**
NBC Thursday Night at the Movies NBC
Program Type TV Movie
130 minutes. Premiere date: 3/11/76. Repeat date: 7/7/77. Based on the book by Jeanne Wakatsuki Houston and James D. Houston about the Japanese-American internment in detention camps during World War II. Music by Paul Chihara.
Executive Producer George J. Santoro
Producer John Korty
Company Korty Films, Inc. in association with Universal Television and NBC-TV
Director John Korty
Writers Jeanne Wakatsuki Houston, James D. Houston, John Korty
Costume Designer Aggie Guerard Rodgers
Set Decorator Jim Poynter
Technical Advisors Edison Uno, Karl Yoneda

CAST
Ko .... Yuki Shimoda
Misa/Jeanne .... Nobu McCarthy
Chiyoko .... Akemi Kikumura
Teddy .... Clyde Kusatsu
Fukimoto .... Mako
Zenihiro .... Pat Morita
Richard .... James Saito
Jeanne (as a girl) .... Dori Takeshita
Lois .... Gretchen Corbett
Alice .... Momo Yashima

514 **A Farewell Visit With President and Mrs. Ford** ABC
Program Type Documentary/Informational

Special
60 minutes. Premiere date: 1/2/77. A discussion with Pres. Gerald R. Ford and Betty Ford about their years in the White House.
Producer Tom Capra
Company ABC News Public Affairs
Director Richard Armstrong
Interviewer Barbara Walters

515 **Fat Albert and the Cosby Kids** CBS
Program Type Animated Film Series
30 minutes. Saturday mornings. Premiere date: 9/9/72. Fifth season premiere: 9/11/76. Cartoon characters created by Bill Cosby. Most episodes in repeats; a few are new.
Executive Producer William H. Cosby
Producers Norm Prescott, Lou Scheimer
Company Bill Cosby-Filmation Associates
Animation Director Don Christensen
Voices Bill Cosby

516 **The Fatal Weakness**
Hollywood Television Theatre PBS
Program Type Dramatic Special
Two hours. Premiere date: 9/30/76. 1946 drawing room comedy by George Kelly. A conversation between Princess Grace of Monaco, the playwright's niece, and Norman Lloyd is seen following the drama. Music by Robert Prince. Program made possible by grants from the Corporation for Public Broadcasting, the Ford Foundation and Public Television Stations.
Executive Producer Norman Lloyd
Producer Norman Lloyd
Company KCET-TV/Los Angeles
Director Norman Lloyd
Writer George Kelly
Costume Designer Noel Taylor
Scenic Designer Edward Stephenson

CAST

Ollie Espenshade .... Eva Marie Saint
Paul Espenshade .... John McMartin
Penny .... Gretchen Corbett
Vernon Hassett .... Dennis Dugan
Mabel Wentz .... Charlotte Moore
Anna .... Sara Seegar

517 **The Father Knows Best Reunion**
The Big Event NBC
Program Type TV Movie
90 minutes. Premiere date: 5/15/77. Drama based on the "Father Knows Best" series (1954–1960) about the Anderson's 35th wedding anniversary.
Executive Producer Renee Valente
Producer Hugh Benson
Company Columbia Pictures Television
Director Marc Daniels
Executive Story Consultant Eugene Rodney
Writer Paul West

CAST

Jim Anderson .... Robert Young
Margaret .... Jane Wyatt
Betty .... Elinor Donahue
Bud .... Billy Gray
Kathy .... Lauren Chapin
Jeanne .... Susan Adams
Jason Harper .... Hal England
Jennifer .... Cari Anne Warder
Robbie .... Christopher Gardner
Ellen .... Kyle Richard
Frank .... Jim McMullan
Marybeth .... Nellie Bellflower
Rev. Lockwood .... Noel Conlon

518 **Fawlty Towers** PBS
Program Type Comedy Series
30 minutes. Weekly. Premiere date: 7/77. Six-part comedy set in a Devonshire (England) resort hotel. Music by Dennis Wilson.
Producer John Howard Davies
Company British Broadcasting Corporation
Distributor Time-Life Television
Writers John Cleese, Connie Booth
Costume Designer Mary Woods
Scenic Designer Peter Kindred

CAST

Basil Fawlty .... John Cleese
Sybil Fawlty .... Prunella Scales
Manuel .... Andrew Sachs
Polly .... Connie Booth
Maj. Gowen .... Ballard Berkeley
Miss Tibbs .... Gilly Flower
Miss Gatsby .... Renee Roberts

519 **Fawn Story**
ABC Afterschool Specials ABC
Program Type Children's Special
60 minutes. Premiere date: 10/22/75. Repeat date: 6/1/77. Young people's drama of an injured doe, filmed on location in Saugus and Newhall, California. Music by Laurin Rinder and Mike Lewis.
Executive Producers Alan Landsburg, Laurence D. Savadove
Company An Alan Landsburg Production
Director Larry Elikann
Writer Tony Kayden

CAST

John McPhail .... Med Flory
Jenna .... Kristy McNichol
Toby .... Poindexter
Louisa .... Karen Oberdiear
Trooper .... Gordon Jump
Hunter No. 1 .... Skip Lowell
Hunter No. 2 .... Michael Maitland
Technician No. 1 .... James Lough
Ranger .... Cal Haynes
Reporter .... Charles Walker II

The FBI Story: The FBI Versus the Ku Klux Klan *see* Attack on Terror: The FBI Versus the Ku Klux Klan

Fear Is the Key *see* CBS Friday Night Movies

520 **The Feather & Father Gang** ABC
Program Type Crime Drama Series
60 minutes. Mondays/Saturdays (as of 5/21/77). Special preview: 12/6/76. Premiere date: 3/7/77. Last show: 8/6/77. Adventures of an attorney and her ex-con man father. Created by William Driskill. Theme and music by George Romanis.
Executive Producer Larry White
Producers William Driskill, Robert Mintz
Company A Larry White Production in association with Columbia Pictures Television
Directors Various
Script Consultants Simon Muntner, Calvin Clements, Jr.
Writers Various

CAST

Toni "Feather" Danton .... Stefanie Powers
Harry Danton .... Harold Gould
Margo .... Joan Shawlee
Lou .... Lewis Charles
Enzo .... Frank Delfino
Michael .... Monte Landis

521 **The Feather & Father Gang—Never Con a Killer**
The ABC Friday Night Movie ABC
Program Type TV Movie
90 minutes. Premiere date: 5/13/77. Pilot film for series of the same name (*see above*) not previously aired.
Executive Producer Larry White
Producer Buzz Kulik
Company Larry White Productions in association with Columbia Pictures Television
Director Buzz Kulik
Writer William Driskill

CAST

Toni "Feather" Danton .... Stefanie Powers
Harry Danton .... Harold Gould
E. J. Valerian .... John Forsythe
Enzo .... Frank Delfino
Dorothy .... Bettye Ackerman
Stanley .... Jim Backus
Cap .... Severn Darden
Wyatt .... Angus Duncan
Contractor .... Cliff Norton
Schroeder .... Eugene Roche
Margo .... Joan Shawlee
Tim .... Marc Singer
Lilah .... Camilla Sparv
Hadley .... Edward Winter

522 **Fernwood 2-Night** Syndicated
Program Type Comedy Series
30 minutes. Mondays–Fridays. Premiere date: 7/4/77. Last show: 9/30/77. Late-night summer replacement for "Mary Hartman, Mary Hartman." Satirical talk show set in "Fernwood, Ohio."
Producer Alan Thicke
Company TAT Communications Company
Distributor TAT Syndication
Director Louis J. Horvitz
Script Consultant Pat Proft
Writers Tom Moore, Jeremy Stevens, Alan Thicke
Creative Consultant J. Ben Stein

CAST

Barth Gimble .... Martin Mull
Jerry Hubbard .... Fred Willard
Happy Kyne .... Frank Devol

523 **Fidel Castro Speaks** ABC
Program Type Documentary/Informational Special
60 minutes. Premiere date: 6/9/77. A formal interview with Cuban President Fidel Castro conducted 5/19/77.
Senior Producer Richard Richter
Producer Tom Capra
Company ABC News
Researcher Mary Hornickel
Interviewer Barbara Walters

524 **Fiesta Bowl** CBS
Program Type Sports Special
Three hours. Live coverage of the Fiesta Bowl in Tempe, Ariz. between the University of Oklahoma Sooners and the University of Wyoming Cowboys 12/25/76.
Company CBS Television Network Sports
Announcer Lindsey Nelson
Analyst Paul Hornung

525 **50 Grand Slam** NBC
Program Type Game/Audience Participation Series
30 minutes. Mondays–Fridays. Premiere date: 10/4/76. Last show: 12/31/76. Contestants match mental and physical agility trying to win $50,000.
Executive Producer Ralph Andrews
Producer George Vosburgh
Company A Ralph Andrews Production in association with the NBC Television Network
Director Dick McDonough
Art Directors Ed Flesh, Bill Camden
Host Tom Kennedy

526 **The Fight Against Slavery**
Syndicated
Program Type Limited Series
Six hours. Premiere: 11/76. Dramatization of the British slave trade between 1750–1831. Filmed on location in England, Africa and Jamaica. Music by Joseph Horovitz.

Producer Christopher Ralling
Company British Broadcasting Corporation
Distributor Time-Life Television
Director Christopher Ralling
Writer Evan Jones
Cinematographer Tony Pierce-Roberts
Film Editors Michael Goldsmith, Bill Wright, Jonathan Crane
Narrator Evan Jones

CAST

John Newton	John Castle
David Lisle	Dinsdale Landen
Granville Sharp	Terence Scully
Thomas Clarkson	Gareth Thomas
Jonathan Strong	Willie Jonah
William Pitt	Ronald Pickup
William Wilberforce	David Collings
Charles James Fox	Ronald Lacey
Preacher	Bryan Marshall
Mrs. Lisle	Joanna Jones
Capt. Crow	Aubrey Morris
Daddy Sharp	Stanley Irons
King Holiday	David John
Olan Equian	Louis Mahoney
Dr. Alexander	Donald Sumpter
Marie Nugent	Dorian Godwin

527 **The Fight To Be Remembered** PBS
Program Type Documentary/Informational Special
60 minutes. Premiere date: 9/27/76. Profiles of six heroines of the American Revolution. Program funded in part by a grant from the American Revolution Bicentennial Administration.
Producer Rick Hauser
Company WGBH-TV/Boston
Director Rick Hauser

528 **Figuring All the Angles**
Special Treat NBC
Program Type Children's Special
60 minutes. Premiere date: 3/9/76. Repeat dates: 11/25/76 and 4/12/77. An examination of the world of professional stunt men and women. Taped at Lake Piru, Calif.
Executive Producer George A. Heinemann
Producer J. Philip Miller
Director J. Philip Miller
Writer W. W. Lewis
Host Chuck Connors
Guests: Ronny Rondell, Dar Robinson, Craig Baxley, Jack Verbois, Regina Parton

529 **Fine Music Specials**
Great Performances PBS
Program Type Music/Dance Series
Times vary. Wednesdays. Classical music specials of concerts and operas. Programs presented during the 1976–77 season are: "Arthur Rubinstein at 90," "Bernstein Conducts Boston Symphony," "Bernstein Conducts Mahler," "Madama Butterfly," "Rostropovich Performs Haydn," "Rubinstein: Works of Chopin," "Salome," "Solti Conducts Mendelssohn," "Von Karajan Conducts Brahms." (*See* individual titles for credits.)

Finian's Rainbow *see* NBC Thursday Night at the Movies

Fire! *see* Irwin Allen's Production of Fire!

530 **The Fire Next Door**
CBS Reports CBS
Program Type Documentary/Informational Special
60 minutes. Premiere date: 3/22/77. A look at the New York City neighborhood of the South Bronx.
Executive Producer Howard Stringer
Producer Tom Spain
Co-Producer Anne Chambers
Company CBS News
Director Tom Spain
Writers Bill Moyers, Tom Spain
Cinematographer Dan Lerner
Film Editor Peter C. Frank
Researcher Oliver Mobley
Reporter/Editor Bill Moyers

531 **Firing Line** PBS
Program Type Public Affairs Series
60 minutes. Saturdays. Show premiered in 1966. Continuous. Weekly interview show with people in the news. Series funded by grants from the Corporation for Public Broadcasting, the Ford Foundation, and Public Television Stations.
Producer Warren Steibel
Company Southern Educational Communications Association
Director Warren Steibel
Host/Interviewer William F. Buckley, Jr.

532 **The First Breeze of Summer**
Theater in America/Great Performances PBS
Program Type Dramatic Special
90 minutes. Premiere date: 1/28/76. Repeat date: 8/17/77. Portrait of a middle class black family in contemporary society. Production by the Negro Ensemble Company. Program funded by grants from Public Television Stations, the Ford Foundation, the Corporation for Public Broadcasting and Exxon Corporation. (Cast listed in alphabetical order.)
Executive Producer Jac Venza
Producer Lindsay Law
Company WNET-TV/New York

The First Breeze of Summer *Continued*
Directors Douglas Turner Ward, Kirk Browning
Writer Leslie Lee
Host Hal Holbrook

CAST

Hattie .... Ethel Ayler
Nate Edwards .... Charles Brown
Sam Greene .... Carl Crudup
Joe Drake .... Peter DeMaio
Gremmar .... Frances Foster
Milton Edwards .... Moses Gunn
Gloria Townes .... Bebe Drake Hooks
Lucretia .... Janet League
Briton Woodward .... Anthony McKay
Aunt Edna .... Barbara Montgomery
Rev. Mosely .... Lou Leabengula Myers
Hope .... Petronia
Lou Edwards .... Reyno
Harper Edwards .... Douglas Turner Ward

533 The First Christmas NBC

Program Type Animated Film Special
30 minutes. Premiere date: 12/19/75. Repeat date: 12/18/76. Animated musical special about the first Christmas snow using dimensional stop-motion photography. Music and lyrics for original songs by Maury Laws and Jules Bass. "White Christmas" by Irving Berlin.
Producers Arthur Rankin, Jr., Jules Bass
Company A Rankin/Bass Production
Directors Arthur Rankin, Jr., Jules Bass
Writer Julian P. Gardner
Conductor Maury Laws
Narrator Angela Lansbury

VOICES

Sister Theresa .... Angela Lansbury
Father Thomas .... Cyril Ritchard
Lukas .... David Kelley
Sister Catherine .... Iris Rainer
Sister Jean .... Joan Gardner
Children .... Dina Lynn, Hilary Momberger, Sean Manning, Dru Stevens, Greg Thomas, Don Messick
Additional Voices The Wee Winter Singers

534 The First Easter Rabbit

Multi-Special Night NBC
Program Type Animated Film Special
30 minutes. Premiere date: 4/9/76. Repeat date: 4/9/77. Animated musical special using dimensional stop-motion photography about the true meaning of Easter. "There's That Rabbit" by Maury Laws and Jules Bass sung by Burl Ives. "Easter Parade" by Irving Berlin sung by Burl Ives, Robert Morse, Christine Winter.
Producers Arthur Rankin, Jr., Jules Bass
Company A Rankin/Bass Production
Directors Arthur Rankin, Jr., Jules Bass
Writer Julian P. Gardner
Conductor Maury Laws

VOICES

Great Easter Bunny .... Burl Ives
Stuffy .... Robert Morse
Flops .... Stan Freberg
Zero/Spats .... Paul Frees
Mother .... Joan Gardner
Whiskers .... Don Messick
Glinda .... Dina Lynn

535 The First Fifty Years

The Big Event NBC
Program Type Documentary/Informational Special
4 1/2 hours. Premiere date: 11/21/76. NBC celebrating its 50th anniversary in radio and television broadcasting.
Executive Producer Greg Garrison
Producers Lee Hale, Chet Hagan
Company The National Broadcasting Company
Director Greg Garrison
Writers Abby Mann, Jess Oppenheimer, Mike Marmer, Bill Angelos, Orson Welles
Musical Director Jack Elliott
Art Director Robert Fletcher
Hosts Jack Albertson, Milton Berle, David Brinkley, Johnny Carson, John Chancellor, Angie Dickinson, Joe Garagiola, Bob Hope, Gene Kelly, Jerry Lewis, Dean Martin, Don Meredith, Gregory Peck, Freddie Prinze, George C. Scott
Narrator Orson Welles

536 First Lady On the Go ABC

Program Type News Special
30 minutes. Premiere date: 6/13/77. Report on Rosalynn Carter's trip to South and Central America which ended 6/12/77.
Producer Arthur Holch
Company ABC News Special Events
Anchor Margaret Osmer
Correspondent Bernard Shaw

537 The First Night of Pygmalion PBS

Program Type Dramatic Special
60 minutes. Premiere date: 3/12/77. Drama-documentary by Richard Huggett about events preceding the opening of "Pygmalion" by George Bernard Shaw.
Executive Producer Robert Allen
Producer Beverly Roberts
Company Canadian Broadcasting Corporation
Director Eric Tell
Writer Hugh Webster
Narrators Helen Burns, Colin Fox

CAST

George Bernard Shaw .... William Hutt
Mrs. Patrick Campbell .... Elizabeth Shepherd
Sir Herbert Beerbohm-Tree .... Paxton Whitehead

538 Fish ABC

Program Type Comedy Series
30 minutes. Saturdays. Premiere date: 2/5/77.

Spin-off from "Barney Miller" about a detective and his wife who run a group home in New York City. Developed by Tony Sheehan, Danny Arnold and Chris Hayward. Music by Jack Elliott and Allyn Ferguson.
Executive Producer Danny Arnold
Producer Steve Pritzker
Company The Minus Corporation
Directors Various
Executive Story Consultants Barbara Avedon, Barbara Corday
Writers Various

CAST

Phil Fish .... Abe Vigoda
Bernice Fish .... Florence Stanley
Charlie Harrison .... Barry Gordon
Mike .... Lenny Bari
Loomis .... Todd Bridges
Victor .... John Cassisi
Jilly .... Denise Miller
Diane .... Sarah Natoli

A Fistful of Dollars *see* The ABC Sunday Night Movie

539 **Five Red Herrings**
Masterpiece Theatre PBS
Program Type Limited Series
60 minutes. Sundays. Premiere date: 12/19/76. Four-part dramatization of the 1930s mystery by Dorothy Sayers. Filmed on location in Scotland. Presented by WGBH-TV/Boston; Joan Sullivan, series producer. Program made possible by a grant from Mobil Oil Corporation.
Producer Bill Sellars
Company British Broadcasting Corporation
Director Robert Tronson
Writer Anthony Steven
Host Alistair Cooke

CAST

Lord Peter Wimsey .... Ian Carmichael
Bunter .... Glyn Houston
Mr. Alcock .... John Junkin
Sandy Campbell .... Ian Ireland
John Ferguson .... David McKail
Matthew Gowan .... Russell Hunter
Jock Graham .... David Rintoul
Henry Strachan .... Roy Boutcher
Hugh Farran .... Donald Douglas
Michael Waters .... Clive Graham
Betty .... Sally Kinghorn
Fenella Strachan .... July Peasgood
Gilda Farran .... Susan Macready
Sir Maxwell Jamieson .... Robert James
Insp. McPherson .... Michael Sheard

540 **Flight to Holocaust** NBC
Program Type TV Movie
Two hours. Premiere date: 3/27/77. Dramatic pilot about a team of professional troubleshooters called to the 20th floor of a skyscraper where a private plane has crashed. Created by A. C. Lyles. Music composed and performed by Paul Williams. Special effects by Joe Unsun.
Producer A. C. Lyles
Company Aycee Productions and First Artists Production Company in association with NBC-TV
Director Bernie Kowalski
Writer Robert Heverly

CAST

Les Taggart .... Patrick Wayne
Mark Gates .... Christopher Mitchum
Scotty March .... Fawne Harriman
Rick Bender .... Desi Arnaz, Jr.
George Beam .... Sid Caesar
Dr. Evans .... Greg Morris
Wilton Senter .... Lloyd Nolan
Colorado Davis .... Paul Williams
Engineer .... Rory Calhoun
Gordon Stokes .... Robert Patten
Linda .... Anne Schedeen
TV Commentator .... Bill Baldwin

541 **Flood!**
NBC Movie of the Week NBC
Program Type TV Movie
Two hours. Premiere date: 11/24/76. Drama of a small town hit by a flood when a dam collapses. Filmed in part on location in Eugene, Ore. Music by Richard La Salle. Special effects by Cliff Wenger and Cliff Wenger, Jr..
Executive Producer Irwin Allen
Company Irwin Allen Productions in association with NBC-TV
Director Earl Bellamy
Writer Don Ingalls
Costume Designer Paul Zastupnevich

CAST

Steve Banning .... Robert Culp
Paul Blake .... Martin Milner
Abbie Adams .... Carol Lynley
Mary Cutler .... Barbara Hershey
Andy Cutler .... Eric Olson
John Cutler .... Richard Basehart
Alice Cutler .... Teresa Wright
Sam Adams .... Cameron Mitchell
Fisherman .... Roddy McDowall
Dr. Horne .... Whit Bissell
Daisy .... Francine York

542 **Florida Citrus Open** NBC
Program Type Sports Special
Live coverage of the final rounds of the 12th annual Florida Citrus Open from the Rio Pinar Country Club in Orlando, Fla. 3/5/77 and 3/6/77.
Producer Larry Cirillo
Company NBC Sports
Director Harry Coyle
Anchors Jim Simpson, Cary Middlecoff
Commentators John Brodie, Jay Randolph, Fran Tarkenton, Bruce Devlin

543 **The Flying Dutchman**
Opera Theater PBS
Program Type Music/Dance Special
Three hours. Premiere date: 5/11/76. Repeat date: 9/6/77. First full-length television production of the opera by Richard Wagner. English translation by Peter Butler and Brian Large; production design by David Meyerscough-Jones. Features the Ambrosian Opera Chorus and the Royal Philharmonic Orchestra. Program made possible by grants from the Ford Foundation, the Corporation for Public Broadcasting and Public Television Stations. Presented by WNET-TV/New York.
Coordinating Producers Linda Krisel, David Griffiths
Producer Brian Large
Company British Broadcasting Corporation and WNET-TV/New York
Conductor David Lloyd-Jones
Chorus Master John McCarthy

CAST

Vanderdecken .... Norman Bailey
Senta .... Gwyneth Jones
Daland .... Stafford Dean
Eric .... Keith Erwen
Marie .... Joan Davies
The Steersman .... Robert Ferguson

544 **Flying Saucers From Outer Space—What's It All About?**
What's It All About? CBS
Program Type Children's Special
30 minutes. Premiere date: 12/4/76. Informational program for school-age children dealing with flying saucers and outer space.
Executive Producer Joel Heller
Producer Vern Diamond
Company CBS News
Director Vern Diamond
Writer Joel Siegel
Correspondents Christopher Glenn, Carol Martin

545 **The Folk Way** PBS
Program Type Documentary/Informational Special
60 minutes. Premiere date: 10/5/76. A look at a group of folk artists in Maryland. Program made possible by grants from the National Endowment for the Arts and the Maryland Arts Council.
Producer Michael B. Styer
Company Maryland Center for Public Broadcasting in cooperation with the Maryland Arts Council
Director Steve Dubin

546 **Food for All** NBC
Program Type Religious/Cultural Special
60 minutes. Premiere date: 6/13/76. Repeat date: 11/21/76. A study about the need for providing food now and in the future.
Producer Doris Ann
Company NBC Television Religious Programs Unit in association with the Communication Commission of the National Council of Churches
Director Joseph Vadala
Writer Philip Scharper
Cinematographer Joseph Vadala
Film Editor Ed Williams
Narrator Hugh Downs

For a Few Dollars More *see* The ABC Sunday Night Movie

For Pete's Sake *see* The ABC Tuesday Night Movie

547 **The Ford-Carter Debate—Preview and Analysis (First Debate)** PBS
Program Type News Special
60 minutes. 9/23/76. 30-minute debate preview plus 30-minute post-debate analysis. Program made possible by grants from the Corporation for Public Broadcasting, the Ford Foundation and Public Television Stations.
Producer Jim Karayn
Company WETA-TV/Washington and WNET-TV/New York
Hosts Robert MacNeil, Jim Lehrer

548 **The Ford-Carter Debate— Preview and Analysis (Second Debate)** PBS
Program Type News Special
60 minutes. 10/6/76. 30-minute preview and 30-minute post-debate analysis of the second debate. Program made possible by grants from the Corporation for Public Broadcasting, the Ford Foundation and Public Television Stations.
Producer Jim Karayn
Company WETA-TV/Washington and WNET-TV/New York
Hosts Robert MacNeil, Jim Lehrer

549 **The Ford-Carter Debate—Preview and Analysis (Third Debate)** PBS
Program Type News Special
60 minutes. 10/22/76. 30-minute preview and 30-minute post-debate analysis of the final debate between the presidential contenders. Program made possible by grants from the Corporation for Public Broadcasting, the Ford Foundation and Public Television Stations.

Producer Jim Karayn
Company WETA-TV/Washington and WNET-TV/New York
Hosts Robert MacNeil, Jim Lehrer

550 **The Forsyte Saga** PBS
Program Type Limited Series
60 minutes. Premiere date: 10/5/69. Series repeats began: 7/77 (seen four times a week). Twenty-six black-and-white episodes of "The Forsyte Saga" based on "The Man of Property," "In Chancery," "To Let," "The White Monkey," "The Silver Spoon" and "Swan Song" by John Galsworthy. Deals with London in the late 19th and early 20th centuries. Musical theme by Eric Coates.
Producer Donald Wilson
Company British Broadcasting Corporation
Directors David Giles, James Cellan Jones
Story Editor Lenox Phillips
Writer John Galsworthy
Scenic Designers Spencer Chapman, Sally Hulke

CAST

Jo (Young Jolyon) Forsyte .... Kenneth More
Soames .... Eric Porter
Aunt Ann .... Fay Compton
Irene .... Nyree Dawn Porter
Winifred .... Margaret Tyzack
Fleur .... Susan Hampshire
Michael Mont .... Nicholas Pennell
Old Jolyon .... Joseph O'Conor
Helene .... Lana Morris
Jon .... Martin Jarvis

551 **Foster and Laurie**
The CBS Friday Night Movies CBS
Program Type TV Movie
Two hours. Premiere date: 11/13/75. Repeat date: 7/29/77. Based on the book by Al Silverman about the 1972 murder of two New York City policemen. Music by Lalo Schifrin.
Executive Producer Charles Fries
Producer Arthur Stolnitz
Company Charles Fries Productions, Inc.
Director John Llewellyn Moxey
Writer Albert Ruben
Art Director Perry Ferguson

CAST

Rocco Laurie .... Perry King
Gregory Foster .... Dorian Harewood
Adelaide Laurie .... Talia Shire
Jacqueline Foster .... Jonelle Allen
Sims .... Roger Aaron Brown
Dealer .... Victor Campos
Mr. Rosario .... Rene Enriquez
Sgt. Bray .... Charles Haid
Max .... Eric Laneuville
Johnson .... Owen Hithe Pace
Ianucci .... David Proval
Commissioner .... Wallace Rooney
Sgt. Petrie .... Edward Walsh
Addict .... James Woods

The 400 Blows *see* PBS Movie Theater

552 **The Four of Us**
Special Comedy Presentation ABC
Program Type TV Movie
60 minutes. Premiere date: 7/18/77. Pilot about a widow and her three children. Created by Reginald Rose. Music by Morton Gould.
Executive Producer Herbert Brodkin
Producer Robert Berger
Company A Titus-Defenders Production (A Herbert Brodkin Production in association with Reginald Rose)
Director James Cellan Jones
Writer Reginald Rose
Costume Designer Joseph Aulisi
Production Designer Ed Wittstein

CAST

Julie Matthews .... Barbara Feldon
Annie Ray .... Heather MacRae
Mrs. Reilly .... Sudie Bond
Marie .... K Callan
Chrissie .... Vicki Dawson
Walter .... Lawrence Keith
Caroline .... Kathy Jo Kelly
Estelle .... Marcia Jean Kurtz
Mr. Hardy .... Peter Maloney
Andy .... Will McMillan
Harry .... Sam Schact

553 **The Fourth Annual Unofficial Miss Las Vegas Showgirl Pageant**
Thursday Night Special ABC
Program Type Parades/Pageants/Awards Special
90 minutes. Premiere date: 2/17/77. Fourth unofficial comedy pageant from Las Vegas, Nevada.
Producers Jeff Harris, Bernie Kukoff
Company Boiney Stoones, Inc. Production
Director Jeff Harris
Writers Jeff Harris, Bernie Kukoff
Host Steve Allen
Co-Host Brett Somers
Guests Mickey Rooney, Pat Paulsen, Jayne Meadows, Stan Can

554 **Francesca, Baby**
ABC Afterschool Specials ABC
Program Type Children's Special
60 minutes. Premiere date: 10/6/76. Drama of a 15-year-old girl trying to cope with the problems created by her mother's alcoholism. Adapted from the book by Joan Oppenheimer. Music composed by Hod David.
Producer Martin Tahse
Company Martin Tahse Productions, Inc.
Director Larry Elikann
Writer Bob Rodgers

Francesca, Baby *Continued*

CAST

Francesca .... Carol Jones
Lillian .... Melendy Britt
Bix .... Dennis Bowen
Kate .... Tara Talboy
Connie .... Alice Nunn
Gordon .... Peter Brandon
Jo Lynn .... Elizabeth Herbert
Mike .... Benny Medina
Patty .... Doney Oatman
Greg .... Scot Marc Sovie
Marion .... Mona Tera
Mrs. Handley .... Lee Kessler
Salesgirl .... Barbara England
Louise .... Jody Britt

555 **Francis Gary Powers: The True Story of the U-2 Spy Incident**
NBC Movie of the Week NBC
Program Type TV Movie
Two hours. Premiere date: 9/29/76. Repeat date: 9/4/77 (with special introduction by Tom Snyder). Dramatization of the events surrounding the shooting down of the American spy plane over the Soviet Union in May 1960 and based on the book "Operation Overflight" by Francis Gary Powers. Music composed by Gerald Fried.
Executive Producer Charles Fries
Producers Edward J. Montagne, John B. Bennett
Company Charles Fries Productions in association with NBC-TV
Director Delbert Mann
Writer Robert E. Thompson
Costume Designer Richard Egan
Art Director Walter Scott Herndon
Consultant Francis Gary Powers

CAST

Francis Gary Powers .... Lee Majors
Rudenko .... Nehemiah Persoff
Oliver Powers .... Noah Beery
Bissell .... William Daniels
Allen Dulles .... Lew Ayres
Mrs. Powers .... Brooke Bundy
Robert Kennedy .... Jim McMullan
McCone .... Biff McGuire
Pres. Eisenhower .... James Flavin
Premier Khrushchev .... Thayer David
Grinev .... David Opatoshu
Wheatley .... Charles Knox Robinson

The French Connection *see* The CBS Wednesday Night Movies

French Connection II *see* The CBS Friday Night Movies

556 **French Open** NBC
Program Type Sports Special
Tape-delayed satellite coverage of the French Open tennis championship from the Roland Garros Stadium in Paris 6/4/77 and 6/5/77.
Producer Dick Auerbach
Company NBC Sports
Director Ted Nathanson
Commentators Bud Collins, John Newcombe

557 **Friends, Romans, Communists**
CBS News Special CBS
Program Type Documentary/Informational Special
60 minutes. Premiere date: 12/10/76. A CBS News Special on the Italian Communist Party.
Executive Producer Perry Wolff
Producer Paul Greenberg
Company CBS News
Director Paul Greenberg
Writer Paul Greenberg
Cinematographer Mario Biasetti
Film Editor Lee Reichenthal
Special Correspondent Luigi Barzini

From Russia With Love *see* The ABC Monday Night Movie

558 **From These Roots**
Americana PBS
Program Type Documentary/Informational Special
30 minutes. Premiere date: 9/24/76. Repeat dates: 11/6/76 and 7/10/77 (as "Americana" special). Award-winning film on black creativity in Harlem during the 1920s. Music by Eubie Blake. Presented by WNET-TV/New York. Program made possible by a grant from the Corporation for Public Broadcasting.
Producer William Greaves
Company William Greaves Productions, Inc.
Director William Greaves
Writer William Greaves
Narrator Brock Peters

The Front Page *see* NBC Monday Night at the Movies/NBC Saturday Night at the Movies

559 **Frosty the Snowman** CBS
Program Type Animated Film Special
30 minutes. Premiere date: 12/7/69. Repeat date: 12/17/76. Based on the song by Jack Rollins and Steve Nelson. Additional music and lyrics by Jules Bass and Maury Laws.
Producers Arthur Rankin, Jr., Jules Bass
Directors Arthur Rankin, Jr., Jules Bass
Writer Romeo Muller
Narrator Jimmy Durante

VOICES

Frosty .... Jackie Vernon

Prof. Hindle .... Billy De Wolfe
Additional Voices Paul Frees, June Foray

560 **Frosty's Winter Wonderland** ABC
Program Type Animated Film Special
30 minutes. Premiere date: 12/2/76. Animated musical sequel to "Frosty the Snowman" using dimensional stop-motion photography.
Producers Arthur Rankin, Jr., Jules Bass
Company Rankin-Bass Productions
Directors Arthur Rankin, Jr., Jules Bass
Writer Romeo Muller
Musical Director Maury Laws
Animators Toru Hara, Tsuguyuki Kubo
Narrator Andy Griffith

VOICES

Mrs. Frosty .... Shelley Winters
Parson Brown .... Dennis Day
Frosty .... Jackie Vernon
Jack Frost .... Paul Frees
Additional Voices Shelley Hines, Erik Stern, Manfred Olea, Barbara Jo Ewing, the Wee Winter Singers

561 **Full Moon Lunch**
Documentary Showcase PBS
Program Type Documentary/Informational Special
60 minutes. Premiere date: 3/25/77. Repeat date: 8/26/77 (captioned for the hearing-impaired). A portrait of a modern Japanese family in the catering business.
Producer John Nathan
Company Hawaii Public Television
Director John Nathan
Cinematographer Shobun An
Film Editor Michio Suwa

562 **The Fun Factory** NBC
Program Type Game/Audience Participation Series
30 minutes. Mondays–Fridays. Premiere date: 6/14/76. Last show: 10/1/76. Comedy-variety game show.
Executive Producers Ed Fishman, Randall Freer
Producer David Fishman
Company Ed Fishman/Randall Freer Productions, Inc., in association with Columbia Pictures Television
Director Walter C. Miller
Host Bobby Van
Regulars Betty Thomas, Deborah Harmon, Jane Nelson, Doug Steckler, Dick Blasucci

563 **Future Cop** ABC
Program Type Limited Series
60 minutes. Premiere date: 3/5/77. Five shows seen irregularly. Last show: 4/30/77. Repeat show: 8/6/77. Crime-drama about a Los Angeles Police Department team of cop and robot. Created by Anthony Wilson and Allen Epstein. Pilot aired 5/1/76 and 7/12/76. Music by J. J. Johnson.
Executive Producers Anthony Wilson, Gary Damsker
Producer Everett Chambers
Company The Culzean Corporation and Tovern Productions in association with Paramount Pictures Corporation
Directors Various
Writers Various

CAST

Off. Joe Cleaver .... Ernest Borgnine
Off. Haven .... Michael Shannon
Off. Bill Bundy .... John Amos

564 **Gabriel Kaplan Presents the Future Stars**
Thursday Night Special ABC
Program Type Music/Comedy/Variety Special
90 minutes. Premiere date: 4/14/77. Showcase for new performers in comedy, music, magic and sports.
Producer Bill Lee
Company Dick Clark Teleshows, Inc.
Director Lee Bernhardi
Host Gabriel Kaplan
Performers Millsenblum, Stallion, Stormin' Norman and Suzy, Dick Arthur, Paul Mooney, Steve Bluestein, Richard Lewis, Ann Meyers, Amber Jim

565 **Galina and Valery Panov**
In Performance at Wolf Trap PBS
Program Type Music/Dance Special
60 minutes. Premiere date: 11/17/75. Repeat dates: 11/8/76 and 7/12/77. Five ballet selections danced by Galina Panov and Valery Panov. Music by the Filene Center Orchestra. Performed at the Wolf Trap Farm Park in Arlington, Va. Program made possible by a grant from the Atlantic Richfield Company.
Executive Producer David Prowitt
Producer Ruth Leon
Company WETA-TV/Washington, D.C.
Director Stan Lathan
Conductor Seymour Lipkin
Hosts Beverly Sills, David Prowitt
Executive-in-Charge Jim Karayn

566 **Galveston: The Gilded Age of the Golden Isle**
Documentary Showcase PBS
Program Type Documentary/Informational Special
60 minutes. Premiere date: 6/24/77. The history of Galveston, an island off the coast of Texas, traced through its architecture. Program made possible by a grant from the Moody Foundation.
Producer Robert Cozens

Galveston: The Gilded Age of the Golden Isle *Continued*
Company KUHT-TV/Houston
Director Robert Cozens
Writer William Colville
Art Director William Colville
Cinematographer Robert Cozens
Film Editor Brian Beasley
Architectural Consultants/Researchers Drexel Turner, Steve Fox
Narrator Richard Kiley

567 **Gambit** CBS
Program Type Game/Audience Participation Series
30 minutes. Mondays-Fridays. Premiere date: 9/4/72. Last show: 12/10/76. Two couples vie for money and prizes.
Executive Producers Merrill Heatter, Bob Quigley
Producer Robert Noah
Company Heatter-Quigley Productions in association with Filmways, Inc.
Director Jerome Shaw
Host Wink Martindale
Hostess/Dealer Elaine Stewart

The Gambler *see* the ABC Sunday Night Movie

568 **The Gardener's Son**
Visions PBS
Program Type Dramatic Special
Two hours. Premiere date: 1/6/77. Drama based on fact about the murder of a South Carolina mill owner by a poor troubled white boy in the 1870s. Concept by Richard Pearce. Music by Charles Gross. Program made possible by grants from the Ford Foundation, the National Endowment for the Arts and the Corporation for Public Broadcasting.
Executive Producer Barbara Schultz
Producers Michael Hausman, Richard Pearce
Company KCET-TV/Los Angeles
Director Richard Pearce
Writer Cormac McCarthy
Costume Designer Ruth Morley
Art Director Patrizia Von Brandenstein
Scenic Designer Carl Copeland

CAST

Robert McEvoy .... Brad Dourif
James Gregg .... Kevin Conway
Mrs. Gregg .... Nan Martin
Patrick McEvoy .... Jerry Hardin
Martha McEvoy .... Anne O'Sullivan
Mrs. McEvoy .... Penelope Allen
Pinky .... Ned Beatty
W. J. Whipper .... Paul Benjamin
Dr. Perceval .... Earl Wynn
Daphne .... Esther W. Tate
Maryellen McEvoy .... Helen Harmon

569 **Gator Bowl** ABC
Program Type Sports Special
Live coverage of the Gator Bowl football game between the Notre Dame Irish and the Penn State Nittany Lions from the Gator Bowl in Jacksonville, Florida 12/27/76.
Executive Producer Roone Arledge
Producer Don Ohlmeyer
Company ABC Sports
Director Andy Sidaris
Play-By-Play Announcer Chris Schenkel
Expert Color Commentator Bud Wilkinson
Sideline Reporter/Feature Reporter Jim Lampley

570 **GE Theater** CBS
Program Type Dramatic Special
Originally premiered as 30-minute series 2/1/53. Returned after a decade 12/18/73 as a series of specials. Two dramas broadcast during the 1976–77 season: "Just an Old Sweet Song" and "The Secret Life of John Chapman." (*See* individual titles for credits.)

571 **Gemini Man** NBC
Program Type Science Fiction Series
60 minutes. Thursdays. Premiere date: 9/23/76. Last show: 10/28/76. Pilot for series aired 5/10/76. Action-adventures of special investigator working for think-tank INTERSECT who has the power to make himself invisible at will. Music by Lee Holdridge.
Executive Producer Harve Bennett
Co-Producers Robert F. O'Neill, Frank Telford
Company Harve Bennett Productions, Inc. in association with Universal Studios and NBC-TV
Directors Various
Writers Various

CAST

Sam Casey .... Ben Murphy
Leonard Driscoll .... William Sylvester
Abby Lawrence .... Katherine Crawford

572 **General Hospital** ABC
Program Type Daytime Drama Series
45 minutes. Mondays-Fridays. Premiere date: 4/1/63. Continuous. Became 45-minute show 7/26/76. Series set in the Port Chester hospital. Created by Frank Hursley and Doris Hursley. John Beradino and Emily McLaughlin are original cast members. Peter Hansen joined the show the first year. Credit information as of March 1977. Cast listed alphabetically.
Producer Tom Donovan
Directors Ken Herman, Jr., Phil Sogard, Tom Donovan

Head Writers Eileen Pollock, Robert Mason Pollock

CAST

Dr. Leslie Faulkner .... Denise Alexander
Audrey Hobart Hardy ....Rachel Ames
Dr. Jeff Webber .... Richard Dean Anderson
Dr. Steve Hardy ....John Beradino
Dr. Gail Adamson ....Susan Brown
Mike Mallon ....Dennis Dimster
Dr. Mark Dante .... Gerald Gordon
Dr. Rick Webber ....Michael Gregory
Dr. Adam Streeter .... Brett Halsey
Lee Baldwin .... Peter Hansen
Dr. Peter Taylor .... Craig Huebing
Terri Arnett ....Bobbi Jordan
Heather Grant .... Georganne LaPierre
Jessie Brewer .... Emily McLaughlin
Dr. Monica Webber .... Patsy Rahn
Diana Taylor .... Valerie Starrett
Dr. Gina Dante .... Anna Stuart
Mary Ellen Dante .... Lee Warrick

573 **The General's Day**
Piccadilly Circus PBS
Program Type Dramatic Special
60 minutes. Premiere date: 1/25/77. Repeat date: 9/4/77. Adaptation of the contemporary drama by William Trevor. Program presented by WGBH-TV/Boston, produced by Joan Sullivan, and made possible by a grant from Mobil Oil Corporation.
Producer Irene Shubik
Company British Broadcasting Corporation
Director John Gorrie
Writer William Trevor
Host Jeremy Brett

CAST

Gen. Suffolk ....Alistair Sim
Miss Lorimer .... Annette Crosbie
Mrs. Hinch .... Dandy Nichols
Mrs. Consitine ....Nan Munro
Mr. Consitine .... Norman Shelly
Muriel .... Julia Goodman
Jock .... Jack Galloway
First Lady .... Lala Lloyd
Second Lady .... Eileen Helsby
Third Lady ....Olive Mercer
Man in Bar ....George Belbin

574 **The George Burns Special** CBS
Program Type Music/Comedy/Variety Special
60 minutes. Premiere date: 12/1/76. Music/variety special taped in November.
Executive Producer Irving A. Fein
Producers Bernard Rothman, Jack Wohl
Company G.B.F. Productions
Director Bill Hobin
Writers Fred S. Fox, Seaman Jacobs, Elon Packard
Musical Directors Jack Elliott, Allyn Ferguson
Star George Burns
Guests Johnny Carson, Madeline Kahn, Walter Matthau, The Osmonds, Chita Rivera

575 **George Foreman Vs. Jimmy Young Heavyweight Fight and World Junior Lightweight Championship** ABC
Program Type Sports Special
2 1/2 hours. Live coverage from San Juan, Puerto Rico 3/17/77 of a heavyweight fight between George Foreman and Jimmy Young and the junior lightweight title fight between Alfredo Escalera and Ronnie McGarvey.
Executive Producer Roone Arledge
Company ABC Sports
Announcer Howard Cosell

576 **The Geraldo Rivera Program**
Thursday Night Special ABC
Program Type Documentary/Informational Series
90 minutes. Thursday. Season premiere: 1/27/77. Last show of season: 6/9/77. Six late-night discussion/interview shows on topics of current interest.
Producer Martin Berman
Director Martin Morris
Host Geraldo Rivera

The Getaway *see* CBS Special Film Presentations/The CBS Wednesday Night Movies

577 **Getting On** PBS
Program Type Educational/Cultural Series
30 minutes. Sundays. Premiere date: 10/17/77. Nine-part magazine-format series about older people. Regular features: "Getting On Portraits," "Getting Together Group" and "Getting Even Comedy Players." Title song by Walter Marks. Captioned for the hearing-impaired. Series made possible by a Model Projects Grant from the U.S. Department of Health, Education and Welfare—Administration on Aging in cooperation with WNYC-TV/New York and further funding from the Equitable Life Assurance Society.
Producer Patricia Reed Scott
Company WNYC-TV/New York and the New York State Network at Albany
Writer Patricia Reed Scott
Hosts Alice Brophy, Paul O'Dwyer

578 **Gianni Schicchi**
The CBS Festival of Lively Arts for Young People CBS
Program Type Children's Special
60 minutes. Premiere date: 11/28/75. Repeat date: 1/9/77. Giacomo Puccini opera, sung in English and performed by the orchestra of The Royal Opera House, Covent Garden.

Gianni Schicchi *Continued*
Executive Producers Herman Krawitz, Robert Weiner
Producer Patricia Foy
Company BBC/Jodav/Ring-Ting-A-Ling Co.
Director Patricia Foy
Conductor Robin Stapleton
Costume Designer Ann Beverley
Set Designer Stanley Morris

CAST

Gianni Schicchi .... Zero Mostel
Lauretta .... Norma Burrowes
Rinuccio .... David Hillman
Zita .... Sheila Rex
Simone .... Don Garrard
La Ciesca .... Margaret Kingsley
Marco .... Richard Van Allan
Nella .... Pauline Tinsley
Gherardo .... Robert Bowman
Gherardino .... Timothy Sprackling
Betto .... Derek Hammond Stroud
Spinelloccio .... Eric Garrett
Amantio .... George MacPherson
Pinellino .... Chris Davies
Guccio .... Paul Statham
Buoso Donati .... Will Edgar Horton

579 **Gibbsville** NBC
Program Type Drama Series
60 minutes. Thursdays. Premiere date: 11/11/76. Last show: 12/30/76. Drama about life in "Gibbsville," Pa. during the 1940s as seen by a young reporter. Based on characters and stories by John O'Hara. Music by Leonard Rosenman. Pilot "The Turning Point of Jim Malloy" show on "NBC Nights at the Movies" 4/12/75.
Executive Producer David Gerber
Producer John Furia, Jr.
Company A David Gerber Production with Columbia Pictures Television in association with NBC-TV
Directors Various
Executive Story Consultant Larry Brody
Writers Various

CAST

Jim Malloy .... John Savage
Ray Whitehead .... Gig Young
Dr. Malloy .... Biff McGuire
Mrs. Malloy .... Peggy McCay

580 **The Girl in the Empty Grave**
NBC Movie of the Week NBC
Program Type TV Movie
Two hours. Premiere date: 9/20/77. Crime drama about a small-town police chief investigating several suspicious deaths. Filmed on location in Big Bear, Calif.
Executive Producer Richard O. Linke
Producers Lane Slate, Gordon Webb
Company MGM-TV Production in association with NBC-TV
Director Lou Antonio
Writer Lane Slate

CAST

Abel .... Andy Griffith
Doc .... Sharon Spelman
John .... Hunter von Leer
Fred .... Claude Jones
Gloria .... Mitzi Hoag
Dr. Peter Cabe .... Edward Winter
Courtland Gates .... Jonathan Banks
David Alden .... George Gaynes
Harry .... Leonard Stone
Gilda .... Mary-Robin Redd
Jedidiah Partridge .... Robert F. Simon
MacAlwee .... Byron Morrow

Giselle *see* American Ballet Theatre's "Giselle"

Give 'Em Hell, Harry! *see* All-Specials Night

581 **Giving Birth**
Documentary Showcase PBS
Program Type Documentary/Informational Special
60 minutes. Premiere date: 12/17/76. Repeat date: 7/8/77 (with captions for the hearing-impaired). A look at different methods of childbirth and the experiences of four different couples. Program made possible by grants from the New York State Council on the Arts and the Rockefeller Foundation.
Executive Producer David Loxton
Coordinating Producer Carol Brandenburg
Producers John Reilly, Julie Gustafson
Company Global Village in association with the Television Laboratory at WNET-TV/New York
Directors John Reilly, Julie Gustafson
Writers John Riley, Julie Gustafson
Film Editors John Riley, Julie Gustafson

582 **Glen Campbell Los Angeles Open Golf Championship** ABC
Program Type Sports Special
Live coverage of the final rounds of the Glen Campbell Los Angeles Open from the Riviera Country Club in Pacific Palisades, Calif. 2/19/77 and 2/20/77.
Executive Producer Roone Arledge
Director Chuck Howard
Company ABC Sports
Directors Jim Jennett, Terry Jastrow
Host Glen Campbell
Anchor Chris Schenkel
Expert Commentators Dave Marr, Bob Rosburg, Jim Lampley, Bill Flemming

583 **The Glory of Their Times** PBS
Program Type Documentary/Informational Special
60 minutes. Premiere date: March 1977. Repeat date: August 1977. A 1969 documentary based on the book by Lawrence S. Ritter about America's legendary baseball players of the early 20th century. Music by Irwin Bazelon.
Executive Producer Cappy Petrash
Producer Bud Greenspan
Company A Cappy Production
Director Bud Greenspan
Conductor Irwin Bazelon.
Writer Bud Greenspan
Narrator Alexander Scourby
Script Consultant Lawrence S. Ritter

584 **God's Country With Marshall Efron** CBS
Program Type Children's Special
30 minutes each. Premiere date: 12/1/74. Repeat dates: 12/5/76 and 12/12/76. Two-part special for young people on how different religious groups helped explore and settle America. Second part repeated 7/3/77.
Executive Producer Pamela Ilott
Producer Ted Holmes
Company CBS News Religious Broadcast
Director Alvin Thaler
Writers Marshall Efron, Alfa-Betty Olsen
Host Marshall Efron

Godzilla Vs. Megalon *see* Multi-Special Night

585 **Going Past Go: An Essay on Sexism**
Documentary Showcase PBS
Program Type Documentary/Informational Special
60 minutes. Premiere date: 1/7/77. Repeat date: 9/9/77 (captioned for the hearing-impaired). Sexism and how it affects men and women in all areas of their lives. Program made possible by a grant from Title I of the Higher Education Act of 1965.
Producers Harry Ratner, Thom Eberhardt
Company KOCE-TV/Huntington Beach, Calif.
Director Thom Eberhardt
Writer Paul Cabbell
Narrator Paul Cabbell

586 **Going Racing** CBS
Program Type Sports Special
60 minutes. Premiere date: 7/10/77. A look at four race track headliners of the season: Seattle Slew, Forego, Willie Shoemaker and Steve Cauthen.
Producers Mike Pearl, E. S. "Bud" Lamoreaux
Company CBS Television Network Sports
Director Bob Fishman
Commentators Gary Bender, Brent Musburger, Frank Wright, Chic Anderson, Charlie Cantey

587 **Gold Watch**
Visions PBS
Program Type Dramatic Special
90 minutes. Premiere date: 11/11/76. Repeat date: 1/20/77. Semi-autobiographical drama about a Japanese-American family in the Pacific Northwest facing internment at the time of Pearl Harbor. Music by Richard Clements. Program made possible by grants from the Ford Foundation, the National Endowment for the Arts and the Corporation for Public Broadcasting.
Producer Barbara Schultz
Company KCET-TV/Los Angeles
Director Lloyd Richards
Writer Momoko Iko
Costume Designer Terence Tam Soon
Art Director Jan Scott

CAST

Masu Murakami .... Mako
Kimiko Murakami .... Shizuko Hoshi
Tadao Murakami .... Jesse Dizon
Chieko Murakami .... Mariel B. Aragon
Abel Hunt .... Hal Bokar
Mr. Tanaka .... Soon-Teck Oh
Mrs. Setsuko Tanaka .... Virginia Wing
Hiroshi Tanaka .... Evan Kim
Mr. Kagawa .... Richard Narita
Mrs. Hawkins .... Danna Hansen
Mr. Shimizu .... Tad Horino
Mrs. Shimizu .... Sachiko Penny Lee
Jeff Shimizu .... Peter Kwong
Rev. Sugano .... Robert Ito
Severson .... Philip Baker Hall
Allen Hunt .... Steve Gustafson
Ralphie Hunt .... Reed Diamond
Markie Goodrich .... Steve Tanner
Teacher .... Mary Robinson
Hunt's Friend .... Dick Sweeney
Soldier .... Tom Baxter

588 **Goldenrod** CBS
Program Type Dramatic Special
Two hours. Premiere date: 4/20/77. Drama of a rodeo hero in western Canada in the early 1950s. Based on the novel by Herbert Harker. Filmed on location in Alberta, Canada.
Executive Producer David Susskind
Producers Lionel Chetwynd, Gerry Arbeid
Company Talent Associates in association with Film Funding Ltd. of Canada
Director Harvey Hart
Writer Lionel Chetwynd
Music Supervisor Franklin Boyd
Technical Advisor Norman Edge

CAST

Jesse Gifford .... Tony Lo Bianco
Shirley Gifford .... Gloria Carlin

Goldenrod *Continued*

John Tyler Jones .... Donald Pleasence
Ethan Gifford .... Will Darrow McMillan
Keno McLaughlin .... Donnelly Rhodes
George Gifford .... Ian McMillan
Mrs. Gunderson .... Patricia Hamilton
Johnson .... Ed McNamara

589 **The Gondoliers**
Opera Theater PBS
Program Type Music/Dance Special
Two hours. Premiere date: 7/12/77. A performance of the operetta by W. S. Gilbert and Arthur Sullivan updated to the early 1900s, with sets patterned after the paintings of Raoul Dufy. Music performed by the Royal Philharmonic Orchestra. Program presented by WNET-TV/New York and made possible by grants from Public Television Stations with additional funding from the Ford Foundation and the Corporation for Public Broadcasting.
Executive Producer Jac Venza
Coordinating Producers David Griffiths, Sam Paul
Producer Cedric Messina
Company British Broadcasting Corporation
Director Bill Hays
Conductor David Lloyd-Jones
Scenic Designer Roger Andrews

CAST

The Grand Inquisitor .... Michael Langdon
Luiz .... Joseph Ward
Casilda .... Beverly Bergen
Duke of Plaza Toro .... Denis Dowling
Duchess of Plaza Toro .... Heather Begg
Inez .... Edith Coates
Marco .... John Brecknock
Tessa .... Delia Wallis
Giuseppe .... Thomas Allen
Gianetta .... Laureen Livingstone
Additional Cast Alan Charles, Sara De Javelin, Cynthia Buchan

Gone With the Wind *see* The Big Event/NBC Monday Night at the Movies

590 **The Gong Show** NBC
Program Type Game/Audience Participation Series
30 minutes. Mondays–Fridays. Premiere date: 6/14/76. Continuous. Talent contest judged by a panel of celebrities and the studio audience. Created by Chuck Barris and Chris Bearde.
Executive Producer Chuck Barris
Producer Gene Banks
Company Chuck Barris/Chris Bearde Production
Director John Dorsey
Musical Director Milton Delugg
Host Chuck Barris
Regular Siv Aberg

591 **The Gong Show (Evening)** Syndicated
Program Type Game/Audience Participation Series
30 minutes. Weekly. Premiere date: 9/76. Evening version of daytime show with a celebrity panel judging offbeat acts. Created by Chuck Barris and Chris Bearde.
Producer Chuck Barris
Company Chuck Barris/Chris Bearde Productions
Distributor Firestone Syndication
Director John Dorsey
Musical Director Milton Delugg
Host Gary Owens

592 **Good Against Evil**
The ABC Sunday Night Movie ABC
Program Type TV Movie
90 minutes. Premiere date: 5/22/77. Drama of the occult about a woman spoken for by the devil. Music by Lalo Schifrin. Filmed in part on location in San Francisco.
Executive Producers Lin Bolen, Ernest Frankel
Company Frankel Productions/Lin Bolen Productions in association with 20th Century-Fox Television
Director Paul Wendkos
Writer Jimmy Sangster
Art Director Richard Y. Haman
Music Supervisor Lionel Newman

CAST

Andy Stuart .... Dack Rambo
Jessica Gordon .... Elyssa Davalos
Mr. Rimmin .... Richard Lynch
Father Kemschler .... Dan O'Herlihy
Father Wheatley .... John Harkins
The Woman .... Jenny O'Hara
Lt. Taggert .... Sandy Ward
Sister Monica .... Lelia Goldoni
Irene .... Peggy McCay
Dr. Price .... Peter Brandon
Linda Isley .... Kim Cattrall
Cindy Isley .... Natasha Ryan
The Doctor .... Richard Sanders
Beatrice .... Lillian Adams
Agnes .... Erica Yohn
Brown .... Richard Stahl
Merlin .... Issac Goz

593 **Good Day!** Syndicated
Program Type Talk/Service/Variety Series
30 minutes. Mondays–Fridays. Premiere date: 9/76. Daytime talk/variety show seen in Boston since September 1973 under the title "Good Morning." Conceived by Bob Bennett.
Executive Producer Bruce Marson
Company WCVB-TV/Boston
Distributor Syndicast Services, Inc.

Hosts John Willis, Janet Langhart
Regular Dr. Timothy Johnson
Stuntman Ken Stahl

594 **Good Morning America** ABC
Program Type News Magazine Series
Two hours. Monday–Friday mornings. Premiere date: 11/3/75. Continuous. Regular features include "Face Off" debates, "Men-Women" segments, "Inside Washington," "People in the News" and the "Good Morning America" baby Paula Kadanoff (on monthly visits). Sandy Hill replaced Nancy Dussault in April 1977. Margaret Osmer left in February 1977.
Executive Producer Woody Fraser
Producers George Merlis, Merrill Mazuer, Michael Krauss
Company The ABC Television Network
Director Jan Rifkinson
Host David Hartman
Co-Host Nancy Dussault/Sandy Hill (as of 4/25/77)
Newscasters Steve Bell, Margaret Osmer
Contributors Jack Anderson, Rona Barrett, Erma Bombeck, Helen Gurley Brown, John Coleman, Howard Cosell, Bruce Jenner, Chrystie Jenner, Dr. Timothy Johnson, John Lindsay, Joan Lunden, Sylvia Porter, Geraldo Rivera, Dr. Lendon Smith, Al Ubell

595 **Good Penny**
Comedy Time NBC
Program Type Comedy Special
30 minutes. Premiere date: 9/1/77. Comedy pilot about a woman in group therapy.
Directors Joe Bologna, Richard Harwood
Writers Renee Taylor, Joe Bologna
CAST
Penny .... Renee Taylor
Al .... Scott Brady
Jerry .... Carmine Caridi
Dr. Forsman .... Roger Bowen
Pauline .... Gloria LeRoy
Herb .... Bobby Alto
Mr. Glazer .... Fredric Franklyn
Receptionist .... Lila Teigh

596 **Good Times** CBS
Program Type Comedy Series
30 minutes. Wednesdays. Premiere date: 2/8/74. Fourth season premiere: 9/22/76. Series created by Eric Monte and Mike Evans; developed by Norman Lear. Theme music by Marilyn Bergman, Alan Bergman and Dave Grusin. Concerns a black family in a Chicago ghetto. Paintings created by Ernie Barnes.
Executive Producer Allan Manings
Producers Austin Kalish, Irma Kalish
Company Tandem Productions, Inc.
Director Gerren Keith
Story Editors John Baskin, Roger Shulman
Writers Various
Story Consultant Bob Peete
CAST
Florida Evans .... Esther Rolle
Willona Woods .... Ja'net DuBois
J.J. .... Jimmie Walker
Michael .... Ralph Carter
Thelma .... BernNadette Stanis
Nathan Bookman .... Johnny Brown

Goodbye, Columbus *see* The ABC Tuesday Night Movie

597 **The Goodies and the Beanstalk**
Piccadilly Circus PBS
Program Type Comedy Special
60 minutes. Premiere date: 3/15/76. Repeat date: 8/28/77. One show of the BBC series "The Goodies" created by Bill Oddie, Tim Brooke-Taylor and Graeme Garden. A satiric version of "Jack and the Beanstalk." Music by Bill Oddie and Michael Gibbs. Program made possible by a grant from Mobil Oil Corporation. Presented by WGBH-TV/Boston; Joan Sullivan, producer.
Producer Jim Franklin
Company British Broadcasting Corporation
Costume Designer Rupert Jarvis
Scenic Designer John Stout
Host Jeremy Brett
Stars Bill Oddie, Tim Brooke-Taylor, Graeme Garden, Alfie Bass, Eddie Waring, John Cleese

Gordon's War *see* The ABC Friday Night Movie

598 **Gospel** PBS
Program Type Music/Dance Special
60 minutes. Premiere date: 12/5/76. Concert of gospel music.
Producer Sharon Litwin
Company WYES-TV/New Orleans
Director Jack Sawyer
Performers The Gospel Soul Children, the Cavalcade of Gospel Stars, Aline White with Wallace Davenport, the McDermott Singers for Christ

599 **Grammy Awards Show** CBS
Program Type Parades/Pageants/Awards Special
Two hours. 19th annual presentation honoring artistic and technical achievement in the recording industry. Live from the Hollywood (Calif.) Palladium 2/19/77. Special musical material by Alan Copeland.
Executive Producer Pierre Cossette

Grammy Awards Show *Continued*
Producer Marty Pasetta
Company Pierre Cossette Company Production
Director Marty Pasetta
Writer Marty Farrell
Musical Director Jack Elliott
Choreographer Alan Johnson
Costume Designer Bill Hargate
Art Director Roy Christopher
Host Andy Williams
Performers Barry Manilow, Starland Vocal Band, Sarah Vaughan, Natalie Cole, Wild Cherry, Chet Atkins and Les Paul

Grand Illusion *see* PBS Movie Theater

Grand Prix of Bowling *see* AMF Grand Prix of Bowling

600 **Grand Prix Tennis: Summer Tour** PBS
Program Type Limited Sports Series
Times vary. Sundays and Mondays. Season premiere: 7/24/77. Live coverage of semi-finals and finals matches in Grand Prix tennis. Programs made possible by grants from Aetna Life and Casualty Company, Fieldcrest Mills, E. & J. Gallo Winery and American Airlines.
Executive Producer Greg Harney
Company WGBH-TV/Boston
Commentators Bud Collins, Donald Dell, Judy Dixon, Kim Prince

601 **Grand Prix Tennis: Winter Circuit** PBS
Program Type Limited Sports Series
Times vary. Saturdays and Sundays. Season premiere: 2/12/77. Live coverage of six games on the winter circuit of Grand Prix Tennis. Programs made possible by grants from Aetna Life and Casualty Company and Fieldcrest Mills.
Executive Producer Greg Harney
Company WGBH-TV/Boston
Announcers Bud Collins, Donald Dell

602 **Grand Slam of Tennis** CBS
Program Type Sports Special
Live and taped coverage of the $200,000 Grand Slam of Tennis from Boca West, Fla. 1/22/77 and 1/23/77.
Producer Frank Chirkinian
Company CBS Television Network Sports
Director Bob Dailey
Commentators Pat Summerall, Tony Trabert

603 **Grandstand** NBC
Program Type Sports Series
Sundays/Saturdays. Premiere date: 9/21/75 (special preview 9/20/75). Second season premiere: 9/5/76. Based on British Broadcasting Corporation series of the same name. Live program featuring sports news, scores, filmed and taped features and commentary wrapped around NBC's major weekend sports events. Regular features: football matchups (with Fran Tarkenton), endangered birds and animals of North America with Dick Borden.
Executive Producer Don Ellis
Producer Bill Fitts
Company NBC Sports
Host Lee Leonard
Co-Host Bryant Gumbel
Reporters Larry Merchant, Fran Tarkenton, Tim Ryan, Don Meredith, Barbara Hunter

604 **Graymoor Christmas** CBS
Program Type Religious/Cultural Special
30 minutes. Premiere date: 12/24/76. Highlights of Christmas eve activities from the Graymoor Christian Unity Center in Garrison, N.Y.
Executive Producer Pamela Ilott
Producer Alan Harper
Company CBS News Religious Broadcast

The Great American Cowboy *see* The ABC Friday Night Movie

605 **The Great Cherub Knitwear Strike**
Visions PBS
Program Type Dramatic Special
90 minutes. Premiere date: 11/25/76. A love story set in a New York City garment factory during the 1930's depression. Program made possible by grants from the Ford Foundation, the National Endowment for the Arts and the Corporation for Public Broadcasting.
Producer Barbara Schultz
Company KCET-TV/Los Angeles
Director George Tyne
Writer Ethel Tyne
Art Director Ben Edwards

CAST

Ruth Schwartz .... Kathy Beller
Bernie Heller .... Adam Arkin
Sam Breitfeld .... Wil Albert
Rose Breitfeld .... Erica Yohn
Grandma .... Frances Chaney
Mr. Genselheimer .... Leon Askin
Gisella Farkas .... Dinah Manoff
Julie .... Deborah Bernstein
Mrs. Reiner .... Hanna Hertelendy
Norman .... Alan Abelew
Mr. Rodgers .... John Alvin
Stanley Bellman .... Richard Kurtzman
Selma Perelman .... Sylvia Walden
Bertha .... Connie Sawyer

Molly .... Bea Silvern
Passya .... Lillian Adams
Angie .... Ellen Travolta
Young Girl Comrade .... Tracy Bogart
Chick Barnes .... Thad Geer
Madame Principal .... Karen Morley
Mr. Granite .... Lloyd Gough
First Boy .... Gary Garfield
Second Boy .... Darryl Semen
Investigator .... Norma Connolly
Neighbors .... Chevi Colton, Al Ward
Office Workers .... Vincent Milana, Eugene Kross
First Young Man .... Christopher Man
Second Young Man .... Paul Ilmer
Questioner From Floor .... Lynn Tufeld
Gisella's Mother .... Bella Bruck
Harry .... Gary Glanz
Mr. Weitzman .... John Bleifer

606 **Great Day**
The ABC Monday Comedy Special ABC
Program Type Comedy Special
30 minutes. Premiere date: 5/23/77. Comedy pilot about a group of lovable bums living in a Los Angeles mission. Music by Peter Matz.
Executive Producer Aaron Ruben
Producer Gene Marcione
Company An Andomar Production
Director Peter Baldwin
Writer Aaron Ruben
Costume Designer Rita Riggs
Art Director Edward Stephenson

CAST

Peavey .... Al Molinaro
Doc .... Dub Taylor
Boomer .... Guy Marks
Molly .... Alice Nunn
Jabbo .... Spo-De-Odee
Moose .... Josip Elic
Billy .... Billy Barty
Pop .... Pat Cranshaw
Mrs. Graham .... Audrey Christie
Woman in the Bar .... Dorothy Konrad

607 **A Great Day for Bonzo**
Childhood/Great Performances PBS
Program Type Dramatic Special
60 minutes. Premiere date: 2/23/77. Repeat date: 9/7/77. Adaptation of a story by H. E. Bates. Comedy-drama of three children, a dog and a mysterious stranger. Presented by WNET-TV/New York. Program made possible by a grant from Exxon Corporation with additional support from member stations of PBS.
Executive Producer Jac Venza
Coordinating Producer Ann Blumenthal
Producer James Brabazon
Company Granada Television
Director Michael Apted
Writer Ian Curteis
Host Ingrid Bergman

CAST

Herbert .... Julian Wedgery
Janey .... Jennifer Cannock
Biff .... Nicholas Callas
Bonzo .... Toddy
Man .... Maurice O'Connell
Girl .... Barbara Hickmott
Farmer .... Ivor Salter
Butcher .... Danny Dickens
Man With Scythe .... Alan Luxton
Herbert's Father .... Jon T. Rudd
Janey's Father .... Bernard Hill
Woodcutters .... Ken Brooks, Richenda Carey

608 **The Great English Garden Party - Peter Ustinov Looks at 100 Years of Wimbledon** NBC
Program Type Sports Special
60 minutes. Premiere date: 6/18/77. A documentary look at the history of Wimbledon commemorating 100 years of tennis tournaments.
Producers Ken Ashton, Alison Hawkes, Pamela Moncur
Company Trans World International, Inc. in association with NBC Sports
Director Phil Pilley
Film Editor Chris Thompson
Host Peter Ustinov

609 **The Great Houdinis**
The ABC Friday Night Movie ABC
Program Type TV Movie
Two hours. Premiere date: 10/8/76. Drama based on the life of Harry Houdini. Music by Peter Matz.
Company An ABC Circle Film
Director Melville Shavelson
Writer Melville Shavelson
Technical Advisor Harry Blackstone, Jr.

CAST

Harry Houdini (Erich Weiss) .... Paul Michael Glaser
Bess Houdini .... Sally Struthers
Mrs. Weiss .... Ruth Gordon
Minnie .... Vivian Vance
Daisy White .... Adrienne Barbeau
Rev. Arthur Ford .... Bill Bixby
Theo Weiss .... Jack Carter
Conan Doyle .... Peter Cushing
Rev. LeVeyne .... Nina Foch
Supt. Melville .... Wilfrid Hyde-White
Dr. Crandon .... Geoffrey Lewis
Lady Doyle .... Maureen O'Sullivan
Dundas Slater .... Clive Revill
Margery .... Barbara Rhoades

610 **The Great Iowa Bike Ride**
Americana PBS
Program Type Documentary/Informational Special
30 minutes. Premiere date: 6/17/77. A record of the over 3,000 bicyclists who made their way across Iowa in a seven-day marathon in August 1976 as part of the Des Moines *Register's* Fourth Annual Great Bike Ride Across Iowa.

The Great Iowa Bike Ride *Continued*
Producer Martin Zell
Company Iowa Public Broadcasting Network
Director Martin Zell
Cinematographer Neal Brown
Film Editor Neal Brown

The Great Locomotive Chase *see* NBC All-Disney Saturday Night at the Movies

611 **The Great Panama Canal Controversy** ABC
Program Type Public Affairs Special
30 minutes. Premiere date: 9/7/77. ABC News Special on the Panama Canal Treaty.
Producer Jeff Gralnick
Company ABC News
Anchor Barbara Walters
Reporters Frank Reynolds, Geraldo Rivera, John Scali, Tom Jarriel, Don Farmer, Sam Donaldson

612 **Great Performances** PBS
Program Type Miscellaneous Series
Times vary. Wednesdays and/or Sundays. Premiere date: 10/17/74. Third season premiere: 10/13/77. A collection of various series in the arts: "Childhood", "Dance in America," "Fine Music Specials," "Hard Times," "Live from Lincoln Center," "Music in America," "Theater in America" as well as individual programs: "Amazing Grace—America in Song," "The Barber of Seville," "Bernstein and the New York Philharmonic," "Bernstein and the New York Philharmonic in London," "Christmas Chester Mystery Play," "Dance Theatre of Harlem," "Easter Chester Mystery Play," "Herbert von Karajan and the Berlin Philharmonic: Beethovan," "Karl Bohm and the Vienna Philharmonic," "Pagliacci," "The St. Matthew Passion," "Three By Balanchine With the New York City Ballet." (*See* individual titles for credits.)

The Great Waldo Pepper *see* NBC Movie of the Week/NBC Saturday Night at the Movies

613 **Greater Greensboro Open** NBC
Program Type Sports Special
Live coverage of the final rounds of the Greater Greensboro (N.C.) Open 4/2/77 and 4/3/77.
Producer Larry Cirillo
Company NBC Sports
Director Harry Coyle
Anchors Jim Simpson, Cary Middlecoff
Commentators Bruce Devlin, Fran Tarkenton, John Brodie, Jay Randolph

614 **Green Eyes**
The ABC Monday Night Movie/ABC Theatre ABC
Program Type TV Movie
Two hours. Premiere date: 1/3/77. Drama of an American veteran looking for his Vietnamese son. Filmed in the Republic of the Philippines. Music by Fred Karlin.
Executive Producers Lee Rich, Philip Capice
Producers David Seltzer, John Erman
Company Lorimar Productions
Director John Erman
Writer David Seltzer

CAST
Lloyd Dubeck .... Paul Winfield
Margaret Sheen .... Rita Tushingham
Noel Cousins .... Jonathan Lippe
Em Thuy .... Victoria Racimo
Trung .... Lemi
Dubeck's Mother .... Royce Wallace
Hat .... Robert DoQui
V.A. Officer .... Fred Sadoff
Mr. Cousins .... Dabbs Greer
Minh .... Joseph Hieu

615 **Gregory Peck: A Living Biography**
Thursday Night Special ABC
Program Type Documentary/Informational Special
90 minutes. Premiere date: 3/31/77. Repeat date: 7/21/77. A look at the career of Gregory Peck.
Producers Ronald Lyon, Andrew W. Solt
Company Ronald Lyon Production in association with LenJen Productions and 20th Century-Fox
Director Ronald Lyon
Writer Andrew W. Solt
Host/Narrator Peter Lawford

616 **Griffin and Phoenix: A Love Story**
The ABC Tuesday Night Movie ABC
Program Type TV Movie
Two hours. Premiere date: 2/27/76. Repeat date: 8/9/77. Drama of a short-lived love affair. Title song written and performed by Paul Williams. Music score by George Aliceson Tipton.
Executive Producer Paul Junger Witt
Producer Tony Thomas
Company An ABC Circle Film
Director Daryl Duke
Writer John Hill

CAST
Geoffrey Griffin .... Peter Falk
Sarah Phoenix .... Jill Clayburgh
Jean .... Dorothy Tristan
George .... John Lehne
Old Man .... George Chandler

Professor .... Milton Parsons
Jody .... Sally Kirkland
Dr. Feinberg .... Ben Hammer
Dr. Thompson .... Irwin Charone
Dr. Glenn .... John Harkins
Randy Griffin .... Randy Faustino
Bob Griffin .... Steven Rogers
Usher .... Rod Haase
Dr. Harding .... Ken Sansom

617 **Guess Who's Pregnant?**
Documentary Showcase PBS
Program Type Documentary/Informational Special
60 minutes. Premiere date: 6/3/77. Repeat date: 9/30/77 (captioned for the hearing-impaired). A look at pregnancy among teen-aged American girls and the consequences of child-bearing at such an early age. Program made possible by a grant from the Van Amerigen Foundation.
Producers Michael Hirsh, Elayne Goldstein
Company WTTW-TV/Chicago
Director David Erdman
Writers Michael Hirsh, Elayne Goldstein
Cinematographer Dick Sato
Film Editor Michael Morley
Narrator Marty Robinson

618 **The Guiding Light** CBS
Program Type Daytime Drama Series
30 minutes. Mondays–Fridays. Premiere date (on television): 6/30/52 after 15 years on radio. Continuous. Created by Irna Phillips. "La Lumiere" theme by Charles Paul. Drama about the Bauer and Thorpe families set in Springfield, U.S.A. Credits as of 1/5/77. Cast listed alphabetically. Charita Bauer is an original cast member.
Executive Producer Allen M. Potter
Company Procter & Gamble Productions
Directors Harry Eggart, Michael Gliona, John Pasquin
Head Writers Jerome Dobson, Bridget Dobson
Writers Jean Rouverol, Rocci Chatfield

CAST

Dr. Sara McIntyre Werner .... Millette Alexander
Bertha (Bert) Bauer .... Charita Bauer
Barbara Norris Thorpe .... Barbara Berjer
Christina Bauer .... Gina Foy
Holly Norris Bauer .... Maureen Garrett
Eve Stapleton .... Janet Grey
Freddie Bauer .... Garry Hannoch
T.J. .... T. J. Hargrave
Dr. Ed Bauer .... Mart Hulswit
Rita Stapleton .... Lenore Kasdorf
Emmet Scott .... Frank Latimore
Hope Bauer .... Robin Mattson
Adam Thorpe .... Robert Milli
Ann Jeffers .... Maureen Mooney
Peggy Thorpe .... Fran Myers
Dr. Justin Marler .... Tom O'Rourke
Katie Parker .... Denise Pence
Jacqueline Marler .... Cindy Pickett
Dr. Stephen Jackson .... Stefan Schnabel
Michael Bauer .... Don Stewart
Billy Fletcher .... Dai Stockton
Viola Stapleton .... Kate Wilkinson
Ben McFarren .... Stephen Yates
Roger Thorpe .... Michael Zaslow

619 **Guilty or Innocent: The Sam Sheppard Murder Case**
NBC Thursday Night at the Movies NBC
Program Type TV Movie
Three hours. Premiere date: 11/17/75. Repeat date: 8/4/77. Drama about Dr. Sam Sheppard, the Cleveland osteopath convicted of murdering his wife in 1954. Filmed in part at the Correctional Facility at Chino, Calif.
Executive Producer Harve Bennett
Producer Harold Gast
Company Universal Television in association with NBC-TV
Director Robert Michael Lewis
Writer Harold Gast
Costume Designers Carl Garrison, Grady Hunt
Art Director William Campbell

CAST

Dr. Sam Sheppard .... George Peppard
Walt Adamson .... William Windom
Philip J. Madden .... Barnard Hughes
F. Lee Bailey .... Walter McGinn
Ilse Brandt .... Nina Van Pallandt
Prosecutor Simmons .... George Murdock
Additional Cast Paul Fix, William Dozier, Jack Knight

A Gunfight *see* The ABC Friday Night Movie

620 **Hallmark Hall of Fame** NBC
Program Type Drama Series
90 minutes/two hours. 26th season premiere: 11/17/76. First special aired Christmas Eve 1951. Dramatic specials seen during the 1976–77 season are: "All Creatures Great and Small," "Beauty and the Beast," "The Disappearance of AIMEE," "Emily, Emily," "Peter Pan." (*See* individual titles for credits.)

621 **The Hambletonian** CBS
Program Type Sports Special
Highlights of the 52nd running of the Hambletonian trotting race from the Du Quoin (Ill.) State Fair 9/3/77.
Producer Bob Stenner
Company CBS Television Network Sports
Director Tony Verna
Commentators Don Criqui, Heywood Hale Broun

622 **A Handful of Souls** CBS
Program Type Religious/Cultural Special
60 minutes. Premiere date: 12/25/75 (midnight

A Handful of Souls *Continued*
to 1 a.m.) Repeat date: 12/26/76. A Christmas cantata commissioned by CBS News for the Bicentennial and performed at the First Baptist Church in Providence, R.I. Music composed by Ezra Laderman; libretto by Joe Darion.
Producer Pamela Ilott
Company CBS News Religious Broadcast
Director Richard Knox
Conductor Alfredo Antonini
Soloists Ara Berberian, Harry Theyard, Ron Holgate, David Clatworthy, Ray Devoll, Jerold Norman, Hilda Harris, Elaine Bonazzi
Group Vocalists The Providence Singers, Barrington Boys Choir

623 **Handle With Care** CBS
Program Type Comedy Special
30 minutes. Premiere date: 5/9/77. Comedy pilot about the members of a nursing corps during the Korean War.
Production Executive Nancy Malone
Producer Lew Gallo
Company 20th Century-Fox Television in association with the CBS Television Network
Director Alan Rafkin
Writers Woody Kling, Dawn Aldredge, Marion C. Freeman, Jim Parker
Art Director Rodger Maus

CAST

Col. Ted Richardson .... Brian Dennehy
Shirley Nichols .... Betsy Slade
Jacqueline Morse .... Didi Conn
Maj. Charlotte Hinkley .... Mary Jo Catlett
Turk .... Jeannie Wilson
Elizabeth Baker .... Marlyn Mason
Cpl. Carp .... Robert Lussier
Dr. O'Brian .... David Dukes
Dr. Roberts .... Oaky Miller
Dr. Rogers .... Howard George
Cpl. Tillingham .... Ted Wass
Soldier No. 1 .... Dick Yarmy
Soldier No. 2 .... Vernon Weddle

Hands of the Ripper *see* The ABC Friday Night Movie

Hannie Caulder *see* CBS Special Film Presentations

624 **Hanukkah** PBS
Program Type Religious/Cultural Special
30 minutes. Premiere date: 12/2/74. Repeat date: 12/13/76. A look at the history and celebration of the Jewish festival of Hanukkah.
Producers Henry Kline II, Edward Cohen
Company Mississippi Authority for Educational Television
Director Henry Kline II
Writer Edward Cohen
Host/Narrator Edward Asner

625 **Happy Days** ABC
Program Type Comedy Series
30 minutes. Tuesdays. Premiere date: 1/15/74. Fourth season premiere: 9/21/76 (60-minute special.) Jefferson High School student growing up in Milwaukee in the 1950s. Created by Garry K. Marshall. "Happy Days" music by Charles Fox; lyrics by Norman Gimbel.
Executive Producers Thomas L. Miller, Edward K. Milkis, Garry K. Marshall
Producers Tony Marshall, Jerry Paris
Company Miller-Milkis Productions, Inc. and Henderson Production Company in association with Paramount Television
Director Jerry Paris
Writers Various
Executive Consultants Lowell Ganz, Mark Rothman

CAST

Richie Cunningham .... Ron Howard
Arthur "Fonzie" Fonzarelli .... Henry Winkler
Howard Cunningham .... Tom Bosley
Marion Cunningham .... Marion Ross
Potsie Weber .... Anson Williams
Ralph Malph .... Donny Most
Joanie Cunningham .... Erin Moran
Alfred .... Al Molinaro

626 **Happy Days (Daytime)** ABC
Program Type Comedy Series
30 minutes. Mondays-Fridays. Morning reruns of evening show. Premiere date: 9/1/75. Continuous. For credit information, *see* "Happy Days."

Hard Driver *see* The ABC Friday Night Movie

627 **Hard Times**
Great Performances PBS
Program Type Limited Series
60 minutes. Wednesday. Premiere date: 5/11/77. Four-part dramatization of the novel by Charles Dickens about England during the Industrial Revolution. Program made possible by grants from Exxon Corporation, the National Endowment for the Humanities, the Corporation for Public Broadcasting, the Ford Foundation and Public Television Stations.
Executive Producer Jac Venza
Producer Peter Eckersley
Company Granada Television/London and WNET-TV/New York
Director John Irvin
Writer Arthur Hopcraft
Scenic Designer Roy Stonehouse

CAST

Louisa Gradgrind .... Jacqueline Tong

Thomas Gradgrind .... Patrick Allen
Tom Gradgrind .... Richard Wren
Josiah Bounderby .... Timothy West
Sissy Jupe .... Michelle Dibnah
Stephen Blackpool .... Alan Dobie
Capt. Harthouse .... Edward Fox
Mrs. Sparsit .... Rosalie Crutchley
Mrs. Gradgrind .... Ursula Howells
Mr. Sleary .... Harry Markham
Rachel .... Barbara Ewing

628 **Hardy Boys Mysteries** ABC
Program Type Children's Series
60 minutes. Sundays. Premiere date: 1/30/77. Shown every other Sunday alternating with "Nancy Drew Mysteries." Based on "The Hardy Boys" books by Franklin W. Dixon. Adventures of two teenage detective sons of a world-famous investigator. Theme music by Glen A. Larson.
Executive Producer Glen A. Larson
Supervising Producer B. W. Sandefur
Producers Arlene Sidaris, Joyce Brotman
Company A Glen A. Larson Production in association with Universal Television
Directors Various
Writers Various

CAST

Joe Hardy .... Shaun Cassidy
Frank Hardy .... Parker Stevenson
Calley Shaw .... Lisa Eilbacher
Fenton Hardy .... Edmund Gilbert
Aunt Gertrude .... Edith Atwater
Chet Morton .... Gary Springer

Harry In Your Pocket *see* NBC Saturday Night at the Movies

629 **Harry S. Truman: Plain Speaking** PBS
Program Type Dramatic Special
60 minutes. Premiere date: 10/5/76. Repeat date: 8/25/77. One-man show about Harry S. Truman based on the book by Merle Miller. Program made possible by grants from Nathan Cummings, Harmon International Industries, Inc., Richard and Edna Solomon, and the Corporation for Public Broadcasting.
Producer David Susskind
Company Talent Associates, Inc. in association with WQED-TV/Pittsburgh
Director Daniel Petrie
Writer Carol Sobieski
Scenic Designers Cletus Anderson, William Matthews

CAST

Harry S. Truman .... Ed Flanders

630 **The Harvey Korman Show**
Special Comedy Presentation ABC
Program Type Comedy Special
30 minutes. Premiere date: 5/19/77. Comedy pilot about a flamboyant actor who runs an acting class in his home.
Executive Producer Hal Dresner
Producer Don Van Atta
Company Chrisma Productions
Director Alan Myerson
Writer Hal Dresner
Art Director Mary Weaver Dodson

CAST

Francis A. Kavanaugh .... Harvey Korman
Maggie Kavanaugh .... Susan Lawrence
Jake Winkleman .... Milton Selzer
Stuart Stafford .... Barry Van Dyke
Carmine Despiccio .... Dino Natali
Parker Crawford .... Don Sparks
Honey Bushkin .... Penelope Windust
Mrs. Robles-Diaz .... Alma Beltran
Howie Hoff .... Bart Braverman
Dobkin .... Robert E. Ball
Schermerhorn .... Brad Trumbull
Chris .... Donna Ponterotto

631 **The Haunted Trailer**
ABC Short Story Specials ABC
Program Type Children's Special
30 minutes. Premiere date: 3/26/77. Comedy about a college girl trying to live in a trailer inhabited by a group of musical poltergeists. Based on a short story by Robert Arthur.
Executive Producer Allen Ducovny
Producer William Beaudine, Jr.
Company ABC Circle Films
Director Ezra Stone
Writer Robert Specht
Art Director Joe Aubel

CAST

Clifford .... Murray Matheson
Mr. Simpson .... Eddie Bracken
Sharon .... Lauren Tewes
Mickey .... Monie Ellis
The Sheriff .... Stu Gilliam
Woman in Car .... Sara Seegar
Gas Station Owner .... Jim Boles

632 **Having Babies**
The ABC Sunday Night Movie/The ABC Tuesday Night Movie ABC
Program Type TV Movie
Two hours. Premiere date: 10/17/76. Repeat date: 8/30/77. Drama of four couples who experience childbirth by the "natural" Lamaze method. Birth sequence filmed at Valley Presbyterian Hospital in Los Angeles. Music by Earle Hagen. Lyrics to "Paper Bridges" by Al Kasha and Joel Hirschhorn sung by Maureen McGovern.
Executive Producers Gerald I. Isenberg, Gerald W. Abrams
Producer Lew Gallo
Company The Jozak Company
Director Robert Day
Writer Peggy Elliott

Having Babies *Continued*
Technical Advisor Florrie Segelman, R. N.

CAST

Frank Gorman	Desi Arnaz, Jr.
Allie Duggan	Adrienne Barbeau
George McNamara	Ronny Cox
Ralph Bancini	Harry Guardino
Hal Bergstrom	Tom Kennedy
Grace Fontreil	Vicki Lawrence
Max Duggan	Richard Masur
Mickey Paterno	Greg Mullavey
Laura Gorman	Linda Purl
Mrs. Fontreil	Jan Sterling
Beth Paterno	Karen Valentine
Al Schneider	Abe Vigoda
Sally McNamara	Jessica Walter

Hawaii *see* The CBS Friday Night Movies

633 **Hawaii Five-O** CBS
Program Type Crime Drama Series
60 minutes. Thursdays. Premiere date: 9/26/68. Ninth season premiere: 9/30/76 (as two-hour special). Created by Leonard Freeman. Crime drama set and filmed in Hawaii about the adventures of the Hawaiian police.
Supervising Producer Philip Leacock
Producers Jim Heinz, Douglas Green
Company The CBS Television Network
Directors Various
Executive Story Consultant Curtis Kenyon
Writers Various
Musical Director Morton Stevens
Story Consultant Herman Groves

CAST

Steve McGarrett	Jack Lord
Danny Williams	James MacArthur
Chin Ho	Kam Fong
Che Fong	Harry Endo
Duke	Herman Wedemeyer
Doc Bergman	Al Eben

634 **Hawaiian Open Golf Championship** ABC
Program Type Sports Special
Live coverage of the final two rounds of the Hawaiian Open from Waialae Country Club in Honolulu 2/5/77 and 2/6/77.
Executive Producer Roone Arledge
Producer Chuck Howard
Company ABC Sports
Directors Jim Jennett, Terry Jastrow
Anchor Jim McKay
Expert Commentators Dave Marr, Bob Rosburg, Peter Alliss

The Heart Is a Lonely Hunter *see* NBC Saturday Night at the Movies

Hearts of the West *see* NBC Monday Night at the Movies

635 **Heaveweight Championship of Tennis** CBS
Program Type Sports Special
Three hours. Taped coverage of a tennis match between Jimmy Connors and Ilie Nastase at Dorado Beach, Puerto Rico 3/5/77.
Producer Frank Chirkinian
Company CBS Television Network Sports
Director Bob Dailey
Commentators Pat Summerall, Jack Whitaker, Tony Trabert

636 **Hedda Gabler**
Classic Theatre: The Humanities in Drama PBS
Program Type Dramatic Special
Two hours. Premiere date: 11/20/75. Repeat date: 4/14/77. 1890 drama by the Norwegian playwright Henrik Ibsen dealing with the problems women suffer in a world dominated by men. Program made possible by grants from the National Endowment for the Humanities and Mobil Oil Corporation. Presented by WGBH-TV/Boston; Joan Sullivan, producer.
Producer Cedric Messina
Company British Broadcasting Corporation
Director Waris Hussein
Writer Henrik Ibsen

CAST

Hedda Gabler	Janet Suzman
George Tesman	Ian McKellen
Eilert Lovborg	Tom Bell
Mrs. Elvsted	Jane Asher
Aunt Juliana	Dorothy Reynolds
Judge Brack	Brendan Barry

637 **Hee Haw** Syndicated
Program Type Music/Comedy/Variety Series
60 minutes. Weekly. Originally premiered on CBS in 1969. Went into syndication in 1971. Season premiere: 9/76. Produced on location in Nashville, Tenn. Regular features: barber shop, truck stop, cooking, cornfield, Country Dictionary, Grandpa's Almanac.
Executive Producers Frank Peppiatt, John Aylesworth
Producer Sam Lovullo
Company Yongestreet Productions
Director Bob Boatman
Writing Supervisors Frank Peppiatt, John Aylesworth
Hosts Roy Clark, Buck Owens
Featured Performers Archie Campbell, George Lindsey, Minnie Pearl, The Hager Twins, Junior Samples, Grandpa Jones (Louis Marshall), Gordie Tapp, Don Harron, Misty Rowe, Gunilla Hutton, Lisa Todd, Cathy

Baker, Marianne Gordon, Gailard Sartain, Kenny Price, John Henry Faulk, Roni Stoneman, Cathy Barton, Buck Trent

638 **Heidi**
Once Upon a Classic PBS
Program Type Children's Series
30 minutes. Saturdays. Premiere date: 11/20/76. Series repeats began 5/21/77. Six-part dramatization of the Johanna Spyris novel about a Swiss orphan girl. Filmed in England. Captioned for the hearing-impaired. Presented by WQED-TV/Pittsburgh and made possible by grants from McDonald's Local Restaurants Association and McDonald's Corporation.
Executive Producer Jay Rayvid
Coordinating Producer John Coney
Producer John McRae
Company British Broadcasting Corporation and Time-Life Television
Director June Wyndham-Davies
Writer Martin Worth
Host Bill Bixby

CAST
Heidi .... Emma Blake
Grandfather .... Hans Meyer
Grandmother .... Flora Robson
Peter .... Nicholas Lyndhurst
Dete .... Myra Francis
Brigitta .... Kathleen Byron
Clara .... Chloe Franks
Frau Sesemann .... Judy Campbell
Fraulein Rottenmeier .... June Jago
Herr Sesemann .... Terence Skelton
Sebastian .... Barry Lowe

Hello, Dolly! *see* CBS Special Film Presentations

639 **Helter Skelter** CBS
Program Type Dramatic Special
Four hours. Premiere dates: 4/1/76 and 4/2/76 (two hours each night). Repeat dates: 1/24/77 and 1/26/77. Based on the book by Vincent Bugliosi with Curt Gentry about the Tate-LaBianca murders of August 1969. Filmed partly on the sites of the actual events. Music by Billy Goldenberg.
Executive Producers Lee Rich, Philip Capice
Producer Tom Gries
Company Lorimar Productions
Director Tom Gries
Writer J.P. Miller
Art Director Phil Barber
Film Editors Byron Buzz Brandt, Bud Isaacs

CAST
Vincent Bugliosi .... George DiCenzo
Charles Manson .... Steve Railsback
Susan Atkins .... Nancy Wolfe
Linda Kasabian .... Marilyn Burns
Patricia Krenwinkel .... Christina Hart
Leslie Van Houten .... Cathey Paine
Aaron Stovitz .... Alan Oppenheimer
Danny DeCarlo .... Rudy Ramos
Ronnie Howard .... Sondra Blake
Rosner .... George Garro
Lt. Brenner .... Vic Werber
Everett Scoville .... Howard Caine
Paul Watkins .... Jason Ronard
Judge Older .... Skip Homeier
Phil Cohen .... Marc Alaimo
Tex Watson .... Bill Durkin
Sgt. Manuel Gries .... Phillip R. Allen
Harry Jones .... David Clennon
Terrence Milik .... Adam Williams
Hank Charter .... Jonathan Lippe
Mr. Quint .... James E. Brodhead
Mrs. Quint .... Anne Newman Mantee
Gail Bugliosi .... Joyce Easton
Friend .... Wright King
William Garretson .... Jon Gries
Sgt. Hank Druger .... Edward Bell
Punchy .... Roy Jenson
Sgt. O'Neal .... Paul Mantee
Mr. Spahn .... Ray Middleton
Sgt. Smith .... Anthony Herrera
Leno LaBianca .... Al Checco
Sgt. Franklin .... Robert Hoy
Sgt. Ross .... Stanley Ralph Ross
Frank Fowler .... Bart Burns
Newscaster .... Jerry Dunphy
Newscaster .... George Putnam
J. Miller Leavy .... Linden Chiles
Sgt. Broom .... Mary Kay Place
Rosemary LaBianca .... Toni Moss
The Family Girls ......Barbara Mallory, Asta Hansen, Deborah Parsons, Melody Hinkle, Deanne Gwinn, Leila Davis, Sondra Lowell, Kathleen Devlin, Mary Jo Thacher, Tracy Tracton, Eileen Dietz Elber, Patricia Post, Lindsay V. Jones

640 **The Hemingway Play**
Hollywood Television Theatre PBS
Program Type Dramatic Special
90 minutes. Premiere date: 3/11/76. Repeat date: 9/23/76. An exploration of the life of Ernest Hemingway using four different characters to depict different phases of his development. Music by Lee Holdridge. Program made possible by grants from the Corporation for Public Broadcasting, the Ford Foundation and Public Television Stations.
Executive Producer Norman Lloyd
Supervising Producer George Turpin
Producer Norman Lloyd
Company KCET-TV/Los Angeles
Director Don Taylor
Writer Frederic Hunter
Costume Designer Noel Taylor
Art Director Roy Christopher

CAST
Wemedge .... Tim Matheson
Hem .... Perry King
Ernest .... Mitchell Ryan
Papa .... Alexander Scourby
Glynis .... Samantha Eggar

The Hemingway Play *Continued*

Julio .... Robert Carricart
Luisa .... Miriam Colon
Dana .... Pamela Sue Martin
Charlie .... Biff McGuire
Paul Vas Dias .... Kenneth Tigar

641 Henry Winkler Meets William Shakespeare

The CBS Festival of Lively Arts for Young People CBS
Program Type Children's Special
60 minutes. Premiere date: 3/20/77. Excerpts from the works of William Shakespeare taped at the American Shakespeare Theatre, Stratford, Conn.
Producer Daniel Wilson
Company Daniel Wilson Productions
Director Jeff Bleckner
Writer Lee Kalcheim
Costume Designer Fred Voelpel
Art Director Fred Voelpel
Star Henry Winkler

CAST

William Shakespeare .... Tom Aldredge
Romeo .... Henry Winkler
Falstaff .... George Ede
Petruchio .... Kevin Kline
Tybalt .... Robert Phelps
Mercutio .... Jordan Clarke
Kate .... Bruce Bouchard
Fencer .... Erik Fredrickson
Additional Cast Stephan Brennan, William Sadler, Bruce Weitz, Bill McIntyre, David Blessing, Franklin Seales

642 Herbert von Karajan and the Berlin Philharmonic: Beethoven

Great Performances PBS
Program Type Music/Dance Special
90 minutes. Premiere date: 12/31/75. Repeat date: 9/18/77. The Symphony No. 9 in D Minor and the Egmont Overture by Ludwig van Beethoven performed by the Berlin Philharmonic Orchestra. Program presented by WNET-TV/New York and made possible by a grant from Exxon Corporation.
Coordinating Producer David Griffiths
Company Unitel Productions
Conductor Herbert von Karajan

643 Here Comes Peter Cottontail CBS

Program Type Animated Film Special
60 minutes. Repeat date: 4/8/77. Based on the book "The Easter Bunny That Overslept" by Priscilla Friedrich and Otto Friedrich. Music and lyrics by Maury Laws and Jules Bass.
Producers Arthur Rankin, Jr., Jules Bass
Directors Arthur Rankin, Jr., Jules Bass
Writer Romeo Muller
Musical Director Maury Laws
Animation Director Kizo Nagashima

VOICES

Mr. Sassafrass .... Danny Kaye
Irontail .... Vincent Price
Peter .... Casey Kasem
Donna .... Iris Rainer
Additional Voices Paul Frees, Joan Gardner, Greg Thomas, Jeff Thomas

644 Here's Lucy CBS

Program Type Comedy Series
30 minutes. Mondays–Fridays. Originally seen between 1968–1974. Daytime rerun premiere: 5/2/77. Comedy about a widow with two children working at the Unique Employment Agency.
Executive Producer Gary Morton
Producers Tommy Thompson, Cleo Smith
Company A Lucille Ball Production in association with Paramount Television
Directors Various
Writers Various

CAST

Lucy Carter .... Lucille Ball
Uncle Harry .... Gale Gordon
Kim Carter .... Lucie Arnaz
Craig Carter .... Desi Arnaz, Jr.

645 The Hidden Heritage CBS

Program Type Religious/Cultural Special
60 minutes. Premiere date: 7/31/77. Highlights of the art exhibit "Two Centuries of Black American Art" filmed at the High Museum in Atlanta, Ga.
Executive Producer Pamela Ilott
Company CBS News Religious Broadcast
Narrator David C. Driskell

646 The Hidden Universe: The Brain ABC

Program Type Science/Nature Special
60 minutes. Premiere date: 6/12/77. An examination of the brain.
Producer Tom Bywaters
Company ABC News Special
Director Tom Bywaters
Writer Tom Bywaters
Cinematographers Dan Lerner, Larry Mitchell, Anton Wilson
Film Editors Nils Rasmussen, Pat Cook
Consultant Dr. Guy M. McKhann
Host David Janssen

High Plains Drifter *see* The ABC Sunday Night Movie

647 **High Risk**
The ABC Friday Night Movie ABC
Program Type TV Movie
90 minutes. Premiere date: 5/15/76. Repeat date: 7/8/77. Pilot about six former circus performers in a high risk caper. Music by Billy Goldenberg.
Executive Producer Paul Junger Witt
Producer Robert E. Relyea
Company A Danny Thomas Production in association with MGM Television
Director Sam O'Steen
Writer Robert Carrington

CAST

Sebastian .... Victor Buono
Guthrie .... Joseph Sirola
Walker-T .... Don Stroud
Sandra .... JoAnna Cameron
Daisy .... Ronne Troup
Erik .... Wolf Roth
Amb. Henriques .... Rene Enriquez
Quincey .... John Fink
Aide .... George Skaff
Butler .... William Beckley

648 **Highlights of Ringling Bros. and Barnum & Bailey Circus**
Multi-Special Night NBC
Program Type Music/Comedy/Variety Special
60 minutes. Premiere date: 3/15/77. Selected acts from the 107th edition of the Ringling Bros. and Barnum & Bailey Circus. Taped at the Bayfront Center, St. Petersburg, Fla. 1/8/77–1/10/77.
Executive Producers Irvin Feld, Kenneth Feld
Producer John Moffitt
Director John Moffitt
Writer Robert Arthur
Choreographers Bill Bradley, Jerry Fries
Costume Designer Don Foote
Host Gene Kelly

649 **Highlights of the Russian Dance Festival** NBC
Program Type Music/Dance Special
60 minutes. Premiere date: 7/7/77. Dance, music and mime performed by entertainers from the Soviet Union. Taped in Las Vegas during a tour by the troupe.
Producer Mike Gargiulo
Company A United Euram Presentation in association with Gosconcert, Moscow, U.S.S.R.
Distributor Worldvision Enterprises, Inc.
Director Mike Gargiulo
Writer Chuck Horner
Host Orson Welles
Performers Georgian Dance Company, Ukrainian Dance Company, Piatnitsky Folk Choir and Dancers, Natalia Kiriushkin and Oleg Kiriushkin, Komuzisty Chamber Ensemble, Mengo Ensemble of the Northern Peoples, Artists from the Tadzhik Republic

650 **Hijack**
Once Upon a Classic PBS
Program Type Children's Special
60 minutes. Premiere date: 5/14/77. Story about three children forced to take a hijacker to France in their father's yacht. Music by Harry Robinson. Filmed in part on location on the Isle of Wight and in the English Channel. Captioned for the hearing-impaired. Presented by WQED-TV/Pittsburgh and made possible by grants from McDonald's Local Restaurants Association and McDonald's Corporation.
Coordinating Producer John Coney
Producer Michael Forlong
Company Michael Forlong Productions Ltd. for the Children's Film Foundation Ltd.
Director Michael Forlong
Writer Michael Forlong
Host Bill Bixby

CAST

Colin .... Richard Morant
Jack .... James Forlong
Jenny .... Tracey Peel
Lucy .... Sally Forlong
Power Boat Driver .... David Hitchen
Power Boat Mechanic .... Richard Kerrigan
Power Boat Owner .... Derek Bond
Policeman .... Robert Swales

The Hindenburg *see* The Big Event

651 **Hollywood High (Pilot I)** NBC
Program Type Comedy Special
30 minutes. Premiere date: 5/19/77. Comedy pilot about four teenagers and their problems.
Executive Producer Gerald I. Isenberg
Producer Gerald W. Abrams
Company The Jozak Company in association with Paramount Television and NBC-TV
Director Peter Baldwin
Writer Michael Weinberger

CAST

Phoebe .... Annie Potts
Dawn .... Kim Lankford
Wheeler .... Chris Pina
Bill .... Rory Stevens
Dr. Bad .... Sam Kwasman
Ickey .... John Megna

652 **Hollywood High (Pilots II and III)** NBC
Program Type Comedy Special
30 minutes each. Premiere date: 7/21/77. Two segments for a proposed comedy series about two high school journalists.
Executive Producers Gerald I. Isenberg, Gerald W. Abrams

Hollywood High (Pilots II and III) *Continued*
Producers Elias Davis, David Pollock
Company A Jozak Company Production in association with Paramount Television and NBC-TV
Director Burt Brinckerhoff
Writers David Pollock, Elias Davis (pilot II)/ Lloyd Garver (pilot III)

CAST

Paula Lindell	Annie Potts
Eugene Langley	Darren O'Connor
Allison	Roberta Wallach
Stu	John Guerrasio
Judith	Beverly Sanders
Mr. Blaine	Dick O'Neill

653 **Hollywood Out-Takes** NBC
Program Type Documentary/Informational Special
60 minutes. Premiere date: 3/27/77. Out-takes from nine films with 1977 Oscar nominations plus interviews with people connected with the films. Show created by Marilyn Beck.
Executive Producer Dick Schneider
Producer Herman S. Saunders
Company A Frederick-Miner-Saunders Production
Director Dick Schneider
Writers Bill Richmond, Gene Perret
Musical Director Milton Delugg
Art Director Hub Braden
Host Marilyn Beck
Guests Jenny Agutter, David Carradine, Blake Edwards, Bob Evans, William Holden, Bob Hope, Alan Pakula, Jon Peters, Michael Phillips, Talia Shire, Sylvester Stallone, Burt Young

654 **The Hollywood Squares** NBC
Program Type Game/Audience Participation Series
30 minutes. Mondays–Fridays. Premiere date: 10/17/66. Continuous. Nine celebrity panelists in a tic-tac-toe board answer questions for contestants.
Executive Producers Merrill Heatter, Bob Quigley
Producer Jay Redack
Company Heatter-Quigley Productions in association with NBC-TV
Director Jerome Shaw
Host Peter Marshall
Announcer Ken Williams
Regulars Rose Marie, George Gobel, Paul Lynde

655 **The Hollywood Squares (Evening)** Syndicated
Program Type Game/Audience Participation Series
30 minutes. Twice weekly. Season premiere: 9/76. Evening version of daytime game with nine celebrities in tic-tac-toe box.
Executive Producers Merrill Heatter, Bob Quigley
Producer Jay Redack
Company Heatter-Quigley Productions
Distributor Rhodes Productions
Director Jerome Shaw
Host Peter Marshall
Announcer Ken Williams
Regulars Rose Marie, George Gobel, Paul Lynde

656 **Hollywood Television Theatre** PBS
Program Type Drama Series
90 minutes/120 minutes. Thursdays. Premiere date: 5/17/70. Season premiere: 9/16/76. Contemporary plays by American and European dramatists. Plays shown during the 1976–77 season are: "The Fatal Weakness," "The Hemingway Play," "The Last of Mrs. Lincoln," "Philemon," "Six Characters in Search of an Author." (*See* individual titles for credits.)

657 **Holmes and Yoyo** ABC
Program Type Comedy Series
30 minutes. Saturdays. Premiere date: 9/25/76. Last regular show: 12/11/76. Two shows seen on "The ABC Monday Comedy Special" on 8/1/77 and 8/8/77. Comedy about a police detective and his rookie computer partner. Created by Jack Sher and Lee Hewitt. Title changed to "Holmes & Yoyo" in October 1976.
Executive Producer Leonard B. Stern
Producer Arne Sultan
Company Heyday Productions, Inc. in association with Universal Television
Directors Various
Writers Various

CAST

Alexander Holmes	Richard B. Shull
Gregory "Yoyo" Yoyonovich	John Schuck
Capt. Harry Sedford	Bruce Kirby
Off. Maxine Moon	Andrea Howard

658 **Home for Passover**
Eternal Light NBC
Program Type Religious/Cultural Special
30 minutes. Premiere date: 4/3/66. Repeat date: 3/27/77. Drama based on the short story of the same name by Sholom Aleichem about a Hebrew teacher's efforts to spend Passover with his family.
Executive Producer Doris Ann
Producer Martin Hoade

Company NBC Television Religious Programs Unit in association with the Jewish Theological Seminary of America
Director Martin Hoade
Writer James Yafee

CAST

Fishel ..... Boris Tumarin
Yankel ..... Gene Wilder
Fisherman ..... George Mathews
Bath-Sheba ..... Sada Thompson
Son ..... Alan Howard

659 The Homecoming—A Christmas Story CBS

Program Type Dramatic Special
Two hours. Premiere date: 12/19/71. Repeat date: 12/24/76. Based on the novel by Earl Hamner. Music by Jerry Goldsmith. Led to series "The Waltons." Focuses on the events of Christmas Eve, 1933.
Executive Producer Lee Rich
Producer Robert L. Jacks
Company CBS Television Network Production
Director Fielder Cook
Writer Earl Hamner
Costume Designers Betsy Cox, Bob Harris, Jr.
Art Director Robert Smith

CAST

Olivia Walton ..... Patricia Neal
Grandpa ..... Edgar Bergen
Grandma ..... Ellen Corby
John Walton ..... Andrew Duggan
Miss Mamie Baldwin ..... Josephine Hutchinson
Hawthorne Dooley ..... Cleavon Little
Miss Emily Baldwin ..... Dorothy Stickney
John-Boy Walton ..... Richard Thomas
Charlie Sneed ..... William Windom
Jason Walton ..... Jon Walmsley
Mary Ellen Walton ..... Judy Norton
Erin Walton ..... Mary McDonough
Ben Walton ..... Eric Scott
Jim-Bob Walton ..... David Harper
Elizabeth Walton ..... Kami Cotler
Sheriff Bridges ..... David Huddleston
Ike Godsey ..... Woodrow Parfrey
City Lady ..... Sally Chamberlain
Claudie Dooley ..... Donald Livingston

660 Homer and the Wacky Doughnut Machine

ABC Short Story Specials ABC
Program Type Children's Special
30 minutes. Premiere date: 4/30/77. Comedy about a boy who saves his uncle's business. Adapted from the short story by Robert McCloskey.
Executive Producer Allen Ducovny
Producer Robert Chenault
Company ABC Circle Films
Director Larry Elikann
Writer Mark Fink

CAST

Uncle Ulysses ..... David Doyle
Mr. Gabby ..... Jesse White
Homer ..... Michael LeClair
Kelly ..... Tara Talboy
Additional Cast Natalie Schafer, Cliff Norton, Bob Hastings, Dodo Denney, Roy Stuart

661 Hometown Saturday Night PBS

Program Type Music/Dance Special
60 minutes. Premiere date: 12/10/75. Repeat date: 12/31/76. A nostalgic recreation of a turn-of-the-century small-town band concert with the new Jack Daniel's Original Silver Cornet Band. Concert staged in the Nashville Opryhouse in February 1975. Program made possible by a grant from Marquette Corporation.
Producer Bob Sabel
Company WDCN-TV/Nashville, Tenn.
Director Bob Boatman
Conductor Dave Fulmer
Narrator Dave Fulmer

662 The Horrible Honchos

ABC Afterschool Specials ABC
Program Type Children's Special
60 minutes. Premiere date: 3/9/77. Story of a group of kids who ostracize a new boy in the neighborhood. Based on "The Seventeenth Street Gang" by Emily Cheney Neville. Original music by Joe Weber.
Executive Producer Daniel Wilson
Producer Fran Sears
Company Daniel Wilson Productions, Inc.
Director Larry Elikann
Writer Thomas Baum

CAST

Minnow ..... Kim Richards
Hollis ..... Christian Juttner
Louise ..... Tara Talboy
Ivan ..... Billy Jacoby
C. C. ..... Christopher Maleki
Hollis' Dad ..... Laurence Haddon
Hollis' Mom ..... Davey Davison
Louise's Mom ..... Pat Delany
Louise's Dad ..... Jack Knight

A Horse Named Comanche *see* NBC All-Disney Saturday Night at the Movies

663 The Hostage Heart

The CBS Friday Night Movies CBS
Program Type TV Movie
Two hours. Premiere date: 9/9/77. Drama of terrorism and ransom during a heart operation. Based on the novel by Gerald Green. Music by Fred Karlin.
Producer Andrew J. Fenady
Company An A. J. Fenady Associates Production in association with MGM Television
Director Bernard McEveety

The Hostage Heart *Continued*

Writers Andrew J. Fenady, Charles Sailor, Eric Kaldor
Art Director Marvin Summerfield
Medical Advisor Chris Hutson, R.N.

CAST

Dr. Eric Lake	Bradford Dillman
Chris LeBlanc	Loretta Swit
Steve Rockewicz	Vic Morrow
Martha Lake	Sharon Acker
John Trask	Stephen Davies
Chief Reinhold	George DiCenzo
Arnold Stade	Cameron Mitchell
Fiona	Belinda J. Montgomery
Dr. Licata	Peter Palmer
Don Harris	Harry Rhodes
Dr. Motzkin	Allan Rich
James Cardone	Paul Shenar
Brian O'Donnell	Robert Walden
Bateman Hooks	Carl Weathers
Dr. Charles Michaels	Brendon Boone
Habib Rashid	Aharon Ipale
Walker Bench	Gregg Palmer
Dr. Harvey Fess	Philip Baker Hall
Jimmy Baggs	Arnold Johnson
Carl Olsen	Ted Markland
Flor Aquino	Kieu-Chinh
Cho Park	Frank Michael Liu
Miller	Steven Marlo

664 **Hot Seat** ABC

Program Type Game/Audience Participation Series
30 minutes. Mondays-Fridays. Premiere date: 7/12/76. Last show: 10/22/76. Game based on measured emotional responses recorded on a Galvanic Skin Response (GSR) Machine with two couples competing against each other.
Executive Producer Robert Noah
Producer Bob Synes
Company Heatter-Quigley Productions
Director Jerome Shaw
Host Jim Peck

665 **Hour of Power** Syndicated

Program Type Religious/Cultural Series
60 minutes. Weekly. Premiere date: 2/70. Continuous. Taped on the campus of the Garden Grove Community Church, Garden Grove, Calif.
Executive Producer Michael C. Nason
Company Mascom Advertising
Director Michael Conley
Musical Director Don G. Fontana
Organist Richard Unfreid
Ministers Dr. Robert H. Schuller, Dr. Raymond Beckering, Rev. Kenneth Van Wyk, Rev. Calvin Rynbrandt

666 **Houston Open** NBC

Program Type Sports Special
Live coverage of the final rounds of the Houston Open from the Woodlands Country Club 4/30/77 and 5/1/77.
Producer Larry Cirillo
Company NBC Sports
Director Harry Coyle
Anchor Jim Simpson, Cary Middlecoff
Commentators John Brodie, Fran Tarkenton, Jay Randolph

667 **How Green Was My Valley**

Masterpiece Theatre PBS
Program Type Limited Series
60 minutes. Sundays. Premiere date: 11/7/76. Six-part series, set in a Welsh mining village, dramatizing the novel by Richard Llewellyn. Presented by WGBH-TV/Boston; Joan Sullivan, series producer. Program made possible by a grant from Mobil Corporation.
Producer Martin Lisemore
Company British Broadcasting Corporation in association with 20th Century-Fox Television
Distributor 20th Century-Fox Television
Director Ronald Wilson
Writer Elaine Morgan
Host Alistair Cooke

CAST

Gwilym Morgan	Stanley Baker
Beth Morgan	Sian Phillips
Bronwen	Nerys Hughes
Huw Morgan (as a child)	Rhys Powys
Huw Morgan (as an adult)	Dominic Guard
Ianto Morgan	Keith Drinkel
Owen Morgan	Mike Gwilym
Angharad Morgan	Sue Jones-Davies
Rev. Gruffydd	Gareth Thomas
Marged	Victoria Plucknett
Ifor Morgan	Norman Comer
Mr. Jonas	Clifford Rose
Blodwen	Sheila Ruskin

668 **How the West Was Won**

The ABC Sunday Night Movie/The ABC Monday Night Movie ABC
Program Type Limited Series
Six hours. Three part series shown 2/6/77, 2/7/77 and 2/14/77. A continuation of the saga of "The Macahans" (shown 1/19/76) and based on the motion picture "How the West Was Won." Developed for television by Albert S. Ruddy and Jim Byrnes. Filmed primarily on location in Kanab, Utah and in part in Southern California. Music by Jerrold Immel.
Executive Producer John Mantley
Producers Jeffrey Hayden, John G. Stephens
Company An Albert S. Ruddy Production in association with MGM-TV
Directors Burt Kennedy, Daniel Mann

Writers Jim Byrnes, William Kelley, John Mantley, Earl W. Wallace, Ron Bishop
Set Decorator Herman N. Schoenbrun
Narrator William Conrad

CAST

Zeb Macahan	James Arness
Kate Macahan	Eva Marie Saint
Luke Macahan	Bruce Boxleitner
Josh Macahan	William Kirby Cullen
Laura Macahan	Kathryn Holcomb
Jessie Macahan	Vicki Schreck
Capt. Martin Grey	Anthony Zerbe
Erika Hanks	Brit Lind
Elam Hanks	Royal Dano
Bishop Benjamin	John Dehner
Jim Anderson	Don Murray
Christy Judson	David Huddleston
Cully Madigan	Jack Elam
Chief Claw	Richard Angarola
Willy Judson	John Lisbon Wood
Charley Judson	Sander Johnson
Jake Judson	Herman Poppe
Lt. Cartwright	Howard McGillin
Sheriff Rose	Med Flory
Joshua Hanks	Todd Lookinland
Macklin	Roy Jenson
Mountain-Is-Long	Robert Padilla
Little Tree	Linda Redfearn
Jeremiah	Guillermo San Juan
Maj. Drake	Peter Hansen
Col. Caine	John Pickard
Mother Tice	Peggy Rea

669 **How to Break Up a Happy Divorce**
NBC Movie of the Week NBC
Program Type TV Movie
90 minutes. Premiere date: 10/6/76. Comedy about a divorcee trying to win back her ex-husband. Music by Nelson Riddle.
Executive Producer Charles Fries
Producers Gerald Gardner, Dee Caruso
Company Charles Fries Productions in association with NBC-TV
Director Jerry Paris
Writers Gerald Gardner, Dee Caruso

CAST

Ellen	Barbara Eden
Tony	Hal Linden
Carter	Peter Bonerz
Eve	Marcia Rodd
Mr. Henshaw	Harold Gould
Mrs. Henshaw	Betty Bresler
Jennifer	Liberty Williams
Lance	Fred Willard

670 **How to Follow the Campaign**
Political Spirit of '76 ABC
Program Type Children's Special
25 minutes. Premiere date: 10/24/76. An ABC News political special on the tradition, composition and nature of the campaign process in the United States.
Producer Sid Darion
Company ABC News
Host Steve Bell

671 **How to Follow the Election**
Political Spirit of '76 ABC
Program Type Children's Special
25 minutes. Premiere date: 10/31/76. An ABC News special on the history, meaning and importance of the Presidential election process.
Producer Sid Darion
Company ABC News
Host Steve Bell

672 **The Hudson Brothers Razzle Dazzle Show** CBS
Program Type Children's Series
30 minutes. Sundays. Premiere date: 9/7/74. Reruns began 9/12/76. Last show: 4/3/77. Repeat shows starring the Hudson Brothers.
Executive Producers Allan Blye, Chris Bearde
Producers Bob Arnott, Coslough Johnson, Stan Jacobson
Company A Blye-Bearde Production
Director Art Fisher
Writers George Burditt, Bob Einstein, David Panich, Ronny Graham, Chris Bearde, Allan Blye
Musical Director Jack Eskew
Choreographer Jaime Rogers
Stars Bill Hudson, Mark Hudson, Brett Hudson
Regulars Ronny Graham, Stephanie Edwards, Gary Owens, Katie McClure

673 **Human Rights—A Soviet-American Debate**
NBC News Special NBC
Program Type Public Affairs Special
90 minutes. Live coverage of a debate between Americans and Russians from Georgetown University, Washington, D.C. on the subject of human rights 6/12/77.
Executive Producer Gordon Manning
Producer Ray Lockhart
Company NBC News
Moderator Edwin Newman
Debaters The Rev. Theodore M. Hesburgh, Robert G. Kaiser, Prof. Alan M. Dershowitz/ Prof. Samuel Zivs, Prof. August Mishin, Ghenrih Borovik

674 **The Hunchback of Notre Dame**
NBC Monday Night at the Movies NBC
Program Type Dramatic Special
Two hours. Premiere date: 7/18/77. Dramatization of the classic novel by Victor Hugo about the hunchback bellringer of the Cathedral of Notre Dame in 15th-century Paris. Music by Wilfred Josephs sung by the Ambrosian Singers with

The Hunchback of Notre Dame
Continued
John McCarthy. Make-up by Maureen Winslade. Filmed in England.
Producer Cedric Messina
Company British Broadcasting Corporation
Director Alan Cooke
Writer Robert Muller
Conductor Marcus Dods
Choreographer Geraldine Stephenson
Costume Designer Dorothea Wallace
Scenic Designer Don Taylor
Script Editor Alan Shallcross

CAST

Archdeacon Claude Frollo .... Kenneth Haigh
Quasimodo .... Warren Clarke
Esmeralda .... Michelle Newell
Pierre .... Christopher Gable
Jehan .... David Rintoul
Phoebus .... Richard Morant
Fleur-de-Lys .... Henrietta Baynes
Madame Gondelaurier .... Ruth Goring
Clopin .... Tony Caunter
La Falourdel .... Liz Smith
Robin .... John Ratcliff
Cardinal .... Terence Bayler

675 **Hunter** CBS
Program Type Crime Drama Series
60 minutes. Fridays. Premiere date: 2/18/77. Last regular show: 4/22/77. Final show: 5/27/77. Mystery-adventure about a U.S. secret agent. Created by William Blinn. Music by Richard Shores.
Executive Producers Lee Rich, Philip Capice
Producer Christopher Morgan
Company Lorimar Productions, Inc.
Directors Various
Executive Story Consultant David Shaw
Story Editor George Bellak
Writers Various
Art Director Phil Barber

CAST

James Hunter .... James Franciscus
Marty Shaw .... Linda Evans

676 **Husbands and Wives** CBS
Program Type Comedy Special
60 minutes. Premiere date: 7/18/77. Comedy pilot about married people in a typical American suburb. Created by Hal Dresner and Joan Rivers. Music by Jack Elliott and Allyn Ferguson.
Executive Producers Edgar Rosenberg, Hal Dresner
Producer Don Van Atta
Company 20th Century-Fox Television in association with the CBS Television Network
Director Bill Persky
Writers Hal Dresner, Joan Rivers.

CAST

Murray Zuckerman .... Alex Rocco
Paula Zuckerman .... Cynthia Harris
Harry Bell .... Ed Barth
Joy Bell .... Suzanne Zenor
Lennie Bell .... Mark Lonow
Rita Bell .... Randee Heller
Ron Cutler .... Ron Rifkin
Helene Cutler .... Linda Miller
Dixon Carter Fielding .... Charles Siebert
Courtney Fielding .... Claudette Nevins

677 **I Am a Woman** PBS
Program Type Dramatic Special
60 minutes. Premiere date: 3/77. One-woman show using excerpts of material showing different personalities of women.
Producer Norman Campbell
Company Canadian Broadcasting Corporation
Director Norman Campbell
Production Designer Robert Lawson
Star Viveca Lindfors

I Never Sang For My Father *see* The ABC Sunday Night Movie

678 **I Regret Nothing** PBS
Program Type Documentary/Informational Special
80 minutes. Premiere date: 3/76. Repeat dates: 12/76 and 3/77. Biography of Edith Piaf filmed in black and white. Film includes songs sung by her, Charles Aznavour, Yves Montand and Les Compagnons de la Chanson.
Producer Michael Houldey
Company British Broadcasting Corporation
Director Michael Houldey
Cinematographer William Lubtchansky
Film Editor Allan Tyrer
Narrator Louis Jourdan

679 **I Want to Keep My Baby!**
The CBS Friday Night Movies CBS
Program Type TV Movie
Two hours. Premiere date: 11/19/76. Repeat date: 9/2/77. Drama of a pregnant teenager. Filmed on location in Denver, Colorado. Music by George Aliceson Tipton. "Child With a Child" music by Craig Lee, lyrics by Hermine Hilton; sung by Salli Terri.
Executive Producer Jerry Thorpe
Producer Joanna Lee
Company The CBS Television Network
Director Jerry Thorpe
Writer Joanna Lee
Art Director Ray Beal

CAST

Sue Ann Cunningham .... Mariel Hemingway
Donna Jo Martelli .... Susan Anspach
Ralph Martelli .... Jack Rader
Don De Reda .... Vince Begatta
Renee De Reda .... Dori Brenner
Rae Finer .... Rhea Pearlman

Chuck Ryan .... Jonathan Jones
Gregg .... Herb Williams
Miranda .... Lisa Pelikan
Andy .... John Megna

680 **I.F. Stone's Weekly**
Documentary Showcase PBS
Program Type Documentary/Informational Special
60 minutes. Premiere date: 11/5/76. Repeat date: 9/16/77. 1973 profile of I.F. Stone, the Washington political journalist. Program made possible by a grant from the Corporation for Public Broadcasting.
Producer Jerry Bruck, Jr.
Company WNYC-TV/New York
Director Jerry Bruck, Jr.
Cinematographer Jerry Bruck, Jr.
Film Editor Jerry Bruck, Jr.
Narrator Tom Wicher

I'm a Fool *see* Bernice Bobs Her Hair/I'm a Fool

681 **The Image Makers: The Environment of Arnold Newman** PBS
Program Type Documentary/Informational Special
30 minutes. Premiere date: 8/31/77. A look at the work of portrait photographer Arnold Newman. Program made possible by a grant from the Nebraska Educational Television Network.
Producer Gene Bunge
Company Nebraska Educational Television Network
Director Linda Elliott

The Importance of Being Ernest *see* PBS Movie Theater

682 **In and Out of Maine: The New People**
Americana PBS
Program Type Documentary/Informational Special
30 minutes. Premiere date: 6/24/77. Five families of young people talk about their new lives in rural surroundings after leaving urban homes and careers. Program made possible in part through a grant from the Maine Council for the Humanities and Public Policy.
Producer Eton Churchill
Company Maine Public Broadcasting Network
Cinematographer Michel Chalufour
Film Editor Michel Chalufour

683 **In Performance at Wolf Trap** PBS
Program Type Music/Dance Series
Times vary. Mondays. Premiere date: 10/14/74. Third season premiere: 9/20/76. Music/dance series from the Wolf Trap Park Farm for the Performing Arts in Arlington, Va. Programs shown during the 1976–77 season are: "Andre Kostelanetz—Nutcracker," "Bonnie Raitt and Mose Allison," "Cleo Laine and John Dankworth," "Dionne Warwick," "Galina and Valery Panov," "Kostelanetz and Menuhin," "La Traviata," "Mikhail Baryshnikov," "The New England Conservatory Ragtime Ensemble and the Katherine Dunham Dancers," "Preservation Hall Jazz Band," "Roberto Devereux," "Sarah Vaughan & Buddy Rich," "The Verdi Requiem," "The World Series of Jazz." (*See* individual titles for credits.) Series made possible by a grant from the Atlantic Richfield Company.

684 **In Search Of ...** Syndicated
Program Type Documentary/Informational Series
30 minutes. Weekly. Premiere date: 9/76. Documentary series dealing with mysterious subjects and phenomena, e.g. Atlantis, the Loch Ness monster, UFOs.
Executive Producer Alan Landsburg
Producer Bob Long
Company Alan Landsburg Productions
Distributor Bristol-Myers
Host/Narrator Leonard Nimoy

In Search of Noah's Ark *see* NBC Monday Night at the Movies

685 **In Search of the Real America** PBS
Program Type Educational/Cultural Series
30 minutes. Monthly. Premiere date: 2/15/77. Six-part series examining America's institutions, attitudes and future. Regular feature: rebuttal arguments by guest critics. Series made possible by grants from the Corporation for Public Broadcasting, the M. L. Annenberg Foundation, Smith Richardson Foundation, Scaife Family Charitable Trusts, Bethlehem Steel Corporation, American Telephone and Telegraph Company and the J.M. Foundation.
Executive Producer Austin Hoyt
Producer Elizabeth Deane
Company WGBH-TV Boston
Director Bruce Shah
Host Ben Wattenberg

686 **In the Glitter Palace**
The Big Event NBC
Program Type TV Movie
Two hours. Premiere date: 2/27/77. Drama of a

In the Glitter Palace *Continued*
lesbian accused of murder. Filmed in part on locations in Los Angeles. Music by John Parker.
Executive Producer Stanley Kallis
Producers Jerry Ludwig, Jay Daniel
Company Columbia Pictures Television in association with NBC-TV
Director Robert Butler
Writer Jerry Ludwig

CAST

Vince Halloran	Chad Everett
Ellen Lange	Barbara Hershey
Casey Walker	Diana Scarwid
Roy Danko	Anthony Zerbe
Raymond Travers	Howard Duff
Nathan Redstone	David Wayne
Grace Mayo	Tisha Sterling
Roger	Ron Rifkin
Judge Kendis	Salome Jens
Fred Ruggiero	Ron Masak
Daisy Dolon	Carole Cook

In the Heat of the Night *see* The CBS Wednesday Night Movies

687 **In the News** CBS
Program Type Children's Series
2 1/2 minutes each. Ten segments shown Saturday mornings; two Sunday mornings. Premiere date: 9/11/71. Sixth season premiere: 9/11/76. Topical news broadcasts for school-age children. Sunday segments are repeats. As of 5/21/77, metric measurements used.
Executive Producer Joel Heller
Producer Judy Reemtsma
Company CBS News
Writer Judy Reemtsma
Reporter/Narrator Christopher Glenn

688 **In the Shadow of the General** PBS
Program Type Documentary/Informational Special
30 minutes. Premiere date: 10/22/76. Repeat date: 3/24/77. The impact of a new power plant - the Gen. George M. Gavin Plant in Cheshire, Ohio - on the economy and life style of the surrounding rural communities. Program made possible by grants from the Ohio Educational Television Network Commission, the Central Educational Network and the Corporation for Public Broadcasting.
Executive Producer David B. Liroff
Producer Gregory Hill
Company WOUB-TV/Athens, Ohio
Director Gregory Hill
Cinematographer Barry Mowat

689 **INA U.S. Pro Indoor Tennis Championship** NBC
Program Type Sports Special
Two hours. Live coverage of the singles final of the INA U.S. Pro Indoor Tennis Championship from the Spectrum in Philadelphia 1/30/77.
Producer Dick Auerbach
Company NBC Sports
Director Ken Fouts
Commentators Bud Collins, John Newcombe

690 **Inauguration Ceremonies**
NBC News Special NBC
Program Type News Special
6 1/2 hours. Live coverage of the inauguration of Jimmy Carter as President of the United States 1/20/77.
Executive Producer Frank Jordan
Producers Lester M. Crystal, Paul Friedman
Company NBC News
Anchor Teams John Chancellor and David Brinkley/Tom Brokaw and Jane Pauley
Correspondents Carl Stern, Catherine Mackin, Linda Ellerbee, John Hart, Tom Pettit, Marilyn Berger, Bob Jamieson, Judy Woodruff, Douglas Kiker

691 **Inaugural Eve Gala Performance** CBS
Program Type Music/Comedy/Variety Special
2 1/2 hours. Premiere date: 1/19/77. Pre-inaugural salute to President-elect Jimmy Carter and Vice President-elect Walter F. Mondale from the John F. Kennedy Center for the Performing Arts in Washington, D.C.
Executive Producer James Lipton
Producer Bob Wynn
Company James Lipton Productions in association with Time-Life Television
Director Marty Pasetta
Writers James Lipton, Herb Sargent, Chevy Chase, Freddie Prinze and the writers of "All in the Family" and "Chico and the Man"
Musical Director Donn Trenner
Scenic Designer Bob Keene
Stars Hank Aaron, Donnie Ray Albert, Jack Albertson, Muhammad Ali, the Alvin Ailey American Dance Theatre, Armed Forces Color Guard, Dan Aykroyd, Warren Beatty, Leonard Bernstein, Elaine Bonazzi, Chevy Chase, Clamma Dale, Bette Davis, James Dickey, Redd Foxx, Aretha Franklin, Dobie Grey, Howard University Choir, Loretta Lynn, Shirley MacLaine, Elaine May, the National Symphony Orchestra, Paul Newman, Mike Nichols, Jack Nicholson, Freddie Prinze, Linda Ronstadt, Robert Shaw, Beverly Sills, Paul Simon, Jean Stapleton, U.S. Army Herald Trumpets, Benita Valente, Frederica

Von Stade, John Wayne, Nancy Williams, Joanne Woodward and the voice of Carroll O'Connor

692 **The Inauguration of Jimmy Carter** PBS

Program Type News Special
90 minutes. Live coverage (in the East) of the inauguration of Jimmy Carter as 39th President of the United States 1/20/77. Taped evening replay plus replay captioned for the hearing-impaired shown 1/22/77. Program made possible by grants from the Corporation for Public Broadcasting, the Ford Foundation and Public Television Stations.
Executive Producer Christie Basham
Company WETA-TV/Washington
Narrator Paul Duke

693 **Inauguration '77: Jimmy Carter Comes To Washington** ABC

Program Type News Special
Seven hours. Live coverage of events highlighted by the inauguration of Jimmy Carter as 39th President of the United States 1/20/77. 6 1/2 hours during the day (10 a.m.-4:30 p.m.) and 30 minutes at night (11:30 p.m.-12 midnight) covering the inaugural parties in progress.
Senior Producer Elliot Bernstein
Producer Jeff Gralnick
Company ABC News Special Events Unit
Director Marvin Schlenker
Anchors Harry Reasoner, Barbara Walters, Howard K. Smith
Reporters Frank Reynolds, Sam Donaldson, Tom Jarriel, Barrie Dunsmore, Ann Compton, Herbert Kaplow, Don Farmer, Roger Peterson, Bill Downes, Jim Kincaid, Margaret Osmer, Charles Gibson
Guest Commentator Art Buchwald

694 **The Incredible Machine**

National Geographic Special PBS
Program Type Science/Nature Special
60 minutes. Premiere date: 10/28/75. Repeat date: 3/29/77. A look at the inner workings of the human body. Music by Billy Goldenberg. Program funded by a grant from Gulf Oil Corporation and presented by WQED-TV/Pittsburgh.
Executive Producer Dennis B. Kane
Production Executive Nicholas Clapp
Producer Irwin Rosten
Company National Geographic Society in association with Wolper Productions
Director Irwin Rosten
Writer Irwin Rosten
Cinematographers Erik Daarstad, John Morrill, Lennart Nilsson, Rokuru Hayashi
Film Editor Hyman Kaufman
Host E. G. Marshall
Narrator E. G. Marshall

695 **Indianapolis "500"** ABC

Program Type Sports Special
Two hours. 5/29/77. Same-day coverage of the Indianapolis "500" from the Indianapolis Motor Speedway.
Executive Producer Roone Arledge
Producer Chuck Howard
Company ABC Sports
Directors Chet Forte, Larry Kamm
Announcers jim McKay, Chris Schenkel
Expert Commentators Jackie Stewart, Bill Flemming, Chris Economaki

696 **Indianapolis "500" Time Trials** ABC

Program Type Sports Special
60 minutes. Live coverage of the final day of time trials for the Indianapolis "500" ("Bumping Day") 5/22/77.
Executive Producer Roone Arledge
Producer Bob Goodrich
Company ABC Sports
Director Larry Kamm
Announcer Jim McKay
Expert Commentators Chris Economaki, Sam Posey

697 **Infinity Factory** PBS

Program Type Children's Series
30 minutes. Mondays and Wednesdays. Premiere date: 9/20/76. Twice-weekly magazine-format show designed to help (primarily black and Latino) children 8-11 years old learn mathematics. Regular features: "Scoops' Place," "City Flats" (filmed at Julio's Panaderia in East Los Angeles) and "Brownstone" plus math-in-the-street interviews, animated cartoons and filmed documentaries. "Scoops' Place" produced by Gregory Brown and Michael Johnson of Family of Man Films, Ltd. in New York; "City Flats" produced by Rosemary Alderette, Gilbert Duron III and Adolfo Vargas in Los Angeles. Music by Webster Lewis and Walter Bland. Series made possible by a grant from the U.S. Office of Education under the Emergency School Aid Act plus additional funding from the Carnegie Corporation of New York, John and Mary R. Markle Foundation, JDR 3rd Fund, National Science Foundation and Alfred P. Sloan Foundation.
Executive Producer Jesus Salvador Trevino
Producers Terri Payne Francis, d. b. Roderick
Company Education Development Center, Inc.
Director Allan Muir
Senior Advisor Jerrold Zacharias

698 **Inner Tennis** PBS
Program Type Limited Sports Series
30 minutes. Mondays. Premiere date: 5/16/76. Program repeats: 8/8/77. Six-part series of tennis lessons based on "The Inner Game of Tennis" written by Tim Gallwey. Funded by a grant from GAF Corporation.
Producer Mark Waxman
Company KCET-TV/Los Angeles
Director Jerry Hughes
Host/Instructor Tim Gallwey

699 **Inside CBS News**
CBS News Special CBS
Program Type Public Affairs Special
A series of broadcasts allowing the public access to the decision-makers at CBS News and produced by CBS affiliated stations.

Part III
60 minutes. Premiere date: 12/16/76 (on national television). Originally produced and broadcast by KOOL-TV/Phoenix. Third program in the series.
Company CBS News
Moderator Homer Lane

Part IV
60 minutes. Premiere date: 5/7/77 (on national television). Originally produced and broadcast by WBTV-TV/Charlotte, N.C. Fourth program in the series.
Company CBS News
Moderator John Wilson

700 **Inside O.U.T.** NBC
Program Type Comedy Special
30 minutes. Premiere date: 3/22/71. Repeat date: 5/9/77. Comedy pilot about a secret agent of O.U.T. (Office of Unusual Tactics.) Created by Lawrence J. Cohen and Fred Freeman.
Executive Producer Harry Ackerman
Producers Lawrence J. Cohen, Fred Freeman
Company Screen Gems Production
Director Reza Badiyi
Writers Lawrence J. Cohen, Fred Freeman

CAST
Pat Bouillon .... Farrah Fawcett (Farrah Fawcett-Majors)
Ron Hart .... Bill Daily
Finance Director .... Edward Andrews
Agent Winston .... Alan Oppenheimer
Agent Dandy .... Mike Henry

701 **Inside the Cuckoo's Nest** PBS
Program Type Documentary/Informational Special
90 minutes. Premiere date: 9/8/77. An in-depth look at the 90-year old Oregon State Hospital in Salem, Oregon that provided the background for the film "One Flew Over the Cuckoo's Nest." Clips from the film are juxtaposed with scenes of hospital routine. Program made possible by grants from the National Institute of Mental Health, the Oregon Committee for the Humanities and the Maurice Falk Fund.
Executive Producer Zev Putterman
Producers Martin Fink, Paul Kaufman
Company KQED-TV/San Francisco
Director Robert N. Zagone

702 **Insight** Syndicated
Program Type Religious/Cultural Series
30 minutes. Weekly. Sixteenth year of weekly dramatic shows.
Executive Producer Rev. Ellwood E. Kieser
Producer Michael Rhodes
Company Paulist Productions
Directors Various
Writers Various

703 **Instant Family**
Comedy Time NBC
Program Type Comedy Special
30 minutes. Premiere date: 7/28/77. Comedy pilot about two bachelor fathers with differing views of child-rearing sharing the same home.
Executive Producer Lila Garrett
Company Lila Garrett Productions
Director Russ Petranto
Writers Mort Lachman, Ray Brenner

CAST
Clifford Beane .... William Daniels
Frank Boyle .... Lou Criscuolo
Robbie Boyle .... Brad Wilkin
Kevin Beane .... Jeff Harlan
Ernie Boyle .... Robbie Rist
Lisa Boyle .... Wendy Fredericks
Alexander Beane .... Sparky Marcus
Steve Fisher .... Jonathan Goldsmith

704 **International Animation Festival** PBS
Program Type Animated Film Series
30 minutes. Tuesdays. Premiere date: 4/1/75. Second season premiere: 1/17/76. Series repeats began 5/17/77. 13-weeks of animated films from around the world emphasizing the work of the Zagreb studies of Yugoslavia and the Canadian National Film Board. Funded by the Corporation for Public Broadcasting, the Ford Foundation and Public Television Stations.
Producers Various
Company KQED-TV/San Francisco
Host Jean Marsh

705 **International Rugby: Ireland vs. England** PBS
Program Type Sports Special
90 minutes. Premiere date: 2/6/77. Ireland vs. England in the 1976 International Rugby Title taped at Lansdowne Stadium in Dublin, Ireland 2/5/77. Program made possible by grants from Aer Lingus and Guiness Breweries.
Executive Producer Greg Harney
Company WGBH-TV/Boston
Announcer Fred Cogley
Commentator Bud Collins

706 **International Soccer—West Germany vs. Northern Ireland** PBS
Program Type Sports Special
60 minutes. Premiere date: 5/8/77. Taped coverage of a soccer game between West Germany and Northern Ireland held at Mungersdorfer Stadium in Cologne, West Germany 4/27/77.
Producer Jim Scalem
Company KQED-TV/San Francisco
Director Jim Scalem
Announcer Leo Weinstein

707 **International Tennis Tournament** CBS
Program Type Sports Special
Live and taped coverage of the fifth International Tennis Tournament from Mt. Washington Valley in North Conway, N.H. 8/6/77 and 8/7/77.
Producer Perry Smith
Company CBS Television Network Sports
Director Sandy Grossman
Commentators Tony Trabert, Rick Barry

708 **Iowa Girls' High School Basketball Championship** PBS
Program Type Sports Special
Two hours. Live coverage of the 58th annual state tournament from Veterans Memorial Auditorium in Des Moines, Iowa 3/20/77. Program made possible in part by a grant from the Land O' Lakes Corporation.
Producer Joseph P. Zesbaugh
Company KAET-TV/Phoenix
Director Dick Siley
Announcers Frosty Mitchell, Jim Zabel

709 **Irwin Allen's Production of Fire**
The Big Event NBC
Program Type TV Movie
Two hours. Premiere date: 5/8/77. Drama about a forest fire threatening a mountain community. Based on a story by Norman Katkov. Music by Richard La Salle. Filmed on location in Oregon. Special effects by Cliff Wenger.
Executive Producer Irwin Allen
Company An Irwin Allen Production in association with Warner Bros. Television and NBC-TV
Director Earl Bellamy
Writers Norman Katkov, Arthur Weiss
Art Director Ward Preston

CAST

Sam Brisbane .... Ernest Borgnine
Martha Wagner .... Vera Miles
Peggy Wilson .... Patty Duke Astin
Alex Wilson .... Alex Cord
Harriet Malone .... Donna Mills
Doc Bennett .... Lloyd Nolan
Larry Durant .... Neville Brand
Fleming .... Ty Hardin
Dan Harter .... Gene Evans
Judy .... Michelle Stacy
Frank .... Erik Estrada

710 **. . . Is a Candidate, Too** PBS
Program Type Public Affairs Series
30 minutes. Premiere date: 10/8/76. Twelve reports on minority party candidates for the U.S. presidency shown prior to the election. Series made possible by a grant from the Corporation for Public Broadcasting.
Producer John Larkin
Company WETA-TV/Washington, D.C. and WNET-TV/New York
Host Paul Duke

711 **Isis**
The Shazam!/Isis Hour CBS
Program Type Children's Series
30 minutes. Saturday mornings. Premiere date: 9/6/75. Second season premiere: 9/11/76. Live-action series about a high school science teacher/crime fighter with extraordinary powers.
Executive Producers Lou Scheimer, Norm Prescott
Producer Arthur H. Nadel
Company Filmation Associates
Directors Various
Writers Various

CAST

Isis/Andrea Thomas .... JoAnna Cameron
Rick Mason .... Brian Cutler
Rennie .... Ronalda Douglas

712 **Israel: A Search for Faith**
James Michener's World PBS
Program Type Documentary/Informational Special
60 minutes. Premiere date: 6/21/77. First in a series of four specials about different places Michener has written about. Program presented by KCET-TV/Los Angeles and made possible by a grant from Mrs. Paul's Kitchens, Inc.
Producer Albert Waller
Co-Producer Ken Golden

Israel: A Search for Faith *Continued*
Company Reader's Digest Association, Inc.
Director Albert Waller
Writer Albert Waller
Host James Michener

713 **The Israel Museum: A Living Legacy**
Eternal Light NBC
Program Type Religious/Cultural Special
60 minutes. Premiere date: 5/28/72. Repeat date: 7/24/77. Documentary taped at the Israel Museum in Jerusalem and at archaeological sites in Israel showing the spectrum of Jewish life and experience in that country.
Executive Producer Doris Ann
Producer Martin Hoade
Company NBC Television Religious Programs Unit in association with the Jewish Theological Seminary of America
Director Martin Hoade
Writer Marc Siegel
Narrator Norman Rose

714 **Issues and Answers** ABC
Program Type Public Affairs Series
30 minutes. Sundays. Premiere date: 10/60. 17th season premiere: 9/19/76. Live interview show with newsmakers; generally from Washington. Six special 60-minute shows preceding the 1976 election; several special shows from southern Africa and the Middle East.
Producer Peggy Whedon
Company ABC News Public Affairs
Director W. P. Fowler
Chief Correspondent Bob Clark

715 **It Must Be Love, ('Cause I Feel So Dumb!)**
ABC Afterschool Specials ABC
Program Type Children's Special
60 minutes. Premiere date: 10/8/75. Repeat date: 1/12/77. Young people's drama about love, filmed on location on Manhattan's Upper West Side.
Producers Arthur Barron, Evelyn Barron
Company Verite Productions
Director Arthur Barron
Writer Arthur Barron
Costume Designer Judith W. Pressburger

CAST

Eric .... Alfred Lutter
Cathy .... Denby Olcott
Lisa .... Vicki Dawson
Father .... Michael Miller
Mother .... Kay Frye
LeRoy .... P. R. Paul

716 **Italian Open** NBC
Program Type Sports Special
Tape delayed satellite coverage of the semi-final and final matches of the Italian Open tennis championship from Rome 5/21/77 and 5/22/77.
Producer Dick Auerbach
Company NBC Sports
Director Ted Nathanson
Commentators Bud Collins, John Newcombe

717 **It's a Brand New World**
Special Treat NBC
Program Type Animated Film Special
60 minutes. Premiere date: 3/8/77. Repeat date: 4/9/77. Animated musical based on the Biblical stories of Noah and Samson. Original music and lyrics by Al Elias, Andy Badale and Murray Semos. "Noah's Ark" written by Romeo Muller and Max Wilk; "Young Samson" by Romeo Muller.
Executive Producer Eddie Elias
Producer Al Elias
Company An Elias Production
Writers Romeo Muller, Max Wilk
Animation Directors Ronald Fritz, Dan Hunn
Animators Martin Taras, Lucifer B. Guarnier, Paul Sparagano, Charles Harriton
Dialogue Director Jon Surgal

VOICES

Teacher/Noah .... Joe Silver
Elijah/Samson .... Malcolm Dodd
Aaron .... Dennis Cooley
Jezebel .... Boni Enten
Barnabas .... George Hirsch
Samson's Mother .... Charmaine Harma
Additional Voices Sylvester Fields, Hilda Harris, Maeretha Stewart

718 **It's a Lovely Day Tomorrow**
Piccadilly Circus PBS
Program Type Dramatic Special
90 minutes. Premiere date: 2/16/76. Repeat date: 7/31/77. Docu-drama about London life during the blitz. Set in the Bethnal Green underground station. Program made possible by a grant from Mobil Oil Corporation. Presented by WGBH-TV/Boston; Joan Sullivan, producer.
Producer John Goldschmidt
Company ATV (England)
Writer Bernard Kops
Host Jeremy Brett

CAST

Jenny .... Cheryl Kennedy
John .... Ralph Mort
Maureen .... Marjorie Yates

It's a Mad, Mad, Mad, Mad World *see* The CBS Friday Night Movies

719 It's a Whole New Thing on CBS CBS

Program Type Music/Comedy/Variety Special
15 minutes. Premiere date: 9/8/77. Special preview of ten new series to be seen on CBS during the 1977–78 season.
Producer Harvey Kornspan
Director Ken Luber
Writer Ken Luber
Film Editor Ken Luber
Hosts Gregory Harrison, Heather Menzies, Donald Moffat

720 It's Anybody's Guess NBC

Program Type Game/Audience Participation Series
30 minutes. Mondays-Fridays. Premiere date: 6/13/77. Contestants trying to guess whether a studio panel will come up with a predetermined reply to questions.
Executive Producer Stu Billett
Producer Steve Feke
Company Stefan Hatos-Monty Hall Production
Director Joseph Behar
Art Director Scott Ritenour
Host Monty Hall

721 It's Arbor Day, Charlie Brown CBS

Program Type Animated Film Special
30 minutes. Premiere date: 3/8/76. Repeat date: 3/14/77. Created by Charles M. Schulz. Music by Vince Guaraldi.
Executive Producer Lee Mendelson
Producer Bill Melendez
Company A Lee Mendelson-Bill Melendez Production in cooperation with United Feature Syndicate, Inc., and Charles M. Schulz Creative Associates
Director Phil Roman
Musical Director Vince Guaraldi

VOICES

Charlie Brown .... Dylan Beach
Lucy .... Sarah Beach
Sally .... Gail M. Davis
Peppermint Patty .... Stuart Brotman
Schroeder .... Greg Felton
Linus .... Liam Martin
Re-Run .... Vinnie Dow
Frieda .... Michelle Muller

722 It's Hard To Be a Penguin PBS

Program Type Documentary/Informational Special
50 minutes. Premiere date: 3/76. Repeat date: 12/76. A look at the lifestyle of the penguin during its four-month breeding cycle. Filmed in Antarctica.
Producer R. H. Materna
Company Materna Productions
Director R. H. Materna
Writer Don Davis
Cinematographer R. H. Materna
Narrator Don Davis

723 It's the Easter Beagle, Charlie Brown CBS

Program Type Animated Film Special
30 minutes. Premiere date: 4/9/74. Repeat date: 4/4/77. Created by Charles M. Schulz. Music composed by Vince Guaraldi.
Executive Producer Lee Mendelson
Producer Bill Melendez
Company Lee Mendelson-Bill Melendez Production in cooperation with United Feature Syndicate, Inc. and Charles M. Schulz Creative Associates
Director Phil Roman
Writer Charles M. Schulz
Musical Director Vince Guaraldi
Music Supervisor John Scott Trotter

VOICES

Charlie Brown .... Todd Barbee
Lucy .... Melanie Kohn
Linus .... Stephen Shea
Peppermint Patty .... Linda Ercoli
Sally .... Lynn Mortensen
Marcie .... Jimmy Ahrens

724 It's the Great Pumpkin, Charlie Brown CBS

Program Type Animated Film Special
30 minutes. Premiere date: 10/27/66. Repeat date 10/23/76. Halloween special created by Charles M. Schultz. Music composed by Vince Guaraldi; arranged by John Scott Trotter.
Executive Producer Lee Mendelson
Company A Lee Mendelson-Bill Melendez Production in cooperation with United Feature Syndicate, Inc.
Director Bill Melendez
Writer Charles M. Schulz
Musical Director Vince Guaraldi

VOICES

Charlie Brown .... Peter Robbins
Lucy .... Sally Dryer
Linus .... Christopher Shea
Sally .... Cathy Steinberg

Ivan the Terrible *see* PBS Movie Theater

725 Jabberjaw ABC

Program Type Animated Film Series
30 minutes. Saturday mornings. Premiere date: 9/11/76. Comedy-adventure series set in an underwater civilization in 2021 A.D. about a lovable shark who is the mascot of four teenagers. Created by Joe Ruby and Ken Spears.
Executive Producers Joseph Barbera, William Hanna
Producer Iwao Takamoto

Jabberjaw *Continued*
Company Hanna-Barbera Productions, Inc.
Story Editor Ray Parker
Writers George Atkins, Haskell Barkin, John Bates, Larz Bourne, Tom Dagenais, Robert Fisher
Animation Director Charles A. Nichols
Voices Tommy Cook, Regis J. Cordic, Ron Feinberg, Barry Gordon, Gay Hartwig, Hettie Lynn Hurtes, Casey Kasem, Keye Luke, Julie McWhirter, Don Messick, Pat Parris, Vic Perrin, Barney Phillips, Hal Smith, John Stephenson, Janet Waldo, Lennie Weinrib, Frank Welker

726 **Jack: A Flash Fantasy**
Opera Theater PBS
Program Type Music/Dance Special
60 minutes. Premiere date: 7/26/77. First rock opera musical-variety show commissioned for television. Music by Peter Mann. Program presented by WNET-TV/New York and made possible by grants from the Corporation for Public Television, the Ford Foundation and Public Television Stations.
Executive Producer Neil Sutherland
Coordinating Producers David Griffiths, Sam Paul
Producers Rob Iscove, Peter Mann
Company Canadian Broadcasting Corporation
Director Rob Iscove
Writers Rob Iscove, Peter Mann
Musical Director Rick Wilkins
Choreographer Rob Iscove
Costume Designer Csilla Marki
Scenic Designer Arthur Herriot

CAST

Jack (Spirit)	Jeff Hyslop
Jill (Spirit)	Laurie Hood
Jack of Hearts	Victor Garber
Jill of Hearts	Gilda Radner
Jack of Spades	William Daniel Grey
Jill of Spades	Vera Biloshisky
Jack of Diamonds	Alan Thicke
Jill of Diamonds	Patricia Gaul
Jack of Clubs	Jerry Sroka
Jill of Clubs	Valri Bromfield

727 **The Jack Benny Show** CBS
Program Type Comedy Series
30 minutes. Tuesdays. Four repeats of shows that originally ran between 1961 and 1964. Repeats began 8/2/77. Last show: 8/30/77. In black and white.
Executive Producer Irving A. Fein
Producer Fred de Cordova
Director Fred de Cordova
Writers Sam Perrin, George Balzer, Al Gordon, Hal Goldman
Star Jack Benny
Regulars Eddie (Rochester) Anderson, Don Wilson

728 **Jack Nicklaus & Friends** ABC
Program Type Sports Special
60 minutes. Premiere date: 4/3/77. Jack Nicklaus, Ben Crenshaw, Tom Weiskopf and Hubert Green playing golf at New St. Andrews golf course in Togichi, Japan co-designed by Jack Nicklaus.
Executive Producer Roone Arledge
Producer Bob Goodrich
Company ABC Sports
Director John Wilcox
Host Jim McKay

729 **Jackie Gleason Inverrary Classic** CBS
Program Type Sports Special
Coverage of the Jackie Gleason Inverrary Classic from the Inverrary Golf & Country Club in Lauderhill, Fla. 2/26/77 and 2/27/77.
Producer Frank Chirkinian
Company CBS Television Network Sports
Directors Bob Dailey, Frank Chirkinian
Commentators Vin Scully, Pat Summerall, Jack Whitaker, Ben Wright, Frank Glieber, Ken Venturi

730 **The Jacksons** CBS
Program Type Music/Comedy/Variety Series
30 minutes. Wednesdays. Premiere date: 1/26/77. Last show: 3/23/77. Musical/variety show. Closing theme: "I'll Be There." Successor to summer show seen between 6/16/76–7/7/76.
Executive Producers Joe Jackson, Richard Arons
Producer Bill Davis
Co-Producers Bonnie Burns, Jim Mulligan
Company Jackson TV Productions
Director Bill Davis
Head Writer Jim Mulligan
Writers Wayne Kline, Biff Manard, David H. Smilow, James W. Tisdale
Musical Director Rick Wilkins
Choreographers Anita Mann, The Jacksons
Costume Designer Warden Neil
Art Director Bill Camden
Creative Consultant Ray Jessel
Stars Michael Jackson, Marlon Jackson, Randy Jackson, Jackie Jackson, Tito Jackson, Rebie Jackson, LaToya Jackson, Janet Jackson

731 **Jade Snow**
Ourstory PBS
Program Type Dramatic Special
30 minutes. Premiere date: 5/10/76. Repeat date: 12/17/76. Dramatization of the early years of ceramicist/author Jade Snow Wong in San

Francisco's Chinatown in the 1920s. Based on her book "Fifth Chinese Daughter." Funded by a grant from the National Endowment for the Humanities.
Executive Producer Don Fouser
Producer Nola Safro
Company WNET-TV/New York
Director Ron Finley
Writer Stephen Jennings
Costume Designer John Boxer
Host Bill Moyers

CAST

Jade Snow Wong	Freda Foh Shen
Father	James Hong
Mother	Mary Mon Toy
Jade Snow (age 5)	Jodi Wu
Jade Snow (age 11)	Amy Mah
Joe	Calvin Jung
Peg Milligan	Claudette Sutherland
Al Milligan	Joe Ponazecki
Nancy Milligan	Denby Olcott
Richie Milligan	Douglas Grober
Uncle Jan	Conrad Yama
Blessing (age 14)	Don Wang
Admiral Kelly	Vincent O'Brien

732 **James Michael Curley: He Did It For a Friend**
Americana PBS
Program Type Documentary/Informational Special
30 minutes. Premiere date: 8/27/76 (with title "He Did It For a Friend: Boston Remembers James Michael Curley.") Repeat date: 2/18/77 (as "Americana" special). A recollection of Boston politician James Michael Curley.
Producer Nancy Porter
Company WGBH-TV/Boston
Directors Nancy Porter, Alan G. Raymond
Writer Alan G. Raymond

733 **James Michener's World** PBS
Program Type Documentary/Informational Special
60 minutes. A series of four specials of which the first aired during the 1976–77 season: "Israel: A Search for Faith." (*See* title for credits.)

Janis *see* NBC Night at the Movies

734 **Jeanne Wolf With . . .** PBS
Program Type Educational/Cultural Series
30 minutes. Thursdays. Third season premiere: 10/14/76. 17-part series of on-location interviews with celebrities in many fields. Series made possible by grants from the Ben Tobin Foundation and Hillcrest Corporation.
Executive Producer Shep Morgan
Producer Jeanne Wolf
Company WPBT-TV/Miami
Director Tom Donaldson
Host/Interviewer Jeanne Wolf

735 **The Jeffersons** CBS
Program Type Comedy Series
30 minutes. Saturdays/Wednesdays (as of 11/10/76)/Mondays (as of 1/17/77). Premiere date: 1/18/75. Third season premiere: 9/25/76. Spin-off from "All in the Family." Created by Don Nicholl, Michael Ross and Bernie West; developed by Norman Lear. Theme song "Movin' On Up" by Jeff Barry and Ja'net Dubois. Self-made success (owner of dry cleaning stores) and family on Manhattan's fashionable East Side.
Producers Don Nicholl, Michael Ross, Bernie West
Company T.A.T. Communications Company in association with NRW Productions
Director Jack Shea
Story Editors Lloyd Turner, Gordon Mitchell, Mike Milligan, Jay Moriarty
Writers Various

CAST

Louise Jefferson	Isabel Sanford
George Jefferson	Sherman Hemsley
Lionel Jefferson	Damon Evans
Helen Willis	Roxie Roker
Tom Willis	Franklin Cover
Mother Jefferson	Zara Cully
Jenny Willis	Berlinda Tolbert
Harry Bentley	Paul Benedict
Florence Johnson	Marla Gibbs
Ralph (Doorman)	Ned Wertimer

Jenny *see* The ABC Friday Night Movie

Jeremiah Johnson *see* The ABC Sunday Night Movie/NBC Night at the Movies

736 **Jerusalem: A Delicate Balance** PBS
Program Type Documentary/Informational Special
90 minutes. Premiere date: 6/7/77. An in-depth look at the troubled situation in Jerusalem plus a face-to-face debate between Israeli and Arab representatives. Program made possible by a grant from the Corporation for Public Broadcasting.
Producer Clete Roberts
Company A co-production of KCET-TV/Los Angeles and the British Broadcasting Corporation
Writer Clete Roberts
Reporter Clete Roberts

737 **Jerusalem Symphony** CBS
Program Type Religious/Cultural Special
60 minutes. Premiere date: 4/3/77. Premiere performance of the "Jerusalem Symphony" composed by Ezra Laderman and performed by the Jerusalem Symphony Orchestra in Jerusalem.
Executive Producer Pamela Ilott
Producer Pamela Ilott
Company CBS News Religious Broadcast
Conductor Alfredo Antonini
Host Abraham Kaplan

738 **Jerusalem: Walls of Witness** CBS
Program Type Religious/Cultural Special
60 minutes. Premiere date: 10/3/76. An examination of recent archaeological discoveries in Jerusalem.
Executive Producer Pamela Ilott
Producer Joseph Clement
Company CBS News Religious Broadcast
Guests Dan Bahat, Dr. Megan Broshi, Dr. Nohmán Avigad, Dr. Yael Israeli

Jesus Christ Superstar *see* NBC Monday Night at the Movies

739 **Jesus of Nazareth**
The Big Event NBC
Program Type Dramatic Special
6 hours 37 minutes. Premiere dates: 4/3/77 and 4/10/77. Dramatization of the life of Jesus. Music by Maurice Jarre performed by the National Philharmonic Orchestra. Filmed in part in Tunisia and Morocco.
Executive Producer Bernard J. Kingham
Producer Vincenzo Labella
Company An ITC-RAI Production
Director Franco Zeffirelli
Writers Anthony Burgess, Suso Cecchi d'Amico, Franco Zeffirelli
Conductor Maurice Jarre
Choreographer Alberto Testa (for Salome's Dance)
Costume Designers Marcel Escoffier, Enrico Sabbatini
Art Director Gianni Quaranta
Scenic Designer Francesco Fedeli

CAST

Jesus .... Robert Powell
Mary Magdalene .... Anne Bancroft
The Centurion .... Ernest Borgnine
The Adulteress .... Claudia Cardinale
Herodias .... Valentina Cortese
Simon Peter .... James Farentino
Balthasar .... James Earl Jones
Barabbas .... Stacy Keach
Quintilius .... Tony Lo Bianco
Joseph of Arimathea .... James Mason
Judas .... Ian McShane
Nicodemus .... Laurence Olivier
Melchior .... Donald Pleasence
Herod Antipas .... Christopher Plummer
Caiaphas .... Anthony Quinn
Gaspar .... Fernando Rey
Simeon .... Ralph Richardson
Pontius Pilate .... Rod Steiger
Herod the Great .... Peter Ustinov
John the Baptist .... Michael York
The Virgin Mary .... Olivia Hussey
Rabbi Yehuda .... Cyril Cusack
Zerah .... Ian Holm
Joseph .... Yorgo Voyagis
Amos .... Ian Bannen
Anna .... Regina Bianchi
Elizabeth .... Marina Berti
Joel .... Oliver Tobias
Martha .... Maria Carta
Habbukuk .... Lee Montague
The Blind Man .... Renato Rascel
Saturninus .... Norman Bowler
Proculus .... Robert Beatty
Naso .... John Phillips
Jotham .... Ken Jones
Abigail .... Nancy Nevinson
Abel .... Renato Terra
Enoch .... Roy Holder
Adam .... Jonathan Adams
Circumsicion Priest .... Christopher Reich
Jesus at 12 years .... Lorenzo Monet
Daniel .... Robert Davey
Saul .... Oliver Smith
Hosias .... George Camiller
Simon the Zealot .... Murray Salem
Andrew .... Tony Vogel
Salome .... Isabel Mestres
Eliphaz .... Michael Cronin
Jonas .... Forbes Collins
Philip .... Steve Gardner
John the Evangelist .... John Duttine
Nahum .... Michael Haughey
Obsessed Boy .... Keith Skinner
Obsessed Boy's Father .... Cyril Shaps
James .... Jonathan Muller
Malachi .... John Tordoff
Matthew .... Keith Washington
James II .... Sergio Nicolai
Ircanus .... Antonello Campodifiori
Jairus .... Renato Montalbano
Thomas .... Bruce Liddington
Thaddeus .... Mimmo Crao
Elihu .... Derek Godfrey

740 **Joe Garagiola Tucson Open** NBC
Program Type Sports Special
Live coverage of the final rounds of the Tucson Open from the Tucson National Golf Club 1/15/77 and 1/16/77.
Producer Larry Cirillo
Company NBC Sports
Director Harry Coyle
Host Joe Garagiola
Anchors Jim Simpson, Cary Middlecoff
Commentators John Brodie, Jay Randolph, Fran Tarkenton, Bruce Devlin

741 **John Berryman: I Don't Think I Will Sing Any More Just Now** PBS
Program Type Documentary/Informational Special
30 minutes. Premiere date: 9/1/76. Repeat date: 5/4/77. A documentary on the life and work of poet John Berryman. Program made possible in part by a grant from the Corporation for Public Broadcasting. Presented by KTCA-TV/St. Paul, Minn.
Producer Carol Johnsen
Company Univ. of Minnesota Dept. of University Relations
Cinematographer Paul Eide
Narrator Allen Hamilton

742 **The John Davidson Christmas Show**
All-Specials Night NBC
Program Type Music/Comedy/Variety Special
60 minutes. Premiere date: 12/15/76. Christmas family special taped on location at the Davidson ranch in Hidden Hills, Calif. Special musical material by Bill Lee and Jack Elliott. Vocal arrangements by Allan Davies.
Executive Producers Dick Clark, Alan Bernard
Producer Bill Lee
Company Hidden Hills Production in association with Dick Clark Teleshows, Inc.
Director Norman Campbell
Writers Phil Hahn, Jonnie Johns
Conductors Jack Elliott, Allyn Ferguson
Choreographer Ron Poindexter
Art Director Ray Klausen
Star John Davidson
Guests The Davidson Family, the Lennon Sisters and their families

743 **John Denver Rocky Mountain Christmas** ABC
Program Type Music/Comedy/Variety Special
60 minutes. Premiere date: 12/10/75. Repeat date: 12/14/76. Holiday special filmed in Aspen, Colorado.
Executive Producer Jerry Weintraub
Producers Al Rogers, Rich Eustis
Company A Jon-Jer Production
Director Bill Davis
Writers Jim Mulligan, April Kelly, Tom Chapman, Dave O'Malley, Steve Martin, Rich Eustis, Al Rogers
Art Director Ken Johnson
Star John Denver
Guest Stars Valerie Harper, Olivia Newton-John, Steve Martin

744 **The John Denver Special** ABC
Program Type Music/Comedy/Variety Special
60 minutes. Premiere date: 11/17/76. Music/variety special taped in part at the Universal Amphitheater in Hollywood. Special musical material by Dick De Benedictis and Bill Dyer.
Executive Producer Jerry Weintraub
Producers Rich Eustis, Al Rogers
Co-Producer Harry Waterson
Company Jon-Jer Production
Director Bill Davis
Writers Marty Farrell, Ray Jessel, Rich Eustis, Al Rogers
Musical Director Milt Okin
Conductors Eddie Karam, Lee Holdridge
Choreographer Danny Daniels
Costume Designers Bill Belew, Anna Zapp
Star John Denver
Special Guest Star Joanne Woodward
Guest Stars Dennis Weaver, the Starland Vocal Band

745 **John Denver—Thank God I'm a Country Boy** ABC
Program Type Music/Comedy/Variety Special
60 minutes. Premiere date: 3/2/77. Variety special highlighting John Denver's country background. Musical routines by Ray Charles. "Red Ball Express" animation by Steven Smith.
Executive Producer Jerry Weintraub
Producers Rich Eustis, Al Rogers
Company Jon-Jer Productions, Inc.
Director Walter C. Miller
Writers Rich Eustis, Al Rogers
Conductors Eddie Karam, Lee Holdridge
Costume Designer Bill Belew
Art Director Ken Johnson
Star John Denver
Guest Stars Glen Campbell, Roger Miller, Mary Kay Place
Special Guest Star Johnny Cash

746 **John Henry Faulk: Conversations Down On the Farm** PBS
Program Type Documentary/Informational Special
30 minutes. Premiere date: 9/3/76. Repeat date: 2/20/77. John Henry Faulk in conversation with John Davenport. Program made possible in part by a grant from the Association for Community Television.
Producer Robert Cozens
Company KUHT-TV/Houston

747 **Johnny Cash Christmas Special** CBS
Program Type Music/Comedy/Variety Special
60 minutes. Premiere date: 12/6/76. Christmas special taped at the Cash family farm in Bon Aqua, Tenn. and the Cash home in Hendersonville, Tenn.
Producer Joseph Cates
Company Joseph Cates Company, Inc.
Director Walter C. Miller

Johnny Cash Christmas Special
Continued
Writers Chet Hagan, Frank Slocum, Larry Markes
Musical Director Bill Walker
Art Director Don Shirley
Star Johnny Cash
Special Guest Stars Roy Clark, Tony Orlando, the Rev. Billy Graham
Guests June Carter Cash, the Carter Family, Barbara Mandrell, Merle Travis, Tommy Cash

748 **Johnny, We Hardly Knew Ye**
All-Specials Night NBC
Program Type Dramatic Special
Two hours. Premiere date: 1/27/77. A dramatization of John F. Kennedy's first primary election in 1946. Based in part on the book by Kenneth P. O'Donnell and David F. Powers with Joe McCarthy. Music by Garry Sherman. Filmed on Location in Bridgeport, Conn.
Executive Producer David Susskind
Co-Producer Lionel Chetwynd
Company A Talent Associates, Ltd. Production in association with Jamel Productions, Inc.
Director Gilbert Cates
Writer Lionel Chetwynd
Conductor Garry Sherman
Costume Designer Anna Hill Johnstone
Set Decorator Richard Merrell
Research Consultant David F. Powers

CAST

John F. Kennedy .... Paul Rudd
Amb. Joseph P. Kennedy .... William Prince
John F. ("Honey Fitz") Fitzgerald .... Burgess Meredith
David F. Powers .... Kevin Conway
Joe Kane .... Richard Venture
Mrs. Rose Kennedy .... Shirley Rich
Billy Sutton .... Tom Berenger
Legion Commander .... David F. Powers
Father Robinson .... Joe Bova
Powers' Sister .... Paddy Croft
Mrs. Murphy .... Mary Diveny
Softy McNamara .... Kenneth McMillan
Sullivan .... Sean Griffin
Bubba .... Ron McLarty
Tip Tobin .... John Ramsey
O'Brien .... Bob O'Connell
Longshoreman .... Brian Dennehy
Sully .... Bernie McInerney
McGraw .... E. Brian Dean
Shorty .... Chip Olcott
Mrs. Gallagher .... Elizabeth Moore
June Neville .... Rebecca Sand
Heather Van Watt .... Joanne Dusseau
Moe Shapiro .... Bernie Passeltiner

The Jolly Corner *see* Parker Adderson, Philosopher/The Jolly Corner

Journey Back to Oz *see* Special Movie Presentation

749 **Judge Horton and the Scottsboro Boys**
NBC Monday Night at the Movies NBC
Program Type Dramatic Special
Two hours. Premiere date: 4/22/76. Repeat date: 1/3/77. A dramatization of the 1931 civil rights case involving nine Alabama black men accused of raping two white women. Filmed entirely on location in central Georgia.
Executive Producer Thomas W. Moore
Producer Paul Leaf
Company A Tomorrow Entertainment Production
Director Fielder Cook
Writer John McGreevey
Costume Designer Ruth Morley
Art Director Frank Smith
Technical Consultant Charles Bennett

CAST

Judge James Horton .... Arthur Hill
Mrs. Horton .... Vera Miles
Sam Liebowitz .... Lewis J. Stadlen
Knight .... Ken Kercheval
Victoria Price .... Ellen Barber
Ruby Bates .... Suzanne Lederer
Lester Carter .... Tom Ligon
Haywood Patterson .... David Harris
Andy Wright .... Ronnie Clanton
Willie Roberson .... Wallace Thomas
Olen Montgomery .... Gregory Wyatt
Leroy Wright .... Larry Butts
Ramsey .... Paul Benjamin
Capt. Burleson .... Barry Snider
Orville Gilley .... Bruce Watson

Juggernaut *see* CBS Special Film Presentations

Jules and Jim *see* PBS Movie Theater

750 **Junior Almost Anything Goes** ABC
Program Type Children's Series
30 minutes. Saturday mornings/Sunday mornings (as of 1/9/77). Premiere date: 9/11/76. Last show: 9/4/77. Three teams of youngsters 12–14 years old in outlandish outdoor competions. Based on the format of "Almost Anything Goes." Developed by Jeff Harris and Bernie Kukoff. Games written by Bill Shinkai and Rowby Goren. Special effects by John Frazier.
Executive Producers Bob Banner, Beryl Vertue
Producer Kip Walton
Company Bob Banner Associates and the Robert Stigwood Organization, Ltd.
Director Kip Walton
Writer Trustin Howard
Costume Designer Rickie Hansen

Art Director Archie Sharp
Host Soupy Sales
Announcer Eddie Alexander (Fast Eddie)

751 **Junior Davis Cup** PBS
Program Type Sports Special
Four hours. Live coverage of the singles finals of the 19th annual Junior Davis Cup Tennis Tournament from Flamingo Park in Miami Beach, Florida 12/26/76. Program made possible by a grant from the Miami Beach Tourist Development Authority.
Executive Producer Ed Waglin
Producer Tom Donaldson
Company WPBT-TV/Miami
Director Tom Donaldson
Announcers Billy Talbert, Donna Floyd Fales

Junior Olympic National Multi-Sport Championships *see* AAU Junior Olympic National Multi-Sport Championships

752 **Junior Orange Bowl Parade** NBC
Program Type Parades/Pageants/Awards Special
45 minutes. 1/1/77. The 28th annual Junior Orange Bowl Parade from Coral Gables, Fla. Special musical material by Anne Delugg; music coordinator: Chuck Bird.
Producer Elmer Gorry
Company NBC Television Network
Director Peter Fatovich
Writer Frank Slocum
Musical Director Milton Delugg
Hosts Anita Bryant, Chuck Barris, Big Bird
Guest Star David Houston

753 **Junior World Curling Championships** PBS
Program Type Sports Special
Two hours. Live coverage of the Junior World Curling Championships from Quebec, Canada 3/6/77. Program made possible by grants from Uni-Royal and Air Canada.
Executive Producer Greg Harney
Company WGBH-TV/Boston
Hosts/Commentators Doug Maxwell, Don Chevrier
Analyst Don Duguid

754 **Just an Old Sweet Song**
GE Theater CBS
Program Type Dramatic Special
90 minutes. Premiere date: 9/14/76. Repeat date: 8/25/77. Original drama about a Detroit family vacationing in the South. Title song by Melvin Van Peebles sung by Ira Hawkins. Other music by Peter Matz.
Producer Philip Barry
Company MTM Enterprises, Inc.
Director Robert Ellis Miller
Writer Melvin Van Peebles
Costume Designers Bob Harris, Jr., Aida Swinson
Art Director Ray Beal
Set Decorator Warren Welch
Special Effects Aubrey Pollard

CAST

Priscilla Simmons .... Cicely Tyson
Nate Simmons .... Robert Hooks
Grandma .... Beah Richards
Joe Mayfield .... Lincoln Kilpatrick
Aunt Velvet .... Minnie Gentry
Mr. Claypool .... Edward Binns
Trunk .... Sonny Jim Gaines
Helen Mayfield .... Mary Alice
Darlene .... Tina Rance
Junior .... Kevin Hooks
Highpockets .... Eric Hooks

JW Coop *see* The ABC Sunday Night Movie

755 **The Kallikaks** NBC
Program Type Comedy Series
30 minutes. Wednesdays. Premiere date: 8/3/77. Last show: 8/31/77. Five-week summer series about poor whites from Appalachia who migrate west to Nowhere, Calif. in search of a better life running a two-pump gas station. Created by Stanley Ralph Ross and Roger Price. "Beat the System" composed by Stanley Ralph Ross and sung by Roy Clark. Other music by Tom Wells and Stanley Ralph Ross.
Executive Producer Stanley Ralph Ross
Production Executive Leonard Friedlander
Producer George Yanok
Company Neila Productions in association with NBC-TV
Directors Various
Writers Various
Art Director Mary Weaver Dodson

CAST

Jasper T. Kallikak .... David Huddleston
Venus Kallikak .... Edie McClurg
Bobbi Lou Kallikak .... Bonnie Ebsen
Junior Kallikak .... Pat Petersen
Oscar Heinz .... Peter Palmer

756 **Kaptain Kool and the Kongs Present All-Star Saturday** ABC
Program Type Children's Special
60 minutes. Premiere date: 9/9/77. Comedy-variety primetime special previewing the 1977–78 ABC children's programs.
Executive Producer Albert J. Tenzer
Producers Sid Krofft, Marty Krofft

Kaptain Kool and the Kongs Present All-Star Saturday *Continued*
Company Sid and Marty Krofft Productions
Director Jack Regas
Writers Frank Karamazoff, Harry Karamazoff
Conductor Tom Oliver
Choreographer Joe Cassini
Costume Designer Madeline Graneto
Art Director Sherman Loudermilk
Stars Kaptain Kool and the Kongs: Michael Lembeck (Kaptain Kool), Debby Clinger (Superchick), Louise Duart (Nashville), Mickey McMeel (Turkey)
Guest Stars Shaun Cassidy, Meadowlark Lemon, Robert Hegyes, Pamela Sue Martin, Parker Stevenson, Lennie Weinrib, Kermit Eller (Darth Vader), Billy Barty, Krofftettes

757 **Karl Bohm and the Vienna Philharmonic**
Great Performances PBS
Program Type Music/Dance Special
60 minutes. Premiere date: 12/17/75. Repeat date: 9/11/77. The Vienna Philharmonic Orchestra in a performance of Mozart's Symphony No. 34 in C Major and Symphony No. 40 in G Minor. Presented by WNET-TV/New York. Program made possible by a grant from Exxon Corporation.
Coordinating Producer David Griffiths
Company Unitel Productions
Conductor Karl Bohm

758 **The Keane Brothers Show** CBS
Program Type Music/Comedy/Variety Series
30 minutes. Fridays. Premiere date: 8/12/77. Last show: 9/2/77. Four-week musical/variety summer series starring the Keane Brothers. Film sequences by Stu Bernstein and Eytan Keller.
Executive Producer Pierre Cossette
Producer Buz Kohan
Company Pierre Cossette Productions, Inc.
Director Tony Charmoli
Writers Bob Arnott, Garry Ferrier, Aubrey Tadman
Musical Director Alan Copeland
Choreographer Anita Mann
Costume Designer Bill Hargate
Stars Tom Keane, John Keane
Regulars The Anita Mann Dancers

CAST

Mr. Goober .... Jimmy Caesar

759 **Keeping Fit** NBC
Program Type Religious/Cultural Special
60 minutes. Premiere date: 1/23/77. A conversation with Dr. Kenneth H. Cooper and Mildred Cooper about aerobics.
Producer Doris Ann
Company NBC Television Religious Programs Unit in association with the Southern Baptist Radio and Television Commission
Director Jack Dillon
Interviewer Betty Rollin

760 **Kemper Open** CBS
Program Type Sports Special
Coverage of the final two rounds of the $250,000 Kemper Open from the Quail Hollow Country Club, Charlotte, N.C. 6/4/77 and 6/5/77.
Producer Frank Chirkinian
Company CBS Television Network Sports
Directors Bob Dailey, Frank Chirkinian
Commentators Vin Scully, Jack Whitaker, Pat Summerall, Frank Glieber, Ben Wright, Ken Venturi

761 **The Kentucky Derby** ABC
Program Type Sports Special
60 minutes. Live coverage of the 103rd running of the Kentucky Derby from Churchill Downs in Louisville, Ky. 5/7/77.
Executive Producer Roone Arledge
Producer Chuck Howard
Company ABC Sports
Director Chet Forte
Announcers Howard Cosell, Jim McKay
Expert Commentator Eddie Arcaro

762 **The Kentucky Derby Special ... A Run for the Roses** ABC
Program Type Sports Special
60 minutes. Premiere date: 5/6/77. Highlights of pre-Derby celebrations plus a filmed segment on the birth of a thoroughbred.
Executive Producer Roone Arledge
Producer Ned Steckel
Company ABC Sports
Director Roger Goodman
Host Frank Gifford
Reporters Jim McKay, Heywood Hale Broun

763 **The Key To the Universe** PBS
Program Type Science/Nature Special
Two hours. Premiere date: 5/24/77. Repeat date: 9/1/77. A look at recent scientific breakthroughs shedding new light on the origins and laws of the universe. Program made possible by a grant from Hoffman–La Roche, Inc.
Producer Alec Nisbett
Company British Broadcasting Corporation and WTTW–TV/Chicago
Writer Nigel Calder
Narrators Nigel Calder, James Ruddle

764 **The Kids from C.A.P.E.R.** NBC
Program Type Children's Series
30 minutes. Saturday mornings. Premiere date: 9/11/76. Last regular show: 11/20/76. Returned: 4/16/77. Last show: 9/3/77. Musical comedy-adventure about four boys who work for their local police department as the Civilian Authority for the Protection of Everyone—Regardless. Created by Romeo Muller; developed and supervised by Merrill Grant. Title song by Ron Dante and Jake Holmes.
Executive Producers Alan Landsburg, Don Kirshner
Producer Stan Cherry
Company Alan Landsburg Productions in association with Don Kirshner Productions
Directors Stan Cherry, Roger Duchowney
Writer Romeo Muller
Music Supervisor Don Kirshner

CAST

P.T. .... Steve Bonino
Bugs .... Cosie Costa
Doomsday .... Biff Warren
Doc .... John Lansing
Chief Vinton .... Robert Emhardt
Klinsinger .... Robert Lussier

765 **The Killers** PBS
Program Type Educational/Cultural Series
90 minutes. Monday mornings. Premiere date: 11/19/73. Series repeats began 9/20/76. Five-part health series dealing with trauma, heart disease, genetic defects, pulmonary disease and cancer. Programs made possible by a grant from Bristol Myers Company.
Executive Producer David Prowitt
Company WNET-TV Science Program Group/New York
Host David Prowitt

Kind Hearts and Coronets *see* PBS Movie Theater

766 **King of the Beasts**
Multi-Special Night NBC
30 minutes. Premiere date: 4/9/77. Animated musical in which a bumbling lion becomes king of the beasts after leaving Noah's Ark. Music by Michael Colicchio; lyrics by Wiley Gregor.
Executive Producer Charles G. Mortimer, Jr.
Company Westfall Productions, Inc.
Director Shamus Culhane
Writers John Culhane, Charles G. Mortimer, Jr., Shamus Culhane

VOICES

The Croc .... Paul Soles
Female Baby Croc .... Judy Sinclair
Female Elephant .... Bonnie Brooks
Male Giraffe/Camel .... Jay Nelson
Polar Bear .... Don Mason
Noah .... Henry Ramer
The Lion .... Carl Banas
Ostrich/Female Penguin .... Ruth Springford
Walrus .... Jack Mather
Male Elephant .... Murray Westgate
Mouse/Male Baby Croc .... Cardie Mortimer

767 **King Orange Jamboree Parade** NBC
Program Type Parades/Pageants/Awards Special
60 minutes. Live coverage of the 43rd annual King Orange Jamboree Parade from Miami, Fla. 12/31/76. Special musical material by Anne Delugg; music coordinator: Chuck Bird.
Producer Elmer Gorry
Company NBC Television Network
Director Peter Fatovich
Writer Frank Slocum
Musical Director Milton Delugg
Hosts Joe Garagiola, Anita Bryant
Guest Stars Lou Rawls, Jaye P. Morgan, K.C. and the Sunshine Band
Featured Guests Margery Johns, Rebecca Ann Reid, the Westchester Wranglerettes

768 **Kingston: Confidential** NBC
Program Type Drama Series
60 minutes. Wednesdays. Premiere date: 3/23/77. Last show: 8/10/77. Drama about investigative reporters for The Frazier Group, owners and operators of newspapers and radio and television stations. Created by David Victor, Dick Nelson, Raymond Burr and Guy Della Cioppa. Pilot "Kingston: The Power Play" aired 9/15/76. Theme music by Henry Mancini.
Executive Producer David Victor
Producer Joe L. Cramer
Company Groverton Productions, Ltd. and R.B. Productions in association with Universal Television and the NBC Television Network
Directors Various
Writers Various
Art Director Ira Diamond
Set Decorator Joseph J. Stone

CAST

R.B. Kingston .... Raymond Burr
Tony Marino .... Art Hindle
Beth Kelly .... Pamela Hensley
Jessica Frazier .... Nancy Olson

769 **Kissinger in Retrospect** PBS
Program Type Documentary/Informational Special
90 minutes. Premiere date: 1/11/77. A retrospective on former Secretary of State Henry Kissinger. Program made possible by grants from the Corporation for Public Broadcasting, the Ford Foundation and Public Television Stations.
Producer Wallace Westfeldt
Company WETA-TV/Washington

Kissinger in Retrospect *Continued*
Writer Stanley Karnow
Hosts Martin Agronsky, Stanley Karnow

770 **Kitty Hawk to Paris**
Directors Documentary Showcase PBS
Program Type Documentary/Informational Special
50 minutes. Premiere date: 5/20/77. 1969 documentary about early aviation history (originally seen on ABC). Program made possible by a grant from the Sperry Rand Corporation and presented by KPBS-TV/San Diego.
Producer John H. Secondari
Company John H. Secondari Productions, Ltd.
Director Helen Jean Rogers
Cinematographer Richard Kuhne
Film Editor Gerard Klein
Narrator John H. Secondari

771 **Kojak** CBS
Program Type Crime Drama Series
60 minutes. Sundays/Tuesdays (as of 1/11/77). Premiere date: 10/24/73. Fourth season premiere: 9/26/76. Police series about a New York City homicide squad. Created by Abby Mann. Music by John Cacavas. George Savalas previously acted in the series under the name Demosthenes. Filmed in part on location in New York City.
Executive Producer Matthew Rapf
Supervising Producer Jack Laird
Producer James McAdams
Company Universal Television
Directors Various
Story Editor Chester Krumholz
Writers Various

CAST

Lt. Theo Kojak .... Telly Savalas
Capt. Frank McNeil .... Dan Frazer
Det. Crocker .... Kevin Dobson
Det. Stavros .... George Savalas

772 **Kojak (Late Night)**
The CBS Late Movie CBS
Program Type Crime Drama Series
60 minutes. Late night repeats of the prime-time police drama. Seen Tuesday and Thursday nights as of 9/14/76; moved to Monday and Thursday nights as of 1/10/77. For credit information, *see* "Kojak."

773 **Korea and the Power Blackout** ABC
Program Type News Special
30 minutes. Premiere date: 7/14/77. Special report on the downing of an Army helicopter in North Korea and the power blackout in New York City.
Executive Producer Elliot Bernstein
Company ABC News Special Events Unit
Anchors Barbara Walters, Roger Grimsby
Reporters Jules Bergman, Don Farmer, Jim Mitchell, Geraldo Rivera, Irv Chapman, Sam Donaldson, Ted Koppel

774 **Kosciuszko: An American Portrait** PBS
Program Type Dramatic Special
60 minutes. Premiere date: 4/5/76. Repeat date: 9/11/77. A dramatization of the contributions to the American Continental Army of Thaddeus Kosciuszko. Filmed on location at Fort Ticonderoga in New York State. Program made possible by a grant from Mrs. Paul's Kitchens, Inc.; presented by KCET-TV/Los Angeles.
Producer Paul Asselin
Company Reader's Digest Films by Guenette-Asselin Productions
Director Paul Asselin
Writers Ray Sipherd, Robert Guenette

CAST

Kosciuszko .... William Lyman
Soldier .... Craig Wasson
Col. James Wilkinson .... Gregory Abels

775 **Kostelanetz and Menuhin**
In Performance at Wolf Trap PBS
Program Type Music/Dance Special
60 minutes. Premiere date: 10/4/76. Repeat date: 8/9/77. Originally shown as part of the 90-minute special "Happy Birthday to U.S." which aired live at the Wolf Trap Farm Park for the Performing Arts in Arlington, Va. 7/4/76. Concert performed by the National Symphony Orchestra. Program made possible by a grant from the Atlantic Richfield Company.
Executive Producer David Prowitt
Producer Ruth Leon
Company WETA-TV/Washington, D.C.
Director Jack Sameth
Conductor Andre Kostelanetz
Guest Soloist Yehudi Menuhin

776 **The Krofft Supershow** ABC
Program Type Children's Series
90 minutes/60 minutes (as of 12/4/76). Saturday mornings. Premiere date: 9/11/76. Live-action comedy adventures.
Executive Producers Sid Krofft, Marty Krofft
Company Sid & Marty Krofft Productions
Hosts Kaptain Kool and the Kongs: Michael Lembeck (Kaptain Kool), Debby Clinger (Superchick), Louise Duart (Nashville), Mickey McMeel (Turkey)

Dr. Shrinker
Three youngsters are miniaturized by a likable villain.
Producer Jack Regas

Director Jack Regas
Script Consultant Donald Boyle
Writers Donald Boyle, Ed Jurist, Bernard Kahn, Leo Rifkin, Si Rose, Greg Strangis

CAST

Dr. Shrinker .... Jay Robinson
Hugo .... Billy Barty
Youngsters .... Ted Eccles, Susan Lawrence, Jeff MacKay

Electrawoman
Serialized story of two magazine reporters who become Electrawoman and Dynagirl to combat crime.
Producer Walter C. Miller
Director Walter C. Miller
Story Editors Dick Robbins, Duane Poole
Writers Gerry Day, Bethel Leslie, Duane Poole, Dick Robbins, Greg Strangis

CAST

Mara/Electrawoman .... Deidre Hall
Lori/Dynagirl .... Judy Strangis

Wonderbug
Three teenagers and their magical car.
Producer Al Schwartz
Director Al Schwartz
Writing Supervisors Dick Robbins, Duane Poole
Writers Jim Brochu, Earle Doud, Mark Fink, Fred S. Fox, Seaman Jacobs, Lee Maddux, Chuck McCann, Jack Mendelsohn, Duane Poole, Dick Robbins
Cast David Levy, Carol Anne Sefflinger, John Anthony Bailey

The Lost Saucer
Re-edited repeats of science fiction comedy about two androids and a boy and his babysitter in space.
Executive Producer Si Rose
Producers Sid Krofft, Marty Krofft
Directors Various
Writers Various

CAST

Fum .... Jim Nabors
Fi .... Ruth Buzzi
Alice .... Alice Playten
Jerry .... Jarrod Johnson

777 **Kup's Show** PBS
Program Type Public Affairs Series
60 minutes. Weekly. Premiere date: 2/58 (as local show carried by WBBM-TV/Chicago). Now carried over the PBS network by WTTW-TV/Chicago as of 3/5/77. Interview show with people in the news. Funded (on PBS) by the Sears-Roebuck Foundation.
Producer Paul Frumkin
Company An Irv Kupcinet Production
Director William Heitz
Host Irv Kupcinet

778 **La Boheme** PBS
Program Type Music/Dance Special
Three hours. Premiere date: 3/15/77. First live telecast from the Metropolitan Opera House at Lincoln Center. A performance of the 1896 opera by Giacomo Puccini sung by the Metropolitan Opera Company and played by the Metropolitan Opera Symphony. Stereo-simulcast on local FM radio stations. Program made possible through a grant from Texaco.
Company WNET-TV/New York in collaboration with the Metropolitan Opera
Conductor James Levine
Host Tony Randall

CAST

Mimi .... Renata Scotto
Rodolfo .... Luciano Pavarotti
Musetta .... Maralin Niska
Marcello .... Ingvar Wixell
Colline .... Paul Plishka
Schaunard .... Allan Monk
Benoit .... Italo Tajo

La Strada *see* PBS Movie Theater

779 **La Traviata (English)**
Opera Theater PBS
Program Type Music/Dance Special
2 1/2 hours. Premiere date: 4/27/76. Repeat date: 8/23/77. A performance of "La Traviata" by Giuseppe Verdi. English language translation by Eric Crozier and Joan Cross. Production designed by David Meyerscough-Jones featuring the New Philharmonic Orchestra and the Ambrosian Opera Chorus. Program made possible by grants from the Ford Foundation, the Corporation for Public Broadcasting and Public Television Stations and presented by WNET-TV/New York.
Coordinating Producers Linda Krisel, David Griffiths
Producer Cedric Messina
Company British Broadcasting Corporation and WNET-TV/New York
Director Brian Large
Conductor Alexander Gibson
Choreographer Ronald Hynd
Costume Designer Elizabeth Waller

CAST

Violetta Valery .... Elisabeth Harwood
Alfredo Germont .... John Brecknock
Georgio Germont .... Norman Bailey
Flora .... Ann Howard
Baron Douphol .... Alan Opie
Marchese D'Obigny .... Alan Charles
Dr. Grenvil .... Michael Rippon
Gastone de Letorieres .... Phillip Langridge
Annina .... Sheila Squires

780 **La Traviata (Italian)**
In Performance at Wolf Trap PBS
Program Type Music/Dance Special
2 1/2 hours. Premiere date: 9/20/76. Repeat date: 9/27/77. A new production by the San Diego Opera Company and the Filene Center Orchestra and Filene Center Chorus of the tragic opera by Giuseppe Verdi with libretto by Francesco Maria Peave. Conceived and staged by Tito Capobianco at the Wolf Trap Farm Park in Arlington, Va. Program made possible by a grant from the Atlantic Richfield Company.
Executive Producer David Prowitt
Producer Ruth Leon
Company WETA-TV/Washington, D.C.
Director Kirk Browning
Conductor Julius Rudel
Costume Designer Carl Toms
Scenic Designer Carl Toms
Host Beverly Sills

CAST

Violetta .... Beverly Sills
Flora Bervoix .... Fredda Rakusin
Dr. Grenvil .... John Cheek
Marquis d'Obigny .... Keith Kibler
Baron Douphol .... Robert Orth
Gastone .... Neil Rosenshein
Alfredo .... Henry Price
Annina .... Evelyn Petros
Giuseppe .... Roger Lucas
Georgio Germont .... Richard Fredricks
Gardener .... Christopher Deane

Ladies Professional Golf Association Championship *see* LPGA Championship

The Lady Killers *see* PBS Movie Theater

781 **Lamp Unto My Feet** CBS
Program Type Religious/Cultural Series
30 minutes. Sunday mornings. Premiere date: 11/21/48. Continuous. Programs of a religious nature.
Executive Producer Pamela Ilott
Producers Ted Holmes, Chalmers Dale, Bernard Seabrooks, Joseph Clement, Marlene Didonato and others
Company CBS News Religious Broadcast
Directors Various

782 **The Land** NBC
Program Type Religious/Cultural Special
60 minutes. Premiere date: 12/12/76. Repeat date: 5/29/77. An examination of land development in the United States. Filmed on location in Louisiana, Kansas, Nebraska, Wyoming and Montana.
Executive Producer Doris Ann
Producer Martin Hoade
Company NBC Television Religious Programs Unit in association with the Office for Film and Broadcasting of the United States Catholic Conference
Director Martin Hoade
Writer Philip Scharper
Narrator Richard Kiley

783 **Land of the Lost** NBC
Program Type Children's Series
30 minutes. Saturday mornings. Premiere date: 9/7/74. Third season premiere: 9/11/76. Last show: 9/3/77. Live-action and animation fantasy of a family in an alternate universe. Music by Larry Neiman and Jack Tillar.
Executive Producers Sid Krofft, Marty Krofft
Producer Jon Kubichan
Company Sid and Marty Krofft Productions
Directors Joseph L. Scanlan, Rick Bennewitz
Story Editor Sam Roeca
Writers Various
Animation Director Gene Warren

CAST

Will Marshall .... Wesley Eure
Holly Marshall .... Kathy Coleman
Uncle Jack .... Ron Harper

The Land That Time Forgot *see* NBC Saturday Night at the Movies

784 **Lanigan's Rabbi**
NBC Sunday Mystery Movie NBC
Program Type Crime Drama Series
90 minutes. Sundays. Premiere date: 1/30/77. Last show: 7/3/77. Broadcast irregularly as part of "NBC Sunday Mystery Movie." Drama of a crime-solving rabbi and a police chief in a New England town. Characters based on the novels of Harry Kemelman. Pilot aired 6/17/76.
Executive Producer Leonard B. Stern
Supervising Producers Don M. Mankiewicz, Gordon Cotler
Company Heyday Productions in association with Universal Television and NBC-TV
Directors Various
Writers Various

CAST

Chief Paul Lanigan .... Art Carney
Rabbi David Small .... Bruce Solomon
Kate Lanigan .... Janis Paige
Miriam Small .... Janet Margolin
Bobbie Whittaker .... Barbara Carney
Lt. Osgood .... Robert Doyle

785 **Las Vegas Entertainment Awards** NBC
Program Type Parades/Pageants/Awards Special
60 minutes. Premiere date: 3/3/77. Sixth annual

awards given by the Academy of Variety and Cabaret Artists to entertainers in the Las Vegas variety and cabaret field. Taped 2/24/77 at the Las Vegas Hilton Hotel.
Executive Producer George LeFave
Producers Norman Sedawie, Conrad Holzgang
Company Sed-Bar Productions, Inc.
Director Steve Binder
Writers Marty Farrell, Donald Ross
Musical Director Joe Buercio
Choreographer Jerry Jackson
Hosts Barbara Eden, Gabriel Kaplan, Wayne Newton
Entertainers/Presenters Jack Albertson, Ann-Margret, David Brenner, Sammy Davis, Jr., Bobbie Gentry, Robert Goulet, Sally Kellerman, Rich Little, Judy Pace Mitchell, Siegfried and Roy, Fred Travalena, David Clayton Thomas, Leslie Uggams, and cast members of Bare Touch of Vegas, Bottoms Up '77, and Folies Bergere

The Last American Hero *see* The ABC Friday Night Movie ("Hard Driver")

786 **The Last Ballot**
Ourstory PBS
Program Type Dramatic Special
30 minutes. Premiere date: 12/16/75. Repeat date: 11/19/76. Dramatization of the election of Thomas Jefferson. Funded by a grant from the National Endowment for the Humanities.
Executive Producer Don Fouser
Company WNET-TV/New York
Director Don Fouser
Costume Designer John Boxer
Art Director Warren Clymer
Host Bill Moyers
Set Decorator Hubert J. Oakes, Jr.

CAST

Bayard	Lee Richardson
Sedgwick	Gil Rogers
Lyon	Roy Poole
Livingston	Joseph Lambie
Smith	Thomas Toner
Jefferson	Jack Ryland
Burr	Edward Zang
Randolph	Noel Craig
Nicholson	Alan Langer
Clerk	Paul Nevins
Inebriate	George Hall

787 **The Last Dinosaur**
The ABC Friday Night Movie ABC
Program Type TV Movie
Two hours. Premiere date: 2/11/77. Drama of a contemporary tycoon hunting a dinosaur in a prehistoric world. Music by Maury Laws with lyrics by Jules Bass sung by Nancy Wilson. Special effects by Tsuburaya Productions Co., Ltd.
Producers Arthur Rankin, Jr., Jules Bass
Company A Rankin/Bass Production
Directors Alex Grasshoff, Tom Kotani
Writer William Overgard

CAST

Masten Thrust	Richard Boone
Frankie Banks	Joan Van Ark
Bunta	Luther Rackley
Chuck Wade	Steven Keats
Dr. Kawamoto	Tatsu Nakamura
Barney	Carl Hansen
Prehistoric Girl	Mamiya Sekia

Last Holiday *see* PBS Movie Theater

788 **The Last of Mrs. Lincoln**
Hollywood Television Theatre PBS
Program Type Dramatic Special
Two hours. Premiere date: 9/16/76. Dramatization of the last 17 years in the life of Mary Todd Lincoln. Music by Lyn Murray. Program made possible by grants from the Corporation for Public Broadcasting, the Ford Foundation and Public Television Stations.
Executive Producer Norman Lloyd
Producer George Schaefer
Company KCET-TV/Los Angeles
Director George Schaefer
Writer James Prideaux
Costume Designer Noel Taylor
Art Director Roy Christopher

CAST

Mary Lincoln	Julie Harris
Tad Lincoln	Robby Benson
Robert Lincoln	Michael Cristofer
Sen. Austin	Denver Pyle
Ninian Edwards	Ford Rainey
Elizabeth Edwards	Priscilla Morrill
Lizzie Keckley	Royce Wallace
Mary Harlan	Linda Kelsey
Porter	Jack Furlong
Man in Park	Jay M. Riley
His Grandson	Kurtis Lee
Lewis Baker	Patrick Duffy
Mrs. McCullough	Kate Wilkinson
Attendant	Macon McCalman
Young Tad	Billy Simpson

Last of the Wild *see* Lorne Greene's Last of the Wild

789 **The Last Voyage of the Argo Merchant**
NBC Reports/Multi-Special Night NBC
Program Type Documentary/Informational Special
60 minutes. Premiere date: 3/15/77. A look at the disastrous last voyage of the oil tanker *Argo Merchant* that went aground 12/15/76.
Producer Thomas Tomizawa
Company NBC News

The Last Voyage of the Argo Merchant *Continued*
Director Darold Murray
Writers John Dancy, Thomas Tomizawa
Set Decorator Don Shirley
Cinematographers Gregory Andracke, Aaron Fears, Dean Gaskill, Henry Kokojan, Steve Petropoulos
Film Editors Frank DeMeo, Louis Giacchetto, Timothy Gibney, Mary Ann Martin
Researchers Louise Linder, Susan Drury, Elliott Anna Jones, Joan Pierce, Leslie Redlich
Reporter John Dancy

790 **Laurence Olivier Presents a Tribute to the American Theatre** NBC
Program Type Dramatic Special
Specials produced by Granada Television of Britain in association with NBC-TV with Laurence Olivier as creative and artistic director. One special seen during the 1976–77 season: "Cat on a Hot Tin Roof." (*See* title for credits.)

791 **Laverne and Shirley** ABC
Program Type Comedy Series
30 minutes. Tuesdays. Premiere date: 1/27/76. Second season premiere: 9/28/76. Characters introduced on "Happy Days." Created by Garry K. Marshall, Mark Rothman and Lowell Ganz. Concerns two young women working in the bottle cap division of the Shotz Brewery in Milwaukee during the late 1950s. "Making Our Dreams Come True" music by Charles Fox; lyrics by Norman Gimbel. Lowell Ganz and Mark Rothman were replaced as producers by Monica Johnson and Eric Cohen.
Executive Producers Garry K. Marshall, Thomas L. Miller, Edward K. Milkis
Producers Tony Marshall, Lowell Ganz, Mark Rothman/Monica Johnson, Eric Cohen
Company Miller-Milkis Productions, Inc. and Henderson Production Company, Inc. in association with Paramount Studios
Directors Various
Writers Various

CAST

Laverne De Fazio	Penny Marshall
Shirley Feeney	Cindy Williams
Frank De Fazio	Phil Foster
Carmine Ragusa	Eddie Mekka
Andrew "Squiggy" Squiggman	David L. Lander
Lenny Kolowski	Michael McKean
Mrs. Babish	Betty Garrett
Big Rosie Greenbaum	Carole Ita White

L'Avventura *see* PBS Movie Theater

Lawrence of Arabia *see* The ABC Sunday Night Movie

792 **The Lawrence Welk Show** Syndicated
Program Type Music/Dance Series
60 minutes. Weekly. Premiere date: 7/2/55 as "The Dodge Dancing Party." In syndication since 9/71.
Executive Producer Sam J. Lutz
Producer James Hobson
Company Teleklew Productions, Inc.
Distributor Don Fedderson Productions, Inc.
Director James Hobson
Musical Director George Cates
Host Lawrence Welk
Regulars Anaconi, Ava Barber, Bobby Burgess, Henry Cuesta, Dick Dale, Ken Delo, Arthur Duncan, Gail Farrell, Jo Feeney, Myron Floren, Sandi Griffiths, Charlotte Harris, Larry Hooper, Guy Hovis, Ralna Hovis, Jack Imel, Cissy King, Bob Lido, Mary Lou Metzger, Tom Netherton, Bob Ralston, Jim Roberts, the Six Semonski Sisters, Tanya Welk, Norma Zimmer

Le Mans *see* NBC Saturday Night at the Movies

793 **A Leaf From a Town Record** PBS
Program Type Documentary/Informational Special
30 minutes. Premiere date: 9/7/77. A look at a small town with large economic problems—Hudson, N.Y. Program made possible by a grant from the New York Council for the Humanities and the Corporation for Public Broadcasting.
Company WMHT-TV/Schenectady, N.Y.

L'Eclisse *see* PBS Movie Theater

794 **Legacy: The Year of the Bicentennial** PBS
Program Type Documentary/Informational Special
60 minutes. Premiere date: 7/4/77. Bicentennial year activities in Pennsylvania. Program presented by the Pennsylvania Public Television Network and made possible by a grant from the Pennsylvania Bicentennial Commission.
Producer John P. Hudak

The Legend of Hell House *see* The ABC Friday Night Movie

795 **The Legend of Rudolph Valentino** PBS
Program Type Documentary/Informational Special
45 minutes. Premiere: 12/76. Repeat date: 3/77.

Documentary exploring the life and death of the silent screen star.
Producers Saul J. Turell, Paul Killian

796 **L'eggs World Series of Women's Tennis** ABC
Program Type Sports Special
Live coverage of the third annual tournament from the Racquet Club Ranch in Tucson, Ariz. 4/16/77 and 4/17/77.
Executive Producer Roone Arledge
Producer Ned Steckel
Company ABC Sports
Director Larry Kamm
Announcer Frank Gifford
Expert Commentator Arthur Ashe

A Lesson in Love *see* PBS Movie Theater

797 **Let's Make a Deal** Syndicated
Program Type Game/Audience Participation Series
30 minutes. Twice weekly. Premiere date (as evening show): 9/71. Last season premiere: 9/76. Evening version of long-running daytime game where player "traders" in strange costumes wheel and deal for prizes.
Executive Producer Stefan Hatos
Producer Alan Gilbert
Company A Stefan Hatos-Monty Hall Production
Distributor Worldvision Enterprises, Inc.
Director Joseph Behar
Musical Director Ivan Ditmars
Host Monty Hall
Announcer Jay Stewart

Let's Scare Jessica to Death *see* The ABC Friday Night Movie

798 **The Liars Club** Syndicated
Program Type Game/Audience Participation Series
30 minutes. Mondays–Fridays. Premiere date: 9/7/74 (KTLA-TV/Los Angeles). In syndication since 1975–76 season. Four celebrity guests make up stories about strange objects.
Executive Producer Ralph Andrews
Producer Larry Hovis
Company Ralph Andrews Productions
Distributor 20th Century-Fox Television
Director Bill Rainbolt
Host Allen Ludden
Regulars Larry Hovis, Dody Goodman
Semi-Regulars Betty White, Alan Sues, Dick Gautier, Buddy Hackett

799 **Liberty Bowl** ABC
Program Type Sports Special
Live coverage of the Liberty Bowl game between the UCLA Bruins and the Alabama Crimson Tide from Memorial Stadium in Memphis, Tenn. 12/20/76.
Executive Producer Roone Arledge
Producer Chuck Howard
Company ABC Sports
Director Andy Sidaris
Play-by-Play Announcer Keith Jackson
Expert Color Commentator Bud Wilkinson
Sideline Reporter/Halftime Host Bill Flemming
Special Features/Sideline Reporter Jim Lampley

800 **Life Among the Lowly**
Visions PBS
Program Type Dramatic Special
90 minutes. Premiere date: 12/2/76. Drama of a 19th century slave trader haunted by his past. Performed by the Trinity Square Repertory Company of Providence. Music composed by Richard Cumming. Program made possible by grants from the Ford Foundation, the National Endowment for the Arts and the Corporation for Public Broadcasting.
Executive Producer Barbara Schultz
Producers Adrian Hall, Robin Miller
Company KCET-TV/Los Angeles
Directors Adrian Hall, Robin Miller
Writers Adrian Hall, Richard Cumming
Costume Designer Betsey Potter
Production Designer Eugene Lee
Set Decorator Sandra Nathanson

CAST

Abram .... Richard Kneeland
Young Abram .... Robert Black
Mother .... Marguerite Lenert
Abigail .... Rose Weaver
Helen .... Margo Skinner
Martha Sue .... Nancy Nichols
Dorothea Dix .... Mina Manente
Mr. Whitney .... William Cain
Slave Buyer .... Timothy Crowe
Capt. Wells .... William Damkoehler
Guard .... Ed Hall
Officer .... Richard K. Jenkins
Official .... David C. Jones
Crippled Man .... Richard Kavanaugh
Slave Buyer .... Howard London
Masterson .... George N. Martin
Guards .... Barbara Meek, Barbara Orson, Daniel Von Bargen

801 **The Life and Assassination of the Kingfish**
NBC Monday Night at the Movies NBC
Program Type Dramatic Special
Two hours. Premiere date: 3/21/77. Dramatization of the events leading to the 1935 assassination of Huey Long. Filmed entirely on location in and around Baton Rouge, La.

The Life and Assassination of the Kingfish *Continued*
Executive Producer Thomas W. Moore
Producer Paul Leaf
Company Tomorrow Entertainment, Inc. in association with NBC-TV
Director Robert Collins
Writer Robert Collins
Costume Designer Ruth Morley
Set Decorator Joanne MacDougall

CAST

Huey Long .... Edward Asner
Manners .... Nicholas Pryor
Rose Long .... Diane Kagan
Earl Long .... Fred Cook
Alice Grosjean .... Dorrie Kavanaugh
J. R. .... Gary Allen
Bozeman .... Donegan Smith
Seymour Weiss .... Stanley Reyes
Murphy Roden .... Rod Masterson
Russell Long .... Steven Ramay

802 **Life and the Structure of Hemoglobin** PBS
Program Type Science/Nature Special
30 minutes. Premiere date: 10/1/75. Repeat date: 1/11/77. A history of hemoglobin and its study. Program made possible by a grant from the National Science Foundation.
Executive Producer Dr. Richard S. Scott
Producer Bert Shapiro
Company KCET-TV/Los Angeles in cooperation with the American Institute of Physics
Director Bert Shapiro
Narrator Dr. John Hopfield

803 **The Life and Times of Elvis Presley**
NBC News Special NBC
Program Type News Special
30 minutes. Live report on the impact of Elvis Presley on America 8/16/77 following his death.
Executive Producer Gordon Manning
Producer Ray Lockhart
Company NBC News
Anchor David Brinkley
Commentators Jackson Bain, Brian Ross

804 **The Life and Times of Grizzly Adams** NBC
Program Type Drama Series
60 minutes. Wednesdays. Premiere date: 2/9/77. Fictionalized portrait of an 1880s fugitive wildlife adventurer whose constant companion is a grizzly bear named Ben. Created by Charles E. Sellier, Jr. in the 1974 film of the same name. (Film shown 5/25/77 as two-hour special.) Theme music written and performed by Thom Pace. Other music by Don Perry. Filmed on location in the Uinta Mountains, Utah and in Arizona.
Executive Producer Charles E. Sellier, Jr.
Producer Arthur Stolnitz
Company Schick Sunn Classic Productions, Inc.
Directors Various
Story Editor Paul Hunter
Writers Various
Wildlife Advisers Steve Martin, Ralph Benton, Terry Rowland

CAST

James "Grizzly" Adams .... Dan Haggerty
Mad Jack .... Denver Pyle
Nakuma .... Don Shanks

The Life and Times of Judge Roy Bean
see CBS Special Film Presentations

805 **Life Goes to the Movies**
The Big Event NBC
Program Type Documentary/Informational Special
Three hours. Premiere date: 10/31/76. Repeat date: 8/29/77. The outstanding stars, films and legends of Hollywood (from 1936–1972) based on the 1975 book, "Life Goes to the Movies." Original music composed by Fred Karlin. Newsreel animated montages by Phillip Savenick.
Executive Producer Jack Haley, Jr.
Producers Mel Stuart, Richard Schickel
Co-Producer Malcolm Leo
Company 20th Century-Fox Television and Time-Life Television
Director Mel Stuart
Writer Richard Schickel
Film Editor Robert K. Lambert
Hosts Henry Fonda, Shirley MacLaine, Liza Minnelli

806 **Lilias, Yoga and You** PBS
Program Type Educational/Cultural Series
30 minutes. Mondays–Fridays. Season premiere: 9/24/76. Physical fitness and mental well-being through hatha yoga exercises demonstrated by Lilias Folan. New shows seen Fridays; repeats seen Monday–Thursdays. Programs funded by the Corporation for Public Broadcasting, the Ford Foundation and Public Television Stations.
Executive Producer Charles Vaughan
Producer Len Goorian
Company WCET-TV/Cincinnati
Director Bill Gustin
Writer Lilias Folan

807 **The Lindbergh Kidnapping Case**
NBC Thursday Night at the Movies NBC
Program Type Dramatic Special
Three hours. Premiere date: 2/26/76. Repeat date: 5/26/77. A dramatization of the 1932 kidnapping, capture and trial. Music composed by

Billy Goldenberg. Filmed in part in Colusa, Calif.
Executive Producer David Gerber
Producer Buzz Kulik
Company A David Gerber Production in association with Columbia Pictures Television and NBC-TV
Director Buzz Kulik
Writer J. P. Miller
Costume Designers Bob Christenson, Denita Cavett
Art Director Carl Anderson

CAST

Charles Lindbergh .... Cliff De Young
Bruno Richard Hauptmann .... Anthony Hopkins
Dr. Condon .... Joseph Cotten
Judge Trenchard .... Walter Pidgeon
Anne Morrow Lindbergh .... Sian Barbara Allen
Edward Reilly .... Martin Balsam
Violet Sharpe .... Denise Alexander
Col. Schwarzkopf .... Peter Donat
Gov. Hoffman .... Laurence Luckinbill
Koehler .... Dean Jagger
Huisache .... Keenan Wynn
Sgt. Finn .... Tony Roberts
Wilentz .... David Spielberg
Betty Gow .... Kate Woodville

808 **The Lion and Androcles** PBS
Program Type Children's Special
60 minutes. Premiere date: 6/16/74. Repeat date: 12/27/76. A comic opera by John Eaton based on the Greek fable and performed by 75 fourth graders in a concert in Bethel, Ohio. Program made possible by grants from the Indiana Arts Commission and the Corporation for Public Broadcasting.
Producer Herbert Seltz
Company WTIU-TV/Indiana University and the Indiana University School of Music
Directors Ross Allen, Mickey Klein
Musical Director Carmon DeLeone

809 **A Little Bit Different**
Special Treat NBC
Program Type Children's Special
60 minutes. Premiere date: 2/8/77. Drama about a 12-year-old boy with bone cancer.
Producer Rift Fournier
Director Rift Fournier
Writer Rift Fournier

CAST

Jamie Burke .... Dai Stockton
Mrs. Burke .... Linda Miller
Mr. Burke .... Pirie MacDonald
Dr. Ryder .... Michael Tolan
Billy Hansen .... David Stambough
Gibbs .... T. J. Hargrave
Coach .... Donegan Smith
Doctor .... Millette Alexander
Jackie Burke .... Regina Scott
Noel Burke .... Paul Blom

810 **The Little Drummer Boy Book II**
All-Specials Night NBC
Program Type Animated Film Special
30 minutes. Premiere date: 12/13/76. Sequel to "The Little Drummer Boy." A new Christmas story using dimensional stop-motion photography. Title song by Katherine Davis, Henry Onorati and Harry Simeone. Original music and lyrics by Maury Laws and Jules Bass. "Do You Hear What I Hear?" by Noel Regney and Gloria Shayne.
Producers Arthur Rankin, Jr., Jules Bass
Company Rankin/Bass Productions, Inc.
Directors Arthur Rankin, Jr., Jules Bass
Writer Julian P. Gardner
Narrator Greer Garson

VOICES

Brutus .... Zero Mostel
Little Drummer Boy .... David Jay
Melchior .... Allen Swift
Simeon .... Ray Owens
Plato .... Robert McFadden

Little Fauss and Big Halsy *see* The ABC Sunday Night Movie

811 **Little House on the Prairie** NBC
Program Type Drama Series
60 minutes. Wednesdays. Premiere date: 9/11/74. Third season premiere: 9/27/76. Based on the "Little House" books by Laura Ingalls Wilder about her life in the West 100 years ago. Set in and around Walnut Grove, Minn., in the 1870s. Music by David Rose.
Executive Producer Michael Landon
Producers John Hawkins, B. W. Sandefur
Company An NBC Production in association with Ed Friendly
Directors Michael Landon, William F. Claxton, Victor French
Writers Various
Art Director Walter M. Jeffries

CAST

Charles Ingalls .... Michael Landon
Caroline Ingalls .... Karen Grassle
Mary Ingalls .... Melissa Sue Anderson
Laura Ingalls .... Melissa Gilbert
Carrie Ingalls .... Lindsay Greenbush, Sidney Greenbush
Mr. Edwards .... Victor French
Grace Edwards .... Bonnie Bartlett
Nellie Oleson .... Alison Arngrim
Mrs. Oleson .... Katherine MacGregor
Mr. Oleson .... Richard Bull
Dr. Baker .... Kevin Hagen

812 **Little Ladies of the Night**
The ABC Sunday Night Movie ABC
Program Type TV Movie
Two hours. Premiere date: 1/16/77. Drama of teenage prostitution. Filmed in part in Los Ange-

Little Ladies of the Night *Continued*
les and Long Beach, Calif. Music by Jerry Fielding.
Executive Producers Aaron Spelling, Leonard Goldberg
Producer Hal Sitowitz
Company Spelling-Goldberg Productions
Director Marvin Chomsky
Writer Hal Sitowitz
Costume Designers Robert Harris, Maddie Sylos
Art Director Paul Sylos

CAST

Lyle York .... David Soul
Russ Garfield .... Lou Gossett
Hailey Atkins .... Linda Purl
Comfort .... Clifton Davis
Mrs. Atkins .... Carolyn Jones
Mr. Atkins .... Paul Burke
Maureen .... Lana Wood
Karen .... Kathleen Quinlan
Finch .... Vic Tayback
Mrs. Colby .... Katherine Helmond
Maggie .... Dorothy Malone
Matron .... Bibi Osterwald
Mrs. Brodwick .... Sandra Deel
Wally .... Claude Earl Jones
Brady .... David Hayward
First Senator .... James Ray
Second Senator .... Tom McDonald
Third Senator .... Byron Morrow
First John .... Matt Bennett
Female Guard .... Connie Sawyer

813 Little Lord Fauntleroy
Once Upon a Classic PBS
Program Type Children's Series
30 minutes. Saturdays. Premiere date: 4/2/77. Series repeats began 8/13/77. Six-part dramatization of the Victorian novel by Frances Hodgson Burnett about a young boy who becomes the heir to a title and an English estate. Music by Kenny Clayton. Captioned for the hearing-impaired. Presented by WQED-TV/Pittsburgh and made possible by grants from McDonald's Local Restaurants Association and McDonald's Corporation.
Executive Producer Jay Rayvid
Coordinating Producer John Coney
Producer Barry Letts
Company British Broadcasting Corporation and Time-Life Television
Director Paul Annett
Story Editor Alistair Bell
Host Bill Bixby

CAST

Cedric Errol .... Glenn Anderson
Earl of Dorincourt .... Paul Rogers
Mrs. Errol .... Jennie Linden
Havisham .... Preston Lockwood
Higgins .... Ian Thompson
Mr. Hobbs .... Ray Smith
Dick .... Paul D'Amato

814 Little Vic
Syndicated
Program Type Children's Series
30 minutes. Weekly. Premiere date: 2/20/77. Six-part series based on the novel by Doris Gates about a Harlem-born orphaned teenager involved with a thoroughbred horse named Little Vic.
Executive Producer Daniel Wilson
Producer Linda Marmelstein
Company Daniel Wilson Productions/ABC Owned Television Stations
Director Harvey Herman
Writer Art Wallace

CAST

Gillie Walker .... Joey Green
Stevens .... Jack Collins
George Gordon .... Med Flory
Julie Sawyer .... Doney Oatman
Lawson .... Charles Stewart
Hammer .... Del Hinkley
Winkler .... Bobby Howard
Richie Miller .... David Levy
Fred Amble .... Myron Natwick
Hiller .... Laurence Haddon

815 Little Women
Special Treat NBC
Program Type Children's Special
60 minutes. Premiere date: 12/14/76. Ballet version of the novel by Louisa May Alcott danced by members of the New York City Ballet with an original score by Robert Maxwell. Masks by Barbara Sexton.
Executive Producer George A. Heinemann
Producer June Reig
Director Sidney Smith
Writer June Reig
Choreographers Edward Villella, Richard Tanner
Costume Designer Anne deVelder
Art Director George Bockman

CAST

Narrator/Mother .... Joanne Woodward
Brooke .... Edward Villella
Meg .... Anna Aragno
Amy .... Judith Fugate
Jo .... Susan Hendl
Beth .... Susan Pilarre
Laurie .... Nolan T'Sani
Mother-Dancer .... Carol Sumner
Father .... Bart Cook
Teacher .... David Richardson
Poor Mother .... Laura Flagg
Minister .... Richard Tanner

816 Liv Ullmann With Dick Cavett PBS
Program Type Documentary/Informational Special
30 minutes. Premiere date: 3/2/77. An interview with Liv Ullmann featuring a discussion of "Scenes From a Marriage."
Producer Jack Sameth

Company WNET-TV/New York
Director Jack Sameth
Interviewer Dick Cavett

Live and Let Die *see* The ABC Sunday Night Movie

817 **Live From Lincoln Center**
Great Performances PBS
Program Type Music/Dance Series
Four live performances from Lincoln Center for the Performing Arts in New York City: "American Ballet Theatre's 'Giselle,'" "Andre Watts," "The Barber of Seville," "The New York Philharmonic." (*See* individual titles for credits.) Programs made possible by grants from Exxon Corporation, the National Endowment for the Arts, the Corporation for Public Broadcasting and the Charles A. Dana Foundation.

Live From the Mardi Gras, It's Saturday Night on Sunday *see* The Big Event/NBC's Saturday Night

Living Free *see* NBC Night at the Movies

818 **Liza's Pioneer Diary**
Visions PBS
Program Type Dramatic Special
90 minutes. Premiere date: 11/18/76. Historical drama about a young woman crossing the plains with a wagon train on its way to the Oregon Territory. Filmed entirely on location in the Southwest. Program made possible by grants from the Ford Foundation, the National Endowment for the Arts and the Corporation for Public Broadcasting.
Executive Producer Barbara Schultz
Producer Nell Cox
Company KCET-TV/Los Angeles
Director Nell Cox
Writer Nell Cox

CAST

Liza Stedman .... Ayn Ruymen
Eben Stedman .... Dennis Redfield
Hiram Stedman .... Patrick Burke
Martha Stedman .... Fran Ryan
Aunt Sara .... Katherine Helmond
Tyler Stedman .... Steven Wick
Buzzy Stedman .... Michael Harvey
Harrod .... Tim Scott
Kate Scofield .... Andra Akers
Jake Scofield .... David Ross
Jennie Scofield .... Kim Buss
Mrs. Zink .... Lucille Benson
Mr. Zink .... Luke Jones
Cousin Emma Zink .... Margaret Roberts
Mrs. Meece .... Cory Cudia
Mr. Meece .... Duke Sundt
Mr. Dunster .... Nobel Willingham
Mrs. Dunster .... Maralyn Millar
Dunster Children .... Glenna Picket, Patty Picket, Lisa Williams, Sean Williams
Zeke Trueblood .... Dixon Newberry
Trueblood Brother .... Jay Quintana
Mr. Johnson .... Rex King
Mrs. Johnson .... Helen Picket
Johnson Children .... Chris Williams, David Williams
Indian Girl .... Angie Espinoza

Logan's Run *see* CBS Special Film Presentations

Lolly-Madonna XXX *see* NBC Monday Night at the Movies

819 **The Loneliest Runner**
NBC Monday Night at the Movies NBC
Program Type TV Movie
90 minutes. Premiere date: 12/20/76. Repeat date: 7/14/77. Drama about a teen-age bed-wetter.
Producer Michael Landon
Company NBC Television Production
Director Michael Landon
Writer Michael Landon

CAST

John Curtis (as a youth) .... Lance Kerwin
John Curtis (as an adult) .... Michael Landon
Arnold Curtis .... Brian Keith
Alice Curtis .... DeAnn Mears
Nancy Rizzi .... Melissa Sue Anderson
Rafer Johnson .... Rafer Johnson

The Long Goodbye *see* The ABC Sunday Night Movie

820 **Look Out World**
Comedy Time/Multi-Speical Night NBC
Program Type Comedy Special
30 minutes. Premiere date: 7/27/77. Comedy pilot about four young men working in a California car wash. Based on the feature film "Car Wash." Filmed on location in a Santa Monica (Calif.) car wash.
Executive Producer Perry Lafferty
Producer Richard Rosenbloom
Company Filmways Television Production
Director Hy Averback
Writers Hal Goldman, Al Gordon, Duke Vincent

CAST

Cannonball .... Michael Huddleston
Benny .... Justin Lord
Delfi .... Bart Braverman
Beau .... Steve Doubet
Gus .... Arnold Soboloff
Darcy .... Maureen Arthur

Look Out World *Continued*

Byron .... Damon Raskin
Byron's Mother .... Susan Bay

821 **Look Up and Live** CBS
Program Type Religious/Cultural Series
30 minutes. Sunday mornings. Premiere date: 1/3/54. Continuous. Cultural programs of a religious nature.
Executive Producer Pamela Ilott
Producers Chalmers Dale, Ted Holmes, Joseph Clement, Alan Harper, Bernard Seabrooks and others
Company CBS News
Directors Various

822 **Look What's Happened to Rosemary's Baby**
The ABC Friday Night Movie ABC
Program Type TV Movie
Two hours. Premiere date: 10/29/76. A sequel to the 1968 motion picture "Rosemary's Baby." Music by Charles Bernstein. Special effects by Joe Mercurio.
Producer Anthony Wilson
Company The Culzean Corporation in association with Paramount Television
Director Sam O'Steen
Writer Anthony Wilson
Art Director Lester D. Gobruegge

CAST

Adrian/Andrew .... Stephen McHattie
Minnie Castavet .... Ruth Gordon
Roman Castevet .... Ray Milland
Rosemary .... Patty Duke Astin
Sheriff Holtzman .... Broderick Crawford
Guy Woodhouse .... George Maharis
Marjean .... Tina Louise
Dr. Ellen Davison .... Donna Mills
Laykin .... Lloyd Haynes
Peter Simon .... David Huffman
Adrian/Andrew (age 8) .... Philip Boyer
Dr. Lister .... Brian Richards

823 **Lorenzo & Henrietta Music Show** Syndicated
Program Type Music/Comedy/Variety Series
60 minutes. Mondays–Fridays. Premiere date: 9/13/76. Last show: 10/15/76. Musical numbers, comedy sketches and interviews with guest celebrities.
Executive Producers Lorenzo Music, Lewis Arquette
Producer Albert J. Simon
Company MTM Enterprises, Inc.
Distributor Metromedia Producers Corporation
Director Bob Lally
Writers Lorenzo Music, John Gibbons, Sandy Helberg, Richard Philip Lewis, Ira Miller, Dennis Reagan, Lewis Arquette
Hosts Lorenzo Music, Henrietta Music

824 **Lorne Greene's Last of the Wild** Syndicated
Program Type Science/Nature Series
30 minutes. Premiere date: 9/74. Third season premiere: 9/76. Based on "Animal Lexicon" created and produced by Ivan Tors.
Executive Producer Skip Steloff
Producer Lawrence Neiman
Company Heritage Enterprises, Inc.
Distributor Y & R Ventures
Directors Various
Writers Various
Narrator Lorne Greene

825 **The Lou Rawls Special**
Thursday Night Special ABC
Program Type Music/Dance Special
90 minutes. Premiere date: 4/21/77. First special for Lou Rawls. Taped in part at the Liberty Church of God and Christ in Watts.
Executive Producer Dick Clark
Producer Bill Lee
Company Dick Clark Teleshows, Inc.
Director Barry Glazer
Writers Robert Illes, James R. Stein
Star Lou Rawls
Guest Stars Lola Falana, Crystal Gayle, the Emotions, Kip Addotta

826 **The Love Boat**
The ABC Friday Night Movie ABC
Program Type TV Movie
Two hours. Premiere date: 9/17/76. Repeat date: 4/29/77. Four interrelated stories of the passengers and crew aboard a cruise ship. Suggested by the novel, "The Love Boat" by Jeraldine Saunders. Filmed in part aboard the *Sun Princess.* "Mona Lisa Speaks" and " 'Til Death Do Us Part" was directed by Richard Kinon and written by Carl Kleinschmitt. "Mr. and Mrs. Havlicek Aboard" was directed by Richard Kinon and Alan Myerson and written by Robert Illes and James R. Stein. "Are There Any Real Love Stories?" was directed by Richard Kinon and Alan Myerson and written by Dawn Aldredge and Marion C. Freeman. Music by Charles Fox.
Producer Douglas S. Cramer
Company 20th Century-Fox Television
Directors Richard Kinon, Alan Myerson
Writers Carl Kleinschmitt, Robert Illes, James R. Stein, Dawn Aldredge, Marion C. Freeman

CAST

Donald Richardson .... Don Adams
George Havlicek .... Tom Bosley
Monica Richardson .... Florence Henderson
Stan .... Gabriel Kaplan
Willard .... Harvey Korman
Iris Havlicek .... Cloris Leachman
Andrew .... Hal Linden
Ellen .... Karen Valentine

The Captain ..... Ted Hamilton
The Doctor ..... Dick Van Patten
The Bartender ..... Theodore Wilson
Richard Garrett III ..... Ric Carrott
Momma ..... Montana Smoyer
Yeoman Purser ..... Sandy Helberg
Steward ..... Joseph Sicari
Lounge Guests ..... Kathryn Ish, Richard Stahl
Cruise Director ..... Terri O'Mara
Arnold ..... Jimmy Baio
Louella ..... Joyce Jameson
Rita ..... Beverly Saunders
1st Officer ..... William H. Bassett
Photographer ..... David Man
Juanita Havlicek ..... Laurette Spang
Binaca ..... Jette Seear

827 **The Love Boat II**
The ABC Friday Night Movie/The ABC Tuesday Night Movie ABC
Program Type TV Movie
Two hours. Premiere date: 1/21/77. Repeat date: 6/28/77. Sequel to "The Love Boat" (*see above*). Four interrelated stories of the passengers and crew aboard a cruise ship. Filmed in part aboard the *Sun Princess.* "Unfaithfully Yours" written by Carl Kleinschmitt; "Here's Looking At You, Love" by Dawn Aldredge and Marion C. Freeman; "For the Love of Sandy" by Dawn Aldredge, Marion C. Freeman and Leonora Thuna; "The Heckler" by Steve Pritzker.
Executive Producers Aaron Spelling, Douglas S. Cramer
Producer Henry Colman
Company Aaron Spelling Productions
Director Hy Averback
Writers Carl Kleinschmitt, Dawn Aldredge, Marion C. Freeman, Leonora Thuna, Steve Pritzker

CAST
Jim Berkley ..... Ken Barry
Donna Morley ..... Diana Canova
Ralph Manning ..... Bert Convy
Eva McFarland ..... Celeste Holm
Elaine Palmer ..... Hope Lange
Linda Morley ..... Kristy McNichol
Stephen Palmer ..... Robert Reed
Robert Grant ..... Craig Stevens
Pat McFarland ..... Marcia Strassman
Angela ..... Tracy Brooks Swope
Roger ..... Lyle Waggoner
Dr. Livingstern ..... Wesley Addy
Amy ..... Candy Azzara
Gopher ..... Fred Grandy
Dr. O'Neill ..... Bernie Kopell
Isaac ..... Ted Lange
Capt. Madison ..... Quinn Redecker
Sandy Summers ..... Diane Stilwell

828 **Love of Life** CBS
Program Type Daytime Drama Series
25 minutes. Mondays–Fridays. Premiere date: 9/24/51 (as 15-minute show). Expanded to 25 minutes 4/14/58. Continuous. The second longest-running daytime drama on television. Story of the Sterling and Aleata-Hart families set in Rosehill, U.S.A. Theme "The Life You Love" by Carey Gold. Credit information as of 2/77. Cast listed alphabetically.
Executive Producer Darryl Hickman
Producer Jean Arley
Company CBS Television
Directors Larry Auerbach, John Desmond
Head Writer Gabrielle Upton
Announcer Kenneth Roberts

CAST
Ian Russell ..... Michael Allinson
Edouard Aleata ..... John Aniston
Ray Slater ..... Lloyd Battista
Dr. Joe Cusack ..... Peter Brouwer
Vivian Carlson ..... Helene Dumas
Lynn Henderson ..... Amy Gibson
Mia Marriott ..... Veleka Gray
Cal Aleata Latimer ..... Roxanne Gregory
Ben Harper ..... Chandler Hill Harben
Betsy Crawford ..... Elizabeth Kemp
Rick Latimer ..... Jerry Lacy
Felicia Flemming Lamont ..... Pamela Lincoln
Charles Lamont ..... Jonathan Moore
Carrie Johnson Lovett ..... Peg Murray
Vanessa Dale Sterling ..... Audrey Peters
Johnny Prentiss ..... Trip Randall
Sarah Caldwell ..... Joanna Roos
Diana Lamont ..... Diane Rousseau
Hank Latimer ..... David Carlton Stambaugh
Arlene Lovett ..... Birgitta Tolksdorf
Bruce Sterling ..... Ron Tomme
Tom Crawford ..... Richard K. Weber
Meg Dale Hart ..... Tudi Wiggins
Jamie Rollins ..... Ray Wise

Love Story *see* The ABC Tuesday Night Movie

829 **Lovers and Friends** NBC
Program Type Daytime Drama Series
30 minutes. Mondays–Fridays. Premiere date: 1/3/77. Last show: 5/6/77. Drama about the Cushing and Saxton families in a wealthy suburb of Chicago. Created by Harding Lemay. Cast list is alphabetical. David Ramsey replaced Bob Purvey in February 1977.
Executive Producer Paul Rauch
Company Procter & Gamble Productions
Directors Peter Levin, Jack Hofsiss, Kevin Kelly
Head Writer Harding Lemay
Writer Tom King
Scenic Designer Otis Riggs, Jr.

CAST
Bentley Saxton ..... David Abbott
Austin Cushing ..... Rod Arrants
Jason Saxton ..... Richard Backus
Sophia Slocum ..... Margaret Barker
Tessa Saxton ..... Vicki Dawson
Josie Saxton ..... Patricia Englund
Megan Cushing ..... Patricia Estrin
Connie Ferguson ..... Susan Foster

Lovers and Friends *Continued*

Laurie Brewster .... Dianne Harper
Lester Saxton .... John Heffernan
Amy Gifford .... Christine Jones
George Kimball .... Stephen Joyce
Desmond Hamilton .... David Knapp
Edith Slocum Cushing .... Nancy Marchand
Barbara Manners .... Karen Philipp
Eleanor Saxton Kimball .... Flora Plumb
Rhett Saxton .... Bob Purvey/David Ramsey
Richard Cushing .... Ron Randell

830 **Loves Me, Loves Me Not** CBS
Program Type Limited Series
30 minutes. Wednesdays. Preview: 3/20/77. Premiere date: 3/23/77. Last show: 4/27/77. Comedy about the romance of a young couple. Music by Charles Fox; lyrics by Norman Gimbel.
Producers Paul Junger Witt, Tony Thomas
Company Witt/Thomas/Harris Productions in association with 20th Century-Fox Television
Directors Various
Writers Various
Art Director Rodger Maus

CAST

Jane .... Susan Dey
Dick .... Kenneth Gilman
Sue ...... Phyllis Glick/Udana Power (preview show)
Tom .... Art Metrano

Lovin' Molly *see* The ABC Friday Night Movie

831 **Lowell Thomas Remembers** PBS
Program Type Documentary/Informational Series
30 minutes. Saturdays. Premiere data: 10/5/75. Second season premiere: 1/8/77. 39-part series of reminiscences by Lowell Thomas covering 1963–1975, aviation between 1929–1939, and various world-famous personalities. Put together with newsreel films from the Movietone News Library. Series funded by the Corporation for Public Broadcasting, the Ford Foundation and Public Television Stations.
Executive Producer James W. Jackson, Jr.
Producer James McQuinn
Company South Carolina ETV Network/ Columbia, S.C.
Director Marc Mangus
Writer Mackie Quavie
Film Editor Bryan Heath

832 **The Loyal Opposition** NBC
Program Type Public Affairs Series
60 minutes each. Sundays. The Republican position on matters of current interest in four special reports—three shown during the 1976–77 series: 3/27/77, 6/19/77 and 9/11/77.
Producer Robert Asman
Company NBC News
Anchors Douglas Kiker, Catherine Mackin

833 **LPGA Championship** NBC
Program Type Sports Special
Live coverage of the final rounds of the 1977 LPGA Championship from the Bay Tree Golf Plantation in Myrtle Beach, S.C. 6/11/77 and 6/12/77.
Producer Larry Cirillo
Company NBC Sports
Director Harry Coyle
Anchors Jim Simpson, Cary Middlecoff, Carol Mann
Commentators Jay Randolph, John Brodie, Fran Tarkenton, Bruce Devlin, Mary Bea Porter

Lt. Robin Crusoe, U.S.N. *see* NBC All-Disney Saturday Night at the Movies

834 **Lucan**
The ABC Sunday Night Movie/The ABC Friday Night Movie ABC
Program Type TV Movie
90 minutes. Premiere date: 5/22/77. Repeat date: 8/5/77. Pilot for 1977–78 series about a 20-year-old raised by wolves in search of his identity. Filmed in part at various southern California locations. Music by Fred Karlin.
Executive Producer Barry Lowen
Producer David Greene
Company Metro-Goldwyn-Mayer Television Production
Director David Greene
Writer Michael Zagor
Production Designer Brian Eatwell
Set Decorator Jacqueline S. Price

CAST

Lucan .... Kevin Brophy
Mickey .... Stockard Channing
Larry McElwaine .... Ned Beatty
Gene Boone .... William Jordan
Dr. Hoagland .... John Randolph
Casey .... Lou Frizzell
Coach Dalton .... Ben Davidson
Rantzen .... George Wyner
Pres. Davis .... Hedley Mattingly
Jess .... John Finnegan
Coffin .... Richard C. Adams
Lucan (age 10) .... Todd Olsen
Policeman .... George Reynolds
Woman .... Virginia Hawkins

835 **Luke Was There**
Special Treat NBC
Program Type Children's Special
60 minutes. Premiere date: 10/5/76. Dramatization of the novel by Eleanor Clymer about a

young boy in a children's shelter. Music by Joseph Horowitz.
Executive Producer Linda Gottlieb
Producer Richard Marquand
Company Learning Corporation of America
Director Richard Marquand
Writer Richard Marquand

CAST

Julius .... Scott Baio
Luke .... David Pendleton
Max .... Matthew Anton
Ricardo .... Kip Ford
Mrs. Cronkite .... Polly Holliday
Lady With a Quarter .... Estelle Omens
Lady With a Handbag .... Alice Yourman
Lady Traveller .... Harriet Sappington
Mother .... Tanya Berezin

836 **Lure of the Dolphins** PBS
Program Type Documentary/Informational Special
52 minutes. Premiere: 12/76. Repeat date: 3/77. A study of dolphins filmed at the Dutch Hardewijk and the English Morecambe dolphinariums, with additional film from the U.S. Navy.
Producer Robin Brown
Company ATV Colour Production
Distributor ITV
Director Robin Brown
Writers Anthony Grey, Robin Brown
Cinematographers Charles Lagus, Jan Morgan
Film Editor Colin Slade
Host/Narrator Anthony Grey

M *see* PBS Movie Theater

837 **The Mac Davis Christmas Special . . . When I Grow Up**
All-Specials Night NBC
Program Type Music/Comedy/Variety Special
60 minutes. Premiere date: 12/15/76. The holiday season as seen through the eyes of 16 children. Special musical material by Ray Charles. Choral director: Bill Cole.
Executive Producers Gary Smith, Dwight Hemion
Producers Mike Post, Steve Binder
Company Cauchemar Productions, Inc.
Director Steve Binder
Writers Buz Kohan, Alan Thicke
Musical Directors Mike Post, Velton Ray Bunch
Choreographers Jim Bates, Rob Iscove
Costume Designers Al Lehman, Ron Talsky
Art Director Romain Johnston
Star Mac Davis
Guest Stars Richard Thomas, Raquel Welch
Featured Performers The Beverly Hills Youth Orchestra, the Valley Master Chorale

838 **Mac Davis . . . Sounds Like Home**
All-Specials Night NBC
Program Type Music/Comedy/Variety Special
60 minutes. Premiere date: 4/26/77. A look at the musical roots of the performers. Special musical material by Ray Charles.
Executive Producers Raymond Katz, Sandy Gallin
Producers Gary Smith, Dwight Hemion
Company Cauchemar Productions, Inc.
Director Dwight Hemion
Writers Buz Kohan, Rod Warren
Musical Director Velton Ray Bunch
Costume Designer Sandy Slepak
Art Director Tom H. John
Star Mac Davis
Guest Stars George Carlin, Furry Lewis, Dolly Parton, Donna Summer
Special Guest Star Tom Jones

839 **Macbeth**
Classic Theatre: The Humanities in Drama PBS
Program Type Dramatic Special
2 1/2 hours. Premiere date: 9/25/75. Repeat date: 2/17/77. The play by William Shakespeare. Program made possible by grants from the National Endowment for the Humanities and Mobile Oil Corporation. Presented by WGBH-TV/Boston; Joan Sullivan, producer.
Producer Cedric Messina
Company British Broadcasting Corporation
Director John Gorrie
Writer William Shakespeare
Costume Designer John Bloomfield
Set Designer Natasha Kroll

CAST

Macbeth .... Eric Porter
Lady Macbeth .... Janet Suzman
Malcolm .... John Alderton
Duncan .... Michael Goodliffe
Banquo .... John Thaw
Macduff .... John Woodvine
Lady Macduff .... Rowena Cooper

840 **MacNamara's Band**
The ABC Monday Comedy Special/Special Comedy Presentation ABC
Program Type Comedy Special
60 minutes. Premiere date: 5/14/77. Repeat dates: 8/29/77 and 9/5/77 (30 minutes each). Spoof of World War II adventure movies set in Norway behind enemy lines.
Executive Producers Jeff Harris, Bernie Kukoff
Producer Darrell Hallenbeck
Co-Producer Hal Cooper
Company Boiney Stoones, Inc.
Director Hal Cooper
Writers Jeff Harris, Bernie Kukoff

CAST

Johnny MacNamara .... John Byner

MacNamara's Band *Continued*

Gaffney .... Bruce Kirby, Sr.
Zoltan .... Sid Haig
Aggie .... Lefty Pedroski
Milgrim .... Joseph Sicari
Hedy .... Denise Galik
Schnell .... Henry Polic II
Dr. Fuchtenstein .... Joseph Mell
Gen. Grosshtecker .... Ben Wright

841 **The MacNeil-Lehrer Report** PBS
Program Type Public Affairs Series
30 minutes. Mondays–Fridays. Continuous. Premiere date: 1/5/76. (Began locally in New York City in November 1975.) An in-depth look at one major news story per day. Series made possible by grants from Public Television Stations, the Corporation for Public Broadcasting and Exxon Corporation.
Executive Producer Ray Weiss
Producers Howard Weinberg, Shirley Wershba, Linda Winslow
Company WNET-TV/New York and WETA-TV/Washington, D.C.
Director Duke Struck
Host Robert MacNeil
Co-Host Jim Lehrer

Macon County Line *see* NBC Monday Night at the Movies/NBC Saturday Night at the Movies

842 **Macy's Thanksgiving Day Parade** NBC
Program Type Parades/Pageants/Awards Special
Two hours. Live coverage of the 50th annual parade from New York City 11/25/76. Music coordinated by Chuck Bird.
Producer Dick Schneider
Company An NBC Television Network Production
Director Dick Schneider
Writer Joseph Scher
Musical Director Milton Delugg
Choreographer James Starbuck
Hosts Della Reese, McLean Stevenson, Ed McMahon

843 **The Mad Mad Mad Mad World of the Super Bowl!** NBC
Program Type Music/Comedy/Variety Special
Two hours. Premiere date: 1/8/77. A spoof of football and the super bowl.
Producer Norman Rosemont
Company Antoinette Productions, Inc.
Director Tim Kiley
Writers Marc London, Paul Pumpian and Harvey Weitzman, Terry Hart
Musical Directors Jack Elliott, Allyn Ferguson
Choreographer Donald McKayle
Costume Designer Pete Menefee
Art Directors Brian Bartholomew, Keaton S. Walker
Hosts Kate Jackson, Jaclyn Smith, Joe Namath
Stars Steve Allen, Foster Brooks, Ruth Buzzi, Charlie Callas, George Carlin, Ray Charles, Charo, Pat Cooper, Irwin Corey, Norm Crosby, Rodney Dangerfield, Jamie Farr, Rosey Grier, Arte Johnson, Harvey Korman, Marc London, Dick Martin, Ed McMahon, Anne Meara, Pat Morita, Lorenzo Music, Dan Rowan, Billy Saluga, Doc Severinsen, Jerry Stiller, Rip Taylor, Fred Travalena, Jimmie Walker, Jonathan Winters, Henny Youngman, the Donald McKayle Dancers

844 **Madama Butterfly**
Fine Music Specials/Great Performances PBS
Program Type Music/Dance Special
Three hours. Premiere date: 10/20/76. 1903 opera by Giacomo Puccini. Music performed by the Vienna Philharmonic Orchestra. Program presented by WNET-TV/New York and made possible by grants from Public Television Stations, the Corporation for Public Broadcasting, the Ford Foundation and Exxon Corporation.
Executive Producer Fritz Buttenstedt
Producer David Griffiths
Company Unitel Productions
Director Jean-Pierre Ponnelle
Conductor Herbert von Karajan

CAST

Butterfly .... Mirella Freni
Benjamin Franklin Pinkerton .... Placido Domingo
Suzuki .... Christa Ludwig
Consul Sharpless .... Robert Kerns

845 **Madame Bovary**
Masterpiece Theatre PBS
Program Type Limited Series
60 minutes. Sundays. Premiere date: 10/10/76. Four-part dramatization of the 19th-century French novel by Gustave Flaubert. Filmed in England. Music by Dudley Simpson. Presented by WGBH-TV/Boston, Joan Sullivan, series producer. Series made possible by a grant from Mobil Oil Corporation.
Producer Richard Beynon
Company British Broadcasting Corporation in association with Time-Life
Director Rodney Bennett
Writer Giles Cooper
Host Alistair Cooke

CAST

Emma Bovary .... Francesca Annis
Charles Bovary .... Tom Conti
Rouault .... Richard Beale
Charles' Mother .... Kathleen Helme
Felicite .... Gabrielle Lloyd

Father Bournisien ..... David Waller
Leon ..... Brian Stirner
Rodolphe ..... Dennis Lill
Apothecary ..... Ray Smith

Made for Each Other *see* The CBS Wednesday Night Movies

846 **Magazine** CBS
Program Type News Magazine Series
60 minutes. Originally premiered in May 1974. Six editions presented during the 1976–77 season: 10/19/76, 12/9/76, 1/18/77, 3/24/77, 4/21/77, 6/9/77.
Executive Producer Joel Heller
Producers Various
Company CBS News
Editor Sylvia Chase

847 **The Magic of ABC Starring David Copperfield** ABC
Program Type Music/Comedy/Variety Special
60 minutes. Premiere date: 9/7/77. Preview of the ABC 1977–78 primetime season.
Executive Producer Joseph Cates
Co-Producers Sandy Krinski, Chet Dowling
Company A Cates Brothers Production
Director Walter C. Miller
Writers Sandy Krinski, Chet Dowling
Musical Director Peter Matz
Choreographer Jaime Rogers
Star David Copperfield
Guest Stars Fred Berry, Shaun Cassidy, Howard Cosell, Kate Jackson, Hal Linden, Kristy McNichol, Penny Marshall, Donny Osmond, Marie Osmond, Parker Stevenson, Adam Rich, Dick Van Patten, Abe Vigoda, Cindy Williams

848 **Magnificat—Mary's Song of Liberation** NBC
Program Type Religious/Cultural Special
60 minutes. Premiere date: 11/16/75. Repeat date: 8/21/77. Mary, as reflected in the art and cultures of 2,000 years. Filmed in England, France, Italy and the U.S.
Executive Producer Doris Ann
Producer Martin Hoade
Company NBC Television Religious Programs Unit in association with the U.S. Catholic Conference Division for Film and Broadcasting
Director Martin Hoade
Writer Philip Scharper
Narrator Marian Seldes

849 **Magnificent Magical Magnet of Santa Mesa** NBC
Program Type TV Movie
90 minutes. Premiere date: 6/19/77. Comedy pilot about a young scientist who invents a disk that can solve the world's energy crisis.
Executive Producer David Gerber
Producers Hy Averback, James H. Brown
Company Columbia Pictures Television
Director Hy Averback
Writer Gerald Gardner

CAST
Freddie Griffith ..... Michael Burns
Marcie ..... Susan Blanchard
J. J. Strange ..... Harry Morgan
Bensinger ..... Tom Poston
Mr. Undershaft ..... Keene Curtis
Cal Bixby ..... Dick Blasucci
Ida Griffith ..... Jane Connell
Mr. Kreel ..... Conrad Janis

The Magnificent Seven Ride! *see* The CBS Wednesday Night Movies

Magnum Force *see* The CBS Friday Night Movies

850 **A Maid at Eaton Place** PBS
Program Type Documentary/Informational Special
30 minutes. Premiere date: 1/16/77. An interview with Alice Willis, who was a maid at Eaton Place in the 1920s.
Producer Bill Varney
Company WITF-TV/Hershey, Pa.
Director Gary Shrawder
Interviewer Bill Varney

Major Barbara *see* PBS Movie Theater

Major League Baseball Championships *see* American League Championship/National League Championship

Major League Baseball Game-of-the-Week *see* Baseball Game-of-the-Week

851 **The Making of "A Bridge Too Far"** NBC
Program Type Documentary/Informational Special
60 minutes. Premiere date: 8/31/77. A behind-the-scenes look at the filming of "A Bridge Too Far." Filmed in various locales in Holland.

The Making of "A Bridge Too Far"
Continued
Company Utopia Production
Writers Jeff Kanew, Barry Schoor
Film Editor R. A. Smith
Narrator Robert Perry

852 **The Making of "The Deep"** CBS
Program Type Documentary/Informational Special
60 minutes. Premiere date: 9/11/77. A look at the production of the motion picture "The Deep." Music by Jimmie Haskell adapted from original music by John Barry.
Executive Producer Peter Guber
Producers Peter Lake, Chuck Workman
Company Casablanca Records and FilmWorks, Inc. for Columbia Pictures Television
Director Chuck Workman
Writer Peter Lake
Narrator Robert Shaw

853 **Making Pictures With Music**
The CBS Festival of Lively Arts for Young People CBS
Program Type Children's Special
60 minutes. Premiere date: 2/13/77. A New York Philharmonic Young People's Concert from Avery Fisher Hall at Lincoln Center for the Performing Arts in New York City demonstrating how music can form pictures in the mind of the listener.
Producer Joshua White
Company The CBS Television Network
Director Joshua White
Writer Sean Kelly
Conductor Michael Tilson Thomas
Narrator Michael Tilson Thomas

Mame *see* NBC Saturday Night at the Movies

A Man Called Horse *see* The CBS Wednesday Night Movies

854 **The Man From Atlantis** NBC
Program Type Limited Series
90 minutes/two hours. Premiere date: 3/4/77. Four episodes presented irregularly as forerunner of the 1977–78 series. 5/7/77 episode shown as part of "NBC Saturday Night at the Movies." Science-fiction drama about the last surviving citizen of Atlantis who works with the Foundation for Oceanic Research. Music by Fred Karlin. Special effects created by Tom Fisher. Filmed in part off the coast of Catalina in Southern California.
Executive Producer Herbert F. Solow
Producer Robert H. Justman
Company Solow Production Company in association with NBC-TV
Directors Various
Writers Various
Stunt Coordinator Paul Stader

CAST

Mark Harris .... Patrick Duffy
Dr. Elizabeth Merrill .... Belinda J. Montgomery
C. W. Crawford .... Alan Fudge
Miller Simon .... Kenneth Tigar

855 **The Man From Nowhere**
Once Upon a Classic PBS
Program Type Children's Special
60 minutes. Premiere date: 3/19/77. Gothic mystery about a man in black stalking an orphan girl in 1860. Music by John Cameron. Filmed on location in Berkshire, England. Captioned for the hearing-impaired. Presented by WQED-TV/Pittsburgh and made possible by grants from McDonald's Local Restaurants Association and McDonald's Corporation.
Coordinating Producer John Coney
Producer Jean Wadlow
Company Charles Barker Films Ltd. for the Children's Film Foundation Ltd.
Director James Hill
Writer John Tully
Art Director Hazel Peiser
Host Bill Bixby

CAST

William .... Shane Franklin
Spikey .... Anthony McCaffery
Nobby .... Reginald Winch
Jim .... Robin Keston
Mr. Freeman .... John Forbes-Robertson
George Harvey .... Ronald Adam
Joe .... Edmund Thomas
Mrs. Smee .... Gabrielle Hamilton
Alice .... Sarah Hollis-Andrews

856 **The Man in the Iron Mask**
Bell System Special NBC
Program Type Dramatic Special
Two hours. Premiere date: 1/17/77. Repeat date: 9/1/77. Adaptation of the novel by Alexandre Dumas filmed in part at various chateaus in France and in Dorset, England. Original music by Allyn Ferguson.
Producer Norman Rosemont
Company A Norman Rosemont Production in association with ITC Entertainment Ltd.
Director Mike Newell
Writer William Bast
Conductor Allyn Ferguson
Costume Designer Olga Lehmann
Stunt Coordinator Romo Gorrara

CAST

King Louis XIV/Philippe .... Richard Chamberlain
Fouquet .... Patrick McGoohan

D'Artagnan .... Louis Jourdan
Louise de la Valliere .... Jenny Agutter
Duval .... Ian Holm
Colbert .... Ralph Richardson
Queen Maria Theresa .... Vivien Merchant
Anne of Austria .... Brenda Bruce
Armand .... Esmond Knight
Baisemeaux .... Godfrey Quigley
Percerin .... Emrys James
Claude .... Denis Lawson
Henriette .... Anne Zelda
Blacksmith .... Stacy Davies

The Man in the White Suit *see* PBS Movie Theater

Man on a Swing *see* The CBS Friday Night Movies

857 **The Man on the Rock**
Piccadilly Circus PBS
Program Type Dramatic Special
90 minutes. Premiere date: 7/12/76. Repeat date: 8/21/77. A portrayal of Napoleon's last years of exile on St. Helena, using his own words from letters and diaries. Settings and costumes modernized. Program made possible by a grant from Mobil Oil Corporation. Presented by WGBH–TV/Boston; Joan Sullivan, producer.
Producer Michael Pearce
Company ATV (England)
Director Michael Pearce
Writer Kenneth Griffith
Cinematographer Grenville Middleton
Film Editor Roger James
Host Jeremy Brett

CAST

Napoleon .... Kenneth Griffith

The Man Who Loved Cat Dancing *see* NBC Saturday Night at the Movies

The Man With the Golden Gun *see* The ABC Monday Night Movie

858 **The Man With the Power**
ABC Movie of the Week NBC
Program Type TV Movie
Two hours. Premiere date: 5/24/77. Action pilot about a man who inherited strange powers from his father—a native of another planet.
Producer Allan Balter
Company Universal Television in association with NBC–TV
Director Nicholas Sgarro
Writer Allan Balter

CAST

Eric Smith .... Bob Neill
Princess Siri .... Persis Khambatta
Agent Bloom .... Tim O'Connor
Paul .... Vic Morrow
Farnsworth .... Roger Perry
Maj. Sajid .... Rene Assa
Shanda .... Noel de Souza
Driver .... James Ingersoll
Dilling .... Bill Fletcher

859 **The Marilyn McCoo & Billy Davis, Jr. Show** CBS
Program Type Music/Comedy/Variety Series
30 minutes. Wednesdays. Premiere date: 6/15/77. Last show: 7/20/77. Six-week musical/variety show.
Executive Producer Dick Broder
Producers Ann Elder, Ed Scharlach
Company Junebug Production
Director Gerren Keith
Head Writers Ann Elder, Ed Scharlach
Writers Thomas Leopold, Jim Ritz
Stars Marilyn McCoo, Billy Davis, Jr.

CAST

Jay Hooper .... Jay Leno
The Rudeen Brothers .... Lewis Arquette, Tim Reid

860 **The Mark Russell Comedy Special** PBS
Program Type Comedy Series
30 minutes. Tuesdays. Four comedy specials of political/topical humor aired live 11/23/76, 2/22/77, 4/12/77 and 6/21/77 at the State University of New York at Buffalo. Fifth show seen 1/4/77 recapped highlights of previous specials. Programs made possible by grants from the Corporation for Public Broadcasting, the Ford Foundation and Public Television Stations.
Executive Producer John L. Hutchinson, Jr.
Producer Wiley Hance
Company WNED–TV/Buffalo
Director Will George
Scenic Designer Bryon Young
Star Mark Russell

861 **Marshall Efron's Illustrated, Simplified and Painless Sunday School** CBS
Program Type Children's Series
30 minutes. Sunday mornings. Premiere date: 1/6/74. First series repeat: 1/2/77. Four more repeats seen between 8/7/77–8/28/77. Religious program for children.
Executive Producer Pamela Ilott
Producer Ted Holmes
Company CBS News
Director Alvin Thaler
Writers Marshall Efron, Alfa-Betty Olsen
Host Marshall Efron

862 Martha Graham Dance Company

Dance in America/Great Performances PBS
Program Type Music/Dance Special
60 minutes. Premiere date: 4/7/76. Repeat date: 7/6/77. Six works choreographed and introduced by Martha Graham performed by the Martha Graham Dance Company: "Appalachian Spring" with music by Aaron Copland, "Diversion of Angels" with music by Norman Dello Joio, "Adorations" with music by Mateo Albeniz, Domenico Cimarosa, John Dowland and Girolamo Frescobaldi, "Frontier" with music by Louis Horst, "Lamentation" with music by Zoltan Kodaly, and "Medea's Dance of Vengeance" from "Cave of the Heart" with music by Samuel Barber. Program made possible by grants from Exxon Corporation, the National Endowment for the Arts and the Corporation for Public Broadcasting.
Executive Producer Jac Venza
Producer Emile Ardolino
Company WNET–TV/New York
Director Merrill Brockway
Choreographer Martha Graham
Costume Designer Martha Graham
Host Gregory Peck

Appalachian Spring

Scenic Designer Isamu Noguchi
Dancers Jessica Chao, Janet Eilber, Bonnie Oda Homsey, Yuriko Kimura, Lucinda Mitchell, Elisa Monte, David Hatch Walker, Tim Wengerd

Diversion of Angels

Dancers Takako Asakawa, Jessica Chao, Mario Delamo, Bonnie Oda Homsey, Peggy Lyman, Susan McGuire, Lucinda Mitchell, Elisa Monte, Peter Sparling, David Hatch Walker, Tim Wengerd

Adorations

Costume Designer Halston
Scenic Designer Leandro Locsin
Dancers Takako Asakawa, Mario Delamo, Janet Eilber, Diane Gray, Elvind Harum, Bonnie Oda Homsey, Yuriko Kimura, Peggy Lyman, Susan McGuire, Daniel Maloney, Peter Sparling, David Hatch Walker, Tim Wengerd, Henry Yu

Frontier

Scenic Designer Isamu Noguchi
Dancer Janet Eilber

Lamentation

Dancer Peggy Lyman

Medea's Dance of Vengeance

Dancer Takako Asakawa

863 Martinelli: Outside Man CBS

Program Type TV Movie
60 minutes. Premiere date: 4/8/77. Crime-drama pilot about a federal undercover agent. Music by Tom Scott. Filmed in part on location in San Francisco.
Executive Producer Paul Magistretti
Producer William F. Phillips
Company MTM Enterprises, Inc.
Director Russ Mayberry
Writer Paul Magistretti
Conductor Tom Scott

CAST

Richie Martinelli .... Ron Leibman
Shaker Thompson .... Woody Strode
Rosalie .... Janet Margolin
Stelio .... Nicholas Colasanto
Sal .... Al Ruscio
Leo .... Pepper Martin
Armand .... Robert Donner
Rasputin .... Ray Vitte
Morgan .... William Wintersole
Ellsworth Howard .... Nicholas Pryor
The Professor .... Alan Haufrect
Larry Trace .... Jack Thibeau
Turino .... Franco Corsaro
Sgt. Mitchell .... John Dennis Johnston
Sully .... Pat Corley
Bank Manager .... Fred Stuthman
Roger Elks .... Michael Frost
Ben .... Neil O'Neill
Alberto .... Dante D'Andre
Ms. Mendoza .... Karmin Murcelo

864 Mary Hartman, Mary Hartman

Syndicated
Program Type Comedy Series
30 minutes. Mondays–Fridays. Premiere date: 1/6/76. Second season premiere: 10/4/76. Last show: 7/3/77. Satiric (evening) soap opera set in the fictional town of Fernwood, Ohio. Created by Gail Parent, Ann Marcus, Jerry Adelman, Daniel Gregory Browne; developed by Norman Lear. Music by Earle Hagen. Succeeded by "Forever Fernwood" in the 1977–78 season.
Executive Producer Norman Lear
Producer Viva Knight
Company T.A.T. Communications Company
Distributor T.A.T. Communications Company/Vidtronics, Inc.
Directors Jim Drake, Nessa Hyams, Harlene Kim Friedman
Script Consultant Daniel Gregory Browne
Writers Various
Program Consultants Elizabeth Hailey, Oliver Hailey

CAST

Mary Hartman .... Louise Lasser
Tom Hartman .... Greg Mullavey
Loretta Haggers .... Mary Kay Place
Charlie Haggers .... Graham Jarvis
Martha Shumway .... Dody Goodman
Cathy Shumway .... Debralee Scott

Grandpa Larkin ....Victor Kilian
Heather Hartman ....Claudia Lamb

865 **The Mary Tyler Moore Show** CBS
Program Type Comedy Series
30 minutes. Saturdays. Premiere date: 9/19/70. Seventh season premiere 9/25/76. Last show: 9/3/77. Series, set mainly in the WJM-TV/Minneapolis newsroom was created by James L. Brooks and Allan Burns. Music by Pat Williams.
Executive Producers James L. Brooks, Allan Burns
Producers Ed. Weinberger, Stan Daniels
Company MTM Enterprises, Inc.
Directors Jay Sandrich and others
Executive Story Consultant David Lloyd
Writers Various

CAST

Mary Richards .... Mary Tyler Moore
Lou Grant ....Edward Asner
Ted Baxter .... Ted Knight
Murray Slaughter .... Gavin MacLeod
Sue Ann Nivens
(The Happy Homemaker) .... Betty White
Georgette Baxter ....Georgia Engel

866 **M*A*S*H** CBS
Program Type Comedy Series
30 minutes. Tuesdays. Premiere date: 9/17/72. Fifth season premiere: 9/21/76 (one-hour special). Based on the 1970 motion picture "M*A*S*H." Adventures of the 4077th Mobile Army Surgical Hospital during the Korean War. Theme music by Johnny Mandel.
Executive Producer Gene Reynolds
Producers Don Reo, Allan Katz, Burt Metcalfe
Company 20th Century-Fox Television
Directors Various
Executive Story Consultant Jay Folb
Writers Various
Art Director Rodger Maus
Music Supervisor Lionel Newman

CAST

Hawkeye .... Alan Alda
Capt. B. J. Hunnicut .... Mike Farrell
Col. Sherman Potter .... Harry Morgan
Maj. "Hot Lips" Houlihan .... Loretta Swit
Maj. Frank Burns .... Larry Linville
Radar O'Reilly .... Gary Burghoff
Corp. Klinger ....Jamie Farr
Father Mulcahy ....William Christopher

867 **Mason**
The ABC Monday Comedy Special ABC
Program Type Music/Comedy/Variety Special
30 minutes. Premiere date: 7/4/77. Comedy pilot about a child genius.
Producer Ira Barmak
Company Filmways TV Productions, Inc.
Director Jack Shea
Writers Austin Kalish, Irma Kalish
Art Director Charles Lisanby

CAST

Mason Bennett ....Mason Reese
Howard Bennett ....Barry Nelson
Peggy Bennet .... Barbara Stuart
Linc .... Keith Charles
Joyce Bennett ....Lee Lawson
Bernice .... Lee Meredith

868 **Master of the World**
Famous Classic Tales CBS
Program Type Animated Film Special
60 minutes. Premiere date: 10/23/76. Based on the novel of the same name by Jules Verne. Music composed by Richard Bowden; background by Peter Connell.
Producer Walter J. Hucker
Company Air Programs International
Writer John Palmer
Animation Director Leif Gram
Voices John Ewart, Tim Eliott, Matthew O'Sullivan, Ron Haddrick, Judy Morris

869 **Masterpiece Theatre** PBS
Program Type Drama Series
60 minutes. Sundays. Umbrella title for a variety of limited dramas differing each season. Series premiered 9/69. Eighth season premiere: 10/10/76. Musical theme "Fanfare" by J. J. Mouret. Programs presented during the 1976–77 season: "Dickens of London," "Five Red Herrings," "How Green Was My Valley," "Madame Bovary," "Poldark," "Upstairs, Downstairs." (*See* individual titles for credits.) Funded by a grant from the Mobil Oil Corporation.
Producer Joan Sullivan
Company WGBH-TV/Boston
Host Alistair Cooke

870 **The Masters Tournament** CBS
Program Type Sports Special
Highlights of early round action and live coverage of the final two rounds of the Masters from the Augusta (Ga.) National Golf Club 4/8/77–4/10/77.
Producer Frank Chirkinian
Company CBS Television Network Sports
Directors Bob Dailey, Frank Chirkinian
Commentators Vin Scully, Jack Whitaker, Pat Summerall, Ben Wright, Henry Longhurst, Frank Glieber, Jim Thacker

871 **Match Game PM** Syndicated
Program Type Game/Audience Participation Series
30 minutes. Weekly. Premiere date: 9/75. Second season premiere: 9/76. Evening version of daytime game.
Producer Ira Skutch

Match Game PM *Continued*
Company Goodson-Todman Productions
Distributor Jim Victory Television, Inc.
Director Marc Breslow
Host Gene Rayburn
Announcer Johnny Olson
Regulars Richard Dawson, Brett Somers, Charles Nelson Reilly

872 **Match Game '76–77** CBS
Program Type Game/Audience Participation Series
30 minutes. Mondays–Fridays. Premiere date: 7/2/73. Continuous. Title changes yearly. Six celebrities seen each week; three are regulars.
Producer Ira Skutch
Company Goodman-Todman Productions
Director Marc Breslow
Host Gene Rayburn
Regulars Richard Dawson, Brett Somers, Charles Nelson Reilly

873 **A Matter of Size**
Americana PBS
Program Type Documentary/Informational Special
30 minutes. Premiere date: 10/29/76. Repeat date: 7/17/77 ("Americana" special). A report on people in a era of increasing bigness. Program made possible by grants from the New York Council for the Humanities and the Corporation for Public Broadcasting.
Producer Joan Lapp
Company WMHT-TV/Schenectady, N.Y.
Director Michael Marton
Film Editor Ted Zborowski

874 **Maude** CBS
Program Type Comedy Series
30 minutes. Mondays. Premiere date: 9/12/72. Fifth season premiere: 9/20/76. Series created by Norman Lear. An offshoot of "All in the Family" about a much-married liberal, Maude Findlay. Set in Tuckahoe, New York. Theme "And Then There's Maude" by Marilyn Bergman, Alan Bergman, Dave Grusin sung by Donny Hathaway.
Executive Producers Rod Parker, Hal Cooper
Producer Charlie Hauck
Company Tandem Productions
Director Hal Cooper
Story Editors William Davenport, Arthur Julian
Writers Various
Story Consultant Charlie Hauck
Script Supervisor Rod Parker

CAST

Maude Findlay .... Beatrice Arthur
Walter Findlay .... Bill Macy
Carol .... Adrienne Barbeau
Dr. Arthur Harmon .... Conrad Bain
Vivian Harmon .... Rue McClanahan
Mrs. Naugatuck .... Hermione Baddeley
Phillip .... Brian Morrison
Bert Beasley .... J. Pat O'Malley

875 **Mayday at 40,000 Feet**
The CBS Friday Night Movies CBS
Program Type TV Movie
Two hours. Premiere date: 11/12/76. Repeat date: 9/17/77. Suspense drama adapted from the novel "Jet Stream" by Austin Ferguson. Music by Richard Markowitz. Filmed on location in Salt Lake City, Utah and Los Angeles, California.
Producer Andrew J. Fenady
Company A.J. Fenady Associates in association with Warner Bros. Television
Director Robert Butler
Writers Austin Ferguson, Dick Nelson, Andrew J. Fenady
Art Director Robert Kinoshita

CAST

Capt. Pet Douglas .... David Janssen
Mike Fuller .... Don Meredith
Stan Burkhart .... Christopher George
Dr. Mannheim .... Ray Milland
Cathy Armello .... Lynda Day George
Susan Mackenzie .... Maggie Blye
Greco .... Marjoe Gortner
Marshall Riese .... Broderick Crawford
Harry Jensen .... Tom Drake
Cindy Weston .... Christopher Norris
Belsen .... Harry Rhodes
Glen Meyer .... Warren Vanders
Terry Dunlap .... Shani Wallis
Kitty Douglas .... Jane Powell
Kent .... William Bryant
Wynberg .... John Pickard
Controller .... Steven Marlo
Doctor .... Jim Chandler
Surgeon .... Phillip Mansour
Forenzo .... Al Molinaro
Julia .... Kathleen Bracken
Dowling .... Bill Catching
Jerry .... Norland Benson
Reporter .... Philip Baker Hall
Lars .... Bert Williams
Guard .... Buck Henry
2nd Reporter .... Bill Harlow
3rd Reporter .... Alan Foster
Carmichael .... Gary McLarty

876 **The Maze—The Story of William Kurelek** PBS
Program Type Documentary/Informational Special
30 minutes. Premiere date: 9/15/76. Repeat date: 3/10/77. The story of painter William Kurelek, a former mental patient. Presented by WNET-TV/New York.
Producer Dr. James B. Mass
Company Houghton-Mifflin Co.
Narrator William Kurelek

McCabe & Mrs. Miller *see* The CBS Wednesday Night Movies

877 **McCloud**
NBC Sunday Mystery Movie NBC
Program Type Crime Drama Series
90 minutes. Sundays. Shown irregularly as part of the "NBC Sunday Mystery Movie." Premiere date: 9/16/70 (as part of "Four-in-One" series). Seventh season premiere: 10/10/76. Last show: 8/28/77. A Taos, N.M. lawman on temporary assignment with the New York Police Department. Based on "World Premiere: 'McCloud: Who Killed Miss U.S.A.?' " broadcast 2/17/70.
Executive Producer Glen A. Larson
Producer Ron Satlof
Company Universal Television in association with the NBC Television Network
Directors Various
Story Editor Michael Sloan
Writers Various

CAST
Marshal Sam McCloud .... Dennis Weaver
Chief Peter B. Clifford .... J. D. Cannon
Sgt. Joe Broadhurst .... Terry Carter
Chris Coughlin ....Diana Muldaur

878 **McDuff, the Talking Dog** NBC
Program Type Children's Series
30 minutes. Saturday mornings. Premiere date: 9/11/76. Last show: 11/20/76. Comedy about a 100-year old English sheepdog ghost in a Victorian home with a veterinarian. Created by William Raynor and Myles Wilder.
Executive Producers William P. D'Angelo, Harvey Bullock, Ray Allen
Producers William Raynor, Myles Wilder
Company William Raynor/Myles Wilder Productions, Inc. in association with D'Angelo/Bullock/Allen Productions, Inc. and NBC-TV
Directors Various
Writers William Raynor, Myles Wilder

CAST
Dr. Calvin Campbell ....Walter Willison
Kimmy .... Michelle Stacy
Mr. Ferguson .... Gordon Jump
Squeaky ....Johnnie Collins
Housekeeper .... Monty Margetts

VOICES
McDuff .... Jack Lester

879 **McLaren's Riders** CBS
Program Type TV Movie
60 minutes. Premiere date: 5/17/77. Action-adventure pilot about two federal law-enforcement officers on "loan-out" to small-town police departments around the country. Music by Fred Karlin.
Producer Herbert F. Solow
Company Solow Production Company
Director Lee H. Katzin
Writer Cliff Gould
Art Director Joe Altadonna
Stunt Coordinator Bill Catching

CAST
Sam Downing ....George DiCenzo
T. Wood .... Ted Neeley
Sheriff Billy Willett .... Harry Morgan
Bobby John Britian .... Brad Davis
Lamarr Skinner .... James Best
Kate Britian .... Hilary Thompson
Wanda ....Joan Goodfellow
Pete Sunfighter ....Geno Silva
Mechanic .... Arch Archambault

880 **The McLean Stevenson Show** NBC
Program Type Comedy Series
30 minutes. Wednesdays. Premiere date: 12/1/76. Last show: 3/9/77. Comedy about the owner of a hardware store and his family.
Executive Producer Monty Hall
Producers Norman Barasch, Carroll Moore, Don Van Atta
Company M & M Production
Directors Various
Writers Various

CAST
Mac Ferguson .... McLean Stevenson
Peggy Ferguson .... Barbara Stuart
Janet Ferguson .... Ayn Ruymen
Chris Ferguson .... Steven Nevil
Grandma .... Madge West
David ....David Hollander
Jason .... Jason Whitney

881 **McMillan**
NBC Sunday Mystery Movie NBC
Program Type Crime Drama Series
90 minutes. Sundays. Shown irregularly as part of the "NBC Sunday Mystery Movie." Premiere date: 9/29/71. Sixth season premiere: 12/5/76. Last show: 8/7/77. Based on "World Premiere: 'Once Upon a Dead Man' " shown 9/17/71. Mystery drama of police commissioner in San Francisco. Created by Leonard B. Stern. Series title changed as Susan Saint James left the show and McMillan was "widowed."
Executive Producer Leonard B. Stern
Producer Jon Epstein
Company Heyday Productions in association with Universal Television and the NBC Television Network
Directors Various
Executive Story Consultant Howard Berk
Writers Various

CAST
Commissioner Stewart McMillan .... Rock Hudson
Lt. Charles Enright .... John Schuck
Agatha ....Martha Raye
Sgt. Dimaggio .... Richard Gilliland
Chief Paulson .... Bill Quinn
Maggie .... Gloria Stroock

McMillan & Wife *see* McMillan

McQ *see* NBC Saturday Night at the Movies

882 **MD** PBS
Program Type Educational/Cultural Series
30 minutes. Wednesdays. Premiere date: 6/8/77. Series repeat began 9/7/77. 13-part medical information series with guest specialists in each field. Programs funded by a grant from Cecil and Ida Green.
Producer Pat Alexander
Company KERA-TV/Dallas-Fort Worth in cooperation with the University of Texas Health Science Center at Dallas
Director George Zimmermann
Host Dr. Daniel W. Foster

883 **Me & Dad's New Wife**
ABC Afterschool Specials ABC
Program Type Children's Special
60 minutes. Premiere date: 2/18/76. Repeat date: 12/15/76. Based on the novel "A Smart Kid Like You" by Stella Pevsner. Young people's drama of a junior high school student and her father's new wife.
Producer Daniel Wilson
Company Daniel Wilson Productions
Director Larry Elikann
Writers Pat Nardo, Gloria Banta

CAST

Nina Beckwith .... Kristy McNichol
Buzz .... Lance Kerwin
Roger .... Leif Garrett
Dolores Beckwith .... Melendy Britt
Charlotte Beckwith .... Betty Beaird
George Beckwith .... Ned Wilson
Laura .... Susannah Mars
Merlaine .... Alice Playten
Additional Cast Jimmy McNichol, Tommy Crebbs, Alexa Kenin, Orlando Ruiz, Debbi Coss

Mean Streets *see* NBC Saturday Night at the Movies

884 **Meat** PBS
Program Type Documentary/Informational Special
Two hours. Premiere date: 11/13/76. Repeat date: 7/11/77. A look at the process by which Americans get their beef and lamb. Filmed in black and white at Monfort of Colorado, Inc., a company which owns feed lots and meat packing facilities. Program made possible by a grant from the Ford Foundation.
Producer Frederick Wiseman
Company WNET-TV/New York
Director Frederick Wiseman
Film Editor Frederick Wiseman

885 **Meet the New Congress**
NBC News Special NBC
Program Type Public Affairs Special
60 minutes. Premiere date: 1/22/77. A look at the 95th Congress and a discussion of domestic and foreign problems and policies.
Producer Robert Asman
Company NBC News
Anchors Catherine Mackin, Linda Ellerbee
Commentator John Hart

886 **Meet the New Senators**
CBS News Special CBS
Program Type Public Affairs Special
90 minutes. Premiere date: 1/16/77. Interviews with the newly elected senators and their families from the Sheraton-Carlton Hotel in Washington, D.C.
Producers Mary O. Yates, Frank Fitzpatrick
Company CBS News
Anchor Roger Mudd

887 **Meet the Press** NBC
Program Type Public Affairs Series
30 minutes. Sundays. Premiere date: 11/6/47 (in New York). Network premiere: 11/20/47. Continuous. The longest-running show on television. Live program, generally from Washington, D.C., with outstanding guests in the news questioned by a panel of newspeople. Created by Lawrence Spivak in October 1945 as a radio promotion for *American Mercury* magazine. Several 60-minute shows produced during the 1976–77 season.
Executive Producer Bill Monroe
Producer Betty Cole Dukert
Company NBC News
Director Max Schindler
Moderator/Panelist Bill Monroe

888 **Meeting of Minds** PBS
Program Type Educational/Cultural Series
60 minutes. Mondays. Premiere date: 1/10/77. Six-part series created by Steve Allen in which important personalities from various periods throughout history discuss major issues. Music composed by Steve Allen. Series made possible by a grant from E. F. Hutton & Company, Inc.
Executive Producer Loring d'Usseau
Producers Perry Rosemond, Loring d'Usseau
Company KCET-TV/Los Angeles
Directors Peter Levin, Bruce Franchini
Writer Steve Allen
Art Director John Retsek
Historical Consultant Dr. Robert L. Phillips
Host/Moderator Steve Allen

CAST

Theodore Roosevelt/Ulysses S. Grant ...... Joe Earley
Cleopatra/Marie Antoinette .... Jayne Meadows
St. Thomas Aquinas .... Peter Bromilow
Thomas Paine .... Joseph Sirola
Dr. Karl Marx .... Leon Askin
Sir Thomas More .... Bernard Behrens
Attila the Hun .... Khigh Dhiegh
Emily Dickinson .... Katherine Helmond
Galileo Galilei .... Alexander Scourby
Charles Darwin .... Murray Matheson

889 **Memorial Tournament** CBS
Program Type Sports Special
Live and taped coverage of the final rounds of the second Memorial Golf Tournament from Muirfield Village Golf Club, Dublin, Ohio 5/21/77 and 5/22/77.
Producer Frank Chirkinian
Company CBS Television Network Sports
Directors Bob Dailey, Frank Chirkinian
Commentators Vin Scully, Jack Whitaker, Pat Summerall, Frank Glieber, Ben Wright, Bob Halloran, Ken Venturi

890 **Menotti: Landscapes and Remembrances** PBS
Program Type Music/Dance Special
60 minutes. Premiere date: 11/14/76. The world premiere performance of the nine-part cantata "Landscapes and Remembrances" by Gian Carlo Menotti performed in May 1976 by the Bel Canto Chorus and the Milwaukee Symphony Orchestra. Program made possible by grants from Exxon Corporation and the National Endowment for the Arts.
Producer Tom Frey
Company WMVS-TV/Milwaukee
Conductor James A. Keeley
Guest Stars Judith Blegan, Gary Kendall, Vahan Khanzadian, Ani Yervanian

891 **Merce Cunningham and Dance Company**
Dance in America/Great Performances PBS
Program Type Music/Dance Special
60 minutes. Premiere date: 1/5/77. Selections from nine works performed by Merce Cunningham and Dance Company. Music composed by John Cage and David Tudor; scenery and costume design by Robert Rauschenberg, Andy Warhol, Jasper Johns, Frank Stella, Remy Charlip, Mark Lancaster. Program made possible by grants from Exxon Corporation, the National Endowment for the Arts and the Corporation for Public Broadcasting.
Executive Producer Jac Venza
Producer Emile Ardolino
Company WNET-TV/New York
Director Merrill Brockway
Choreographer Merce Cunningham

892 **The Merv Griffin Show** Syndicated
Program Type Talk/Service/Variety Series
90 minutes. Mondays–Fridays. Show first produced in 1964. Current syndication started in 1972. Continuous. Daytime talk/variety series.
Producer Bob Murphy
Company Merv Griffin Productions in association with Metromedia Producers Corporation
Director Dick Carson
Writers Merv Griffin, Bob Murphy, Tony Garofalo
Musical Director Mort Lindsay
Host Merv Griffin

893 **Michael Landon's Sounds of the West Rose Parade Preview** NBC
Program Type Music/Comedy/Variety Special
45 minutes. Premiere date: 1/1/77. Entertainment previewing the 88th annual Rose Parade with stars of the parade.
Producer Dick Schneider
Company NBC-TV Network Production
Director Dave Caldwell
Writer Barry Downes
Choreographer Tad Tadlock
Host Michael Landon

894 **Microbes and Men** PBS
Program Type Drama Series
60 minutes. Mondays. Premiere date: 2/21/77. Six-part series dramatizing the lives and accomplishments of 19th-century medical pioneers based on the book by Robert Reid. Regular feature: "Epilogue," produced at the Salk Institute by KCET-TV/Los Angeles, in which research scientists at the institute discuss new frontiers in medical research. Series presented by KCET-TV/Los Angeles and made possible by grants from Hoffman-La Roche, Inc. and the Arthur Vining Davis Foundations.
Producer Peter Goodchild
Company British Broadcasting Corporation and Time-Life Films
Host Dr. Jonas Salk

The Invisible Enemy
Director John Glenister
Writer Martin Worth

CAST

Ignaz Semmelweis .... Robert Lang
Hebra .... David Garfield
Skoda .... Wolfe Morris
Klein .... John Gill
Marcusovsky .... Nigel Lambert
Beck .... Tim Meats
Marie .... Sandra Payne
Hildenbrand .... Donald Bisset

Microbes and Men *Continued*

Rokitansky .... Leonard Maguire

A Germ Is Life

Director Peter Jones
Writer Martin Worth

CAST

Louis Pasteur .... Arthur Lowe
Robert Koch .... James Grout
Marie Pasteur .... Antonia Pemberton
Biot .... Donald Eccles
Raulin .... Richard Kane
Emmy Koch .... Patricia Heneghan

Men of Little Faith

Director Peter Jones
Writer John Wiles

CAST

Louis Pasteur .... Arthur Lowe
Robert Koch .... James Grout
Emile Roux .... Charles Kay
Chamberland .... Michael Griffiths
Marie Pasteur .... Antonia Pemberton
Emmy Koch .... Patricia Heneghan
Thuillier .... Ioan Meredith
Loir .... Keith Drinkel

Certain Death

Director Peter Jones
Writer Bruce Norman

CAST

Louis Pasteur .... Arthur Lowe
Emile Roux .... Charles Kay
Metchnikoff .... Jacob Witkin
Prof. Peter .... Aubrey Richards
Loir .... Keith Drinkel
Grancher .... John Normington
Vulpian .... Geoffrey Lumsden

A Tuberculin Affair

Writer Martin Worth

CAST

Robert Koch .... James Grout
Paul Ehrlich .... Milo O'Shea
Emil Behring .... David Swift
Von Gossler .... Geoffrey Toone
Emmy Koch .... Patricia Heneghan
Bergmann .... Charles Morgan

The Search for the Magic Bullet

Director Denis Postle
Writer Martin Worth

CAST

Paul Ehrlich .... Milo O'Shea
Sir Almroth Wright .... Michael Gough
Hedwig Ehrlich .... Stephanie Bidmead
Herxheimer .... Clifford Rose
Bertheim .... Vernon Dobtcheff
Wasserman .... Jack Woolgar

895 The Midnight Special NBC

Program Type Music/Comedy/Variety Series
90 minutes. Saturdays (1 a.m.). Premiere date: 2/3/73. Fifth season premiere: 2/4/77. First "Midnight Special" broadcast 8/19/72. Musical show featuring top acts in rock, pop, soul, country, and comedy.
Executive Producer Burt Sugarman
Producer Stan Harris
Company Burt Sugarman, Inc. Productions
Director Stan Harris
Announcer Wolfman Jack

896 Mighty Moose and the Quarterback Kid

ABC Afterschool Specials ABC
Program Type Children's Special
60 minutes. Premiere date: 12/1/76. Comedy-drama based on a story by Jeff Millar about a 12-year old who prefers photography to football. Music by Glen Ballard.
Executive Producer Alex Karras
Producer Harry Bernsen
Co-Producer Nick Frangakis
Company Harry Bernsen Productions, Inc. in association with Karavan Productions, Inc.
Director Tony Frangakis
Writers Gerald Gardner, Kay Cousins Johnson

CAST

Benny Singleton .... Brandon Cruz
Coach Puckett .... Dave Madden
Mr. Singleton .... Joseph Mascolo
Alex "Mighty Moose" Novak .... Alex Karras
Suzy .... Nancy Puthuff
L. J. .... Charles Everett
Morris .... Peter Halton
Robbie .... Matthew Robert
Luncheonette Owner .... Larry Gelman
Additional Cast The Northridge Knights Junior Midget Team

897 The Mikado

Opera Theater PBS
Program Type Music/Dance Special
Two hours. Premiere date (on PBS): 5/18/76. Repeat date: 8/16/77. 1967 film of the D'Oyly Carte Opera Company production of the operetta by W. S. Gilbert and Arthur Sullivan. Features the City of Birmingham Symphony Orchestra. Program funded by grants from the Ford Foundation, the Corporation for Public Broadcasting and Public Television Stations. Presented by WNET-TV/New York.
Coordinating Producers Linda Krisel, David Griffiths
Producers Anthony Havelock-Allan, John Brabourne
Company BHE Production released through Warner Brothers
Director Stuart Burge

CAST

Nanki-Poo .... Philip Potter
Yum-Yum .... Valerie Masterson
Ko-Ko .... John Reed
Pooh-Bah .... Kenneth Sandford
The Mikado .... Donald Adams
Pitti-Sing .... Peggy Ann Jones

Pish-Tush	Thomas Lawlor
Go-To	George Cook
Peep-Bo	Pauline Wales
Katisha	Christene Palmer

898 **The Mike Douglas Show** Syndicated
Program Type Talk/Service/Variety Series
90 minutes. Mondays–Fridays. Premiered in 1961. Continuous. Show has new guest co-host each week. Celebrated 15th anniversary with special shows throughout November 1976.
Producer Jack Reilly
Company Group W/Westinghouse Broadcasting Company, Inc. in association with Mike Douglas Entertainments, Inc.
Distributor Group W/Westinghouse Broadcasting Company, Inc.
Director Don King
Host Mike Douglas

899 **Mikhail Baryshnikov**
In Performance at Wolf Trap PBS
Program Type Music/Dance Special
60 minutes. Premiere date: 12/6/76. Repeat date: 7/26/77. Selections from five ballets in a concert at the Wolf Trap Center for the Performing Arts in Arlington, Va.: "Pas de Deux" from "Coppelia" with music by Leo Delibes; "Le Spectre de la Rose" with music by Carl Maria von Weber and staged by Andre Eglevsky; "Vestris" with music by G. Banshchikov; "Prelude and First Movement" from "Push Comes to Shove" with music by Franz Joseph Haydn and Joseph Lamb arranged by David E. Bourne; "Pas de Deux" from "Don Quixote" with music by Leon Minkus. Music performed by the Filene Center Orchestra Program made possible by a grant from the Atlantic Richfield Company.
Executive Producer David Prowitt
Producer Ruth Leon
Company WETA-TV/Washington, D.C.
Director Stan Lathan
Conductor Akiro Endo

Pas de Deux—Coppelia
Choreographer Arthur Saint-Leon
Dancers Mikhail Baryshnikov, Gelsey Kirkland

Le Spectre de la Rose
Choreographer Michel Fokine
Costume Designers Leon Bakst, Stanley Simmons
Dancers Mikhail Baryshnikov, Marianna Tcherkassky

Vestris
Choreographer Leonid Jacobson
Dancer Mikhail Baryshnikov

Prelude and First Movement—Push Comes to Shove
Choreographer Twyla Tharp
Costume Designer Santo Loquasto
Dancers Mikhail Baryshnikov, Marianna Tcherkassky, Martine Van Hamel

Pas de Deux—Don Quixote
Choreographer Marius Petipa
Dancers Mikhail Baryshnikov, Gelsey Kirkland

900 **The Million Dollar Rip-Off**
NBC Movie of the Week NBC
Program Type TV Movie
90 minutes. Premiere date: 9/22/76. Repeat date: 6/23/77. Drama about the payroll heist of a big city's mass transit system. Story by Andrew Peter Marin based on a screenplay by William DeVane and John Pleshette. Music by Vic Mizzy. Filmed in Los Angeles and Chicago.
Producer Edward J. Montagne
Company Charles Fries Productions in association with NBC-TV
Director Alexander Singer
Writer Andrew Peter Marin
Costume Designer Frank Novak

CAST

Muff Novak	Freddie Prinze
Ralph Fogherty	Allen Garfield
Kitty	Brooke Mills
Jessie	Joanna de Varona
Lil	Christine Belford
Helene	Linda Scruggs Bogart
Lubeck	James Sloyan
Jarrett	Bob Hastings

901 **Minstrel Man**
Mobil Showcase Presentation CBS
Program Type Dramatic Special
Two hours. Premiere date: 3/2/77. Drama about black minstrels in 1885. Filmed on location in Mississippi. Original music and music arrangement by Fred Karlin.
Executive Producers Roger Gimbel, Edward L. Rissien
Producers Mitchell Brower, Robert Lovenheim
Company A Roger Gimbel Production for First Artists
Director William A. Graham
Script Consultant Toni Morrison
Writers Richard Shapiro, Esther Mayesh Shapiro
Choreographer Donald McKayle
Art Director Hilyard Brown

CAST

Harry Brown, Jr.	Glynn Turman
Charlie Bates	Ted Ross
Rennie Brown	Stanley Clay
Jessamine	Saundra Sharp
Tambo	Art Evans
Harry Brown, Sr./Fat Man	Gene Bell
George	Earl Billings
Young Harry Brown, Jr.	Anthony Amos
Young Rennie Brown	Amechi Uzodinma

Minstrel Man *Continued*

Robert	Arthur Rooks
Tess	Carol Sutton
Finch	Wilbur Swartz
Turpin	Robert Earle
Carmichael	Don Lutenbacher
Pitchman	Billy Holliday
Fair Manager	Robert L. Harper

Miracle in Milan *see* PBS Movie Theater

902 **Miss America Pageant** CBS
Program Type Parades/Pageants/Awards Special
Two hours. Finale of the 1977 Miss America Pageant live from Convention Hall, Atlantic City, N.J. 9/10/77. Production numbers produced, directed and written by George Cavalier. Original music and lyrics by Edna Osser and Glenn Osser.
Executive Producer Albert A. Marks, Jr.
Producer John L. Koushouris
Director Dave Wilson
Writer Angela Osborne
Choreographer Ron Poindexter
Hosts Bert Parks, Phyllis George
Entertainers Dorothy Benham, Terry Meeuwsen, Debbie Ward, Michele Sisk, John Lamont, Scott Hayden, Miss America USO Troupe

903 **Miss Black America Pageant** NBC
Program Type Parades/Pageants/Awards Special
Two hours. Live coverage of the 10th annual Miss Black America Pageant from the Santa Monica (Calif.) Civic Auditorium 9/9/77.
Executive Producer Burt Sugarman
Producer Lee Miller
Company Burt Sugarman, Inc.
Director Sidney Smith
Musical Director Phil Moore
Executive Consultant Bob Finkel
Host Billy Dee Williams
Special Guest Stars LeVar Burton, Lou Gossett, Diahann Carroll, Twanna Kilgore

904 **Miss, Mrs., or Ms.—What's It All About?**
What's It All About? CBS
Program Type Children's Special
30 minutes. Premiere date: 5/21/77. Informational program for school-age children examining the roles of women in America today.
Executive Producer Joel Heller
Producer Vern Diamond
Company CBS News
Director Vern Diamond
Writer Ellen Schecter
Correspondents Sylvia Chase, Christopher Glenn

905 **Miss Teenage America Pageant** NBC
Program Type Parades/Pageants/Awards Special
90 minutes. Live coverage of the 16th annual pageant from the Maybee Center, Oral Roberts University, Tulsa, Okla. 11/27/76.
Producer Joseph Cates
Company A Joseph Cates Company, Inc. Production
Director Sidney Smith
Writer Frank Slocum
Musical Director James Gaertner
Art Director Don Shirley
Star Bob Hope
Host Cathy Durden
Featured Guests Gary Moore Singers

906 **Miss Universe Beauty Pageant** CBS
Program Type Parades/Pageants/Awards Special
Two hours. Live coverage via satellite of the finale of the Miss Universe Pageant from the National Theater in Santo Domingo, Dominican Republic 7/16/77.
Executive Producers Bob Finkel, Harold L. Glasser
Producer Bob Finkel
Director Sidney Smith
Writer Donald K. Epstein
Musical Director Elliot Lawrence
Choreographer Gene Bayliss
Art Director Don Shirley
Hosts Bob Barker, Helen O'Connell
Featured Guest Rina Messinger

907 **Miss USA Beauty Pageant** CBS
Program Type Parades/Pageants/Awards Special
Two hours. Live coverage of the finals of the 26th annual Miss USA Beauty Pageant from Gaillard Municipal Auditorium, Charleston, S.C. 5/14/77.
Executive Producers Bob Finkel, Harold L. Glasser
Producer Bob Finkel
Company Miss Universe, Inc.
Director Sidney Smith
Writer Donald K. Epstein
Musical Director Elliot Lawrence
Choreographer Gene Bayliss
Art Director Don Shirley
Hosts Bob Barker, Helen O'Connell
Special Guest Bobby Vinton
Featured Guests Barbara Elaine Peterson, Rina Messinger

908 **Miss World 1976** NBC
Program Type Parades/Pageants/Awards Special
77 minutes. Premiere date: 4/23/77. Highlights of the 26th Miss World Contest from the Royal Albert Hall in London, England. Taped in November 1976.
Executive Producers Seymour Sietz, Hal Blake; Phil Lewis
Producer Michael Begg
Company BBS Productions in association with the British Broadcasting Corporation
Director Michael Begg
Writer Herbert L. Strock
Hosts Jo Ann Pflug, Chuck Woolery
Announcer Herb Kerns
Special Guest Star Sasha Distel

909 **Missa Solemnis** PBS
Program Type Music/Dance Special
90 minutes. Premiere date (on PBS): 4/16/76. Repeat date: 3/22/77. A performance of "Missa Solemnis" by Ludwig van Beethoven taped at St. Peter's Basilica in Rome in May 1970 to commemorate the 200th anniversary of his birth and the 50th anniversary of Pope Paul VI to the priesthood. Music performed by the Symphony Orchestra of RAI with Angelo Stefanato solo violinist. Originally shown over the Eurovision network in 1970. Program made possible by a grant from Alitalia Airlines. Presented by WGBH-TV/Boston; Henry Morgenthau, executive producer.
Company Radiotelevisione Italiana
Director Franco Zeffirelli
Conductor Wolfgang Sawallisch
Choral Director Josef Schmidthurber
Guest Performers Ingrid Bjorner, Christa Ludwig, Placido Domingo, Kurt Moll

Mister *see also* Mr.

910 **Mister Rogers' Neighborhood** PBS
Program Type Children's Series
30 minutes. Monday mornings-Friday mornings. Premiere date: 5/22/67. Title changed from "Misterogers' Neighborhood" in Sept. 1970. The longest-running children's show on PBS. Created by Fred Rogers. Regular feature: visits to the puppet-populated Neighborhood of Make-Believe. Series funded by grants from Sears Roebuck Foundation, the Corporation for Public Broadcasting, the Ford Foundation, Public Television Stations and Johnson and Johnson Baby Products.
Executive Producer Fred Rogers
Producer Bill Moates
Company Family Communications, Inc. in association with WQED-TV/Pittsburgh
Director Bill Moates
Writer Fred Rogers
Musical Director John Costa
Art Director Jack Guest
Host Fred Rogers
Puppeteers Fred Rogers, William P. Barker, Robert Trow

CAST

Lady Aberlin .... Betty Aberlin
Chef Brockett .... Don Brockett
Francois Clemmons .... Francois Clemmons
Pilot Ito .... Yoshi Ito
Mrs. McFeely .... Betsy Nadas
Elsie Neal .... Elsie Neal
Handyman Negri .... Joe Negri
Mr. McFeely .... David Newell
Audrey Cleans Everything (A.C.E.)/Audrey Paulifficate .... Audrey Roth
Robert Troll/Bob Dog/Bob Trow .... Robert Trow

VOICES

X the Owl/King Friday XIII/Queen Sara Saturday/ Cornflake S. Pecially/Lady Elaine Fairchilde/ Henrietta Pussycat/Grandpere/Edgar Cooke/ Daniel Striped Tiger/Doneky Hodie .... Fred Rogers
Dr. Duckbill Platypus/Mrs. Elsie Jean Platypus .... William P. Barker
Harriett Elizabeth Cow .... Robert Trow

911 **Mitzi ... Zings Into Spring** CBS
Program Type Music/Comedy/Variety Special
60 minutes. Premiere date: 3/29/77. Musical-comedy special with a spring theme. Special musical material by Marvin Laird.
Executive Producer Jack Bean
Company Green Isle Enterprises, Inc.
Director Tony Charmoli
Writer Jerry Mayer
Choreographer Tony Charmoli
Costume Designer Bob Mackie
Scenic Designer Robert Kelly
Star Mitzi Gaynor
Special Guests Roy Clark, Wayne Rogers

912 **Mixed Nuts**
Special Comedy Presentation ABC
Program Type Comedy Special
30 minutes. Premiere date: 5/12/77. Comedy pilot about patients in a psychiatric hospital.
Executive Producers Jerry Belson, Mark Carliner
Producer Michael Leeson
Company Viacom Enterprises
Director Peter H. Hunt
Writers Jerry Belson, Michael Leeson

CAST

Dr. Sarah Allgood .... Zohra Lampert
Nurse Cassidy .... Conchata Ferrell
Bugs .... Dan Barrows
Logan .... Richard Karron
Moe .... Morey Amsterdam
Gato .... James Victor
Jamie .... Ed Begley, Jr.
Dr. Folder .... Emory Bass

Mobil Showcase Presentation *see* Doug Henning's World of Magic/Minstrel Man/Ten Who Dared

913 **Mobile Medics** CBS
Program Type Dramatic Special
30 minutes. Premiere date: 5/10/77. Medical action pilot about three men operating a mobile medical unit. Created by Robert Hamilton. Special effects by Dick Albain,
Producer Bruce Lansbury
Company Bruce Lansbury Productions, Ltd. in association with Columbia Pictures Television
Director Paul Krasny
Writer Robert Hamilton
Art Director John Beckman

CAST

Craig Bryant .... Ben Masters
Robb Spencer .... Jack Stauffer
Pete Vasquez .... Jaime Tirelli
Liz Rheiner .... Ellen Weston
Foreman .... Robert DoQui
Cheryl .... Julie Cobb
Nurse .... Maggie Malooly
Fire Captain .... John Pickard

Monday Night Baseball *see* ABC's Monday Night Baseball

914 **The Moneychangers**
The Big Event/NBC Saturday Night at the Movies NBC
Program Type Limited Series
6 1/2 hours. Sundays (except premiere). Premiere date: 12/4/76. Last show: 12/19/76. Dramatization of the novel by Arthur Hailey about a power struggle in a banking empire. Music composed by Henry Mancini. Filmed in part on locations in Los Angeles.
Producers Ross Hunter, Jacque Mapes
Company Ross Hunter Productions, Inc. in association with Paramount Television and NBC-TV
Director Boris Sagal
Writers Dean Riesner, Stanford Whitmore
Art Director Jack DeShields

CAST

Alex Vandervoort .... Kirk Douglas
Roscoe Heyward .... Christopher Plummer
Miles Eastin .... Timothy Bottoms
Margot Bracken .... Susan Flannery
Edwina Dorsey .... Anne Baxter
Nolan Wainwright .... Percy Rodrigues
Jerome Patterton .... Ralph Bellamy
Avril Devereaux .... Joan Collins
Tony Bear .... Robert Loggia
Beatrice Heyward .... Jean Peters
Harold Austin .... Patrick O'Neal
George Quartermain .... Lorne Greene
Dr. McCartney .... Helen Hayes
Juanita .... Amy Tivell
Lewis Dorsey .... Hayden Rorke

Monika *see* PBS Movie Theater

915 **A Monster Concert** PBS
Program Type Music/Dance Special
30 minutes. Premiere date: 1/18/76. Repeat date: 9/28/76. Ten grand pianos and twenty pianists perform in a "monster concert."
Senior Producer Gene Bunge
Producer Ron Nicodemus
Company Nebraska Educational Television Network
Director Ron Nicodemus
Conductor George Koutzen
Host Harold Shiffler
Guest Artists Eugene List, Russell Riepe, Vincent Savant, Arthur Easley

916 **The Monster Squad** NBC
Program Type Children's Series
30 minutes. Saturday mornings. Premiere date: 9/11/76. Last show: 9/3/77. Teen-age caretaker and his wax museum monsters who "come alive" fighting crime. Music by Richard La Salle.
Executive Producers William P. D'Angelo, Harvey Bullock, Ray Allen
Producer Michael McLean
Company D'Angelo/Bullock/Allen Productions in association with NBC-TV
Directors Herman Hoffman, William P. D'Angelo and others
Story Editor Stanley Ralph Ross
Writers Various
Art Director Keaton S. Walker

CAST

Dracula .... Henry Polic II
Frankenstein .... Michael Lane
Bruce Wolfman .... Buck Kartalian
Walt .... Fred Grandy

917 **MONSTERS! Mysteries or Myths?**
All-Specials Night NBC
Program Type Documentary/Informational Special
60 minutes. Premiere date: 11/25/74 (on CBS). Repeat date: 1/20/77. A look at the legends of the Abominable Snowman, the Loch Ness Monster and Bigfoot.
Executive Producer George Lefferts
Producer Robert Guenette
Company Wolper Productions in association with the Smithsonian Institution
Director Robert Guenette
Writer Robert Guenette
Narrator Rod Serling

918 **Monte Carlo Circus Festival** CBS
Program Type Music/Comedy/Variety Special
60 minutes. Premiere date: 2/16/77. A presenta-

tion of the best of 45 circus acts from the annual Monte Carlo circus festival.
Producers Joseph Cates, Gilbert Cates
Company Joseph Cates Company, Inc. in association with Son et Lumiere, Jean Paul Blondeau Productions
Directors Joseph Cates, Gilbert Cates
Writers Joseph Cates, Gilbert Cates
Host Chad Everett

More Dead Than Alive *see* NBC Saturday Night at the Movies

919 **Most Wanted** ABC
Program Type Crime Drama Series
60 minutes. Saturdays/Mondays (as of 3/7/77). Premiere date: 10/16/76. Last regularly scheduled show: 4/25/77. Two Saturday shows: 8/13/77 and 8/20/77. Action-adventures of a semi-autonomous unit of the Los Angeles Police Department that handles crimes on the Mayor's "Most Wanted" list. Series created by Laurence Heath. Pilot aired 3/21/76. Music composed by Lalo Schifrin.
Executive Producer Quinn Martin
Supervising Producer Russell Stoneham
Producer Harold Gast
Company A Quinn Martin Production
Directors Virgil Vogel and others
Writers Various

CAST
Capt. Linc Evers .... Robert Stack
Sgt. Charlie Benson .... Shelly Novack
Off. Kate Manners .... Jo Ann Harris
Mayor Dan Stoddard .... Harry Rhodes

Mother *see* PBS Movie Theater

920 **Mother's Little Network** PBS
Program Type Comedy Special
30 minutes. Premiere date: 2/8/77. Skits, animated sequences and takeoffs in an American version of "Monty Python's Flying Circus." Program made possible by grants from the Corporation for Public Broadcasting, the National Endowment for the Arts and the Rockefeller Foundation.
Producer Fred Barzyk
Company WGBH-TV/Boston
Performers Tony Kahn, Arnie Reisman, Ernie Fosselius, Nancy Spiller

921 **The Mound Builders**
Theater in America/Great Performances PBS
Program Type Dramatic Special
90 minutes. Premiere date: 2/11/76. Repeat date: 8/3/77. 1975 play written specifically for and produced by the Circle Repertory Company, New York City. Program made possible by funds from Exxon Corporation, Public Television Stations, the Corporation for Public Broadcasting and the Ford Foundation. Cast listed in alphabetical order.
Executive Producer Jac Venza
Producer Ken Campbell
Company WNET-TV/New York and New Jersey Public Television/Trenton
Directors Marshall W. Mason, Ken Campbell
Writer Lanford Wilson
Costume Designer Jennifer Von Mayrhauser
Host Hal Holbrook
Set Designer John Lee Beatty

CAST
D. K. Eriksen .... Tanya Berezin
Chad Jasker .... Brad Dourif
Cynthia .... Stephanie Gordon
Dr. Jean Loggins .... Trish Hawkins
Dr. Dan Loggins .... Jonathan Hogan
Kirsten .... Lauren Jacobs
Dr. August Howe .... Rob Thirkield

922 **Mowgli's Brothers** CBS
Program Type Animated Film Special
30 minutes. Premiere date: 2/11/76. Repeat date: 5/6/77. Third in a series of adaptations from "The Jungle Books" by Rudyard Kipling. Music by Dean Elliott.
Producers Chuck Jones, Oscar Dufau
Company Chuck Jones Enterprises
Directors Chuck Jones, Hal Ambro
Writer Chuck Jones
Narrator Roddy McDowall

VOICES
Mowgli/Shere Khan/Akela/Tabaqui/Bagheera/Baloo .... Roddy McDowall
Mother Wolf .... June Foray

923 **Mozart in Seattle** PBS
Program Type Music/Dance Special
60 minutes. Premiere date: 6/21/76. Repeat date: 9/5/77. A behind-the-scenes look at two artists preparing for a concert of Mozart's Sinfonia Concertante for Violin, Viola and Orchestra performed with the Seattle Symphony Orchestra. Program made possible by grants from Gull Industries, Inc., the King County Arts Commission, the Seattle Arts Commission, the Seattle Symphony Orchestra, the Sam and Althea Stroum Foundation and Members of Nine.
Producer Robert Hagopian
Company KCTS-TV/Seattle, Wash.
Director Robert Hagopian
Conductor Milton Katims
Soloists Henryk Szeryng, Milton Katims

Mr. Majestyk *see* The CBS Wednesday Night Movies

Mr. Ricco *see* NBC Saturday Night at the Movies

924 **Mr. Rooney Goes to Work**
CBS News Special CBS
Program Type Documentary/Informational Special
60 minutes. Premiere date: 7/5/77. A look at Americans at work across the country.
Executive Producer Perry Wolff
Producer Andrew A. Rooney
Company CBS News
Director Andrew A. Rooney
Writer Andrew A. Rooney
Cinematographer Walter Dombrow
Film Editor Robert R. Forte
Reporter Andrew A. Rooney

925 **Mr. T & Tina** ABC
Program Type Comedy Series
30 minutes. Saturdays. Premiere date: 9/25/76. Last show: 10/30/76. An East-meets-West comedy, set in Chicago, about the transplanted family of a Japanese inventor-widower and a Nebraska-born governess. Created by James Komack; developed for television by Stan Cutler. Theme song "Chicago" adapted by George Aliceson Tipton.
Executive Producer James Komack
Producers Bob Carroll, Jr., Madelyn Davis
Co-Producer Gary Shimokawa
Company The Komack Company, Inc.
Directors Various
Executive Story Consultant David Panich
Script Consultant George Tibbles
Writers Various
Creative Consultant Eric Cohen

CAST
Taro Takahashi .... Pat Morita
Tina Kelly .... Susan Blanchard
Michi .... Pat Suzuki
Harvard .... Ted Lange
Miss Llewellyn .... Miriam Byrd-Nethery
Uncle Matsu .... Jerry Hatsuo Fujikawa
Sachi .... June Angela
Aki .... Gene Profanato

926 **Mrs. Gandhi's India** PBS
Program Type Documentary/Informational Special
60 minutes. Premiere date: 9/21/76. Repeat date: 10/29/76. An interview with Prime Minister Indira Gandhi of India plus a studio segment anchored by Martin Agronsky.
Producer Frank Phillippi
Company WETA-TV/Washington
Interviewer Anthony Mayer

927 **Mrs. Warren's Profession**
Classic Theatre: The Humanities in Drama PBS
Program Type Dramatic Special
Two hours. Premiere date: 12/18/75. Repeat date: 5/12/77. George Bernard Shaw's 1902 comedy/drama about prostitution. Taped in 1972. Program made possible by grants from the National Endowment for the Humanities and the Mobil Oil Corporation. Presented by WGBH-TV/Boston; Joan Sullivan, producer.
Producer Cedric Messina
Company British Broadcasting Corporation
Director Herbert Wise
Writer George Bernard Shaw

CAST
Mrs. Warren .... Coral Browne
Vivie Warren .... Penelope Wilton
Sir George Crofts .... James Grout
Mr. Praed .... Derek Godfrey
Frank Gardner .... Robert Powell
The Rev. Samuel Gardner .... Richard Pearson

928 **Muggsy** NBC
Program Type Children's Series
30 minutes. Saturdays. Premiere date: 9/18/76. Last show: 4/2/77. Drama set in an urban ghetto about a teen-age girl, her cab-driver stepbrother and their garage-owner friend. Taped on location in Bridgeport, Conn. Theme "Keepin' It Together" music by David Collins; lyrics by J. Philip Miller sung by Blood, Sweat and Tears.
Executive Producer George A. Heinemann
Producer Joseph F. Callo
Company An NBC Television Production
Directors J. Philip Miller, Tad Danielewski, Bert Salzman, Sidney Smith
Story Editor Jon Surgal
Writers Various
Art Director Leon Munier

CAST
Muggsy .... Sarah MacDonnell
Nick .... Ben Masters
Gus .... Paul Michael
Clytemnestra .... Star-Shemah
T.P. .... Donny Cooper
Lil Man .... Jimmy McCann

929 **Mulligan's Stew** NBC
Program Type TV Movie
90 minutes. Premiere date: 6/20/77. Comedy about the family of the high school coach who inherit four orphans. Pilot for 1977–78 series of the same name.
Producer Joanna Lee
Company Christiana Production in association with Paramount Television
Director Noel Black
Writer Joanna Lee

CAST
Michael Mulligan .... Lawrence Pressman
Jane Mulligan .... Elinor Donahue

Mark	Johnny Whitaker
Mr. Hollenbeck	Alex Karras
Jimmy	K. C. Martel
Melinda	Julie Haddock
Stevie	Suzanne Crough
Adam	Christopher Ciampa
Polly	Lory Kochheim
Kimmy	Sunshine Lee

Multi-Special Night *see* All-Specials Night/Multi-Special Night

930 **The Muppet Show** Syndicated
Program Type Music/Comedy/Variety Series
30 minutes. Weekly. Premiere date: 9/76. The Muppets plus guests in a comedy-variety show emceed by Kermit the Frog. Developed in cooperation with the CBS-TV owned and operated stations.
Executive Producer Jim Henson
Producer Jack Burns
Company ITC Entertainment and Henson Associates
Distributor ITC Entertainment
Director Jerry Juhl
Head Writer Jack Burns
Writers Jack Burns, Jim Henson, Jerry Juhl
Musical Director Jack Parnell

931 **Murder at the World Series**
The ABC Sunday Night Movie ABC
Program Type TV Movie
Two hours. Premiere date: 3/20/77. Drama of a kidnapping during the World Series in Houston. Music by John Cacavas. Filmed on location in Houston and Los Angeles.
Producer Cy Chermak
Company ABC Circle Films
Director Andrew V. McLaglen
Writer Cy Chermak
Art Director Elayne Barbara Ceder

CAST

Margo Mannering	Lynda Day George
Harvey Murkison	Murray Hamilton
Lois Marshall	Karen Valentine
Moe Gold	Gerald S. O'Loughlin
Larry Marshall	Michael Parks
Karen Weese	Janet Leigh
Governor	Hugh O'Brian
Alice Dakso	Nancy Kelly
Severino	Johnny Seven
Liza	Tamara Dobson
Sam	Joseph Wiseman
Cisco	Bruce Boxleitner
Vawn	Larry Mahan
Frank Gresham	Cooper Huckabee
Kathy	Maggie Wellman
Jane Torres	Cynthia Avila
Barbara Gresham	Monica Gayle

932 **Murder One**
Documentary Showcase PBS
Program Type Documentary/Informational Special
60 minutes. Premiere date: 5/13/77. Repeat date: 9/23/77 (captioned for the hearing-impaired). Documentary focusing on six men convicted of first degree murder in North Carolina and Georgia as well as a look at their families and the families of their victims. Program made possible by grants from the Corporation for Public Broadcasting, the Harvard Center for Criminal Justice and the Mary Reynolds Babcock Foundation.
Executive Producer Patricia Sides
Producers Fleming Barnes "Tex" Fuller, John R. Haney, Hugh Fisher
Company WNET-TV/New York, Georgia Educational Television and South Carolina Educational Television
Writer Fleming Barnes "Tex" Fuller
Narrator Fleming Barnes "Tex" Fuller

933 **The Murderer** PBS
Program Type Dramatic Special
25 minutes. Premiere date: 10/12/76. Repeat date: 7/10/77. Dramatization of a story by Ray Bradbury.
Producer Andrew Silver
Company WGBH New Television Workshop/Boston
Director Andrew Silver

CAST

Brock	Paul Guilfoyle
Nordau	Frederic Kimball

934 **Music for Young Performers**
The CBS Festival of Lively Arts for Young People CBS
Program Type Children's Special
60 minutes. Premiere date: 2/8/76. Repeat date: 5/14/77. A New York Philharmonic Young People's Concert of music written for and performed by young musicians.
Producer Roger Englander
Company CBS Television Network
Director Roger Englander
Writer Michael Tilson Thomas
Conductor Michael Tilson Thomas
Narrator Michael Tilson Thomas
Boy Sopranos Todd Butt, Gavin Maloney
Musicians Gary Schocker, John Senior, Ethan Bauch, Carleton Greene, Chan Hee Kim

935 **Music Hall America** Syndicated
Program Type Music/Comedy/Variety Series
60 minutes. Weekly. Premiere date: 9/76. One-season country music/comedy/variety show

Music Hall America *Continued*
taped at Opryland, USA in Nashville. Different guest hosts weekly.
Executive Producers Roy Smith, Henry Gillespie
Producer Lee Miller
Company Viacom Enterprises in association with Opryland Productions
Distributor Viacom Enterprises
Director Lee Bernhardi
Writers Wally Dalton, Mike Kagan

936 **Music in America**
Great Performances PBS
Program Type Music/Dance Series
Two classical music shows seen as part of the "Great Performances" series: "Copland Conducts Copland" and "The Music of Ernest Bloch." (*See* individual titles for credits.)

937 **Music in Jerusalem** PBS
Program Type Music/Dance Special
60 minutes. Premiere date: 8/16/77. A look at the Jerusalem Music Center. Filmed over four years. Program made possible by a grant from Automatic Data Processing, Inc.
Executive Producer Ruth Leon
Producer Paul Salinger
Company WETA-TV/Washington, D.C.
Director Paul Salinger
Host/Narrator Isaac Stern

938 **The Music of Christmas** PBS
Program Type Music/Dance Special
30 minutes. Premiere date: 12/21/75. Repeat date: 12/20/76. Christmas concert from the Mormon Tabernacle in Salt Lake City. Performed by the Mormon Youth Symphony and Chorus. Program made possible by a grant from Bonneville International.
Company KUED-TV/Salt Lake City
Conductor Jay Welch
Assistant Conductor Had Gundersen

939 **The Music of Ernest Bloch**
Music in America/Great Performances PBS
Program Type Music/Dance Special
60 minutes. Premiere date: 5/19/76. Repeat date: 8/7/77. The Cleveland Symphony Orchestra performing the works of Ernest Bloch. Program funded by a grant from Exxon Corporation.
Executive Producer Jac Venza
Producers David Griffiths, Klaus Hallig
Company WNET-TV/New York and the International Television Trading Corporation
Conductor Lorin Maazel
Guest Soloist Leonard Rose

940 **The Music School**
The American Short Story PBS
Program Type Dramatic Special
60 minutes. Premiere date: 5/10/77. Adaptation of the short story by John Updike about a middle-aged writer in contemporary society. Music by Ed Bogas. Program presented by South Carolina Educational Television and made possible by a grant from the National Endowment for the Humanities.
Executive Producer Robert Geller
Producer Dan McCann
Company Learning in Focus, Inc.
Director John Korty
Writer John Korty
Host Colleen Dewhurst

CAST

Alfred Schweigen .... Ronald Weyand
Schweigen's Wife .... Dana Larsson
Scientist .... Tom Dahlgren
Scientist's Wife .... Vera Stough
Country Priest .... Frank Albertson
Maggie Johns .... Elizabeth Huddle Nyberg
Divorced Woman .... Anne Lawder

Mutual of Omaha's Wild Kingdom *see* Wild Kingdom

941 **My Dear Uncle Sherlock**
ABC Short Story Specials ABC
Program Type Children's Special
30 minutes. Premiere date: 4/16/77. Story of a 12-year-old boy and his uncle who solve a mystery using deductive reasoning. Based on the short story by Hugh Pentecost.
Executive Producer Allen Ducovny
Producer William Beaudine, Jr.
Company ABC Circle Films
Director Arthur H. Nadel
Writer Manya Starr

CAST

Joey Trimble .... Robbie Rist
Uncle "Sherlock" George .... Royal Dano
Bill Leggett .... John Karlen
Off. Gilligan .... Vaughn Armstrong
Dave Taylor .... John Milford
Mr. Trimble .... John Carter
Mrs. Trimble .... Inga Swenson

942 **My Father Calls Me Son: Racism and Native Americans** PBS
Program Type Documentary/Informational Special
30 minutes. Premiere date: 10/8/76. A look at racism and its effect on American Indians.
Producers Paul Cabbell, David Fanning
Company KOCE-TV/Huntington Beach, Calif.
Directors David Fanning, Harry Ratner
Reporter Paul Cabbell

943 **My Kingdom for Love: Abdication** PBS

Program Type Documentary/Informational Special

60 minutes. Premiere date: 8/77. Documentary on King Edward VIII using film clips and first-hand accounts.

Producer Gordon Watkins
Company British Broadcasting Corporation and Time-Life Films
Distributor Time-Life Films through the Eastern Educational Television Network
Director Philip Geddes
Writer James Cameron
Narrator James Cameron

944 **My Mom's Having a Baby**

ABC Afterschool Specials ABC

Program Type Children's Special

60 minutes. Premiere date: 2/16/77. Repeat date: 5/8/77 (evening special). Story explaining the facts of human reproduction using drama, animation and a videotaped birth sequence showing Candace Farrell giving birth to her child. Music by Dean Elliott; lyrics by John Bradford.

Executive Producers David H. DePatie, Friz Freleng
Producer Robert Chenault
Company DePatie-Freleng Enterprises
Director Larry Elikann
Writers Susan Fichter Kennedy, Elaine Evans Rushnell
Art Director Ray Markham
Animation Director Tom Yakutis
Animators Don Williams, Nelson Shin, Bob Richardson, John Gibbs

CAST

Dr. Lendon Smith	Lendon Smith, M.D.
Petey Evans	Shane Sinutko
Oscar	Jarrod Johnson
Kelly	Rachel Longaker
Anne Evans	Candace Farrell
Peter's Father	Ed Rombola
Nurse	Karen Glow Carr
Receptionist	Dodo Denney

Mysteries From Beyond Earth *see* NBC Night at the Movies

945 **Mysteries of the Great Pyramid** CBS

Program Type Documentary/Informational Special

60 minutes. Premiere date: 4/20/77. Examination of the Pyramid of Cheops at Giza, Egypt. Music by Lyn Murray.

Producer William Kronick
Co-Producer Jeffrey Pill
Company Wolper Productions
Director William Kronick
Writer William Kronick
Cinematographers Andre Gunn, Gilbert Hubbs, Peter Hoving, Patrick Turley
Film Editor David Saxon
Researcher Vicke-Leigh Yarwood
Host/Narrator Omar Sharif

946 **The Mysterious Island**

Famous Classic Tales CBS

Program Type Animated Film Special

60 minutes. Premiere date: 11/15/75. Repeat date: 11/25/76. Based on the novel by Jules Verne about five refugees from a Confederate prison during the Civil War. Music by Richard Bowden. Backgrounds by Peter Connell and Milan Zahorsky.

Executive Producer Walter J. Hucker
Company Air Programs International
Writer John Palmer
Animation Director Leif Gram
Voices John Llewellyn, Mark Kelly, Alastair Duncan, Ron Haddrick, Tim Eliott

947 **Nadia—From Romania With Love** CBS

Program Type Music/Comedy/Variety Special

60 minutes. Premiere date: 11/23/76. A behind-the scenes look at Nadia Comaneci. The first entertainment co-production between the United States and Romania, filmed on location in Romania.

Executive Producers Dick Foster, Monte Kay
Producers Bill Innes, Tom Egan
Company Clerow Productions, Inc. in association with Radioteleviziunea Romana
Directors Dick Foster, Sterling Johnson
Writers Tom Egan, Dumitru Udrescu
Conductor Everett Gordon
Host Flip Wilson

948 **Name That Tune** NBC

Program Type Game/Audience Participation Series

30 minutes. Mondays-Fridays. Premiere date: 1/3/77. Last show: 6/10/77. Originally created by Harry Salter 9/2/54. New daytime show ran on NBC 7/29/74–1/3/75. Musical quiz game with contestants trying to guess the "mystery tune."

Executive Producer Ralph Edwards
Producer Ray Horl
Company Ralph Edwards Productions in association with the NBC Television Network
Director Richard Gottlieb
Conductor Tommy Oliver
Art Director Ed Flesh
Musicologist Harvey Bacal
Host Tom Kennedy
Announcer John Harlan

Name That Tune (Evening) *see* $100,000 Name That Tune

949 **Nancy Drew Mysteries** ABC
Program Type Children's Series
60 minutes. Sundays. Premiere date: 2/6/77. Seen every other Sunday alternating with "Hardy Boys Mysteries." Based on the "Nancy Drew" books by Carolyn Keene. Adventures of an all-American teenage detective. Each episode entitled "The Mystery of the. . . ." Theme music by Glen A. Larson.
Executive Producer Glen A. Larson
Supervising Producer B. W. Sandefur
Producers Arlene Sidaris, Joyce Brotman
Company A Glen A. Larson Production in association with Universal Television
Directors Various
Writers Various

CAST
Nancy Drew ....Pamela Sue Martin
Carson Drew .... William Schallert
Ned Nickerson ....George O'Hanlon, Jr.
George Fayne .... Jean Rasey

950 **The Nancy Walker Show** ABC
Program Type Comedy Series
30 minutes. Thursdays. Premiere date: 9/30/76. Last show: 12/23/76. Show created and developed by Norman Lear and Rod Parker about a talent agent and her family. "Nancy's Blues" music by Marvin Hamlisch; lyrics by Marilyn Bergman and Alan Bergman.
Executive Producer Rod Parker
Producers Arnie Rosen, Jerry Davis
Company A Norman Lear T.A.T. Communications Company, Inc. Production
Directors Various
Writers Various

CAST
Nancy Kitteridge ....Nancy Walker
Lt. Comdr. Kenneth Kitteridge ...... William Daniels
Terry Folson .... Ken Olfson
Lorraine .... Beverly Archer
Glen .... James Cromwell
Michael Futterman .... Sparky Marcus
Teddy Futterman .... William Schallert

951 **Nashville 99** CBS
Program Type Limited Series
60 minutes. Fridays. Premiere date: 4/1/77. Last show: 4/22/77. Four-week action drama about a Nashville policeman. Created by Ernest Frankel. Weekly guest appearances by country and western stars. "Nashville 99" music by Earle Hagen; lyrics by Jerry Reed; sung by Jerry Reed. Series filmed on location in and around Nashville, Tenn.
Executive Producer Ernest Frankel
Company Frankel Productions in association with 20th Century-Fox Television
Directors Various
Writers Various

CAST
Det. Lt. Stonewall ("Stoney") Jackson Huff .... Claude Akins
Det. Trace Mayne ....Jerry Reed
Birdie Huff .... Lucille Benson

952 **A Nation of Nations** CBS
Program Type Religious/Cultural Special
30 minutes. Premiere date: 12/24/75. Repeat date: 12/19/76. Different ethnic groups in Chicago in a festival celebrating "Christmas Around the World."
Executive Producer Pamela Ilott
Producer Alan Harper
Company CBS News Religious Broadcast

953 **National Basketball Association East-West All-Star Classic** CBS
Program Type Sports Special
2 1/4 hours. Live coverage of the 27th annual All-Star Classic from the Milwaukee (Wisc.) Arena 2/13/77.
Executive Producer E. S. "Bud" Lamoreaux
Producer Chuck Milton
Company CBS Television Network Sports
Director Sandy Grossman
Announcer Brent Musburger
Analyst Billy Cunningham

National Basketball Association Games *see* NBA on CBS

National Collegiate Athletic Association *see* NCAA

954 **The National Disaster Survival Test** The Big Event NBC
Program Type Documentary/Informational Special
90 minutes. Premiere date: 5/1/77. Home-participation test on how to survive various disasters. Special effects by Conrad Rothman.
Executive Producer Warren V. Bush
Producers Robert Guenette, Paul Asselin
Company A Warren V. Bush Production in association with Guenette/Asselin Productions, Inc. and in cooperation with the National Safety Council
Director Don Horan
Writer Robert Guenette
Production Designer Edward Stephenson
Stunt Coordinator Ted Duncan
Researcher Jane Rockman
Test Coordinator Diane Asselin

Host Tom Snyder
Co-Hosts Shana Alexander, John Amos, Kate Jackson, Wally Schirra

National Football Conference *see* NFC

955 **National Geographic Special** PBS
Program Type Documentary/Informational Series
60 minutes/90 minutes. Tuesdays. Premiere date: 10/28/75. Second season premiere: 12/7/76. Monthly specials produced by the National Geographic Society. Programs shown during the 1976–77 season: "The Animals Nobody Loved," "The Incredible Machine," "The New Indians," "Search for the Great Apes," "This Britain: Heritage of the Sea," "Treasure," "The Volga," "Voyage of the Hokule'a." (*See* individual titles for credits.)

956 **National League Championship (Baseball)** ABC
Program Type Sports Special
Live coverage of the National League Championship games between the Cincinnati Reds and the Philadelphia Phillies beginning 10/9/76. Special features: "Up Close and Personal" profiles of the athletes.
Executive Producer Roone Arledge
Producer Chuck Howard
Company ABC Sports
Director Don Ohlmeyer
Announcer Al Michaels
Color Commentator Warner Wolf
Expert Analyst Tom Seaver

957 **National Tractor Pull 1976**
Americana PBS
Program Type Documentary/Informational Special
30 minutes. Premiere date: 3/25/77. Highlights of the National Tractor Pull competition taped in August 1976 at the Wood County Fairgrounds in Bowling Green, Ohio. Program made possible by a grant from Ohio Educational Broadcasting.
Producer Dal Neitzel
Company WBGU-TV/Bowling Green, Ohio
Director Dal Neitzel
Host Dave Grimm

958 **Nations Challenge Cup** CBS
Program Type Sports Special
Two hours. Live coverage of the Challenge Cup game between the University of Arizona Wildcats and the U.S.S.R. Red Army Basketball Team 3/6/77 from McKale Center at the University of Arizona at Tucson.
Company Trans World International
Director Tony Verna
Announcer Brent Musburger
Expert Analyst Mendy Rudolph

959 **The Nations Challenge Cup: World Series of Skiing** CBS
Program Type Sports Special
60 minutes. Premiere date: 2/13/77. Top amateur skiers from ten nations in competition in St. Moritz, Switzerland.
Producer Bob Stenner
Company CBS Television Network Sports
Director Jim Cross
Commentators Jack Whitaker, Hank Tauber

960 **The Natural Look**
Comedy Time NBC
Program Type Comedy Special
30 minutes. Premiere date: 7/6/77. Comedy pilot about an executive at Contessa Toiletries whose husband is a pediatrician.
Executive Producer Lillian Gallo
Producers Leonora Thuna, Pamela Chais
Company MTM Enterprises, Inc.
Director Robert Moore
Writer Leonora Thuna

CAST

Reedy Harrison .... Barbara Feldon
Dr. Bud Harrison .... Bill Bixby
Countess .... Brenda Forbes
Edna .... Sandy Sprung
Jane .... Caren Kaye
Arthur .... Michael MacRae

961 **The Naturalists** PBS
Program Type Documentary/Informational Series
30 minutes. Premiere date: 3/11/73. Program repeats began 9/24/76 (Friday mornings). Four-part series about famous American naturalists: Henry Thoreau, Theodore Roosevelt, John Muir and John Burroughs. Made possible by a grant from the Corporation for Public Broadcasting.
Producer James Case
Company Special Projects Cine Unit of KRMA-TV/Denver
Director James Case
Film Editor James Case

Nature's Half Acre *see* NBC All-Disney Saturday Night at the Movies

962 **NBA on CBS (National Basketball Association Games)** CBS
Program Type Limited Sports Series
Live coverage of regular-season, play-off and championship games. Fourth season premiere: 10/22/77. Regular Sunday games began 1/2/77.

NBA on CBS (National Basketball Association Games) *Continued*

Playoffs began 4/17/77. Championship games began 5/22/77 between the Philadelphia '76ers and the Portland Trail Blazers. Half-time features include the second season of "Red on Roundball" with Red Auerbach, "The Greek's Grapevine on Basketball" hosted by Jimmy "The Greek" Snyder and "CBS Slam Dunk" with commentary by Don Criqui.
Executive Producer E. S. "Bud" Lamoreaux
Producers Chuck Milton, Bob Stenner, Tom O'Neill, Bill Barnes
Company CBS Television Network Sports
Directors Sandy Grossman, Tony Verna, John McDonough, Bob Dunphy, Peter Bleckner
Announcers Brent Musburger, Don Criqui, Gary Bender, Jerry Gross, Bob Costas, Frank Glieber
Expert Analysts Mendy Rudolph, Billy Cunningham, Steve Jones, Jeff Mullins, Lenny Wilkins, John Andariese, Pete Maravich (play-offs)
Basketball Editor/Analyst Sonny Hill

963 NBC All-Disney Saturday Night at the Movies NBC

Program Type Feature Film Specials
Three hours. Saturdays. Theatrically released feature films and shorts produced by Disney Studios and presented at various times during the year. Films broadcast during the 1976–77 season are "The Great Locomotive Chase" (1956) shown 10/16/76 in conjunction with "Nikki, Wild Dog of the North" (1961), "A Horse Named Comanche" (1958—released commercially as "Tonka") shown 1/29/77 in conjunction with "Wonders of the Water World" (1961) and "Lt. Robin Crusoe, U.S.N." (1966) shown 12/11/76 in conjunction with "Nature's Half Acre" (1951).

964 NBC Forum: Choosing Our Government

NBC News Special NBC
Program Type Public Affairs Special
Two hours. Premiere date: 3/20/77. Excerpts from the NBC Forum which examined the American election process. Taped in Washington, D.C. 3/4/77 and 3/5/77.
Executive Producer A. H. Perlmutter
Coordinating Producer Lou Solomon
Producer Robert Asman
Company NBC News
Director Max Schindler
Host John Chancellor

965 NBC Late Night Movie NBC

Program Type Feature Film Series
Times vary. Sundays. Premiere date: 4/3/77. Theatrically-released feature films shown late Sunday evenings.

966 NBC Midday News NBC

Program Type News Series
Five minutes. Mondays–Fridays. Continuous. Last show: 12/31/76. Replaced by "NBC News Update" (daytime).
Executive Producer Lester M. Crystal
Company NBC News
Director Jack Dillon
Anchor Edwin Newman

967 NBC Monday Night at the Movies NBC

Program Type Feature Film Series – TV Movie Series
Two hours (generally). Mondays. Season premiere: 9/20/76. A combination of theatrically released feature films and made-for-television movies. The TV movies are: "Alexander: The Other Side of Dawn," "Amelia Earhart," "Cat on a Hot Tin Roof," "Dark Victory," "Dawn: Portrait of a Teenage Runaway," "The Death of Richie," "The Hunchback of Notre Dame," "Judge Horton and the Scottsboro Boys," "The Life and Assassination of the Kingfish," "The Loneliest Runner," "Night Terror," "Rosetti and Ryan: Men Who Love Women," "The Savage Bees," "A Sensitive, Passionate Man," "Sherlock Holmes in New York," "Sybil" (Part II), "Terraces," "The War Between the Tates." (*See* individual titles for credits.) The feature films are: "Airport 1975" (1974) shown 9/20/76, "Breakout" (1975) shown 7/11/77, "Breezy" (1973) shown 4/11/77, "Buona Sera, Mrs. Campbell" (1969) shown 8/15/77, "Camelot" (1967) Part II shown 12/27/76, "The Eiger Sanction" (1975) shown 5/9/77, "The Family Way" (1967) shown 8/8/77, "The Front Page" (1974) shown 11/29/76, "Gone With the Wind" (1939) Part II shown 11/8/76, "Hearts of the West," (1975) shown 1/31/77, "In Search of Noah's Ark" (1976) shown 5/2/77, "Jesus Christ Superstar" (1973) shown 10/11/76, "Lolly-Madonna XXX" (1973) shown 8/1/77, "Macon County Line" (1974) shown 4/18/77, "Never Give an Inch" (1971—released theatrically as "Sometimes a Great Notion") shown 10/4/76, "Rafferty and the Highway Hustlers" (1975—released theatrically as "Rafferty and the Gold Dust Twins") shown 3/14/77, "Shamus" (1973) shown 8/22/77, "Sssssss" (1973) shown 7/25/77, "The Sunshine Boys" (1975) shown 2/14/77, "Westworld" (1973) shown 1/24/77, The Wind and the Lion" (1975) shown 3/7/77.

968 **NBC Movie of the Week** NBC
Program Type Feature Film Series – TV Movie Series
90 minutes/two hours. Wednesdays (through 11/24/76, then irregularly). Premiere date: 9/22/76. Last show: 11/24/76. Returned: 1/12/77. Last show: 9/20/77. A combination of theatrically released feature films and made-for-television movies. The TV movies are: "Benny and Barney: Las Vegas Undercover," "Charlie Cobb: Nice Night for a Hanging," "The City," "Corey: For the People," "Cover Girls," "Danger in Paradise," "The Deadly Triangle," "Flood!" "Francis Gary Powers: The True Story of the U-2 Spy Incident," "The Girl in the Empty Grave," "How to Break Up a Happy Divorce," "The Man With the Power," "The Million Dollar Rip-Off," "Night Terror," "No Where to Hide," "Pine Canyon Is Burning," "The Possessed," "Richie Brockelman: The Missing 24 Hours," "The Savage Bees," "Scott Free," "Sex and the Married Woman," "The Silence," "The Spell," "Stalk the Wild Child," "Stonestreet," "The Strange Possession of Mrs. Oliver," "The 3,000 Mile Chase," "Yesterday's Child." (*See* individual titles for credits.) The feature films are: "The Adventures of Frontier Fremont" (1976) shown 2/2/77, "The Great Waldo Pepper" (1975) shown 11/10/76, "The Outer Space Connection" (1975) shown 3/3/77, "The Owl and the Pussycat" (1970) shown 3/16/77, "A Touch of Class" (1973) shown 6/30/77, "When the North Wind Blows" (1974) shown 4/5/77.

NBC News Specials *see* NBC Reports/NBC News Specials

969 **NBC News Update** NBC
Program Type News Series
60 seconds. Daily. Premiere date: 8/6/75. Continuous. First regularly scheduled news summary in prime time. Anchored Monday–Friday nights by Tom Snyder, then by Lloyd Dobyns as of February 1977. John Schubeck anchors the report in the West. Saturdays and Sundays the program originates from Washington, D.C. with various newscasters.
Company NBC News
Anchors Tom Snyder/Lloyd Dobyns, John Schubeck

970 **NBC News Update (Daytime)** NBC
Program Type News Series
60 seconds each. Mondays–Fridays. Premiere date: 1/3/77. Five-times-a-day daytime updates on the news. Anchored by Jane Pauley, Edwin Newman and Chuck Scarborough in the Eastern time zone; by Jess Marlow, Paul Moyer and Kelly Lange in the Pacific and Central zones. Successor to the "NBC Midday News."
Executive Producer Joseph Angotti
Company NBC News
Anchors Jane Pauley, Edwin Newman, Chuck Scarborough/Jess Marlow, Paul Moyer, Kelly Lange

971 **NBC Night at the Movies** NBC
Program Type Feature Film Specials
Times vary. Irregular showings of theatrically released motion pictures. Films shown during 1976–77 season are: "Ali the Fighter" (1975) shown 3/28/77, "Big Jake" (1971) shown 5/4/77, "Bigfoot, the Mysterious Monster" (1975) shown 2/28/77, "Elvis on Tour" (1972) shown 9/7/77, "Janis" (1974) shown 9/3/77 (1–2:30 a.m.), "Jeremiah Johnson" (1972) shown 5/10/77, "Living Free" (1972) shown 6/1/77, "Mysteries From Beyond Earth" (1976) shown 4/30/77, "The Ra Expeditions" (1974) shown 6/8/77, "Salty" (1974) shown 6/2/77, "The Spirit of St. Louis" (1957) shown 5/20/77. (*See also* also "NBC All-Disney Saturday Night at the Movies," "NBC Monday Night at the Movies," "NBC Saturday Night at the Movies," "NBC Thursday Night at the Movies.")

972 **NBC Nightly News** NBC
Program Type News Series
30 minutes. Mondays–Fridays. Premiere date: 8/1/70 (as a seven-nights-a-week expansion of "The Huntley-Brinkley Report"). Continuous. John Chancellor became Chief Reporter and Writer on 8/16/71. David Brinkley became co-anchor 6/7/76. Joseph Angotti became executive producer 12/76. On 9/6/77, David Brinkley began co-anchoring from Washington, D.C. Regular feature: "Special"—a daily series of background and investigative reports.
Executive Producer Lester M. Crystal/Joseph Angotti
Company NBC News
Anchors John Chancellor, David Brinkley

973 **NBC Reports/NBC News Specials** NBC
Program Type Documentary/Informational Series
Live and taped coverage of special events and reports. Programs shown during the 1976–77 season are: "Africa's Defiant White Tribe," "Blackout in New York City," "Carter Abroad: An Assessment," "Danger! Radioactive Waste," "A Day With President Carter," "Energy: Another View," "The Enterprise," "Failing to Learn—Learning to Fail," "Human Rights—A Soviet-American Debate," "Inauguration Ceremonies," "The Last Voyage of the Argo Mer-

NBC Reports/NBC News Specials *Continued*
chant," "The Life and Times of Elvis Presley," "Meet the New Congress," "NBC Forum: Choosing Our Government," "Passport to the Unknown," "President Carter's Address to the Nation on Domestic Matters," "President Carter's Address to the United Nations," "The President's Energy Message to Congress," "The Sometime Soldiers," "State of the Union Address," "The Struggle for Freedom," "Violence in America," "Year End Report." (*See* individual titles for credits.)

974 **NBC Saturday Night at the Movies** NBC
Program Type Feature Film Series – TV Movie Series
Two hours (generally). Saturdays. Season premiere: 9/25/76. A combination of theatrically released feature films and made-for-television movies. The TV films are: "The Deadly Tower," "Exo-Man," "Man from Atlantis" (one episode), "The Moneychangers" (one episode), "Spectre." (*See* individual titles for credits.) The feature films are: "Against a Crooked Sky" (1975) shown 4/23/77, "Airport 1975" (1974) shown 4/30/77, "Big Jake" (1971) shown 9/25/76, "Billy Jack" (1971) shown 11/20/76, "Blue Water, White Death" (1971) shown 11/27/76, "Born Losers" (1967) shown 2/5/77, "Breakout" (1975) shown 10/2/76, "Camelot" (1967) shown 12/25/76 (part I), "The Day of the Dolphin" (1973) shown 11/6/76 and 6/25/77, "Dirty Harry" (1972) shown 10/23/76 and 9/10/77, "Earthquake" (1974) shown 5/14/77, "The Front Page" (1974) shown 8/6/77, "The Great Waldo Pepper" (1975) shown 7/2/77, "Harry In Your Pocket" (1973) shown 7/30/77, "The Heart Is a Lonely Hunter" (1968) shown 7/23/77, "The Land That Time Forgot" (1975) shown 2/26/77, "Le Mans" (1971) shown 5/28/77, "Macon County Line" (1974) shown 11/13/76, "Mame" (1974) shown 12/18/76, "The Man Who Loved Cat Dancing" (1973) shown 3/19/77, "Mean Streets" (1973) shown 3/12/77, "McQ" (1974) shown 10/30/76 and 4/6/77, "More Dead Than Alive" (1969) shown 6/11/77, "Mr. Ricco" (1975) shown 1/22/77, "Never Give an Inch" (1971—released theatrically as "Sometimes a Great Notion") shown 7/9/77, "The Outfit" (1974) shown 4/2/77, "Paper Lion" (1968) shown 8/13/77, "Rio Lobo" (1970) shown 2/19/77, "Sidecar Racers" (1975) shown 6/4/77, "Sssssss" (1973) shown 10/9/76, "The Stone Killer" (1973) shown 3/26/77, "The Sugarland Express" (1974) shown 9/3/77, "They Came to Rob Las Vegas" (1969) shown 7/16/77, "The Train Robbers" (1973) shown 8/20/77, "Where the Red Fern Grows" (1974) shown 4/9/77, "The Wild Party" (1974) shown 2/12/77, "The Wrath of God" (1972) shown 3/5/77.

975 **NBC Saturday Night News** NBC
Program Type News Series
30 minutes. Saturdays. Continuous. John Hart replaced Tom Brokaw as anchor and Joseph Angotti replaced Lester M. Crystal as executive producer in December 1976.
Executive Producer Lester M. Crystal/Joseph Angotti
Company NBC News
Anchor Tom Brokaw/John Hart

976 **NBC Sunday Mystery Movie** NBC
Program Type Crime Drama Series
90 minutes/two hours. Sundays. Five series shown on an irregularly rotating basis: "Columbo," "Lannigan's Rabbi," "McCloud," "McMillan," "Quincy." (*See* individual titles for credits.)

977 **NBC Sunday Night News** NBC
Program Type News Series
30 minutes. Sundays. Continuous. Catherine Mackin replaced Tom Brokaw 12/76. Joseph Angotti replaced Lester M. Crystal as executive producer 12/76. Regular feature: "Sunday Profile."
Executive Producer Lester M. Crystal/Joseph Angotti
Company NBC News
Anchor Tom Brokaw/Catherine Mackin

978 **NBC Thursday Night at the Movies** NBC
Program Type Feature Film Series – TV Movie Series
Two hours/three hours. Thursdays. One show 1/6/77, then regularly from 4/28/77. Last show: 8/25/77. A combination of theatrically released feature films and made-for-television movies. The TV movies are: "The Call of the Wild," "Eric," "Farewell to Manzanar," "Guilty or Innocent: The Sam Sheppard Murder Case," "The Lindbergh Kidnapping Case," "Robinson Crusoe," "Snowbeast." (*See* individual titles for credits.) The feature films are: "Eight on the Lam" (1976) shown 7/28/77, "Escape from Colditz" (1972) shown 8/25/77, "Finian's Rainbow" (1968) shown 8/11/77.

979 **NBC's Best Seller** NBC
Program Type Drama Series
60 minutes/two hours. Thursdays. Premiere date: 9/30/76. Last show: 4/25/77. Dramatizations of best-selling novels: "Captains and the

Kings," "Once an Eagle," "The Rhinemann Exchange," "Seventh Avenue." (*See* individual titles for credits.)
Production Executive Charles Engel
Company Universal Television

980 **NBC's Saturday Night Live** NBC
Program Type Music/Comedy/Variety Series
90 minutes. Saturdays. Premiere date: 10/11/75. Second season premiere: 9/18/76. Live comedy-variety show with different guest hosts and entertainers. Shown weekly except for the first Saturday of each month. Title changed from "NBC's Saturday Night" as of 5/14/77. Bill Murray joined the Not Ready for Prime Time Players as a replacement for Chevy Chase 2/26/77. Ralph Nader hosted the show 1/15/77; Julian Bond 4/9/77. Primetime show, "Live From the Mardi Gras, It's Saturday Night on Sunday" seen as a "Big Event" 2/20/77. Regular features: "Weekend Update," "The Coneheads," "Samurai Warrior."
Producer Lorne Michaels
Company NBC-TV
Director Dave Wilson
Script Consultant Herb Sargent
Writers Dan Aykroyd, Anne Beatts, John Belushi, Chevy Chase, Tom Davis, James Downey, Al Franken, Lorne Michaels, Marilyn Suzanne Miller, Bill Murray, Michael O'Donoghue, Herb Sargent, Tom Schiller, Rosie Shuster, Alan Zweibel
Musical Director Howard Shore
Costume Designers Eugene Lee, Franne Lee
Announcer Don Pardo
Regulars Dan Aykroyd, John Belushi, Chevy Chase, Jane Curtin, Garrett Morris, Bill Murray, Laraine Newman, Gilda Radner

NCAA Basketball *see also* College Basketball '77

981 **NCAA Basketball Championship** NBC
Program Type Sports Special
Live coverage of the NCAA championship between the Marquette Warriors and the University of North Carolina Tar Heels from the Omni in Atlanta 3/28/77.
Producer George Finkel
Company NBC Sports in association with TVS
Director Harry Coyle
Announcers Dick Enberg, Curt Gowdy
Color Analyst Billy Packer

982 **NCAA Basketball Semi-Finals** NBC
Program Type Sports Special
Live coverage of doubleheader semifinals from the Omni in Atlanta 3/26/77 between the University of North Carolina-Charlotte 49ers and the Marquette Warriors and the University of Nevada-Las Vegas Running Rebels and the University of North Carolina Tar Heels.
Producer George Finkel
Company NBC Sports and TVS
Director Harry Coyle
Announcers Dick Enberg, Curt Gowdy
Color Analyst Billy Packer

983 **NCAA Basketball Tournament** NBC
Program Type Sports Special
Live coverage of regional play-offs, semi-finals and finals 3/12/77–3/19/77.
Executive Producer Scotty Connal
Producers George Finkel, Roy Hammerman, Mike Weisman, Jim Marooney
Company NBC Sports in association with TVS
Directors Harry Coyle, Ken Fouts, Charlie Sieg, Jim Holmes
Announcers Dick Enberg, Curt Gowdy, Marv Albert, Jim Simpson
Color Analysts Billy Packer, John Wooden, Gary Thompson, Tom Hawkins

984 **NCAA Football (NCAA Game of the Week)** ABC
Program Type Limited Sports Series
Live coverage of national, regional and doubleheader college football games. Saturdays (except Thanksgiving weekend coverage and premiere game on Thursday night). 11th season premiere: 9/9/76. Last show of season: 12/11/76. Keith Jackson is the principal play-by-play announcer. "NCAA Football" includes coverage of the Pioneer Bowl, Grantland Rice Bowl, Knute Rockne Bowl and Amos Alonzo Stagg Bowl.
Executive Producer Roone Arledge
Producers Chuck Howard and others
Company ABC Sports
Directors Andy Sidaris and others
Play-by-Play Announcers Keith Jackson, Chris Schenkel, Verne Lundquist, Chris Lincoln, Bob Murphy
Expert Commentators Ara Parseghian, Bud Wilkinson, Lee Grosscup, Steve Davis, Rick Forzano, Ron Johnson
Sideline Reporter Bill Flemming
Special Features Reporter Jim Lampley
Pre-Game/Halftime Host Bill Flemming

985 **NCAA-Japan International Volleyball Championship** PBS
Program Type Sports Special
Two hours. Premiere date: 4/3/77. The Japanese All-Stars vs. the UCLA Bruins from Pauley Pavilion at UCLA in Los Angeles.
Producer Robert Cozens

NCAA-Japan International Volleyball Championship *Continued*
Company WGBH-TV/Boston
Director Robert Cozens
Announcer Chick Hearn

986 **The Neil Diamond Special** NBC
Program Type Music/Dance Special
60 minutes. Premiere date: 2/21/77. A Neil Diamond concert taped in Fall, 1976 at the Greek Theatre in Los Angeles. Program stereosimulcast on local FM radio stations.
Executive Producer Jerry Weintraub
Producers Gary Smith, Dwight Hemion
Company A Smith-Hemion Production/An Arch Angel Television Presentation
Director Dwight Hemion
Writer Buz Kohan
Star Neil Diamond

987 **Nepal—Where the Gods Are Young** PBS
Program Type Documentary/Informational Special
30 minutes. Premiere date: 12/7/76. A look at the art of Nepal through an exhibition of works from the 8th–19th centuries. Presented by KTCA-TV/St. Paul-Minneapolis. Program made possible by a grant from the Jerome Foundation.
Executive Producer Russell Connor
Company Cable Arts Foundation in cooperation with the Asia Society
Director Russell Connor
Narrator Russell Connor

The Neptune Disaster *see* The ABC Friday Night Movie

The Nepture Factor *see* The ABC Friday Night Movie ("The Neptune Disaster")

Never Give an Inch *see* NBC Monday Night at the Movies/NBC Saturday Night at the Movies

988 **The New Adventures of Batman** CBS
Program Type Animated Film Series
30 minutes. Saturday mornings. Premiere date: 2/12/77. Animated adventures of Batman and Robin based on the primetime series.
Executive Producers Lou Scheimer, Norm Prescott
Producer Don Christensen
Company Filmation Associates Production
Supervising Director Don Towsley
Writers Various
Animation Directors Rudy Larriva, Lou Zukor, Glen Wetzler

VOICES

Batman .... Adam West
Robin .... Burt Ward

989 **The New Adventures of Gilligan** ABC
Program Type Animated Film Series
30 minutes. Sunday mornings. Premiere date: 9/7/74. Third season premiere (in reruns): 9/12/76. Last show: 9/4/77. Based on the characters in the nighttime series "Gilligan's Island." Created by Sherwood Schwartz.
Executive Producers Norm Prescott, Lou Scheimer
Company Filmation Productions
Directors Don Towsley, Lou Zukor, Rudy Larriva, Bill Reed
Writers Various
Creative Director Don Christensen
Executive Consultant Sherwood Schwartz
Series Consultant Dr. Nathan Cohen

VOICES

Gilligan .... Bob Denver
Skipper .... Alan Hale
Howell .... Jim Backus
Lovey .... Natalie Schafer
Professor .... Russell Johnson
Ginger .... Jane Webb
Maryann .... Jane Edwards

990 **The New Candid Camera** Syndicated
Program Type Game/Audience Participation Series
30 minutes. Weekly. Premiere date: 9/74. Third season premiere: 9/76. Originated as "Candid Microphone" on radio in 1947. "Candid Camera" premiered on television 9/12/49.
Producer Allen Funt
Company Allen Funt Productions, Inc.
Distributor Firestone Program Syndication Company
Hosts Allen Funt, Jo Ann Pflug

991 **A New England Christmas** PBS
Program Type Dramatic Special
30 minutes. Premiere date: 12/20/72. Repeat date: 12/24/76. Drama of a man returning to a Maine Christmas with his father. Program made possible by a grant from the Corporation for Public Broadcasting.
Producer John R. Morison
Company Maine Public Broadcasting Network
Director Richard Zimmerman
Writer Lyn Marschner

CAST

Jon Emery (as an adult) .... Dave Osgood

Jon Emery (as a child) .... Norman Wilkinson
Mrs. Emery .... Dorothy Wilkinson
Sue Emery .... Susan Wilkinson
Mr. Emery (in the past) .... J. Norman Wilkinson
Granny .... Ginny Palmer
Storekeeper .... Orrin P. Kimball
Mr. Emery (in the present) .... John Riley

992 **The New England Conservatory Ragtime Ensemble and the Katherine Dunham Dancers**
In Performance at Wolf Trap PBS
Program Type Music/Dance Special
60 minutes. Premiere date: 11/3/75. Repeat date: 11/22/76. A performance of American ragtime music and dance performed at the Wolf Trap Farm Park in Arlington, Va. by the New England Conservatory Ragtime Ensemble and the Katherine Dunham Dancers. Program made possible by a grant from the Atlantic Richfield Company.
Executive Producer David Prowitt
Producer Ruth Leon
Company WETA-TV/Washington, D.C.
Director Clark Santee
Conductor Gunther Schuller
Choreographer Katherine Dunham
Hosts Beverly Sills, David Prowitt
Executive-in-Charge Jim Karayn

993 **A New Generation: Shades of Gray**
Americana PBS
Program Type Documentary/Informational Special
30 minutes. Premiere date: 12/3/76. An examination of the attitudes of today's college students as compared to those of the 1960s.
Producer Paula Brody
Company WMHT-TV/Schenectady, N.Y.
Director Timothy Patryk

994 **New Howdy Doody Show** Syndicated
Program Type Children's Series
30 minutes. Mondays–Fridays. Premiere date: 9/76. Last show: 10/76. Revival of 1947–1960 children's show with Howdy Doody an electronic marionette.
Executive Producer E. Roger Muir
Producer Ronnie Wayne
Company Nicholson-Muir Productions for Buffalo Bill Enterprises
Distributor Jim Victory Television
Director Nick Nicholson
Writers Willie Gilbert, Lydia Wilen, Nick Nicholson
Host Buffalo Bob Smith

CAST

Clarabell Hornblow .... Lew Anderson
Mr. Cornelius Cobb .... Nick Nicholson
Happy Harmony .... Marilyn Patch
Fletcher-the-Sketcher .... Milt Neil
Mr. Nicholson Muir .... Bill LeCornec
Guy Mann .... Guy Mann
Jackie Davis .... Jackie Davis

995 **The New Indians**
National Geographic Special PBS
Program Type Documentary/Informational Special
60 minutes. Premiere date: 2/15/77. An in-depth look at four Native Americans working to revive interest in their Indian heritage. Program made possible by a grant from the Gulf Oil Corporation.
Executive Producers Dennis B. Kane, Thomas Skinner
Producers Terry Sanders, Freida Lee Mock
Company The National Geographic Society and WQED-TV/Pittsburgh
Director Terry Sanders
Writers Freida Lee Mock, Terry Sanders, Arthur Bramble
Host E. G. Marshall
Narrator Robert Redford

996 **The New Love Boat** ABC
Program Type TV Movie
90 minutes. Premiere date: 5/5/77. Repeat date: 8/31/77. Pilot for the 1977–78 series "The Love Boat" about the passengers and crew of the *Pacific Princess.* Filmed in part on location on the *Queen Mary* in Long Beach, California.
Executive Producers Aaron Spelling, Douglas S. Cramer
Producer Henry Colman
Company Aaron Spelling Productions
Director Richard Kinon
Writers Brad Buckner, Rick Hawkins, Liz Sage, Michael Norell

CAST

Capt. Merrill Stubing .... Gavin MacLeod
Dr. Adam Bricker .... Bernie Kopell
Burl "Gopher" Smith .... Fred Grandy
Isaac Washington .... Ted Lange
Julie McCoy .... Lauren Tewes
Cleo .... Georgia Engel
Leonora Klopman .... Stella Stevens
Ernie Klopman .... Pat Harrington
Morris Beekman .... Phil Silvers
Mae Allen .... Audra Lindley
Stanley Adams .... Gary Frank
Joyce Adams .... Melanie Mayron

997 **New Mickey Mouse Club** Syndicated
Program Type Children's Series
30 minutes. Mondays–Fridays. Premiere date: 1/17/77. Revival of old "Mickey Mouse Club" of the 1950s with theme of the day: "Who, What, Where, When and How Day," "Let's Go Day," "Surprise Day," "Talent Showcase Day," "Showtime Day."

New Mickey Mouse Club *Continued*
Executive Producer Ron Miller
Producers Ed Ropolo, Michael Wuergler
Company Walt Disney Productions
Distributor SFM Media Services Corporation
Directors John Tracy, Dick Krown, Dick Amos, James Field
Writers Marc Ray, Ron Bastone, Tedd Anasti, David Talisman
Mouseketeers Pop Attmore, Scott Craig, Nita DiGiampaolo, Mindy Feldman, Angelo Florez, Allison Fonte, Shawnte Northcutte, Kelly Parsons, Julie Piekarski, Todd Turquand, Lisa Whelchel, Curtis Wong

998 **The New Treasure Hunt** Syndicated
Program Type Game/Audience Participation Series
30 minutes. Weekly. Premiere date (in syndication): 9/74. Last season premiere: 9/76. Syndicated evening version of defunct daytime network show created by Jan Murray and originally produced 8/12/57.
Producer Michael J. Metzger
Company Chuck Barris Productions
Distributor Sandy Frank Film Syndication, Inc.
Director John Dorsey
Host Geoff Edwards
Announcer Johnny Jacobs

999 **New Year's at Pops** PBS
Program Type Music/Dance Special
75 minutes. Premiere date: 12/31/75. Repeat date: 12/31/76. The Boston Pops Orchestra in a New Year's celebration from Symphony Hall in Boston. Program made possible by a grant from the Martin Marietta Corporation.
Producer William Cosel
Company WGBH-TV/Boston
Conductor Arthur Fiedler

1000 **New Year's Eve With Guy Lombardo** CBS
Program Type Music/Dance Special
90 minutes. Premiere date: 12/31/76. Live broadcast (in the East) from the Grand Ballroom of the Waldorf-Astoria Hotel and Times Square in New York City.
Executive Producer Kevin O'Sullivan
Producer Albert Hartigan
Company Worldvision Enterprises, Inc.
Director Robert Myhrum
Stars Guy Lombardo, the Royal Candaians
Guest Stars Billy Eckstine, Carol Lawrence
Times Square Host Ben Grauer

1001 **New Year's Rockin' Eve 1977** ABC
Program Type Music/Dance Special
90 minutes. Premiere date: 12/31/76. Live New Year's Eve celebration from the Coconut Grove in Los Angeles and Times Square in New York City.
Executive Producer Dick Clark
Producer Bill Lee
Company Dick Clark Teleshows
Director John Moffitt
Writer Robert Arthur
Hosts Dick Clark, Frankie Valli
Guests Frankie Valli and the Four Seasons, K.C. and the Sunshine Band, Bachman Turner Overdrive, Donna Summer

1002 **The New York Philharmonic**
Live from Lincoln Center/Great Performances PBS
Program Type Music/Dance Special
Two hours. Premiere date: 11/20/76. Live performance of the New York Philharmonic Orchestra in a regularly scheduled concert from Avery Fisher Hall in Lincoln Center for the Performing Arts, New York City. Stereo-simulacst on local FM radio stations. Program made possible by grants from Exxon Corporation, the National Endowment for the Arts, the Corporation for Public Broadcasting and the Charles A. Dana Foundation.
Producer John Goberman
Company WNET-TV/New York in collaboration with Lincoln Center
Conductor Raphael Kubelik
Host Dick Cavett
Announcer Martin Bookspan
Guest Soloist Claudio Arrau

1003 **Newsbreak** CBS
Program Type News Series
60 seconds. Nightly. Premiere date: 1/1/77. Nightly 60-second news headline service. Stephani Shelton succeeded Sylvia Chase in September 1977 as Saturday correspondent.
Producer Ralph Paskman
Company CBS News
Anchors Morton Dean (Sundays–Fridays), Sylvia Chase/Stephani Shelton (Saturdays)

1004 **Next Door** PBS
Program Type Dramatic Special
21 minutes. Premiere date: 7/12/76. Repeat date: 8/21/77. Adaptation of a story by Kurt Vonnegut.
Producer Andrew Silver
Company WGBH-TV/Boston
Director Andrew Silver
Writer Andrew Silver
Film Editor Andrew Silver

CAST

Boy .... Matthew Brady

1005 **NFC Championship** CBS
Program Type Sports Special
Three hours. Live coverage of the National Football Conference championship game between the Minnesota Vikings and the Los Angeles Rams from Metropolitan Stadium, Bloomington, Minn. 12/26/76.
Producer Chuck Milton
Company CBS Television Network Sports
Director Sandy Grossman
Announcer Pat Summerall
Analyst Tom Brookshier

1006 **NFC Play-Offs (Game I)** CBS
Program Type Sports Special
Three hours. Live coverage of the National Football Conference play-off between the Washington Redskins and the Minnesota Vikings from Metropolitan Stadium in Bloomington, Minn. 12/18/76.
Producer Bob Stenner
Company CBS Television Network Sports
Director Tony Verna
Announcer Vin Scully
Analyst Paul Hornung

1007 **NFC Play-Offs (Game II)** CBS
Program Type Sports Special
Three hours. Live coverage of the National Football Conference play-off between the Los Angeles Rams and the Dallas Cowboys from Texas Stadium in Irving, Tex. 12/19/76.
Producer Chuck Milton
Company CBS Television Network Sports
Director Sandy Grossman
Announcer Pat Summerall
Analyst Tom Brookshier

1008 **NFL Game of the Week** NBC
Program Type Limited Sports Series
Live coverage of 90 regular-season NFL games including seven doubleheaders. Season premiere: 9/12/76. Last regular season game: 12/12/76. Curt Gowdy and Don Meredith broadcast national games.
Executive Producer Scotty Connal
Producers Dick Auerbach, Larry Cirillo, George Finkel, Joe Gallagher, Roy Hammerman, Jim Marooney, Ted Nathanson, David Stern, Mike Weisman
Company NBC Sports
Directors Dave Caldwell, Harry Coyle, Jim Cross, Ken Fouts, Jim Holmes, Craig Janoff, Ted Nathanson, Charlie Sieg, Barry Stoddard
Announcers Jack Buck, Curt Gowdy, Charlie Jones, Ross Porter, Jay Randolph, Tim Ryan, Jim Simpson, Dick Stockton
Color Analysts Lionel Adridge, John Brodie, Len Dawson, Sam DeLuca, Mike Haffner, Floyd Little, Paul Maguire, Don Meredith

1009 **NFL Game of the Week (Syndicated)** Syndicated
Program Type Limited Sports Series
30 minutes. Weekly. Season premiere: 9/15/76. 18-week series showing highlights of the outstanding NFL game of the preceding week.
Company NFL Films Inc.
Distributor Pro Sports Entertainment

1010 **NFL on CBS** CBS
Program Type Limited Sports Series
Three hours. Sundays (some Saturdays). 21st season premiere: 9/12/76. Last regular show: 12/12/76. Live coverage of 91 regular-season national and regional games.
Producers Various
Company CBS Sports
Directors Various
Announcers Pat Summerall, Frank Glieber, Al Michaels, Gary Bender, Paul Hornung, Lindsey Nelson, Don Criqui, Vin Scully, Jim Thacker, Bob Costas
Analysts Tom Brookshier, Alex Hawkins, Johnny Unitas, Sonny Jurgensen, Johnny Morris, Tim Van Galder, Emerson Boozer, Paul Hornung, Tom McDonald, Tom Matte, Dick Butkus, Bob Lilly

1011 **NFL Pre-Season Games (CBS)** CBS
Program Type Sports Special
Three hours each. Sundays. Live coverage of three pre-season NFL games 8/14/77, 8/21/77 and 8/28/77.
Producer Chuck Milton
Company CBS Television Network Sports
Director Sandy Grossman
Announcers Pat Summerall, Brent Musburger
Analyst Tom Brookshier

1012 **NFL Pre-Season Games (NBC)** NBC
Program Type Sports Special
Live coverage of three pre-season football games 8/19/77, 8/27/77 and 9/8/77.
Executive Producer Scotty Connal
Producers George Finkel, Ted Nathanson
Producer NBC Sports
Director Ted Nathanson
Announcers Jim Simpson, Curt Gowdy
Analysts John Brodie, Merlin Olsen

1013 **The NFL Today** CBS

Program Type Limited Sports Series

Live pre-game, half-time and post-game show presented during regular season games and National Football Conference playoffs and championship. Season premiere: 9/12/76. Last show of season: 12/26/76. Series covers the major NFL games played that day, other sports events during the weekend, and features such as "The Greek's Grapevine" with Jimmy "the Greek" Snyder.

Producers Sid Kaufman, Hal Classon, Mike Pearl

Company CBS Television Network Sports

Director Joel Banow

Hosts Brent Musburger, Phyllis George, Irv Cross

Analyst Jimmy "The Greek" Snyder

1014 **The Night That Panicked America**

The ABC Friday Night Movie ABC

Program Type TV Movie

Two hours. Premiere date: 10/31/75. Repeat date: 7/22/77. Dramatization of the events resulting from Orson Welles' *Mercury Theatre* radio broadcast on 10/30/38 of "The War of the Worlds" by H. G. Wells. Includes the original radio transcript by Howard W. Koch.

Executive Producer Anthony Wilson

Producer Joseph Sargent

Company Paramount Television

Director Joseph Sargent

Writers Nicholas Meyer, Anthony Wilson

Conductor Frank Comstock

Creative Consultant Paul Stewart

CAST

Orson Welles .... Paul Shenar
Hank Muldoon .... Vic Morrow
Stefan Grubowski .... Cliff De Young
Jess Wingate .... Michael Constantine
Paul Stewart .... Walter McGinn
Ann Muldoon .... Eileen Brennan
Linda Davis .... Meredith Baxter
Norman Smith .... Tom Bosley
Rev. Davis .... Will Geer
Tom .... Granville Van Dusen
Tex .... Burton Gilliam
Howard Koch .... Joshua Bryant
Radio Actor No. 1 .... Ron Rifkin
Radio Actor No. 2 .... Walker Edmiston
Charlie .... Liam Dunn
Radio Actor No. 3 .... Casey Kasem
Radio Actor No. 4 .... Marcus J. Grapes
Announcer .... Art Hannes
Toni .... Shelley Morrison

1015 **Night Terror**

NBC Monday Night at the Movies/NBC Movie of the Week NBC

Program Type TV Movie

90 minutes. Premiere date: 2/7/77. Repeat date: 7/17/77. Suspense drama of woman fleeing for her life.

Executive Producer Charles Fries

Producers Joel Glickman, Daniel Selznick

Company Charles Fries Production in association with NBC-TV

Director E. W. Swackhamer

Writers Carl Gabler, Richard DeNeut

CAST

Carol .... Valerie Harper
The Killer .... Richard Romanus
Walter .... Michael Tolan
Aunt Vera .... Beatrice Manley
Carolyn .... Quinn Cummings
Buddy .... Damon Raskin
Man in Sports Car .... Nicholas Pryor
Old Derelict .... John Quade
Indian Woman .... Madeleine Taylor Holmes
Indian Man .... John War-Eagle

1016 **Nightmare in Badham County**

The ABC Friday Night Movie ABC

Program Type TV Movie

Two hours. Premiere date: 11/5/76. Drama about two college girls unjustly sentenced to a primitive women's prison farm. Music by Charles Bernstein.

Executive Producer Douglas S. Cramer

Producer W.L. Baumes

Company An ABC Circle Film

Director John Llewellyn Moxey

Writer Jo Heims

CAST

Cathy Phillips .... Deborah Raffin
Diane Emery .... Lynne Moody
Sheriff Dannen .... Chuck Connors
Dulcie .... Fionnuala Flanagan
Greer .... Tina Louise
Supt. Deaner .... Robert Reed
Sarah .... Della Reese
Smitty .... Lana Wood
Emiline .... Kim Wilson
Judge .... Ralph Bellamy

Nikki, Wild Dog of the North *see* NBC All-Disney Saturday Night at the Movies

1017 **1976–77: What Was, What Will Be** ABC

Program Type Public Affairs Special

60 minutes. Premiere date: 1/2/77. Year-end correspondents roundtable discussion focusing on the major news stories of 1976 and their impact on 1977.

Producer Jeff Gralnick

Company ABC News Public Affairs

Director Robert Delaney

Anchors Harry Reasoner, Barbara Walters

Correspondents Howard K. Smith, Frank Reynolds, Tom Jarriel, Sam Donaldson, Peter Jennings, Dan Cordtz

1018 **The Nixon Interviews: Lessons Learned** ABC
Program Type Public Affairs Special
30 minutes. Premiere date: 5/26/77. Discussion following the syndicated Nixon-Frost interviews.
Producer Elliot Bernstein
Company ABC News Special Events Unit
Director Marvin Schlenker
Hosts Frank Reynolds, Sam Donaldson
Guests David Frost, John Scali, Tom Jarriel

1019 **The Nixon Interviews With David Frost** Syndicated
Program Type Documentary/Informational Special
90 minutes each. Weekly. Premiere date: 5/4/77. Four interviews with former Pres. Richard M. Nixon taped between 3/23/77–4/20/77 near San Clemente, California. Fifth 90-minute interview aired 9/6/77.
Executive Producer David Frost
Producers John Birt, David Frost
Company Paradine Productions, RAI (Italy), TFI (France), Channel 9 (Australia), Polygram (Germany)
Distributor Syndicast Services
Director Jorn Winther
Executive Editor C. Robert Zelnick
Interviewer David Frost

1020 **No Room at the Table** PBS
Program Type Documentary/Informational Special
30 minutes. Premiere date: 10/1/76. A look at pollution in Orange County, California. Song by Malvina Reynolds. Program made possible by a grant from Title I of the Higher Education Act.
Producer Harry Ratner
Company KOCE-TV/Huntington Beach, Ca.
Directors Thom Eberhardt, Harry Ratner
Writer Paul Cabbell
Reporter Paul Cabbell

1021 **No Where to Hide**
NBC Movie of the Week NBC
Program Type TV Movie
90 minutes. Premiere date: 6/5/77. Crime drama pilot about a contemporary U.S. marshall assigned to protect a former syndicate hit man who is testifying against his ex-boss.
Executive Producer Mark Carliner
Producers Rift Fournier, Edward Anhalt
Company Mark Carliner Production for Viacom Enterprises
Director Jack Starrett
Writer Edward Anhalt

CAST

Insp. Ike Scanlan	Lee Van Cleef
Charles Montague	Russell Johnson
Dep. Ted Willoughby	Charlie Robinson
Joey Faber	Tony Musante
Alberto Amarici	Edward Anhalt
Linda Faber	Lelia Goldoni
Frankie Faber	Noel Fournier
Vittorio	John Alderman
Rick	David Proval

1022 **Norton-Bobick Heavyweight Bout** NBC
Program Type Sports Special
Two hours. Live coverage of the heavyweight fight between Ken Norton and Duane Bobick and the preliminary light-heavyweight fight between Mike Quarry and Mike Rossman from Madison Square Garden 5/11/77. Also shown: a 25-minute segment of boxing scenes from famous motion pictures.
Producer Ted Nathanson
Company NBC Sports
Director Ted Nathanson
Host Joe Garagiola
Announcer Dick Enberg
Expert Analyst Larry Merchant

Nosferatu *see* PBS Movie Theater

1023 **Nova** PBS
Program Type Science/Nature Series
60 minutes. Wednesdays. Premiere date: 3/3/74. Fourth season premiere: 1/5/77. Weekly series focusing on a variety of science-related topics produced with the advice and cooperation of the American Association for the Advancement of Science. Captioned for the hearing-impaired. Series made possible by grants from Exxon Corporation, the National Science Foundation, Public Television Stations, the Ford Foundation and the Corporation for Public Broadcasting.
Executive Producer John Angier
Producers Various
Company WGBH-TV/Boston

1024 **Now** NBC
Program Type News Magazine Special
60 minutes. Premiere date: 6/30/77. Pilot for magazine program combining news and entertainment. Original music by Don Elliott.
Executive Producer Stuart Schulberg
Producer William Cosmas
Company NBC News
Director Sidney A. Vassall
Writers Linda Ellerbee, Jack Perkins
Film Editors Frank DeMeo, Irwin Graf, George Johnson, Mary Ann Martin

Now *Continued*
Project Producers Fred Flamenhaft, Ene Riisna, Jean Venable
Researchers Karen Curry, Susan Drury, Christopher Isham
Co-Anchors Jack Perkins, Linda Ellerbee

1025 **Number Our Days**
Americana PBS
Program Type Documentary/Informational Special
30 minutes. Premiere date: 5/6/77. Repeat date: 9/18/77. Oscar-winning documentary examining a community of elderly Jews in Venice, California. Based on the anthropological field work of Dr. Barbara Myerhoff. Program made possible by a grant from the Corporation for Public Broadcasting.
Executive Producer Loring d'Usseau
Producer Lynne Littman
Company KCET-TV/Los Angeles
Director Lynne Littman
Narrator Dr. Barbara Myerhoff

1026 **The Nutcracker** PBS
Program Type Music/Dance Special
90 minutes. Premiere date: 12/22/75. Repeat date: 12/21/76. A performance of the Christmas classic by Peter Ilich Tchaikovsky performed by Ballet West and the Utah Symphony Orchestra. Program made possible by funds contributed through Friends of KUED-TV plus grants from the Utah Division of Fine Arts and the Corporation for Public Broadcasting.
Producer Byron Openshaw
Company KUED-TV/Salt Lake City
Director Kirk Browning
Musical Director Maurice Abravanel
Choreographer William Christensen

CAST

Sugar Plum Fairy .... Victoria Morgan
Sugar Plum Cavalier .... Tomm Ruud
Dr. Drosselmeyer .... Michael Onstad
Additional Cast Cynthia Young, Bruce Caldwell, Cary Tidyman

October *see* PBS Movie Theater

1027 **The Odd Ball Couple** ABC
Program Type Animated Film Series
30 minutes. Sunday mornings/Saturday mornings (as of 1/8/77). Premiere date: 9/6/75. Second season premiere: 9/12/76 (series in repeats). Last show: 9/3/77. Based on "The Odd Couple" by Neil Simon about two reporters-at-large: Fleabag, a messy dog and Spiffy, a neat cat.
Producers David H. DePatie, Friz Freleng
Company DePatie-Freleng Productions
Story Editor Bob Ogle
Writers Bob Ogle, Joel Kane, Dave Detiege, Earl Kress, John W. Dunn
Supervising Director Lewis Marshall
Voices Paul Winchell, Frank Nelson, Sarah Kennedy, Joe Besser, Bob Holt, Joan Gerber, Frank Welker, Don Messick, Ginny Taylor

1028 **Of Mind and Matter** CBS
Program Type Religious/Cultural Special
60 minutes. Premiere date: 9/5/76. Repeat date: 9/4/77. Profile of Berea College in Kentucky.
Executive Producer Pamela Ilott
Producer Chalmers Dale
Company CBS News Religious Broadcast
Writer Arnold Walton
Narrator Ted Holmes

1029 **Off Campus** CBS
Program Type Comedy Special
30 minutes. Premiere date: 6/8/77. Comedy pilot about college students who share a co-ed rooming house.
Producer Gilbert Cates
Company Jodagi-Elephant Production
Director Burt Brinckerhoff
Writer Marshall Brickman

CAST

Janet .... Marilu Henner
Steve .... Josh Mostel
Stanley .... Peter Riegert
Josh .... Chip Zien
Weineke .... Joe Bova
Additional Cast Ann Risley, Alexa Kenin, Robert Hitt, James Gallery

1030 **Off the Wall** NBC
Program Type Comedy Special
30 minutes. Premiere date: 5/7/77. Comedy pilot about the advisor in a coed dorm at a midwestern university. Music by Mike Post and Peter Carpenter; lyrics by Harry Gold
Executive Producer Franklin Barton
Producers George Tricker, Neil Rosen
Company Universal Television
Director Bob LaHendro
Writers George Tricker, Neil Rosen

CAST

Arthur .... Frank O'Brien
Matthew Bozeman .... Todd Susman
Flash .... Harry Gold
Gordon .... Sean Roche
Melvin .... Sandy Helberg
Jeanie .... Dana House
Mother .... Hal Williams
Lenny .... Barbara Deutsch

1031 **Offshore Onshore** PBS
Program Type Documentary/Informational Special
60 minutes. Premiere date: 7/5/77. The potential

impact of off-shore oil drilling on New England's ecology and economy is assessed. Program funded by grants from the U.S. Department of Interior—Bureau of Land Management and Geodetic Survey, the U.S. Department of Commerce, the Environmental Protection Agency, the Massachusetts Institute of Technology Sea Grants and the States of Maine, Connecticut, Massachusetts, Rhode Island and New Hampshire.
Producer Peter Cook
Company WGBH-TV/Boston

1032 **On the Road With Charles Kuralt**
CBS News Special CBS
Program Type Documentary/Informational Special
60 minutes. Premiere date: 12/24/76. Selected segments of "On the Road to '76" featured on the "CBS Evening News With Walter Cronkite" seen during the 1975–76 television season.
Executive Producer Leslie Midgley
Producers Charles Kuralt, Bernard Birnbaum
Company CBS News
Cinematographer Isadore Bleckman
Film Editors Steve Frankel, Val Lebedeff, Tom Micklas, Al Rausch, Robert Reingold
Reporter/Anchor Charles Kuralt

1033 **On to the Omni** NBC
Program Type Sports Special
30 minutes. Premiere date: 3/12/77. A look at past NCAA Tournaments and a preview of the 1977 tournament.
Producer Jim Marooney
Company NBC Sports
Director Jim Marooney
Host Dick Enberg
Guests Bobby Knight, Dave Gavitt

1034 **Once an Eagle**
NBC's Best Seller NBC
Program Type Limited Series
Nine hours. Thursdays. Premiere date: 12/2/76. Dramatization of the novel by Anton Myrer about two Regular Army officers in the years between 1918–1945. Filmed in part on locations in the Napa Valley and Los Angeles, Calif. and in Hawaii.
Executive Producer William Sackheim
Producer Peter Fischer
Company Universal Television in association with NBC-TV
Directors E. W. Swackhamer, Richard Michaels
Writer Peter Fischer

CAST

Sam Damon .... Sam Elliott
Courtney Massengale .... Cliff Potts
Tommy Damon .... Darleen Carr
Emily Massengale .... Amy Irving
George Caldwell .... Glenn Ford
Lt. Merrick .... Clu Gulager
Marge Krisler .... Lynda Day George
Ben Krisler .... Robert Hogan
Donny Damon (as a boy) .... John Waldron
Jinny Massengale .... Melanie Griffith
Joe Brand .... Kario Salem
Donny Damon (as an adult) .... Andrew Stevens
Ryetower .... Kip Niven

1035 **Once Upon a Classic** PBS
Program Type Children's Series
30 minutes/60 minutes. Saturdays. Premiere date: 10/9/76. Adaptations of literary classics for children plus modern-day original dramas. Captioned for the hearing-impaired. Programs presented during the 1976–77 season are: "Avalanche," "The Battle of Billy's Pond," "David Copperfield," "Heidi," "Hijack," "Little Lord Fauntleroy," "The Man From Nowhere," "The Prince and the Pauper." (*See* individual titles for credits.)

1036 **Once Upon a Time ... Is Now the Story of Princess Grace**
The Big Event NBC
Program Type Documentary/Informational Special
90 minutes. Premiere date: 5/22/77. A look at the life of Princess Grace of Monaco. Music by Ron Grainer. Lyrics for title song by Ian Page; sung by Johnny Mathis. Filmed in London, Paris, Monaco and the United States.
Executive Producer William Allyn
Producers Sandra Smith Allyn, David Lunney
Company An Allyn/Lunney Production
Director Kevin Billington
Host Lee Grant

1037 **One Day at a Time** CBS
Program Type Comedy Series
30 minutes. Tuesdays. Premiere date: 12/16/75. Second season premiere: 9/28/76. Series created by Whitney Blake and Allan Manings and developed by Norman Lear. Comedy about a newly divorced mother of two teen-age daughters.
Executive Producers Norman Paul, Jack Elinson
Producers Dick Bensfield, Perry Grant
Company A Norman Lear T.A.T. Communications Company and Allwhit, Inc. Productions
Director Herbert Kenwith
Writers Various

CAST

Ann Romano .... Bonnie Franklin
Julie Cooper .... Mackenzie Phillips
David Kane .... Richard Masur
Barbara Cooper .... Valerie Bertinelli
Dwayne Schneider .... Pat Harrington
Ginny Wrobliki .... Mary Louise Wilson

1038 **$100,000 Name That Tune** Syndicated

Program Type Game/Audience Participation Series

30 minutes. Weekly. Premiere date: 9/74. Third season premiere: 9/76. Evening version of daytime show that went off the air 1/3/75. Show created by Harry Salter for radio in 1951. Two contestants compete to name the songs being played. Changed name for the 1976–77 season to indicate top prize.

Executive Producer Ralph Edwards
Producer Ray Horl
Company A Ralph Edwards Production
Distributor Sandy Frank Station Syndication, Inc.
Director Richard Gottlieb
Writer Richard Gottlieb
Conductor Tommy Oliver
Host Tom Kennedy
Announcer John Harlan
Musicologist Harvey Bacal
Music Coordinator Richard Gottlieb

1039 **$128,000 Question** Syndicated

Program Type Game/Audience Participation Series

30 minutes. Weekly. Premiere date: 9/76. Revival of the 1950s quiz show "The $64,000 Question" created by Steve Carlin with unlikely experts in specific fields.

Executive Producer Steve Carlin
Producer Willie Stein
Company Cinelar Associates
Distributor Viacom International
Director Dick Schneider
Host Mike Darrow

1040 **One Life to Live** ABC

Program Type Daytime Drama Series

45 minutes. Mondays-Fridays. Premiere date: 7/15/68. Continuous. Became 45-minute show 7/26/76. Set in Llanview, U.S.A. Created by Agnes Nixon. Credit information as of April 1977. Cast list is alphabetical.

Producer Joseph Stuart
Company An ABCTelevision Network Presentation
Directors David Pressman, Don Wallace, Peter Miner
Head Writer Gordon Russell
Writers Sam Hall, Ted Dazan, Don Wallace, Enid Rudd

CAST

Brian Kendall ..... Stephen Austin
Anna Craig ..... Doris Belack
Karen Wolek ..... Kathryn Breech
Vince Wolek ..... Jordan Charney
Patricia Kendall ..... Jacqueline Courtney
Lt. Ed Hall ..... Al Freeman, Jr.
Jenny Wolek ..... Katherine Glass
Dr. Will Vernon ..... Farley Granger
Cathy Lord ..... Jennifer Harmon
Danny Wolek ..... Neail Holland
Carla Hall ..... Ellen Holly
Matt McAllister ..... Vance Jefferis
Naomi Vernon ..... Teri Keane
Kevin Riley ..... Morgan K. Melis
Samantha Vernon ..... Julie Montgomery
Brad Vernon ..... Jameson Parker
Joe Riley ..... Lee Patterson
Dr. Dorian Lord ..... Nancy Pinkerton
Dr. James Craig ..... Nat Polen
Dr. Peter Janssen ..... Jeffrey Pomerantz
Alan Bennett ..... Roger Rathburn
Tony Lord ..... George Reinholt
Victoria Riley ..... Erika Slezak
Dr. Larry Wolek ..... Michael Storm
Lana ..... Jackie Zeman

1041 **One of a Kind: John Prine** PBS

Program Type Music/Dance Special

60 minutes. Premiere date: 10/9/76. A performance by country-folk singer/composer John Prine.

Producer Taylor Hackford
Company KCET-TV/Los Angeles
Director Allan Muir

1042 **One of My Wives Is Missing**

The ABC Friday Night Movie ABC

Program Type TV Movie

Two hours. Premiere date: 3/5/76. Repeat date: 12/31/76. Suspense drama of a small town detective with a missing wife case. Filmed in part on location at Lake Arrowhead, Calif. Music by Billy Goldenberg.

Executive Producers Aaron Spelling, Leonard Goldberg
Producer Barney Rosenzweig
Company A Spelling-Goldberg Production
Director Glenn Jordan
Writer Pierre Marton
Art Director Paul Sylos

CAST

Murray Levine ..... Jack Klugman
Elizabeth Corban ..... Elizabeth Ashley
Daniel Corban ..... James Franciscus
Father Kelleher ..... Joel Fabiani
Mrs. Foster ..... Ruth McDevitt
Sidney ..... Milton Selzer
Bert ..... Tony Costello

1043 **Oneida**

Americana PBS

Program Type Documentary/Informational Special

30 minutes. Premiere date: 2/25/77. Repeat date: 8/14/77. The history and contemporary life of the Oneida tribe of Northeastern Wisconsin. Program made possible by a grant from the Seymour Community Schools and presented by the Wisconsin Educational Television Network.

Producer Brian Schmidlin
Company Northeastern Wisconsin In-School Telecommunications/Educational Communications Office–University of Wisconsin/Green Bay and the Oneida Tribe of Wisconsin
Director Larry Neukum
Writer Brian Schmidlin
Cinematographer Fred Wessel
Film Editor Phil Gries
Narrator Brian Schmidlin

1044 **An Only Child**
Childhood/Great Performances PBS
Program Type Dramatic Special
60 minutes. Premiere date: 3/16/77. Repeat date: 9/28/77. Adaptation of a story by Frank O'Connor about an Irish boy growing up in the slums of Cork at the time of the Irish Rebellion. Presented by WNET-TV/New York. Program made possible by a grant from Exxon Corporation with additional support from member stations of PBS.
Executive Producer Jac Venza
Coordinating Producer Ann Blumenthal
Producer James Brabazon
Company Granda Television
Director Donald McWhinnie
Writer Brian Wright
Host Ingrid Bergman

CAST

Michael (5 years old) .... Paul Carey
Michael (12 years old) .... Brian Frahill
Michael O'Donovan .... Joe Lynch

1045 **Only Then Regale My Eyes** PBS
Program Type Documentary/Informational Special
60 minutes. Premiere date: 1/26/76. Repeat date: 8/2/77. A look at France from 1774–1830 through its art. Filmed almost entirely in Paris at historic landmarks and museums. Produced in cooperation with the Detroit Institute of Arts. Program made possible by a grant from the McGregor Fund.
Executive Producer Jack Costello
Company WTVS-TV/Detroit
Writer Paul Winter
Cinematographer Ron Castorri
Narrator Paul Winter
Art Consultants Linda Downs, Ron Winokur
Music Consultant Martin Herman

1046 **Opera Theater** PBS
Program Type Music/Dance Series
Times vary. Tuesdays. Premiere date: 4/27/76. Second season premiere: 7/5/77. Ten-part series of opera and operetta (five repeats) in English. Shows seen during the 1976–77 season: "Die Fledermaus," "The Flying Dutchman," "The Gondoliers," "Jack: A Flash Fantasy," "La Traviata," "The Mikado," "Santa Fe Opera," "Trouble in Tahiti," "The World of Ivor Novello," "The World of Victor Herbert." (*See* individual titles for credits.)

1047 **Operation Petticoat**
The ABC Sunday Night Movie ABC
Program Type TV Movie
Two hours. Premiere date: 9/4/77. Pilot for the 1977–78 season comedy series of the same name. Based on the 1959 motion picture and on a story by Paul King and Joe Stone.
Executive Producer Leonard B. Stern
Producer David J. O'Connell
Company Heyday Productions and Universal Television
Director John Astin
Writer Leonard B. Stern

CAST

Lt. Cmdr. Matthew Sherman .... John Astin
Lt. Nick Holden .... Richard Gilliland
Maj. Edna Hayward .... Yvonne Wilder
Yeoman Hunkle .... Richard Brestoff
Ensign Stovall .... Christopher J. Brown
Seaman Dooley .... Kraig Cassity
Molumphrey .... Wayne Long
Williams .... Richard Marion
Admiral .... Jackie Cooper
Seaman Gossett .... Michael Mazes
Tostin .... Jack Murdock
Seaman Horwich .... Peter Schuck
Lt. Watson .... Raymond Singer
Seaman Broom .... Jim Varney
Lt. Crandall .... Melinda Naud
Lt. Duran .... Jamie Lee Curtis
Lt. Colfax .... Dorrie Thomson
Lt. Reid .... Bond Gideon

1048 **Oral Roberts and You** Syndicated
Program Type Religious/Cultural Series
30 minutes. Weekly. Sermons by Oral Roberts plus music.
Producer Ron Smith
Company Traco Productions, Inc. in association with Oral Roberts Association
Director Matt Connolly, Jr.
Musical Director Ronn Huff
Featured Singers Richard Roberts, Patti Roberts, Reflection, World Action Singers

1049 **Orange Bowl** NBC
Program Type Sports Special
Live coverage of the 43rd Orange Bowl game between the Colorado Buffaloes and the Ohio State Buckeyes from Miami, Fla. 1/1/77.
Producer Ted Nathanson
Company NBC Sports
Director Ken Fouts
Announcer Jim Simpson
Analyst John Brodie

1050 **The Original Rompin' Stompin' Hot and Heavy, Cool and Groovy All Star Jazz Show**
The CBS Festival of Lively Arts for Young People CBS
Program Type Children's Special
60 minutes. Premiere date: 4/13/76. Repeat date: 12/5/76. A history of jazz created by Gary Keys. Special lyrics by Chris Acemandese Hall.
Executive Producers Ron Kass, Edgar Bronfman, Jr.
Producer Gary Keys
Company Gorilla Films, Ltd. in association with Sagittarius Entertainment, Inc.
Director Jerome Schnur
Writers Gary Keys, Edward Gant
Musical Director Chico O'Farrell
Choreographer George Faison
Costume Designer Carol Luiken
Host Dionne Warwick
Stars Count Basie, Stan Getz, Dizzy Gillespie, Lionel Hampton, Herbie Hancock, Gerry Mulligan, Max Roach, Joe Williams
Accompanying Musicians Seldon Powell, Wally Kane, Chris Woods, Frank Foster, Frank Wess, Sol Yaged, Joe Newman, Victor Paz, John Faddis, Marvin Stamm, Wayne Andra, John Gordon, Eddie Bert, Jack Jeffers, Roland Hanna, George Benson, Richard Davis, Charlie Persip

Orpheus *see* PBS Movie Theater

1051 **Oscar's Best Movies** ABC
Program Type Documentary/Informational Special
2 1/4 hours. Premiere date: 2/13/77. Film clips from the 48 Academy Award-winning motion pictures.
Producer Howard W. Koch
Company The Academy of Motion Picture Arts and Sciences
Director Howard W. Koch
Writers William Ludwig, Leonard Spigelgass
Musical Supervisor Henry Mancini
Hosts Julie Andrews, Goldie Hawn, Walter Matthau, Gregory Peck, Katharine Ross
Special Guest Olivia de Havilland

The Other *see* The CBS Friday Night Movies

1052 **The Others**
Documentary Showcase PBS
Program Type Documentary/Informational Special
60 minutes. Premiere date: 11/19/76. Repeat date: 7/22/77 (with captions for the hearing-impaired). The problems of the mentally retarded and how the Iowa Department of Social Services deals with them.
Producer John Beyer
Company Iowa Public Broadcasting Network
Director John Beyer
Writer John Beyer
Narrator Matthew James Faison

1053 **Our Happiest Birthday**
CBS News Special CBS
Program Type Documentary/Informational Special
60 minutes. Premiere date: 7/11/76. Repeat date: 7/4/77 Highlights of the Bicentennial as seen on the CBS program "In Celebration of US" 7/4/76. Some additional film footage added to the program.
Senior Producer Ernest Leiser
Producer Vern Diamond
Company CBS News
Director Vern Diamond
Writer William Moran
Host Walter Cronkite

1054 **Our Town**
Bell System Special NBC
Program Type Dramatic Special
Two hours. Premiere date: 5/30/77. The Pulitzer Prize-winning play by Thornton Wilder in a production specially designed for TV, about people in a small New England town.
Executive Producer Saul Jaffe
Producer George Schaefer
Company Hartwest Productions, Inc.
Director George Schaefer
Writer Thornton Wilder
Costume Designer Noel Taylor
Production Designer Roy Christopher
Creative Consultant Robert Hartung

CAST
Stage Manager ..... Hal Holbrook
Dr. Gibbs ..... Ned Beatty
Mrs. Webb ..... Barbara Bel Geddes
George Gibbs ..... Robby Benson
Mr. Webb ..... Ronny Cox
Emily Webb ..... Glynnis O'Connor
Mrs. Gibbs ..... Sada Thompson
Mrs. Soames ..... Charlotte Rae
Howie Newsome ..... William Lanteau
Simon Stimson ..... David Cryer
Constable Warren ..... Don Beddoe
Joe Stoddard ..... Ford Rainey
Sam Craig ..... Charles Cyphers
Rebecca Gibbs ..... Elizabeth Cheshire
Joe Crowell, Jr. ..... Allen Price
Si Crowell ..... Michael Sharrett
Wally Webb ..... Scott Atlas

1055 **Ourstory** PBS
Program Type Drama Series
30 minutes. Friday mornings. Historical dramatizations from Colonial times to the present originally designed to coincide with monthly American Issues Forum discussions. Programs shown during the 1976–77 season: "The Devil's Work," "Eliza," "The Erie War," "Jade Snow," "The Last Ballot," "The Peach Gang," "The Queen's Destiny," "The World Turned Upside Down." (*See* individual titles for credits.)

The Outer Space Connection *see* NBC Movie of the Week

The Outfit *see* NBC Saturday Night at the Movies

1056 **Over Easy** PBS
Program Type Educational/Cultural Special
30 minutes each. Premiere dates: 9/13/76 and 9/14/76. Two magazine-variety pilot programs dealing with the interests of senior citizens. Programs made possible by funding from the U.S. Department of Health, Education and Welfare—Administration on Aging and the Corporation for Public Broadcasting.
Executive Producer Richard R. Rector
Producer Jules Power
Company KQED-TV/San Fransicso
Director James Crum
Head Writer Christopher Lukas
Musical Director Arturo Juarez
Scenic Designer Allen Edward Klein
Host Hugh Downs
Stars Rudy Vallee, Phyllis Diller

The Overlanders *see* PBS Movie Theater

The Owl and the Pussycat *see* NBC Movie of the Week

1057 **Pagliacci**
Great Performances PBS
Program Type Music/Dance Special
90 minutes. Premiere date: 3/19/75. Repeat date: 6/8/77. 1968 film version of the opera by Ruggiero Leoncavallo performed at La Scala Opera House in Milan, Italy with the La Scala Opera Orchestra and La Scala Opera Chorus. Program presented by WNET-TV/New York and made possible by a grant from Exxon Corporation.
Coordinating Producer David Griffiths
Producer Paul Hager
Company Cosmotel S.A. Production
Conductor Herbert von Karajan

CAST
Canio/Pagliaccio .... Jon Vickers
Nedda/Columbine .... Raina Corsi-Kabaivanska
Tonio/Taddeo .... Peter Glossop
Beppo/Harlequin .... Sergio Lorenzi
Silvio .... Rolando Panerai

1058 **Paint Along With Nancy Kominsky** PBS
Program Type Educational/Cultural Series
30 minutes. Tuesdays and Thursdays. Premiere date: 6/7/77. Series repeats began 9/6/77. Twice-weekly 26-program series on painting designed for beginners. Funded by a grant from the Commercial Union Assurance Companies.
Producer Patrick Dromgoole
Company Connecticut Public Television in association with SPORTONV
Directors Ron Nicodemus, Ken Horseman
Host Nancy Kominsky

1059 **The Pallisers** PBS
Program Type Limited Series
60 minutes. Mondays. Premiere date: 1/24/77 (90 minutes). 22-part dramatization of six Victorian novels by Anthony Trollope. Filmed in England. Series presented by WNET-TV/New York and made possible by a grant from Prudential Insurance Company of America.
Producer Martin Lisemore
Company British Broadcasting Corporation and Time-Life Television
Directors Hugh David, Ronald Wilson
Writer Simon Raven
Host Sir John Gielgud

CAST
Lady Glencora M'Cluskie Palliser Susan Hampshire
Plantagenet Palliser .... Philip Latham
Alice Vavasor .... Caroline Mortimer
Duke of Omnium .... Roland Culver
Phineas Finn .... Donal McCann
Lady Dumbello .... Rachel Herbert
Burgo Fitzgerald .... Barry Justice
George Vavasor .... Gary Watson
Countess Midlothan .... Fabia Drake
Marchioness of Auld Reekie .... Sonia Dresdel
Mme. Max Goesler (Marie Finn) .... Barbara Murray
Lady Laura Standish .... Anna Massey
Violet Effingham .... Mel Martin
Kennedy .... Derek Godfrey
Mary .... Maire Ni Ghrainne
Lizzie Eustace .... Sarah Badel
Frank .... Martin Jarvis
Lord George .... Terence Alexander
Mrs. Carbuncle .... Helen Lindsay
Rev. Emilius .... Anthony Ainley
Lord Fawn .... Derek Jacobi
Mr. Bonteen .... Peter Sallis
Silverbridge .... Roderick Shaw
Adelaide .... Jo Kendall
Gerard .... Jeremy Clyde
Dolly Longstaffe .... Donald Pickering
Lopez .... Stuart Wilson
Emily .... Sheila Ruskin

The Pallisers *Continued*

Wharton	Brewster Mason
Lady Mary	Kate Nicholls
Frank Tregear	Jeremy Irons
Gerald	Michael Cochrane
Duke of St. Bungay	Roger Livesey
Lord Silverbridge	Anthony Andrews
Isabel	Lynne Frederick
Lady Mabel Grex	Anna Carteret
John Grey	Bernard Brown

1060 **Palm Sunday Liturgy** NBC
Program Type Religious/Cultural Special
60 minutes. Premiere date: 4/3/77. Live coverage of the Palm Sunday Liturgy in the Cathedral of St. Peter in Chains in Cincinnati, Ohio.
Producer Doris Ann
Company NBC Television Religious Programs Unit in association with the Office for Film and Broadcasting of the United States Catholic Conference
Celebrant The Most Rev. Joseph L. Bernardin

1061 **Panic in Echo Park** NBC
Program Type TV Movie
90 minutes. Premiere date: 6/23/77. Dramatic pilot about a doctor in the minority community of Echo Park.
Producers Edgar J. Scherick, Daniel H. Blatt
Company Edgar J. Scherick Associates, Inc.
Director John Llewellyn Moxey
Writer Dalene Young

CAST

Dr. Michael Stoner	Dorian Harewood
Cynthia	Catlin Adams
Dr. Tishman	Robin Gammell
Dickerson	Norman Bartold
Fallen Reilly	Ramon Bieri
Dr. O'Connor	Regis J. Cordic

Paper Chase *see* The ABC Sunday Night Movie

Paper Lion *see* NBC Saturday Night at the Movies

Paper Moon *see* The CBS Friday Night Movies/CBS Special Film Presentations

1062 **Paradise Restored**
Classic Theatre: The Humanities in Drama PBS
Program Type Dramatic Special
90 minutes. Premiere date: 10/16/75. Repeat date: 3/10/77. Modern play about the 17th century poet John Milton. Music by Mathew Locke. Program funded by grants from the National Endowment for the Humanities and Mobil Oil Corporation. Presented by WGBH-TV/Boston; Joan Sullivan, producer.
Company British Broadcasting Corporation
Director Don Taylor
Writer Don Taylor
Costume Designer Elizabeth Moss

CAST

John Milton	John Neville
Mary Milton/Mary Powell	Polly James
Elizabeth Milton	Anne Stallybrass
Anne	Rosemary McHale
Deborah	Jane Hayden
Cromwell	Bernard Hepton

The Parallax View *see* The CBS Wednesday Night Movies

1063 **The Parenthood Game**
All-Specials Night NBC
Program Type Science/Nature Special
60 minutes. Premiere date: 1/27/77. A study of how wild creatures raise their young. Filmed on locations throughout the world. Music by Wilfred Josephs.
Executive Producer Aubrey Buxton
Producer Colin Willock
Company Survival Anglia Ltd. in association with the World Wildlife Fund
Writers Colin Willock, Jim de Kay
Conductor Marcus Dods
Cinematographers Terry Andrewartha, Des Bartlett, Jen Bartlett, Anthony Bomford, Elizabeth Bomford, Rod Borland, Dr. Brian Burke, Ted Channell, Chris Doncaster, Jeff Foott, Richard Kemp, Chris Knights, John Pearson, G. Dieter Plage, Don Renn, Alan Root, Lee Tepley, Christian Zuber, Oxford Scientific Films
Film Editor Leslie Parry
Researcher Paul Willock
Narrator Bob Newhart

1064 **Parker Adderson, Philosopher/The Jolly Corner**
The American Short Story PBS
Program Type Dramatic Special

Parker Adderson, Philosopher
45 minutes. Premiere date: 5/3/77. Adaptation of the short story by Ambrose Bierce about a Yankee spy captured by a Confederate general. Music by Artie Traum. Program presented by South Carolina Educational Television and made possible by a grant from the National Endowment for the Humanities.
Executive Producer Robert Geller
Producer Ozzie Brown
Company Learning in Focus, Inc.
Director Arthur Barron

Writer Arthur Barron
Costume Designer Evelyn Barron
Host Colleen Dewhurst

CAST

Parker Adderson .... Harris Yulin
General .... Douglass Watson
Lieutenant .... Darren O'Connor

The Jolly Corner
45 minutes. Adaptation of the short story by Henry James about an expatriate returning to New York in the 1890s after 35 years in Europe. Music by Charles Gross.
Executive Producer Robert Geller
Producer David B. Appleton
Company Learning in Focus, Inc.
Director Arthur Barron
Writer Arthur Barron
Costume Designer Robert Pusilo
Scenic Designer Stuart Wurtzel
Host Colleen Dewhurst

CAST

Spencer Brydon .... Fritz Weaver
Alice .... Salome Jens
Additional Cast Paul Sparer, Lucy Landau, Sudie Bond, James Greene, George Backman

1065 **Pasadena Tournament of Roses** NBC
Program Type Parades/Pageants/Awards Special
2 1/2 hours. Live coverage of the 88th annual parade from Pasadena, Calif. 1/1/77. Music coordinated by Milton Delugg.
Producer Dick Schneider
Company NBC Television Network
Director Dick Schneider
Writer Barry Downes
Hosts Bryant Gumbel, Michael Landon, Kelly Lange

1066 **Passport to the Unknown**
NBC Reports NBC
Program Type Documentary/Informational Special
60 minutes. Premiere date: 6/29/77. An investigation into the disappearance of Americans in Ecuador.
Producer Paul Altmeyer
Company NBC News
Director Dick Roy
Cinematographer Dick Roy
Film Editor Katherine Field
Researcher Naomi Kaufman
Reporter Paul Altmeyer

1067 **Paths in the Wilderness** PBS
Program Type Documentary/Informational Special
30 minutes. Premiere date: 12/4/76. The life of Jesuit priest Eusebio Francisco Kino in Northern Mexico and Southern Arizona. Program made possible by grants from the American Revolution Bicentennial Administration and the Arizona Bicentennial Commission.
Producer David DuVal
Company KUAT-TV/Tucson
Director David DuVal
Writer Charles Polzer, S.J.
Cinematographer Harry Atwood
Film Editor David DuVal
Narrator Sandy Rosenthal

VOICES

Padre Kino .... Franklin Brown

1068 **The Patsy Awards** Syndicated
Program Type Parades/Pageants/Awards Special
30 minutes. Premiere date: 6/24/77. The 27th annual awards honoring animal actors presented by the American Humane Society. Taped 6/4/77 at Knott's Berry Farm in Buena Park, Calif.
Executive Producer Wally Sherman
Producer Joseph Landis
Company Western International Media Corporation
Distributor Western International Media Corporation
Hosts Betty White, Allen Ludden
Presenters Pat Paulsen, June Lockhart

Patton *see* The ABC Sunday Night Movie

1069 **Paul Anka . . . Music My Way** ABC
Program Type Music/Dance Special
60 minutes. Premiere date: 4/25/77. Musical show taped at the Hollywood Palladium. Special musical material by Alan Copeland. Film sequences by Eytan Keller and Stu Bernstein.
Producer Marty Pasetta
Company Pasetta Productions, Inc.
Director Marty Pasetta
Writer Buz Kohan
Musical Director John Harris
Choreographer Alan Johnson
Costume Designer Bill Hargate
Art Director Ray Klausen
Star Paul Anka
Guest Stars Natalie Cole, Dr. Buzzard's Original Savannah Band, St. Paul's Baptist Church Choir

1070 **The Paul Lynde Comedy Hour** ABC
Program Type Music/Comedy/Variety Special
60 minutes. Premiere date: 4/23/77. Comedy playlets plus music.

The Paul Lynde Comedy Hour
Continued
Executive Producers Raymond Katz, Sandy Gallin
Producers Rich Eustis, Al Rogers
Company Hoysyl Productions
Director Sidney Smith
Writers Chet Dowling, Sandy Krinski, April Kelly, George Geiger, Dave Letterman, Jim Mulligan
Musical Director Eddie Karam
Costume Designer Ret Turner
Art Director Ken Johnson
Comedy Consultant Lawrence Kasha
Star/Host Paul Lynde
Guest Stars Cloris Leachman, Tony Randall, K.C. and the Sunshine Band, LeVar Burton
Other Performers R. G. Brown, Feliz Silla, Tom Biener, April Kelly, Elizabeth Detterich, Ret Turner

1071 **The Paul Lynde Halloween Special** ABC
Program Type Music/Comedy/Variety Special
60 minutes. Premiere date: 10/29/76. A Halloween variety special. Special material by Billy Barnes.
Executive Producers Raymond Katz, Sandy Gallin
Producers Bob Booker, George Foster, Joe Byrne
Director Sidney Smith
Writers Alan David, Sol Weinstein, Howard Albrecht, Bruce Vilanch, Ron Pearlman, Biff Manard, Ronny Graham
Musical Director Artie Butler
Choreographer Marc Breaux
Costume Designer Bill Hargate
Art Director Charles Lisanby
Star Paul Lynde
Guest Stars Tim Conway, Roz Kelly, Margaret Hamilton, Billie Hayes, Billy Barty, Kiss
Special Guest Stars Florence Henderson, Betty White

1072 **PBS Movie Theater** PBS
Program Type Feature Film Series
Times vary. Saturdays/Tuesdays (10/24/76–1/4/77)/Saturdays. Feature films from the Janus Film Collection purchased with the help of a grant from the Exxon Corporation. Films aired during the 1976–77 season are: "Alexander Nevsky" (1938) shown 2/12/77, "Androcles and the Lion" (1953) shown 3/26/77, "Beauty and the Beast" (1946) shown 7/23/77, "The Blue Angel" (1930) shown 10/9/76, "Brief Encounter" (1946) shown 9/10/77, "The Cabinet of Dr. Caligari" (1919) shown 5/14/77, "Caesar and Cleopatra" (1946) shown 3/5/77, "Casque D'Or" (1952) shown 8/6/77, "Dreams" (1955) shown 11/9/76, "Earth" (1930) shown 2/5/77, "The 400 Blows" (1958) shown 8/20/77, "Grand Illusion" (1937) shown 8/13/77, "The Importance of Being Ernest" (1952) shown 11/30/76, "Ivan the Terrible" (1944) shown in two parts 2/19/77 and 2/26/77, "Jules and Jim" (1961) shown 7/16/77, "Kind Hearts and Coronets" (1949) shown 8/27/77, "La Strada" (1954) shown 4/2/77, "The Lady Killers" (1955) shown 12/7/76, "Last Holiday" (1950) shown 9/3/77, "L'Avventura" (1960) shown 4/16/77, "L'Eclisse" (1962) shown 4/30/77, "A Lesson in Love" (1954) shown 11/2/76, "M" (1931) shown 10/2/76, "Major Barbara" (1941) shown 3/19/77, "The Man in the White Suit" (1951) shown 6/18/77, "Miracle in Milan" (1951) shown 4/9/77, "Monika" (1952) shown 10/19/76, "Mother" (1929) shown 1/22/77, "Nosferatu" (1929) shown 5/28/77, "October" (1927) shown 1/15/77, "Orpheus" (1949) shown 7/30/77, "The Overlanders" (1946) shown 9/25/76, "Potemkin" (1925) shown 1/4/77, "Pygmalion" (1938) shown 3/12/77, "Queen of Spades" (1949) shown 6/4/77, "The Red Shoes" (1948) shown 12/21/76, "Richard III" (1955) shown 12/28/76, "The Rocking Horse Winner" (1949) shown 6/11/77, "The Rules of the Game" (1939) shown 7/2/77, "Sawdust and Tinsel" (1953) shown 10/26/76, "The Seventh Seal" (1956) shown 11/23/76, "Shoeshine" (1946) shown 4/23/77, "Smiles of a Summer Night" (1955) shown 11/16/76, "Soft Skin" (1964) shown 7/9/77, "Storm Over Asia" (1929) shown 1/29/77, "Summer Interlude" (1950) shown 1/4/77, "Umberto D" (1952) shown 5/7/77, "The Waltz of the Toreadors" (1949) shown 12/14/76.

1073 **The Peach Gang**
Ourstory PBS
Program Type Dramatic Special
60 minutes. Premiere date: 9/22/75. Repeat dates: 10/22/76 and 10/29/76 (30 minutes each). Dramatizes the conflict between English and Indian concepts of justice in 17th century America. Filmed at Plimoth Plantation, Plymouth, Mass. Music by Wladimir Selinsky. Program funded by the National Endowment for the Humanities.
Executive Producer Don Fouser
Producer Don Fouser
Company WNET-TV/New York
Director William A. Graham
Writer Allan Sloane
Conductor Wladimir Selinsky
Host Bill Moyers

CAST

Arthur Peach .... Daniel Tamm
Canonicus .... Chief Dan George
Roger Williams .... James Tolkan
Thomas Prence .... Gil Rogers

William Bradford .... David Hooks
Miles Standish .... John Carpenter
Miantonomo .... William Wilcox
John Alden .... Patrick Gorman
Young Indian/Penowanyanquis .... Billy Drago
Richard Stinnings .... Michael Kimberly
Thomas Jackson .... Michael L. Barlow
Steven Hopkins .... Ron Faber
Dorothy Temple .... Annie O'Neill
Dr. James .... William Shust
Matthew Fletcher .... Gary Cookson
Strongheart Sekatau .... Eric Thomas
Mudjewis .... John Brown III
Firefly Song of Wind .... Ella Thomas
Princess Evening Star .... Gertrude Aiken

1074 **Peggy Fleming With Holiday on Ice at Madison Square Garden** CBS
Program Type Music/Comedy/Variety Special
60 minutes. Premiere date: 10/26/76. Ice skating special from Madison Square Garden in New York City.
Executive Producer Bob Banner
Producer Bob Shipstad
Company Bob Banner Associates
Director Steve Binder
Musical Director Paul Walberg
Choreographers Bob Maxon, Helen Maxon
Star Peggy Fleming
Special Guest Star Andy Williams
Guest Stars Mark Wilson, The Muppets, Holiday on Ice Skaters

1075 **The Pennsylvania Ballet**
Dance in America/Great Performances PBS
Program Type Music/Dance Special
60 minutes. Premiere date: 6/2/76. Repeat date: 9/4/77. Excerpts from five works taped in Philadelphia and Nashville by the Pennsylvania Ballet. Program made possible by grants from the National Endowment for the Arts, Exxon Corporation and the Corporation for Public Broadcasting.
Executive Producer Jac Venza
Producer Emile Ardolino
Company WNET-TV/New York
Director Merrill Brockway
Narrator Barbara Weisberger
Series Producer Merrill Brockway

Concerto Barocco
Choreographer George Balanchine
Dancers Joanne Danto, Gregory Drotar, Gretchen Warren and Dana Arey, Karen Brown, Marcia Darhower, Tamara Hadley, Sherry Lowenthal, Anya Patton, Constance Ross, Missy Yancey

Grosse Fugue
Choreographer Hans van Manen
Dancers Alba Calzada, Marcia Darhower, Dane LaFontsee, Sherry Lowenthal, Michelle Lucci, Edward Myers, Jerry Schwender, Janek Schergen

Concerto Grosso
Choreographer Charles Czarny
Dancers Karen Brown, Tamara Hadley, Mark Hochman, David Jordan, Dane LaFontsee, Barry Leon, Gretchen Warren, Missy Yancey

Madrigalesco
Choreographer Benjamin Harkarvy
Dancers Alba Calzada, Marcia Darhower, Edward Myers, Jerry Schwender

Adagio Hammerklavier
Choreographer Hans van Manen
Dancers Michelle Lucci, Lawrence Rhodes

1076 **Pennsylvania Lynch**
Visions PBS
Program Type Dramatic Special
90 minutes. Premiere date: 12/9/76. Drama about turn-of-the-century Hungarian immigrants in a small Pennsylvania town caught up in a lynching. Based on a historical incident. Program made possible by grants from the Ford Foundation, the National Endowment for the Arts and the Corporation for Public Broadcasting.
Producer Barbara Schultz
Company KCET-TV/Los Angeles
Directors Jeff Bleckner, Rick Bennewitz
Writer David Epstein
Costume Designer Sandra Stewart
Art Director Lynn Griffin

CAST

Robert Dayka .... Tom Atkins
Eva Dayka .... Lelia Goldoni
Paul Dayka .... Bill Whitaker
Sandor .... Bo Brundin
Gretta .... Lenka Peterson
Sheriff .... Richard Venture
Zachariah Walker .... Robert Walter Delegall
Mr. James .... Jason Wingreen
Nmika .... Fritz Feld
Kosko .... Harry Frazier
Cronin .... Ken O'Brien
Thomson .... Lincoln Demyan
District Attorney .... Herb Armstrong
Stanley Huff .... Will Mackenzie
Grundy .... Ralph Lev Mailer
Village Idiot .... John Megna
Officer .... Herman Poppe
Phillips .... Marius Mazmanian
Reporters .... Robert Chapel, Louis Plant, Frank Coppola, Brett Dunham, Wally Berns
Black Men .... Ken Men'ard, Frenchia Guizon

1077 **The People Vs. Gary Gilmore**
CBS Reports CBS
Program Type Documentary/Informational Special
60 minutes. Premiere date: 1/17/77. A report on

The People Vs. Gary Gilmore *Continued*
how the case of Gary Gilmore affects the United States.
Executive Producer Howard Stringer
Company CBS News
Writer Bill Moyers
Correspondent Bill Moyers

1078 **The People Vs. Inez Garcia** PBS
Program Type Dramatic Special
90 minutes. Premiere date: 5/25/77. Docudrama edited from the trial of Inez Garcia and adapted from the stage production of Rena Down. Program made possible by a grant from the Corporation for Public Broadcasting (unedited version).
Executive Producer Zev Putterman
Producers Rena Down, Christopher Lukas
Company KQED-TV/San Francisco
Directors Rena Down, Christopher Lukas
Writer Rena Down
Scenic Designer Henry May
Narrator Jessica Epstein

CAST

Inez Garcia .... Silvana Gallardo
Charles Garry .... Robert Loggia
Braudrick .... Marc Jacobs
Judge .... Robert Haswell
Luis Castillo .... Jearado Carmona
Dr. Oldden .... Barbara Oliver
Juan Garcia .... Carlos Baron
Raul Garcia .... Julio Rossetti
Worthington .... David Klein
Freddie Medrano .... Manuel Gonzales
Courtroom Interpreter .... Judith Weston
Additional Cast Louis Winfield Bailey, Loretta Sheridan, Patrick Taffe, Raymond L. Lopez

1079 **The People's Choice Awards** CBS
Program Type Parades/Pageants/Awards Special
Two hours. 2/10/77. Third annual awards from the Long Horn Theater in Hollywood.
Executive Producer Bob Stivers
Producer Bob Finkel
Company Bob Stivers Productions
Director Walter C. Miller
Writers Herbert Baker, Dan Kibbee
Musical Director Frank Devol
Scenic Designer Brian Bartholomew
Hosts Dick Van Dyke, Army Archerd
Awards Hostess Summer Bartholomew

1080 **People's Command Performance: 1977** CBS
Program Type Music/Comedy/Variety Special
Two hours. Premiere date: 4/7/77. Repeat date: 8/28/77. Performances by entertainers selected in a public-opinion survey. Special musical material by Artie Malvin.
Executive Producer Bob Stivers
Producers Bernard Rothman, Jack Wohl
Company People Command Performance Production
Director Walter C. Miller
Writer Herbert Baker
Musical Directors Jack Elliott, Allyn Ferguson
Choreographer Dee Dee Wood
Choral Director Artie Malvin
Hosts George Burns, Bernadette Peters
Stars The Ace Trucking Company, George Benson, Edgar Bergen, LeVar Burton, George Carlin, Carol Channing, the Doobie Brothers, Nancy Dussault, Redd Foxx, Robert Goulet, Loretta Lynn, Don Rickles, Red Skelton, Beverly Sills, Dionne Warwick, Paul Williams

1081 **Pepsi Mixed Team Championship** PBS
Program Type Sports Special
Two hours each. Premiere dates: 12/18/76 and 12/19/76. Final two rounds of the professional golfers' mixed team championships covered live from the "Blue Monster" course at the Doral Country Club in Miami, Florida. Program made possible by a grant from the National Golf Foundation.
Producer Renate Cole
Company KERA-TV/Dallas
Director Waid Blair
Announcers Norm Hitzges, Bob Halloran, Ray Scott
Color Commentators Jimmy Demaret, Mary Bea Porter

1082 **Perry Como's Christmas in Austria**
All Specials Night NBC
Program Type Music/Comedy/Variety Special
60 minutes. Premiere date: 12/13/76. A celebration of the Christmas season from various locations in Austria. Special musical material and choral direction by Ray Charles.
Executive Producer Bob Banner
Producer Stephen Pouliot
Company A Roncom Production in association with Bob Banner Associates and ORF
Director Stephen Pouliot
Writer Stephen Pouliot
Musical Director Nick Perito
Costume Designer Gordon Brockway
Art Director Archie Sharp
Star Perry Como
Guest Stars Sid Caesar, Senta Berger, Karl Schranz, the Vienna Boys Choir, the Salzburg Marionette Theatre, the Vienna Waltz Champions

1083 **Perry Como's Music From Hollywood** ABC
Program Type Music/Dance Special
60 minutes. Premiere date: 3/28/77. A tribute to music from the movies. Special musical material and choral direction by Ray Charles.
Producer Bob Henry
Company Roncom Productions, Inc. in association with Bob Henry Productions
Director Bob Henry
Writer George Yanok
Musical Director Nick Perito
Costume Designer Bill Belew
Art Director Romain Johnston
Star Perry Como
Guest Stars Hal Linden, Sandy Duncan, Shirley Jones, Henry Mancini

1084 **Peter and the Wolf** PBS
Program Type Children's Special
30 minutes. Premiere date: 12/27/72. Repeat date: 12/27/76. Puppet production of the children's story.
Producer Bob Rowland
Company Mississippi Authority for Educational Television
Director Ed Van Cleef
Narrator Karen Gilfoy
Puppeteers Peter Zapletal, Jarmila Zapletal

1085 **Peter Marshall Variety Show** Syndicated
Program Type Music/Comedy/Variety Series
90 minutes. Weekly. Premiere date: 9/76. One-season variety show with weekly guests.
Executive Producer David Salzman
Producers Rocco Urbisci, Neal Marshall
Company Group W Productions and Marshall-Lewellen Productions
Distributor Group W/Westinghouse Productions, Inc.
Director Jeff Margolis
Writers George Tricker, Ed Scharlach
Musical Director Alan Copeland
Art Director Rene Lagler
Host Peter Marshall
Regulars Chapter 5, Rod Gist & Denny Evans

1086 **Peter Pan**
The Big Event/Hallmark Hall of Fame NBC
Program Type Dramatic Special
Two hours. Premiere date: 12/12/76. New musical adaptation of the 1904 play by Sir James M. Barrie about a boy who won't grow up. "Once Upon a Bedtime" sung by Julie Andrews. Musical and dramatic sequences supervised by Michael Kidd. Music and lyrics by Anthony Newley and Leslie Bricusse. Stereo-simulcast on local FM radio stations.
Executive Producers Gary Smith, Dwight Hemion
Producer Gary Smith
Company An ATV/ITC Production in association with NBC
Director Dwight Hemion
Writers Jack Burns, Andrew Birkin
Musical Director Ian Fraser
Conductors Ian Fraser, Jack Parnell
Costume Designer Sue Le Cash
Art Director David Chandler
Narrator Sir John Gielgud

CAST

Peter Pan .... Mia Farrow
Capt. Hook/Mr. Darling .... Danny Kaye
Mrs. Darling .... Virginia McKenna
Tiger Lily .... Paula Kelly
Wendy .... Briony McRoberts
John .... Ian Sharrock
Michael .... Adam Stafford
Nana/Crocodile .... Peter O'Farrell
Slightly .... Jerome Watts
Tootles .... Nicky Lyndhurst
Nibs .... Adam Richens
Curly .... Michael Deeks
First Twin .... Simon Mooney
Second Twin .... Andrew Mooney
Smee .... Tony Sympson
Starkey .... Joe Melia
Pirates .... Oscar James, George Harris, Michael Crane, Max Latimer, Fred Evans, Peppi Borza
Wendy (older) .... Jill Gascoine
Jane .... Linsey Baxter

1087 **PGA Championship** ABC
Program Type Sports Special
Live coverage of the final rounds of the PGA Golf Championship from the Pebble Beach (Calif.) Golf Links 8/13/77 and 8/14/77.
Executive Producer Roone Arledge
Producer Chuck Howard
Company ABC Sports
Directors Jim Jennett, Terry Jastrow, Andy Sidaris
Anchor Jim McKay
Expert Commentators Dave Marr, Peter Alliss, Bob Rosburg, Bill Flemming

1088 **The Phantom of the Open Hearth**
Visions PBS
Program Type Dramatic Special
90 minutes. Premiere date: 12/23/76. Comedy about a 1940s Junior Prom. Adapted by the author from his book "Wanda Hickey's Night of Golden Memories, and Other Disasters." Presented by KCET-TV/Los Angeles. Program made possible by grants from the Ford Foundation, the National Endowment for the Arts and the Corporation for Public Broadcasting.
Executive Producer Barbara Schultz
Producers Fred Barzyk, David Loxton
Company WNET Television Laboratory/New

The Phantom of the Open Hearth *Continued*
York and WGBH New Television Workshop/Boston
Directors Fred Barzyk, David Loxton
Writer Jean Shepherd
Costume Designer Jennifer Von Mayrhauser
Art Director John Wright Stevens

CAST

Ralph (as man) .... Jean Shepherd
Ralph (as boy) .... David Elliott
Father .... James Broderick
Mother .... Barbara Bolton
Randy .... Adam Goodman
Daphne Bigelow .... Tobi Pilavin
Wanda Hickey .... Roberta Wallach
Uncle Carl .... Ed Huberman
Schwartz .... Bryan Utman
Flick .... William Lampley
John .... Carlton Power
Halfback .... Steve Nuding
Sherby .... David Pokat
Gertz .... Chris Clark
Awkie .... Joe Mayo
Zudock .... David Howard
Mr. Doppler .... Frank Dolan
Al .... Joey Faye
Morty .... John Peters
Clara Mae .... Andrea McCullough
Budge .... Peter Graham
Arlita .... Leigh Brown
Steelworker .... Michael Stein
Deliveryman .... James Bonnell
Waiter .... Sol Schwade

1089 **Phils Ochs Memorial Celebration** PBS
Program Type Music/Dance Special
90 minutes. Premiere date: 7/9/77. Concert-tribute to Phil Ochs taped at Madison Square Garden in New York City 5/28/76. Program made possible in part by a grant from the Corporation for Public Broadcasting.
Producer Douglas Bailey
Company WHYY-TV/Philadelphia-Wilmington
Directors Douglas Bailey, Russell Kneeland
Performers Dan Van Ronk, Pete Seeger, Fred Hellerman, Eric Andersen, Tim Harden, Tom Rush, Melanie, Oscar Brand, Bob Gibson, Jim Glover, David Blue, Peter Yarrow

1090 **Philemon**
Hollywood Television Theatre PBS
Program Type Dramatic Special
Two hours. Premiere date: 10/7/76. Musical play set in the Roman city of Antioch in 287 A.D. about a clown who becomes a saint. An interview with lyricist Tom Jones and composer Harvey Schmidt follows. Program made possible by grants from the Corporation for Public Broadcasting, the Ford Foundation and Public Television Stations.
Executive Producer Norman Lloyd
Producer Norman Lloyd
Company KCET-TV/Los Angeles
Director Norman Lloyd
Writers Tom Jones, Harvey Schmidt
Musical Director Ken Collins
Costume Designer Charles Blackburn
Art Director Eugene Lourie

CAST

Cockian .... Dick Latessa
Commander .... Howard Ross
Wife .... Leila Martin
Andos .... Michael Glenn-Smith
Kiki .... Kathrin King Segal
Servillus .... Charles Blackburn
Marsyas .... Virginia Gregory
Musicians .. Ken Collins, Bill Grossman, Penna Rose

1091 **Phoenix Open** CBS
Program Type Sports Special
60 minutes each day. Live coverage of the final two rounds of the Phoenix Open from the Phoenix (Ariz.) Country Club 1/8/77 and 1/9/77.
Producer Frank Chirkinian
Company CBS Television Network Sports
Directors Frank Chirkinian, Bob Dailey
Commentators Pat Summerall, Jack Whitaker, Ben Wright, Ken Venturi, Frank Beard

1092 **Photoplay Gold Medal Awards** NBC
Program Type Parades/Pageants/Awards Special
90 minutes. Premiere date: 6/18/77. Live coverage (in the East) of the 56th annual Photoplay Gold Medal Awards in 22 categories of entertainment favorites.
Executive Producers Dick Clark, Dan Lewis
Producer Bill Lee
Company Dick Clark Teleshows, Inc. in association with Photoplay Magazine Enterprises, Inc.
Director John Moffitt
Writer Robert Arthur
Musical Director Lenny Stack
Choreographer Ron Poindexter
Costume Designer Al Lehman
Art Director Ray Klausen
Hosts Angie Dickinson, Elliott Gould
Entertainers Connie Stevens, Stiller and Meara (Anne Meara and Jerry Stiller), Paul Williams
Presenters June Allyson, Desi Arnaz, Richard Anderson, Adrienne Barbeau, Steve Bluestein, James Brolin, LeVar Burton, Mike Connors, Robert Conrad, Mac Davis, Olivia de Havilland, Sandy Duncan, Lola Falana, Donna Fargo, Bonnie Franklin, Eydie Gorme, Richard Hatch, Earl Holliman, Bruce Jenner, Dorothy Lamour, Burgess Meredith, Jane Powell,

Eva Marie Saint, William Shatner, Suzanne Somers, Sissy Spacek, Robert Stack, Abe Vigoda

1093 **Phyllis** CBS
Program Type Comedy Series
30 minutes. Mondays/Sundays (as of 1/16/77)/Tuesdays (as of 8/2/77). Premiere date: 9/8/75. Second season premiere: 9/20/76. Last show: 8/30/77. Spin-off from "The Mary Tyler Moore Show." Series concerns the widowed Phyllis Lindstrom, her daughter and in-laws in San Francisco. Music by Dick De Benedictis.
Producers Ed. Weinberger, Stan Daniels
Company MTM Enterprises, Inc.
Directors Various
Writers Various

CAST

Phyllis Lindstrom .... Cloris Leachman
Jonathan Dexter .... Henry Jones
Audrey Dexter .... Jane Rose
Dan Valenti .... Carmine Caridi
Bess Lindstrom .... Lisa Gerritsen
Mother Dexter .... Judith Lowry
Harriet Hastings .... Garn Stephens
Leonard Marsh .... John Lawlor

1094 **Piccadilly Circus** PBS
Program Type Miscellaneous Series
Times vary. Monthly. Premiere date: 1/19/76. Repeats seen weekly as of 7/10/77. Comedies, dramas, dramatic readings and documentaries produced in England. Programs made possible by a grant from Mobil Oil Corporation. Presented by WGBH-TV/Boston. Shows seen during the 1976–77 season are: "Alice Through the Looking Glass," "The Author of Beltraffio," "Ballet Shoes," "The Circus Moves On in Calabria," "The General's Day," "The Goodies and the Beanstalk," "It's a Lovely Day Tomorrow," "The Man on the Rock," "Plaintiffs and Defendants," "The Stanley Baxter Big Picture Show," "Stocker's Copper," "Time and Time Again." (*See* individual titles for credits.)

1095 **The Picnic** PBS
Program Type Comedy Special
30 minutes. Premiere date: 8/76. Repeat date: 12/76. Comedy without dialogue set in the English countryside.
Producer Terry Hughes
Company BBC-TV

CAST

General .... Ronnie Barker
General's Son .... Ronnie Corbett

1096 **Pilobolus Dance Theatre**
Dance in America/Great Performances PBS
Program Type Music/Dance Special
60 minutes. Premiere date: 5/4/77. A performance by the Pilobolus Dance Theatre of four works from the repertoire: "Ocellus," "Ciona," "Monkshood's Farewell," "Untitled." Program made possible by grants from Exxon Corporation, the National Endowment for the Arts and the Corporation for Public Broadcasting.
Executive Producer Jac Venza
Producers Emile Ardolino, Judy Kinberg
Company WNET-TV/New York
Director Merrill Brockway
Dancers Moses Pendleton, Jonathan Wolken, Alison Chase, Robby Barnett, Martha Clarke, Michael Tracy

1097 **The Pinballs**
ABC Afterschool Specials ABC
Program Type Children's Special
60 minutes. Premiere date: 5/18/77. Drama about three youngsters from different backgrounds placed in a foster home together. Based on the novel by Betsy Byars.
Producer Martin Tahse
Company Martin Tahse Productions, Inc.
Director Richard Bennett
Writer Jim Inman
Art Director Ray Markham

CAST

Carlie Higgins .... Kristy McNichol
Harvey .... Johnny Doran
Thomas J. .... Sparky Marcus
Mrs. Mason .... Priscilla Morrill
Mr. Mason .... Walter Brooke
Harvey's Father .... Barry Coe
Ms. Harris .... Jacque Lynn Colton
Policeman .... James Chandler
Nurse .... Beverly Hope Atkinson

1098 **Pine Canyon Is Burning**
NBC Movie of the Week NBC
Program Type TV Movie
90 minutes. Premiere date: 5/18/77. Dramatic pilot about a small-town firefighter raising his two children alone.
Executive Producer Robert A. Cinader
Producers Gino Grimaldi, Hannah Shearer
Company Universal Television in association with the NBC Television Network
Director Christian Nyby III
Writer Robert A. Cinader
Art Director George Renne

CAST

Capt. William Stone .... Kent McCord
Margaret Stone .... Megan McCord
Michael Stone .... Shane Sinutko
Sandra .... Diana Muldaur
Charlie Edison .... Dick Bakalyan
Anne Walker .... Brit Lind
Capt. Ed Wilson .... Andrew Duggan

Pine Canyon Is Burning *Continued*

Edna Wilson .... Doreen Lang
Whitey Olson .... Curtis Credel

1099 **The Pink Panther Laugh & 1/2 Hour & 1/2 Show** NBC

Program Type Animated Film Series
90 minutes. Saturday mornings. Premiere date: 9/6/69. Eighth season premiere: 9/11/76. Animated adventures of the Pink Panther interspersed with episodes of "The Ant and the Aardvark," "Inspector Clouseau," "Texas Toads," and "Misterjaw" (new show). The Pink Panther created by Blake Edwards. "The Pink Panther Theme" by Henry Mancini.
Producers David H. DePatie, Friz Freleng
Company DePatie-Freleng Enterprises, Inc. and the NBC Television Network
Directors Various
Writers Various

Misterjaw

Adventures of a playful shark. Music by Doug Goodwin and Steve DePatie.
Producers David H. DePatie, Friz Freleng
Directors Bob McKimson, Sid Marcus
Story Editor Bob Ogle
Writers Bob Ogle, Dave Detiege

VOICES

Misterjaw .... Arte Johnson
Catfish the Hunter .... Arnold Stang

1100 **Pinocchio** CBS

Program Type Children's Special
90 minutes. Premiere date: 3/27/76. Repeat date: 4/18/77. Musical version of children's tale by Carlo Collodi; words and music by Billy Barnes.
Producers Bernard Rothman, Jack Wohl
Company Rothman/Wohl Productions
Directors Ron Field, Sidney Smith
Writer Herbert Baker
Musical Director Eddie Karam
Choreographer Ron Field
Costume Designer Bill Hargate
Art Directors Romain Johnston, John Dapper

CAST

Gepetto/Stroganoff/Carlo Collodi .... Danny Kaye
Pinocchio/Theresa .... Sandy Duncan
The Fox .... Flip Wilson
The Cat .... Liz Torres
Candlewick .... Gary Morgan
The Coachman .... Clive Revill
Bad Boy No. 1 .... Don Corriea
Bad Boy No. 2 .... Roy Smith

1101 **P.J. and the President's Son**

ABC Afterschool Specials ABC
Program Type Children's Special
60 minutes. Premiere date: 11/10/76. Update of Mark Twain's "The Prince and the Pauper" about the 15-year-old son of a President of the United States and his middle-class look-alike who exchange life styles for a few days. Music composed by Joe Weber. Filmed in part in Washington, D.C.
Executive Producer Daniel Wilson
Producer Fran Sears
Company Daniel Wilson Productions
Director Larry Elikann
Writer Thomas Baum
Costume Designer Ann Hannon
Special Consultant Jack Ford

CAST

P.J./Preston .... Lance Kerwin
Grandma McNulty .... Irene Tedrow
Mr. Nolan .... Laurence Haddon
Piccard .... Robert Miller Driscoll
Tina .... Patti Cohoon
Bascomb .... Milton Selzer
Reporter .... Carol Worthington
Ambassador's Daughter .... Rosalind Chao
The President .... Peter Brandon
The First Lady .... Jane Brandon
The Ambassador .... Chao-Li Chi
The Chef .... Fritz Feld

1102 **Plaintiffs and Defendants**

Piccadilly Circus PBS
Program Type Dramatic Special
65 minutes. Premiere date: 10/12/76. Repeat date: 7/10/77. English comedy about a middle-aged attorney. Program presented by WGBH-TV/Boston, produced by Joan Sullivan, and made possible by a grant from Mobil Oil Corporation.
Producer Kenith Trodd
Company British Broadcasting Corporation
Director Michael Lindsay-Hogg
Writer Simon Gray
Host Jeremy Brett

CAST

Peter .... Alan Bates
Charles .... Dinsdale Landen
Joanna .... Georgina Hale
Hilary .... Rosemary McHale
Jeremy .... Daniel St. George
Client .... Rosemary Martin

Play It Again, Sam *see* The CBS Friday Night Movies

1103 **The Playboy of the Western World**

Classic Theatre: The Humanities in Drama PBS
Program Type Dramatic Special
Two hours. Premiere date: 12/11/75. Repeat date: 5/5/77. 1908 classic filmed in part on the coast of Western Ireland in 1971. Program funded by grants from the National Endowment for the Humanities and Mobil Oil Corporation.

Presented by WGBH-TV/Boston; Joan Sullivan, producer.
Producer Cedric Messina
Company British Broadcasting Corporation
Director Alan Gibson
Writer J. M. Synge

CAST

Christy Mahon .... John Hurt
Pegeen Mike .... Sinead Cusack
Widow Quinn .... Pauline Delaney
Michael James .... Joe Lynch
Shawn Keogh .... Donal McCann

1104 **Playboy's Playmate Party**
Thursday Night Special ABC
Program Type Music/Comedy/Variety Special
90 minutes. Premiere date: 5/12/77. Introduction of the 1977 Playmate of the Year of *Playboy* Magazine. Taped at the Playboy Mansion West, Holmby Hills, California.
Executive Producer Hugh Hefner
Producer Michael Trikilis
Company Playboy Productions
Director Jack Regas
Host Dick Martin
Performers Barbara Mandrell, Johnnie Taylor, Steve Bluestein, Jay Leno

1105 **Playing the Thing** PBS
Program Type Music/Dance Special
30 minutes. Premiere date: 1/27/76. Repeat date: 11/14/76. A history of the harmonica plus performances by Sonny Terry, Duster Bennett, Brian Chaplin and others. Program made possible by a grant from the Corporation for Public Broadcasting.
Producer Christopher Morphet
Company Maryland Center for Public Broadcasting
Director Christopher Morphet
Cinematographer Christopher Morphet
Film Editor Christopher Morphet

1106 **Pleasant Valley Classic** NBC
Program Type Sports Special
Live coverage of the final rounds of the Pleasant Valley Classic from the Pleasant Valley Country Club in Sutton, Mass. 7/16/77 and 7/17/77. New feature: 60-second instructional piece by golf teacher Bob Toski called "Toski's Tips."
Producer Larry Cirillo
Company NBC Sports
Director Harry Coyle
Anchors Jim Simpson, Cary Middlecoff
Commentators Jay Randolph, Fran Tarkenton, John Brodie, Bruce Devlin

1107 **Pleasure at Her Majesty's: Python & Friends Comedy Special** PBS
Program Type Comedy Special
70 minutes. Premiere date: 3/77. Repeat date: 8/77. Filmed highlights of a gala reunion of British comedians at Her Majesty's Theatre in London's West End in the spring of 1976 over a three night period.
Producer Roger Graef
Director Roger Graef
Cinematographers Charles Stewart, Ernest Vinzce
Narrator Dudley Moore
Performers Peter Cook, Alan Bennett, Michael Palin, John Cleese, John Bird, Terry Gilliam, Barry Humphries, Eleanor Bron, Graham Chapman, John Fortune, Graeme Garden, Neil Innes, Des Jones, Terry Jones, Jonathan Miller, Jonathan Lynn, Bill Oddie, Tim Brooke-Taylor

Pocket Money *see* The CBS Friday Night Movies

1108 **Poldark**
Masterpiece Theatre PBS
Program Type Limited Series
60 minutes. Sundays. Premiere date: 5/8/77. 16-part romantic adventure set in late 18th-century Cornwall adapted from the "Poldark" novels of Winston Graham. Music by Kenyon Emrys-Roberts. Presented by WGBH-TV/Boston; produced by Joan Sullivan. Series made possible by a grant from Mobil Oil Corporation.
Producer Morris Barry
Company British Broadcasting Corporation Production
Directors Christopher Barry, Paul Annett, Kenneth Ives
Story Editor Simon Masters
Writers Jack Pulman, Paul Wheeler, Peter Draper, Jack Russell
Costume Designer John Bloomfield
Production Designer Oliver Bayldon
Host Alistair Cooke

CAST

Ross Poldark .... Robin Ellis
Demelza .... Angharad Rees
Francis Poldark .... Clive Francis
Verity Poldark .... Norma Streader
Elizabeth Poldark .... Jill Townsend
Charles Poldark .... Frank Middlemass
Capt. Blamey .... Jonathan Newth
Caroline Penvenen .... Judy Geeson
Keren .... Sheila White
Dwight Enys .... Richard Morant
George Warleggan .... Ralph Bates
Nicholas Warleggan .... Nicholas Selby
Jud .... Paul Curran
Prudie .... Mary Wimbush
Jinny Carter .... Gillian Bailey

Poldark *Continued*

Capt. MacNeil	Donald Douglas
Penvenen	Patrick Holt
Zacky Martin	Forbes Collins
Mrs. Tabb	Sheelah Wilcocks
Pearce	John Baskcomb
Sir Hugh Bodrugan	Christopher Benjamin
Lady Constance Bodrugan	Cynthia Grenville
Pascoe	Ralph Nossek
Capt. Bray	Denis Holmes

1109 **Police Story** NBC

Program Type Crime Drama Series

60 minutes. Tuesdays. Premiere date: 10/2/73. Fourth season premiere: 9/21/76. Last regular show: 4/19/77. Repeats of shows from previous years seen on "The Best of Police Story" from 5/10/77–8/23/77. Anthology series created by Joseph Wambaugh. Developed for television by E. Jack Neuman. Theme music by Jerry Goldsmith. On 1/4/77 "Police Story" presented a drama based on an incident in the career of Joseph Wambaugh. Show planned for 1977–78 season as irregularly-scheduled two-hour specials.

Executive Producer David Gerber

Producer Liam O'Brien

Company David Gerber Productions in association with Columbia Pictures Television and NBC-TV

Directors Various

Executive Story Consultants Liam O'Brien, Ed Waters

Writers Various

Production Consultant Joseph Wambaugh

1110 **Police Woman** NBC

Program Type Crime Drama Series

60 minutes. Tuesdays. Premiere date: 9/13/74. Third season premiere: 9/28/76. Spin-off from "Police Story" episode entitled "The Gamble." Crime drama of an undercover police woman in a large city. Theme music by Morton Stevens. Special effects by Bill Clove.

Executive Producer David Gerber

Producer Douglas Benton

Company David Gerber Productions in association with Columbia Pictures Television and NBC-TV

Directors Various

Executive Story Editor Ed DeBlasio

Writers Various

Art Director Bob Purcell

CAST

Sgt. Pepper Anderson	Angie Dickinson
Sgt. Bill Crowley	Earl Holliman
Joe Styles	Ed Bernard
Pete Royster	Charles Dierkop

1111 **Political Spirit of '76** ABC

Program Type News Special – Public Affairs Special

A series of news and public affairs specials seen during the election year. Premiere date: 2/24/76. Last show: 11/2/76. Shows seen during the 1976–77 season are: "Battle for the White House," "How to Follow the Campaign," "How to Follow the Election," "Political Spirit of '76: Election Night," "The Presidential Debates—A Perspective," "The Vice-Presidential Debate Analysis." (*See* individual titles for credits.)

1112 **Political Spirit of '76: Election Night** ABC

Program Type News Special

Live coverage of election results 11/2/76–11/3/76 beginning 7p.m. and continuing until 5a.m. (Eastern time).

Senior Producer Daryl Griffin

Producers Ronald Ogle, Bob Roy, Elliot Bernstein, Jeff Gralnick

Company ABC News Special Events Unit

Director Marvin Schlenker

Anchors Harry Reasoner, Barbara Walters, Howard K. Smith

Senate Correspondent Frank Reynolds

Gubernatorial Correspondent Ann Compton

Congressional Correspondent Don Farmer

Cutaway Correspondent Steve Bell

Pollster/Voter Analyst Louis Harris

Special Commentator Theodore H. White

Remote Correspondents Sam Donaldson, Tom Jarriel, Herbert Kaplow, Jim Kincaid

1113 **The Porter Wagoner Show** Syndicated

Program Type Music/Comedy/Variety Series

30 minutes. Weekly. Premiered in 1960. 17th season premiere: 9/76. Country music/variety show.

Executive Producer Bill Graham

Producer J. Reginald Dunlap

Company Show Biz, Inc.

Distributor Show Biz, Inc.

Director Gene Birke

Musical Director Porter Wagoner

Star Porter Wagoner

1114 **A Portrait of Jamie** PBS

Program Type Documentary/Informational Special

30 minutes. Premiere date: 7/5/77. An interview with artist Jamie Wyeth. Program made possible by a grant from the Corporation for Public Broadcasting.

Executive Producer Ken Johnson

Producer Rod Bates

Company Nebraska Educational Television Network
Director Rod Bates
Interviewer Rod Bates

Posse *see* The CBS Wednesday Night Movies

1115 **The Possessed**
NBC Movie of the Week NBC
Program Type TV Movie
90 minutes. Premiere date: 5/1/77. Repeat date: 8/28/77. Pilot drama about a defrocked minister battling the forces of evil in an isolated school for girls. Music by Leonard Rosenman.
Executive Producer Jerry Thorpe
Producer Philip Mandelker
Company Warner Bros. Television in association with the NBC Television Network
Director Jerry Thorpe
Writer John Sacret Young

CAST

Kevin Leahy .... James Farentino
Louise Gelson .... Joan Hackett
Ellen Sumner .... Claudette Nevins
Sgt. Taplinger .... Eugene Roche
Paul Winjam .... Harrison Ford
Weezie .... Ann Dusenberry
Lane .... Diana Scarwid
Celia .... Dinah Manoff
Alex .... Carol Jones
Marty .... P. J. Soles
Barry .... Ethelinn Block
Student .... Susan Walden

1116 **Possessions**
Childhood/Great Performances PBS
Program Type Dramatic Special
60 minutes. Premiere date: 3/9/77. Repeat date: 9/21/77. Adaptation of a story by George Ewart Evans about a Welsh widow and her three sons who must sell their pony to help pay off their debts. Presented by WNET-TV/New York. Program made possible by a grant from Exxon Corporation with additional support from member stations of PBS.
Executive Producer Jac Venza
Coordinating Producer Ann Blumenthal
Producer James Brabazon
Company Granada Television
Director John Irvin
Writer Elaine Morgan
Host Ingrid Bergman

CAST

Cassie Pritchard .... Rhoda Lewis
Dando Hamer .... Anthony Hopkins
Tom Pritchard .... Christopher Jones
Willy Pritchard .... Terry Lock
Gomer Pritchard .... David Holland
Gerrie .... Janet Davies
Auctioneer .... Talfryn Thomas
Glyn .... Alan Luxton
First Customer .... Beryl Hall
Second Customer .... Louise Jervis

Potemkin *see* PBS Movie Theater

1117 **The Practice** NBC
Program Type Comedy Series
30 minutes. Wednesdays. Premiere date: 1/30/76. Second season premiere: 10/13/76. Last show: 1/26/77. Created by Steve Gordon. Show concerns a general practitioner on New York City's West Side. Music by James Di Pasquale; theme by David Shire.
Executive Producer Paul Junger Witt
Supervising Producer Tony Thomas
Producer Ronald Rubin
Company Danny Thomas Productions in association with MGM Television and the NBC Television Network
Directors Bill Persky, Noam Pitlik and others
Script Consultants Joel Kimmel, Ann Gibbs
Story Editor Bernard Kahn
Writers Various

CAST

Dr. Jules Bedford .... Danny Thomas
Dr. David Bedford .... David Spielberg
Nurse Molly Gibbons .... Dena Dietrich
Jenny Bedford .... Shelley Fabares
Helen .... Didi Conn
Lenny .... Mike Evans
Tony Bedford .... Damon Raskin
Paul Bedford .... Allen Price

1118 **The Preakeness** ABC
Program Type Sports Special
60 minutes. Live coverage of the 102nd running of the Preakness from Pimlico Race Course, Baltimore, Md. 5/21/77.
Executive Producer Roone Arledge
Producer Chuck Howard
Company ABC Sports
Director Chet Forte
Announcers Howard Cosell, Jim McKay
Expert Commentator Eddie Arcaro

1119 **The Predators** NBC
Program Type Science/Nature Special
60 minutes. Premiere date: 5/19/77. An examination of predators and their prey in the North American wilderness. Music composed by John Murtaugh.
Producer Marty Stouffer
Company Stouffer Productions, Ltd.
Directors Marty Stouffer, Mark Stouffer
Writer John Savage
Conductor John Murtaugh
Cinematographers Marty Stouffer, Mark Stouffer
Film Editors Tom Kennedy, Mark Stouffer, Ira

The Predators *Continued*
Wohl
Narrator Robert Redford

1120 **Preservation Hall Jazz Band**
In Performance at Wolf Trap PBS
Program Type Music/Dance Special
60 minutes. Premiere date: 11/25/74. Reedited date: 12/29/75. Repeat date: 12/13/76. A Concert of New Orleans jazz by the Preservation Hall jazz Band performed at the Wolf Trap Farm Park in Arlington, Va. Program made possible by a grant from Atlantic Richfield Company.
Executive Producer David Prowitt
Producer Ruth Leon
Company WETA-TV/Washington, D.C.
Director Clark Santee
Hosts Beverly Sills, David Prowitt

1121 **The Presidency: 100 Days of Jimmy Carter** PBS
Program Type Public Affairs Special
30 minutes. Premiere date: 5/3/77. An assessment of the first hundred days of the presidency of Jimmy Carter.
Executive Producer Robert Ferrante
Company WGBH-TV/Boston
Executive Editor Ed Baumeister
Moderator Christopher Lydon
Guests Hubert Humphrey, James Reston, Archibald MacLeish, Thomas Corcoran, Doris Kearns, I. F. Stone

1122 **President Carter's Address to the Joint Session of Congress** ABC
Program Type News Special
60 minutes. Live coverage of Pres. Jimmy Carter's address to Congress outlining his energy proposals plus analysis and interviews of the speech 4/20/77.
Executive Producer Elliot Bernstein
Company ABC News
Anchors Harry Reasoner, Barbara Walters
Correspondents Frank Reynolds, Don Farmer, Sam Donaldson

1123 **President Carter's Address to the Nation** ABC
Program Type News Special
Live coverage of Pres. Jimmy Carter's address to the nation on domestic matters 2/2/77.
Company ABC News
Correspondent Sam Donaldson

1124 **President Carter's Address to the Nation on Domestic Matters**
NBC News Special NBC
Program Type News Special
30 minutes. Live coverage of Pres. Jimmy Carter's address to the nation on domestic matters 2/2/77.
Executive Producer Gordon Manning
Company NBC News
Anchor John Chancellor

1125 **President Carter's Address to the United Nations**
NBC News Special NBC
Program Type News Special
Live coverage of Pres. Jimmy Carter's address before the United Nations General Assembly 3/17/77.
Executive Producer Gordon Manning
Company NBC News
Anchor David Brinkley

1126 **President Carter's Visit to Yazoo City, Mississippi** PBS
Program Type News Special
90 minutes. Premiere date: 7/21/77. A report of the President's town meeting in Yazoo City, Mississippi.
Producer Mike Seymour
Company Mississippi Authority for Educational Television
Director Ron Harris
Narrators Howard Lett, John Pittman

1127 **Presidential Address to a Joint Session of Congress**
CBS News Special CBS
Program Type News Special
40 minutes. Live coverage of Pres. Jimmy Carter's address to Congress on energy 4/20/77.
Producer Sanford Socolow
Company CBS News
Anchor Bob Schieffer
Reporters Nelson Benton, Phil Jones

1128 **Presidential Address to the Nation**
CBS News Special CBS
Program Type News Special
30 minutes. Live coverage of Pres. Jimmy Carter's address to the nation on energy 4/18/77.
Producer Bill Headline
Company CBS News
Anchor Barry Serafin
Analyst Bob Schieffer

1129 **The Presidential Candidates Debate—Post Debate Wrap-Up (First Debate)**
Decision '76 NBC
Program Type News Special
15 minutes. 9/23/76. Analysis and review of the first presidential debate.
Company NBC News
Anchors John Chancellor, David Brinkley
Reporters Kenley Jones, Marilyn Berger, John Hart

1130 **The Presidential Candidates Debate—Post-Debate Wrap-Up (Second Debate)**
Decision '76 NBC
Program Type News Special
15 minutes. 10/6/76. Analysis and review of the second debate between the presidential candidates.
Company NBC News
Anchors John Chancellor, David Brinkley

1131 **The Presidential Candidates Debate—Post-Debate Wrap-Up: (Third Debate)**
Decision '76 NBC
Program Type News Special
15 minutes. 10/22/76. Analysis and wrap-up of the final debate between the presidential candidates.
Producers Lester M. Crystal, Ray Lockhart
Company NBC News
Anchors John Chancellor, David Brinkley
Correspondents Catherine Mackin, Douglas Kiker, Marilyn Berger, Bob Jamieson, Don Oliver, Kenley Jones

1132 **The Presidential Debates (First Debate)** ABC, CBS, NBC, PBS
Program Type News Special
90 minutes. 9/23/76. Live coverage of the first debate between Pres. Gerald R. Ford and Gov. Jimmy Carter from the Walnut Street Theater in Philadelphia. Debate was stretched an additional 23 minutes due to audio difficulties. PBS broadcast was tape-delayed with simultaneous translation in sign language for the hearing-impaired. Repeated 9/24/76 with captions.
Producer Elliot Bernstein (ABC)
Company League of Women Voters Education Fund
Director Richard Armstrong
Moderator Edwin Newman
Panelists Elizabeth Drew, James Gannon, Frank Reynolds

1133 **The Presidential Debates (Second Debate)** ABC, CBS, NBC, PBS
Program Type News Special
90 minutes. 10/6/76. Live coverage of the second debate between Pres. Gerald R. Ford and Gov. Jimmy Carter from the Palace of Fine Arts Theater in San Francisco. PBS broadcast was tape-delayed with simultaneous translation in sign language for the hearing-impaired; later repeat captioned.
Company League of Women Voters Education Fund
Moderator Pauline Frederick
Panelists Max Frankel, Henry L. Trewhitt, Richard Valeriani

1134 **The Presidential Debates (Third Debate)** ABC, CBS, NBC, PBS
Program Type News Special
90 minutes. 10/22/76. Live coverage of the final debate between Pres. Gerald R. Ford and Gov. Jimmy Carter from the College of William and Mary in Williamsburg, Va. Same-day PBS tape-delayed broadcast with simultaneous translation for the hearing-impaired; later broadcast captioned.
Producer Christie Basham (NBC)
Company League of Women Voters Education Fund
Moderator Barbara Walters
Panelists Joseph Kraft, Robert C. Maynard, Jack Nelson

1135 **The Presidential Debates—A Perspective (First Debate)**
Political Spirit of '76 ABC
Program Type News Special
30 minutes. 9/23/76. An ABC News special program of analysis and review of the first Ford-Carter debate.
Producer Phil Lewis
Company ABC News Special Events Unit
Anchors Harry Reasoner, Howard K. Smith
Correspondents Frank Reynolds, Tom Jarriel, Sam Donaldson, Herbert Kaplow
Public Opinion Research Expert Louis Harris

1136 **The Presidential Debates—A Perspective (Second Debate)**
Political Spirit of '76 ABC
Program Type News Special
15 minutes. 10/6/76. An ABC News special program of analysis and review of the second presidential debate.
Senior Producer Jeff Gralnick
Company ABC News Special Events Unit
Anchors Harry Reasoner, Barbara Walters

The Presidential Debates—A Perspective (Second Debate) *Continued*
Analysts Howard K. Smith, Barrie Dunsmore
Correspondents Tom Jarriel, Sam Donaldson

1137 **The Presidential Debates—A Perspective (Third Debate)**
Political Spirit '76 ABC
Program Type News Special
60 minutes. 10/22/76. Analysis of the final debate between the presidential contenders, results of the latest Louis Harris/ABC News poll and interviews with members of the Ford and Carter families.
Senior Producer Jeff Gralnick
Company ABC News Special Events Unit
Anchors Harry Reasoner, Barbara Walters
Correspondents Tom Jarriel, Sam Donaldson

1138 **The Presidential Election—What's It All About?**
What's It All About? CBS
Program Type Children's Special
30 minutes. Premiere date: 10/30/76. Informational broadcast for school-age children explaining the American process of choosing a president and vice-president.
Executive Producer Joel Heller
Producer Vern Diamond
Company CBS News
Animator Jerry Merola
Researcher Pat Olsen
Anchor Correspondent Walter Cronkite
Correspondents Sylvia Chase, Morton Dean, Christopher Glenn

1139 **The Presidential Inauguration**
CBS News Special Report CBS
Program Type News Special
Six hours. 1/20/77. Live coverage of the inauguration of Jimmy Carter as 39th President of the United States. Includes "Inaugural Almanac" (historical stories of past inaugurations produced by Mark Kramer and Louise Durbin and reported by Charles Osgood).
Executive Producer Russ Bensley
Company CBS News
Anchors Walter Cronkite, Roger Mudd, Bob Schieffer
Analysts Eric Sevareid, Bill Moyers
Correspondents/Reporters Nelson Benton, Ed Bradley, Jed Duvall, Phil Jones, Marvin Kalb, Marya McLaughlin, Bruce Morton, Ike Pappas, Bill Plante, Richard Roth, Barry Serafin, Lesley Stahl

1140 **The President's Energy Message to Congress**
NBC News Special NBC
Program Type News Special
60 minutes. Live coverage of Pres. Jimmy Carter's address on energy before a joint session of Congress 4/20/77.
Company NBC News
Anchor John Hart
Reporters Catherine Mackin, Irving R. Levine, Eric Burns, George Lewis, Frank Bourgholtzer

1141 **Previn and the Pittsburgh** PBS
Program Type Music/Dance Series
60 minutes. Sundays. Premiere date: 2/27/77. Series repeats began 4/24/77. Eight-part series of musical discussion and performances with guest artists and the Pittsburgh Symphony. Series made possible by a grant from the Alcoa Foundation.
Executive Producer Jay Rayvid
Producers James A. DeVinney, Virginia K. Bartlett
Company WQED-TV/Pittsburgh
Director Ian Engelmann
Conductor Andre Previn
Host Andre Previn

1142 **The Price is Right** CBS
Program Type Game/Audience Participation Series
60 minutes. Mondays-Fridays. New series premiere: 9/4/72. Continuous. Show originally seen in 1956. Became television's first regularly scheduled 60-minute daytime game show 11/3/75.
Executive Producer Frank Wayne
Producer Jay Wolpert
Company Goodson-Todman Productions
Director Marc Breslow
Host Bob Barker
Announcer Johnny Olson

1143 **The Price is Right (Evening)**
Syndicated
Program Type Game/Audience Participation Series
30 minutes. Weekly. Premiere date: 9/72. Fifth season premiere: 9/76. Evening version of daytime show.
Executive Producer Frank Wayne
Producer Jay Wolpert
Company Goodson-Todman Productions
Distributor Viacom Enterprises
Director Marc Breslow
Host Dennis James
Announcer Johnny Olson

1144 **The Primary English Class**
The ABC Monday Comedy Special ABC
Program Type Comedy Special
30 minutes. Premiere date: 8/15/77. Comedy pilot about an English teacher in a night class for foreign adults. Theme song by Joe Hamilton and Peter Matz.
Executive Producer Joe Hamilton
Company Joe Hamilton Productions, Inc.
Directors Roger Beatty, Tim Conway
Writers Arnie Kogen, Roger Beatty
Set Decorator Bill Harp

CAST

Sandy Lambert .... Valerie Curtin
Hal .... Murphy Dunne
Yosef Ari .... Harvey Jason
Lupe .... Maria O'Brien
Sergio .... Joe Bennett
Wilhelm Ritterman .... Bob Holt
Yoko .... Suesie Elene
Chuma .... Freeman King

1145 **The Prince and the Pauper**
Once Upon a Classic PBS
Program Type Children's Series
30 minutes. Saturdays. Premiere date: 10/9/76. Series repeats began 7/2/77. Six-part dramatization of the Mark Twain classic. Filmed in England. Captioned for the hearing-impaired. Presented by WQED-TV/Pittsburgh and made possible by grants from McDonald's Local Restaurants Association and McDonald's Corporation.
Executive Producer Jay Rayvid
Director John Coney
Producer Barry Letts
Company British Broadcasting Corporation and Time-Life Television
Director Barry Letts
Writer Richard Harris
Costume Designer James Acheson
Host Bill Bixby

CAST

Prince Edward/Tom Canty .... Nicholas Lyndhurst
John Canty .... Ronald Herdman
Miles Hendon .... Barry Stokes
Lord Hertford .... Bernard Kay
Lord Sudbroke .... Martin Friend
Lord Rushden .... Ronald Lacey
Darbon .... Max Faulkner
Mother Canty .... June Brown
Henry VIII .... Ronald Radd

1146 **The Prince of Central Park** CBS
Program Type Dramatic Special
90 minutes. Premiere date: 6/17/77. Drama about two children living in Central Park. Based on the novel by Evan H. Rhodes. Music by Arthur B. Rubinstein. Filmed on location in and around Central Park in New York City.
Executive Producer Philip Capice
Producer Harvey Hart
Company Lorimar Productions
Director Harvey Hart
Writer Jeb Rosebrook
Art Director Hank Aldrich

CAST

Mrs. Miller .... Ruth Gordon
Jay Jay .... T. J. Hargrave
Laurie .... Lisa Richard
Elmo .... Marc Vahanian
Alice .... Eda Reiss Merin
Ardis .... Carol Gustafson
Kristin .... Brooke Shields
Mme. Dupres .... Brenda Currin
Rodney .... Bruce Howard Webster
Rodney's Father .... William Knight
Boy in Cafeteria .... Mike Brown
Bus Boy .... Tony Travis
Girl in Cafeteria .... Kim Webster
Italian Woman .... Jo Flores Chase
Mother in Cafeteria .... Carol Nadell
Preacher .... Estelle Omens
Security Guard .... J. Herbert Kerr
Tour Guide .... Ellin Ruskin
Vendor .... Dan Hedaya

1147 **The Prince of Homburg**
Theater in America/Great Performances PBS
Program Type Dramatic Special
Two hours. Premiere date: 4/27/77. The Chelsea Theater Center of New York in a production of the 1811 psychological drama by Heinrich von Kleist translated by James Kirkup. Taped at the Biltmore House in Asheville, N.C. Program made possible by grants from Exxon Corporation, the Corporation for Public Broadcasting, the Ford Foundation and Public Television Stations.
Executive Producer Jac Venza
Producer Lindsay Law
Company WNET-TV/New York and WRKL-TV/Columbia, S.C.
Directors Robert Kalfin, Kirk Browning
Writer Heinrich von Kleist
Host Hal Holbrook

CAST

Prince .... Frank Langella
Natalia .... Randy Danson
Elector .... K. Lype O'Dell
Col. Kottwitz .... Roger DeKoven
Elector's Wife .... M'El Dowd
Additional Cast George Morfogen, Robert Einekel, Frank Anderson, Jon Peter Benson, William Myers, Larry Swansen

1148 **The Prison Game**
Visions PBS
Program Type Dramatic Special
90 minutes. Premiere date: 1/13/77. Drama about a "To-Tell-the-Truth"-type game show in which three women claim to be a murderer. Program made possible by grants from the Ford Foundation, the National Endowment for the

The Prison Game *Continued*
Arts and the Corporation for Public Broadcasting.
Producer Barbara Schultz
Company KCET-TV/Los Angeles
Director Robert Stevens
Writer Susan Yankowitz
Costume Designer Terence Tam Soon
Art Director John Retsek

CAST

Anna I .... Edith Diaz
Anna II .... Jessica Walter
Anna III .... Cara Williams
Henry Stokes .... Peter Bonerz
Marion Kostine .... Neva Patterson
Marvin Simeon .... Severn Darden
Moderator (Chuck Cooper) .... Bo Kaprall
Husband I .... Chu Chu Malave
Husband II .... David Hayward
Husband III .... Ryan MacDonald
Carrie .... Migdia Varela
Psychiatrist .... Tom Palmer

1149 **Pro Football Hall of Fame Special** NBC
Program Type Sports Special
30 minutes. Premiere date: 9/8/77. The importance of the Pro Football Hall of Fame to the Canton, Ohio community and to football hall-of-famers.
Company NFL Films in association with SFM Media Service Corporation

1150 **Professional Bowlers Association National Championship Tournament** CBS
Program Type Sports Special
Two hours. Live coverage of the finals of the championship tournament from Leilani Lanes in Seattle, Wash. 6/19/77.
Producer Bob Stenner
Company CBS Television Network Sports
Director Tony Verna
Announcer Frank Glieber
Commentator Carmen Salvino

1151 **Professional Bowlers Tour** ABC
Program Type Limited Sports Series
90 minutes. Saturday afternoons. Premiere date: 1/6/62. 16th season premiere: 1/8/77. Last show of season: 4/23/77. 16-week series of live telecasts of bowling tournaments. Regular feature: bowling tips by Nelson Burton, Jr..
Executive Producer Roone Arledge
Producers Bob Goodrich (regular producer), Ned Steckel
Company ABC Sports
Directors Roger Goodman, Jim Jennett
Announcers Chris Schenkel (regular announcer), Dave Diles, Al Michaels
Expert Commentator Nelson Burton, Jr.

Professional Golf Association *see* PGA

1152 **The Puzzle Children** PBS
Program Type Documentary/Informational Special
60 minutes. Premiere date: 10/19/76. A look at learning-disabled children through talk, songs and skits. Music by Peter Knight. "Something" composed by Joe Raposo. Program shown in conjunction with "What's Wrong With My Child?" and made possible by a grant from the 3M Company.
Executive Producer Thomas Skinner
Producer Stephen Dick
Company WQED-TV/Pittsburgh
Director Bill Davis
Writer Stephen Dick
Cinematographer Walt Seng
Film Editor Michael Colonna
Hosts Julie Andrews, Bill Bixby
Cast Jack Riley, Judy Kahan, Elliott Reed

Pygmalion *see* PBS Movie Theater

1153 **Pygmies** PBS
Program Type Documentary/Informational Special
60 minutes. Premiere date: 3/76. Repeat date: 12/76. A look at the daily lives of the Bajaka tribe of Pygmies and an assessment of their chances for survival. Film produced in 1974.
Producer Bethusy Huc
Director Bethusy Huc
Cinematographer Bethusy Huc

1154 **Quark** NBC
Program Type Comedy Special
30 minutes. Premiere date: 5/7/77. Science-fiction comedy pilot about the commander of the United Galaxy Sanitation Patrol in the year 2222 A.D.
Executive Producers David Gerber, Mace Neufeld
Producer Buck Henry
Company David Gerber Productions in association with Columbia Pictures Television
Director Peter H. Hunt
Writer Buck Henry

CAST

Adam Quark .... Richard Benjamin
Gene/Jean .... Timothy Thomerson
O.B. Mudd .... Douglas V. Fowley
Betty I .... Tricia Barnstable
Betty II .... Cyb Barnstable
Otto Palindrome .... Conrad Janis
The Head .... Alan Caillou
Interface .... Misty Rowe
Andy the Robot .... Bobby Porter

Queen of Spades *see* PBS Movie Theater

1155 **The Queen's Destiny**
Ourstory PBS
Program Type Dramatic Special
30 minutes. Premiere date: 4/12/76. Repeat date: 12/10/76. A dramatization of the overthrow of Queen Liliuokalani of Hawaii in 1893. Funded by grants from the National Endowment for the Humanities, the Arthur Vining Davis Foundations and the George Gund Foundation.
Executive Producer Don Fouser
Producer Don Fouser
Company WNET-TV/New York
Director Don Fouser
Writer Robert Pendlebury
Costume Designer John Boxer
Host Bill Moyers

CAST

Queen Liliuokalani .... Miriam Colon
Samuel Parker .... Manu Tupou
A. P. Peterson .... George Pentecost
W. H. Cornwell .... Bill Moor
John F. Colburn .... Wayne Maxwell
Wilson .... Tom Martin
Princess .... Nai Bonet

1156 **The Queen's Silver Jubilee Gala at Covent Garden** PBS
Program Type Music/Dance Special
Two hours. Premiere date: 5/31/77. A command performance by the Royal Opera Company and the Royal Ballet in honor of Queen Elizabeth's 25-year reign in England. Devised and produced by Sir Frederick Ashton and John Copley. Taped at Covent Garden, London 5/30/77. Program presented by WNET-TV/New York and made possible by a grant from IBM Corporation.
Executive Producer Humphrey Burton
Coordinating Producers David Griffiths, Ann Blumenthal
Producer Brian Large
Company British Broadcasting Corporation
Director Brian Large
Conductors Colin Davis, Ashley Lawrence
Performers Margot Fonteyn, Rudolf Nureyev, Placido Domingo, Margaret Price

1157 **The Quest** NBC
Program Type Western Series
60 minutes. Wednesdays. Premiere date: 9/22/76 (90 minutes). Last show: 12/29/76. Pilot aired 5/13/76. Drama of two brothers searching for their sister who is living with Indians. Created by Tracy Kennan Wynn. Music by Richard Shores.
Executive Producer David Gerber
Producers Mark Rodgers, James H. Brown
Company David Gerber Productions in association with Columbia Pictures Television and NBC-TV
Directors Various
Story Editor Jack Miller
Writers Various

CAST

Morgan (Two Persons) Baudine .... Kurt Russell
Quentin Baudine .... Tim Matheson

1158 **Quincy**
NBC Sunday Mystery Movie NBC
Program Type Crime Drama Series
90 minutes/60 minutes. Sundays/Fridays (as of 2/4/77). Premiere date: 10/3/76. Mystery drama involving a medical examiner in the Los Angeles City Coronor's Office. Created by Glen A. Larson and Lou Shaw. Music by Stu Phillips. Shown as part of "NBC Sunday Mystery Movie" from 10/3/76–1/2/77. Became weekly show as of 2/4/77.
Executive Producer Glen A. Larson
Producer Lou Shaw
Company Glen A. Larson Productions in association with Universal Television and NBC-TV
Directors Various
Story Editor Michael Kozoll
Writers Various

CAST

Quincy .... Jack Klugman
Lt. Frank Monahan .... Garry Walberg
Dr. Robert Astin .... John S. Ragin
Lee Porter .... Lynnette Mettey
Sam Fujiyama .... Robert Ito
Sgt. Brill .... Joseph Roman
Danny Tovo .... Val Bisoglio

1159 **The Quinns**
The ABC Friday Night Movie ABC
Program Type TV Movie
90 minutes. Premiere date: 7/1/77. Pilot drama about four generations of New York City firefighters. Created by Sidney Carroll, based on an idea by Phyllis Minoff and Fran Sears. Music by John Scott.
Producer Daniel Wilson
Company Daniel Wilson Productions, Inc.
Director Daniel Petrie
Writer Sidney Carroll
Conductor John Scott
Art Director Mel Bourne

CAST

Bill Quinn .... Barry Bostwick
Elizabeth Quinn .... Susan Browning
Sean Quinn, Sr. .... Liam Dunn
Rita .... Pat Elliott
Peggy Quinn .... Geraldine Fitzgerald
Michael Quinn .... Peter Masterson
Laurie .... Penny Peyser
Tom Quinn .... William Swetland
Eugene Carmody .... Pat Corley
Renee Carmody .... Virginia Vestoff
Millicent Priestley .... Blair Brown

The Ra Expeditions *see* NBC Night at the Movies

Race With the Devil *see* The CBS Wednesday Night Movies

Rafferty and the Gold Dust Twins *see* NBC Monday Night at the Movies ("Rafferty and the Highway Hustlers")

Rafferty and the Highway Hustlers *see* NBC Monday Night at the Movies

1160 **Raid on Entebbe**
The Big Event NBC
Program Type Dramatic Special
Three hours. Premiere date: 1/9/77. Dramatization of the 7/4/76 Israeli raid on Entebbe airport. Music by David Shire.
Executive Producers Edgar J. Scherick, Daniel H. Blatt
Company Edgar J. Scherick Associates in association with 20th Century-Fox Television and NBC-TV
Director Irvin Kershner
Writer Barry Beckerman
Production Designer W. Stewart Campbell
Art Director Kirk Axtell

CAST

Gen. Dan Shomron .... Charles Bronson
Prime Minister Rabin .... Peter Finch
Pres. Idi Amin .... Yaphet Kotto
Gen. Mordechai Gur .... Jack Warden
Dan Cooper .... Martin Balsam
Wilfred Boese .... Horst Bucholz
Capt. Bacos .... Eddie Constantine
Cohen .... Allan Arbus
Gen. Allon .... Robert Loggia
Gen. Peled .... John Saxon
Begin .... David Opatoshu
Dora Block .... Sylvia Sidney
Krieger .... Mariclare Costello
Yonni Netanyahu .... Stephen Macht
Additional Cast Tige Andrews, Warren Kemmerling, James Woods, Lou Gilbert, Alex Colon, Harvey Lembeck, Peter Brocco, Aharon Ipale

1161 **Ransom for Alice** NBC
Program Type TV Movie
90 minutes. Premiere date: 6/2/77. Police-western pilot set in the 1880s about two deputy marshalls. Special effects by Bob Warner.
Producer Franklin Barton
Company Universal Television
Director David Lowell Rich
Writer Jim Byrnes
Art Director David Marshall
Set Decorator Richard Friedman

CAST

Clint Kirby .... Gil Gerard
Jenny Cullen .... Yvette Mimieux
Pete Phelan .... Charles Napier
Alice Halliday .... Laurie Prange
Jess Halliday .... Barnard Hughes
Whitaker Halliday .... Robert Hogan
Isaac Pratt .... Harris Yulin
Nick .... Marc Vahanian
Harry Darew .... Gene Barry
Toby .... Mills Watson

1162 **Razzmatazz** CBS
Program Type Children's Special
60 minutes. Premiere date: 4/16/77. Pilot for young people's news magazine series.
Executive Producer Joel Heller
Producer Vern Diamond
Company CBS News in cooperation with Scholastic Magazines, Inc.
Director Vern Diamond
Writer Joel Heller
Scenic Designer Neil DeLuca
Animation Directors George Smith, Joseph Lagana
Host Barry Bostwick

1163 **Realidades** PBS
Program Type Educational/Cultural Series
30 minutes. Sundays. Premiere date: 10/13/75. Second season premiere: 7/17/77. Ten-part Spanish/English public and cultural affairs program of special interest to the Latino community. Series made possible by a grant from the Corporation for Public Broadcasting.
Executive Producer Humberto Cintron
Producers Various
Company WNET-TV/New York
Host Humberto Cintron

1164 **Rebop** PBS
Program Type Children's Series
30 minutes. Saturdays. Premiere date: 10/9/76. Series repeats began 4/15/77. 26-week multi-cultural series for children ages 9–13. Three weekly film portraits of young people from different cultural backgrounds. Series made possible by grants from the U.S. Department of Health, Education and Welfare, Parker Brothers, Kenner Products and Fundimension Division of General Mills, Inc.
Executive Producer Topper Carew
Producers Lois H. Johnson, Jesus Henrique Maldonaldo, Dasal Banks, Tanya Hart, David K. Liu, Hazel V. Bright, Peter Cook
Company WGBH-TV/Boston
Cinematographers Tim Hill, Werner Bundschuh, Henry Johnson, Elvida Abella

1165 **Red Alert**
The CBS Wednesday Night Movies CBS
Program Type TV Movie
Two hours. Premiere date: 5/18/77. Drama about a threatened nuclear holocaust. Based on the novel "Paradigm Red" by Harold King. Filmed on location near Houston, Texas at the Lyndon B. Johnson Space Center (NASA).
Executive Producer Gerald I. Isenberg, Gerald W. Abrams
Producer Barry Goldberg
Company Jozak Productions/Paramount Pictures
Director William Hale
Writer Sandor Stern
Art Director Jim Spencer

CAST

Frank Brolen .... William Devane
Henry Stone .... Ralph Waite
Carl Wyche .... Michael Brandon
Judy Wyche .... Adrienne Barbeau
Larry Cadwell .... David Hayward
Sheriff Sweeney .... M. Emmet Walsh
Lou Banducci .... Malcolm Whitman
Bill Young .... Don Wiseman
Harry Holland .... Howard Finch
Stover .... Charles Krohn
Mrs. Kerwin .... Dixie Taylor
Howard Ives .... Jim Siedow

The Red Shoes *see* PBS Movie Theater

Red Sun *see* The CBS Wednesday Night Movies

The Reincarnation of Peter Proud *see* The ABC Sunday Night Movie

1166 **Rejoice: An Easter in Greece** CBS
Program Type Religious/Cultural Special
60 minutes. Premiere date: 4/10/77. Easter Holy Week as celebrated in various parts of Greece.
Executive Producer Pamela Ilott
Producer Warren Wallace
Company CBS News Religious Broadcast
Writer Warren Wallace
Cinematographer Warren Wallace
Narrator Warren Wallace
Consultant Helena Yatras

1167 **Remembering Groucho** ABC
Program Type Documentary/Informational Special
30 minutes. Premiere date: 9/2/77. Special report on the career of Groucho Marx.
Executive Producer Elliot Bernstein
Producer Arthur Holch
Company ABC News
Anchor Harry Reasoner
Special Guest Dick Cavett

1168 **Renascence** PBS
Program Type Documentary/Informational Special
30 minutes. Premiere date: 12/27/76. A television essay celebrating the process of rebirth in the natural world. Program made possible by a grant from the Weyerhaeuser Company Foundation.
Producer Richard Gilbert
Company KCTS-TV/Seattle
Director Richard Gilbert
Writer James Halpin

Report to the Commissioner *see* The CBS Friday Night Movies

1169 **The Restless Earth** PBS
Program Type Science/Nature Special
Two hours. Premiere date: 2/28/72. Repeat date: 1/3/77. A look at the current geologic theory of shifting plates in the earth's crust. Program made possible by a grant from Ciba-Geigy Corp.
Executive Producer Philip Daly
Company A co-production of WNET-TV/New York, the British Broadcasting Corporation, Sveriges Radio (Sweden), the Australian Broadcasting Commission and Baverisher Rundfunk (West Germany).
Writer Nigel Calder
Moderator David Prowitt

1170 **The Restoration of Rembrandt's "Night Watch"** PBS
Program Type Documentary/Informational Special
45 minutes. Premiere date: 8/77. A look at the process of restoring Rembrandt's famous painting after it was mutilated on 9/14/75. Filmed at the Rijksmuseum in Amsterdam, Holland.
Company N.C.R.V., Holland
Cinematographers Gerard van den Bergh, Hans Koekoek, Henny van Aurich, Louis Spoelstra

1171 **The Retirement Revolution**
CBS News Special CBS
Program Type Documentary/Informational Special
60 minutes. Premiere date: 7/26/77. An examination of the problems of retired people.
Executive Producer Leslie Midgley
Producer Bernard Birnbaum
Company CBS News
Director Ken Sable

The Retirement Revolution *Continued*
Writer Charles Collingwood
Anchor Charles Collingwood

1172 **Revenge for a Rape**
The ABC Friday Night Movie ABC
Program Type TV Movie
Two hours. Premiere date: 11/19/76. Drama of a man who becomes a vigilante. Based on a story by Albert S. Ruddy. Music by Jerrold Immel. Filmed on location in Vancouver, British Columbia.
Executive Producer Richard R. St. Johns
Producer Alan P. Horowitz
Company Albert S. Ruddy Productions
Director Timothy Galfas
Writer Yabo Yablonsky

CAST

Travis Green .... Mike Connors
Sheriff Paley .... Robert Reed
Amy Green .... Tracy Brooks Swope
Raleigh .... Deanna Lund
Dr. Bird .... Roger Dressler
Curly .... Jock Livingston
Chuck .... Glenn Wilder
Cooper .... Larry Watson
Nurse .... Shirley Barclay
Farley .... Joe Austin

1173 **Rex Humbard World Outreach Ministry** Syndicated
Program Type Religious/Cultural Series
60 minutes. Weekly. Syndicated for over 24 years from the Cathedral of Tomorrow. Sermons by Rex Humbard.
Executive Producer Rex Humbard, Jr.
Producer Bob Anderson
Company The Cathedral of Tomorrow-World Outreach Ministry
Director Bob Anderson
Musical Director Danny Koker
Regulars The Rex Humbard Family Singers, Cathedral Choir
Featured Soloists Maude Aimee Humbard, Elizabeth Humbard

1174 **Rex Mays Classic 150** CBS
Program Type Sports Special
Two hours. Live coverage of the Rex Mays Classic 150 championship race from Milwaukee, Wisc. 6/12/77.
Producer Bernie Hoffman
Company CBS Television Network Sports
Director Bernie Hoffman
Commentators Ken Squier, David Hobbs, Brock Yates

1175 **The Rhinemann Exchange**
NBC's Best Seller NBC
Program Type Limited Series
Five hours. Thursdays. Premiere date: 3/10/77. Dramatization of the novel by Robert Ludlum about espionage during World War II. Filmed on location in Mexico City and Cuernavaca, Mexico.
Executive Producer George Eckstein
Producer Richard Collins
Company Universal Television in association with NBC-TV
Director Burt Kennedy
Writer Richard Collins
Costume Designer Yvonne Wood
Set Decorator Richard Friedman
Art Director William H. Tuntke

CAST

David Spaulding .... Stephen Collins
Dr. Lyons .... Rene Auberjonois
Bobby Ballard .... Roddy McDowall
Dr. Azevedo .... Ben Wright
Col. Pace .... Larry Hagman
Leslie Jenner Hawkewood .... Lauren Hutton
Kendall .... Claude Akins
Irene .... Trisha Noble
Altmuller .... Werner Klemperer
Dietricht .... John van Dreelen
Stoltz .... Bo Brundin
Rhinemann .... Jose Ferrer
Swanson .... Vince Edwards
Asher Feld .... Len Berman
Col. Meehan .... Ramon Bieri
Lt. Funes .... Pedro Armendariz, Jr.
Amb. Granville .... John Huston
Mrs. Cameron .... Kate Woodville
Alex Spaulding .... William Prince
Indian Girl .... Victoria Racimo
Geoffrey Moore .... Jeremy Kemp

1176 **Rhoda** CBS
Program Type Comedy Series
30 minutes. Mondays/Sundays (as of 1/16/77). Premiere date: 9/9/74. Third season premiere: 9/20/76. Spin-off from "The Mary Tyler Moore Show" created by James L. Brooks and Allan Burns. Comedy about a window dresser in New York City. Music by Billy Goldenberg
Executive Producers James L. Brooks, Allan Burns
Producers David Davis, Charlotte Brown
Company MTM Enterprises, Inc.
Directors Various
Executive Story Consultants Geoffrey Neigher, Coleman Mitchell
Story Editors Gloria Banta, Pat Nardo
Writers Various

CAST

Rhoda Morgenstern Gerard .... Valerie Harper
Joe Gerard .... David Groh
Brenda Morgenstern .... Julie Kavner
Gary Levy .... Ron Silver
Sally Gallagher .... Anne Meara
Nick Lobo .... Richard Masur

Johnny Venture .... Michael DeLano
VOICES
Carlton the Doorman .... Lorenzo Music

1177 **Rich Man, Poor Man—Book I**
ABC

Program Type Limited Series
60 minutes/two hours. Tuesdays. Premiere date: 2/1/76. Series repeats began 5/10/77. Last show: 6/21/77. Twelve hour dramatization of the novel by Irwin Shaw tracing the lives of the Jordache family from 1945–1965. Music by Alex North.
Executive Producer Harve Bennett
Producer Jon Epstein
Company Harve Bennett Productions in association with Universal Television
Directors David Greene, Boris Sagal
Writer Dean Riesner
Costume Designer Charles Waldo
Art Director John E. Chilberg II
CAST
Rudy Jordache .... Peter Strauss
Tom Jordache .... Nick Nolte
Julie Prescott .... Susan Blakely
Axel Jordache .... Edward Asner
Mary Jordache .... Dorothy McGuire
Willie Abbott .... Bill Bixby
Teddy Boylan .... Robert Reed
Virginia Calderwood .... Kim Darby
Duncan Calderwood .... Ray Milland
Bill Denton .... Lawrence Pressman
Smitty .... Norman Fell
Teresa Santoro .... Talia Shire
Brad Knight .... Tim McIntire
Marsh Goodwin .... Van Johnson
Kate .... Kay Lenz
Falconetti .... William Smith

1178 **Rich Man, Poor Man—Book II**
ABC

Program Type Drama Series
60 minutes. Tuesdays. Premiere date: 9/21/76 (two-hour special). Last show: 3/8/77. A continuation of "Rich Man, Poor Man" shown during the 1975–76 season and repeated in 1977 *(see above)*. 21 chapters follow the lives of the Jordache family members after the death of Tom Jordache. Music by Alex North.
Executive Producer Michael Gleason
Producer Jon Epstein
Company Universal Television
Directors Various
Writers Various
CAST
Rudy Jordache .... Peter Strauss
Wesley Jordache .... Gregg Henry
Billy Abbott .... James Carroll Jordan
Maggie Porter .... Susan Sullivan
Anthony Falconetti .... William Smith
Marie Falconetti .... Dimitra Arliss
Ramona Scott .... Penny Peyser
Charles Estep .... Peter Haskell
Scotty .... John Anderson
Phil Greenberg .... Sorrell Booke
Annie Adams .... Cassie Yates
Diane Porter .... Kimberly Beck
Claire Estep .... Laraine Stephens
Kate Jordache .... Kay Lenz
Arthur Raymond .... Peter Donat
Sen. Dillon .... G.D. Spradlin
Sen. Paxton .... Barry Sullivan
Al Barber .... Ken Swofford
John Franklin .... Philip Abbott
Vickie St. John .... Colleen Camp

1179 **The Richard Pryor Special?**
Multi-Special Night NBC
Program Type Music/Comedy/Variety Special
60 minutes. Premiere date: 5/5/77. Richard Pryor's first television special. Forerunner of the 1977–78 season series "The Richard Pryor Show."
Executive Producer Burt Sugarman
Producer Bob Ellison
Company Burt Sugarman Production in association with Richard Pryor Enterprises and NBC
Director John Moffitt
Writers Richard Pryor, Bob Ellison, Rocco Urbisci, Paul Mooney, Alan Thicke
Star Richard Pryor
Guest Stars John Belushi, Mike Evans, LaWanda Page, Shirley Hemphill, Maya Angelou, Glynn Turman, Timothy Thomerson, the Pips

Richard III *see* PBS Movie Theater

1180 **Richie Brockelman: The Missing 24 Hours**
NBC Movie of the Week NBC
Program Type TV Movie
90 minutes. Premiere date: 10/27/76. Repeat date: 5/29/77. Mystery-drama pilot about a college-educated private eye. Music composed by Mike Post and Peter Carpenter; lyrics by Stephen Geyer and Herb Pedersen.
Executive Producers Stephen J. Cannell, Steven Bochco
Producer William F. Phillips
Company Universal Television in association with NBC-TV
Director Hy Averback
Writers Stephen J. Cannell, Steven Bochco
CAST
Richie Brockelman .... Dennis Dugan
Elizabeth Morton .... Suzanne Pleshette
Sharon Deterson .... Barbara Bosson
Darcy Davenport .... Sharon Gless
Mr. Davenport .... Lloyd Bochner
Mr. Brockelman .... Norman Fell
Mrs. Brockelman .... Helen Page Camp
Arnold Springfield .... William Windom
Mr. McNeil .... Ned Wilson
Prell .... W. T. Zacha

Richie Brockelman: The Missing 24 Hours *Continued*

Art .... Tom Falk
Dave .... George Fisher
Mitchell Rider .... Harold Sylvester
Hooker .... Gloria LeRoy
Marine .... Hunter von Leer

1181 **Riding High**
Comedy Time NBC
Program Type Comedy Special
30 minutes. Premiere date: 8/25/77. Comedy pilot about a would-be writer who works as an extra at Tumbleweed Productions in the Hollywood of the 1930s. Based on the motion picture "Hearts of the West."
Producer Mark Merson
Company MGM-TV in association with NBC-TV
Director Lee Philips
Writer Larry Gelbart

CAST
Lewis Tater .... Charles Frank
Trout .... Wendy Phillips
Howard Pike .... Lonny Chapman
Bert Kessler .... Allan Miller
Sid .... Don Calfa
Mrs. Stern .... Pearl Shear
Lyle Montana .... Allen Case
Vinegar .... Jim Varney
Bear .... Pat Cranshaw
Wally .... Bill Hart

1182 **Rikki-Tikki-Tavi** CBS
Program Type Animated Film Special
30 minutes. Premiere date: 1/9/75. Repeat date: 4/4/77. Adapted from "The Jungle Books" by Rudyard Kipling.
Producer Chuck Jones
Company Chuck Jones Enterprises, Inc.
Director Chuck Jones
Writer Chuck Jones
Narrator Orson Welles

VOICES
Rikki-Tikki-Tavi .... Orson Welles
Additional Voices June Foray, Les Tremayne, Michael LeClair, Lennie Weinrib, Shep Menken

Rio Lobo *see* NBC Saturday Night at the Movies

1183 **The Rivalry**
Bicentennial Hall of Fame PBS
Program Type Dramatic Special
90 minutes. Premiere date: 12/12/75 (on NBC). Repeat date: 11/16/76. Drama of the 1858 debates between Abraham Lincoln and Stephen Douglas. Adapted from the play by Norman Corwin. Music by Mauro Bruno. Presented by KCPT-TV/Kansas City. Program presented to PBS by Hallmark Cards, Inc. Interview segment between Elie Abel and Dr. Daniel J. Boorstin funded by a grant from the Corporation for Public Broadcasting.
Executive Producer Duane C. Bogie
Producer Walt DeFaria
Company Foote, Cone & Belding Productions
Director Fielder Cook
Writers Donald Carmorant, Ernest Kinoy
Costume Designer Ann Roth
Art Director Ben Edwards
Music Supervisor John Caper, Jr.

CAST
Abraham Lincoln .... Arthur Hill
Sen. Stephen Douglas .... Charles Durning
Adele Douglas .... Hope Lange

1184 **The Rivals**
Classic Theatre: The Humanities in Drama PBS
Program Type Dramatic Special
Two hours. Premiere date: 11/6/75. Repeat date: 3/31/77. 1775 English Restoration comedy. Harpsichord score played by Tom McCall. Funded by grants from the National Endowment for the Humanities and Mobil Oil Corporation. Presented by WGBH-TV/Boston; Joan Sullivan, producer.
Producer Cedric Messina
Company British Broadcasting Corporation
Director Basil Coleman
Writer Richard Brinsley Sheridan
Set Designer Richard Wilmot

CAST
Capt. Absolute .... Jeremy Brett
Bob Acres .... John Alderton
Mrs. Malaprop .... Beryl Reid
Sir Anthony Absolute .... Andrew Cruickshank
Lydia Languish .... Jenny Linden

1185 **Robert F. Kennedy Pro-Celebrity Tennis Tournament** ABC
Program Type Sports Special
90 minutes. Coverage of the sixth annual tournament from the West Side Tennis Club, Forest Hills, N.Y. 8/28/77.
Executive Producer Roone Arledge
Producer Ned Steckel
Company ABC Sports
Director Andy Sidaris
Announcer Howard Cosell
Expert Commentator Arthur Ashe

1186 **Roberto Devereux**
In Performance at Wolf Trap PBS
Program Type Music/Dance Special
2 1/2 hours. Premiere date: 10/6/75. Repeat dates: 10/18/76 and 9/20/77. The opera by Gaetano Donizetti performed by the Wolf Trap Company and the Filene Center Orchestra at the

Wolf Trap Farm Park in Arlington, Va. Program made possible by a grant from the Atlantic Richfield Company.
Executive Producer David Prowitt
Producer Ruth Leon
Company WETA-TV/Washington, D.C.
Director Kirk Browning
Conductor Julius Rudel
Hosts Beverly Sills, David Prowitt
Executive-in-Charge Jim Karayn

CAST

Queen Elizabeth I .... Beverly Sills
Roberto Devereux ....John Alexander
Sara, Duchess of Nottingham .... Susanne Marsee
Nottingham ....Richard Fredricks
Raleigh .... David Rae Smith

1187 **Robinson Crusoe**
NBC Thursday Night at the Movies NBC
Program Type Dramatic Special
Two hours. Premiere date: 11/27/74. Repeat date: 8/18/77. Adaptation of the classic novel by Daniel Defoe. Filmed in Tobago, West Indies. Dog played by Rex.
Producer Cedric Messina
Company British Broadcasting Corporation in association with NBC-TV
Director James MacTaggart
Writer James MacTaggart
Script Editor Alan Shallcross

CAST

Robinson Crusoe .... Stanley Baker
Friday ....Ram John Holder
Sea Captain .... Jerome Willis

1188 **Rock Follies** PBS
Program Type Limited Series
60 minutes. Premiere date: 3/77. Five-part musical-drama series about a female rock singing group "The Little Ladies" trying to make it to the top. Music composed by Andrew Mackay, lyrics by Howard Schuman.
Producer Andrew Brown
Company Thames Television International/London
Directors Brian Farnham, Jon Scoffield
Writer Howard Schuman
Conductor Andrew Mackay
Choreographer David Toguri

CAST

Devonia "Dee" Rhodes ....Julie Covington
Anna Wynd ....Charlotte Cornwell
Nancy "Q" Cunard de Longchamps .... Rula Lenska
Stavros Kuklas .... Michael Angelis
Musical Director .... Emlyn Price

1189 **Rock Music Awards Show** NBC
Program Type Parades/Pageants/Awards Special
Two hours. Live coverage (in the East) of the third annual Rock Music Awards from the Hollywood (Calif.) Palladium 9/15/77.
Executive Producer Don Kirshner
Producer Bob Wynn
Co-Producer David Yarnell
Company A Kirshner Entertainment Corporation Production
Director Don Mischer
Writer April Kelly
Musical Director Bill Conti
Choreographer Jeff Kutash & The Dancin' Machine
Costume Designer Sandy Slepak
Creative Supervisor Merrill Grant
Hosts Peter Frampton, Olivia Newton-John
Entertainers/Presenters Jeff Kutash and The Dancin' Machine, Stevie Wonder, Rod Stewart, Peter Frampton, Dolly Parton, George Benson, Olivia Newton-John, Alice Cooper, Kate Jackson, Mike Love, Martin Mull, Mary Kay Place, R2D2 (Kenny Baker), Shields and Yarnell, Brian Wilson, Dennis Wilson, Gary Wright

1190 **Rock Sonata for Piano and Amplified Cello** PBS
Program Type Music/Dance Special
30 minutes. Premiere date: 2/16/77. Rock concert performed on the piano and amplified cello and written by Paul Schoenfield. Taped before a live audience. Program made possible by a grant from Ohio Educational Broadcasting.
Producer Ronald Gargasz
Company WBGU-TV/Bowling Green, Ohio
Directors Ronald Gargasz, Dal Neitzel
Performers Paul Schoenfield, Peter Howard

1191 **The Rockford Files** NBC
Program Type Crime Drama Series
60 minutes. Fridays. Premiere date: 9/13/74. Third season premiere: 9/24/76. Action drama revolving around an ex-con/private investigator who takes on unsolved police cases. Created by Roy Huggins and Stephen J. Cannell. Theme music by Mike Post and Peter Carpenter.
Executive Producer Meta Rosenberg
Supervising Producer Stephen J. Cannell
Producers David Chase, Charles F. Johnson
Company A Roy Huggins/Public Arts Production in association with Cherokee Productions, Universal Television and NBC-TV
Directors Russ Mayberry, William Wiard and others
Writers Stephen J. Cannell, Juanita Bartlett, David Chase and others

CAST

Jim Rockford .... James Garner
Joseph "Rocky" Rockford ....Noah Beery
Det. Dennis Becker .... Joe Santos

The Rockford Files *Continued*

Angel Martin .... Stuart Margolin
Beth Davenport .... Gretchen Corbett

The Rocking Horse Winner *see* PBS Movie Theater

1192 **Roger & Harry**

The ABC Monday Night Movie ABC

Program Type TV Movie

90 minutes. Premiere date: 5/2/77. Pilot film about men who recover lost and stolen objects and missing people. Music by Jack Elliott and Allyn Ferguson.

Executive Producer Bruce Lansbury
Producer Anthony Spinner
Company Bruce Lansbury Productions. Ltd. in association with Columbia Pictures Television
Director Jack Starrett
Writer Alvin Sapinsley
Art Directors Ross Bellah, Carl Braunger

CAST

Roger Quentin .... John Davidson
Harry Jaworsky .... Barry Primus
Blair .... Richard Lynch
Kate Wilson .... Carole Mallory
Joanna March .... Anne Randall Stewart
Cindy St. Claire ....Susan Sullivan
Arthur Pennington .... Harris Yulin
Sylvester March .... Biff McGuire
Heller ....Vaughn Armstrong
Du Cloche .... Titos Vandis
David Petersen .... Alan McRae
Cutts .... Henry Sutton
Mankowitz ....James O'Connell
Television Reporter .... Fred Holliday
Lt. Shelley ....Robert DoQui

Rollerball *see* The CBS Wednesday Night Movies

1193 **The Romantic Rebellion** PBS

Program Type Educational/Cultural Series

30 minutes. Thursday mornings. Premiere date: 1/13/75. Repeats began: 2/17/77. 15-week series on the Romantic rebellion in art during the late 18th and early 19th centuries. Programs funded by a grant from the American Can Company. Presented by WNET-TV/New York.

Producer Colin Clark
Company Visual Programme Systems
Distributor Reader's Digest Association
Director Colin Clark
Writer Kenneth Clark
Host/Narrator Kenneth Clark

1194 **Rona Looks at Carol Burnett, Valerie Harper, Sally Struthers and Nancy Walker** ABC

Program Type Documentary/Informational Special

60 minutes. Premiere date: 10/27/76. Interviews with four television comediennes.

Executive Producer William Trowbridge
Producer Rona Barrett
Company Miss Rona Enterprises, Inc. in association with Martin Ransohoff Productions, Inc.
Director Lawrence Einhorn
Interviewer Rona Barrett
Guests Carol Burnett, Valerie Harper, Sally Struthers, Nancy Walker

1195 **Rona Looks at Kate Jackson, Penny Marshall, Toni Tennille and Cindy Williams** ABC

Program Type Documentary/Informational Special

60 minutes. Premiere date: 4/14/77. Interviews with four new television stars.

Executive Producer William Trowbridge
Producer Mark Massari
Company Martin Ransohoff Productions, Inc. in association with Miss Rona Enterprises, Inc.
Director Mark Massari
Interviewer Rona Barrett
Guests Kate Jackson, Penny Marshall, Toni Tennille, Cindy Williams

1196 **The Rookies** ABC

Program Type Crime Drama Series

60 minutes. Wednesdays. Season premiere: 9/22/76. Last show: 8/31/77. Late-night repeat presentations of series which aired in primetime on ABC between 9/11/72–6/29/76.

Executive Producers Aaron Spelling, Leonard Goldberg
Producers Various
Company Spelling/Goldberg Productions
Directors Various
Writers Various

CAST

Off. Terry Webster ....Georg Stanford Brown
Off. Mike Danko ....Sam Melville
Off. Chris Owens .... Bruce Fairbairn
Lt. Eddie Ryker ....Gerald S. O'Loughlin
Jill Danko .... Kate Jackson
Willie Gillis .... Michael Ontkean

1197 **Roosevelt and Truman** CBS

Program Type Comedy Special

30 minutes. Premiere date: 5/25/77. Comedy pilot about bail-bond partners. Created by Norman Steinberg and Robert Dimitri.

Executive Producer Norman Steinberg
Producer Richard Dimitri

Company Universal Television
Director James Burrows
Writers Norman Steinberg, Richard Dimitri

CAST

Roosevelt ..... Art Evans
Truman ..... Philip Thomas
Juanita ..... Ilka Payan
Richie ..... Richard Karron
Rev. Davis ..... Hank Rolike
Mrs. Tilson ..... Minnie S. Lindsey
Rodriguez ..... Danny Mora
Garcia ..... Bert Rosario
Savoyan ..... Bob Manuel
Crawford ..... Tim Pelt
Quinn ..... Michael Keaton

1198 **Roots** ABC
Program Type Limited Series
12 hours. Premiere date: 1/23/77. Last show: 1/30/77. Shown on eight consecutive nights. Dramatization based on the book by Alex Haley tracing the lives of his family from Africa in 1750 to Tennessee after the Civil War. Developed for television by William Blinn. Filmed in part in and around Savannah, Ga. and on the ship *Unicorn.* Music by Gerald Fried and Quincy Jones.
Executive Producer David L. Wolper
Producer Stan Margulies
Company A David L. Wolper Production
Directors Marvin Chomsky, John Erman, David Greene, Gilbert Moses
Writers William Blinn, M. Charles Cohen, Ernest Kinoy, James Lee
Costume Designer Jack Martell
Production Designer Jan Scott
Art Director Joseph R. Jennings
Script Supervisor William Blinn
Consultant Alex Haley

CAST

Kunta Kinte ..... LeVar Burton
Kunta Kinte (Toby) ..... John Amos
Binta ..... Cicely Tyson
Capt. Davies ..... Edward Asner
Kadi Touray ..... O. J. Simpson
Third Mate Slater ..... Ralph Waite
Nyo Boto ..... Maya Angelou
The Wrestler ..... Ji-Tu Cumbuka
The Kintango ..... Moses Gunn
Omoro ..... Thalmus Rasulala
Brima Cesay ..... Harry Rhodes
Gardner ..... William Watson
Fanta ..... Ren Woods
Fiddler ..... Louis Gossett, Jr. (Lou Gossett)
John Reynolds ..... Lorne Greene
Mrs. Reynolds ..... Lynda Day George
Ames ..... Vic Morrow
Carrington ..... Paul Shenar
William Reynolds ..... Robert Reed
Bell ..... Madge Sinclair
Grill ..... Gary Collins
Fanta (as an adult) ..... Beverly Todd
The Drummer ..... Raymond St. Jacques
Tom Moore ..... Chuck Connors
Missy Anne ..... Sandy Duncan
Noah ..... Lawrence-Hilton Jacobs
Ordell ..... John Schuck
Kizzy ..... Leslie Uggams
Squire James ..... Macdonald Carey
Matilda ..... Olivia Cole
Mingo ..... Scatman Crothers
Stephen Bennett ..... George Hamilton
Mrs. Moore ..... Carolyn Jones
Sir Eric Russell ..... Ian McShane
Sister Sara ..... Lillian Randolph
Sam Bennett ..... Richard Roundtree
Chicken George ..... Ben Vereen
Evan Brent ..... Lloyd Bridges
Tom ..... Georg Stanford Brown
Ol' George ..... Brad Davis
Lewis ..... Hilly Hicks
Jemmy Brent ..... Doug McClure
Irene ..... Lynne Moody
Martha ..... Lane Binkley
Justin ..... Burl Ives

1199 **Rose Bowl** NBC
Program Type Sports Special
Live coverage of the 63rd Rose Bowl game between the Michigan Wolverines and the USC Trojans from Pasadena, Calif. 1/1/77.
Company NBC Sports
Announcer Curt Gowdy
Analyst Don Meredith

1200 **Rosetti and Ryan: Men Who Love Women**
NBC Monday Night at the Movies NBC
Program Type TV Movie
Two hours. Premiere date: 5/23/77. Pilot for 1977–78 season series "Rosetti and Ryan" about two criminal attorneys who defend a murder suspect.
Executive Producer Leonard B. Stern
Producer Jerry Davis
Company Heyday Productions in association with Universal Television
Director John Astin
Writers Don M. Mankiewicz, Gordon Cotler

CAST

Joseph Rosetti ..... Tony Roberts
Frank Ryan ..... Squire Fridell
Jessica Hornesby ..... Jane Elliot
Sgt. Agopian ..... Bill Dana
Sylvia Crawford ..... Patty Duke Astin
Beverly Dresden ..... Susan Anspach
Judge Hardcastle ..... Dick O'Neill
Drusilla ..... Roberta Leighton
Sister Constanza ..... Andrea Howard
Benny ..... Al Molinaro
Judge Black ..... William Marshall
Greta ..... Barbara Alston

1201 **Rostropovich Performs Haydn**
Fine Music Specials/Great Performances PBS
Program Type Music/Dance Special
60 minutes. Premiere date: 3/30/77. Two cello concertos by Franz Joseph Haydn performed by the Orchestra of the Academy of St. Martin-in-

Rostropovich Performs Haydn *Continued*
the-Field. Program stereo-simulcast on local FM radio stations. Presented by WNET-TV/New York and made possible by grants from Exxon Corporation, the Corporation for Public Broadcasting, the Ford Foundation and Public Television Stations.
Executive Producer Fritz Buttenstedt
Producer David Griffiths
Company Unitel Productions
Conductor Mstislav Rostropovich
Soloist Mstislav Rostropovich

1202 **Royal Jubilee** ABC
Program Type News Special
4 1/2 hours. Live coverage from London of events in the celebration of the silver anniversary of the coronation of Queen Elizabeth 6/7/77. Part of ABC coverage seen on "Good Morning America."
Executive Producer Elliot Bernstein
Producer Daryl Griffin
Company ABC News Special Events
Director Marvin Schlenker
Anchors Peter Jennings, Hilary Brown
Correspondents Robert Trout, Frank Reynolds, David Hartman

1203 **Royce** CBS
Program Type TV Movie
60 minutes. Premiere date: 5/21/76. Repeat date: 7/12/77. Western pilot set in the 1870s, filmed on location in Arizona. Music by Jerrold Immel.
Executive Producer Jim Byrnes
Producer William F. Phillips
Company MTM Enterprises, Inc.
Director Andrew V. McLaglen
Writer Jim Byrnes
Art Director Al Heschong
Set Decorator Robert Bradfield

CAST

Royce .... Robert Forster
Susan Mabry .... Marybeth Hurt
Stephen Mabry .... Moosie Drier
Heather Mabry .... Terri Lynn Wood
Blair Mabry .... Michael Parks
White Bull .... Eddie Little Sky
Dent .... Dave Cass

1204 **The Rubber Gun Squad**
Comedy Time NBC
Program Type Comedy Special
30 minutes. Premiere date: 9/1/77. Comedy pilot about two New York City policemen based at a Central Park precinct. Filmed on location in New York.
Executive Producer Philip D'Antoni
Producer Sonny Grosso
Company Philip D'Antoni Television Production in association with NBC-TV
Director Hy Averback
Writers Sid Dorfman, Simon Muntner

CAST

Chopper .... Andy Romano
Eddie .... Lenny Baker
Sgt. O'Leary .... Tom Signorelli
Rosie .... Betty Buckley
Jerome .... Alan Weeks
Dewey .... Frank Simpson
Mooney .... Don Scardino
Capt. Egan .... Kenneth McMillan
Austin .... Paul Jabara
Mr. Griffin .... William Robertson

1205 **Rubinstein: Works of Chopin**
Fine Music Specials/Great Performances PBS
Program Type Music/Dance Special
60 minutes. Premiere date: 12/24/75. Repeat date: 7/24/77. The London Symphony Orchestra in a Christmas concert of works by Frederic Chopin, Johannes Brahms and Franz Schubert filmed at Fairfield Halls, Croyden, England. Program presented by WNET-TV/New York and made possible by grants from Exxon Corporation, the Corporation for Public Broadcasting, the Ford Foundation and Public Television Stations.
Executive Producer Fritz Buttenstedt
Coordinating Producer David Griffiths
Producers Fritz Buttenstedt, David Griffiths
Company Unitel Productions
Conductor Andre Previn
Guest Artist Arthur Rubinstein

1206 **Rudolph the Red-Nosed Reindeer** CBS
Program Type Animated Film Special
60 minutes. Premiere date: 12/64. Repeat date: 12/1/76. Annual Christmas show based on the song by Johnny Marks. Additional music and lyrics by Johnny Marks; orchestration by Maury Laws. Adapted from a story by Robert L. May.
Producers Arthur Rankin, Jr., Jules Bass
Company Videocraft International Production
Director Larry Roemer
Writer Romeo Muller
Narrator Burl Ives

VOICES

Sam the Snowman .... Burl Ives
Rudolph .... Billie Richards
Yukon Cornelius .... Larry Mann
Santa Claus .... Stan Francis
Hermy the Elf .... Paul Soles
Clarice .... Janet Orenstein
Additional Voices Alfie Scopp, Paul Kligman, Corinne Conley, Peg Dixon

1207 **Rudolph's Shiny New Year** ABC
Program Type Animated Film Special
60 minutes. Premiere date: 12/10/76. A sequel to "Rudolph the Red-Nosed Reindeer" with music and lyrics by Johnny Marks. Filmed in Animagic—dimensional stop-motion photography.
Producers Arthur Rankin, Jr., Jules Bass
Company Rankin-Bass Productions
Directors Arthur Rankin, Jr., Jules Bass
Writer Romeo Muller
Musical Director Maury Laws
Narrator Red Skelton

VOICES

Father Time .... Red Skelton
Sir Tentwothree .... Frank Gorshin
One Million B.C. .... Morey Amsterdam
Big Ben .... Hal Peary
Eon .... Paul Frees
Rudolph .... Billie Richards
Additional Voices Don Messick, Iris Rainer

The Rules of the Game *see* PBS Movie Theater

1208 **Run for the Heisman** ABC
Program Type Sports Special
30 minutes. Premiere date: 11/26/76. A look at the top candidates for the Heisman Trophy.
Executive Producer Roone Arledge
Producer Terry O'Neil
Company ABC Sports
Director Ric LaCivita
Narrator Keith Jackson

The Russians Are Coming, the Russians Are Coming *see* The CBS Friday Night Movies

1209 **Ryan's Hope** ABC
Program Type Daytime Drama Series
30 minutes. Mondays–Fridays. Premiere date: 7/7/75. Continuous. Created by Claire Labine and Paul Avila Mayer. Set in the Riverside section (Upper West Side) of Manhattan. Credit information as of February 1977. Cast listed alphabetically.
Executive Producers Paul Avila Mayer, Claire Labine
Producer Robert Costello
Company A Labine-Mayer Production in association with the ABC Television Network
Directors Lela Swift, Jerry Evans
Head Writers Claire Labine, Paul Avila Mayer
Writer Mary Munisteri

CAST

Jillian Coleridge .... Nancy Addison
Johnny Ryan .... Bernard Barrow
Dr. Buckminster "Bucky" Carter .... Justin Deas
Dr. Seneca Beaulac .... John Gabriel
Maeve Ryan .... Helen Gallagher
Dr. Pat Ryan .... Malcolm Groome
Dr. Roger Coleridge .... Ron Hale
Dr. Faith Coleridge .... Catherine Hicks
Det. Bob Reid .... Earl Hindman
Delia Reid Ryan .... Ilene Kristen
Jack Fenelli .... Michael Levin
Mary Ryan Fenelli .... Kate Mulgrew
Dr. Clem Moultrie .... Hannibal Penney, Jr.
Frank Ryan .... Andrew Robinson

1210 **Salome**
Fine Music Specials/Great Performances PBS
Program Type Music/Dance Special
Two hours. Premiere date: 2/2/77. Filmed version of the 1905 one-act German opera by Richard Strauss based on the play by Oscar Wilde. Music performed by the Vienna Philharmonic Orchestra. Program stereo-simulcast on local FM radio stations. Presented by WNET-TV/New York and made possible by grants from Exxon Corporation, the Corporation for Public Broadcasting, the Ford Foundation and Public Television Stations.
Executive Producer Fritz Buttenstedt
Producer David Griffiths
Company Unitel Productions
Director Goetz Friedrich
Conductor Karl Bohm

CAST

Salome .... Teresa Stratas
Herod .... Hans Beirer
Herodias .... Astrid Varnay
Jokanaan (John the Baptist) .... Bernd Weikl
Narraboth .... Wieslaw Ochman
Page .... Hanna Schwarz

Salty *see* NBC Night at the Movies

1211 **Sam** CBS
Program Type Dramatic Special
30 minutes. Premiere date: 5/24/77. Adventures of a Labrador retriever working with the Los Angeles Police Department. Music by Billy May.
Executive Producers Jack Webb, Paul Donnelly
Producer James Doherty
Company Mark VII Ltd.
Director Jack Webb
Writers John Randolph, Don Noble
Art Director Walter Scott Herndon

CAST

Sam .... Sam (Labrador retriever)
Off. Mike Breen .... Mark Harmon
Capt. Gene Cody .... Gary Crosby
Staff Sergeant .... Edward Winter
Jane .... Kristin Nelson
Sgt. Smith .... James S. Smith
Sergeant No. 2 .... William Boyett
Bomb Squad No. 1 .... Robert Patten
Barney Quinn .... Ron Kelly
Harry .... Gunnar Nelson
Fred .... Matthew Nelson
Holdup Man .... Al Shelly
Hashmarks .... Don Ross

Sam *Continued*

Ice Cream Man .... John Nolan
Sally Young .... Janear Hines
Bomb Squad No. 2 .... Ed Demeer
High No. 1 .... R. A. Rondell
High No. 2 .... Fred Hice
Backup No. 1 .... Tom Scott
Suspect No. 2 .... Raymond Mayo

1212 **Sammy & Company** Syndicated

Program Type Music/Comedy/Variety Series

90 minutes. Weekly. Premiere date: 3/75. Last season premiere: 9/76. Variety show with celebrity interviews.

Executive Producer Pierre Cossette
Producer Eric Lieber
Company Pierre Cossette Company in association with Systel Industries
Distributor Syndicast Services, Inc.
Musical Director George Rhodes
Host Sammy Davis, Jr.

1213 **Sammy Davis Jr.—Greater Hartford Open** CBS

Program Type Sports Special

Live and taped coverage of the final rounds of the 26th Open from the Wethersfield (Conn.) Country Club 8/6/77 and 8/7/77.

Producer Frank Chirkinian
Company CBS Television Network Sports
Directors Bob Dailey, Frank Chirkinian
Commentators Vin Scully, Pat Summerall, Jack Whitaker, Ben Wright, Frank Glieber, Rick Barry, Ken Venturi

1214 **The San Pedro Bums**

The ABC Friday Night Movie ABC

Program Type TV Movie

90 minutes. Premiere date: 5/13/77. Pilot for 1977–78 series "The San Pedro Beach Bums" about five young men who live on an old boat. Music by Pete Rugolo.

Executive Producers Aaron Spelling, Douglas S. Cramer
Producer E. Duke Vincent
Company An Aaron Spelling Production
Director Barry Shear
Writer E. Duke Vincent
Art Director Paul Sylos

CAST

Buddy .... Christopher Murney
Boychick .... Jeffry Druce
Dancer .... John Mark Robinson
Stuf .... Stuart Pankin
Moose .... Darryl McCullough
Turk .... Bill Lucking
Pop .... Titos Vandis
Sgt. Yost .... Ramon Bieri
Mrs. McClory .... Jeanne Cooper
Ramirez .... Jorge Cervera, Jr.
Mr. McClory .... Kevin Hagen
Mr. Donelli .... Dick Balduzzi
Louise .... Louise Hoven
Suzy .... Susan Mullen
Margo .... Lisa Reeves
Pam .... Susan Walden

1215 **Sanford and Son** NBC

Program Type Comedy Series

30 minutes. Fridays. Premiere date: 1/14/72. Sixth season premiere: 9/24/76. Last show: 9/2/77. Based on British TV comedy series "Steptoe and Son" created by Ray Galton and Alan Simpson. Music by Quincy Jones. Concerns a father-and-son junk yard in South Central Los Angeles. 1977–78 season spin-off entitled "Sanford Arms."

Executive Producer Bud Yorkin
Producers Saul Turteltaub, Bernie Orenstein
Company A Bud Yorkin/Norman Lear/Tandem Production through Norbud Productions, Inc. in association with NBC-TV
Directors Various
Writers Various
Costume Designer Lee Smith
Art Director Edward Stephenson

CAST

Fred Sanford .... Redd Foxx
Lamont Sanford .... Demond Wilson
Aunt Esther .... LaWanda Page
Grady Wilson .... Whitman Mayo
Bubba .... Don Bexley
Rollo .... Nathaniel Taylor
Donna Harris .... Lynn Hamilton
Woody .... Raymond Allen
Hoppy .... Howard Platt
Smitty .... Hal Williams
Janet .... Marlene Clark
Roger .... Edward Crawford

1216 **Sanford and Son (Daytime)** NBC

Program Type Comedy Series

30 minutes. Mondays–Fridays. Premiere date: 6/14/76. Continuous. Morning reruns of evening series. For credit information, *see* "Sanford and Son."

1217 **Santa Claus Is Coming to Town** ABC

Program Type Animated Film Special

60 minutes. Premiere date: 12/13/70. Repeat date: 12/12/76. Animated special using dimensional stop-motion photography. Music by Maury Laws; lyrics by Jules Bass. Title song composed by J. Fred Coots; lyrics by Haven Gillespie.

Producers Arthur Rankin, Jr., Jules Bass
Company Rankin/Bass Productions
Directors Arthur Rankin, Jr., Jules Bass
Writer Romeo Muller
Narrator Fred Astaire

VOICES

Postman S. D. Kluger .... Fred Astaire
Kris Kringle .... Mickey Rooney
Winter Warlock .... Keenan Wynn
Burgermeister .... Paul Frees
Tanta Kringle .... Joan Gardner
Jessica .... Robie Lester
Additional Voices Dina Lynn, Andrea Sacino, Greg Thomas, Gary White, Westminster Children's Choir

1218 **Santa Fe Opera**
Opera Theater PBS
Program Type Music/Dance Special
90 minutes. Premiere date: 7/5/77. Documentary-and-performance special celebrating the Santa Fe Opera's 20th year. Taped in the summer of 1976 with excerpts from "The Mother of Us All" with music by Virgil Thomson and text by Gertrude Stein, "The Marriage of Figaro" by Wolfgang Amadeus Mozart, "La Traviata" by Giuseppe Verdi, "L'Egisto" by Francesco Cavalli, and "Salome" by Richard Strauss. Program made possible by grants from Public Television Stations with additional funding from the Ford Foundation and the Corporation for Public Broadcasting.
Executive Producers Jac Venza, Barry Gavin
Producers Humphrey Burton, David Griffiths
Company WNET-TV/New York and the British Broadcasting Corporation
Director David Chesire
Host Donald Gramm
Narrator Donald Gramm

The Mother of Us All
Director Peter Wood
Conductor Raymond Leppard
Costume Designer Robert Indiana
Scenic Designer Robert Indiana

CAST

Susan B. Anthony .... Mignon Dunn
Anne .... Batyah Godfrey
Jo the Loiterer .... James Atherton
Angel More .... Ashley Putnam
John Adams .... William Lewis
Constance Fletcher .... Helen Vanni

The Marriage of Figaro
Conductor Robert Baustian

CAST

Figaro .... Donald Gramm
Cherubino .... Faith Esham
Susanna .... Sheri Greenawald

La Traviata
Conductor John Crosby

CAST

Violetta .... Ellen Shade
Alfredo .... William Lewis

L'Egisto
Conductor Raymond Leppard

CAST

Clori .... Linn Maxwell
Egisto .... Jerold Norman
Climene .... Ellen Shade
Four Seasons .... Susan Peterson, Ashley Putnam, Cheryl Boatwright, Patricia McCaffrey

Salome

CAST

Joakanaan .... William Dooley

1219 **Sarah Vaughan & Buddy Rich**
In Performance at Wolf Trap PBS
Program Type Music/Dance Special
60 minutes. Premiere date: 10/28/74. Repeat dates: 9/27/76 and 8/30/77. Jazz concert performed at the Wolf Trap Farm Park for the Performing Arts in Arlington, Va. Program made possible by a grant from the Atlantic Richfield Company.
Executive Producer David Prowitt
Company WETA-TV/Washington, D.C.
Director Stan Lathan
Host David Prowitt
Guest Stars Sarah Vaughan, Buddy Rich

Saturday Night Live *see* NBC's Saturday Night Live

1220 **The Savage Bees**
NBC Monday Night at the Movies/NBC Movie of the Week NBC
Program Type TV Movie
Two hours. Premiere date: 11/22/76. Repeat date: 4/27/77. Drama about killer bees in New Orleans during Mardi Gras. Produced on locations in and around New Orleans. Music by Walter Murphy.
Executive Producers Alan Landsburg, Merrill Grant, Don Kirshner
Producer Bruce Geller
Company Alan Landsburg/Don Kirshner Production in association with NBC-TV
Director Bruce Geller
Writer Guerdon Trueblood

CAST

Sheriff Donald McKew .... Ben Johnson
Jeff DuRand .... Michael Parks
Rufus .... Paul Hecht
Dr. Meuller .... Horst Bucholz
Jeannie Devereaux .... Gretchen Corbett
Police Lieutenant .... Bruce French
Pelligrino .... James Best
Coast Guard Lieutenant .... David Gray
Coast Guard Chief .... Richard Boyle
Freighter Boatswain .... Elliot Keener

Save the Tiger *see* The CBS Wednesday Night Movies

Sawdust and Tinsel *see* PBS Movie Theater

1221 **Say Brother Pays Tribute to Webster Lewis With a Night on the Town** PBS
Program Type Music/Dance Special
60 minutes. Premiere date: 6/19/77. A concert performed by the 50-member Webster Lewis Orchestra and the Post Pop Space Rock Be-Bop Gospel Tabernacle Chorus.
Producer Barbara Barrow
Company WGBH-TV/Boston
Director David Atwood
Conductor Webster Lewis

The Scalphunters *see* The ABC Sunday Night Movie

Scarecrow *see* The CBS Wednesday Night Movies

1222 **Scenes From a Marriage** PBS
Program Type Limited Series
60 minutes. Wednesdays. Premiere date: 3/9/77. The original six-part television series shown in Sweden in 1973 about a couple whose marriage is dissolving. Shown in Swedish with English subtitles and also dubbed into English in a second version. Series made possible by grants from the Corporation for Public Broadcasting, the Ford Foundation and Public Television Stations. Presented by WNET-TV/New York.
Executive Producer Lars-Owe Carlberg
Coordinating Producer David Griffiths
Producer Ingmar Bergman
Company Swedish Television
Director Ingmar Bergman
Writer Ingmar Bergman
Costume Designer Inger Pehrsson
Scenic Designer Bjorn Thulin
Cinematographer Sven Nykvist
Host Liv Ullmann

CAST
Marianne .... Liv Ullmann
Johan .... Erland Josephson
Peter .... Jan Malmsjo
Katarina .... Bibi Andersson
Eva .... Gunnel Lindblom
Mrs. Jacobi .... Barbro Hiort af Ornas
Mrs. Palm .... Anita Wall

1223 **Scenes From the Middle Class**
Visions PBS
Program Type Dramatic Special
Two hours. Premiere date: 12/16/76. Two one-hour original plays. Program made possible by grants from the Ford Foundation, the National Endowment for the Arts and the Corporation for Public Broadcasting.
Producer Barbara Schultz
Company KCET-TV/Los Angeles
Director Rick Bennewitz
Costume Designer Sandra Stewart
Art Director John Retsek

Monkey in the Middle
60 minutes. Drama of a middle class black couple with a shaky marriage.
Writer Betty Patrick

CAST
Evelyn Burrell .... Mary Alice
Russell Burrell .... Thalmus Rasulala
Gang-Gang .... Royce Wallace
David Burrell .... Carl Franklin
Rudy .... Albert Hall
Vicky .... Lane Bradbury

Winter Tour
60 minutes. Drama of a white upper-middle class family on the way down.
Writer David Trainer

CAST
Leonore Bishop .... Patricia Barry
Brian Bishop .... Wayne Tippit
Jane Bishop .... Jean Rasey
Clifford .... Marc McClure
Peter Melville .... Ted Neeley

1224 **Schoolhouse Rock** ABC
Program Type Animated Film Series
Three minute films. Saturday mornings (five times)/Sunday mornings (twice) during the children's programming time. Premiered in 1972–73 season with "Multiplication Rock." "Grammar Rock" introduced 9/8/73. "America Rock" (Bicentennial-oriented history and government) premiered 9/7/74. Series is based on an idea by David B. McCall; "America Rock" was developed in consultation with Prof. John A. Garraty.
Executive Producer Tom Yohe
Producer Radford Stone
Company McCaffrey and McCall
Musical Director Bob Dorough

1225 **The Scooby-Doo/Dynomutt Hour** ABC
Program Type Animated Film Series
60 minutes/90 minutes (as of 12/4/76). Saturday mornings. Premiere date for "Scooby-Doo" cartoons: 9/71 (on CBS). Series about a dog and his young friends who solve mysteries. "Dynomutt, Dog Wonder" premiere: 9/11/76. Cartoon featuring a robot dog who fights crime with the Blue Falcon. Created by Joe Ruby and Ken Spears.
Executive Producers William Hanna, Joseph Barbera
Producer Iwao Takamoto
Story Editors Norman Maurer, Ray Parker
Writers Haskell Barkin, Larz Bourne, Dick Conway, Donald Glut, Orville Hampton, David Ketchum, Jeff Maurer, Michael Maurer, Norman Maurer, Ray Parker, Lee Orgel, Duane

Poole, Dick Robbins, Dalton Sandifer, Deidre Starlight
Storyboard Director Alex Lovy
Voices Henry Corden, Regis J. Cordic, Mickey Dolenz, Ron Feinberg, Joan Gerber, Virginia Gregg, Bob Holt, Hettie Lynn Hurtes, Linda Hutson, Ralph James, Casey Kasem, Larry McCormick, Julie McWhirter, Allan Melvin, Don Messick, Shirley Mitchell, Heather North

1226 **Scott Free**
NBC Movie of the Week NBC
Program Type TV Movie
90 minutes. Premiere date: 10/13/76. Adventure-drama pilot about a professional gambler who wins a piece of land in a poker game. Music by Mike Post and Peter Carpenter.
Executive Producers Meta Rosenberg, Stephen J. Cannell
Producer Alex Beaton
Company Cherokee Productions and Universal Television in association with NBC-TV
Director William Wiard
Writer Stephen J. Cannell

CAST

Tony Scott	Michael Brandon
Holly Morrison	Susan Saint James
Joseph Donaldson	Robert Loggia
Ed McGraw	Ken Swofford
Santini	Michael Lerner
George Running Bear	Dehl Berti
Al	Paul Koslo
Dave	Tony Giorgio
Max	Allan Rich
Agent	Bart Burns
Little Lion	Cal Bellini
Kevin	Stephen Nathan

1227 **Sea Marks**
Theater in America/Great Performances PBS
Program Type Dramatic Special
Two hours. Premiere date: 5/12/76. Repeat date: 8/10/77. Two-character play, filmed on location in Ireland and performed by the Manhattan Theatre Club. Program made possible by funding from Exxon Corporation, Public Television Stations, the Corporation for Public Broadcasting and the Ford Foundation.
Executive Producer Jac Venza
Producer Ronald F. Maxwell
Company WNET-TV/New York
Directors Ronald F. Maxwell, Steven Robman
Writer Gardner McKay
Host Hal Holbrook

CAST

Colm Primrose	George Hearn
Timothea Stiles	Veronica Castang

1228 **Sea Pines Heritage Classic** CBS
Program Type Sports Special
Final rounds of the 1977 Classic from Harbour Town Golf Links, Hilton Head Island (S.C.) 3/26/77 and 3/27/77.
Producer Frank Chirkinian
Company CBS Television Network Sports
Directors Bob Dailey, Frank Chirkinian
Commentators Vin Scully, Pat Summerall, Jack Whitaker, Frank Glieber, Ben Wright, Ken Venturi

1229 **Search for the Great Apes**
National Geographic Special PBS
Program Type Science/Nature Special
60 minutes. Premiere date: 1/13/76. Repeat date: 5/31/77. Filmed over seven years, program shows Birute M. F. Galdikas-Brindamour studying the orangutan in Borneo, and Dian Fossey working with mountain gorillas in Rwanda. Music composed by Walter Scharf. Program funded by a grant from Gulf Oil Corporation and presented by WQED-TV/Pittsburgh.
Executive Producer Dennis B. Kane
Producers Christine Z. Wiser, David Saxon
Company National Geographic Society in association with Wolper Productions
Directors Robert M. Young, Robert M. Campbell, Christine Z. Wiser
Narrator Richard Kiley

1230 **Search for Tomorrow** CBS
Program Type Daytime Drama Series
30 minutes. Mondays-Fridays. Premiere date: 9/3/51 (in 15-minute format). Continuous. The longest-running daytime drama on television. Created by Agnes Nixon. Drama about the family of Joanne Vincente, the Phillips family and the Bergman family in Henderson, U.S.A. "Search for Tomorrow" theme by Jon Silberman. Mary Stuart is an original cast member. Melissa Manchester guested on the show in four episodes between 12/27/76–1/7/77. Credit information as of February 1977. Cast listed alphabetically.
Producer Mary-Ellis Bunim
Company Procter & Gamble Productions
Director Ned Stark
Head Writer Peggy O'Shea
Announcer Dwight Weist

CAST

Cindy French	Allison Argo
David Sloan	Lewis Arlt
Liza Kaslo	Meg Bennett
Stephanie Pace	Marie Cheatham
Dr. Wade Collins	John Cunningham
John Wyatt	Val Dufour
Jennifer Phillips	Morgan Fairchild
Stu Bergman	Larry Haines
Bruce Carson	Joel Higgins
Woody Reed	Kevin Kline
Dr. Gary Walton	Richard Lohman
Eric Heywood	Chris Lowe
Wendy Wilkins	Andrea McArdle

Search for Tomorrow *Continued*

Steve Kaslo .... Michael Nouri
Dr. Greg Hartford .... Bob Rockwell
Kathy Phillips .... Courtney Sherman
Scott Phillips .... Peter Simon
Ralph Heywood .... Drew Snyder
Joanne Vincent .... Mary Stuart
Janet Collins .... Millee Taggart
Ellie Bergman .... Billie Lou Watt
Amy Carson .... Anne Wyndham

1231 **Second Chance** ABC

Program Type Game/Audience Participation Series

30 minutes. Mondays-Fridays. Premiere date: 3/7/77. Last show: 7/15/77. Three contestants compete for prizes in a question-and-answer game allowing them to change their answers for a second chance. Created by Bill Carruthers and Jan McCormack.

Executive Producer Bill Carruthers
Producer Joel Stein
Company A Carruthers Company Production in association with Warner Bros. Television
Director Chris Darley
Writers Jan McCormack, Bill Mitchell, Ray Reese
Host Jim Peck
Announcer Joe Seiter

1232 **Seconds to Play**
Americana PBS

Program Type Documentary/Informational Special

30 minutes. Premiere date: 12/17/76. Repeat date: 7/24/77. A behind-the-scenes look at the live telecast of the 1975 Ohio State-UCLA football game at the Los Angeles Coliseum. Program made possible by grants from the Corporation for Public Broadcasting and the National Endowment for the Arts.

Producer Patrick Crowley
Company Patrick Crowley Film and Television Production for KQED-TV/San Francisco

1233 **The Secret Life of John Chapman**
GE Theater CBS

Program Type Dramatic Special

90 minutes. Premiere date: 12/27/76. Drama based on the real-life experiences of John R. Coleman taken from his book "Blue Collar Journal." Filmed in part in King County, Wash. and Washington, D.C. Music by Fred Myrow.

Executive Producer Gerald I. Isenberg
Producer Gerald W. Abrams
Company The Jozak Company
Director David Lowell Rich
Writer Albert Rubin
Art Director Trevor Williams

CAST

John Chapman .... Ralph Waite
Wilma .... Susan Anspach
Gus Reed .... Pat Hingle
Meredith Chapman .... Elayne Heilveil
Andy Chapman .... Brad Davis
College Chairman .... Maury Cooper
Charlie .... Charlie Watters
Phil .... Reuben Sierra
Victor .... Gardner Hayes
"Dammit" Stanley .... Bill Treadwell
Al .... Teotha Dennard
Grady .... John Aylward
Wally .... Curtis Jackson
Factory Clerk .... Peter Fisher
Manager .... John Roeder
Secretary .... Zoaunne Leroy
Trustee .... Richard Arnold
Dump Truck Driver .... Thomas Ross
Back Hoe Operator .... Earnest M. Simon
Waiter .... Norman Bernard
Hard Hat .... Richard Hawkins
Boss .... Joe Brazil

The Secret of Santa Vittoria *see* The CBS Wednesday Night Movies

1234 **Secret Service**
Theater in America/Great Performances PBS

Program Type Dramatic Special

Two hours. Premiere date: 1/12/77. The Phoenix Repertory Company of New York in a revival of the turn-of-the-century melodrama of Civil War espionage by William Gillette. Civil War songs arranged by Arthur Miller. Program made possible by grants from the Corporation for Public Broadcasting, Public Television Stations, the Ford Foundation and Exxon Corporation.

Executive Producer Jac Venza
Producer Ken Campbell
Company WNET-TV/New York
Directors Daniel Freudenberger, Peter Levin
Writer William Gillette

CAST

Thorne .... John Lithgow
Edith .... Meryl Streep
Arrelsford .... Charles Kimbrough
Caroline .... Marybeth Hurt
Wilfred .... Don Scardino
Mrs. Varney .... Alice Drummond
Henry Dumont .... Lenny Baker
Lt. Maxwell .... Frederick Coffin
Cpl. Matson .... Joe Grifasi
Jonas .... David Harris
Sgt. Wilson .... Jeffrey Jones
Tel. Mess. B .... Arthur Miller
Cavalry Orderly .... Moultrie Patton
Lt. Allison .... Jonathan Penzner
Gen. Randolph .... Roy Poole
Lt. Foray .... Rex Robbins
Tel. Mess. A .... Hansford Rowe
Martha .... Louise Stubbs
Pvt. Eddinger .... Stuart Warmflash

1235 **Secrets**
The ABC Sunday Night Movie ABC
Program Type TV Movie
Two hours. Premiere date: 2/20/77. Drama of a compulsively promiscuous woman. Music by George Aliceson Tipton. "Dream Away" written by Susan Blakely. Puppets by Bob Baker Marionette Productions. Filmed on location in Southern California.
Executive Producer Gerald I. Isenberg
Producer Gerald W. Abrams
Company The Jozak Company
Director Paul Wendkos
Writer James Henerson

CAST

Andrea Fleming	Susan Blakely
Herb Fleming	Roy Thinnes
Helen Warner	Joanne Linville
Ed Warner	John Randolph
Laura Fleming	Melody Thomas
Dr. Lee	Frances Lee McCain
Phyllis Turner	Charlotte Stewart
Chrissie	Michelle Stacy
Taxi Driver	Brian Cutler
Larry Bleier	Anthony Eisley
Joanne Weese	Rosanne Covy
Joel Corcoran	Andrew Stevens
Phyllis Turner	Charlotte Stewart
Piano Tuner	Paul Itkin
Andrea (age 7)	Elizabeth Cheshire

1236 **See How They Run**
Americana PBS
Program Type Documentary/Informational Special
30 minutes. Premiere date: 2/4/77. A look at the role of reporters in the political process.
Producer Daniel Miller
Company Iowa Public Broadcasting Network
Writer Daniel Miller
Cinematographer John Leiendecker
Film Editor John Leiendecker

1237 **The Seeds** NBC
Program Type Religious/Cultural Special
60 minutes. Premiere date: 12/1/74. Repeat date: 4/10/77. Documentary, filmed in Tunisia, Turkey and Italy, on the first 600 years of Christianity.
Producer Doris Ann
Company NBC Television Religious Programs Unit in association with the National Council of Churches
Director Joseph Vadala
Writer Philip Scharper
Cinematographer Joseph Vadala
Film Editors Ed Williams, Boris Forlini
Reporter Hugh Downs

1238 **Senior Bowl** NBC
Program Type Sports Special
Live coverage of the 28th annual Senior Bowl from Ladd Memorial Stadium in Mobile, Ala. 1/8/77.
Producer Dick Auerbach
Company NBC Sports
Director Jim Holmes
Announcer Jack Buck
Analyst Len Dawson

1239 **A Sensitive, Passionate Man**
NBC Monday Night at the Movies NBC
Program Type TV Movie
Two hours. Premiere date: 6/6/77. Drama about a marriage threatened by a husband's alcoholism. Based on the novel by Barbara Mahoney. "My Sensitive, Passionate Man" lyrics by David Janssen and Carol Connors; music by Carol Connors and Bill Conti; sung by Melba Moore.
Producer Alan Jay Factor
Company Factor-Newland Productions in association with NBC-TV
Director John Newland
Writer Rita Lakin
Art Director Elayne Barbara Ceder

CAST

Marjorie Delaney	Angie Dickinson
Michael Delaney	David Janssen
Dan Delaney	Todd Lookinland
Kerry Delaney	Justin Randi
Pat Morris	Mariclare Costello
Jack Morris	Richard Venture
John Chapin	Rhodes Reason
Dr. Lazerow	Richard Bull

The Sentry Collection Prsents *see* Steve Lawrence and Eydie Gorme From This Moment On . . . Cole Porter

1240 **Serpico** NBC
Program Type Crime Drama Series
60 minutes. Fridays. Premiere date: 9/24/76. Last show: 1/28/77. Based on the character of Frank Serpico, a New York City Police Department undercover agent, from the book by Peter Maas. Pilot for series, "The Deadly Game," aired 4/24/76. Series filmed in part on location in New York City. Music by Elmer Bernstein.
Executive Producer Emmet G. Lavery, Jr.
Producer Don Ingalls
Company An Emmet G. Lavery, Jr. Production in association with Paramount Television and NBC-TV
Directors Various
Writers Various
Creative Consultant Robert Collins

CAST

Frank Serpico	David Birney
Tom Sullivan	Tom Atkins

1241 Sesame Street PBS

Program Type Children's Series

60 minutes. Monday-Friday mornings. Premiere date: 11/10/69. Eighth season premiere: 11/29/76. Magazine format for preschool children. Muppets created by Jim Henson. Series made possible by grants from the U.S. Department of Health, Education and Welfare - Office of Education, Public Television Stations, the Ford Foundation, the Corporation for Public Broadcasting, and the Carnegie Corporation of New York. Wednesday programs include specially prepared segments for children with learning disabilities.

Executive Producer Jon Stone
Producer Dulcy Singer
Company Children's Television Workshop
Directors Robert Myhrum, Jon Stone, Emily Squires, Jimmy Baylor, Bob Schwarz
Writers Ray Sipherd, Emily Perl Kingsley, Joseph Bailey, David Korr, Judy Freundberg, Tony Geiss
Musical Director Sam Pottle
Costume Designer Domingo Rodriguez
Art Director Alan J. Compton
Set Decorator Nat Mongioi

CAST

David .... Northern J. Calloway
Luis .... Emilio Delgado
Mr. Hooper .... Will Lee
Susan .... Loretta Long
Maria .... Sonia Manzano
Bob .... Bob McGrath
Gordon .... Roscoe Orman
Big Bird/Oscar .... Carroll Spinney

Puppeteers Jim Henson, Frank Oz, Jerry Nelson, Richard Hunt, Peter Friedman, Caroly Wilcox

The Seven-Ups *see* The ABC Sunday Night Movie

1242 Seventh Avenue

NBC's Best Seller NBC

Program Type Limited Series

Six hours. Thursdays. Premiere date: 2/10/77. Dramatization of the novel by Norman Bogner about New York City's garment industry. Filmed on location in New York.

Executive Producer Franklin Barton
Producer Richard Irving
Company Universal Television in association with NBC-TV
Directors Richard Irving, Russ Mayberry
Writer Laurence Heath
Production Designer Philip Rosenberg
Art Director Lloyd Papez

CAST

Jay Blackman .... Steven Keats
Rhoda Gold Blackman .... Dori Brenner
Eva Meyers .... Jane Seymour
Myrna Gold .... Anne Archer
Al Blackman .... Kristoffer Tabori
Frank Topo .... Richard Dimitri
Douglas Fredericks .... Ray Milland
Harry Lee .... Alan King
Joe Vitelli .... Herschel Bernardi
Marty Cass .... John Pleshette
Mr. Finkelstein .... Jack Gilford
Gus Farber .... Eli Wallach
John Meyers .... William Windom
Celia Blackman .... Anna Berger
Morris Blackman .... Mike Kellin
Barney Green .... Josh Mostel
Dave Shaw .... Paul Sorvino
Neal Blackman .... Joshua Freund

The Seventh Seal *see* PBS Movie Theater

1243 Sex and the Married Woman

NBC Movie of the Week NBC

Program Type TV Movie

Two hours. Premiere date: 9/13/77. Comedy about a couple whose marriage founders after the wife writes a book about the sexual experiences of married women.

Executive Producer George J. Santoro
Producer Jack Arnold
Company Universal Television in association with NBC-TV
Director Jack Arnold
Writer Michael Norell

CAST

Leslie Fitch .... Joanna Pettet
Alan Fitch .... Barry Newman
Uncle June .... Keenan Wynn
Duke Skaggs .... F. Murray Abraham
Louie Grosscup .... Dick Gautier
Peter Nebben .... Angus Duncan
Virginia Ladysmith .... Fannie Flagg
Irma Caddish .... Jayne Meadows
Arnie .... Larry Hovis
Carolyn .... Jeanne Lange
Hedi Lomax .... Nita Talbot
Jim Cutler .... Chuck McCann

1244 Shadows On the Grass PBS

Program Type Music/Dance Special

30 minutes. Premiere date: 9/14/76. Repeat date: 5/18/77. Contemporary and classical music by the Sheldon Trio filmed in scenic Nebraska locations.

Producer Gene Bunge
Company Nebraska Educational Television Network
Director Ron Nicodemus
Cinematographer Ron Nicodemus
Film Editor Ron Nicodemus
Performers Cary Lewis (pianist), Arnold Schatz (violinist), Dorothy Lewis (cellist)

1245 **The Shakers** PBS
Program Type Documentary/Informational Special
30 minutes. Premiere date: 4/21/75. Repeat date: 1/5/77. A look at the last surviving members of the Shaker sect. Program made possible by grants from Ann Rockefeller Coste, the National Endowment for the Humanities and the Corporation for Public Broadcasting.
Producers Tom Davenport, Frank DeCola
Company Maryland Center for Public Broadcasting in association with the American Crafts Council

1246 **The Shaman's Last Raid**
ABC Afterschool Specials ABC
Program Type Children's Special
60 minutes. Premiere date:11/19/75. Repeat date: 4/20/77. Drama of Apache children in today's world. Based on the novel by Betty Baker. Music by Neiman Tillar.
Producer Jon Kubichan
Company A Lenjen Production in association with 20th Century-Fox
Director H. Wesley Kenney
Writers Tom August, Helen August
Art Director Fred Luff

CAST

Red Eagle .... Ned Romero
Shaman .... Dehl Berti
Mrs. Strong .... Gina Alvarado
Ebon Strong .... Oscar Valdez
Melody Strong .... Monika Ramirez
Woodley .... Angus Duncan
Wrangler .... Clay Tanner

Shamus *see* NBC Monday Night at the Movies

1247 **Shari Lewis, Ed McMahon: Bearly in the Parade** NBC
Program Type Children's Special
60 minutes. Premiere date: 11/25/76. Musical fantasy (with puppets from "The Shari Show.") Original music by Lan O'Kun.
Producer Dick Schneider
Directors Dick Schneider, Jay Miller
Writers Jaie Brashar, Jeremy Tarcher
Musical Director Milton Delugg
Puppeteers Shari Lewis, Ron Martin
Stars Shari Lewis, Ed McMahon

Sharks' Treasure *see* The CBS Friday Night Movies

1248 **Shazam!**
The Shazam!/Isis Hour CBS
Program Type Children's Series
30 minutes. Saturday mornings. Premiere date: 9/7/74. Third season premiere: 9/11/76. Last show: 9/3/77. Based on characters in "Shazam!" Magazine. Live-action adventure/crime series.
Executive Producers Lou Scheimer, Norm Prescott, Richard Rosenbloom
Producer Arthur H. Nadel
Company Filmation Associates
Directors Various
Writers Various

CAST

Billy Batson .... Michael Gray
Mentor .... Les Tremayne
World's Mightiest Mortal .... John Davey

The Shazam!/Isis Hour *see* Isis/Shazam!

1249 **She Stoops to Conquer**
Classic Theatre: The Humanities in Drama PBS
Program Type Dramatic Special
Two hours. Premiere date: 10/23/75. Repeat date: 3/17/77. 18th century English comedy classic. Program made possible by grants from the National Endowment for the Humanities and Mobil Oil Corporation. Presented by WGBH-TV/Boston; Joan Sullivan, producer.
Producer Cedric Messina
Company British Broadcasting Corporation
Director Michael Elliott
Writer Oliver Goldsmith

CAST

Marlow .... Tom Courtenay
Mrs. Hardcastle .... Thora Hird
Kate Hardcastle .... Juliet Mills
Mr. Hardcastle .... Ralph Richardson
Tony Lumpkin .... Trevor Peacock
Hastings .... Brian Cox
Constance Neville .... Elaine Taylor
Mr. Marlow .... Esmond Knight

1250 **Sheehy and the Supreme Machine**
The ABC Monday Comedy Special ABC
Program Type Comedy Special
30 minutes. Premiere date: 8/22/77. Comedy pilot about an ex-Marine apartment building maintenance man and a gang of teenagers.
Executive Producer Harry Colomby
Producers Bernie Kukoff, Jeff Harris
Company Kukoff-Harris/Boiney Stoones, Inc.
Director Howard Storm
Writers Bernie Kukoff, Jeff Harris

CAST

Jack Sheehy .... John Byner
Mr. Cagle .... Tige Andrews
Bogen .... Jimmy Baio
Teddy .... Pierre Daniel
Dirt .... John Cassisi

Sheehy and the Supreme Machine
Continued

Evel .... Moosie Drier
Pantsface .... David Arnott
Loretta Bogen .... Gwynne Gilford

1251 **Sheila** CBS
Program Type Comedy Special
30 minutes. Premiere date: 8/29/77. Comedy pilot about a marriage-minded single woman working for a Broadway composer-producer. Created by Gail Parent and Kenny Solms.
Executive Producer Gail Parent
Producer Martin Cohan
Company Paramount Television
Director Peter Bonerz
Writers Gail Parent, Kenny Solms

CAST

Sheila Levine .... Dori Brenner
Marty Rose .... Milton Berle
Kate .... Barbara Trentham
Stewart Rose .... George Wyner
Joshua .... Larry Breeding
Brad Wooly .... Phillip R. Allen

1252 **Sherlock Holmes in New York**
NBC Monday Night at the Movies NBC
Program Type TV Movie
Two hours. Premiere date: 10/18/76. Drama based on the character created by Sir Arthur Conan Doyle. Music composed by Richard Rodney Bennett.
Executive Producer Nancy Malone
Producer John Cutts
Company 20th Century-Fox Television in association with NBC-TV
Director Boris Sagal
Writer Alvin Sapinsley
Costume Designers Hal Hoff, Shannon Litten
Art Director Lawrence G. Paull

CAST

Sherlock Holmes .... Roger Moore
Prof. Moriarty .... John Huston
Dr. Watson .... Patrick Macnee
Irene Adler .... Charlotte Rampling
Insp. Lafferty .... David Huddleston
Frau Reichenbach .... Signe Hasso
McGraw .... Gig Young
Daniel Furman .... Leon Ames
Heller .... John Abbott
Haymarket Proprietor .... Jackie Coogan

1253 **Shields and Yarnell** CBS
Program Type Music/Comedy/Variety Series
30 minutes. Mondays. Premiere date: 6/13/77. Last show: 7/25/77. Six-part series of mime, singing, dancing and comedy. Regular sketch: "The Clinkers." Special musical material by Hod David. Animation sequences by John Wilson.
Executive Producer Steve Binder
Producers Frank Peppiatt, John Aylesworth
Company A Steve Binder Production, Get the Hook Productions and Yongestreet Entertainment Corp.
Director Steve Binder
Writers Barry Adelman, John Aylesworth, Frank Peppiatt, Don Sandburg, Robert Shields, Barry Silver, Ted Zeigler
Musical Director Norman Mamey
Costume Designer Ret Turner
Art Director Romain Johnston
Stars Robert Shields, Lorene Yarnell (Shields and Yarnell)
Regulars Ted Zeigler, Joanna Cassidy

1254 **The Shirley MacLaine Special: Where Do We Go From Here?** CBS
Program Type Music/Comedy/Variety Special
60 minutes. Premiere date: 3/12/77. A look at the U.S. in the next 200 years. Special musical material by Marvin Laird; special lyrics by Digby Wolfe.
Producer George Schlatter
Company A George Schlatter Production in association with MacLaine Enterprises, Inc.
Director Tony Charmoli
Writer Digby Wolfe
Musical Director Donn Trenner
Choreographer Alan Johnson
Costume Designer Pete Menefee
Art Director Robert Kelly
Star Shirley MacLaine
Guest Stars Les Ballets Trockadero de Monte Carlo, Don Ellis and the Don Ellis Electric Orchestra, Laserium, Sergio Aragones

Shoeshine *see* PBS Movie Theater

1255 **Shoot for the Stars** NBC
Program Type Game/Audience Participation Series
30 minutes. Mondays-Fridays. Premiere date: 1/3/77. Word-association paraphrase game with teams of contestants and celebrities.
Executive Producer Bob Stewart
Producer Bruce Burmester
Company A Bob Stewart Production
Director Mike Gargiulo
Host Geoff Edwards
Announcer Bob Clayton

Sidecar Racers *see* NBC Saturday Night at the Movies

1256 **The Silence**
NBC Movie of the Week NBC
Program Type TV Movie
90 minutes. Premiere date: 11/6/75. Repeat

date: 7/31/77. True-life drama of a West Point cadet who was subject to total exile after being accused of violating the honor code. Music by Maurice Jarre. Filmed entirely on location in New York.
Executive Producer Edgar J. Scherick
Producer Bridget Potter
Company A Palomar Pictures International Production
Director Joseph Hardy
Writer Stanley R. Greenberg
Costume Designer Ann Roth
Art Director Mel Bourne

CAST

Cadet James Pelosi .... Richard Thomas
Stanley Greenberg .... Cliff Gorman
Capt. Nichols .... George Hearn
Capt. Harris .... Percy Granger
Col. Mack .... James Mitchell
Court President .... John Kellogg
Cadet Captain .... Charles Frank
Mr. Pelosi .... Andrew Duncan
Andy .... Malcolm Groome
Red Sash .... Peter Weller
Tom .... Michael Cooke
Mr. Keane .... John Carpenter

1257 **Sills and Burnett at the Met** CBS
Program Type Music/Comedy/Variety Special
60 minutes. Premiere date: 11/25/76. Music, comedy and dance taped before a live audience at the Metropolitan Opera House in New York City. Special musical material by Ken Welch and Mitzi Welch.
Producer Joe Hamilton
Company Jocar Productions
Director Dave Powers
Writers Kenny Solms, Gail Parent
Musical Director Peter Matz
Choreographer Ernest Flatt
Costume Designer Bob Mackie
Art Director Paul Barnes
Set Decorator Bill Harp
Stars Carol Burnett, Beverly Sills

1258 **The Silver Broom World Curling Championship** PBS
Program Type Sports Special
2 1/2 hours. Premiere date: 4/3/77. Live coverage of the World Curling Championship from Carlstadt, Sweden.
Executive Producer Greg Harney
Company WGBH-TV/Boston
Commentators Don Duguid, Don Chevrier, Doug Maxwell

1259 **The Silver Jubilee** ABC
Program Type Documentary/Informational Special
30 minutes. Premiere date: 6/3/77. Preview of celebrations from London in honor of Queen Elizabeth's 25th anniversary on the throne.
Executive Producer Elliot Bernstein
Producer Arthur Holch
Company ABC News Special Events
Director Marvin Schlenker
Writer Arthur Holch
Host Peter Jennings

1260 **Sinatra and Friends** ABC
Program Type Music/Dance Special
60 minutes. Premiere date: 4/21/77. All-music special. Production numbers by Hugh Lambert.
Producer Paul W. Keyes
Co-Producer Marc London
Company A Paul W. Keyes Production
Director Bill Davis
Writers Paul W. Keyes, Marc London
Musical Director Nelson Riddle
Art Director E. Jay Krause
Music Coordinator Irving Weiss
Star/Host Frank Sinatra
Guest Stars Tony Bennett, Natalie Cole, John Denver, Loretta Lynn, Dean Martin, Robert Merrill, Leslie Uggams

1261 **Sirota's Court** NBC
Program Type Comedy Series
30 minutes. Wednesdays. Premiere date: 12/1/76. Last show: 1/26/77. Returned with two episodes 4/6/77 and 4/13/77. Comedy set in a night court.
Producers Harvey Miller, Peter Engel
Company Peter Engel Productions in association with Universal Studios and NBC-TV
Director Mel Ferber
Writers Various

CAST

Judge Matthew Sirota .... Michael Constantine
Maureen O'Connor .... Cynthia Harris
Gail Goodman .... Kathleen Miller
Sawyer Dabney .... Ted Ross
Asst. D.A. Bud Nugent .... Fred Willard
John the Bailiff .... Owen Bush

1262 **Sit Down, Shut Up Or Get Out** NBC
Program Type Religious/Cultural Special
60 minutes. Premiere date: 5/9/71. Repeat date: 3/27/77. Drama about an intellectually gifted 13-year old and his problems at school.
Executive Producer Doris Ann
Producer Martin Hoade
Company NBC Television Religious Programs Unit in association with the National Council of Churches
Director Martin Hoade
Writer Allan Sloane

CAST

Christopher Bright .... Freddie James

Sit Down, Shut Up Or Get Out
Continued
Mr. Newman .... James Karen
Principal .... Sorrell Booke
Teacher .... Miriam Colon
Coach .... Peter DeAnda
Bolton .... Frank Moon
Wadley .... Bill Herndon

1263 **Six American Families** PBS
Program Type Documentary/Informational Series
60 minutes. Mondays. Premiere date: 4/4/77. Six documentaries looking at contemporary family life in the United States. Series presented by KQED-TV/San Francisco and made possible by a grant from the Travelers Insurance Companies.
Executive Producer George Moynihan
Producers Bill Jersey, Albert Maysles and David Maysles, Arthur Barron, Mark Obenhaus
Company Group W (Westinghouse Broadcasting Company) in association with the United Church of Christ and the United Methodist Church
Directors Bill Jersey, Albert Maysles and David Maysles, Arthur Barron, Mark Obenhaus
Host Paul Wilkes

1264 **Six Characters in Search of an Author**
Hollywood Television Theatre PBS
Program Type Dramatic Special
90 minutes. Premiere date: 10/14/76. Television studio staging of the 1921 play by Luigi Pirandello. Program made possible by grants from the Corporation for Public Broadcasting, the Ford Foundation and Public Television Stations.
Executive Producer Norman Lloyd
Producer Norman Lloyd
Company KCET-TV/Los Angeles
Director Stacy Keach
Writer Paul Avila Mayer
CAST
Father .... Andy Griffith
Director .... John Houseman
Mother .... Julie Adams
Stepdaughter .... Beverly Todd
Son .... James Keach
Madam Pace .... Pat Ast
Children .... H. B. Barnum III, Claire Touchstone
Additional Cast Laurence Hugo, Timothy Blake, Pat Hitchcock, Deborah Winters, Jeremy Foster, Leon Charles, Philip Epstein, Harold Oblong

1265 **The Six Million Dollar Man** ABC
Program Type Crime Drama Series
60 minutes. Sundays. Premiere date: 1/14/74. Fourth season premiere: 9/19/76 (in conjunction with "The Bionic Woman.") Based on the novel "Cyborg" by Martin Caidin and pilot "The Six Million Dollar Man" originally broadcast 3/7/73. Action-adventures of bionic man working for the U.S. Office of Scientific Information (O.S.I.).
Executive Producer Harve Bennett
Producers Lionel E. Siegel Allan Balter
Company A Harve Bennett Production in association with Universal Television
Directors Various
Writers Various
CAST
Steve Austin .... Lee Majors
Oscar Goldman .... Richard Anderson

1266 **6 Rms Riv Vu** CBS
Program Type Dramatic Special
90 minutes. Premiere date: 3/17/74. Repeat date: 6/13/77. Adaptation of the Broadway play by Bob Randall. Taped before a live audience at the Ed Sullivan Theater in New York City.
Producer Joe Hamilton
Company Punkin Productions, Inc.
Directors Alan Alda, Clark Jones
Writer Bob Randall
CAST
Anne Miller .... Carol Burnett
Paul Friedman .... Alan Alda
Janet Friedman .... Millie Slavin
Richard Miller .... Lawrence Pressman
Superintendent .... Jose Ocasio
Pregnant Woman .... Maureen Silliman
Woman in 4-A .... Francine Beers

1267 **The Sixth David Frost Presents the Guinness Book of World Records**
Thursday Night Special ABC
Program Type Music/Comedy/Variety Special
90 minutes. Premiere date: 2/10/77. Sixth program based on facts and feats authenticated in "The Guinness Book of World Records." Taped at Circus Circus in Las Vegas, Nevada.
Producer David Frost, Marvin Minoff
Producer Jorn Winther
Director Jorn Winther
Writers Mike Smollins, Kathy Gori
Host David Frost
Celebrity Guest George Gobel

1268 **Sixty Minutes** CBS
Program Type News Magazine Series
60 minutes. Sundays. Premiere date: 9/24/68. Ninth season premiere: 9/19/76. Became 52-week primetime show 12/7/75. Three reports weekly. Regular features: "Mail" (viewer response) and "Point-Counter-Point" with Shana Alexander and James J. Kilpatrick.
Executive Producer Don Hewitt
Senior Producer Palmer Williams
Producers Richard Clark, Joseph De Cola, Grace Diekhaus, Marion Goldin, Norman Gorin, Imre Horvath, Jim Jackson, Barry

Lando, Paul Loewenwarter, William McClure, Harry Moses, Igor Oganesoff, Philip Scheffler, Jeanne Solomon, John Tiffin, Al Wasserman, Joseph Wershba and others
Company CBS News
Director Arthur Bloom
Co-Editors Mike Wallace, Morley Safer, Dan Rather

1269 **A Skating Spectacular '76** PBS
Program Type Sports Special
60 minutes. Premiere date: 12/31/76. Figure skating exhibition taped 11/20/76 and 11/21/76 at the Rochester Institute of Technology. Program made possible by grants from the Gannett Foundation, S. Ritter Sumway, Xerox Corporation, R. T. French, Champion Products, Gleason Memorial Fund, Sybron Corporation and the Rochester Telephone Corporation.
Executive Producer James A. DeVinney
Producer Jim Dauphinee
Company WXXI-TV/Rochester, N.Y.
Director Jim Dauphinee
Performers Tai Babilonia and Randy Gardner, Linda Fratianne, Dee Oseroff, Craig Bond and members of the Genesee Figure Skating Club

Sky Terror *see* The ABC Sunday Night Movie

Skyjacked *see* The ABC Sunday Night Movie ("Sky Terror")

Sleeper *see* The ABC Tuesday Night Movie

Sleuth *see* The ABC Sunday Night Movie

1270 **Smash-Up on Interstate 5**
The ABC Friday Night Movie/The ABC Tuesday Night Movie ABC
Program Type TV Movie
Two hours. Premiere date: 12/3/76. Repeat date: 8/23/77. Drama revolving around a massive crash on a Southern California freeway. Based on the novel "Expressway" by Elleston Trevor. Music by Bill Conti. Filmed in and around Los Angeles.
Executive Producer Edward S. Feldman
Producer Roger Lewis
Company A Filmways Production
Director John Llewellyn Moxey
Writers Eugene Price, Robert Presnell, Jr.
Production Designer W. Stewart Campbell
Stunt Coordinator Charles Picerni

CAST

Sgt. Marcum ..... Robert Conrad
Al Pearson ..... Buddy Ebsen
Erica ..... Vera Miles
Dale ..... David Groh
June Pearson ..... Harriet Nelson
Burnsey ..... Sue Lyon
Lee ..... Scott Jacoby
Laureen ..... Donna Mills
Danny ..... Herb Edelman
Barbara ..... Sian Barbara Allen
Penny ..... Bonnie Ebsen
Pete ..... George O'Hanlon, Jr.
Trudy ..... Terry Moore
Off. Berman ..... David Nelson
Off. Hutton ..... Tommy Lee Jones
Estevez ..... Joe Kapp
Andy ..... Joel Parks
Randy ..... Barry Hamilton

Smile *see* The CBS Wednesday Night Movies

1271 **Smile, Jenny, You're Dead**
The CBS Friday Night Movies CBS
Program Type TV Movie
Two hours. Premiere date: 2/3/74 (on ABC). Repeat date: 8/12/77. Second pilot for "Harry O" series.
Producer Jerry Thorpe
Company Warner Bros. Television
Director Jerry Thorpe
Writer Howard Rodman

CAST

Harry Orwell ..... David Janssen
Jennifer English ..... Andrea Marcovicci
Col. John Lockport, Ret. ..... John Anderson
Lt. Humphrey Kenney ..... Howard da Silva
Meade De Ruyter ..... Martin Gabel
Det. Milt Bosworth ..... Clu Gulager
Roy St. John ..... Zalman King
Charley English ..... Tim McIntire
Liberty ..... Jodie Foster
Portrait Photographer ..... Harvey Jason
Mildred ..... Barbara Leigh
Lt. Richard Marum ..... Victor Arco
Julia ..... Ellen Weston
Asst. Photographer ..... Chet Winfield

Smiles of a Summer Night *see* PBS Movie Theater

1272 **Snoopy at the Ice Follies** CBS
Program Type Music/Comedy/Variety Special
60 minutes. Premiere date: 10/24/71 (on NBC). Repeat date: 1/14/77. Musical comedy-on-ice. Colorado film sequences directed by Walt Defaria.
Executive Producer Lee Mendelson
Producers Walt Defaria, Warren Lockhart
Company Lee Mendelson Productions Inc. in association with Charles M. Schulz Creative De-

Snoopy at the Ice Follies *Continued*
velopment Corporation and Walt Defaria Productions
Director Walter C. Miller
Musical Director Paul Walberg
Host Charles M. Schulz
Featured Skaters Karen Kresge, Richard Dwyer, Susan Berens, Atoy Wilson, Mr. Frick, Tim Wood, Kathy Miller, Nancy and Leandre

CAST

Stage Manager .... Laurie Braude

Snoopy, Come Home *see* CBS Special Film Presentations

1273 **Snowbeast**
NBC Thursday Night at the Movies NBC
Program Type TV Movie
Two hours. Premiere date: 4/28/77. Drama about a ski resort terrorized by a killer beast. Music by Robert Prince. Special effects by Marlowe Newkirk. Filmed on location in Bunnison County, Colorado.
Executive Producer Douglas S. Cramer
Producer W. L. Baumes
Company Douglas Cramer Productions in association with NBC-TV
Director Herb Wallerstein
Writer Joseph Stefano
Art Director Steven Sardanis

CAST

Gar Seberg .... Bo Svenson
Ellen Seberg .... Yvette Mimieux
Tony Rill .... Robert Logan
Sheriff Paraday .... Clint Walker
Carrie Rill .... Sylvia Sidney
Snowbeast .... Michael J. London
Buster .... Thomas Babson
Jennifer .... Kathy Christopher
Heidi .... Anne McEncroe

Soft Skin *see* PBS Movie Theater

1274 **Solar Energy** PBS
Program Type Science/Nature Series
30 minutes. Monday mornings. Premiere date: 3/25/75. Repeats shown as of 12/13/76. Six-part series on solar energy possibilities. Funded by grants from the Corporation for Public Broadcasting, the Ford Foundation and Public Television Stations.
Producer Carl Manfredi
Company KNME-TV/Albuquerque
Host David Prowitt

1275 **Soldier's Home/Almos' a Man**
The American Short Story PBS
Program Type Dramatic Special

Soldier's Home
45 minutes. Premiere date: 4/26/77. Adaptation of the short story by Ernest Hemingway about a soldier who returns to his home town after World War I. Music by Dick Hyman. Program presented by South Carolina Educational Television and made possible by a grant from the National Endowment for the Humanities.
Executive Producer Robert Geller
Producer David B. Appleton
Company Learning in Focus, Inc.
Director Robert Young
Writer Robert Geller
Costume Designer Robert Pusilo
Scenic Designer Michael Molly
Host Colleen Dewhurst

CAST

Harold Krebs .... Richard Backus
Mrs. Krebs .... Nancy Marchand
Kenner .... Mark LaMura
Additional Cast Robert McIlwaine, Lisa Essary, Lane Binkley, Robert Hitt, Philip Oxnam, Robert Nichols, Mark Hall, Tom Kubiak, Bryan Utman

Almos' a Man
45 minutes. Adaptation of the short story by Richard Wright about growing up black in the South of the 1930s. Music by Taj Mahal.
Executive Producer Robert Geller
Producer Dan McCann
Company Learning in Focus, Inc.
Director Stan Lathan
Writer Leslie Lee
Costume Designer Marianne DeFina
Scenic Designer Don DeFina
Host Colleen Dewhurst

CAST

Dave Glover .... LeVar Burton
Mrs. Glover .... Madge Sinclair
Bob Glover .... Robert DoQui
Hawkins .... Gary Goodrow
Additional Cast Christopher Brooks, Roy Andrews

1276 **Solti Conducts Mendelssohn**
Fine Music Specials/Great Performances PBS
Program Type Music/Dance Special
60 minutes. Premiere date: 12/8/76. The Chicago Symphony Orchestra taped at Orchestra Hall in Chicago performing the music of Felix Mendelssohn. Program stereo-simulcast on local FM stations. Presented by WNET-TV/New York and made possible by grants from Exxon Corporation and Public Television Stations.
Executive Producer Klaus Hallig
Producer David Griffiths
Company Unitel Productions
Director Humphrey Burton
Conductor Sir Georg Solti

1277 **Somerset** NBC
Program Type Daytime Drama Series
30 minutes. Mondays–Fridays. Premiere date: 3/30/70. Last show: 12/31/76. Began as "Another World—Somerset;" about families living in the town of the same name. Credits as of December 1976. Cast list is alphabetical.
Executive Producer Lyle B. Hill
Producer Sid Sirulnick
Company Procter & Gamble Productions
Directors Jack Coffey, Bruce M. Minnix
Head Writer Russell Kubec
Musical Director Chet Kingsbury
Announcer Bill Wolff

CAST

Steve Slade ... Gene Bua
Julian Cannell ... Joel Crothers
Tom Conway ... Ted Danson
Dan Briskin ... Bernard Grant
Vicki Paisley ... Veleka Gray
Dr. Teri Kurtz ... Gloria Hoye
Ellen Grant ... Georgann Johnson
Heather Kane ... Audrey Landers
Dr. Stanley Kurtz ... Michael Lipton
Jill Farmer ... Susan MacDonald
Dr. Jerry Kane ... James O'Sullivan
Lt. Will Price ... Eugene Smith
Carrie Wheeler ... Jobeth Williams

1278 **Something for Joey** CBS
Program Type Dramatic Special
Two hours. Premiere date: 4/6/77. Dramatization of the true-life relationship between Heisman Trophy winner John Cappelletti and his brother Joey. Music by David Shire.
Producer Jerry McNeely
Company MTM Enterprises, Inc.
Director Lou Antonio
Writer Jerry McNeely
Art Director Sydney Z. Litwack

CAST

Anne Cappelletti ... Geraldine Page
John Cappelletti, Sr. ... Gerald S. O'Loughlin
John Cappelletti ... Marc Singer
Joey Cappelletti ... Jeff Lynas
Joyce Cappelletti ... Linda Kelsey
Marty Cappelletti ... Brian Farrell
Jean Cappelletti ... Kathy Beller
Mike Cappelletti ... Steven Guttenberg
Joe Paterno ... Paul Picerni
Eddie O'Neil ... Stephen Parr
Archbishop ... David Hooks
Mrs. Frone ... June Dayton
Dr. Wingreen ... James Karen
Dr. Klunick ... David Garfield
Mark ... Kevin McKenzie

1279 **Something Personal** PBS
Program Type Documentary/Informational Series
30 minutes. Saturdays. Premiere date: 7/16/77. Nine-part series of documentary films showing the variety and uniqueness of American women. Series made possible by grants from the National Endowment for the Arts and the Corporation for Public Broadcasting.
Executive Producer Nancy Porter
Producers Nancy Porter, Joyce Chopra, Ann Hershey, Miriam Weinstein, Mitchell Block, Mirra Bank, Lynne Littman
Company WGBH-TV/Boston

1280 **The Sometime Soldiers**
NBC Reports NBC
Program Type Documentary/Informational Special
60 minutes. Premiere date: 12/3/76. An examination of the U.S. military reserves.
Producer Robert Rogers
Company NBC News
Director Robert Rogers
Writer Robert Rogers
Reporter Ford Rowan

Sometimes a Great Notion *see* NBC Monday Night at the Movies/NBC Saturday Night at the Movies ("Never Give an Inch")

1281 **Song at Twilight: An Essay on Aging**
Documentary Showcase PBS
Program Type Documentary/Informational Special
60 minutes. Premiere date: 1/21/77. A look at the aging process and society's attitude toward older people.
Producer Paul Cabbell
Company KOCE-TV/Huntington Beach, Calif.
Director Thom Eberhardt
Writer Paul Cabbell
Narrator Paul Cabbell

1282 **The Sonny and Cher Show** CBS
Program Type Music/Comedy/Variety Series
60 minutes. Sundays/Fridays (as of 1/14/77). Premiere date: 2/1/76. Second season premiere: 9/26/76. Last regular show: 3/18/77. Rebroadcasts began 5/30/77 (Mondays). Last show: 8/29/77. Recurrent sketches: the Egyptian soap opera, the "Cutesy News" and Mother Goose tales. Show was a revival of "The Sonny and Cher Comedy Hour" (1971–1974) and a successor to "Cher" (1975–1976).
Executive Producer Nick Vanoff
Producers Frank Peppiatt, Phil Hahn
Company Apis Productions, inc., in association with Yongestreet Entertainment Corp.
Director Tim Kiley
Writers Barry Adelman, Bob Arnott, Jeannine

The Sonny and Cher Show *Continued*
Burnier, Stuart Gillard, Coslough Johnson, Iris Rainer, Barry Silver
Musical Director Harold Battiste
Choreographer Jaime Rogers
Costume Designers Bob Mackie, Ret Turner
Stars Cher, Sonny Bono
Regulars Ted Zeigler, Shields and Yarnell

1283 **Soul Train** Syndicated
Program Type Music/Comedy/Variety Series
60 minutes. Weekly. Premiere date: 8/17/70 (WCIU-TV/Chicago). In syndication since 10/71. Black variety show created by Don Cornelius.
Producer Don Cornelius
Company Don Cornelius Productions
Director B. J. Jackson
Host Don Cornelius
Announcer Sid McCoy

Sounder *see* Special Movie Presentation

1284 **The Sounds of Christmas Eve** NBC
Program Type Music/Dance Special
30 minutes. Premiere date: 12/73. Repeat date: 12/24/76. A concert of Christmas music and readings. Musical arrangements by Tommy Newsom.
Producer Dick Schneider
Co-Producer Bud Robinson
Company NBC-TV Network Presentation
Director Dick Schneider
Writer Shelly Cohen
Host Doc Severinsen
Guests Henry Mancini, Victor Buono, St. Charles Borromeo Church Choir, NBC Orchestra

1285 **Soundstage** PBS
Program Type Music/Dance Series
60 minutes. Mondays. Premiere date: 11/12/74. Third season premiere: 10/25/76. Weekly contemporary music series featuring guest stars. Funded by the Corporation for Public Broadcasting, the Ford Foundation and Public Television Stations.
Producers William Heitz, Charles Mitchell
Company WTTW-TV/Chicago
Director Richard Carter

1286 **South Africa: The White Laager**
Documentary Showcase PBS
Program Type Documentary/Informational Special
60 minutes. Premiere date: 5/27/77. Repeat date: 9/2/77 (captioned for the hearing-impaired). An examination of apartheid in South Africa.
Producers Peter Davis, Barry Callaghan
Company Swedish Television, United Nations Television and WGBH-TV/Boston

Soylent Green *see* The CBS Wednesday Night Movies

1287 **Space Ghost/Frankenstein Jr.** NBC
Program Type Animated Film Series
30 minutes. Saturday mornings. Return date: 11/27/76. Last show: 9/3/77. Two cartoon features: "Space Ghost" about an interplanetary crime fighter and his two young assistants and "Frankenstein Jr." about a not-altogether reliable character and a young scientific genius in a series of misadventures.
Executive Producers William Hanna, Joseph Barbera
Company Hanna-Barbera Productions
Director Charles A. Nichols
Writers Various
Musical Director Hoyt Curtin

1288 **Space: 1999** Syndicated
Program Type Science Fiction Series
60 minutes. Premiere date: 9/75. Second (last) season premiere: 9/76. Weekly. Scientists on Moonbase Alpha in outer space adventures. Created by Gerry Anderson and Sylvia Anderson. Special effects by Brian Johnson. Music composed by Barry Gray and Vic Elms.
Executive Producer Gerry Anderson
Producer Fred Freiberger
Company A Gerry Anderson Production
Distributor International Television Corporation
Directors Various
Story Editor Fred Freiberger
Conductor Barry Gray
Costume Designer Rudi Gernreich

CAST

Cmdr. John Koenig .... Martin Landau
Dr. Helena Russell .... Barbara Bain
Maya .... Catherine Schell

1289 **Space Shuttle: The First Voyage**
CBS News Special CBS
Program Type News Special
30 minutes. Live coverage of the landing of the manned space shuttle orbiter "Enterprise" in the Mojave Desert 8/12/77. Broadcast from NASA's Dryden Flight Research Center, Edwards Air Force Base in California.
Executive Producer Russ Bensley
Producer Jack Kelly
Co-Producers Ron Bonn, David Buksbaum, Mark Kramer, Dick Sedia
Company CBS News

Directors Jack Kelly, Joseph Yaklovitch
Anchor Morton Dean
Reporter Richard Wagner

1290 **The Spaceship Enterprise** ABC
Program Type News Special
60 minutes. Live coverage of the first manned separation-flight of the space shuttle 8/12/77.
Executive Producer Elliot Bernstein
Producer Daryl Griffin
Company ABC News Special Events
Anchors Frank Reynolds, Jules Bergman

1291 **Sparrow** CBS
Program Type TV Movie
60 minutes. Premiere date: 1/12/77. Mystery drama pilot of a mailroom clerk turned detective in an insurance company. Created and written by Larry Cohen and Paul Bauman with a revised story by Walter Bernstein.
Executive Producer Herbert B. Leonard
Producers Sam Manners, Charles Russell
Company Tori Productions, Inc.
Director Stuart Hagmann
Writer Walter Bernstein

CAST

Sparrow .... Randy Herman
Medwick .... Don Gordon
Tammy .... Beverly Sanders
Harriet .... Karen Sedgley
Bruce .... Jeff Holland
Brady .... Tom Quinn
Bennett .... Jack Wallace
Marty .... Lenny Baker
Karen .... Dori Brenner

1292 **Special Comedy Presentation** ABC
Program Type Comedy Special
30 minutes/60 minutes. Five special presentations of comedy pilots: "The Four of Us," "The Harvey Korman Show," "MacNamara's Band," "Mixed Nuts," "Tabitha." (*See* individual titles for credits.)

1293 **Special Movie Presentation** ABC
Program Type Feature Film Specials
Times vary. Theatrically released motion pictures shown irregularly. Films shown during the 1976–77 season are: "Butch Cassidy and the Sundance Kid" (1969) shown 9/26/76, "The Effect of Gamma Rays on Man-in-the-Moon Marigolds" (1973) shown 7/18/77, "Journey Back to Oz" (1971) shown 12/5/76, "Sounder" (1972) shown in two parts 11/14/76 and 11/21/76, "Thoroughly Modern Millie" (1967) shown 7/16/77, "Thunderball" (1965) shown 5/7/77, "Winnie the Pooh and Tigger Too" (1974) shown 11/25/76.

1294 **A Special Olivia Newton-John** ABC
Program Type Music/Comedy/Variety Special
60 minutes. Premiere date: 11/17/76. A country and western music variety special. Special material by Ken Welch and Mitzi Welch.
Executive Producers Raymond Katz, Sandy Gallin, Danny Cleary
Producer Joe Layton
Company Katz-Gallin-Cleary Enterprises, Inc.
Director Norman Campbell
Writers Gerald Gardner, Dee Caruso, Fred Smoot
Musical Director Peter Matz
Costume Designers Pete Menefee, Fleur Timeyer
Art Director Tom H. John
Star Olivia Newton-John
Special Guest Star Elliott Gould
Guest Stars Lee Majors, Lynda Carter, Ron Howard, Tom Bosley, Rona Barrett

1295 **Special Treat** NBC
Program Type Children's Series
60 minutes each. Tuesdays. Premiere date: 10/21/75. Second season premiere: 10/5/76. Monthly programs seen Tuesday afternoons. Specials shown during the 1976–77 season are: "Big Henry and the Polka Dot Kid," "The Day After Tomorrow," "Figuring All the Angles," "It's a Brand New World," "A Little Bit Different," "Little Women," "Luke Was There." (*See* individual titles for credits.)

1296 **Spectre**
NBC Saturday Night at the Movies NBC
Program Type TV Movie
Two hours. Premiere date: 5/21/77. Pilot drama of criminologist and physician companion investigating the power of supernatural forces on international crime. Filmed on location in England. Music by John Cameron.
Executive Producer Gene Roddenberry
Producer Gordon L. T. Scott
Company 20th Century-Fox Production in association with NBC-TV
Director Clive Donner
Writers Gene Roddenberry, Sam Peeples
Costume Designer Judy Moorcroft

CAST

Sebastian .... Robert Culp
Dr. Hamilton .... Gig Young
Insp. Cabell .... Gordon Jackson
Mitri .... John Hurt
Anitra .... Ann Bell
Sir Geoffrey Cyon .... James Villiers
Lilith .... Majel Barrett
Synda .... Jenny Runnacre
Butler .... Angela Grant
Maid .... Linda Benson

1297 **Speed Buggy** NBC
Program Type Animated Film Series
30 minutes. Saturday mornings. Premiere date: 9/8/73 (on CBS). Season premiere on NBC: 11/27/76. (reruns). Last show: 9/3/77. Animated adventure-comedy of three teenagers and their remote-controlled car.
Executive Producers William Hanna, Joseph Barbera
Producer Iwao Takamoto
Company Hanna-Barbera Productions
Director Charles A. Nichols
Writers Jack Mendelsohn, Larz Bourne, Len Janson, Joel Kane, Jack Kaplan, Woody Kling, Norman Maurer, Chuck Menville, Ray Parker, Larry Rhine
Musical Director Hoyt Curtin
Voices Chris Allen, Mike Bell, Mel Blanc, Ron Feinberg, Arlene Golonka, Virginia Gregg, Phil Luther, Jr., Jim MacGeorge, Sid Miller, Alan Oppenheimer, Mike Road, Charlie Martin Smith, Hal Smith, John Stephenson, Janet Waldo

1298 **The Spell**
The Big Event/NBC Movie of the Week NBC
Program Type TV Movie
90 minutes. Premiere date: 2/20/77. Repeat date: 7/3/77. Supernatural story of overweight adolescent. Music by Gerald Fried.
Executive Producers Charles Fries, Dick Berg
Producer David Manson
Company Charles Fries Productions/Stonehenge Productions in association with NBC-TV
Director Lee Philips
Writer Brian Taggert

CAST

Marion Matchett .... Lee Grant
Glenn Matchett .... James Olson
Rita Matchett .... Susan Myers
Jill .... Barbara Bostock
Kristina Matchett .... Helen Hunt
Jo Standish .... Lelia Goldoni
Dale Boyce .... Jack Colvin
Stan .... James Greene
Rian .... Wright King

1299 **Spencer's Pilots** CBS
Program Type Drama Series
60 minutes. Fridays. Premiere date: 9/17/76. Last show: 11/19/76. Adventure series about charter service pilots working for Spencer Aviation. Based on TV-movie pilot which aired 4/9/76.
Executive Producers Bob Sweeney, Edward H. Feldman
Producer Larry Rosen
Company CBS Television Network
Directors Various
Story Editor Bill Froug
Writers Various
Art Director Robert Bradfield
Stunt Coordinator Art Scholl

CAST

Cass Garrett .... Christopher Stone
Stan Lewis .... Todd Susman
Spencer Parish .... Gene Evans
Linda Dann .... Margaret Impert
Mickey Wiggins .... Britt Leach

The Spirit of St. Louis *see* NBC Night at the Movies

1300 **Spoleto: The Festival of Two Worlds** PBS
Program Type Documentary/Informational Special
30 minutes. Premiere date: 5/22/77. A look at the Festival of Two Worlds in Spoleto, Italy and in Charleston, South Carolina. Program made possible by a grant from the Corporation for Public Broadcasting.
Producer Sidney Palmer
Company South Carolina Educational Television Network
Director Sidney Palmer
Writer Sidney Palmer

Ssssss *see* **NBC Monday Night at the Movies/NBC Saturday Night at the Movies**

1301 **SST - Death Flight**
The ABC Friday Night Movie ABC
Program Type TV Movie
Two hours. Premiere date: 2/25/77. Drama about sabotage aboard the first flight of a U.S. supersonic transport. Based on a story by Guerdon Trueblood. Music by John Cacavas. Filmed in and around Los Angeles and Ventura County, Calif.
Producer Ron Roth
Company ABC Circle Films
Director David Lowell Rich
Writers Robert L. Joseph, Meyer Dolinsky
Art Director Peter Wooley

CAST

Carla Stanley .... Barbara Anderson
Tim Vernon .... Bert Convy
Paul Whitley .... Peter Graves
Marshall Cole .... Lorne Greene
Anne Redding .... Season Hubley
Mae .... Tina Louise
Les Phillips .... George Maharis
Willy Basset .... Burgess Meredith
Hank Fairbanks .... Doug McClure
Lyle Kingman .... Martin Milner
Dr. Ralph Therman .... Brock Peters
Capt. Walsh .... Robert Reed
Nancy Kingman .... Susan Strasberg

Angela Garland ....Misty Rowe
David .... Billy Crystal
Bob Connors .... John de Lancie
Kathy ....Chrystie Jenner

1302 **The St. Matthew Passion**
Great Performances PBS
Program Type Music/Dance Special
3 1/2 hours. Premiere shown in two parts: 4/14/76 (90 minutes) and 4/15/76 (two hours.) Repeat date: 4/10/77. The "Passion According to St. Matthew" by Johann Sebastian Bach performed by the Munich Bach Orchestra, the Munich Bach Choir, and the Munich Boys' Choir. Program presented by WNET-TV/New York and made possible by a grant from Exxon Corporation.
Executive Producer Fritz Buttenstedt
Coordinating Producer David Griffiths
Company Unitel Productions
Conductor Dr. Karl Richter

CAST

Evangelist .... Peter Schreier
Jesus .... Ernst Gerold Schramm
Judas/Pilate .... Siegmund Minsgern
Additional Cast Helen Donath, Julia Hamari, Horst R. Laubenthal, Walter Berry

1303 **The Stages of Preston Jones** PBS
Program Type Documentary/Informational Special
30 minutes. Premiere date: 6/28/77. A look at the career of playwright Preston Jones. Filmed in New York, Dallas and West Texas. Program made possible by grants from the Texas Commission for the Arts and Humanities, the National Endowment for the Arts and the Corporation for Public Broadcasting.
Executive Producer Bill Porterfield
Producers Patsy Swank, Kenneth Harrison
Company KERA-TV/Dallas-Fort Worth
Director Kenneth Harrison
Cinematographer Kenneth Harrison
Film Editor Kenneth Harrison

1304 **Stalk the Wild Child**
NBC Movie of the Week NBC
Program Type TV Movie
90 minutes. Premiere date: 11/3/76. Repeat date: 7/14/77. Based on true stories of children found living wild. Filmed on location in Carmel and southern California. Music by John Rubinstein.
Executive Producer Charles Fries
Producers Stanley Bass, Paul Wendkos
Company Charles Fries Productions in association with NBC-TV
Director William Hale
Writer Peter Packer
Costume Designers Kent James, Carol James

CAST

Dr. James Hazard .... David Janssen
Maggie ....Trish Van Devere
Cal (as youth) .... Benjamin Bottoms
Cal (as young man) ....Joseph Bottoms
Gault .... Allan Arbus
Andrea .... Jamie Smith Jackson
Ellen ....Fran Ryan
Secretary .... Marcia Warner
Menzies .... Jerome Thor

1305 **The Stanley Baxter Big Picture Show**
Piccadilly Circus PBS
Program Type Music/Comedy/Variety Special
60 minutes. Premiere date: 9/6/76. Repeat date: 7/24/77. One-man show of sketches and songs by Stanley Baxter. Program made possible by a grant from Mobil Oil Corporation. Presented by WGBH-TV/Boston; Joan Sullivan, producer.
Producer Jon Scoffield
Director Jon Scoffield
Writer Ken Hoare
Choreographer Norman Maen
Host Jeremy Brett
Star Stanley Baxter

1306 **Star Soccer** PBS
Program Type Limited Sports Series
60 minutes. Weekly. Season premiere: 11/76. 28-week series of soccer matches from the top two divisions of the English Football League. 90-minute games are taped, edited and aired one week later on U.S. television.
Company Incorporated Television Company, Ltd. (I.T.C.)
Distributor Eastern Educational Network through KCET-TV/Los Angeles
Host/Announcer Mario Machado

Star Spangled Girl *see* The ABC Friday Night Movie

1307 **The Starland Vocal Band Show** CBS
Program Type Music/Comedy/Variety Series
30 minutes. Sundays/Fridays (as of 8/19/77). Premiere date: 7/31/77. Last show: 9/2/77. Six-week music-variety summer show. Weekly report on the Washington scene by Mark Russell.
Executive Producer Jerry Weintraub
Producer Al Rogers
Company Star-Jer Productions
Director Rick Bennewitz
Writers April Kelly, George Geiger, Dave Letterman, Phil Proctor, Peter Bergman
Musical Director Milt Okin
Conductor Eddie Karam
Costume Designer David Doucette

The Starland Vocal Band Show
Continued
Art Director Ken Johnson
Stars The Starland Vocal Band (Bill Danoff, Taffy Danoff, Margot Chapman, Jon Carroll)
Regulars Mark Russell, Dave Letterman, Jeff Altman, Phil Proctor, Peter Bergman

1308 **Starsky and Hutch** ABC
Program Type Crime Drama Series
60 minutes. Saturdays. Premiere date: 9/10/75. Second season premiere: 9/25/76. Police drama about two plainclothes detectives. Series created by William Blinn. 90-minute pilot originally telecast 4/30/75. Music by Lalo Schifrin.
Executive Producers Aaron Spelling, Leonard Goldberg
Producer Joseph T. Naar
Company Spelling/Goldberg Productions
Directors Various
Story Editor Michael Fisher
Writers Various

CAST

Ken "Hutch" Hutchinson	David Soul
Dave Starsky	Paul Michael Glaser
Capt. Harold Dobey	Bernie Hamilton
Huggy Bear	Antonio Fargas

1309 **State Fair America** CBS
Program Type Music/Comedy/Variety Special
Two hours. Premiere date: 9/10/77. Entertainment special taped on location at four state fairs: the San Luis Obispo Fair in Paso Robles, Calif., the Illinois Fair in Peoria, Ill., Cheyenne frontier days in Cheyenne, Wyo. and the Allentown Fair in Allentown, Pa. Music by Jack Elliott and Allyn Ferguson.
Executive Producers Bernard Rothman, Jack Wohl
Producer Eric Lieber
Company Rothman/Wohl Productions
Director Jeff Margolis
Writers Aubrey Tadman, Garry Ferrier
Choreographer Kevin Carlisle
Costume Designer Bill Hargate
Stars Lynn Anderson, Roy Clark, Steven Ford, Kansas, Gabriel Kaplan, Alan King, Robert Klein, Hal Linden, Mary MacGregor, Marilyn McCoo, and Billy Davis, Jr., Mel Tillis, Jimmie Walker

1310 **State of the Union Address (ABC)** ABC
Program Type News Special
60 minutes. Live coverage of the State of the Union Address to Congress by Pres. Gerald R. Ford 1/12/77.
Company ABC News Special Events Unit

1311 **State of the Union Address (CBS)**
CBS News Special CBS
Program Type News Special
60 minutes. Live coverage of Pres. Gerald R. Ford's State of the Union Address to a joint session of Congress 1/12/77.
Producer Sanford Socolow
Company CBS News

1312 **State of the Union Address (NBC)**
NBC News Special NBC
Program Type News Special
60 minutes. Premiere date: 1/12/77. Live coverage of the State of the Union Address by Pres. Gerald R. Ford.
Company NBC News
Anchor John Hart

The Stepford Wives *see* The ABC Sunday Night Movie

1313 **Steve Allen's Laugh Back** Syndicated
Program Type Music/Comedy/Variety Series
90 minutes. Weekly. Premiere date: 6/76. Last show: 12/76. Clips showing highlights of Steve Allen's old shows, plus new routines and guest celebrities.
Producer Jerry Harrison
Company IPS Productions
Distributor Hughes Television Network
Musical Director Terry Gibbs
Host Steve Allen
Regular Jayne Meadows

1314 **Steve Lawrence and Eydie Gorme From This Moment On ... Cole Porter**
The Sentry Collection Presents ABC
Program Type Music/Dance Special
60 minutes. Premiere date: 3/10/77. A tribute to Cole Porter and his music. Special musical material by Larry Grossman.
Producers Gary Smith, Dwight Hemion
Director Dwight Hemion
Writers Harry Crane, Buz Kohan
Musical Director Jack Parnell
Choreographer Norman Maen
Art Director Bryan Holgate
Stars Steve Lawrence, Eydie Gorme
Special Guest Stars Bob Hope, Ethel Merman, Natalia Makarova, Swingle Singers II

1315 **Stick Around**
The ABC Monday Comedy Special ABC
Program Type Comedy Special
30 minutes. Premiere date: 5/30/77. Comedy pi-

lot set in 2055 about a young couple with an out-of-date robot.
Producers Fred Freeman, Lawrence J. Cohen
Company TAT Communications Company Production in association with Humble Productions, Inc.
Director Bill Hobin
Writers Fred Freeman, Lawrence J. Cohen

CAST

Vance Keefer .... Fred McCarren
Elaine Keefer .... Nancy New
Andy .... Andy Kaufman
Earl .... Craig Richard Nelson
Joe Burkus .... Cliff Norton
Ed .... Jeffrey Kramer
Lisa .... Liberty Williams
Woman Customer .... Priscilla Morrill
Man Customer .... Alan Haufrect

1316 **Stocker's Copper**
Piccadilly Circus PBS
Program Type Dramatic Special
90 minutes. Premiere date: 4/19/76. Repeat date: 7/17/77. Dramatization of a 1913 strike in Cornwall, England. Filmed on location in St. Austell, Cornwall, where the strike took place. Program made possible by a grant from Mobil Oil Corporation. Presented by WGBH-TV/Boston; Joan Sullivan, producer.
Producer Graeme McDonald
Company British Broadcasting Corporation
Director Jack Gold
Writer Tom Clarke
Host Jeremy Brett

CAST

Manuel Stocker .... Bryan Marshall
Alice Stocker .... Jane Lapotaire
Herbert Griffith .... Gareth Thomas
Glamorgan Sergeant .... Dominic Allan
Engine Man .... William Moore
Stocker Children .... Angela Billing, Barry Hawken
Cornish P.C. .... Don McKillop
Clayworker .... Harry Littlewood
Vincent .... Tony Caunter
Rev. Booth Coventry .... Malcolm Tierney
Chief Supt. .... Michael Beint

The Stone Killer *see* NBC Saturday Night at the Movies

1317 **Stonestreet**
NBC Movie of the Week NBC
Program Type TV Movie
90 minutes. Premiere date: 1/16/77. Repeat date: 7/10/77. Pilot drama centered on a private investigator. Music by Pat Williams.
Production Executive David J. O'Connell
Producer Leslie Stevens
Company Universal Television in association with NBC-TV
Director Russ Mayberry
Writer Leslie Stevens
Costume Designer George R. Whittaker
Art Director John E. Chilberg II
Set Decorator Peg Cummings

CAST

Liz Stonestreet .... Barbara Eden
Elliot Osborn .... Richard Basehart
Jessica Hilliard .... Joan Hackett
Mrs. Shroeder .... Louise Latham
Arlene .... Elaine Giftos
Eddie Shroeder .... James Ingersoll
Chuck Voit .... Val Avery
Della .... Sally Kirkland
Max Pierce .... Joseph Mascolo
Dale Anderson .... Robert Burton
Erna .... LaWanda Page
Amory Osborn .... Ann Dusenberry

1318 **Stonewall Joe**
Americana PBS
Program Type Documentary/Informational Special
30 minutes. Premiere date: 12/10/76. A profile of country singer Joe Robinson who supports himself by building stone walls. Photographed in black and white. Program made possible by grants from the New York State Council for the Arts and the Corporation for Public Broadcasting.
Producer Michael Marton
Company WMHT-TV/Schenectady, N.Y.
Director Michael Marton
Cinematographer Michael Marton

1319 **Stop the Presses** CBS
Program Type Comedy Special
30 minutes. Premiere date: 7/15/77. Comedy pilot about investigative reporters working on a small New England newspaper. Created by Allan Katz and Don Reo. Music by Dion.
Executive Producer Mark Carliner
Producers Allan Katz, Don Reo
Company Mark Carliner Productions for Viacom Enterprises
Director Joan Darling
Writers Allan Katz, Don Reo

CAST

Adam Brooks .... John Rubinstein
Dave Schuster .... Bryan Gordon
Ed Reynolds .... James Gregory
Herman Simmons .... Allan Rich
Barbara Pinski .... Kit McDonough
Leon Vanderschmidt .... Basil Hoffman
Caleb White .... Leonard Barr
Mary Louise Donovan .... Sharon Farrell

Storm Over Asia *see* PBS Movie Theater

1320 **A Storyteller's Town**
Americana PBS
Program Type Documentary/Informational Special
30 minutes. Premiere date: 3/18/77. A look at Clyde, Ohio, Sherwood Anderson's boyhood home and the setting for "Winesburg, Ohio." Program made possible by grants from the Ohio College Bicentennial Program and the George Gund Foundation.
Producer Patrick Fitzgerald
Company WBGU-TV/Bowling Green, Ohio
Director Patrick Fitzgerald
Writer Gene Dent
Narrator Leonard Slominski

CAST
Sherwood Anderson .... Eric Vaughn

1321 **Strange New World**
The ABC Friday Night Movie ABC
Program Type TV Movie
90 minutes. Premiere date: 7/13/75. Repeat date: 6/3/77. Science fiction drama of three astronauts who return to earth after surviving in suspended animation for 180 years.
Executive Producers Walon Green, Ronald F. Graham
Producer Robert Larson
Company Warner Bros. Television Production
Director Robert Butler
Writers Walon Green, Ronald F. Graham, Al Ramrus

CAST
Capt. Anthony Vico .... John Saxon
Dr. Allison Crowley .... Kathleen Miller
Dr. Scott .... Keene Curtis
The Surgeon .... James Olson
Tana .... Martine Beswick
Sprang .... Reb Brown
Sirus .... Ford Rainey
Badger .... Bill McKinney
Daniel .... Gerrit Graham

1322 **The Strange Possession of Mrs. Oliver**
NBC Movie of the Week NBC
Program Type TV Movie
90 minutes. Premiere date: 2/28/77. Repeat date: 7/24/77. Mystery drama about a woman possessed with the personality of another woman long dead. Filmed on locations in Los Angeles.
Production Executive Robert A. Papazian
Producer Stan Shpetner
Company A Shpetner Production in association with NBC-TV
Director Gordon Hessler
Writer Richard Matheson

CAST
Miriam Oliver .... Karen Black
Greg Oliver .... George Hamilton
Mark .... Robert F. Lyons
Housekeeper .... Lucille Benson
Mrs. Dempsey .... Jean Allison
Saleslady .... Gloria LeRoy

1323 **Strangers in the Homeland**
Under God NBC
Program Type Religious/Cultural Special
60 minutes. Premiere date: 3/21/76. Repeat date: 8/7/77. Original play following the Slater family from 1775 to 1976.
Executive Producer Doris Ann
Producer Martin Hoade
Company NBC Television Religious Programs Unit in association with the National Council of Churches
Director Martin Hoade
Writer Michael de Guzman

CAST
Jane Slater .... Beatrice Straight
William Slater .... James Noble
Arthur Slater .... Gary Cookson
Jonathan Dodge .... Bill Moor
The Speaker .... Clarence Felder
Rev. Hatch .... Roberts Blossom

1324 **The Streets of San Francisco** ABC
Program Type Crime Drama Series
60 minutes. Thursdays. Premiere date: 9/16/72. Fifth season premiere: 9/30/76. Last show: 6/30/77. Police drama set in San Francisco. Based on characters from a novel by Carolyn Weston. Developed for television by Edward Hume.
Executive Producer Quinn Martin
Producer William Robert Yates
Company Quinn Martin Productions
Directors Various
Script Consultant Jack Sowards
Writers Various

CAST
Lt. Mike Stone .... Karl Malden
Insp. Dan Robbins .... Richard Hatch

1325 **The Streets of San Francisco (Late Night)** ABC
Program Type Crime Drama Series
60 minutes. Thursdays/Mondays (as of 1/3/77). Late-night programming of repeat shows of the primetime series. Premiere date: 9/23/76. For credit information, *see* "The Streets of San Francisco."

1326 **The Struggle for Freedom**
NBC Reports NBC
Program Type Documentary/Informational Special
60 minutes. Premiere date: 6/14/77. Report on human rights on the eve of a conference in Belgrade, Yugoslavia assessing the 1975 Helsinki Agreement.
Executive Producer Gordon Manning

Producers Kenneth Donoghue, Thomas Tomizawa
Company NBC News
Director Walter Kravetz
Writers John Dancy, Kenneth Donoghue, Thomas Tomizawa, Garrick Utley
Film Editors Brian Gallagher, Irwin Graf, Mary Ann Martin
Researchers Joan Carrigan, Leslie Redlich
Anchor Garrick Utley
Reporter/Analyst John Dancy

1327 **Studio See** PBS
Program Type Children's Series
30 minutes. Tuesdays. Premiere date: 1/25/77. 26-week magazine-format series for youngsters 10–15 years old created by Jayne Adair and produced at locations throughout the country. Three-four features weekly plus regular "poetry power" and animation segments contributed by children. Series made possible by grants from the Corporation for Public Broadcasting, the Ford Foundation and Public Television Stations.
Executive Producer Gene Upright
Producer Jayne Adair
Company South Carolina Educational Television Network
Supervising Director Hugh Martin

1328 **Stumpers** NBC
Program Type Game/Audience Participation Series
30 minutes. Mondays–Fridays. Premiere date: 10/4/76. Last show: 12/31/76. Word-clue game played by contestants teamed with celebrities.
Executive Producer Lin Bolen
Producer Walt Case
Company Lin Bolen Productions in association with NBC-TV
Director Jeff Goldstein
Host Allen Ludden

1329 **Sugar Bowl** ABC
Program Type Sports Special
Live coverage of the Sugar Bowl football game between the Pittsburgh Panthers and the Georgia Bulldogs from the Superdome in New Orleans, La. 1/1/77.
Executive Producer Roone Arledge
Producer Chuck Howard
Company ABC Sports
Director Andy Sidaris
Play-By-Play Announcer Keith Jackson
Expert Color Commentator Ara Parseghian
Feature Reporter/Sideline Reporter Jim Lampley

1330 **Sugar Time!** ABC
Program Type Comedy Series
30 minutes. Saturdays. Premiere date: 8/13/77. Last show: 9/3/77. Four-part comedy series about three aspiring rock singers in a group called "Sugar" who work at the Tryout Room. Series created by James Komack and developed for television by Hank Bradford. Music supervised by Paul Williams.
Executive Producer James Komack
Producers Hank Bradford, Martin Cohan
Company James Komack Company, Inc.
Directors Bill Hobin, Stan Cutler
Story Editors Iris Rainer, Dawn Aldredge
Writers Various

CAST

Maxx .... Barbi Benton
Diane .... Didi Carr
Maggie .... Marianne Black
Al Marks .... Wynn Irwin
Paul Landson .... Mark Winkworth
Lightning Jack Rappaport .... Charles Fleischer

The Sugarland Express *see* NBC Saturday Night at the Movies

Suicide Run *see* The ABC Sunday Night Movie

Summer Interlude *see* PBS Movie Theater

Summer of '42 *see* The ABC Friday Night Movie

1331 **Summer Semester** CBS
Program Type Educational/Cultural Series
30 minutes/three times a week. 14th season premiere: 5/23/77. Last show: 9/17/77. Two courses 17 weeks in length three times a week. "Latin America: The Restless Colossus" shown Mondays/Wednesdays/Fridays. Produced under the auspices of Bergen Community College in Paramus, N.J. with Dr. Philip C. Dolce as coordinator. "Aging" shown Tuesdays/Thursdays/Saturdays. Produced under the auspices of St. John's University, New York City with Winston L. Kirby as coordinator.
Producer Roy Allen
Company WCBS-TV/New York
Director Roy Allen

1332 **Sun Bowl** CBS
Program Type Sports Special
Three hours. Live coverage of the 42nd Sun Bowl football game between the University of Texas A

Sun Bowl *Continued*
& M Aggies and the University of Florida Gators from El Paso, Tex. 1/2/77.
Company CBS Television Network Sports
Announcer Pat Summerall
Analyst Tom Brookshier

1333 **Sunrise Semester** CBS
Program Type Educational/Cultural Series
30 minutes each day. Monday-Saturday mornings. Premiered locally (WCBS-TV/New York): 9/23/57. Network premiere: 9/22/63. Fall season premiere: 9/20/76. Two courses given each semester by professors at New York University. "Communication, the Invisible Environment" presented by Dr. Neil Postman shown Mondays/Wednesdays/Fridays. "The Novel and Theater of Contemporary France" presented by Prof. Thomas Bishop shown Tuesdays/Thursdays/Saturdays. Spring season premiere: 1/24/77. "Teaching the Learning Disabled" presented by Dr. D. Kim Reid shown Mondays/Wednesdays/Fridays. "Religions and Civilizations of the Near East" presented by Prof. Bernard Lewis shown Tuesdays/Thursdays/Saturdays.
Producer Roy Allen
Company WCBS-TV/New York
Director Roy Allen
Supervisors for New York University Myron Price, Hope Chasin

1334 **The Sunshine Boys** NBC
Program Type Comedy Special
60 minutes. Premiere date: 6/9/77. Comedy pilot about a long-retired team of vaudeville comics who fight each other. Based on the play and feature film by Neil Simon.
Executive Producer Michael Levee
Producer Sam Denoff
Company Ray Stark Productions and MGM Television in association with NBC-TV
Director Robert Moore
Writer Neil Simon

CAST

Willie Clark .... Red Buttons
Al Lewis .... Lionel Stander
Ben Clark .... Michael Durrell
Myrna Navazio .... Bobbie Mitchell
Muriel Green .... Sarina Grant
Ray Banks .... George Wyner
Sylvia Banks .... Barra Grant
Gary Banks .... Philip Tanzani
Bobby Banks .... Tony Sherman
Julio .... Danny Mora
Mrs. Krause .... Bella Bruck
Anita DeVane .... Ann Cooper

The Sunshine Boys (Feature Film) *see* NBC Monday Night at the Movies

1335 **Super Bowl XI** NBC
Program Type Sports Special
Live coverage of the 11th Super Bowl game between the Minnesota Vikings and the Oakland Raiders From Pasadena, Calif. 1/9/77.
Executive Producer Scotty Connal
Company NBC Sports
Announcer Curt Gowdy
Analyst Don Meredith

1336 **Super Bowl Pre-Game Show/Post-Game Show** NBC
Program Type Sports Special
60 minutes/30 minutes. Live coverage of activities preceding and following the 11th Super Bowl from the Rose Bowl in Pasadena, Calif. 1/9/77.
Executive Producer Scotty Connal
Company NBC Sports
Host Lee Leonard
Co-Host Bryant Gumbel
Commentators/Reporters Don Meredith, John Brodie, Len Dawson, Lionel Aldridge, Paul Maguire, Larry Merchant, Barbara Hunter, Tim Ryan

Super Cops *see* CBS Special Film Presentations

1337 **Super Friday** CBS
Program Type Children's Special
90 minutes. Premiere date: 11/26/76. Thanksgiving holiday rebroadcast of three regular shows: "Ark II," "Fat Albert and the Cosby Kids," "Isis." (*See* individual titles for credits.)

1338 **Super Friends** ABC
Program Type Animated Film Series
30 minutes. Saturday mornings. Originally broadcast between 9/73–9/75. Reruns revived between 2/21/76–9/4/76. Re-edited reruns revived as of 12/4/76. Became "The All New Superfriends Hour" during the 1977–78 season. Comedy-adventure about Superman, Batman, Wonder Woman and Aquaman and their adventures with two teenagers, Wendy and Marvin.
Executive Producers William Hanna, Joseph Barbera
Producer Iwao Takamoto
Company Hanna-Barbera Productions
Director Charles A. Nichols
Writers Fred Freiberger, Willie Gilbert, Bernard Kahn, Dick Robbins, Ken Rotcop, Henry Sharp, Arthur Weiss, Marshall Williams
Musical Director Hoyt Curtin
Story Advisor Dr. Haim Ginott
Voices Sherry Alberoni, Norman Alden, Danny Dark, Shannon Farnon, Casey Kasem, Ted

Knight, Olan Soule, John Stephenson, Frank Welker

1339 **Super Night at Forest Hills** CBS
Program Type Music/Comedy/Variety Special
60 minutes. Premiere date: 9/9/77. Entertainment special saluting the sport of tennis. Taped at the West Side Tennis Club in Forest Hills, N.Y. Special musical material by Alan Copeland.
Executive Producer Pierre Cossette
Producer Marty Pasetta
Company Pierre Cossette Productions
Director Marty Pasetta
Writers Buz Kohan, Aubrey Tadman, Garry Ferrier
Musical Director Alan Copeland
Choreographer Alan Johnson
Costume Designer Bill Hargate
Art Director Charles Lisanby
Hosts Sammy Davis, Jr., Sandy Duncan, Andy Williams
Guest Stars Arthur Ashe, Tracy Austin, Foster Brooks, Vitas Gerulaitis, Buddy Hackett, Lainie Kazan, the Keane Brothers, Alan King, Billie Jean King, Ethel Merman, Ilie Nastase, Stan Smith, Virginia Wade, Kelly the Chimp

1340 **Super Night at the Super Bowl** CBS
Program Type Music/Comedy/Variety Special
90 minutes. Premiere date: 1/8/77. A salute to football and Super Bowl XI from Pasadena, California. Live broadcast in the East. Film sequence produced by Stu Bernstein and Eytan Keller. Special musical material by Billy Barnes.
Executive Producer Pierre Cossette
Producer Marty Pasetta
Company Pierre Cossette Productions
Director Marty Pasetta
Writers Buz Kohan, Alan Thicke, Pat McCormick
Musical Director George Wyle
Choreographer Alan Johnson
Costume Designer Bill Hargate
Art Director Ray Klausen
Hosts Sammy Davis, Jr., Elliott Gould, Andy Williams
Guest Stars Jack Albertson, Johnny Bench, the Borden Twins, Natalie Cole, Angie Dickinson, Joe Frazier, Phyllis George, the Marquis Chimps, Ken Norton, Roger Owens, Charley Pride, Don Rickles, Sha-Na-Na, O. J. Simpson, University of Southern California Marching Band, the Sylvers, John Wayne

1341 **Super Visions** PBS
Program Type Comedy Series
4–10 minutes (approximately). Thursdays. Premiere date: 10/21/76. Satiric filler sketches about television following showings of "Visions."
Company TVTV Productions

1342 **The Superstars** ABC
Program Type Limited Sports Series
90 minutes. Sundays. Series premiered in 1973 (with men only). Fifth season premiere: 1/2/77. Last show of season: 3/27/77. Ten programs pitting championship athletes against each other in competitions outside their specialties. "The Superstars (male athletes—five programs): 1/2/77–1/30/77 plus two-hour final 2/20/77; "The Women Superstars" (third season—one program): 2/6/77; "The Superteams" (third season —three programs): 2/27/77–3/13/77; "The World Superstars" (first season—one program): 3/27/77.
Executive Producer Roone Arledge
Producer Don Ohlmeyer
Company ABC Sports
Director Larry Kamm
Host Keith Jackson/Al Michaels (women's competition only)
Expert Commentators Reggie Jackson, Bruce Jenner/Hilary Hilton, Andrea Kirby (women's competition only)

Support Your Local Gunfighter *see* The CBS Friday Night Movies

Survive! *see* The ABC Sunday Night Movie

1343 **Susan and Sam**
Comedy Time NBC
Program Type Comedy Special
30 minutes. Premiere date: 7/13/77. Comedy pilot about magazine reporters in love.
Co-Producers Alan Alda, Mark Merson
Company Helix Production
Director Jay Sandrich
Writer Alan Alda

CAST

Susan	Christine Belford
Sam	Robert Foxworth
Doug Braden	Lee Bergere
Hilly	Alan Oppenheimer
Percy	Jack Bannon
Felix	Maurice Sneed
Barbara	Christina Hart
Waiter	Dick Balduzzi

1344 Suzy Visits: Ol' Blue Eyes and Ol' Brown Eyes . . .Frank Sinatra and Muhammad Ali NBC

Program Type Documentary/Informational Special

60 minutes. Premiere date: 5/24/77. Interviews with Frank Sinatra and Muhammad Ali.

Producer Lucy Jarvis

Company Creative Projects, Inc. Production in association with NBC-TV

Interviewer Aileen Mehle (Suzy Knickerbocker)

1345 S.W.A.T. ABC

Program Type Crime Drama Series

60 minutes. Fridays. Late-night repeats of series that ran from 2/24/75–6/29/76. Premiere date: 9/24/76. Went off the air 4/15/77; returned Thursdays as of 5/5/77.

Executive Producers Aaron Spelling, Leonard Goldberg

Company Spelling/Goldberg Productions

Directors Various

Writers Various

CAST

Lt. Dan "Hondo" Harrelson .... Steve Forrest
Jim Street .... Robert Urich
Sgt. David "Deacon" Kay .... Rod Perry
Dominic Luca .... Mark Shera
T. J. McCabe .... James Coleman

1346 Sweet Hostage

The ABC Friday Night Movie ABC

Program Type TV Movie

Two hours. Premiere date: 10/10/75. Repeat date: 4/15/77. Based on the novel "Welcome to Xanadu" by Nathaniel Benchley. Filmed entirely on location in New Mexico. "Strangers on a Carousel" music by George Barrie; lyrics by Bob Larimer; sung by Steven Michael Schwartz. Music score by Luchi De Jesus.

Executive Producer George Barrie

Producers Richard E. Lyons, Sidney D. Balkin

Company Brut Productions

Director Lee Philips

Writer Edward Hume

Art Director Phil Barber

CAST

Doris Mae Withers .... Linda Blair
Leonard Hatch .... Martin Sheen
Mrs. Withers .... Jeanne Cooper
Sheriff Emmet .... Lee de Broux
Mr. Withers .... Bert Remsen
Harry Fox .... Dehl Berti
Mr. Smathers .... Al Hopson
Hank Smathers .... Bill Sterchi
Juan .... Roberto Valentino DeLeon
Tom Martinez .... Michael C. Eiland
Dry Goods Clerk .... Mary Michael Carnes
Liquor Store Proprietor .... Don Hann
Hospital Attendant .... Ross Elder
Man in Bungalow .... Chris Williams

1347 Sweet Land of Liberty

Americana PBS

Program Type Documentary/Informational Special

30 minutes. Premiere date: 1/7/77. Repeat date: 7/31/77. Award-winning documentary focusing on the fight for gay legal and civil rights in small American communities.

Executive Producer Joyce Campbell

Producer Mike Kirk

Company KUID-TV/Moscow, Idaho

Cinematographer Tom Coggins

1348 Switch CBS

Program Type Crime Drama Series

60 minutes. Tuesdays/Sundays (as of 1/16/77)/Saturdays (as of 7/23/77). Premiere date: 9/9/75. Second season premiere: 9/21/76. Crime drama about a retired cop and an ex-con man in private eye partnership. Created by Glen A. Larson.

Executive Producer Matthew Rapf

Supervising Producer James McAdams

Producer Jack Laird

Company Universal Television in association with Glen Larson Productions

Directors Various

Executive Story Consultant Jack Guss

Story Editor Stephen Kandel

Writers Various

CAST

Pete Ryan .... Robert Wagner
Frank "Mac" MacBride .... Eddie Albert
Malcolm .... Charlie Callas
Maggie .... Sharon Gless

1349 Sybil

The Big Event/NBC Monday Night at the Movies NBC

Program Type Dramatic Special

Four hours. Premiere dates: 11/14/76 and 11/15/76 (two hours each night). Drama of a real woman with 16 personalities. Based on the book by Flora Rheta Schreiber about the experiences of Dr. Cornelia B. Wilbur. Music by Leonard Rosenman; lyrics by Alan Bergman and Marilyn Bergman.

Executive Producers Peter Dunne, Philip Capice

Producer Jacqueline Babbin

Company Lorimar Productions, Inc. in association with NBC-TV

Director Daniel Petrie

Writer Stewart Stern

CAST

Dr. Cornelia B. Wilbur .... Joanne Woodward
Sybil .... Sally Field
Richard .... Brad Davis
Hattie .... Martine Bartlett
Frieda Dorsett .... Jane Hoffman
Dr. Quinoness .... Charles Lane

Grandma Dorsett .... Jessamine Milner
Willard Dorsett .... William Prince

1350 **Sylvester and Tweety** CBS
Program Type Animated Film Series
30 minutes. Saturday mornings. Premiere date: 9/11/76. Last show: 9/3/77. Animated cartoon classics about the cat and bird couple from the Warner Bros. library
Company Warner Bros., Inc.
Voices Mel Blanc

1351 **Synthesis** PBS
Program Type Music/Dance Special
30 minutes. Premiere date: 10/6/76. Concert of contemporary music performed on electronic synthesizers. Program made possible by a grant from the Ohio Educational Television Network.
Executive Producer David B. Liroff
Producer John Harnack
Company WOUB-TV/Athens, Ohio
Director John Harnack
Performer Tom Piggott

1352 **Szysznyk** CBS
Program Type Limited Series
30 minutes. Mondays. Premiere date: 8/1/77. Last show: 9/5/77. Six-week comedy summer series about an ex-Marine sergeant who is the playground supervisor at the Northeast Community Center in Washington, D.C. Created by Jim Mulligan and Ron Landry. Music by Doug Gilmore.
Executive Producer Jerry Weintraub
Producers Rich Eustis, Michael Elias
Company Four's Company Productions
Director Peter Bonerz
Writers Jim Mulligan, Ron Landry, Michael Elias
Costume Designer Bill Belew
Art Director Ken Johnson
Consultant Al Rogers

CAST

Nick Szysznyk .... Ned Beatty
Ms. Harrison .... Olivia Cole
Sandi Chandler .... Susan Lanier
Leonard Kriegler .... Leonard Barr
Ralph .... Jarrod Johnson
Fortwengler .... Barry Miller
Tony La Placa .... Scott Colomby
Ray Gun .... Thomas Carter

1353 **Tabitha**
Special Comedy Presentation ABC
Program Type Comedy Special
30 minutes. Premiere date: 5/7/77. Comedy pilot about the grown-up daughter of Samantha, the witch of "Bewitched." Special effects by Robert Peterson.
Executive Producer Jerry Mayer
Producer Robert Stambler
Company Columbia Pictures Television
Director Bruce Bilson
Writer Jerry Mayer
Art Directors Ross Bellah, Robert Peterson

CAST

Tabitha .... Lisa Hartman
Paul .... Robert Urich
Marvin .... Mel Stewart
Adam .... David Ankrum
Aunt Minerva .... Karen Morrow
Roger .... Barry Van Dyke
Andrew .... Eric Server
Sherry .... Timothy Blake

1354 **Tail Gunner Joe**
The Big Event NBC
Program Type Dramatic Special
Three hours. Premiere date: 2/6/77. A dramatization of the rise and fall of Sen. Joseph R. McCarthy.
Producer George Eckstein
Company Universal Television in association with NBC-TV
Director Jud Taylor
Writer Lane Slate
Musical Director Billy May
Art Director Lawrence G. Paull

CAST

Joseph McCarthy .... Peter Boyle
Joseph Welch .... Burgess Meredith
Sen. Margaret Chase Smith .... Patricia Neal
Paul Cunningham .... John Forsythe
Logan .... Heather Menzies
Sylvester .... Ned Beatty
Eliot .... Charles Cioffi
Jean Kerr .... Karen Carlson
Pres. Eisenhower .... Andrew Duggan
Roy Cohn .... George Wyner
Mrs. DeCamp .... Jean Stapleton
Drew Pearson .... Robert F. Simon
Pres. Truman .... Robert Symonds
Sen. Symington .... Lin McCarthy
Sen. Lucas .... Philip Abbott
Middleton .... Wesley Addy
Armitage .... Henry Jones
Gen. Lamkin .... John Randolph
Mrs. Gates .... Kelly Jean Peters

The Taking of Pelham One Two Three
see CBS Special Film Presentations

1355 **Tales of the Unexpected** NBC
Program Type Drama Series
60 minutes. Wednesdays. Premiere date: 2/2/77. Last show: 3/13/77 (two-hour special). One extra episode seen 8/17/77. Suspense anthology series.
Executive Producer Quinn Martin
Producer John Wilder
Company Quinn Martin Productions in association with NBC-TV

Tales of the Unexpected *Continued*
Directors Various
Writers Various
Narrator William Conrad

1356 **The Taming of the Shrew**
Theater in America/Great Performances PBS
Program Type Dramatic Special
Two hours. Premiere date: 11/10/76. Repeat date: 8/24/77. The American Conservatory Theatre of San Francisco in a commedia dell'arte production of the comedy by William Shakespeare. Music by Lee Hoiby. Program made possible by grants from Exxon Corporation, the Corporation for Public Broadcasting, the Ford Foundation and Public Television Stations.
Executive Producer Jac Venza
Producer Ken Campbell
Company WNET-TV/New York
Directors William Ball, Kirk Browning
Costume Designer Robert Fletcher
Scenic Designer Ralph Funicello
CAST
Katherina .... Fredi Olster
Petruchio .... Marc Singer
Baptista .... William Peterson
Bianca .... Sandra Shotwell
Gremio .... Raye Birk
Grumio .... Ronald Boussom
Tranio .... Rick Hamilton
Biondello .... Daniel Kern
Lucentio .... Stephen St. Paul
Hortensio .... James R. Winker

1357 **The Taming of the Shrew (Ballet)** PBS
Program Type Music/Dance Special
90 minutes. Premiere date: 3/76. Repeat date: 3/77. The Stuttgart Ballet Company in "The Taming of the Shrew" based on the play by William Shakespeare with music by Domenico Scarlatti arranged by Kurt-Heinz Stolze.
Company Zweites Deutsches Ferensehen (ZDF), Stuttgart
Director Herbert Junkers
Conductor Bernhard Kontarsky
Choreographer John Cranko
CAST
Katharina .... Marcia Haydee
Petrucchio .... Richard Cragun
Bianca .... Brigit Keil
Baptista .... Gerd Praast
Lucentio .... Jan Stripling
Gremio .... Egon Madsen

1358 **The Tapestry/Circles**
Visions PBS
Program Type Dramatic Special
90 minutes. Premiere date: 12/30/76. Two plays about ambitious black women and the pressures to make them conform. Program made possible by grants from the Ford Foundation, the National Endowment for the Arts and the Corporation for Public Broadcasting.
Producer Barbara Schultz
Company KCET-TV/Los Angeles
Director Maya Angelou
Writer Alexis DeVeaux
Production Designer Ralph Holmes

The Tapestry
CAST
Jet .... Gloria Jones Schultz
Axis .... Glynn Turman
Lavender .... Ebony Wright
Rev. Paradise .... Alvin Childress
Momma .... Ruth Beckford-Smith
Daddie/Man in Legal Office .... Raymond Allen
Sister Lott/Woman in Legal Office .... Lareyn Carole
Prof. Wane/Other Man .... Rai Tasco
Woman .... Tamu

Circles
CAST
Retha .... Tamu
Mrs. Burden .... Ruth Beckford-Smith
Jeremiah .... Raymond Allen

1359 **Tarzan—Lord of the Jungle** CBS
Program Type Animated Film Series
30 minutes. Saturday mornings. Premiere date: 9/11/76. Animated childrens series based on the books by Edgar Rice Burroughs.
Executive Producers Lou Scheimer, Norm Prescott
Producer Don Christensen
Company Filmation Associates
Writers Chuck Menville, Len Janson
Animation Director Don Christensen
VOICES
Tarzan .... Robert Ridgely

1360 **Tattletales** CBS
Program Type Game/Audience Participation Series
30 minutes. Mondays-Fridays. Premiere date: 2/18/74. Continuous. Three guest celebrity couples each week winning cash prizes divided among the studio audience.
Executive Producer Ira Skutch
Producer Paul Alter
Company Goodson-Todman Productions
Director Paul Alter
Host Bert Convy
Announcer Gene Wood

1361 **The Ted Knight Musical Comedy Variety Special Special** CBS
Program Type Music/Comedy/Variety Special
60 minutes. Premiere date: 11/30/76. A recreaction of a visit by Ted Knight to his home of Terryville, Conn.

Executive Producer Ned Shankman
Producer Bob Finkel
Company Kono Productions
Director Sidney Smith
Writers Herbert Baker, Mike Marmer, Stan Burns
Musical Director Peter Matz
Choreographer Tom Hansen
Costume Designer Bill Belew
Art Director Ray Klausen
Star Ted Knight (as Ted Baxter)
Guest Stars Edward Asner, Fred MacMurray, Rue McClanahan, Ethel Merman, Phil Silvers, Loretta Swit
Guests Robbie Rist, Joe Ross, Claude Stroud

1362 **The Television Critics Circle Awards** CBS
Program Type Parades/Pageants/Awards Special
Two hours. Live coverage of the first Television Critics Circle Awards from KTTV-TV/Los Angeles 4/11/77. Special musical material by Ken Welch and Mitzi Welch.
Executive Producer David Susskind
Producers Gary Smith, Dwight Hemion
Company Talent Associates, Ltd.
Director Dwight Hemion
Writers Marty Farrell, Pat Proft, Lennie Ripps
Musical Director Ian Fraser
Choreographer Ron Field
Costume Designer Frank Thompson
Art Director Charles Lisanby
Hosts Beverly Sills, Steve Lawrence
Performers/Presenters Jane Alexander, Ann-Margret, Edward Asner, Ken Berry, LeVar Burton, Diahann Carroll, Sandy Duncan, Edward Herrmann, Harvey Korman, Louise Lasser, Linda Lavin, Jean Marsh, Mary Tyler Moore, Lou Rawls, Shields and Yarnell, Neil Simon, Ben Vereen

1363 **Television: For Better or For Worse** PBS
Program Type Documentary/Informational Special
30 minutes. Premiere date: 5/13/77. The future of television discussed by industry executives. Special drawn from the book "Television: Ethics For Hire" by Dr. Robert S. Alley. Program made possible by a grant from the Virginia Endowment for the Humanities and Public Policy.
Producer Dr. Robert S. Alley
Company WCVE-TV/Richmond, Va.
Director Ernest Skinner
Cinematographers Ernest Skinner, Robert Bruce
Host Dr. Robert S. Alley

1364 **Television Grows Up** ABC
Program Type Documentary/Informational Special
15 minutes. Premiere date: 9/6/77. A look at television in a changing world as seen in ABC programming.
Producers Larry Sullivan, Harry Marx
Company Sullivan and Marx, Inc.
Host Dick Van Patten

1365 **Tell Me If Anything Ever Was Done** PBS
Program Type Documentary/Informational Special
60 minutes. Premiere date: 1/4/77. Repeat date: 6/20/77. A look at the scientific contributions of Leonardo da Vinci. Program made possible by grants from the Arthur Vining Davis Foundation and Mobil Oil Corporation.
Producer Adrian Malone
Company WGBH-TV/Boston and the British Broadcasting Corporation
Director Adrian Malone
Writer Jacob Bronowski
Host Jacob Bronowski

The Ten Commandments *see* The ABC Sunday Night Movie.

1366 **Ten Who Dared**
Mobil Showcase Presentation Syndicated
Program Type Limited Series
60 minutes. Weekly. Premiere date: 1/77. Ten-week series of docu-dramas filmed on location around the world recreating famous explorations.
Producer Michael Latham
Company British Broadcasting Corporation in cooperation with Time-Life Films
Distributor SFM Media Services
Directors Various
Writers Various
Host Anthony Quinn

CAST

Christopher Columbus .... Carlos Ballesteos
Francisco Pizarro .... Francisco Cordova
James Cook .... Dennis Burgess
Alexander von Humboldt .... Matthias Fuchs
Jedediah Smith .... Richard Clark
Robert Burke .... Martin Shaw
William Wills .... John Bell
Henry Morton Stanley .... Sean Lynch
Charles Doughty .... Paul Chapman
Mary Kingsley .... Penelope Lee
Roald Amundsen .... Per Theodore Haugen

1367 **Tennessee Williams' South** PBS
Program Type Documentary/Informational Special
80 minutes. Premiere date: 12/76. Repeat date: 8/77. Documentary about the south of Tennessee Williams plus excerpts from his plays
Producer Harry Rasky
Company Canadian Broadcasting Corporation
Distributor Eastern Educational Television Network
Director Harry Rasky
Performers Burl Ives, Colleen Dewhurst, Jessica Tandy, Michael York, John Colicos, Maureen Stapleton, William Hutt, Tennessee Williams

The Terminal Man *see* The CBS Friday Night Movies

1368 **Terraces**
NBC Monday Night at the Movies NBC
Program Type TV Movie
90 minutes. Premiere date: 6/27/77. Dramatic pilot about residents who share adjoining terraces in a high rise apartment building.
Executive Producer Charles Fries
Company Charles Fries Productions in association with NBC-TV
Director Lila Garrett
Writers Lila Garrett, George Kirgo

CAST

Dr. Roger Cabe .... Lloyd Bochner
Chalan Turner .... Julie Newmar
Gregg Loomis .... Bill Gerber
Julie Borden .... Kit McDonough
Beth Loomis .... Eliza Garrett
Alex Bengston .... James Phipps
Roberta Robbins .... Jane Dulo
Martin Robbins .... Arny Freeman
Dorothea Cabe .... Lola Albright
Steve .... Timothy Thomerson

1369 **Testimony of Two Men** Syndicated
Program Type Limited Series
Six hours. Premiere date: 5/77. Dramatization of the novel by Taylor Caldwell about two brothers from Hambledon, Pa. in the second half of the 19th century.
Producer Jack Laird
Company MCA Television
Distributor MCA Television
Directors Larry Yust, Leo Penn
Writers William Hanley, James M. Miller, Jennifer Miller

CAST

Jonathan Ferrier .... David Birney
Harald Ferrier .... David Huffman
Martin Eaton .... Steve Forrest
Marjorie/Hilda Eaton .... Barbara Parkins
Adrian Ferrier .... William Shatner
Kenton Campion .... J. D. Cannon
Jeremiah Hadley .... Cameron Mitchell
Jonas Witherby .... Ray Milland
Mavis Eaton .... Linda Purl
Jenny Heger .... Laurie Prange
Howard Best .... Barry Brown
Flora Eaton .... Margaret O'Brien
Myrtle Heger .... Kathleen Nolan
Louis Hedler .... Tom Bosley
Father McNulty .... Randolph Mantooth
Francis Campion .... Kario Salem
Priscilla Madden .... Devon Ericson
Father McGuire .... Dan Dailey
David Paxton .... Leonard Frey
Peter Heger .... Theodore Bikel
Jim Spaulding .... Ralph Bellamy
Amelia Forster .... Inga Swenson
Jon (age 10) .... Paul David
Mavis (age 6) .... Missy Gold
Jerome Eaton .... John de Lancie
Henrietta Campion .... DeAnn Mears

1370 **Teton: Decision and Disaster**
Documentary Showcase PBS
Program Type Documentary/Informational Special
60 minutes. Premiere date: 2/18/77. An examination of the political and economic circumstances surrounding the contruction of the Teton Dam Project which collapsed on June 5, 1976. Program made possible by a grant from the Rocky Mountain Public Broadcasting Network Program Fund.
Producers Mike Kirk, Mindy Cameron
Company KAID-TV/Boise, Idaho and KUID-TV/Moscow, Idaho
Director Mike Kirk
Cinematographers Tom Coggins, Erich Korte
Film Editor Tom Coggins
Narrator Joe Stanosch

1371 **Texaco Presents Bob Hope's All-Star Comedy Spectacular From Lake Tahoe** NBC
Program Type Music/Comedy/Variety Special
90 minutes. Premiere date: 1/21/77. Comedy/variety special taped at various locations in Lake Tahoe.
Executive Producer Bob Hope
Producer Sheldon Keller
Co-Producer Jack Watson
Company Hope Enterprises
Director Dick McDonough
Writers Charles Lee, Gig Henry, Jeffrey Barron, Katherine Green, Howard Albrecht, Sol Weinstein, Sheldon Keller
Musical Director Les Brown
Star Bob Hope
Guest Stars Ann-Margret, Charo, Mac Davis, Sammy Davis, Jr., Dean Martin
Special Guest Appearances Muhammad Ali, Howard Cosell

1372 **Texaco Presents Bob Hope's All-Star Comedy Tribute to Vaudeville** NBC
Program Type Music/Comedy/Variety Special
90 minutes. Premiere date: 3/25/77. A salute to comedy, music and personalities of vaudeville.
Executive Producer Bob Hope
Producer Sheldon Keller
Company Hope Enterprises
Director Dick McDonough
Writers Charles Lee, Gig Henry, Jeffrey Barron, Katherine Green, Howard Albrecht, Sol Weinstein, Sheldon Keller
Musical Director Les Brown
Star Bob Hope
Guest Stars Lucille Ball, Jack Albertson, Bernadette Peters, The Captain & Tennille, Vivian Reed

1373 **Texaco Presents Bob Hope's Comedy Christmas Special** NBC
Program Type Music/Comedy/Variety Special
90 minutes. Premiere date: 12/13/76. A holiday season musical/variety special.
Executive Producer Bob Hope
Producer Sheldon Keller
Co-Producer Jack Watson
Company Hope Enterprises
Director Dick McDonough
Writers Charles Lee, Gig Henry, Jeffrey Barron, Katherine Green, Howard Albrecht, Sol Weinstein
Musical Director Les Brown
Costume Designer Sal Anthony
Star Bob Hope
Guest Stars John Wayne, Neil Sedaka, Dyan Cannon, Lola Falana, Kate Jackson
Featured Guests Associated Press All-American Football Team, Dorothy Benham, Diane Ramaker, Rebecca Ann Reid, John Robinson, Bo Schembechler

1374 **Texaco Presents Bob Hope's World of Comedy** NBC
Program Type Music/Comedy/Variety Special
Two hours. Premiere date: 10/29/76. Highlights of 26 years of Bob Hope television shows.
Executive Producer Bob Hope
Producer Jack Haley, Jr.
Company Hope Enterprises
Director Jack Haley, Jr.
Writers Charles Lee, Gig Henry, Jeffrey Barron, Katherine Green
Musical Director Les Brown
Art Director E. Jay Krause
Star Bob Hope
Guest Stars Lucille Ball, Don Rickles, Norman Lear, Neil Simon, Big Bird

1375 **Texas 200** CBS
Program Type Sports Special
Two hours. Live coverage of the Texas 200 from the Texas World Speedway in College Station, Texas 7/31/77.
Producer Bernie Hoffman
Company CBS Television Network Sports
Director Bernie Hoffman
Announcer Ken Squier

1376 **That Was the Year That Was**
The Big Event NBC
Program Type Music/Comedy/Variety Special
90 minutes. Premiere date: 12/26/76. A satirical look at 1976. Music composed by Joe Raposo. Film sequences by Mel Stuart and Gary Weis.
Executive Producers Irv Wilson, Herman Rush, Burt Shevelove
Producer Frank Badami
Company A Rush/Wilson Production
Director Don Mischer
Writing Supervisors Tony Geiss, Tom Meehan
Writers Art Buchwald, Jules Feiffer, Buck Henry, Gloria Steinem, Mike Barrie, Jim Mulholland, Tony Geiss, Herb Hartig, Harvey Jacobs, Tom Meehan, Jane Richmond, Lynn Roth, Jonathan Reynolds
Conductor Joe Raposo
Production Designers Eugene Lee, Franne Lee
Creative Consultant Diane Silver
Historian Walter Pincus
Hosts Blythe Danner, Buck Henry, Robert Klein, Brenda Vaccaro
Guest Stars Art Buchwald, James Coco, William Daniels, Charles Durning, Jules Feiffer, Ruth Gordon, Tammy Grimes, George S. Irving, Melba Moore, Edwin Newman, Estelle Parsons, Rex Reed, Cyril Ritchard, Gloria Steinem

That's Entertainment! *see* CBS Special Film Presentations

1377 **Theater in America**
Great Performances PBS
Program Type Drama Series
Times vary (generally two hours). Wednesdays. Premiere date: 1/23/74. Fourth series premiere: 10/13/76. Classic and contemporary plays performed by different American repertory companies. Plays shown during the 1976–77 season are: "Ah, Wilderness!" "Beyond the Horizon," "Cyrano de Bergerac," "Eccentricities of a Nightingale," "End of Summer," "Enemies," "The First Breeze of Summer," "The Mound Builders," "The Prince of Homburg," "Sea Marks," "Secret Service," "The Taming of the Shrew," "Waiting for Godot," "Zalmen or the

Theater in America *Continued*
Madness of God." (*See* individual titles for credits.)

1378 **There's Always Room** CBS
Program Type Comedy Special
30 minutes. Premiere date: 4/24/77. Comedy pilot set in a Los Angeles rooming house. Music by Bill Conti.
Executive Producers Robert W. Christiansen, Rick Rosenberg
Producer Michael Leeson
Company Chris-Rose Productions, Inc.
Director Robert Moore
Writer Michael Leeson
Art Director Ken Johnson

CAST

Madelyn Fairchild	Maureen Stapleton
Stewart Dennis	Conrad Janis
Annette Enderby	Debbie Zipp
Bob Enderby	Barry Nelson
Valerie	Leland Palmer
Buck Burke	Roy Applegate
Mr. McRaven	Woodrow Chambliss

1379 **These Faces I've Seen**
Americana PBS
Program Type Documentary/Informational Special
30 minutes. Premiere date: 5/20/77. A look at the Puerto Rican community of Springfield, Massachusetts. Program made possible in part by a grant from the Massachusetts Foundation for Humanities and Public Policy.
Producer Daniel Kain
Company WGBY-TV/Springfield, Mass.
Director Daniel Kain
Cinematographer Kirk Smallman

They Call Me Mister Tibbs *see* The CBS Friday Night Movies

They Came to Rob Las Vegas *see* NBC Saturday Night at the Movies

1380 **They Said It With Music: Yankee Doodle to Ragtime** CBS
Program Type Music/Dance Special
Two hours. Premiere date: 7/4/77. Musical salute to America and American songwriters. Created and conceived by Goddard Lieberson. Film and animation sequences by Jerome Rosenfeld.
Executive Producer Goddard Lieberson
Producer Bob Henry
Director Bob Henry
Writers Goddard Lieberson, Max Wilk
Musical Director Fred Karlin
Choreographer Rob Iscove
Costume Designer Bill Belew
Art Directors Romain Johnston, John Dapper
Set Decorator Robert Checci
Animation Director Stan Smith
Music Researcher Fred Karlin
Stars Bernadette Peters, Tony Randall, Jason Robards, Jean Stapleton, Flip Wilson
Guests Ladd Anderson, Robert Babb, Teddy Buckner and His Group, Tammi Bula, Michael Dees, Avril M. Chown, Paul De Korte, Art Evans, Donna Fein, Guy Finley, Kathy Gale, Tammy Glenn, Leeyan Granger, Bessie Griffin, Jimmy Griffin, Helen Hudson, Marty Kaniger, Kathleen Kernohan, Bill Lee, Jay Meyer, Thurl Ravenscroft, Vi Redd

1381 **The Thin Edge** PBS
Program Type Educational/Cultural Series
60 minutes. Monday mornings. Premiere date: 3/31/75. Series repeats shown from 11/8/76. Five programs on mental health covering depression, aggression, guilt, anxiety and sexuality. Series made possible by a grant from Bristol Myers Company.
Executive Producer David Prowitt
Company WNET Science Program Group/New York
Director Al Miselow
Host David Prowitt

1382 **A Third Testament** PBS
Program Type Educational/Cultural Series
60 minutes. Sundays. Premiere date: 3/28/76. Series repeat began 1/2/77. Six-part series examining the lives and writings of six men of faith to determine whether a modern Biblical "third testament" exists. Programs focus on St. Augustine, Blaise Pascal, William Blake, Soren Kierkegaard, Leo Tolstoy and Dietrich Bonhoeffer. Funded by the Arthur Vining Davis Foundations and the Lilly Endowment, Inc. Presented by KCET-TV/Los Angeles.
Producers Richard Nielsen, Pat Ferns
Company Time-Life Films, the Canadian Broadcasting Corporation, and Societe Radio-Canada
Writer Malcolm Muggeridge
Host Malcolm Muggeridge

1383 **A Thirst in the Garden**
Americana PBS
Program Type Documentary/Informational Special
30 minutes. Premiere date: 3/11/77. Repeat date: 8/28/77. Award-winning film examining the plight of Mexican-American farmworkers in the Lower Rio Grande Valley who exist without safe drinking water.

Producer Steve Singer
Company KERA-TV/Dallas-Fort Worth
Cinematographer Travis Rhodes
Film Editor Travis Rhodes
Reporter Steve Singer

1384 **This Britain: Heritage of the Sea**
National Geographic Special PBS
Program Type Documentary/Informational Special
60 minutes. Premiere date: 12/9/75. Repeat date: 5/17/77. Documentary special based on the book "This England" by the National Geographic Society. Program funded by a grant from Gulf Oil Corporation and presented by WQED-TV/Pittsburgh.
Executive Producer Dennis B. Kane
Producer Terry Sanders
Company National Geographic Society in association with Wolper Productions
Director Terry Sanders
Writer Nicolas Noxon
Narrator Richard Basehart

1385 **This Far By Faith** PBS
Program Type Documentary/Informational Special
60 minutes. Premiere date: 2/22/77. Repeat date: 6/27/77. Special tracing the evolution of the black church in America. Filmed in Los Angeles, New York and Louisiana. Presented by KCET-TV/Los Angeles. Program made possible by a grant from American Telephone and Telegraph Company.
Executive Producer Chris Petersen
Producers Brock Peters, Alan Belkin
Company UniWorld Group, Inc., New York and the Petersen Company, Los Angeles
Director Eric Karson
Musical Director Coleridge-Taylor Perkinson
Narrator Brock Peters
Guests/Performers Roscoe Lee Browne, Beah Richards, Glynn Turman, the Edwin Hawkins Singers, Carmen de Lavallade, the Louis Cotrell Heritage Hall Jazz Band, Donald Byrd, the Grant African Methodist Episcopal Church Choir, Geoffrey Holder, James Baldwin, Jacob Lawrence

1386 **This Is My Son** NBC
Program Type Religious/Cultural Special
60 minutes. Premiere date: 6/19/77. Drama about a family's struggle to adjust to their retarded son.
Producer Doris Ann
Company NBC Television Religious Programs Unit in association with the National Council of Churches
Director Lynwood King
Writer Allan Sloane
Costume Designer George Drew
Production Designer Leon Munier
Consultant Emily Perl Kingsley

CAST

Emily Kingston	Carolee Campbell
Jay Kingston	Don Gantry
Joe	Glenn Zachar
Jennifer	Taryn Grimes
Doctor	Maurice Copeland
Fathers	Joel Colodner, Michael Sedgwick
Interns	George Patterson, William Schultz
Nurse	Elinor Mays

1387 **This Is the Life** Syndicated
Program Type Religious/Cultural Series
30 minutes. Weekly. Premiere date: 9/52. 25th season premiere: 9/76. Dramatic anthology series.
Producer Ardon Albrecht
Company Chaparral Productions and Lutheran Television
Directors Various
Writers Various

1388 **Thomas Hart Benton's "The Sources of Country Music"**
Americana PBS
Program Type Documentary/Informational Special
30 minutes. Premiere date: 5/27/77. A chronicle of the creation of the last major work of the artist, "The Sources of Country Music." Program presented by KCPT-TV/Kansas City, Missouri and made possible by grants from the Kansas City Life Insurance Company, the National Endowment for the Arts, and the Corporation for Public Broadcasting.
Producer John Altman, Mary Nelson
Company Pentacle Productions, Inc.

Thoroughly Modern Millie *see* Special Movie Presentation

1389 **Three American Goldsmiths** PBS
Program Type Documentary/Informational Special
30 minutes. Premiere date: 12/15/76. An examination of the work of Mary Scheer, William Neumann and Heikki Seppa.
Producer Joseph Ordos
Company KTCA-TV/Minneapolis-St. Paul
Cinematographer Paul Eide
Film Editor Paul Eide
Narrator Joseph Ordos

1390 **Three Artists in the Northwest** PBS
Program Type Documentary/Informational Special
30 minutes. Premiere date: 3/1/77. The words and visions of painter Guy Anderson, sculptor George Tsutakawa and poet Theodore Roethke featuring the music of Alan Hovhaness. Roethke poetry read by Roberta Byrd Barr. Program made possible by grants from the Washington State Arts Commission, the National Endowment for the Arts, the Members of Nine and the Corporation for Public Broadcasting.
Producer Jean Walkinshaw
Company KCTS-TV/Seattle
Cinematographer Wayne Sourbeer

1391 **Three By Balanchine With the New York City Ballet**
Great Performances PBS
Program Type Music/Dance Special
60 minutes. Premiere date: 5/21/75. Repeat date: 7/31/77. Taped in Europe in 1973 featuring three works choreographed by George Balanchine: "Serenade," "Tarantella," "Duo Concertant." Music played by the Orf Symphony Orchestra and danced by the New York City Ballet. Piano solo performed by Gordon Boelzner. Program made possible by a grant from Exxon Corporation. Presented by WNET-TV/New York.
Executive Producer Jac Venza
Coordinating Producer Emile Ardolino
Producer Dr. Reiner E. Mortiz
Company RM Productions in cooperation with Unitel
Director Hugo Niebeling
Conductor Robert Irving
Choreographer George Balanchine
Guest Artists Peter Martins, Kay Mazzo, Patricia McBride, Edward Villella

1392 **3 Girls 3** NBC
Program Type Limited Series
60 minutes. Wednesdays. First show: 3/30/77. Three more shows seen between 6/15/77–6/29/77. Musical-variety mini-series about a trio determined to make it in show business. Regular feature: "Singles" spot.
Executive Producers Gary Smith, Dwight Hemion
Producers Kenny Solms, Gail Parent
Company 3 Girls 3 Productions, Inc.
Directors Tony Mordente (first show)/Tim Kiley
Head Writers Kenny Solms, Gail Parent
Musical Director Marvin Laird
Choreographer Alan Johnson
Stars Debbie Allen, Ellen Foley, Mimi Kennedy

1393 **The Three Sisters**
Classic Theatre: The Humanities in Drama PBS
Program Type Dramatic Special
2 1/2 hours. Premiere date: 12/4/75. Repeat date: 4/28/77. 1901 Russian classic by Anton Chekhov. Program made possible by grants from the National Endowment for the Humanities and Mobil Oil Corporation. Presented by WGBH-TV/Boston; Joan Sullivan, producer.
Producer Gerald Savory
Company British Broadcasting Corporation
Director Cedric Messina
Writer Anton Chekhov
Set Designer Natasha Kroll

CAST

Masha .... Janet Suzman
Olga .... Eileen Atkins
Irina .... Michele Dotrice
Vershinin .... Michael Bryant
Chebutykin .... Joss Ackland
Natasha .... Sarah Badel
Toozenbach .... Ronald Hines
Andrey .... Anthony Hopkins
Soliony .... Donald Pickering
Koolyghin .... Richard Pearson
Servant .... Maeve Leslie

1394 **The 3,000 Mile Chase**
NBC Movie of the Week NBC
Program Type TV Movie
Two hours. Premiere date: 6/16/77. Action drama pilot about a professional courier and an importer chased cross-country by gangsters. Based on a story by Roy Huggins. Filmed in part in Antelope Valley, Calif.
Executive Producer Roy Huggins
Producer Jo Swerling, Jr.
Company Universal Television in association with NBC-TV
Director Russ Mayberry
Writer Philip DeGuere, Jr.

CAST

Matthew Considine/Marty Scanlon .. Cliff De Young
Paul Dvorak/Leonard Staveck .... Glenn Ford
Rachel Kane .... Blair Brown
Frank Oberon .... David Spielberg
Emma Dvorak .... Priscilla Pointer
Livingston .... Lane Allan
Inspector .... John Zenda
Santeen .... Carmen Argenziano
Richette .... Tom Bower
Prosecutor .... Roger Aaron Brown

1395 **Three Times Daley** CBS
Program Type Comedy Special
30 minutes. Premiere date: 8/3/76. Repeat date: 4/20/77. Comedy pilot about a divorced newspaper columnist and his father and son. Created by John Rappaport.
Executive Producer Leonard B. Stern
Producer John Rappaport

Company Heyday Productions in association with Universal Television
Director Jay Sandrich
Writer John Rappaport
Musical Director Don Costa

CAST

Bob Daley .... Don Adams
Alex Daley .... Liam Dunn
Wes Daley .... Jerry Houser
Stacy .... Bibi Besch
Jenny .... Ayn Ruymen

1396 **Three's Company** ABC
Program Type Comedy Series – Limited Series
30 minutes. Thursdays. Preview: 3/15/77. Premiere date: 3/24/77. Originally scheduled as a five-week limited series with run ending 4/21/77. Repeats began 8/11/77. Comedy about two women sharing their Santa Monica, Calif. apartment with a man. Based on the Thames (England) television program "Man About the House" created by Johnnie Mortimer and Brian Cooke. Developed by Don Nicholl, Michael Ross and Bernie West. Theme music by Joe Raposo; lyrics by Don Nicholl.
Producers Don Nicholl, Michael Ross, Bernie West
Company The NRW Company in association with TTC Productions, Inc.
Director Bill Hobin
Executive Story Consultants Paul Wayne, George Burditt
Writers Various

CAST

Jack Tripper .... John Ritter
Janet Wood .... Joyce DeWitt
Chrissy Snow .... Suzanne Somers
Helen Roper .... Audra Lindley
Stanley Roper .... Norman Fell

1397 **Through All Time**
Americana PBS
Program Type Documentary/Informational Special
30 minutes each. Part I: "Traditional Small Towns" shown 4/8/77. Part II: "Pleasure Domes and Money Mills" shown 4/15/77. A look at the traditional influence of small towns on American life as well as a look at company towns and boom towns (resorts and tourists areas). Programs made possible by grants from the Corporation for Public Broadcasting and the National Endowment for the Humanities.
Producer James Case
Company KPBS-TV/San Diego, Calif.
Director James Case
Writer Peggy Clifford
Narrator Carl Swenson

Thunderball *see* Special Movie Presentation

Thunderbolt and Lightfoot *see* The ABC Sunday Night Movie

1398 **Thursday Night Special** ABC
Program Type Miscellaneous Series
90 minutes. Thursdays. Season premiere: 1/6/77. A combination of new and repeat presentations of awards shows, documentary reports and variety shows seen as late-night presentations. The new shows seen during the 1976–77 season are: "Academy of Country Music Awards," "Alan King's Pleasures of Rome," "David Hartman . . . Gamblers: Winners and Losers," "Elton John: In Concert," "The Fourth Annual Unofficial Miss Las Vegas Showgirl Pageant," "The Geraldo Rivera Program," "Gabriel Kaplan Presents the Future Stars," "Gregory Peck: A Living Biography," "The Lou Rawls Special," "Playboy's Playmate Party," "The Sixth David Frost Presents the Guinness Book of World Records." (*See* individual titles for credits.)

1399 **Tiger, Tiger** CBS
Program Type Science/Nature Special
60 minutes. Premiere date: 4/28/77. Documentary on the Bengal tiger. Filmed on location in the forests of India and Nepal. Music by Frank Corrdell.
Executive Producer Aubrey Buxton
Company Survival Anglia Ltd.
Writer Colin Willock
Cinematographers G. Dieter Plage, Mike Price
Film Editor Leslie Parry
Narrator Richard Widmark

1400 **Time and Time Again**
Piccadilly Circus PBS
Program Type Dramatic Special
90 minutes. Premiere date: 6/14/76. Repeat date: 8/14/77. Television adaptation of the English stage comedy by Alan Ayckbourn. Program made possible by a grant from Mobil Oil Corporation. Presented by WGBH-TV/Boston; Joan Sullivan, producer.
Producer Cecil Clarke
Company ATV/London
Director Casper Wrede
Writer Casper Wrede
Host Jeremy Brett

CAST

Leonard .... Tom Courtenay
Anna .... Bridget Turner
Graham .... Michael Robbins
Peter .... Peter Egan
Joan .... Cheryl Kennedy

1401 **Time Travelers**
The ABC Friday Night Movie ABC
Program Type TV Movie
90 minutes. Premiere date: 3/19/76. Repeat date: 7/29/77. Pilot about scientists sent back in time to 1871 at the time of the Chicago fire. Based on a story by Irwin Allen and Rod Sterling. Music by Morton Stevens.
Producer Irwin Allen
Company An Irwin Allen Production in association with 20th Century-Fox Television
Director Alex Singer
Writer Jackson Gillis
Costume Designer Paul Zastupnevich
Art Director Eugene Lourie

CAST

Dr. Clinton Earnshaw .... Sam Groom
Jeff Adams .... Tom Hallick
Dr. Henderson .... Richard Basehart
Jane Henderson .... Trish Stewart
Dr. Helen Sanders .... Francine York
Dr. Cummings .... Booth Colman
Dr. Stafford .... Walter Burke
Sharkey .... Dort Clark
Irish Girl .... Kathleen Bracken
Betty .... Victoria Meyerink
Chief Williams .... Baynes Barron
News Vendor .... Albert Cole

1402 **The Tiny Tree**
Bell System Family Theatre NBC
Program Type Animated Film Special
30 minutes. Premiere date: 12/14/75. Repeat date: 12/12/76. Created by Chuck Couch. Theme songs "To Love and Be Loved" and "When Autumn Comes" by Johnny Marks sung by Roberta Flack. Characters designed by Louis Schmitt. Story development by Bob Ogle and Lewis Marshall.
Executive Producers David H. DePatie, Friz Freleng
Producer Chuck Couch
Company DePatie-Freleng Enterprises, Inc.
Director Chuck Couch
Music Supervisor Dean Elliott

VOICES

Squire Badger .... Buddy Ebsen
Hawk .... Allan Melvin
Turtle .... Paul Winchell
Lady Bird/Little Girl .... Janet Waldo
Boy Bunny/Girl Raccoon .... Stephen Manley
Groundhog/Father Bird/ Beaver/Mole .... Frank Welker

1403 **To Expect To Die: A Film About Living**
Documentary Showcase PBS
Program Type Documentary/Informational Special
60 minutes. Premiere date: 2/25/77. The story of the Robert Hardgrove family in the months before his death.
Executive Producer Joseph H. Russin
Producer Trevor Thomas
Company KQED-TV/San Francisco
Cinematographer Blair Stapp
Film Editor Blair Stapp
Reporter Trevor Thomas

1404 **To Tell the Truth** Syndicated
Program Type Game/Audience Participation Series
30 minutes. Mondays–Fridays. Premiere date: 9/74. Third season premiere: 9/76. Revival of show which was originally produced in 1956. Three regular panelists plus one guest celebrity each week.
Producer Bruno Zirato, Jr.
Company Goodson-Todman Productions
Distributor Firestone Program Syndication Company
Director Lloyd Gross
Host Garry Moore
Regulars Kitty Carlisle, Bill Cullen, Peggy Cass

1405 **To the Queen! A Salute to Elizabeth II** ABC
Program Type Documentary/Informational Special
60 minutes. Premiere date: 6/11/77. A look at the reign of Queen Elizabeth II and the Royal Family.
Executive Producer Elliot Bernstein
Co-Producers Gary Herman, Penelope Fleming
Company ABC News Special Events
Director Jack Sameth
Writer Harvey Jacobs
Host Peter Jennings
Guests Jean Marsh, Peter Cook and Dudley Moore, Jackie Stewart

1406 **To the Top of the World: An Assault on Everest** CBS
Program Type Sports Special
60 minutes. Premiere date: 1/7/77. Repeat date: 7/10/77. The conquest of Mount Everest by a team of Americans in the fall of 1976. Three 10-minute segments of the climb were shown on the "CBS Sports Spectacular" during August, September and October 1976.
Producers Ed Goren, Mike Hoover
Company CBS Television Network Sports
Director Mike Hoover
Writer Paul Boorstin
Cinematographers Peter Smokler, Pete White, Jonathan Wright, Peter Pilafian
Film Editors Tim Huntley, Norman Smith
Narrator Jack Whitaker

1407 **Today** NBC
Program Type News Magazine Series
Two hours. Monday-Friday mornings. Premiere date: 1/14/52. Continuous. Live program of news, weather reports, sports results, interviews, discussions, reviews and occasional special entertainment. Regular features: "Critic's Corner," "Family Doctor," and consumer reports. Twenty-five year retrospective shown 1/14/77. Jane Pauley became regular 10/11/76.
Executive Producer Paul Friedman
Producer Douglas P. Sinsel
Company NBC News
Directors Marvin D. Einhorn, James W. Gaines
Host Tom Brokaw
Regulars Gene Shalit, Jane Pauley, Betty Furness, Dr. Art Ulene
Newscaster Floyd Kalber
Weather/Sports Reporter Lew Wood
Traveling Co-Host Jim Hartz

1408 **The Tom & Jerry/Grape Ape/Mumbly Show** ABC
Program Type Animated Film Series
60 minutes/30 minutes (as of 12/4/76). Saturday mornings. Premiere date: 9/6/75. Second season premiere: 9/11/76. Cartoons about Tom and Jerry, a giant purple gorilla, The Grape Ape, and a new comedy-adventure about a sleuthing dog named Mumbly added 9/11/76. Last show for "Grape Ape": 11/27/76. "The Tom & Jerry/Mumbly Show" became a 30 minute series 12/4/76.
Executive Producers Joseph Barbera, William Hanna
Producer Iwao Takamoto
Company Hanna-Barbera Productions, Inc.
Director Charles A. Nichols
Writers Bill Ackerman, Larz Bourne, Tom Dagenais, Alan Dinehart, Don Jurwich, Joel Kane, Dick Kinney, Jack Mendelsohn, Ray Parker, Duane Poole, Howard Post, Frank Ridgeway, Dick Robbins
Musical Director Hoyt Curtin
Storyboard Editor Alex Lovy
Voices Norman Alden, Henry Corden, Joan Gerber, Kathy Gori, Virginia Gregg, Bob Hastings, Bob Holt, Marty Ingels, Allan Melvin, Don Messick, Alan Oppenheimer, Joe E. Ross, Hal Smith, John Stephenson, Lurene Tuttle, Jean VanderPyl, Janet Waldo, Lennie Weinrib, Frank Welker, Paul Winchell

The Tom & Jerry/Mumbly Show *see* The Tom & Jerry/Grape Ape/Mumbly Show

Tom Sawyer *see* CBS Special Film Presentations

1409 **Tom Wolfe's Los Angeles** PBS
Program Type Comedy Special
60 minutes. Premiere date: 1/10/77. A satirical look at Los Angeles. Program made possible by grants from the Corporation for Public Broadcasting, the Ford Foundation and the National Endowment for the Arts. Presented by WETA-TV/Washington.
Producers Eugene N. Aleinikoff, Richard O. Moore
Company PTV Production, Inc.
Director Richard O. Moore
Writer Tom Wolfe

CAST

Rudy .... Isaac Ruiz
Observer .... Tom Wolfe

1410 **Toma** ABC
Program Type Crime Drama Series
60 minutes. Mondays. Premiere date: 4/25/77. Late-night repeat presentations of primetime show which originally aired on ABC between 10/4/73–9/6/74.
Executive Producer Roy Huggins
Producers Stephen J. Cannell, Jo Swerling, Jr.
Company Universal Television/Public Arts, Inc.
Directors Various
Writers Various

CAST

Dave Toma .... Tony Musante
Insp. Spooner .... Simon Oakland
Patty Toma .... Susan Strasberg

1411 **Tomorrow** NBC
Program Type Talk/Service/Variety Series
60 minutes. Tuesday–Friday mornings (1–2 a.m.). Premiere date: 10/15/73. Continuous. Early-morning talk show with guests covering a broad range of topics. Show originated in Burbank, Calif., went to New York City 12/2/74 and returned to Burbank 6/6/77.
Co-Producers Pamela Burke, Bruce McKay
Company NBC Television Network Production
Director George Paul
Art Director Scott Ritenour
Host Tom Snyder

1412 **The Tonight Show Starring Johnny Carson** NBC
Program Type Talk/Service/Variety Series
90 minutes. Mondays–Fridays. Premiere date: 12/27/54. Continuous. Johnny Carson became host 10/1/62. Two-hour 14th anniversary show 10/1/76. Late-night entertainment program. Guest hosts each Monday.
Producer Fred de Cordova

The Tonight Show Starring Johnny Carson *Continued*
Company NBC Television Network
Director Bobby Quinn
Writing Supervisor Hal Goodman
Musical Director Doc Severinsen
Host Johnny Carson
Announcer Ed McMahon
Assistant Music Conductor Tommy Newsom

Tonka *see* NBC All-Disney Saturday Night at the Movies ("A Horse Named Comanche")

1413 **The Tony Awards** ABC
Program Type Parades/Pageants/Awards Special
Live coverage of the 31st annual Tony Awards presented by the American Theatre Wing on 6/5/77 from the Shubert Theatre in New York City.
Executive Producer Alexander H. Cohen
Producer Hildy Parks
Company Brentwood Television Corporation Production
Director Clark Jones
Writer Hildy Parks
Hosts Jack Albertson, Beatrice Arthur, Buddy Ebsen, Damon Evans, Jean Stapleton, Leslie Uggams
Presenters Jane Alexander, Alan Arkin, Lauren Bacall, Valerie Harper, Robert Preston, Tony Randall

Tony Orlando and Dawn *see* Tony Orlando & Dawn Rainbow Hour

1414 **Tony Orlando & Dawn Rainbow Hour** CBS
Program Type Music/Comedy/Variety Series
60 minutes. Tuesdays. Premiere date: 12/4/74. Third season premiere: 9/21/76. Last show: 12/28/76. Name of show changed for third season from "Tony Orlando and Dawn." Regular feature: "The George Carlin Report."
Producers Saul Ilson, Ernest Chambers
Company Ilson/Chambers Productions, Inc., in association with Yellow Ribbon Productions, Inc.
Directors Peter Calabrese, Bill Foster
Head Writers Al Gordon, Hal Goldman
Writing Supervisors Saul Ilson, Ernest Chambers
Musical Director Bob Rozario
Choreographer Walter Painter
Costume Designer Michael Travis
Stars Tony Orlando and Dawn (Telma Hopkins and Joyce Vincent Wilson)
Regulars George Carlin, Bob Holt, Susan Lanier, Jimmy Martinez, Edie McClurg, Nancy Steen, Adam Wade

1415 **The Tony Randall Show** ABC
Program Type Comedy Series
30 minutes. Thursdays. Premiere date: 9/23/76. Comedy about a widowed Philadelphia judge with two children. Each episode entitled "Case: . . ." Created by Tom Patchett and Jay Tarses. Music by Pat Williams. Last regular show on ABC: 3/10/77. Went to CBS for the 1977–78 season.
Producers Tom Patchett, Jay Tarses
Company An MTM Enterprises Production
Directors Various
Writers Various
Creative Consultant Michael Zinberg

CAST

Judge Walter Franklin .... Tony Randall
Jack Terwilliger .... Barney Martin
Miss Janet Reubner .... Allyn Ann McLerie
Roberta (Bobby) Franklin .... Devon Scott
Oliver Wendell Franklin .... Brad Savage
Mrs. Bonnie McClellan .... Rachel Roberts
Mario Lanza .... Zane Lasky

A Touch of Class *see* NBC Movie of the Week

1416 **A Touch of the Renaissance at Christmas** PBS
Program Type Music/Dance Special
30 minutes. Premiere date: 12/24/74. Repeat date: 12/23/76. Christmas music and rites originating in the Renaissance performed by the West Virginia University Camerata Singers. Program made possible by a grant from the Corporation for Public Broadcasting.
Producer David R. Hopfer
Company WWVU-TV/Morgantown, W. Va.
Director David R. Hopfer
Conductor Scott Stringham
Host Jack Hollahan

1417 **Tournament of Champions Golf Championship** ABC
Program Type Sports Special
Live coverage of the final two rounds of the 25th Tournament of Champions Golf Championship from the La Costa Country Club in Carlsbad, Calif. 4/16/77 and 4/17/77.
Executive Producer Roone Arledge
Producer Terry Jastrow
Company ABC Sports
Directors Jim Jennett, Andy Sidaris
Anchor Chris Schenkel
Expert Analysts Dave Marr, Bob Rosburg, Bill Flemming, Dan Jenkins

1418 **The Tournament of Roses Parade and Pageant** CBS
Program Type Parades/Pageants/Awards Special
2 1/2 hours. Live coverage of the 88th annual parade from Pasadena, Calif. 1/1/77.
Producer Vern Diamond
Company CBS Television
Director Vern Diamond
Writer Sandra Harmon
Hosts/Commentators Bob Barker, David Groh, Esther Rolle, Loretta Swit

1419 **Tournament Players Championship** ABC
Program Type Sports Special
Live coverage of the final rounds of the Tournament Players Championship from the Sawgrass Golf Club in Jacksonville, Fla. 3/19/77 and 3/20/77.
Executive Producer Roone Arledge
Producer Bob Goodrich
Company ABC Sports
Directors Jim Jennett, Terry Jastrow
Anchor Jim McKay
Expert Commentators Dave Marr, Bob Rosburg, Bill Flemming, Peter Alliss

1420 **Trailblazers of Modern Dance**
Dance in America/Great Performances PBS
Program Type Music/Dance Special
60 minutes. Premiere date: 6/22/77. The development of modern dance—from the turn-of-the-century through the 1930s. Program includes two reconstructions of Isadora Duncan's "Scriabin Etudes" danced by Annabelle Gibson, "Five Brahms Waltzes in the Manner of Isadora Duncan" choreographed and introduced by Sir Frederick Ashton and danced by Lynn Seymour, "Japanese Spear Dance" choreographed by Ted Shawn and danced by Clif da Raita and "Soaring" choreographed by Doris Humphrey and danced by the Trisler Danscompany. Program made possible by grants from Exxon Corporation, the National Endowment for the Arts and the Corporation for Public Broadcasting.
Executive Producer Jac Venza
Producer Emile Ardolino
Company WNET-TV/New York
Director Merrill Brockway
Choreographers Isadora Duncan, Martha Graham, Ruth St. Denis, Doris Humphrey, Ted Shawn, Frederick Ashton
Narrator Michael Tolan

VOICES

Isadora Duncan .... Rosemary Harris

The Train Robbers *see* NBC Saturday Night at the Movies

1421 **Treasure**
National Geographic Special PBS
Program Type Documentary/Informational Special
60 minutes. Premiere date: 12/7/76. The story of Mel Fisher's search for the lost Spanish galleon *Atocha* sunk off the Florida Keys on Sept. 6, 1622. Program made possible by a grant from Gulf Oil Corporation.
Executive Producers Dennis B. Kane, Thomas Skinner
Producer Nicolas Noxon
Company The National Geographic Society and WQED-TV/Pittsburgh
Director Nicolas Noxon
Writer Nicolas Noxon
Host E. G. Marshall
Narrator Alexander Scourby

1422 **Trelawney of the "Wells"**
Classic Theatre: The Humanities in Drama PBS
Program Type Dramatic Special
Two hours. Premiere date: 11/27/75. Repeat date: 4/21/77. Classic Victorian melodrama. Program made possible by grants from the National Endowment for the Humanities and Mobil Oil Corporation. Presented by WGBH-TV/Boston; Joan Sullivan, producer.
Producer Cedric Messina
Company British Broadcasting Corporation
Director Herbert Wise
Writer Arthur Wing Pinero

CAST

Tom Wrench .... John Alderton
Rose Trelawny .... Elaine Taylor
Mrs. Telfer .... Lally Bowers
James Telfer .... Graham Crowden
Sir William Gower .... Roland Culver
Arthur Gower .... Ian Ogilvy
Miss Trafalgar Gower .... Rachel Kempson
Avonia Bunn .... Elizabeth Seal
Imogen Parrott .... Moira Redford

1423 **The Tribal Eye** PBS
Program Type Educational/Cultural Series
60 minutes. Wednesdays. Premiere date: 10/15/75. Program repeats shown from 4/6/77. Seven-part series examining 16 tribal cultures as seen through the eyes of their artists. (Produced with open and closed captions for the hearing impaired.) Funded by a grant from the IBM Corporation; presented by WNET-TV/New York.
Producer David Attenborough
Company British Broadcasting Corporation in association with Warner Bros. Television
Director David Attenborough
Writer David Attenborough
Narrator David Attenborough

1424 A Tribute to Johann Strauss PBS

Program Type Music/Dance Special
60 minutes. Premiere date: 3/10/75. Repeat date: 12/76. 1975 New Year's Eve Concert performed by the Vienna Philharmonic Orchestra.
Company ORF (Austrian Television Network) and ZDF (The Second German Television Network)
Conductor Willi Boskovsky
Performers The Vienna State Opera Ballet Corps, the Vienna Volksoper Ballet, the Vienna Men's Choir

Trick Baby *see* The ABC Friday Night Movie ("The Double Con")

1425 Trouble in Tahiti

Opera Theater PBS
Program Type Music/Dance Special
60 minutes. Premiere date: 5/4/76. Repeat date: 8/9/77. Television version of the jazz-based one-act opera by Leonard Bernstein featuring the London Symphonic Wind Band. Program made possible by grants from the Ford Foundation, the Corporation for Public Broadcasting and Public Television Stations and presented by WNET-TV/New York.
Executive Producer Humphrey Burton
Coordinating Producers Linda Krisel, David Griffiths
Producer David Griffiths
Company Amberson Video, Inc. and London Weekend Television
Director Bill Hays
Conductor Leonard Bernstein

CAST

Sam	Julian Patrick
Dinah	Nancy Williams
Greek Chorus	Antonia Butler, Michael Clarke, Mark Brown

1426 Truman at Potsdam

Bicentennial Hall of Fame PBS
Program Type Dramatic Special
90 minutes. Premiere date: 4/8/76 (on NBC). Repeat date: 11/23/76. Drama based on the book "Meeting at Potsdam" by Charles L. Mee, Jr. about the historic 1945 conference. Presented by KCPT-TV/Kansas City. Program presented to PBS by Hallmark Cards, Inc. Interview segment between Elie Abel and Dr. Daniel J. Boorstin funded by a grant from the Corporation for Public Broadcasting
Producer David Susskind
Company Talent Associates Ltd., in association with MacLean and Co.
Director George Schaefer
Writer Sidney Carroll
Costume Designer Jane Robinson
Art Director Ellen Schmidt
Narrator David Schoenbrun

CAST

Harry Truman	Ed Flanders
Winston Churchill	John Houseman
Josef Stalin	Jose Ferrer
Henry L. Stimson	Alexander Knox
James F. Byrnes	Barry Morse
Charles E. Bohlen	Karl Held
Joseph E. Davies	Tony Steedman
Gen. George C. Marshall	Kevin Stoney
Adm. William D. Leahy	Leo McCabe
Adm. Ernest J. King	Robert O'Neill
Gen. H. H. Arnold	Lindsay Campbell
James K. Vardaman	Lionel Murton
Maj. Gen. Harry Vaughan	Guy Doleman
Charles G. Ross	Percy Herbert
Sir Anthony Eden	Dennis Burgess
Sir Alexander Cadogan	Bruce Taylor
Clement Attlee	Kenneth Waller
Lord Moran	David Markham
V. I. Molotov	Alexander Boettcher

1427 Truth or Consequences Syndicated

Program Type Game/Audience Participation Series
30 minutes. Mondays-Fridays. In syndication since 1967. Program began on radio in 1948; went to television in 1952.
Executive Producer Ralph Edwards
Producer Ed Bailey
Company A Ralph Edwards Production
Distributor Metromedia Producers Corporation
Director Bill Chestnut
Musical Director Hal Hidy
Host Bob Barker

Tucson Open *see* Joe Garagiola Tucson Open

1428 Tuesday Movie of the Week ABC

Program Type Feature Film Series – TV Movie Series
Times vary. Tuesdays. Premiere date: 9/21/76. Late-night presentations of theatrically released motion pictures and repeat presentations of made-for-television films.

1429 Tut: The Boy King

Multi-Special Night NBC
Program Type Documentary/Informational Special
60 minutes. Premiere date: 7/27/77. The art treasures from the tomb of Tutankhamun. Taped at the National Gallery of Art in Washington, D.C. Music composed by Robert Maxwell.
Executive Producer George A. Heinemann
Producer Joseph F. Callo
Director Sidney Smith
Writer W.W. Lewis
Conductor Robert Maxwell

Art Director Norman Davidson
Narrator Orson Welles

1430 **TVTV Looks at the Oscars**
Documentary Showcase PBS
Program Type Documentary/Informational Special
60 minutes. Premiere date: 3/18/77. A humorous look behind the scenes of the 1976 Academy Awards presentation.
Producers Wendy Apple, David Axelrod, Paul Goldsmith, Hudson Marquez, Tom Morey, Allen Rucker, Michael Shamberg, Megan Williams
Company TVTV and KCET-TV/Los Angeles
Directors Wendy Apple, David Axelrod, Paul Goldsmith, Hudson Marquez, Tom Morey, Allen Rucker, Michael Shamberg, Megan Williams

CAST

Judy Beasley .... Lily Tomlin

1431 **The TVTV Show** NBC
Program Type Comedy Special
90 minutes. Premiere date: 5/1/77 (12 midnight-1:30 a.m.). A look at America's addiction to television. Taped with minicams.
Producer Michael Shamberg
Company TVTV Production Co.
Director Alan Myerson
Writers Mary Kay Brown, Peter Elbling, Brian McConnachie, Billy Murray, Michael Shamberg

CAST

Ralph Buckler .... Howard Hesseman
Mary Kay .... Mary Frann
George .... Carl Gottlieb
Mother .... Mina Kolb
Father .... Gary Goodrow
Nancy .... Annie Poth
Tommy .... Mike Darnell

1432 **'Twas the Night Before Christmas** CBS
Program Type Animated Film Special
30 minutes. Premiere date: 12/8/74. Repeat date: 12/17/76. Adapted from "A Visit from St. Nicholas" by Clement Moore. Music by Maury Laws; lyrics by Jules Bass.
Producers Arthur Rankin, Jr., Jules Bass
Company Rankin-Bass Productions
Directors Arthur Rankin, Jr., Jules Bass
Writer Jerome Coopersmith
Narrator Joel Grey

VOICES

Albert Mouse .... Tammy Grimes
Mayor of Junctionville .... John McGiver
Father Mouse .... George Gobel
Additional Voices Patricia Bright, Allen Swift, Robert McFadden, Christine Winter, Scott Firestone

1433 **The $25,000 Pyramid** Syndicated
Program Type Game/Audience Participation Series
30 minutes. Weekly. Premiere date: 9/74. Third season premiere: 9/76. Evening version of "The $20,000 Pyramid."
Producer Anne Marie Schmitt
Company A Bob Stewart Production
Distributor Viacom International, Inc.
Director Mike Gargiulo
Host Bill Cullen

1434 **21 Hours at Munich**
The ABC Sunday Night Movie ABC
Program Type TV Movie
Two hours. Premiere date: 11/7/76. Repeat date: 4/17/77. A dramatization of the Palestinian attack on Israeli athletes at the 1972 Olympics. Filmed on the actual sites in Munich, Germany. Based on the book "The Blood of Israel" by Serge Groussard. Music by Laurence Rosenthal. Song "Osse Shalom" by Nurit Hirsh.
Executive Producer Edward S. Feldman
Producers Frank von Zerneck, Robert Greenwald
Company A Filmways Production filmed in association with Moonlight Productions, Inc.
Director William A. Graham
Writers Edward Hume, Howard Fast
Art Director Herta Pischinger

CAST

Chief of Police Manfred Schreiber .. William Holden
Annaliese Graes .... Shirley Knight
Issa .... Franco Nero
Gen. Zvi Zamir .... Anthony Quayle
Merk .... Noel Willman
Genscher .... Georg Marischka
Gutfreund .... Paul Smith
Weinberger .... Martin Gilat
Chancellor Willy Brandt .... Richard Basehart

1435 **The $20,000 Pyramid** ABC
Program Type Game/Audience Participation Series
30 minutes. Mondays–Fridays. Premiere date (on CBS): 3/26/73. Moved to ABC 5/6/74. Continuous. Name (and prizes) changed from "The $10,000 Pyramid" 1/19/76. Two celebrities and two contestants team up to test their word power.
Producer Anne Marie Schmitt
Company A Bob Stewart Production
Director Mike Gargiulo
Host Dick Clark

1436 **Two Ball Games**
Americana PBS
Program Type Documentary/Informational Special
30 minutes. Premiere date: 1/14/77. Repeat

Two Ball Games *Continued*
date: 8/7/77. Structured and unstructured play among youngsters contrasted in an official Little League game and a pick-up sandlot game among neighborhood children.
Company WGBH-TV/Boston
Director David H. Gluck

1437 **Two Brothers**
Visions PBS
Program Type Dramatic Special
90 minutes. Premiere date: 10/21/76. Repeat date: 1/27/77. Story about one man's attempts to prevent the suicide of his younger brother. Filmed in part in Watts and at other locations in Los Angeles. Program made possible by grants from the Corporation for Public Broadcasting, the National Endowment for the Arts and the Ford Foundation.
Producer Barbara Schultz
Company KCET-TV/Los Angeles
Director Burt Brinckerhoff
Writer Conrad Bromberg
Costume Designer Elizabeth Manny
Art Director John Retsek

CAST

Joe Morris	Judd Hirsch
David Morris	David Spielberg
Mrs. Morris	Sarah Cunningham
Dr. Markle	Stephen Elliott
Agnes Morris	Diane Shalet
Dr. Horlick	Tom Rosqui
Sylvia	Zina Jasper
Maj. Yang	George Chiang
Col. Files	Bard Stevens
Maj. Huntley	Ronnell Bright
Mrs. Cruz	Karmin Murcelo
Atkins	Napoleon Whiting
Mrs. Pickett	Kathryn Jackson
Mexican Boy	Raphael Vega
Lizzie Morris	Ariane Heller
Pharmacist	Alan Lurie

1438 **Two Stones**
Documentary Showcase PBS
Program Type Documentary/Informational Special
60 minutes. Premiere date: 2/11/77. Repeat date: 8/20/77. A look at disabled people and society's attitudes towards them.
Producer Fritz Williams
Company WITF-TV/Hershey, Pa.
Director Ray Priest
Writer Fritz Williams
Cinematographer Ray Priest
Film Editor Ray Priest
Narrator Fritz Williams

2001: A Space Odyssey *see* The Big Event

1439 **Twyla Tharp & Dancers**
Dance in America/Great Performances PBS
Program Type Music/Dance Special
60 minutes. Premiere date: 3/24/76. Repeat date: 4/13/77. A performance of "Sue's Leg" created by Twyla Tharp and danced to the music of Fats Waller. Program made possible by grants from the National Endowment for the Arts, the Corporation for Public Broadcasting and the Exxon Corporation.
Executive Producer Jac Venza
Company WNET-TV/New York
Choreographer Twyla Tharp
Series Producer Merrill Brockway
Dancers Twyla Tharp, Rose Marie Wright, Kenneth Rinker, Tom Rawe

Umberto D *see* PBS Movie Theater

1440 **U.N. Day Concert (1976)** PBS
Program Type Music/Dance Special
90 minutes. Premiere date: 10/24/76. Repeat date: 5/22/77. Annual concert honoring the founding of the United Nations from the U.N. General Assembly Hall. Music performed by the National Symphony Orchestra. Program made possible by grants from the Corporation for Public Broadcasting and IBM Corporation.
Company United Nations Television in cooperation with WNET-TV/New York
Conductor Antal Dorati
Guest Performers Lazar Berman, Marian Anderson

1441 **Under God** NBC
Program Type Religious/Cultural Special
60 minutes. Sundays. Two programs of a religious-cultural nature presented during the 1976–77 season: "Faces of Hope" and "Strangers in the Homeland." (*See* individual titles for credits.)

United Nations *see* U.N.

United States *see also* U.S.

1442 **United States Boxing Championships** ABC
Program Type Limited Sports Series
60 minutes/90 minutes. Premiere date: 1/16/77. Last show: 4/10/77. Conceived and arranged by Don King Productions in association with Ring Magazine as a series of bouts over six months to determine U.S. boxing champions in all major weight divisions, series was cancelled due to allegations of fight-fixing and kickbacks. One show

seen as part of "ABC's Wide World of Sports." Chris Schenkel announced the final program.
Executive Producer Roone Arledge
Producer Chet Forte
Company ABC Sports
Directors Various
Announcer Howard Cosell
Expert Commentator George Foreman

United States Golf Association *see* USGA

1443 **United States Open Tennis Championships** CBS
Program Type Sports Special
26 1/2 hours. Live coverage of the U.S. Open from the West Side Tennis Club in Forest Hills, N.Y. 9/3/77, 9/4/77, 9/5/77, 9/10/77 and 9/11/77. (*See also* "U.S. Open Update.")
Producers Bernie Hoffman, Frank Chirkinian
Company CBS Television Network Sports
Director Bob Dailey
Commentators Pat Summerall, Tony Trabert, Virginia Wade, Gary Bender, Cliff Drysdale, Jack Whitaker (final day)

1444 **Upstairs, Downstairs**
Masterpiece Theatre PBS
Program Type Limited Series
60 minutes. Sundays. Premiere date: 1/6/74. Fourth (last) season premiere: 1/16/77. Series repeats began 9/5/77 (four times a week). Last 16 episodes following the fortunes of the Bellamy household of 165 Eaton Place, Belgravia, London from 1919–1929. Series created by Jean Marsh and Eileen Atkins. Music by Alexander Faris. Funded by a grant from Mobil Oil Corporation. Presented by WGBH-TV/Boston; Joan Sullivan, producer.
Executive Producer Rex Firkin
Producer John Hawkesworth
Company London Weekend Television
Story Editor Alfred Shaughnessy
Writers Various
Host Alistair Cooke

CAST

Richard Bellamy .... David Langton
James Bellamy .... Simon Williams
Hudson .... Gordon Jackson
Rose .... Jean Marsh
Mrs. Bridges .... Angela Baddeley
Edward .... Christopher Beeny
Daisy .... Jacqueline Tong
Ruby .... Jenny Tomasin
Georgina Worsley .... Leslie-Anne Down
Sir Geoffrey .... Raymond Huntley
Lady Prudence .... Joan Benham
Virginia Hamilton .... Hannah Gordon
William Hamilton .... Jonathan Seely
Alice Hamilton .... Anne Yarker
Lily .... Karen Dotrice
Frederick .... Gareth Hunt
Lady Diana Newbury .... Celia Bannerman

1445 **Upstairs, Downstairs Farewell—A Million Dollar Party** PBS
Program Type Telethon
Two hours. Premiere date: 5/1/77. Telethon to raise money for public television presented as a farewell party for "Upstairs, Downstairs." Telecast live from Boston before the final episode of the series. Participants included many members of the cast.
Producers Dighton Spooner, Joan Sullivan
Company WGBH-TV/Boston
Director Russ Fortier
Host Alistair Cooke

U.S. *see also* United States

1446 **US Against the World**
The Big Event NBC
Program Type Sports Special
Two hours. Premiere date: 9/7/77. Teams of American, British and "rest of the world" celebrities in various athletic competitions. Filmed at the University of California at Los Angeles.
Executive Producers Howard Katz, Rudy Tellez
Producer Don Ohlmeyer
Company Trans World International, Inc. with the cooperation of the UCLA Alumni Association in association with the NBC Television Network
Director Don Ohlmeyer
Host Don Rickles
Co-Hosts Ed McMahon, Jack Klugman
Stars from the U.S.: Gabriel Kaplan (captain), Linda Blair, Angel Cordero, Jr., Dan Haggerty, Kristy McNichol, Rob Reiner, Susan Saint James, Suzanne Somers, Flip Wilson
Stars from Great Britain: Marty Feldman (captain), Roger Daltry, Richard Dawson, Susan George, Andy Gibb, Olivia Hussey, Jane Seymour, Bill Shoemaker, Twiggy
Stars from the Rest of the World: Rich Little (captain), Susan Blakely, LeVar Burton, Susan Clark, Britt Ekland, Sergio Mendes, Michael Ontkean, Lafitt Pincay, Jr., Elke Sommer

1447 **U.S. Amateur Golf Championship** ABC
Program Type Sports Special
90 minutes. Live coverage of the final round of the 1977 U.S. Amateur Golf Championship from the Aronimink Golf Club in Newton Square, Pa. 9/5/77.
Executive Producer Roone Arledge
Producer Bob Goodrich
Company ABC Sports

U.S. Amateur Golf Championship
Continued
Director Jim Jennett
Anchor Chris Schenkel
Expert Commentators Dave Marr, Bob Rosburg

1448 **U.S. Grand Prix West** CBS
Program Type Sports Special
Two hours. Live coverage of the Long Beach (Calif.) Grand Prix 4/3/77.
Producer Bernie Hoffman
Company Lirol Productions
Director Bernie Hoffman
Announcer Ken Squier
Expert Commentators David Hobbs, Bobby Unser, Dan Gurney, Brock Yates

U.S. Olympic Invitational Track and Field Meet *see* Vitalis/U.S. Olympic Invitational Track and Field Meet

1449 **U.S. Open Golf Championship** ABC
Program Type Sports Special
Live and taped coverage of the U.S. Open Championship from the Southern Hills Country Club in Tulsa, Okla. 6/17/77, 6/18/77 and 6/19/77 including complete coverage of the final 18 holes.
Executive Producer Roone Arledge
Producer Chuck Howard
Company ABC Sports

1450 **U.S. Open Update** CBS
Program Type Sports Special
15 minutes. Nine evenings of highlights of the United States Open Tennis Championships 8/31/77–9/9/77 (except 9/4/77). (*See also* "United States Open Tennis Championships.")
Producers Bernie Hoffman, Frank Chirkinian
Company CBS Television Network Sports
Director Bob Dailey
Hosts Pat Summerall, Tony Trabert

U.S. Pro Indoor Tennis Championship *see* INA U.S. Pro Indoor Tennis Championship

1451 **U.S. Women's Open Golf Championship** ABC
Program Type Sports Special
Live coverage of the final rounds of the U.S. Women's Open Golf Championship from the Hazeltine National Golf Club in Chaska, Minn. 7/23/77 and 7/24/77.
Executive Producer Roone Arledge
Producer Bob Goodrich
Company ABC Sports
Director Jim Jennett
Anchors Jim McKay, Andrea Kirby
Expert Commentators Dave Marr, Bill Flemming, Bob Rosburg

1452 **USA: People and Politics** PBS
Program Type Public Affairs Series
30 minutes. Mondays/Fridays (as of 7/9/76). Premiere date: 2/23/76. 37-week political series debuting on the eve of the first (New Hampshire) presidential primary and continuing until 11/1/76. Broadcast live from Washington, D.C. Special 60-minute interview with Jimmy Carter which originally aired 7/16/76 updated and shown 1/19/77 on the eve of the inauguration. Series funded by grants from the Ford Foundation, the Corporation for Public Broadcasting and Public Television Stations.
Executive Producer Wallace Westfeldt
Producers Jerome Toobin, Gerald Slater
Company WNET-TV/New York and WETA-TV/Washington, D.C.
Anchor/Commentator Lynn Sherr
Correspondents Paul Duke, Lee Clark, Robert Sam Anson, Lisa Feiner, Charles Rose

1453 **USGA Highlights 1976** ABC
Program Type Sports Special
30 minutes. Premiere date: 12/19/76. Highlights of the 1976 United States Golf Association tournaments.
Executive Producer Roone Arledge
Producer Bob Goodrich
Company ABC Sports
Director Jim Jennett
Host Jim McKay

1454 **USTA National Men's 35 Hardcourt Championships** PBS
Program Type Sports Special
Four hours. Live coverage of the final matches in singles and doubles competition of men over 35 from San Antonio, Texas 6/19/77. Program made possible by a grant from the Texas Tennis Association.
Executive Producer Larry White
Producer Bob Vaughan
Company KLRN-TV/San Antonio-Austin
Director John Crowe
Announcer Kim Prince

1455 **Valentine's Second Chance**
ABC Short Story Specials ABC
Program Type Children's Special
30 minutes. Premiere date: 1/29/77. Repeat dates: 5/28/77 and 8/27/77. Story of a reformed safecracker risking his new status to save a boy

from a time-locked safe. Based on "A Retrieved Reformation" by O. Henry. Music by Ray Ellis.
Executive Producer Allen Ducovny
Producer William Beaudine, Jr.
Company ABC Circle Films
Director Hollingsworth Morse
Writer Alvin Boretz
Art Director Joe Altadonna

CAST

Jimmy Valentine .... Ken Berry
Det. Ben Price .... Greg Morris
Annabel .... Elizabeth Baur
Joe Willie .... Sean Marshall
Fergus .... Ham Larsen
Dawson .... Max Showalter
Sheriff .... Burke Byrnes

1456 **Valley Forge**
Bicentennial Hall of Fame PBS
Program Type Dramatic Special
90 minutes. Premiere date: 12/3/75 (on NBC). Repeat date: 11/9/76. Adapted from the play by Maxwell Anderson about the plight of the Continental Army in the winter of 1777–78. Music by Vladimir Solinsky. Presented by KCPT-TV/Kansas City. Program presented to PBS by Hallmark Cards, Inc. Interview segment between Elie Abel and Dr. Daniel J. Boorstin funded by a grant from the Corporation for Public Broadcasting.
Executive Producer Duane C. Bogie
Producer Fielder Cook
Company Clarion Productions and Columbia Pictures Television
Director Fielder Cook
Writer Sidney Carroll
Costume Designer Ann Roth
Art Director Ben Edwards

CAST

Gen. George Washington .... Richard Basehart
Gen. William Howe .... Harry Andrews
Maj. John Andre .... Simon Ward
Gen. Lafayette .... Victor Garber
Brig. Gen. Varnum .... Josef Sommer
Brig. Stirling .... Paul Sparer
Lt. Col. Trench .... Michael Tolan
The Hessian .... Christopher Walken
Lt. Cutting .... David Dukes
Spad .... Lane Smith
Congressman Folsom .... Edward Herrmann
Congressman Harvie .... John Heard
Auntie .... Nancy Marchand
Tavis .... Lisa Pelikan

1457 **Van Dyke and Company** NBC
Program Type Music/Comedy/Variety Series
60 minutes. Thursdays. Premiere date: 9/20/76 (special Monday program). Last show 12/30/76. Regular sketch: "The Bright Family."
Executive Producer Byron Paul
Producers Allan Blye, Bob Einstein
Company A Blye-Einstein Production in association with Catspaw Productions
Director John Moffitt
Writers Dick Van Dyke, Allan Blye, Bob Einstein, George Burditt, Garry Ferrier, Ken Finkelman, Mitch Markowitz, Don Novello, Pat Proft, Lennie Ripps, Mickey Rose, Aubrey Tadman
Musical Director Lex De Azevedo
Choreographer Lester Wilson
Star Dick Van Dyke
Regulars Andy Kaufman, the Los Angeles Mime Company, Marilyn Sokol, Pat Proft

Vanishing Point *see* CBS Special Film Presentations

1458 **The Verdi Requiem**
In Performance at Wolf Trap PBS
Program Type Music/Dance Special
90 minutes. Premiere date: 12/15/75. Repeat date: 10/11/76. The National Symphony Orchestra and University of Maryland Chorus in a performance of the "Requiem" by Giuseppe Verdi at the Wolf Trap Farm Park in Arlington, Va. Program made possible by a grant from the Atlantic Richfield Company.
Executive Producer David Prowitt
Producer Ruth Leon
Company WETA-TV/Washington, D.C.
Director Jack Sameth
Conductor Julius Rudel
Hosts Beverly Sills, David Prowitt
Executive-in-Charge Jim Karayn
Guest Soloists Rachel Mathes, Gwendolyn Killebrew, Ermano Mauro, Samuel Ramey

1459 **Very Good Friends**
ABC Afterschool Specials ABC
Program Type Children's Special
60 minutes. Premiere date: 4/6/77. Drama of a teenager coping with the death of her younger sister. Based on the novel "Beat the Turtle Drum" by Constance Greene.
Producer Martin Tahse
Company Martin Tahse Productions, Inc.
Director Richard Bennett
Writer Arthur Heinemann

CAST

Kate .... Melissa Sue Anderson
Joss .... Katy Kurtzman
Father .... William H. Bassett
Mother .... Pamela Nelson
Tootie .... Sparky Marcus
Miss Pemberthy .... Anne Seymour
Essig .... William Lanteau
Mrs. Essig .... Montana Smoyer
Harry .... Joshua Davis

1460 **Vibrations Encore** PBS
Program Type Music/Dance Series
30 minutes. Tuesday mornings. Premiere date: 9/26/74. Repeats shown as of 1/4/77. Seven-part music series based on the original "Vibrations" programs. Funded by a grant from Exxon Corporation.
Executive Producer Donald Skelton
Producer Bud Myers
Company WNET-TV/New York
Director Bud Myers
Host Noel Harrison

1461 **The Vice-Presidential Debate** ABC, CBS, NBC, PBS
Program Type News Special
75 minutes. 10/15/76. Live coverage of the debate between vice-presidential candidates Sen. Robert Dole and Sen. Walter Mondale from the Alley Theater in Houston, Texas. Same-day PBS tape-delayed broadcast with simultaneous translation in sign language for the hearing-impaired; second repeat captioned.
Producer Wallace Westfeldt (PBS)
Company League of Women Voters Education Fund
Moderator James Hoge
Panelists Marilyn Berger, Hal Bruno, Walter Mears

1462 **The Vice-Presidential Debate Analysis**
Political Spirit of '76 ABC
Program Type News Special
15 minutes. 10/15/76. Same night review and analysis of the debate between the vice-presidential candidates.
Senior Producer Jeff Gralnick
Company ABC News Special Events Unit
Anchors Harry Reasoner, Barbara Walters
Analyst Howard K. Smith
Correspondents Herbert Kaplow, Don Farmer

1463 **The Vice-Presidential Debate—Preview and Analysis** PBS
Program Type News Special
60 minutes. 10/15/76. 30-minute preview plus 30-minute post-debate analysis of the confrontation between the vice-presidential candidates. Program made possible by grants from the Corporation for Public Broadcasting, the Ford Foundation and Public Television Stations.
Producer Jim Karayn
Company WETA-TV/Washington and WNET-TV/New York
Host Lynn Sherr

1464 **The Vice-Presidential Debate—Wrap-Up**
Decision '76 NBC
Program Type News Special
15 minutes. 10/15/76. Analysis and review of the debate between the vice-presidential contenders.
Company NBC News
Anchors John Chancellor, David Brinkley

1465 **Victory at Entebbe** ABC
Program Type Dramatic Special
Three hours. Premiere date: 12/13/76. Dramatization of the Israeli raid on Entebbe Airport July 4, 1976.
Executive Producer David L. Wolper
Producer Robert Guenette
Company David L. Wolper Productions
Director Marvin Chomsky
Writer Ernest Kinoy
Scenic Designer Edward Stephenson

CAST

Shimon Peres	Burt Lancaster
Yitzhak Rabin	Anthony Hopkins
Idi Amin Dada	Julius Harris
Benyamin Wise	David Groh
Mrs. Wise	Helen Hayes
Chana Vilnofsky	Linda Blair
Edra Vilnofsky	Elizabeth Taylor
Hershel Vilnofsky	Kirk Douglas
German Terrorist	Helmut Berger
Yakov Shlomo	Theodore Bikel
Yonni	Richard Dreyfuss
Nurse	Jessica Walter
Gur	Stefan Gierasch
Gen. Shomron	Harris Yulin

1466 **Video Visionaries** PBS
Program Type Educational/Cultural Series
30 minutes. Tuesdays. Premiere date: 8/7/74. Repeats shown as of 1/11/77. 13-part series. A compilation of work from experimental television projects at WGBH-TV/Boston, the Television Laboratory at WNET-TV/New York and the National Center for Experiments in Television (NCET)/San Francisco. Series made possible by grants from the National Endowment for the Arts and the Corporation for Public Broadcasting.
Producers Dorothy Chiesa, Fred Barzyk, David Loxton, Ann Turner
Company WGBH-TV/Boston, WNET-TV/New York, KQED-TV/San Francisco

1467 **Vienna Philharmonic New Year's Concert** PBS
Program Type Music/Dance Special
60 minutes. Premiere date: 3/77. Repeat date: 8/77. The annual (1976) New Year's all-Strauss family concert performed by the Vienna Philhar-

monic Orchestra with dancing by the Vienna State Opera Corps de Ballet.
Company ORF (Austrian Television System) and ZDF (Second German Television Network)
Conductor Willi Boskovsky

1468 **Villa Alegre** PBS
Program Type Children's Series
30 minutes. Monday-Friday mornings. Premiere date: 9/23/74. New season premiere: 9/20/76. Spanish/English show set in Villa Alegre (Happy Village) stressing themes of human relations, food and nutrition, the natural environment, energy and man-made objects. Series funded by grants from the U.S. Department of Health, Education and Welfare Department of Education and the Exxon U.S.A. Foundation.
Executive Producer Claudio Guzman
Producer Larry Gottlieb
Company Bilingual Childrens Television, Inc.
Director Charles Ed Rickey
Head Writer Barbara Chain
Writers Ken Clark, John Figueroa, Richard Kletter, Alex Nogales, Eyvind Rodriguez
Musical Director Dr. Moises Rodriguez
Production Designer Michael Baugh
Regulars Nono Arsu, Linda Dangcil, Sam Edwards, Maria Grimm, Darryl Henriquez, Julio Medina, Federico Roberto, Wilfredo H. Rodriquez, Hal Smith, Catana Tully, Carmen Zapata

1469 **Violence in America**
NBC Reports NBC
Program Type Documentary/Informational Special
3 1/2 hours. Premiere date: 1/5/77. An examination of the causes and manifestations of violent behavior in the United States (three hours) plus a half hour of discussion moderated by Edwin Newman.
Executive Producer Stuart Schulberg
Producers William Cosmas, Adrienne Cowles
Company NBC News
Directors Darold Murray, Ivan Cury
Cinematographers Aaron Fears, Steve Petropoulos, Dick Smith, Alicia Weber
Supervising Film Editor Timothy Gibney
Film Editors Frank DeMeo, Brian Gallagher, Louis Giacchetto, Irwin Graf, Mary Ann Martin, George Zicarelli
Researchers Susan Drury, Christopher Isham, Sara Pecker, Mamye Smith, Jeff Strickler
Anchor Edwin Newman
Correspondents Linda Ellerbee, Floyd Kalber, Carl Stokes

1470 **Visions** PBS
Program Type Drama Series
90 minutes/two hours. Thursdays. Premiere date: 10/21/76. Weekly series of original television dramas. Programs shown during the 1976–77 season are: "El Corrido," "The Gardener's Son," "Gold Watch," "The Great Cherub Knitwear Strike," "Life Among the Lowly," "Liza's Pioneer Diary," "Pennsylvania Lynch," "The Phantom of the Open Hearth," "The Prison Game," "Scenes from the Middle Class," "The Tapestry/Circles," "Two Brothers," "The War Widow." (*See* individual titles for credits.) Series made possible by grants from the Ford Foundation, the National Endowment for the Arts and the Corporation for Public Broadcasting.
Producer Barbara Schultz
Company KCET-TV/Los Angeles

1471 **Vitalis/U.S. Olympic Invitational Track and Field Meet** NBC
Program Type Sports Special
90 minutes. Premiere date: 2/12/77. The ninth Track and Field Meet from New York City's Madison Square Garden.
Producer George Finkel
Company NBC Sports
Director Ken Fouts
Announcers Charlie Jones, Barbara Hunter, Noel Montruccio

1472 **The Volga**
National Geographic Special PBS
Program Type Documentary/Informational Special
60 minutes. Premiere date: 3/8/77. Film documentary of life along the Volga River through the heart of Russia. Filmed aboard the cruise ship *Lenin.* Program produced with the cooperation of Novosti Television, Moscow, and the captain and crew of the *Lenin,* Volga Passenger Lines. Funded by a grant from Gulf Oil Corporation.
Executive Producers Dennis B. Kane, Thomas Skinner
Producer Irwin Rosten
Company National Geographic Society and WQED-TV/Pittsburgh
Director Irwin Rosten
Writer Irwin Rosten
Host E. G. Marshall
Narrator Jack Palance

1473 **Volleyball: USA vs. China** PBS
Program Type Sports Special
Two hours. Premiere date: 12/5/76. Coverage of women's and men's volleyball competitions between the U.S. and China taped 10/9/76 in Pasadena, Texas. Program made possible by a

Volleyball: USA vs. China *Continued*
grant from the Association for Community Television.
Executive Producer James L. Bauer
Producer Robert Cozens
Company KUHT-TV/Houston
Director Robert Cozens
Announcer Dick Beeler
Color Commentators Rosalie Kuntz, Doug Beal

1474 **Von Karajan Conducts Brahms**
Fine Music Specials/Great Performances PBS
Program Type Music/Dance Special
60 minutes. Premiere date: 11/17/76. Repeat date: 8/14/77. The Berlin Philharmonic Orchestra in performances of the Symphony No. 1 in C Minor by Johannes Brahms and the Coriolan Overture by Ludwig van Beethoven. Performance broadcast simultaneously in FM stereo. Presented by WNET-TV/New York and made possible by grants from Exxon Corporation, the Ford Foundation, the Corporation for Public Broadcasting, and Public Television Stations.
Executive Producer Fritz Buttenstedt
Producer David Griffiths
Company Unitel Productions
Conductor Herbert von Karajan

1475 **Voyage of the Hokule'a**
National Geographic Special PBS
Program Type Documentary/Informational Special
90 minutes. Premiere date: 1/18/77. Repeat date: 3/19/77. Documentary recounting the reproduction and 3,000-mile voyage of modern Hawaiians from Hawaii to Tahiti and back in a double-hulled canoe re-enacting a feat of ancient Polynesia. Program made possible by a grant from Gulf Oil Corporation.
Executive Producers Dennis B. Kane, Thomas Skinner
Producer Dale Bell
Company The National Geographic Society and WQED-TV/Pittsburgh
Writer Theodore Strauss
Host E. G. Marshall
Narrator E. G. Marshall

1476 **Voyage to the Ends of the Earth**
PBS
Program Type Documentary/Informational Special
30 minutes. Premiere date: 1/25/77. Repeat date: 5/28/77. The story of Norwegian explorer Fridtjof Nansen and his crew in their expedition to the North Pole. Program presented by WETA-TV/Washington and made possible by a grant from the Autolite Division of the Bendix Company.
Executive Producer Charles Keller
Producer Michael Bortmann
Company Capital Cities Television Production
Narrator Sir John Gielgud

CAST

Fridtjof Nansen .... Knut Wigert

1477 **The Wacko Saturday Morning Preview and Other Good Stuff Special**
CBS
Program Type Children's Special
60 minutes. Premiere date: 9/8/77. Musical-variety primetime special previewing new and returning children's series on the 1977–78 CBS schedule.
Executive Producers Chris Bearde, Bob Wood
Producers Coslough Johnson, Richard Adamson, Kathe Connolly
Company Payson-Odin Productions
Director Stanley Dorfman
Writers Rick Kellard, Bob Comfort, Bo Kaprall
Musical Director Alexander Hamilton
Art Director Jack McAdam
Guest Stars Soupy Sales, the Sylvers, the Dwight Twilly Band, Julie McWhirter, Bo Kaprall, Charles Fleischer
Cameo Guests Marty Allen, Jim Backus, Carol Burnett, Jonathan Harris, Harry Nilsson, Gary Owens, Loretta Swit, Kermit Eller (Darth Vader)

1478 **Waiting for Fidel**
Documentary Showcase PBS
Program Type Documentary/Informational Special
60 minutes. Premiere date: 11/12/76. Repeat date: 7/1/77. The record of a journey to Cuba by three North Americans in 1974 and their fruitless attempts to interview Castro. Presented by WNYC-TV/New York. Program made possible by a grant from the Corporation for Public Broadcasting.
Producer Michael Rubbo
Company National Film Board of Canada
Director Michael Rubbo

1479 **Waiting for Godot**
Theater in America/Great Performances PBS
Program Type Dramatic Special
2 1/2 hours. Premiere date: 6/29/77. The Los Angeles Actors' Theatre production of the 1953 tragicomedy by Samuel Beckett. Program made possible by grants from Exxon Corporation, the Corporation for Public Broadcasting, the Ford Foundation and Public Television Stations.
Executive Producer Jac Venza
Producer Ken Campbell
Company WNET-TV/New York
Directors Gwen Arner, Charles S. Dubin

Writer Samuel Beckett

CAST

Vladimir/Didi	Dana Elcar
Estragon/Gogo	Donald Moffat
Pozzo	Ralph Waite
Lucky	Bruce French

1480 **Walk a Country Mile** PBS
Program Type Documentary/Informational Special
30 minutes. Premiere date: 1/15/76. Repeat date: 5/1/77. A look at rural New Jersey's Ramapo Mountain people
Executive Producer Kenneth Stein
Producer Brian Kellman, Emily Van Ness
Company WNJT-TV/Trenton

1481 **The Walker Cup Golf Match** ABC
Program Type Sports Special
30 minutes. Premiere date: 9/4/77. Highlights of the international golf competition between the U.S., Great Britain and Ireland from the Shinnecock Hills Golf Club in Southampton, Long Island.
Executive Producer Roone Arledge
Producer Ric LaCivita
Company ABC Sports
Director Brice Weisman
Announcers Alistair Cooke, Pat Ward Thomas

1482 **Walkin' Walter**
The ABC Monday Comedy Special ABC
Program Type Comedy Special
30 minutes. Premiere date: 6/13/77. Comedy pilot about an ex-vaudevillian songwriter. Created by Garry K. Marshall.
Executive Producers Garry K. Marshall, Edward K. Milkis, Thomas L. Miller
Producer Arnold Margolin
Company Miller-Milkis and Garry Marshall Productions in association with Paramount Television
Director Arnold Margolin
Writers Lowell Ganz, Mark Rothman

CAST

Walkin' Walter	Spo-De-Odee
Rosabelle Hoxie	Madge Sinclair
Booker Brown	Christoff St. John
Jackie Onassis Orlando	Denise Marcia
Loud Leon	David Yanez
Wendell Henderson	Jack Dodson
Rev. Tucker Tooley	Theodore Wilson

Walking Tall-Part II *see* The ABC Friday Night Movie

1483 **Wall Street Week** PBS
Program Type Educational/Cultural Series
30 minutes. Fridays. Premiere date: 1/7/72. Continuous. Theme "Twelve Bars for TWX" by Donald Swartz. Weekly guests and panel of stock market experts analyze economic trends and developments. Series made possible by grants from the Corporation for Public Broadcasting, the Ford Foundation and Public Television Stations.
Executive Producer Anne Truax Darlington
Producer John H. Davis
Company Maryland Center for Public Broadcasting
Director George Beneman
Host/Moderator Louis Rukeyser

1484 **Walt Disney World Golf Classic** ABC
Program Type Sports Special
Live coverage of the final two rounds of the Walt Disney World Golf Classic from Lake Buena Vista, Fla. 11/6/76 and 11/7/76.
Executive Producer Roone Arledge
Company ABC Sports

1485 **The Waltons** CBS
Program Type Drama Series
60 minutes. Thursdays. Premiere date: 9/14/72. Fifth season premiere: 9/23/76. Family drama set in Walton's Mountain, W. Va. during the 1930s depression. Created by Earl Hamner and based on his novel and the television special "The Homecoming." Standard sign-off: the Walton's bedroom lights go off as they bid each other goodnight. Theme music by Jerry Goldsmith. Summer reruns called "The Best of 'The Waltons' " (*see* entry).
Executive Producers Lee Rich, Earl Hamner
Producer Andy White
Company Lorimar Productions
Directors Various
Executive Story Consultant Earl Hamner
Writers Various

CAST

John-Boy	Richard Thomas
John	Ralph Waite
Olivia	Michael Learned
Grandma	Ellen Corby
Grandpa	Will Geer
Mary Ellen	Judy Norton-Taylor
Erin	Mary McDonough
Jason	Jon Walmsley
Ben	Eric Scott
Jim-Bob	David Harper
Elizabeth	Kami Cotler
Ike Godsey	Joe Conley
Corabeth	Ronnie Claire Edwards
Curtis Willard	Tom Bower
Emily Baldwin	Mary Jackson
Mamie Baldwin	Helen Kleeb

The Waltz of the Toreadors *see* PBS Movie Theater

1486 Wanted: The Sundance Woman
The ABC Friday Night Movie ABC
Program Type TV Movie
Two hours. Premiere date: 10/1/76. Action drama about Etta Place. Filmed in part in Old Tucson, Arizona. Music by Fred Karlin.
Executive Producer Stan Hough
Producer Ron Preissman
Company 20th Century-Fox Television
Director Lee Philips
Writer Richard Fielder
Art Director Arch Bacon

CAST

Etta Place .... Katharine Ross
Charlie Siringo .... Steve Forrest
Lola Wilkins .... Stella Stevens
Dave Riley .... Michael Constantine
Mattie Riley .... Katherine Helmond
Pancho Villa .... Hector Elizondo
Fierro .... Hector Elias
Sheriff .... Warren Berlinger
Maj. Vasquez .... Jorge Cervera
Elsie .... Lucille Benson
Ben Lant .... Redmond Gleeson

1487 The War Between the Tates
NBC Monday Night at the Movies NBC
Program Type TV Movie
Two hours. Premiere date: 6/13/77. Comedy-drama of a marriage threatened by marital infidelity. Based on the novel by Alison Lurie. Music by John Barry. Filmed in Toronto, Canada.
Executive Producer David Susskind
Producer Frederick Brogger
Company Talent Associates Ltd. in association with NBC-TV
Director Lee Phillips
Writer Barbara Turner
Art Director Earl Preston

CAST

Brian Tate .... Richard Crenna
Erica Tate .... Elizabeth Ashley
Danielle .... Ann Wedgeworth
Wendy .... Annette O'Toole
Sanford Finkelstein .... Granville Van Dusen
Mathilda .... Laura Patrick
Jeffrey .... Shawn Campbell
Leonard .... Colin Fox
Roo .... Julie Philips
Celia .... Mina Badiyi

1488 The War Widow
Visions PBS
Program Type Dramatic Special
90 minutes. Premiere date: 10/28/76. Repeat date: 2/10/77. An original television play dramatizing the relationship between two women during World War I. Program made possible by grants from the Ford Foundation, the National Endowment for the Arts and the Corporation for Public Broadcasting.
Producer Barbara Schultz
Company KCET-TV/Los Angeles
Director Paul Bogart
Writer Harvey Perr
Costume Designer Sandra Stewart
Production Designer Ralph Holmes

CAST

Amy .... Pamela Bellwood
Jenny .... Frances Lee McCain
Sarah .... Katharine Bard
Emily .... Maxine Stuart
Kate .... Barbara Cason
Annie .... Nan Martin
Beth .... Stephanie Retsek

VOICES

Leonard .... Tim Matheson

A Warm December *see* The CBS Wednesday Night Movies

1489 Washington: City Out of Wilderness PBS
Program Type Documentary/Informational Special
30 minutes. Premiere date: 7/12/76. Repeat date: 1/18/77. A history of Washington, D.C. tracing its growth and the parallel growth of the Capitol building. Presented by WETA-TV/Washington, D.C.
Producer Francis Thompson
Company Francis Thompson, Inc. for the Washington Capitol Historical Society
Film Editor Nicolas Kaufman

1490 Washington Week in Review PBS
Program Type Public Affairs Series
30 minutes. Fridays. Premiere date: 2/22/67. Continuous. Regular and guest reporters discuss the top national and international stories of the week. Series funded by grants from the Corporation for Public Broadcasting, the Ford Foundation and Public Television Stations.
Producer Elvera Riley
Company WETA-TV/Washington, D.C.
Director Jim Eddins
Moderator Paul Duke
Regulars Peter Lisagor (died 12/76), Neil McNeil, Charles Corddry

1491 The Way It Was PBS
Program Type Limited Sports Series
30 minutes. Saturdays. Premiere date: 10/3/74. Third season premiere: 2/19/77. 13-week sports nostalgia series with guest co-hosts and celebrities. Series funded by a grant from the Mobil Oil Corporation.
Executive Producer Gerry Gross
Producers Gary Brown, Dick Enberg
Company Gerry Gross Productions in association with KCET-TV/Los Angeles

Director Jerry Hughes
Host Curt Gowdy

1492 **Way Out Games** CBS
Program Type Children's Series
30 minutes. Saturday mornings/Sunday mornings (as of 4/10/77). Premiere date: 9/11/76. Last show: 9/4/77. Teenagers 12-15 years old from different states competing in athletic games. Pilot "W.O.G." aired 1/10/76.
Producers Jack Barry, Dan Enright
Company Barry & Enright Productions, Inc. in association with MGM Television
Director Richard Kline
Host Sonny Fox

The Way We Were *see* The ABC Sunday Night Movie

The Way West *see* CBS Special Film Presentations

1493 **WCT Challenge Cup** NBC
Program Type Sports Special
2 1/2 hours. Live coverage of the WCT Challenge Cup match from Caesars Palace in Las Vegas 4/10/77.
Company NBC Sports
Commentators Bud Collins, John Newcombe

1494 **WCT Doubles Championship** NBC
Program Type Sports Special
Three hours. Live coverage of the doubles championship from the Municipal Auditorium in Kansas City 5/8/77.
Producer Dick Auerbach
Company NBC Sports
Director Ken Fouts
Commentators Bud Collins, John Newcombe

1495 **WCT Singles Championship** NBC
Program Type Sports Special
Three hours. Live coverage of the WCT Singles Championship from Moody Coliseum at Southern Methodist University in Dallas 5/15/77.
Producer Dick Auerbach
Company NBC Sports
Director Ken Fouts
Commentators Bud Collins, John Newcombe

1496 **We Will Freeze in the Dark** Syndicated
Program Type Documentary/Informational Special
60 minutes. Premiere date: 4/12/77. A report on the energy crisis and energy conservation in the U.S.
Producer Av Westin
Company Capital Cities Communications
Distributor Capital Cities Communications
Director Av Westin
Anchor Nancy Dickerson

1497 **The Weather Machine** PBS
Program Type Science/Nature Special
Two hours. Premiere date: 2/24/75. Repeat date: 10/31/76. A look at the science of weather prediction around the world. A coproduction of six broadcasting organizations. Program made possible by a grant from Champion International Corporation; presented by WNET-TV/New York.
Executive Producer Alec Nisbett
Company WNET-TV/New York, British Broadcasting Corporation, KRO (Holland), OECA (Canada), SR 1 (Sweden), ZDF (Germany)
Writer Nigel Calder
Correspondent David Prowitt

1498 **Wednesday Mystery of the Week** ABC
Program Type TV Movie Series
90 minutes. Wednesdays. Season premiere: 9/22/76. Last-night repeat presentations of made-for-television mystery movies.

1499 **Weekend** NBC
Program Type News Magazine Series
90 minutes. Monthly (the first Saturday each month). Premiere date: 10/19/74. Third season premiere: 10/9/76. Late-night television magazine with three or more topics each edition. Created by Reuven Frank.
Executive Producer Reuven Frank
Producers William B. Hill, Peter Jeffries, Clare Crawford-Mason, Sy Pearlman, James Gannon, Karen Lerner, Anthony Potter, Craig Leake, Bill Brown, Peter Poor, Patrick Trese, Eliot Frankel, Vernon Hixson, Rosemary Short
Company NBC News
Director Gerald Polikoff
Head Writer Lloyd Dobyns
Anchor Lloyd Dobyns

1500 **Welcome Back, Kotter** ABC
Program Type Comedy Series
30 minutes. Thursdays. Premiere date: 9/9/75. Second season premiere: 9/23/76. Comedy about a teacher assigned to his old high school in Brooklyn to teach the "sweathogs." Series created by Gabriel Kaplan and Alan Sacks; de-

Welcome Back, Kotter *Continued*
veloped for television by Peter Meyerson. Music by John B. Sebastian. "Sweathog Back-to-School Special" broadcast 9/10/77.
Executive Producer James Komack
Producers Eric Cohen, George Yanok
Company The Komack Company, Inc. and Wolper Productions
Directors Bob LaHendro and others
Writers Various

CAST

Gabe Kotter .... Gabriel Kaplan
Julie Kotter .... Marcia Strassman
Mr. Woodman .... John Sylvester White
Juan Epstein .... Robert Hegyes
Freddie (Boom Boom) Washington .... Lawrence-Hilton Jacobs
Arnold Horshack .... Ron Palillo
Vinnie Barbarino .... John Travolta

West Side Story *see* The CBS Friday Night Movies

1501 **Westchester Classic** CBS
Program Type Sports Special
Live and taped coverage of the final rounds of the $300,000 Westchester Classic from the Westchester Country Club in Rye, N.Y. 8/20/77 and 8/21/77.
Producer Frank Chirkinian
Company CBS Television Network Sports
Directors Bob Dailey, Frank Chirkinian
Commentators Vin Scully, Pat Summerall, Jack Whitaker, Ben Wright, Rick Barry, Frank Glieber, Ken Venturi

1502 **Western Open** CBS
Program Type Sports Special
Live and taped coverage of the final rounds of the 74th Open from the Butler National Golf Club, Oak Brook, Ill. 6/25/77 and 6/26/77.
Producer Frank Chirkinian
Company CBS Television Network Sports
Directors Bob Dailey, Frank Chirkinian
Commentators Vin Scully, Pat Summerall, Jack Whitaker, Frank Glieber, Ben Wright, Ken Venturi

1503 **Westside Medical** ABC
Program Type Drama Series – Limited Series
60 minutes. Thursdays. Preview date: 3/15/77. Premiere date: 3/24/77. Originally scheduled as a four-week limited series. Last show: 4/14/77. Return date: 6/30/77. Last show: 8/25/77. Drama about three young doctors in their own clinic. Created by Barry Oringer. Music by Billy Goldenberg.
Executive Producer Martin Starger
Producer Alan A. Armer
Company Marstar Productions, Inc.
Directors Various
Script Consultant James Menzies
Story Editor Worley Thorne
Writers Various
Technical Consultant Walter D. Dishell, M.D.
Technical Advisor Chris Hutson, R.N.

CAST

Dr. Sam Lanagan .... James Sloyan
Dr. Janet Cottrell .... Linda Carlson
Dr. Philip Parker .... Ernest Thompson
Carrie .... Alice Nunn

Westworld *see* NBC Monday Night at the Movies

1504 **What Are the Loch Ness and Other Monsters All About?**
What's It All About? CBS
Program Type Children's Special
30 minutes. Premiere date: 2/14/76. Repeat date: 3/26/77. Special informational report on movie, mythical and "maybe" monsters such as the Loch Ness monster and Bigfoot.
Executive Producer Joel Heller
Producer Walter Lister
Company CBS News
Director Alvin Thaler
Writer Walter Lister
Researcher Barbara Flack
Reporters Christopher Glenn, Carol Martin, Joel Siegel

1505 **Whatever Happened to Dobie Gillis?** CBS
Program Type Comedy Special
30 minutes. Premiere date: 5/10/77. Comedy pilot based on the 1960s series "The Adventures of Dobie Gillis" with characters created by Max Shulman. Music by Randy Newman.
Executive Producer James Komack
Producer Michael Manheim
Company The Komack Company in association with the CBS Television Network
Directors James Komack, Gary Shimokawa
Writers Peter Meyerson, Nick Arnold
Art Director Michael Baugh

CAST

Dobie Gillis .... Dwayne Hickman
Maynard G. Krebs .... Bob Denver
Zelda Gillis .... Sheila James
Herbert T. Gillis .... Frank Faylen
Georgie Gillis .... Steven Paul
Lucky .... Lorenzo Lamas
Henshaw .... Wynn Irwin
Mrs. Lazlo .... Alice Backes
Mrs. Tucker .... Susan Davis

1506 **What's Happening!!** ABC
Program Type Comedy Series
30 minutes. Saturdays/Thursdays (as of 12/30/76.) Premiere date: 8/5/76 (as a four-week summer series). Return date: 11/13/76 Series about three middle class high school students in a black neighborhood. Music by Henry Mancini.
Producers Bud Yorkin, Saul Turteltaub, Bernie Orenstein
Company TOY Productions
Directors Various
Writers Various

CAST

Roger "Raj" Thomas	Ernest Thomas
Dwayne	Haywood Nelson
Rerun	Fred Berry
Mrs. Thomas	Mabel King
Dee Thomas	Danielle Spencer
Shirley	Shirley Hemphill

1507 **What's It All About?** CBS
Program Type Children's Series
30 minutes. Saturdays. Series premiered in July 1972. Four informational broadcasts for young people shown during the 1976–77 season: "Flying Saucers From Outer Space—What's It All About?" "Miss, Mrs., or Ms.—What's It All About?" "The Presidential Election—What's It All About?" "What Are the Loch Ness and Other Monsters All About?" (*See* individual titles for credits.)

What's Up, Doc? *see* The ABC Friday Night Movie

1508 **What's Wrong With My Child?** PBS
Program Type Documentary/Informational Special
60 minutes. Premiere date: 10/19/76. Answers to questions about children's learning disabilities —shown in conjunction with "The Puzzle Children." Program made possible by a grant from the 3M Company.
Producer Stephen Dick
Company WQED-TV/Pittsburgh
Director John Cosgrove
Host Naomi Zigmond

When Legends Die *see* The CBS Wednesday Night Movies

1509 **When Television Was Live**
CBS News Special CBS
Program Type Documentary/Informational Special
Two hours. Premiere date: 4/28/77. A look at television in the 1950s.
Executive Producer Perry Wolff
Producer Max Wilk
Co-Producer Judith Hole
Company CBS News
Writer Perry Wolff
Researcher Gail Eisen
Reporter Charles Kuralt

When the North Wind Blows *see* NBC Movie of the Week

Where the Red Fern Grows *see* NBC Saturday Night at the Movies

White Lightning *see* CBS Special Film Presentations

1510 **The White Seal** CBS
Program Type Animated Film Special
30 minutes. Premiere date: 3/24/75. Repeat date: 5/13/77. Adapted from "The Jungle Books" by Rudyard Kipling. Music arranged by Dean Elliott from Beethoven's Sixth Symphony.
Producer Chuck Jones
Company Chuck Jones Enterprises, Inc.
Director Chuck Jones
Writer Chuck Jones
Musical Director Dean Elliott
Narrator Roddy McDowall
Master Animators George Nicholas, Hal Ambro

VOICES

Kotick/Sea Catch/ Sea Cow/Whale/Walrus	Roddy McDowall
Matkah	June Foray

1511 **Who Knows One?: The National Theatre of the Deaf Celebrates the Passover Seder** PBS
Program Type Religious/Cultural Special
30 minutes. Premiere date: 4/5/77. Highlights of a seder held by the National Theatre of the Deaf in sign language, speech and song. Captioned for the hearing-impaired at WGBH-TV/Boston. Program made possible by grants from the National Theatre of the Deaf and the Bureau of Education for the Handicapped.
Producer Lucy Winslow
Company WGBH-TV/Boston and the National Theatre of the Deaf
Director David Atwood

1512 **Who's Ahead? The Debate Over Defense**
CBS News Special CBS
Program Type Documentary/Informational

Who's Ahead? The Debate Over Defense *Continued*
Special
60 minutes. Premiere date: 4/20/77. A look at U.S. and Russian military preparedness.
Senior Producer Ernest Leiser
Company CBS News
Anchor Charles Collingwood
Correspondent Ike Pappas

1513 **Who's Got a Right to Rhodesia**
CBS News Special CBS
Program Type Documentary/Informational Special
60 minutes. Premiere date: 3/28/77. An examination of the war in Rhodesia.
Producer Irv Drasnin
Company CBS News
Writer Irv Drasnin
Reporter Irv Drasnin

1514 **Who's Who** CBS
Program Type News Magazine Series
60 minutes. Tuesdays/Sundays (as of 6/5/77). Premiere date: 1/4/77. Last show: 6/26/77. Magazine series about people in the news. Regular feature: "On the Road" with Charles Kuralt. John Sharnik replaced Don Hewitt as executive producer.
Executive Producer Don Hewitt/John Sharnik
Senior Producer Grace Diekhaus
Producers Various
Company CBS News
Director Arthur Bloom
Editor/Chief Reporter Dan Rather
Correspondents Charles Kuralt, Barbara Howar

1515 **Why Me?** PBS
Program Type Documentary/Informational Special
60 minutes. Premiere date (on PBS): 11/24/75. Repeat date 10/31/76. Originally shown on KNXT-TV in May 1974. A look at how ten women coped with breast cancer, an exploration of the controversy over surgical treatment of operable cancer, and an on-camera demonstration of self-examination. Program made possible by a grant from 3M Company; presented by KCET-TV/Los Angeles.
Executive Producer Dan Gingold
Producer Joe Saltzman
Company KNXT-TV/Los Angeles
Writer Joe Saltzman
Cinematographers Chuck Stokes, Vic Nastasia
Film Editor Robert Heitmann
Narrator Lee Grant
Reporter Joe Saltzman

Wide World of Sports *see* ABC's Wide World of Sports

The Wilby Conspiracy *see* CBS Special Film Presentations

1516 **The Wild Duck**
Classic Theatre: The Humanities in Drama PBS
Program Type Dramatic Special
Two hours. Premiere date: 11/13/75. Repeat date: 4/7/77. Comic tragedy by the Norwegian playwright Henrik Ibsen. Program made possible by grants from the National Endowment for the Humanities and Mobil Oil Corporation. Presented by WGBH-TV/Boston; Joan Sullivan, producer.
Producer Cedric Messina
Company British Broadcasting Corporation
Director Alan Bridges
Writer Henrik Ibsen

CAST
Hjalmar Ekdal .... Denholm Elliott
Gregers Werle .... Derek Godfrey
Haakon Werle .... Mark Dignam
Gina Ekdal .... Rosemary Leach
Old Ekdal .... John Robinson
Hedvig Ekdal .... Jenny Agutter

1517 **Wild Kingdom** Syndicated
Program Type Science/Nature Series
30 minutes. Weekly. Show premiered in 1962. Season premiere: 9/76. Oldest of the animal documentary shows.
Producer Don Meier
Company Don Meier Productions, Inc.
Distributor Mutual of Omaha
Director Don Meier
Host Marlin Perkins
Regular Jim Fowler

The Wild Party *see* NBC Saturday Night at the Movies

1518 **Wild, Wild World of Animals**
Syndicated
Program Type Science/Nature Series
30 minutes. Weekly. Premiere date: 9/73. Fourth season premiere: 9/76. Animals in their natural habitats fighting for survival.
Producer Stanley Joseph
Company Time-Life Television Productions
Narrator William Conrad

1519 **Wimbledon** NBC
Program Type Sports Special
10 1/2 hours. Tape-delayed satellite coverage of

early-round and finals matches in the 100th Wimbledon Tennis Championships from the All-England Lawn Tennis and Croquet Club outside London 6/25/77, 6/26/77 and 7/2/77.
Producers Dick Auerbach, Ted Nathanson
Company NBC Sports
Director Ted Nathanson
Commentators Bud Collins, Jim Simpson, John Newcombe

The Wind and the Lion *see* NBC Monday Night at the Movies

1520 **Winner Take All** CBS
Program Type TV Movie
60 minutes. Premiere date: 4/1/77. Crime drama pilot about a police lieutenant and a free-lance insurance investigator. Music by John Elizalde.
Executive Producer Quinn Martin
Supervising Producer Russell Stoneham
Producer John Wilder
Company Quinn Martin Productions
Director Robert Day
Writer Cliff Gould
Art Director Herman Zimmerman

CAST

Charlie Quigley	Michael Murphy
Allison Nash	Joanna Pettet
E. P. Woodhouse	Clive Revill
Mo Rellis	Mark Gordon
Hiram Yerby	David Huddleston
Maria von Alsburg	Signe Hasso
Solange Dupree	Martine Beswick
Room Clerk	John Fiedler
Clarence Woo	James Hong
Claude Villemont	Alain Patrick
Mae Burt	Dorothy Meyer
Swenson	Loni Anderson
Hank	James McCallion
Maitre D'	Maurice Marsac
Waiter	Roger Etienne
Herbie	Robert Walter Delegall
Fireman	Dave Cass
Hood	Frank Michael Liu
Second Hood	Byron Chung
Third Hood	Ken Endoso
Doyle	Stephen Farr
Officer	Phil Adams

1521 **Winners and Losers: Poverty in California**
Documentary Showcase PBS
Program Type Documentary/Informational Special
60 minutes. Premiere date: 1/14/77. The causes and effects of poverty examined in a 1975 award-winning documentary.
Producers Paul Cabbell, David Fanning
Company KOCE-TV/Huntington Beach, Calif.
Director David Fanning
Writer Paul Cabbell
Narrator Paul Cabbell

Winnie the Pooh and Tigger Too *see* Special Movie Presentation

1522 **The Winter That Was . . . The Energy That Wasn't** ABC
Program Type Documentary/Informational Special
75 minutes. Premiere date: 3/4/77. An examination of the U.S. energy problem.
Executive Producer Elliot Bernstein
Producer Daryl Griffin
Company ABC News Special Events Unit
Director Robert Delaney
Anchor Tom Jarriel

The Wizard of Oz *see* CBS Special Film Presentations

1523 **Wodehouse Playhouse** PBS
Program Type Comedy Series
30 minutes. Weekly. Premiere date: 7/77. Thirteen dramatizations of short stories by P. G. Wodehouse. Theme music by Raymond Jones. Introductions by Cyril Luckham with film of P. G. Wodehouse.
Producers Michael Mills, David Askey
Company British Broadcasting Corporation and Time-Life Films
Distributor Eastern Educational Network
Writer David Climie
Stars Pauline Collins, John Alderton

1524 **Woman** PBS
Program Type Public Affairs Series
30 minutes. Thursdays. Fourth season premiere: 9/23/76. Discussions on the changing options and consciousness of women. Funded by grants from the Corporation for Public Broadcasting, the Ford Foundation and Public Television Stations.
Producer Sandra Elkin
Company WNED-TV/Buffalo
Director Will George
Interviewer/Moderator Sandra Elkin

1525 **Woman Alive!**
Documentary Showcase PBS
Program Type Documentary/Informational Series
60 minutes. Fridays. Premiere date: 10/21/75. Second season premiere: 4/8/77. Five shows exploring different perspectives on the status of women. Programs made possible by a grant from the Corporation for Public Broadcasting.

Woman Alive! *Continued*
Executive Producer Joan Shigekawa
Producers Various
Company WNET-TV/New York in collaboration with *Ms.* Magazine
Directors Various
Hosts Lynn Sherr, Gloria Steinem

1526 **Woman of Valor**
Eternal Light NBC
Program Type Religious/Cultural Special
60 minutes. Premiere date: 3/20/77. Drama about Jewish settlers in New York City in the late 18th century based on a work by Morton Wishengrad.
Executive Producer Doris Ann
Producer Martin Hoade
Company NBC Television Religous Programs Unit in association with the Jewish Theological Seminary of America
Director Martin Hoade
Writer Virginia Mazer

CAST

Jessy Judah .... Carol Teitel
Walter Judah .... Donald Warfield

1527 **The Woman Who Cried Murder**
The ABC Friday Night Movie ABC
Program Type TV Movie
Two hours. Premiere date: 9/26/75. Repeat date: 3/18/77. Aired originally as "Death Scream." Drama about the murder of a young woman whose 15 neighbors did nothing to help. Filmed on location in Los Angeles. Music by Gil Melle.
Executive Producer Ron Bernstein
Producer Deanne Barkley
Company RSO Films
Director Richard T. Heffron
Writer Stirling Silliphant

CAST

Det. Rodriguez .... Raul Julia
Det. Lambert .... John Ryan
Det. Bellen .... Phillip Clark
Judy .... Lucie Arnaz
Mr. Singleton .... Edward Asner
Mr. Jacobs .... Art Carney
Betty May .... Diahann Carroll
Carol .... Kate Jackson
Mrs. Singleton .... Cloris Leachman
Hilda Murray .... Tina Louise
Mrs. Jacobs .... Nancy Walker
Mr. Kosinsky .... Eric Braeden
Mrs. Whitmore .... Allyn Ann McLerie
Mrs. Kosinsky .... Dimitra Arliss
Mr. Whitmore .... William Bryant
Mrs. Daniels .... Joan Goodfellow
Lady Wing Ding .... Thelma Houston
Det. Ross .... Bert Freed
Det. Hughes .... Don Pedro Colley
Joey .... Tony Dow
Mary .... Sally Kirkland
Jimmy .... Todd Susman
Jenny Storm .... Belinda Balaski
Teila .... Helen Hunt

1528 **Women's International Golf Tournament** NBC
Program Type Sports Special
Live coverage of the final rounds of the second annual Women's International Golf Tournament from Moss Creek Plantation at Hilton Head Island, S.C. 4/16/77 and 4/17/77.
Producer Larry Cirillo
Company NBC Sports
Director Harry Coyle
Anchors Jim Simpson, Cary Middlecoff
Commentators John Brodie, Fran Tarkenton, Jay Randolph, Bruce Devlin, Carol Mann, Marlene Floyd, Mary Bea Porter

1529 **Wonder Anew** PBS
Program Type Music/Dance Special
60 minutes. Premiere date: 12/22/76. 63rd annual Christmas Festival performed by members of the St. Olaf Choir, the Chapel Choir, the Campus Choir, the Viking Chorus, the Manitou Singers and the St. Olaf College Orchestra. Program made possible by a grant from the Jerome Foundation.
Executive Producer Dick Vogl
Producer David Allen Silvian
Company KTCA-TV/St. Paul
Director David Allen Silvian
Conductors Kenneth Jennings, Robert Scholz, Alice Larsen, Donald Berglund
Scenic Designer John Maakestad
Cinematographer Kirk Hokanson
Film Editor Kirk Hokanson

1530 **Wonder Woman** ABC
Program Type Drama Series
60 minutes. Saturdays (generally). Premiere date: 10/13/76. Regular run began 12/18/76 after irregular scheduling. Last show on ABC: 7/30/77. (Series on CBS for the 1977–78 season.) Adventures of Amazon princess from Paradise Island fighting the Nazis during World War II. Based on the comic book characters created by Charles Moulton and developed for television by Stanley Ralph Ross in three specials which aired during the 1975–76 season. "Wonder Woman" music by Charles Fox; lyrics by Norman Gimbel.
Executive Producer Douglas S. Cramer
Producer W. L. Baumes
Company Douglas S. Cramer Company in association with Warner Bros. Television
Directors Various
Writers Various

CAST

Wonder Woman/Diana Prince .... Lynda Carter
Maj. Steve Trevor .... Lyle Waggoner

Gen. Blankenship .... Richard Eastham
Corp. Etta Candy .... Beatrice Colen

1531 **The Wonderful Kangaroo** NBC
Program Type Science/Nature Special
60 minutes. Premiere date: 4/13/77. A look at different types of kangaroos. Filmed in various parts of Australia.
Executive Producer Aubrey Buxton
Company A Survival Anglia Ltd. Production in association with the World Wildlife Fund
Writer Malcolm Penny
Cinematographers Des Bartlett, Jen Bartlett
Film Editor Leslie Parry
Narrator Peter Ustinov

1532 **The Wonderful World of Disney** NBC
Program Type Children's Series
60 minutes. Sundays. Premiere date: 9/24/61. 16th season premiere: 9/26/76. The longest-running prime-time program on television. Anthology series of nature stories, adventures, cartoons, dramas and comedies—some made-for-television and others originally released as theatrical features by Disney Studios. Several two-hour shows presented during the 1976–77 season including Disney Studio's first made-for-television feature "The Ghost of Cypress Swamp" 3/13/77.
Executive Producer Ron Miller
Producers Various
Company Walt Disney Productions in association with NBC-TV

Wonders of the Water World *see* NBC All-Disney Saturday Night at the Movies

1533 **Woody** PBS
Program Type Documentary/Informational Special
90 minutes. Premiere date: 11/2/76. Repeat date: 6/28/77. A look at the career of Woody Herman. Filmed and taped in Iowa, Wisconsin, California, Minnesota and Illinois. Concert taped at Adventureland, Des Moines, Iowa 4/20/76. Program made possible by a grant from the Miller Brewing Company.
Executive Producer John Beyer
Company Iowa Public Broadcasting Network
Director John Beyer
Writer John Beyer
Cinematographer Ron Burnell
Film Editor Ron Burnell

1534 **Woody Woodpecker** NBC
Program Type Animated Film Series
30 minutes. Saturday mornings. Premiere date: 9/11/76. Last show: 9/3/77. The character of Woody Woodpecker introducing his own cartoons as well as those of Chilly Willy and Andy Panda.
Executive Producer Walter Lantz
Company A Walter Lantz Production in association with Universal
Directors Various
Writers Various

VOICES

Woody Woodpecker ....Gracie Lantz

1535 **Work, Work, Work**
Documentary Showcase PBS
Program Type Documentary/Informational Special
60 minutes. Premiere date: 6/17/77. Repeat date: 8/12/77 (captioned for the hearing-impaired). Prize-winning documentary examining workers and their attitudes towards their jobs throughout history. Program made possible in part by a grant from the New Jersey Committee for the Humanities.
Producers Kenneth Stein, Art Ciocoo, Paul Buck
Company New Jersey Public Television

World Championship Tennis *see* WCT

1536 **The World Famous Moscow Circus** CBS
Program Type Music/Comedy/Variety Special
60 minutes each. Premiere dates: 7/22/77 and 7/29/77. Highlights of the best acts of the Moscow Circus. Taped at the Moscow Circus in the U.S.S.R.
Executive Producer Lothar Bock
Producer Charles Andrews
Company U.S.S.R. State Committee for Radio and Television in association with Teleglob AG and the British Broadcasting Corporation
Director Ian Smith
Writer Charles Andrews
Hosts William Conrad (Part I)/Shirley Jones (Part II)

1537 **World Heavyweight Championship —Muhammad Ali Vs. Alfredo Evangelista** ABC
Program Type Sports Special
2 1/2 hours. Live coverage of three fights from the Capital Centre in Landover, Maryland 5/16/77: the World Heavyweight Championship between Muhammad Ali and Alfredo Evangelista; the World Junior Lightweight Championship between Alfredo Escalera and Carlos Becer-

World Heavyweight Championship—Muhammad Ali Vs. Alfredo Evangelista *Continued*
ril; a non-title fight between Roberto Duran and Javier Muniz.
Executive Producer Roone Arledge
Producer Chuck Howard
Company ABC Sports
Director Chet Forte
Announcers Howard Cosell, Chris Schenkel

1538 **World Hockey Association Fifth Annual All-Star Game** PBS
Program Type Sports Special
Three hours. Premiere date: 1/18/77. The all-star teams from the Eastern and Western Divisions of the World Hockey Association in a game played at the Hartford (Conn.) Civic Center. Program made possible by grants from Avco Financial Service and Connecticut General Life Insurance Company.
Executive Producer Al Binford
Producer Ken Horseman
Company Connecticut Public Television
Director Craig Janoff

1539 **The World Invitational Tennis Classic** ABC
Program Type Limited Sports Series
90 minutes. Sundays. Series broadcast for the first time in 1974. Fourth season premiere: 5/1/77. Last show of season: 7/10/77. 11 weeks of singles, doubles and mixed doubles matches between world class tennis players. Games played at the Sea Pines Plantation on Hilton Head Island, South Carolina.
Executive Producer Roone Arledge
Company ABC Sports
Anchor Chris Schenkel
Expert Commentator Pancho Gonzalez/Andrea Kirby (one game)

1540 **The World of Darkness** CBS
Program Type TV Movie
60 minutes. Premiere date: 4/17/77. Occult-adventure pilot about a sportswriter with a special connection to the supernatural. Created by Art Wallace. Music by Fred Karlin. Filmed in part on location in Toronto.
Executive Producer David Susskind
Producer Diana Kerew
Company Talent Associates Ltd.
Director Jerry London
Writer Art Wallace
Production Designer Ben Edwards
Art Director Karen Bromley

CAST

Paul Taylor .... Granville van Dusen
Joanna Sanford .... Beatrice Straight
Clara Sanford .... Tovah Feldshuh
Dr. Thomas Madsen .... Gary Merrill
John Sanford .... James Austin
Matty Barker .... Shawn Mcann
Helen .... Jane Eastwood
Max .... Al Bernardo

1541 **The World of Franklin and Jefferson** PBS
Program Type Documentary/Informational Special
30 minutes. Premiere date: 5/10/77. A mixed-media look at 18th century America and the accomplishments of Benjamin Franklin and Thomas Jefferson. Music by Elmer Bernstein. Program made possible by a grant from the IBM Corporation.
Producers Charles Eames, Ray Eames
Company KCET-TV/Los Angeles and the Office of Charles and Ray Eames for the American Revolution Bicentennial Administration
Narrators Orson Welles, Nina Foch

1542 **The World of Ivor Novello**
Opera Theater PBS
Program Type Music/Dance Special
60 minutes. Premiere date: 8/2/77. A salute to Ivor Novello, the British musical theater composer during the war years. Filmed in part at the Drury Lane Theatre, London with a cast headed by Mary Costa. Program presented by WNET-TV/New York and made possible by grants from Public Television Stations, the Ford Foundation and the Corporation for Public Broadcasting.
Coordinating Producers David Griffiths, Sam Paul
Producer Neil Sutherland
Company Canadian Broadcasting Corporation
Conductor Richard Bonynge
Host Ian Wallace

1543 **The World of Survival** Syndicated
Program Type Science/Nature Series
30 minutes. Weekly. Premiere date: 9/71. Sixth (last) season premiere: 9/76. Animals fighting for survival against natural enemies and man.
Executive Producer Aubrey Buxton
Company Survival Anglia Ltd. in association with the World Wildlife Fund
Distributor J.W.T. Syndication
Directors Various
Writers Various
Host John Forsythe

1544 **The World of Victor Herbert**
Opera Theater PBS
Program Type Music/Dance Special
60 minutes. Premiere date: 7/19/77. A salute to the music of Victor Herbert in selections from his

operettas with a 12-member vocal chorus and ten dancers plus guest stars. Program presented by WNET-TV/New York and made possible by grants from Public Television Stations, the Ford Foundation and the Corporation for Public Broadcasting.
Coordinating Producers David Griffiths, Sam Paul
Producer Neil Sutherland
Company Canadian Broadcasting Corporation, Vancouver
Choreographer Don Gillies
Costume Designer Suzanne Mess
Scenic Designer Jimmy Jones
Choral Director John Fenwick
Featured Performers Barbara Shuttleworth, Christine Chandler, Robert Jeffrey, Allan Stewart Coates, Cynthia Dale, Vincent Dale

1545 **World Press** PBS
Program Type Public Affairs Series
30 minutes. Sundays. Seventh series began 7/18/76. Roundup of international commentary on news events by a rotating group of experts. Program made possible by grants from the Corporation for Public Broadcasting, the Ford Foundation and Public Television Stations.
Executive Producer Zev Putterman
Producer Andrew Stern
Company KQED-TV/San Francisco
Director Tom Cohen
Moderator Marshall Windmiller
Panelists William Brinner, Elizabeth Farnsworth, Gerald Feldman, Desmond Fitz-Gerald, Maurice Jonas, Mark Mancall, John Marcum, Michel Nabti, Phiroze Nagarvala, John Searle, Paola Sensi-Isolani, Paul Zinner

1546 **The World Racquets Championship** CBS
Program Type Sports Special
60 minutes. Premiere date: 5/29/77. Highlights of the World Racquets Championship Tournament.
Producer Peter Bleckner
Company CBS Television Network Sports
Commentators Don Criqui, Tony Trabert

1547 **World Series** NBC
Program Type Sports Special
Live coverage of the 1976 World Series between the Cincinnati Reds and the New York Yankees 10/16/76–10/20/76. Game two 10/17/76 seen as part of "The Big Event."
Executive Producer Scotty Connal
Producer Roy Hammerman
Company NBC Sports
Director Harry Coyle
Announcers Joe Garagiola, Tony Kubek

1548 **World Series of Golf** CBS
Program Type Sports Special
Live and taped coverage of the three final days of play from the Firestone Country Club in Akron, Ohio 9/3/77–9/5/77.
Producer Frank Chirkinian
Company CBS Television Network Sports
Director Frank Chirkinian
Commentators Vin Scully, Jack Whitaker, Ben Wright, Rick Barry, Frank Glieber, Ken Venturi

1549 **The World Series of Jazz**
In Performance at Wolf Trap PBS
Program Type Music/Dance Special
60 minutes. Premiere date: 10/25/76. Three jazz artists in concert with their own groups at the Wolf Trap Farm Park for the Performing Arts in Arlington, Va.: Earl "Fatha" Hines with Marva Josie and Eddie Graham, Rudy Rutherford and Harley White; Dizzy Gillespie with Rodney Jones, Earl May and Mickey Roker; Billy Eckstine and his 14-piece orchestra. Program made possible by a grant from the Atlantic Richfield Company.
Producers David Prowitt
Producer Ruth Leon
Company WETA-TV/Washington, D.C.
Director Stan Lathan
Conductor Bobby Tucker

World Team Tennis *see* WTT

1550 **The World Turned Upside Down**
Ourstory PBS
Program Type Dramatic Special
30 minutes. Premiere date: 11/4/75. Repeat date: 11/12/76. Story of slave who spied on the British in order to win his freedom. Music by Benjamin Lees. Filmed in part at Richmondtown Restoration, Richmondtown, Staten Island, N.Y. Special effects by Ed Drohan. Funded by a grant from the National Endowment for the Humanities.
Executive Producer Don Fouser
Producer Ron Finley
Company WNET-TV/New York
Director Ron Finley
Writer Beverly Cross
Costume Designer John Boxer
Art Director Stephen Hendrickson
Host Bill Moyers

CAST

Armistead .... David Harris
Lafayette .... Richard Brestoff
Abercrombie .... Michael Ebert
Stevens .... Frank Raiter
Cornwallis .... Louis Turenne
Rush .... Saylor Creswell
Hessian Major .... Kenneth Tigar

The World Turned Upside Down *Continued*

O'Hara .... Gregor Roy
Hand .... Ronald Frazier
Washington .... David Hooks
Gimat .... Ian Thomson
Thacher .... Don Plumley
British Soldier No. 1 .... Sam McMurray
British Soldier No. 2 .... Dermot McNamara
Black Girl .... Shelley Fann
Field Hand No. 1 .... Nat Jonas
Field Hand No. 2 .... Tim Pelt
Drummer Boy .... Charles Brennan
Black Boy .... Al "Jocko" Fann
British Sentry .... Neil Hunt
Orderly .... Tazewell Thompson
British and American Soldiers .... The Brigade of the American Revolution

1551 **The World's Worst Air Crash: The Avoidable Accident?**
Documentary Showcase PBS
Program Type Documentary/Informational Special
90 minutes. Premiere date: 5/5/75. Repeat date: 3/4/77 (as "Documentary Showcase" special). An expanded and updated version of the 1975 documentary covering the latest developments in the continuing story of the aftermath of the crash.
Producers Gail Macandrew, Peter Williams
Company WNET-TV/New York, Thames Television, London and the *Sunday Times of London*
Reporter Peter Williams
Correspondent Robert Sam Anson

The Wrath of God *see* NBC Saturday Night at the Movies

The Wrecking Crew *see* The ABC Tuesday Night Movie

1552 **WTT All-Star Match** NBC
Program Type Sports Special
Live coverage (in the East) of the World Team Tennis All-Star Match from the San Diego (Calif.) Sports Arena 7/9/77.
Producer George Finkel
Company NBC Sports
Director Ken Fouts
Commentators Bud Collins, John Newcombe, Barbara Hunter

W.W. and the Dixie Dancekings *see* The ABC Sunday Night Movie

1553 **Yazoo City Asks the President** ABC
Program Type News Special
Two hours. Premiere date: 7/21/77. Tape-delayed coverage of the 7/21/77 town meeting in Yazoo City, Mississippi with Pres. Jimmy Carter.
Executive Producer Elliot Bernstein
Company ABC News Special Events Unit
Anchors Frank Reynolds, Sam Donaldson

1554 **A Year at the Top** CBS
Program Type Comedy Series
30 minutes. Fridays/Sundays (as of 8/21/77). Premiere date: 8/5/77 (60 minute show). Last show: 9/4/77. Five-week musical comedy summer series about aspiring songwriters who unwittingly hook up with the son of the Devil. Created by Woody Kling; developed in association with Don Kirshner; developed by Norman Lear. "A Year at the Top" theme by Paul Shaffer and Howard Greenfield.
Executive Producer Norman Lear
Producer Darryl Hickman
Company T.A.T. Communications Company in association with Don Kirshner Productions
Director Marlena Laird
Writers Various
Music Supervisor Don Kirshner

CAST

Greg .... Greg Evigan
Paul .... Paul Shaffer
Miss Worley .... Priscilla Morrill
Grandma Belle Durbin .... Nedra Volz
Frederick J. Hanover .... Gabriel Dell
Trish .... Julie Cobb

1555 **Year End Report**
NBC News Special NBC
Program Type Public Affairs Special
90 minutes. Premiere date: 12/26/76. A report on the results of a poll about America's moods and attitudes at the end of 1976.
Executive Producer Gordon Manning
Producers Earl Ubell, Ray Lockhart
Company NBC News
Anchor John Chancellor
Correspondents Irving R. Levine, Marilyn Berger, Richard Valeriani, Tom Pettit, John Hart, Jane Pauley

1556 **The Year 1200** CBS
Program Type Religious/Cultural Special
60 minutes. Premiere date: 3/29/70. Repeat date: 5/29/77. Poetry and prose from the early 13th century plus an exibit of religious art from the Metropolitan Museum in New York City. Music arranged by Susan Block.
Producer Pamela Ilott
Company CBS News Religious Broadcast

Writer Pamela Ilott
Narrator Alfred Drake
Readers Beatrice Straight, Michael Tolan, William Prince

1557 The Year Without a Santa Claus ABC

Program Type Animated Film Special
60 minutes. Premiere date: 12/10/74. Repeat date: 12/14/76. Animated special using dimensional stop-motion photography. Based on the book by Phyllis McGinley. Music by Maury Laws; lyrics by Jules Bass.
Producers Arthur Rankin, Jr., Jules Bass
Company Rankin/Bass Productions
Directors Arthur Rankin, Jr., Jules Bass
Writer William Keenan

VOICES

Mrs. Santa (Narrator)	Shirley Booth
Santa Claus	Mickey Rooney
Snowmiser	Dick Shawn
Heatmiser	George S. Irving
Jingle Bells	Robert McFadden
Jangle Bells	Bradley Bolke
Mother Nature	Rhoda Mann
Ignatius Thistlewhite	Colin Duffy
Mr. Thistlewhite	Ron Marshall
"Blue Christmas" Girl	Christine Winter

Additional Voices The Wee Winter Singers

1558 Yesterday's Child

NBC Movie of the Week NBC
Program Type TV Movie
90 minutes. Premiere date: 2/3/77. Repeat date: 8/7/77. Mystery drama based on "Night of Clear Choice" by Doris Miles Disney.
Producer William Kayden
Company William Kayden Productions in association with Paramount Pictures Corp. and NBC-Tv
Directors Corey Allen, Bob Rosenbaum
Writer Michael Gleason

CAST

Laura Talbot	Shirley Jones
John Talbot	Ross Martin
Henley	Claude Akins
Emma Talbot	Geraldine Fitzgerald
Ann	Stephanie Zimbalist
Noel Talbot	Terence Scammell
Seth Talbot	Daniel Zippi
Marie	Carol Lawson Locatell

1559 You Be the Judge CBS

Program Type Sports Special
90 minutes. Premiere date: 10/22/76. Heavyweight title bout between Muhammad Ali and Ken Norton taped 9/28/76 at Yankee Stadium in New York City.
Producer Frank Chirkinian
Company CBS Television Network Sports
Director Frank Chirkinian
Host Jack Whitaker
Anchor Brent Musburger
Commentators Tom Brookshier, Jerry Quarry

You Only Live Twice *see* The ABC Sunday Night Movie

1560 You Should See What You're Missing

Documentary Showcase PBS
Program Type Documentary/Informational Special
60 minutes. Premiere date: 11/26/76. Ten people in the television industry criticizing the medium.
Producer Michael Hirsh
Company WTTW-TV/Chicago
Director William Heitz

1561 The Young and the Restless CBS

Program Type Daytime Drama Series
30 minutes. Mondays–Fridays. Premiere date: 3/26/73. Continuous. Created by William J. Bell and Lee Phillip Bell. Story about the Brooks and Foster families in Genoa City, U.S.A. Cast listed alphbetically.
Executive Producer John Conboy
Producer Patricia Wenig
Company Columbia Pictures Television
Directors Dick Dunlap, Bill Glenn
Head Writer William J. Bell

CAST

Lorie Brooks	Jaime Lyn Bauer
Nancy Becker	Cathy Carricaburu
Stuart Brooks	Robert Colbert
Kay Chancellor	Jeanne Cooper
Ron Becker	Dick DeCoit
Jill Foster	Brenda Dickson
Jennifer Brooks	Dorothy Green
Brad Eliot	Tom Hallick
Snapper Foster	David Hasselhoff
JoAnn Curtzinsky	Kay Heberle
Jack Curtis	Anthony Herrera
Brock Reynolds	Beau Kayzer
Greg Foster	Brian Kerwin
Leslie Brooks Eliot	Janice Lynde
Liz Foster	Julianna McCarthy
Lance Prentiss	John McCook
Peggy Brooks	Pamela Solow
Vanessa Prentiss	K. T. Stevens
Chris Foster	Trish Stewart

1562 Young Pioneers ABC

Program Type TV Movie
Two hours. Premiere date: 3/1/76. Repeat date: 1/9/77 and 1/16/77 (60 minutes each). Pilot film based on the novel, "Young Pioneers," by Rose Wilder Lane about teenage newlyweds in the Dakota wilderness of the 1870s. Filmed partly in the San Rafael Valley, Ariz. Music by Laurence Rosenthal.
Executive Producer Ed Friendly

Young Pioneers *Continued*
Producer Ed Friendly
Company An ABC Circle Film
Director Michael O'Herlihy
Writer Blanche Hanalis

CAST

David Beaton	Roger Kern
Molly Beaton	Linda Purl
Dan Gray	Robert Hays
Nettie Peters	Shelly Juttner
Mr. Peters	Robert Donner
Mr. Swenson	Frank Marth
Doyle	Brendan Dillon
Mr. Beaton	Charles Tyner
Dr. Thorne	Jonathan Kidd
Clerk	Arnold Soboloff
Mrs. Swenson	Bernice Smith
Eliza	Janis Famison
Man in Land Office	Dennis Fimple

1563 **Young Pioneers' Christmas**
The ABC Friday Night Movie ABC
Program Type TV Movie
Two hours. Premiere date: 12/17/76. Sequel to "Young Pioneers" (*see* above) about a young couple in the Dakota wilderness of the 1870s who put aside their grief to extend friendship during the Christmas season. Filmed in part in Southern Arizona. Music by Laurence Rosenthal.
Executive Producer Ed Friendly
Producer Ed Friendly
Company An ABC Circle Film
Director Michael O'Herlihy
Writer Blanche Hanalis
Art Director Jan M. Van Tamelen

CAST

Molly Beaton	Linda Purl
David Beaton	Roger Kern
Dan Gray	Robert Hays
Nettie Peters	Kay Kimler
Mr. Peters	Robert Donner
Loftus	Britt Leach
Yancy	Arnold Soboloff
Doyle	Brendan Dillon
Pike	Rand Bridges
Charlie Peters	Brian Melrose
Flora Peters	Sherri Wagner

1564 **You're a Poet and Don't Know It! . . . The Poetry Power Hour**
The CBS Festival of Lively Arts for Young People CBS
Program Type Children's Special
60 minutes. Premiere date: 11/14/76. Recitations, dramatizations and discussions of 200 years of American poetry.
Executive Producers Lester Gottlieb, Robert Stolfi
Producer Burt Shevelove
Director John Desmond
Writer Thomas Baum
Costume Designer Leslie Renfield
Scenic Designer J. Newton White
Stars Frank Converse, Blythe Danner, Rosemary Harris, Leonard Nimoy, Tom Seaver, Jack Weston
Children Kelly Jordan, John McCurry, Gladys Moore, David Moskin, Julie Newman, Tony Perez, David Stambough

1565 **You're Gonna Love It Here** CBS
Program Type Comedy Special
30 minutes. Premiere date: 6/1/77. Comedy pilot about a Broadway star, her press agent son and 11-year-old grandson. Title song by Mitzi Welch and Peter Matz; sung by Ethel Merman.
Executive Producer Frank Konigsberg
Producer Mel Farber
Company A Silliphant-Konigsberg Production in association with Warner Bros. Television
Directors Gordon Risgby, Bruce Paltrow
Writer Bruce Paltrow

CAST

Lolly Rogers	Ethel Merman
Harry	Austin Pendleton
Peter	Chris Barnes

Additional Cast Matthew Anton, Jerome Dempsey, Tony Holmes, Joanne Jonas, Glenn Scarpelli

1566 **You're Not Elected, Charlie Brown** CBS
Program Type Animated Film Special
30 minutes. Premiere date: 10/29/72. Repeat date: 9/23/76. Animated special based on the "Peanuts" comic strip about Charlie Brown's race for the class presidency. Musical score by Vince Guaraldi.
Producers Lee Mendelson, Bill Melendez
Company Lee Mendelson-Bill Melendez Production in cooperation with United Feature Syndicate, Inc.
Director Bill Melendez
Writer Charles M. Schulz
Music Supervisor John Scott Trotter

VOICES

Charlie Brown	Chad Webber
Linus Van Pelt	Stephen Shea
Lucy Van Pelt	Robin Kohn
Russell Anderson	Todd Barbee
Sally	Hilary Momberger
Violet	Linda Ercoli
Schroeder	Brian Kazanjian

Yours, Mine and Ours *see* The ABC Friday Night Movie

1567 **Zalmen or the Madness of God**
Theater in America/Great Performances PBS
Program Type Dramatic Special
Two hours. Premiere date: 1/8/75. Repeat date: 7/27/77. Mystical drama of religious persecution in Russia. Performed by members of the Arena Stage Company in Washington, D.C. Pro-

gram funded by grants from Exxon Corporation and the Corporation for Public Broadcasting.
Executive Producer Jac Venza
Producer Ken Campbell
Company WNET-TV/New York
Directors Alan Schneider, Peter Levin
Writer Elie Wiesel
Costume Designer Marjorie Slaiman
Host Hal Holbrook
Set Designer William Ritman

CAST

Zalmen	Richard Bauer
Rabbi	Joseph Wiseman
Chairman	Robert Prosky
Srul	Sanford Seeger
Smuel	Leib Lensky
Motke	Michael Mertz
Chaim	David Reinhardsen
Zender	Glenn Taylor
Doctor	Mark Hammer
Inspector	Howard Witt
Nina	Dianne Wiest
Alexei	Gary Bayer
Misha	John Koch, Jr.
Commissar	Scott Schofield
Secretary	Nancy Dutton
Avrom	Michael Gorrin
Feige	Leslie Carr
Guards	Michael Haney, Ken Kantor
Cantor	John Jellison

1568 **Zoom** PBS
Program Type Children's Series
30 minutes. Monday-Friday afternoons. Premiere date: 1/9/72. Fifth season premiere: 10/9/76. Magazine-format series produced for, by, and about youngsters 8-12 years old. Regular features: ZOOMgames and ZOOMbarrells, ZOOMplays, ZOOMraps, ZOOMphenomenon, ZOOMgoody, ZOOMguests, ZOOMdo. Thursday programs captioned for the hearing-impaired by WGBH-TV/Boston. Series made possible by grants from the Corporation for Public Broadcasting, the Ford Foundation, Public Television Stations, General Foods, and the U.S. Bureau of Education for the Handicapped (Thursday programs).
Executive Producer C. Susheel Bibbs
Producers Monia Joblin, Mary Benjamin Blau
Company WGBH-TV/Boston
Director Richard Heller
Musical Director Newton Wayland
Scenic Designer Clint Heitman

Who's Who in TV 1976-1977